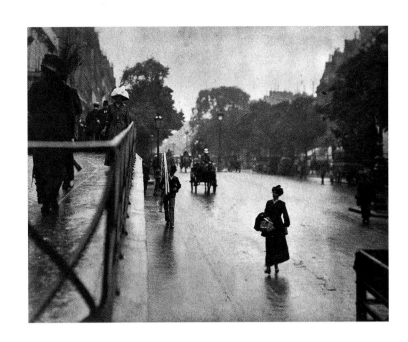

Bystander: A History of Street Photography

Conversation

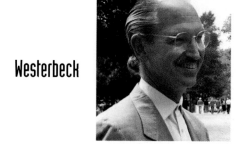

Westerbeck **Winograd seemed to be ha humanity surging down the**

Meyerowitz *Yes! It's like going into the sea and lettir the sea. On the street each successive wo wave after wave, you bathe in it. There i all that chance and change — it's tough something will reveal itself — just a spli picture!*

Westerbeck **I remember hearing Garry and the "beautiful." Why was "tough" such**

Meyerowitz *"Tough" meant it was an uncompromisir instinct, raw, of the moment, something was TOUGH. Tough to like, tough to see tougher they were the more beautiful th*

piest when he confronted a wall of
reet. He threw himself into it.

the waves break over you. You feel the power of
brings a whole new cast of characters. You take
omething exciting about being in the crowd, in
t there — but if you can keep paying attention
cond — and then there's a crazy cockeyed

t of you often calling pictures "tough" or
key word for you?

mage, something that came from your gut, out of
t couldn't be described in any other way. So it
ugh to make, tough to understand. The
ecame. It was our language.

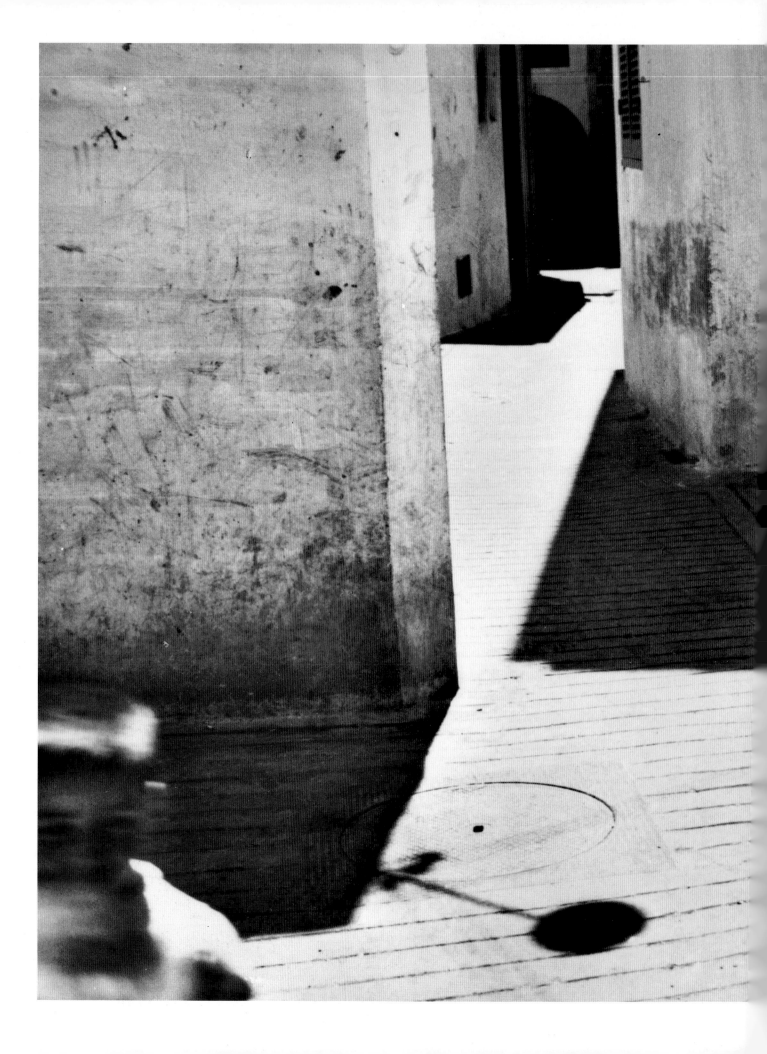

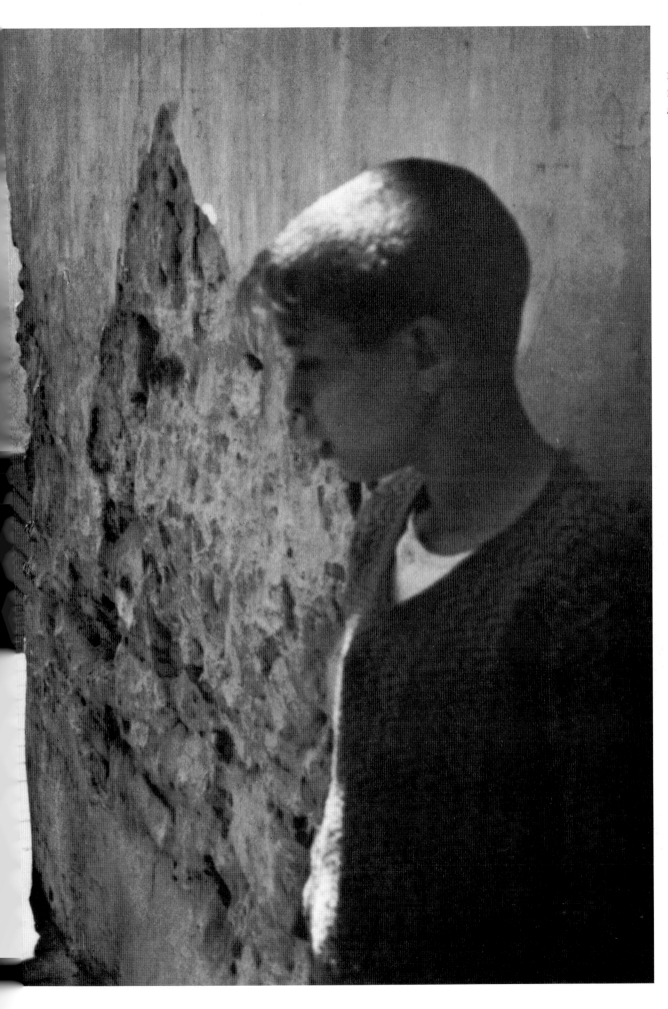

6

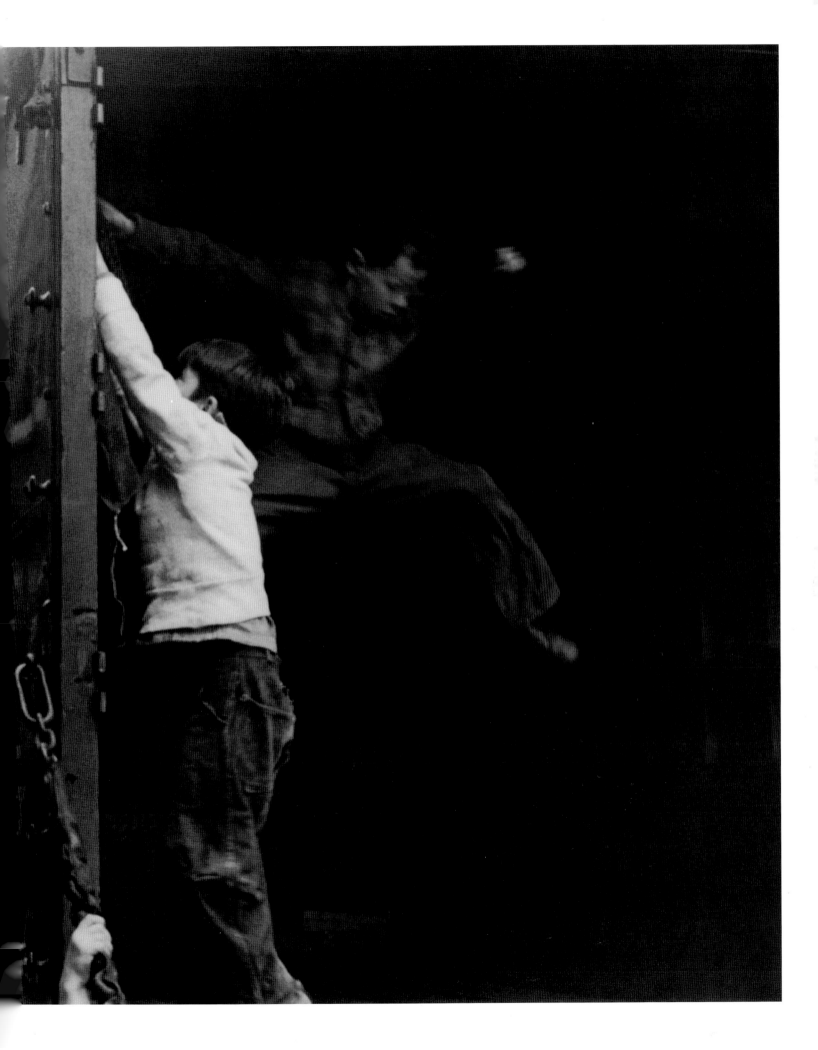

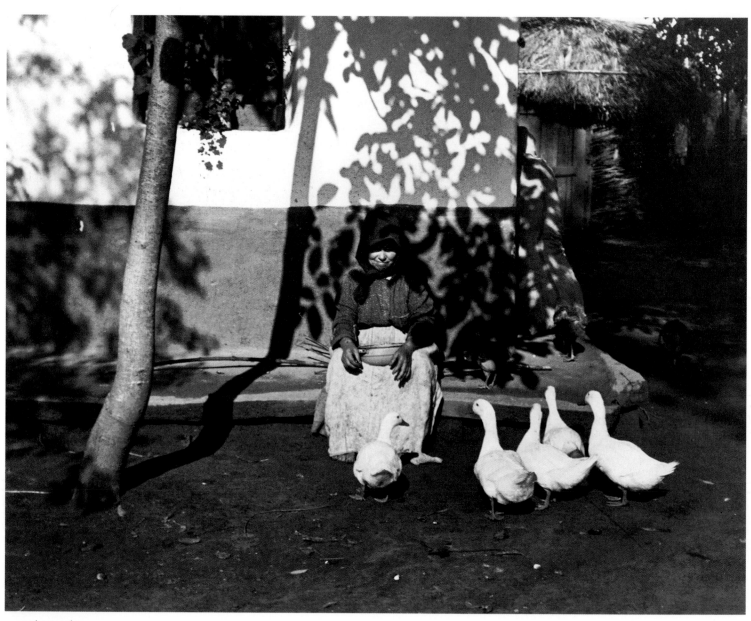

ANDRÉ KERTÉSZ
Feeding the Ducks in the
Late Afternoon, Tisza
Szalka, 1924

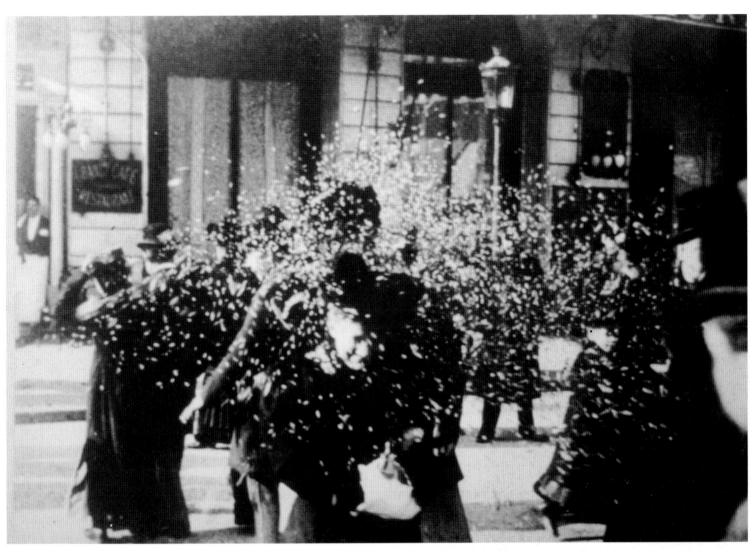

MAURICE BUCQUET
Untitled, n.d.

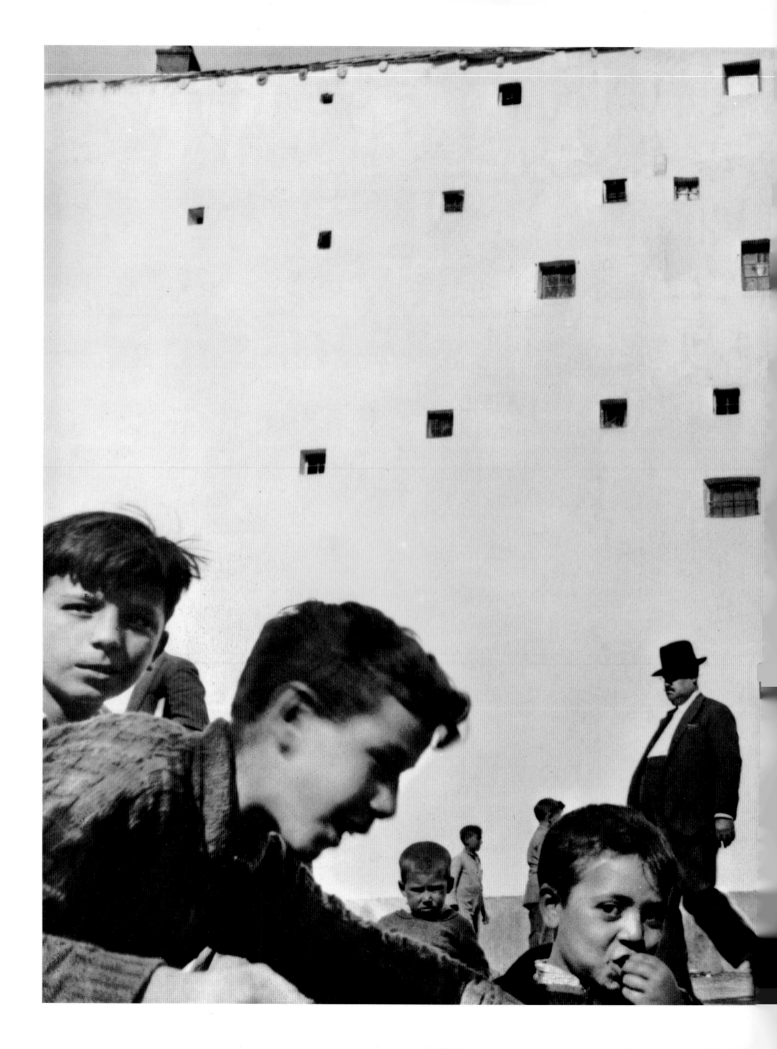

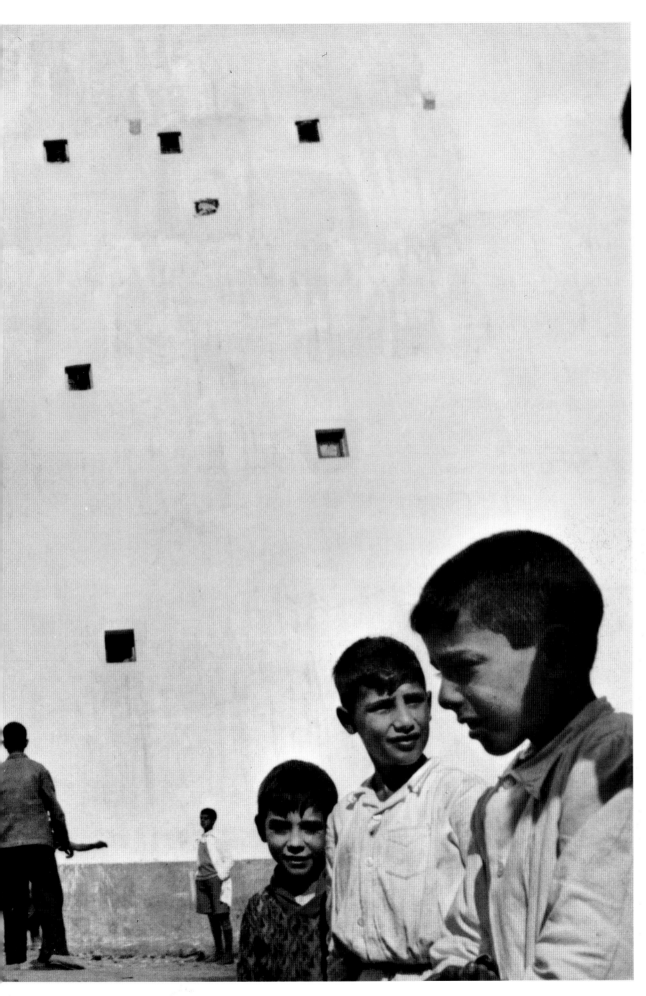

HENRI CARTIER-BRESSON
Madrid, 1933

11

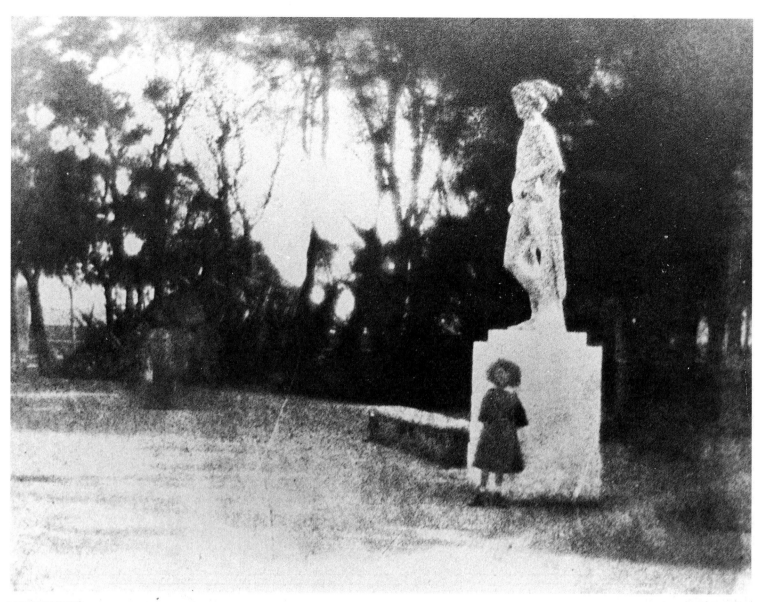

THE REVEREND
CALVERT JONES or
CHRISTOPHER
TALBOT
Villa Reale, Naples,
1846

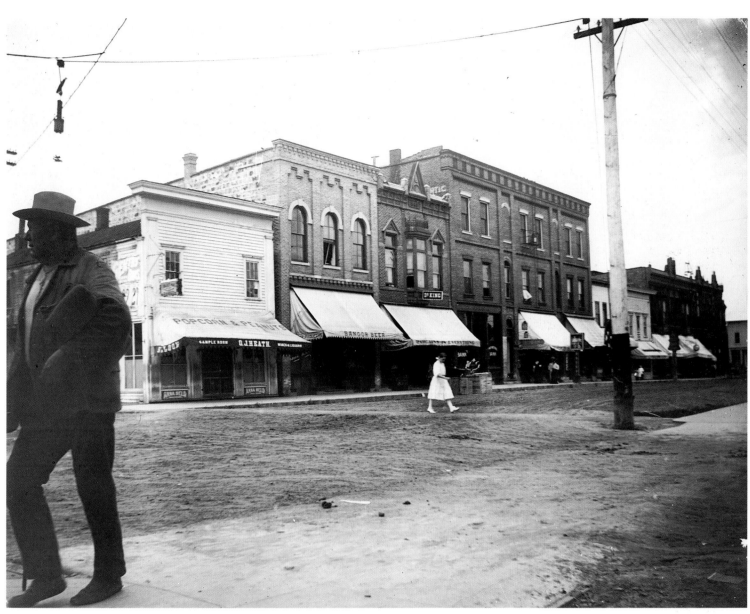

CHARLES J. VAN
SCHAICK
Black River Falls,
Wisconsin,
c. 1890–1910

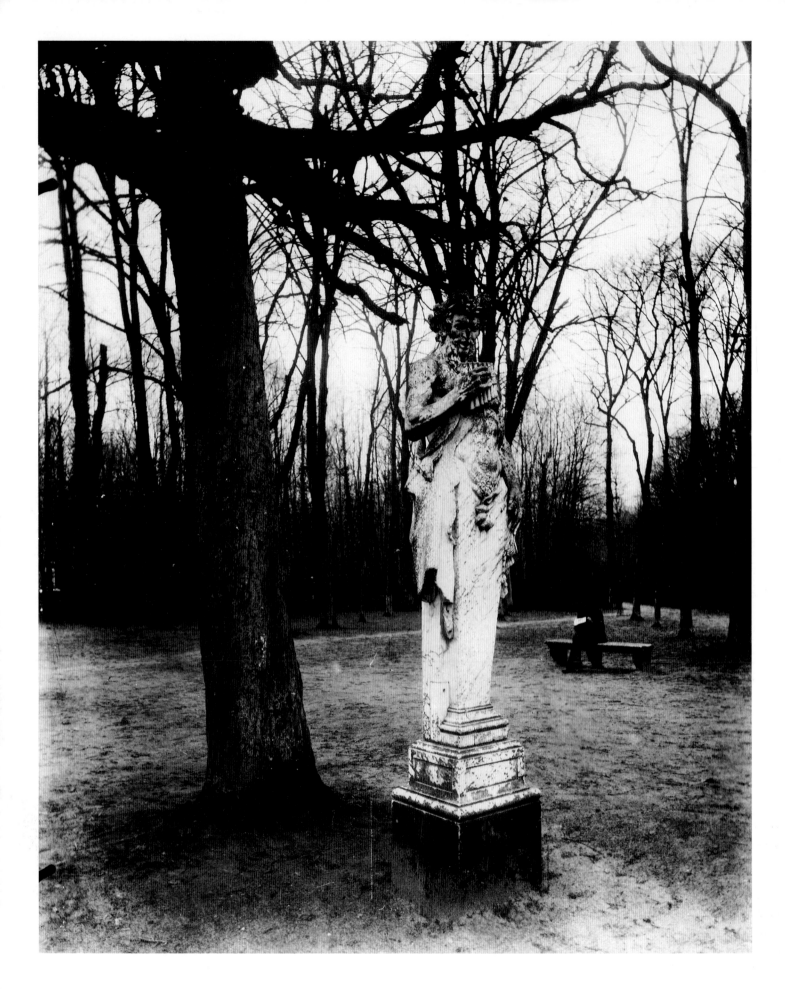

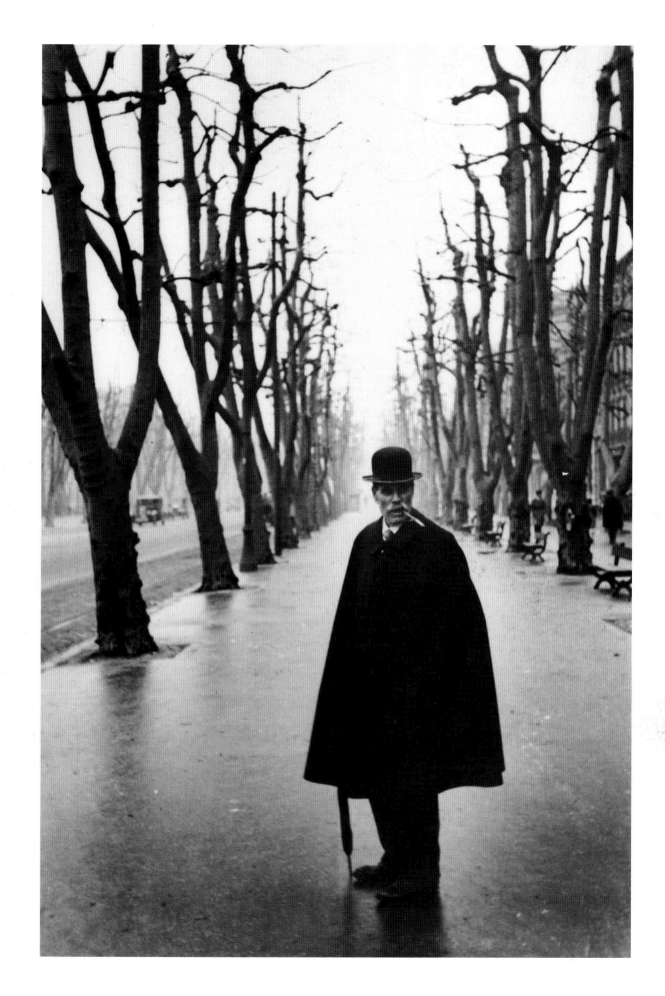

15

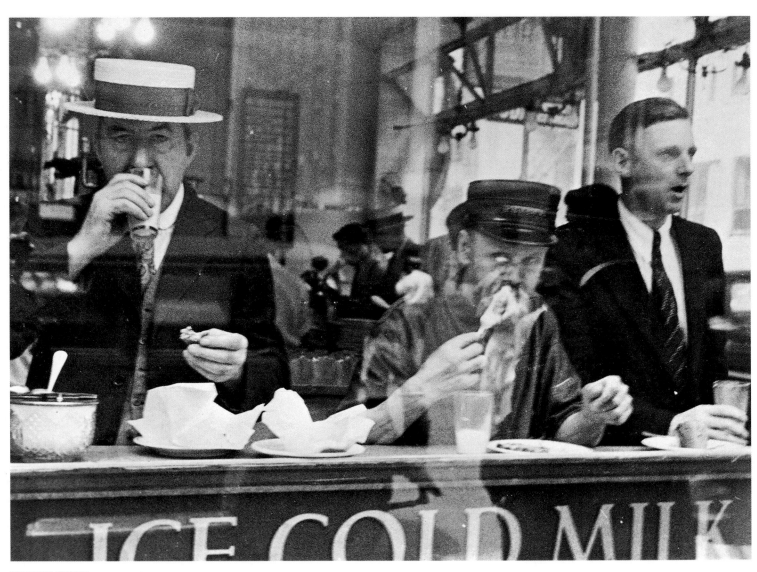

WALKER EVANS

New York, c. 1930

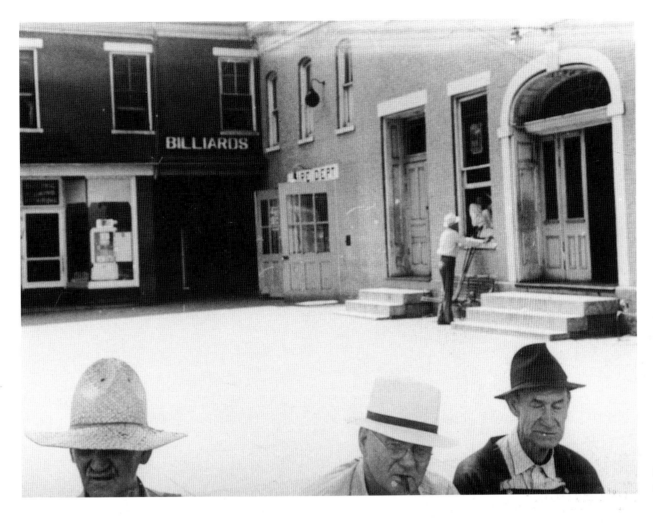

BEN SHAHN
Untitled, 1935–38

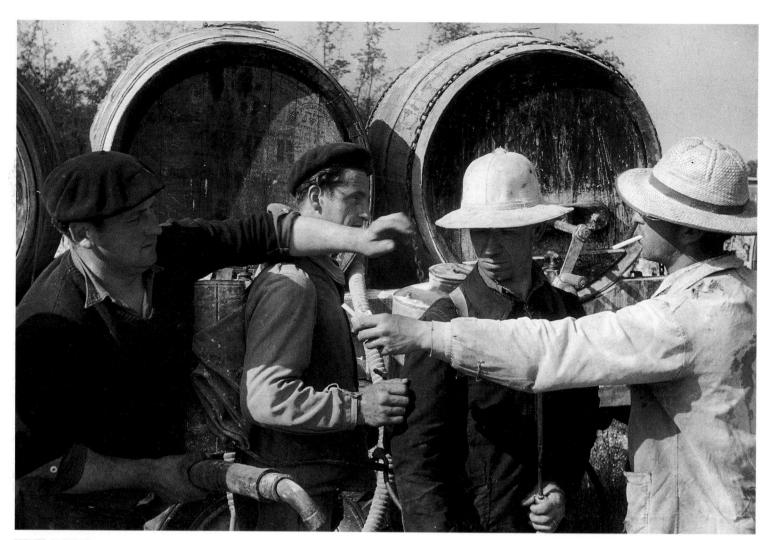

HENRI CARTIER-
BRESSON
Sauternes, Gironde,
1950–55

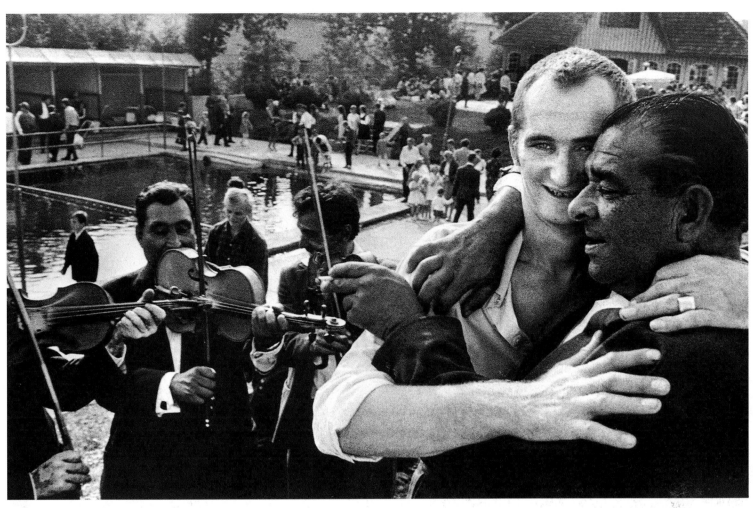

JOSEF KOUDELKA
Czechoslovakia, 1966

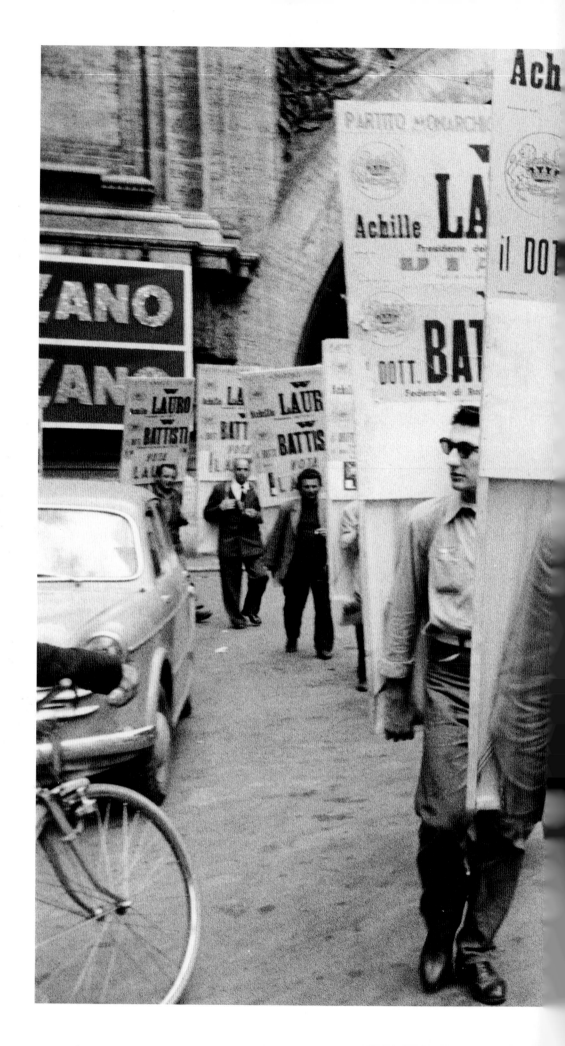

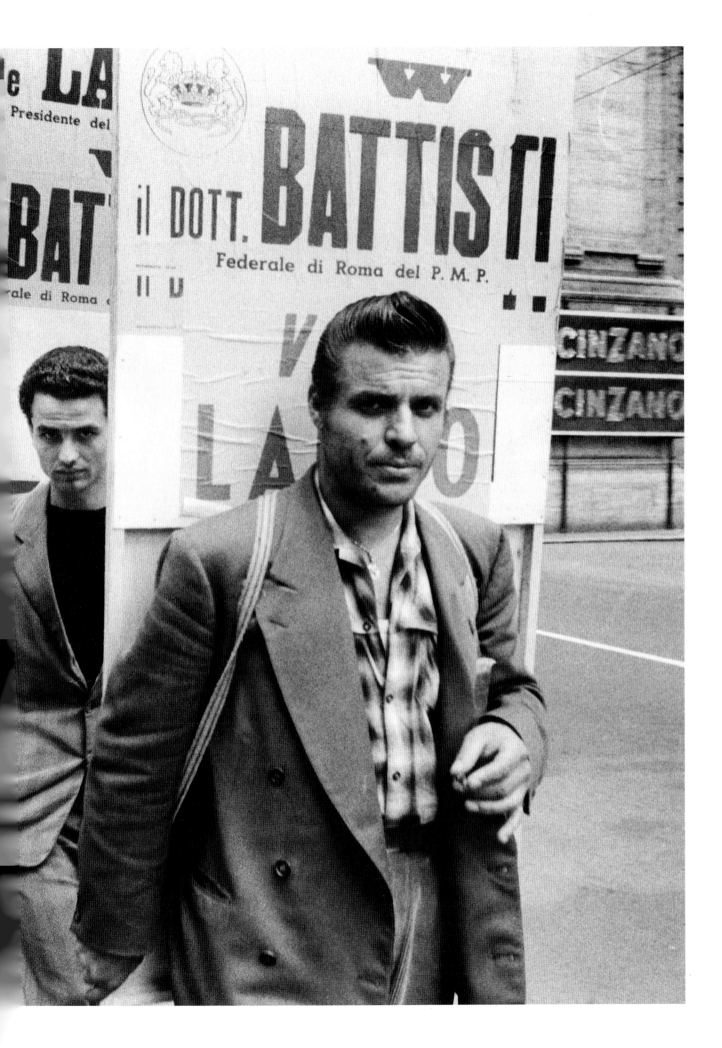

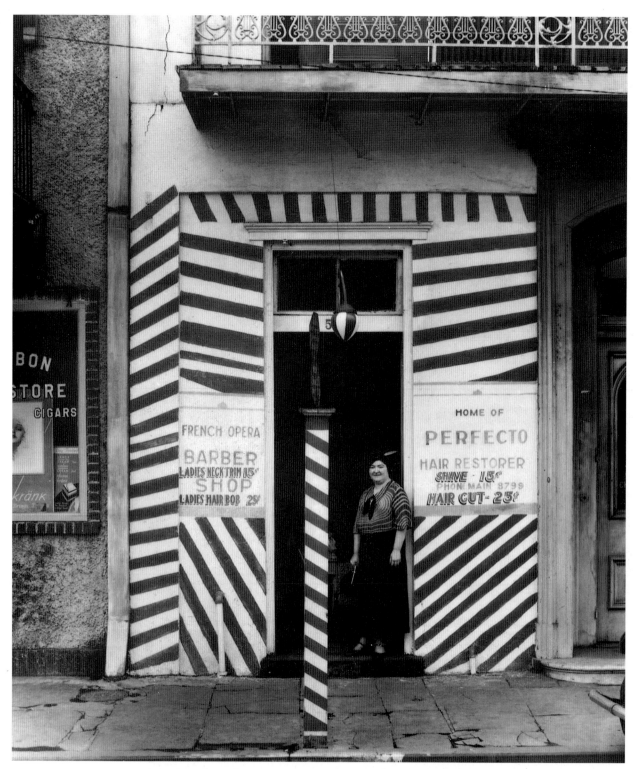

WALKER EVANS
Sidewalk and
Shopfront, New Orleans,
1935

22

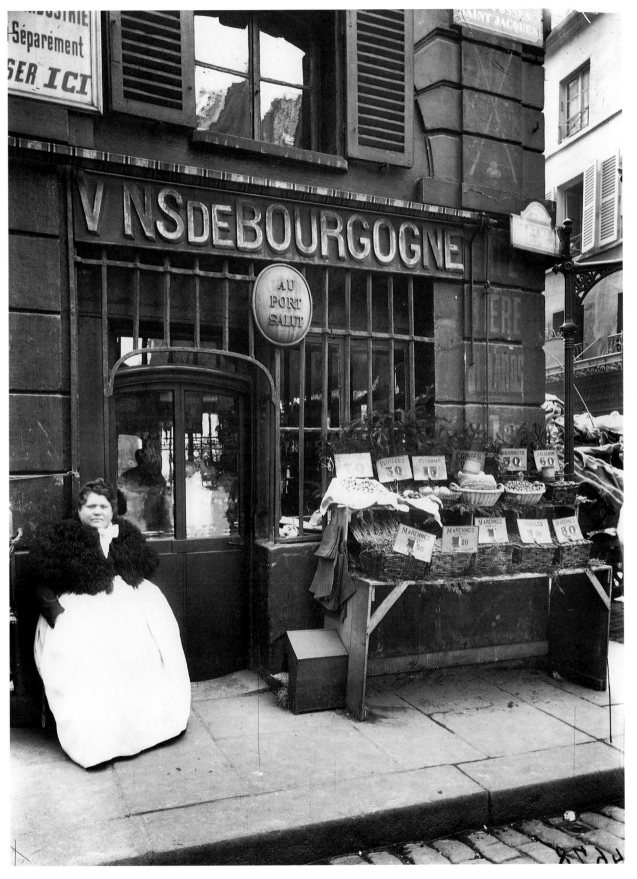

EUGÈNE ATGET
Paris, n.d.

23

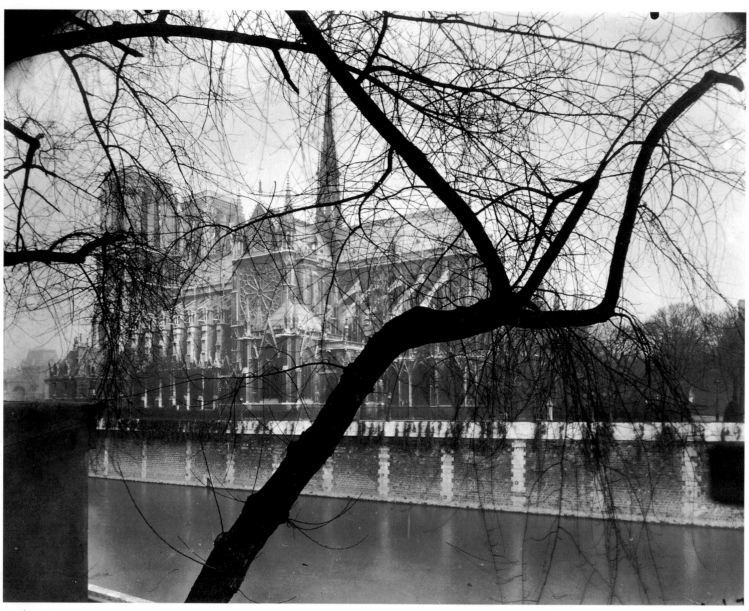

EUGÈNE ATGET

Notre Dame, 1915

24

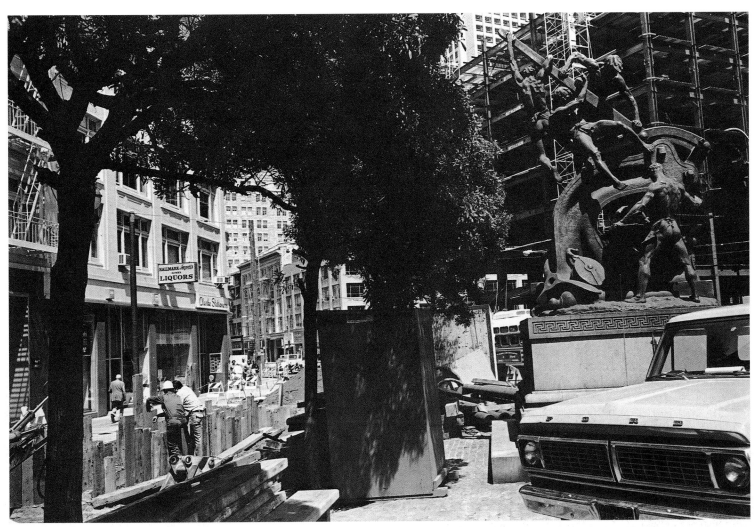

LEE FRIEDLANDER
Mechanics' Monument,
San Francisco, 1972

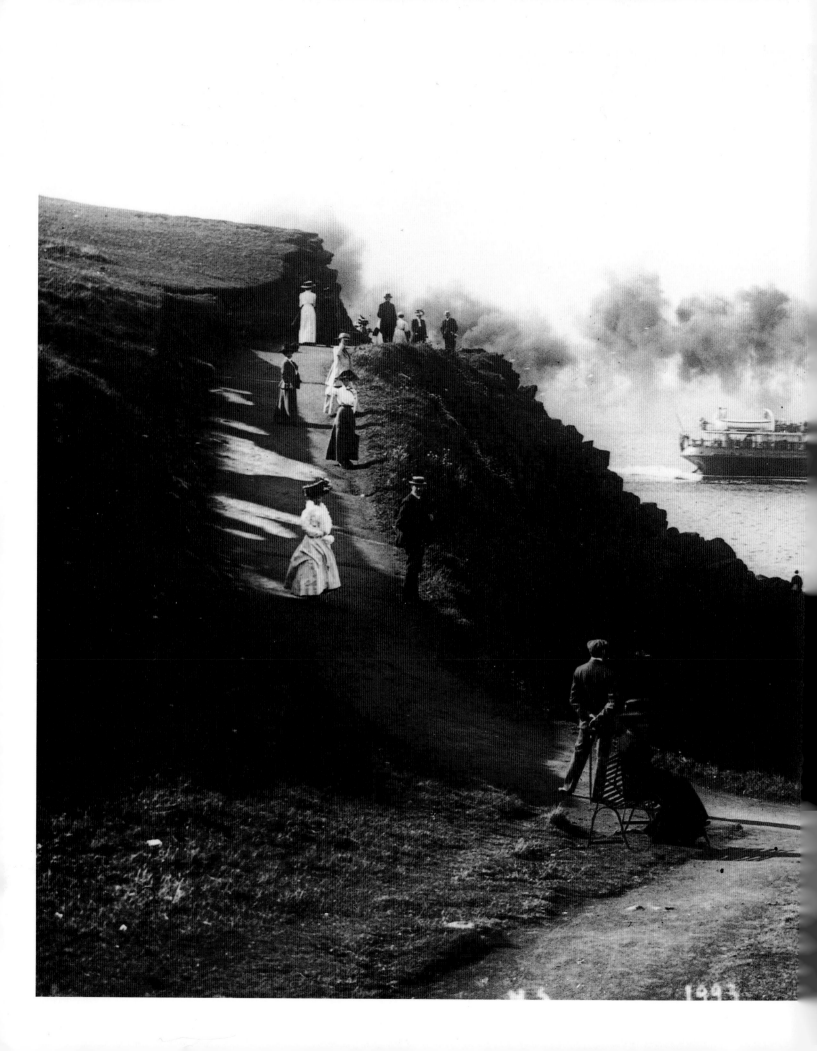

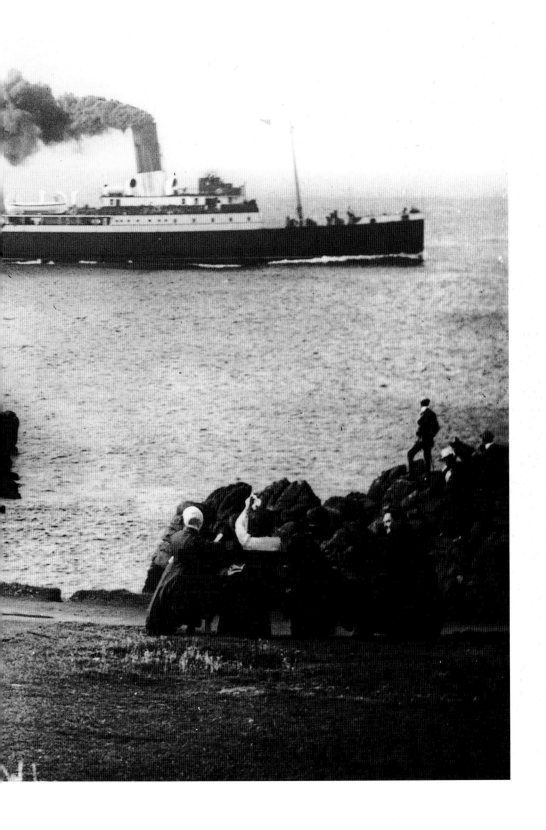

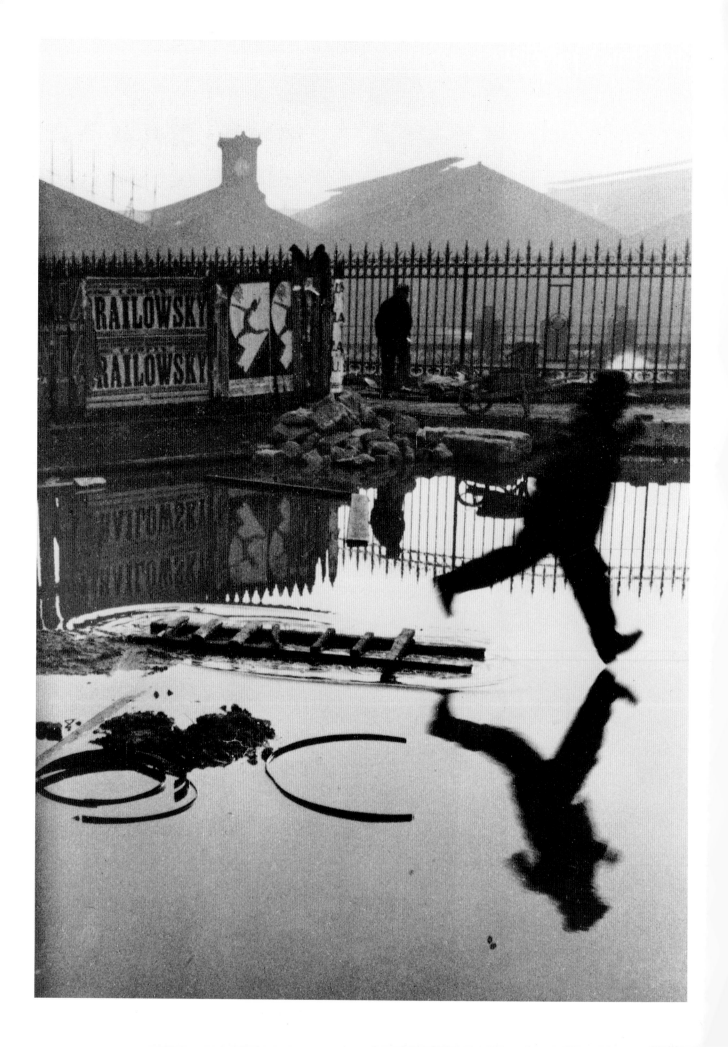

Bystander: ◆
A History of
Street Photography

Colin Westerbeck
Joel Meyerowitz

A Bulfinch Press Book
Little, Brown and Company
Boston New York Toronto London

Page 1: ALFRED STIEGLITZ, *A Snapshot, Paris,* 1911
Page 28: HENRI CARTIER-BRESSON, *Behind the Gare Saint-Lazare, Paris,* 1932

First Edition

Additional copyright information and a complete listing of the credits for the
photographs reproduced in this book appear on pages 407–409.

LIBRARY OF CONGRESS CATALOGING-IN-PUBLICATION DATA
Westerbeck, Colin.
Bystander: a history of street photography / Colin Westerbeck, Joel Meyerowitz. — 1st ed.
p.   cm.
Includes bibliographical references and index.
ISBN 0-8212-1755-0
1. Documentary photography — History. 2. Public spaces — Pictorial works.
3. Streets — Pictorial works. I. Meyerowitz, Joel. II. Title.
TR820.5.W46 1993   770'.9 — dc20   93-14900

Designed by Caroline Rowntree

Bulfinch Press is an imprint and trademark of Little, Brown and Company (Inc.)
Published simultaneously in Canada by Little, Brown & Company (Canada) Limited

PRINTED IN HONG KONG

The authors dedicate this book to their children —
Kate Westerbeck and Sasha and Ariel Meyerowitz

Contents

Introduction

To most people a street photographer is someone in Times Square or Piccadilly Circus who will take your picture for a fee and send you the print later (or, since the adoption of the Polaroid by such vendors, give it to you right on the spot). In at least one prominent instance, a photographer discussed in this book — Weegee — did begin his career by plying that trade; and from John Thomson to Manuel Alvarez Bravo to Diane Arbus, there are certainly others here who made a practice of soliciting subjects for impromptu portraits done on the street. For the most part, however, the photographers discussed in these pages have tried to work without being noticed by their subjects. They have taken pictures of people who are going about their business unaware of the photographer's presence. They have made candid pictures of everyday life in the street. That, at its core, is what street photography is.

It is a kind of photography that tells us something crucial about the nature of the medium as a whole, about what is unique to the imagery that it produces. The combination of this instrument, a camera, and this subject matter, the street, yields a type of picture that is idiosyncratic to photography in a way that formal portraits, pictorial landscapes, and other kinds of genre scenes are not.

Among the properties particular to the medium that street photography explores and exploits, by its nature, are instantaneity and multiplicity. Since its earliest days, photography has held out a promise no other medium could match, of being faster than the hand, or even the eye, at capturing physical detail. While the experiments of Eadweard James Muybridge and Etienne-Jules Marey or certain moments in photojournalism may yield more information, street photographers use the capacity for information more imaginatively.

They *think about* this attribute of photography more profoundly than anyone else. Similarly, their art has a special reliance on the multiplicity of photography, its ability to create serial imagery and sequences of pictures.

In this aspect of the medium a paradox is implicit to which street photographers are very sensitive. On the one hand, the many shots that they can get at even a rapidly moving, changing subject allow them to strive for the singular image, some one, perfect composition into which all the other possibilities are condensed. On the other hand, they might make purposely open-ended, unbalanced pictures that can't stand alone and need to be played off one another in groups or runs in books. The choice between the two ideas is, in large measure, the choice between Henri Cartier-Bresson's work and Robert Frank's.

While stop-action images of people are bound to figure prominently in any collection of street photographs, this book also contains many pictures in which there are no people at all. The most salient examples are to be found among the pictures of Eugène Atget. Yet even he was, through implication and inference, trying to show us life on the street. Suggesting presence in the midst of absence, he was attempting to reveal the life *of* the street as it inhered in the setting itself. Like every other practitioner of this genre, he wandered the streets with his camera, looking for what would today be called photo opportunities. More important, he was also like every other street photographer in his readiness to respond to errant details, chance juxtapositions, odd non sequiturs, peculiarities of scale, the quirkiness of life in the street.

Atget's career might remind us that the photographers included here are often not the ones who thought of themselves as artists or hoped to see signed prints of their work hung in museums. On the contrary, a fundamental part of the photography in this book is anonymous, and most of it is imagery of a strictly personal and sometimes casual sort done by photographers who subscribed to no aesthetic theory or artistic school. They discovered their idea of what a photograph should be by looking into the camera itself, improvising their art form as they went along. This is how many of street photography's motifs, as art historians would call them, came about.

Motion blur, for instance, is something that the photographers, since they were unable to prevent it under many circumstances, learned to use to their advantage. It became a way to express the energy of the street. An unfixed image can suggest either the fidgeting and fussing of a child too excited to sit still while its picture is taken or the wooziness of an old derelict too far gone to focus anymore, or any human condition in between. Whatever it evokes, the evanescence of the image might be thought of as reflecting the anonymity of the photographer himself. Like the subject of the picture, the photographer who took it frequently proves a rather elusive, transient figure.

Street photographs have an imaginative life all their own, one that sometimes seems quite independent of whatever intentions the photographer may have had. This book is an attempt to describe that life, to articulate the appeal that this sort of imagery has had for modern viewers. The street as it is defined here might be a crowded boulevard or a country lane, a park in the city or a boardwalk at the beach, a lively café or a deserted hallway in a tenement, or even a subway car or the lobby of a theater. It is any public place where a photographer could take pictures of subjects who were unknown to him and, whenever possible, unconscious of his presence.

At the same time that the street, as subject matter, is dealt with almost as if it had its own personality, imposing itself upon (or perhaps seducing) any photographer who confronts it,

the sensibilities of the photographers themselves are also obviously too varied for their individuality to be denied. This is why we examine the career of any photographer who is essential to this tradition in full, rather than just in regard to street photographs. The attempt is always to reveal the extent to which these images have been the center, the motor, the inspiration of the career as a whole.

The tradition of street photography is a diffuse, fragmented, intermittent one. But it is a tradition nonetheless — a succession of influences and inheritances — because these photographers have made their work available both to posterity and to each other through publication, which they have favored over exhibition. There are certain pictures, such as Paul Strand's *Blind Woman* of 1916, that everybody who took up street photography thereafter appears to have seen and been affected by. Among curators and editors of photographic books, a prejudice sometimes exists against a picture like this because it's so familiar. But the contrary desire always to find something new with which to impress the audience can lead, in excess, to a misrepresentation of photographic history. While this book does contain, it is hoped, some interesting discoveries, an effort has been made to give the pictures that everybody has seen before their fair due, recognizing that having been seen by everyone is what makes them indispensable.

This book came out of conversations that the authors began having more than a decade ago. Ultimately, Colin Westerbeck wrote the text, based on a lot of traveling and looking at pictures that he and Joel Meyerowitz did together, and Meyerowitz acted as editor of the text and shaper of the selection of pictures. At the time that we met, some years before our collaboration on this project began, Meyerowitz was himself a street photographer in New York working with a 35mm Leica camera in both color and black-and-white. His enthusiasm for what he was doing and the quality of his results were what originally attracted Westerbeck to this subject, as the last chapter, which takes the form of a conversation between the authors, reflects.

The term "bystander" is most familiar in the phrase "innocent bystander," somebody who gets swept up in events because he or she chanced to be present when, as Joseph Heller said, "something happened." But bystanders are also people who come to bear witness. They are those who are there expressly for the purpose of making observations, which in this context is almost the same thing as making observances, as if taking the photograph were a ritual fulfillment of a moral obligation. That certainly is something that almost all the figures in this study seem to share: a compulsion to take pictures, an irresistible need to do it, an imperative that reaches from Eugène Atget to Henri Cartier-Bresson, from amateurs to professionals, and from the most famous among them to (one suspects) the most completely anonymous and secretive.

PART ONE
Eugène Atget
& the Nineteenth Century

1: Before Photography

A photograph of life on the street by Henri Cartier-Bresson reveals an astonishing beauty, drama, and formal order that we usually feel we would have missed completely without his help. He sees so many things we cannot that we wonder whether the street itself isn't just the product of his imagination, as if he had invented it the way other Surrealist photographers invent their visions in their studios or their darkrooms. Yet in a sense it is the street that has invented him. Life in the street, especially in Paris, has created a modern sensibility that photographers like Cartier-Bresson embody. To appreciate fully the photographic imagery to be found in the chapters that follow, it would be a good idea to consider first the importance — indeed, the urgency — with which the subject matter in such pictures has presented itself to the camera.

Perhaps because so much of the modern history of France was made in the Paris streets, from the revolution of 1789 to the student rebellion of 1968, life there developed a certain intensity, an air of expectation, even during periods of quiet. At the same time, life also appears to have taken on a kind of calmness, or at least an insouciance, amid destruction and death. It became difficult to tell a crisis from the everyday. Upheaval became a way of life. This is the atmosphere that Victor Hugo captured in *Les Misérables* when he described the events of 1832:

> There is shooting at a crossroads or in a street or alleyway, barricades are besieged, captured and recaptured, houses are pockmarked with bullets, blood flows, corpses litter the pavement — and two streets away one may hear the click of billiard-balls in a cafe. . . . [F]iacres proceed along the street with parties on their way to dine, sometimes in the very quarter where the battle is in progress. In 1831 the firing stopped to allow a wedding to pass.[1]

The universality of Hugo's account is evident from the fact that Gustave Flaubert wrote, in *Sentimental Education*, a nearly identical description of 1848. Flaubert's narrative of the June days has not only the same ping of bullets, streams of blood, and litter of corpses underfoot, but the same curious mixture of hostilities with civility that Hugo saw:

> Fresh bands of people continually came up, pushing on the combatants at the guard-house. The firing became quicker. The wineshops were open; people went into them from time to time to smoke a pipe and drink a glass of beer, and then came back again to fight. A lost dog began to howl. This made the people laugh.[2]

Notice how Flaubert and Hugo even tried to give the same rhythm to events. There is a certain jerkiness in what happened, a distinct lack of transition, which Flaubert's style is better suited to convey. In Hugo's passage, we are aware of the writer writing. He is a rhetorician who builds up the tempo with a grammatical series. In *Sentimental Education*, the language becomes as abrupt as the events. It is as if reality itself had written the passage.

At the heart of Flaubert's novel is a moment when his young hero, Frédéric, awakens to musket fire and goes out into the streets. Events have been set in motion by a disturbance in which the "trees on the boulevards, the urinals, the benches, the gratings, the gasburners, everything was torn off and thrown about." Again the atmosphere is a mélange where all the transitions that give life its natural order have been omitted. As he approaches the thick of the battle, Frédéric comes upon a couple arguing over whether the man should join the fray. Appealing to the crowd because he has participated in so many public disturbances before, the man remonstrates with his wife, saying, "Now they're fighting again! I must fight! Go away!" At last Frédéric himself ascends the barricades, from which he is "fascinated and entertained by the scene around him. . . . The impression left on him was that he was looking on at a show."[3]

Flaubert 's approach is not to characterize events but merely to select them, as a photographer does, so that the event itself implies the interpretation. The history of 1848 is made vivid by an argument between a husband and wife, a domestic squabble carried on in the street. This is what the revolution is: the nation's private disagreements dragged out in public for everyone to see. No wonder Frédéric should feel as if he were "at a show." The theater is where we are used to seeing man's private life publicly displayed.

Public indiscretion continued in the nineteenth century even when civil disorders abated. People threw themselves into their social life with the same abandon with which they had entered into the violence. By the 1830s, according to historian Roger Williams, "the world of pleasure . . . was expanding from salon and boudoir to the boulevard, the racetrack, and the club."[4] A few decades later the diarists the Goncourts, remarking that whole families now went out to the cafés to dine, complained in their journal, "The home is dying. Life is threatening to become public."[5] Under these social conditions, the idea that the street was a theater occurred to many nineteenth-century observers.

Thus the metaphor was far from new when it popped into Frédéric's mind in *Sentimental Education*. But the image was being given a new aptness by the Paris of his day. Napoléon III would want life in his capital to be a grand show, and Baron Haussmann would be his scenic designer. He created a permanent set on which the street theater of Paris could be performed, as it were, in repertory. As architectural historian Norma Evenson said,

> In the years following Haussmann's renovations, the boulevard became the symbol of modern Paris. City life was essentially a public life, and the street was the stage on which the urban drama was played. All the variety and vitality of Paris — its social range, its material abundance, its sense of fashion — seemed to be visible in the streets. To artists the boulevard was an abundantly stimulating subject; probably no other city sat for its portrait as often as the French capital.[6]

In 1858 a journalist named Victor Fournel published a remarkable book, *Ce qu'on voit dans les rues de Paris* (What one sees on the streets of Paris), in which the metaphor of the street as theater was sustained for several hundred pages. To take a walk was to "take my seat in the pit of this improvised theater," Fournel declared. He imagined that everyone he encountered "carries an impression of some sort affixed on his brow, in his bearing and the tone of his voice." From such indications someone's "daily occupation" and "intimate domestic life" could be surmised. Simply by "rubbing shoulders" with people or being able to "catch a glimpse of a profile," Fournel said, "I place in all their breasts [a] window . . . and through the open pane I look into the bottom of each heart with a curious eye."[7]

The playgoer who attended the performance that Fournel was describing was a *flâneur*, a walker in the city. He was a connoisseur of the street, someone with an appreciation for its drama that he expressed through his *flânerie*. Hannah Arendt claimed that *flânerie* was "the nineteenth century's secret style" not only of "walking," but of "thinking." She wrote that "like the dandy and the snob, the *flâneur* had his home in the nineteenth century."[8] Fournel devoted a whole chapter to the subject — "The Art of *Flânerie*" — in which he explained that "the *flâneur* observes and reflects. . . . He is always in full possession of his individuality."[9] He is the boulevardier who sits self-consciously in the café of an afternoon, like Maurice Chevalier in *Gigi.* He is there to be seen as well as to see.

The *theatrum mundi,* the idea that all the world's a stage, had a long tradition. The boulevardier might be thought of as a modern revival of a role that had been created early in the eighteenth century in the *fêtes galantes.* These were outings on which fashionable people, frequently dressed in theatrical costume, would go to the countryside and parade around, admiring one another. Jean-Antoine Watteau's paintings of such occasions are in a sense forerunners of a kind of street photography done two centuries later by Jacques-Henri Lartigue along the smart promenades in the Bois de Boulogne.

The street theater that Fournel described was first envisioned exactly one hundred years before the publication of his 1858 volume, in Jean-Jacques Rousseau's *Letter to d'Alembert.* This treatise on politics and the arts condemned the conventional theater of the eighteenth century, proposing in its place public spectacles where there would be no separation between the stage and the gallery. It was more suitable to a republic, Rousseau felt, to "let the spectators become an entertainment to themselves; make them actors themselves; do it so that each sees and loves himself in the others so that all will be better united."[10] In the aftermath of the French Revolution this scene actually came to pass, much as Rousseau imagined it, when Robespierre produced a festival in which all the citizens of Paris participated.

Taking his place on the stage of the nineteenth century, the *flâneur* played the part that Rousseau had written for him as both actor and audience. He became a bystander of the kind that the chorus had originally been in Greek drama, in the early development of which the spectators and the protagonist were one and the same. Both were embodied by a band of choral dancers who sang and mimed the hero's story for their own edification. In effect, Rousseau had adapted this classical theater to the modern world, in which the primitive and maenadic element was preserved.

If one side of the *flâneur* was the self-possessed Apollonian, the boulevardier, the other side was a more Dionysian sort of character, a *badaud.* No English term renders this French word precisely. A *badaud* is a gawker, a gaper, a rubbernecker. But he is also someone for whom looking becomes participation, a way to be drawn into the scene. Fournel said that in the crowd "the *badaud* disappears, absorbed by the external world which carries him away from himself, which smites him with elation and ecstasy. . . . A nature apart, a naive and ardent spirit, transported by his revery, his passion, his quiet enthusiasm, [he is] by instinct and temperament an artist."[11]

There was in Paris a painter who was the very embodiment of the artist Fournel described: Constantin Guys, "The Painter of Modern Life," as he is referred to in the title of an essay Charles Baudelaire wrote about him. "Observer, philosopher, *flâneur* — call him what you will," Baudelaire wrote of Guys. Then he proceeded to depict the painter in terms that closely resemble Fournel's account of the *badaud.* "The crowd is his element," Baudelaire said, "as the air is that of birds and water of fishes. His passion and his profession are to become one flesh with the crowd. . . . [They are] to see the world, to be at the centre of the world, and yet to remain hidden from the world."[12]

Guys was "a passionate lover of . . . incognitos," according to Baudelaire, who didn't identify the painter by name in his essay. His subject, he said, "carries originality to the point of shyness."[13] Manic shyness and a desire for anonymity are traits typical of street photographers, not only of Eugène Atget and other contemporaries of Guys in the nineteenth century, but of modern figures like Cartier-Bresson and Helen Levitt as well. The street photographer is a kind of Guys with a camera. He is the artist to whom Fournel looked forward, metaphorically speaking, when he at one point dropped his favorite image of the stage to try out a new analogy.

Fournel wrote,

> *An intelligent and conscientious* badaud *who scrupulously does his duty — that is to say, who observes everything and forgets nothing — can play the leading roles in the republic of art. This man is a roving and impassioned daguerreotype that preserves the least traces, and on which are reproduced, with their changing reflections, the course of things, the movement of the city, the multiple physiognomy of the public spirit, the confessions, antipathies and admirations of the crowd.*[14]

The "republic of art" of which Fournel spoke was the one founded by Rousseau, to whom Fournel's phrase seems an intentional allusion. The first citizen of this revolutionary state, which was more a state of being than a political entity, was the nineteenth-century man in the street.

The poet Czeslaw Milosz, who came to live in the French capital after World War II, said he felt that walking there was like breasting waves of sensation that washed over you from the street. He spoke of his "joyous immersion in the reservoir of universal life"; diving into the crowd was like being "a swimmer who trusts himself to the wave, and senses the immensity of the element that surrounds him." This oceanic feeling is the one that Fournel identified with the *badaud* and that Baudelaire associated with Constantin Guys. Milosz found the Paris streets to be an aesthetic experience, one from which he received directly the sort of stimulation we as a rule attribute to art. "The experiences which we clumsily call aesthetic . . . ," he said, "are associated with works of art for only an insignificant number of individuals."[15] In his opinion, life on the street was our mass art.

Milosz's prose echoes that of earlier writers, as if life in the street imposed a particular style on whoever wrote about it. Everything he sees is in "heaps," and the impressions he has of it all get piled on top of each other as well. Sights are covered up with sounds ("snatches of arias, the throbbing of motors . . . the warble of birds, called greetings, laughter"), and sounds are buried under smells ("coffee, gasoline, oranges, ozone, roasting nuts, perfumes"). The aesthetic arising from the street is one of "constant unexpectedness."[16] This makes the prose itself into a jumble; the words have to spill out in a rush to keep pace with their subject. When Flaubert or Hugo describes street fighting, when Baudelaire writes about Guys or Fournel about *flânerie*, the effect is the same.

Like the metaphor of the street as theater, the street scene as endless chance juxtapositions, a cornucopia of imagery, carried over from periods of murder and mayhem into the everyday life of the city. This aesthetic was reflected even in the architecture of nineteenth-century Paris, which displayed an unprecedented eclecticism. The classical tradition with its "abstract perfection of balance, order, and harmony," as Norma Evenson put it, still dominated the city in 1800. "As the century advanced, however," Evenson said, "a series of new major landmarks appeared, almost like human presences: awkward, vulgar, daring, imperfect, and capable of inspiring love."[17] These were the Paris Opera, the Church of Sacré-Coeur, the Trocadero Palace, and, as the century's pièce de résistance, the Eiffel Tower. When scanning the skyline, as when watching humanity parade through the streets, one was struck by the abrupt leaps in style.

New commercial institutions like the tabloid newspaper and the department store contributed to this urban aesthetic too. Both were expressly designed to compel their audience to jump from one subject to another without transition. The dailies put a story of a lurid murder next to one about a statesman concluding a treaty, an account of a debutante ball beside a shipping report, an ad for soap by a dispatch from abroad. Everything was thrown together at random as it was in the street. Department stores were organized — or, rather, disorganized — along similar lines. The jolts as one went from opera glasses or umbrellas to intimate apparel were made that much greater by the breakdown in the distinction between private and public. Stores began featuring display windows in which first merchandise, then mannequins, and eventually whole scenes from domestic life could be set up. When one passed along the street and looked into a drawing room, kitchen, or boudoir, the line between private and public experience began to get hazy.

Historian Rosalind Williams claimed that the "chaotic-exotic style" of decor in department stores was inspired by the success of the panoramas in Paris.[18] These were amusements open to the public in which walk-in stage sets of extraordinary realism, often in three dimensions, re-created famous historical scenes or cities in distant lands. At the frequent expositions held during the nineteenth century, panoramas transported visitors to a series of far-off countries in rapid succession. Only an age conditioned by non sequiturs, by disorienting transitions from one reality to another, could have been entertained by such spectacles. At the Paris Exposition of 1900, almost two thirds of the attractions were panoramic voyages. The most ingenious, a reporter of the day thought, was one in which painted canvas backdrops were replaced by photographs.

One of the most popular panoramas in Paris was a version called the diorama, which opened in 1822 under the management of Louis-Jacques-Mandé Daguerre. The essayist Walter Benjamin said he felt that there was a continuity, aesthetically, between the diorama and the daguerreotype. In an essay entitled "Paris, Capital of the Nineteenth Century" he said,

The panoramas, which declare a revolution in the relation of art to technology, are at the same time an expression of a new feeling about life. . . . In the panoramas the city dilates to become a landscape, as it does in a subtler way for the flâneur. Daguerre is a pupil of the panorama painter Prevost, whose establishment is situated in the Passage des Panoramas. . . . In 1839 Daguerre's panorama burns down. In the same year he announces the invention of the daguerreotype.[19]

Benjamin was one of our most perceptive commentators on photography, although he often approached the medium in an oblique way. His essay "On Some Motifs in Baudelaire" voiced a profound insight into photography's significance when it observed,

The invention of the match around the middle of the nineteenth century brought forth a number of innovations which have one thing in common: one abrupt movement of the hand triggers a process of many steps. . . . Of the countless movements of switching, inserting, pressing, and the like, the "snapping" of the photographer has had the greatest consequences. . . . The camera gave the moment a posthumous shock, as it were. Haptic experiences of this kind were joined by optic ones, such as are supplied by the advertising pages of a newspaper or the traffic of a big city. Moving through this traffic involves the individual in a series of shocks and collisions. . . . Baudelaire speaks of the man who plunges into the crowd as into a reservoir of electric energy. Circumscribing the experience of the shock, he calls this man "a kaleidoscope equipped with consciousness."[20]

Benjamin saw a connection between photography and what might be called the psychoaesthetics of Baudelaire's poetry. In the conclusion to the same essay, he noted that Baudelaire believed his essential formative experience was "having been jostled by the crowd."[21] This was perhaps photography's most important formative experience as well. Pioneers like Charles Nègre were to anticipate the entire range of imagery that street photographs would eventually contain, just as

Baudelaire anticipated the modern sensibility that those images, along with a great deal of other art, would reflect. Baudelaire's was the original split personality. In the midst of the crowd he was, like the *flâneur*, both a euphoric participant and a cold observer. He was our premier poet of alienation; yet chagrin in his work is never far from wild enthusiasm. Bitter irony is close to amusement, and revulsion to wonder.

What makes his voice as a poet the first modern one is this neurotic tone, the sudden shifts of mood it conveys through abrupt juxtapositions of images like those in street photographs. The stimulating ambivalence of his experience in the street, the two-minded edginess of it, was apparent when he proclaimed, "The man who is unable to people his solitude is equally unable to be alone in a bustling crowd." [22] Merely taking a stroll became for him a "divine prostitution of the soul giving itself entire . . . to the unexpected as it comes along, to the stranger as he passes." [23] His work is filled with strangers glimpsed on the street, such as the "lovely fugitive" with whom he has a chance encounter, à la Garry Winogrand, in the poem "In Passing." Because she is a total stranger — "Of me you know nothing, I nothing of you" — the enigmatic woman in this poem is a presence all the more poignant to Baudelaire. [24]

The only creature of the crowd who might prefigure the street photographer better than Baudelaire would be somebody who literally lives his life in the street. Such a character is the urchin Gavroche of *Les Misérables:*

> When it comes to repartee the urchin is as gifted as Talleyrand, no less cynical but more honest. He has a talent for unpredictable mirth. . . . [He] haunts the street corners with his ribaldry, his laughter and his malice, whistles, sings, applauds, derides, finds without seeking, knows what he does not know, is at once a Spartan and a pickpocket, mad to the point of wisdom, lyrical to the point of lewdness, squatting on

> Olympus, wallowing in the mire and emerging decked with stars.

> Paris begins with its strollers and ends with its street-urchins, two species produced by no other town. Passive acceptance content merely to look on, and inexhaustible enterprise; Respectability and Riot. In no other town are these so much a part of the natural scene. All monarchy is in the stroller, all anarchy in the urchin. [25]

Gavroche is killed in the uprising of 1832 while capering in front of one of the barricades. He is truly a child of the century. Only someone born into the Paris produced by the many nineteenth-century aftershocks of the French Revolution could feel completely at home there, as he does. He is at once both boisterous and sneaky, sentimental and alienated. He is a mass of contradictions happily lumped together. Hugo could describe him only in oxymorons, which force our perceptions to leap from each quality to its opposite without transitions, just as life on the street does. Gavroche is an urchin-*flâneur*, a prototype of the street photographer.

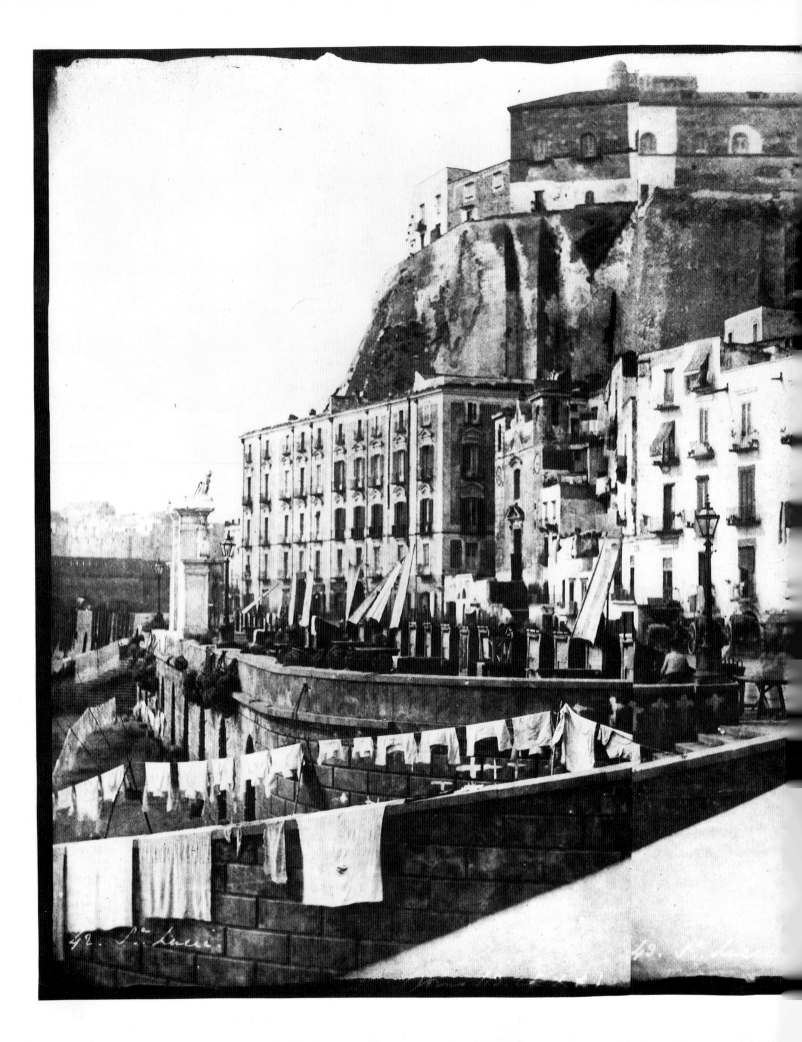

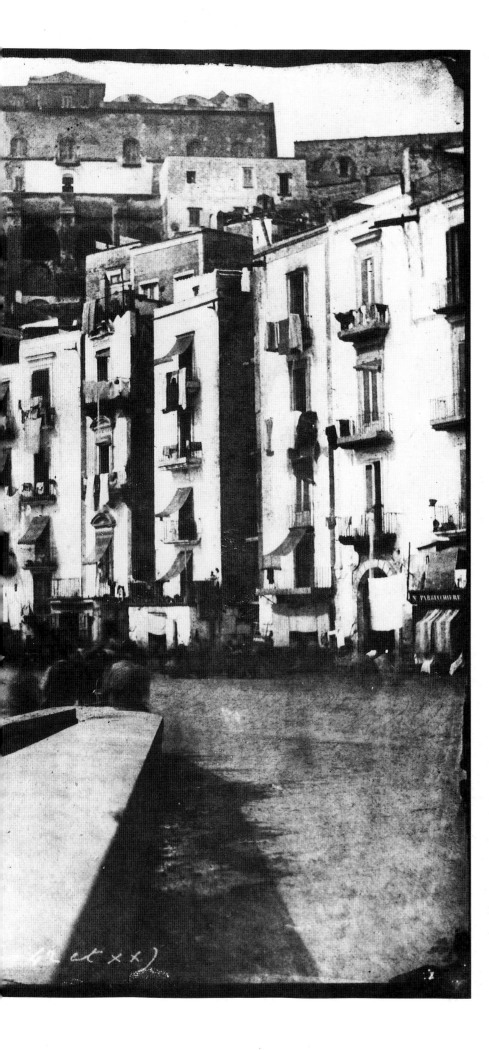

**THE REVEREND
CALVERT JONES**
*Panorama of Santa
Lucia, Naples*, c. 1846

CHARLES NÈGRE
*Market Scene at the
Port de l'Hôtel de Ville,*
1851

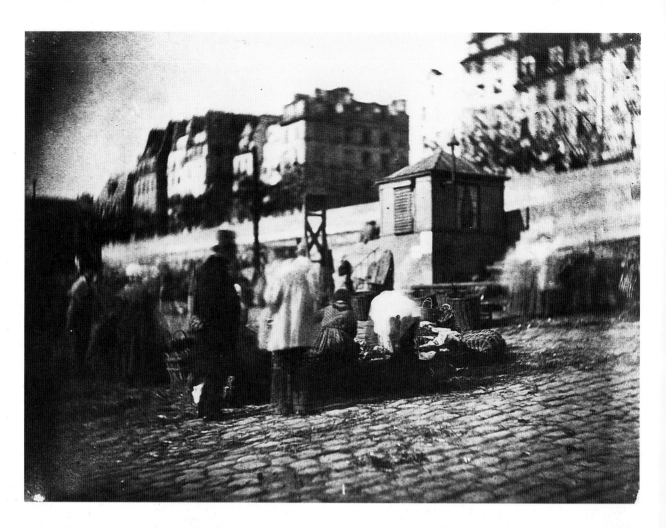

CHARLES NÈGRE
*A Fallen Horse, Quai de
Bourbon,* c. 1855

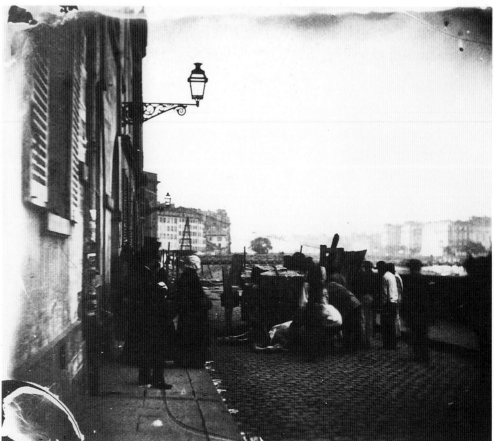

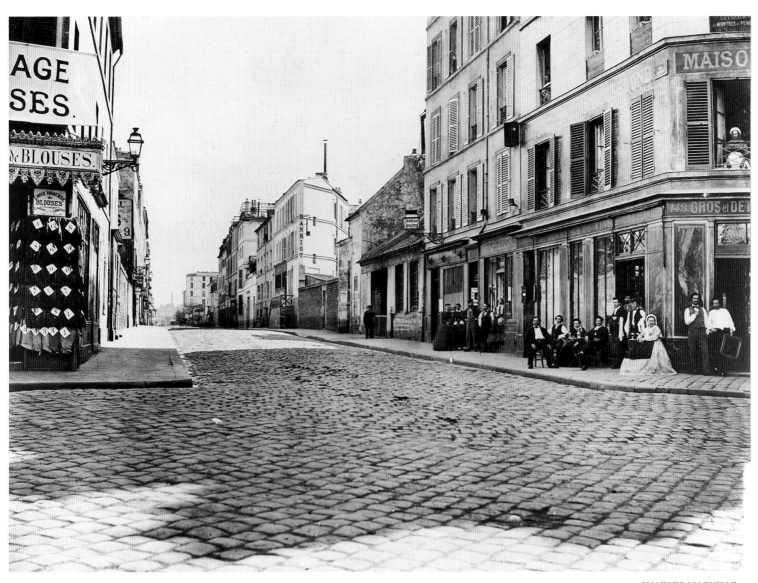

CHARLES MARVILLE
Rue Pascal from Rue
Moufftard, 1865

EUGÈNE ATGET
Rue du Maure, c. 1908

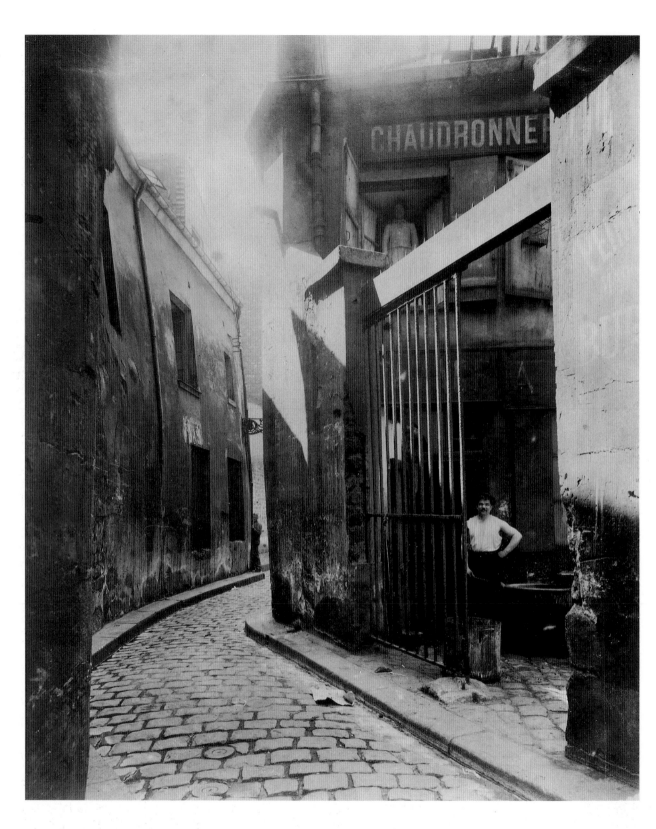

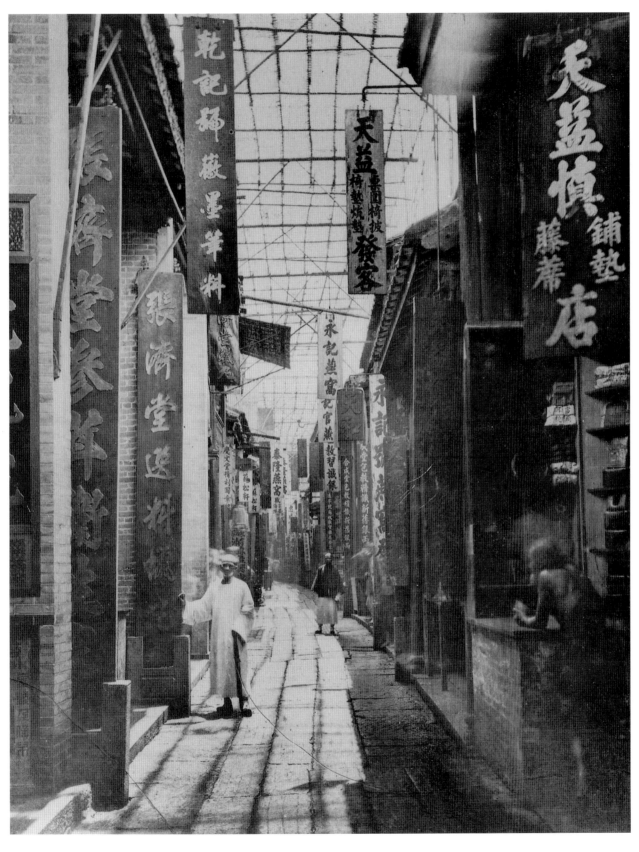

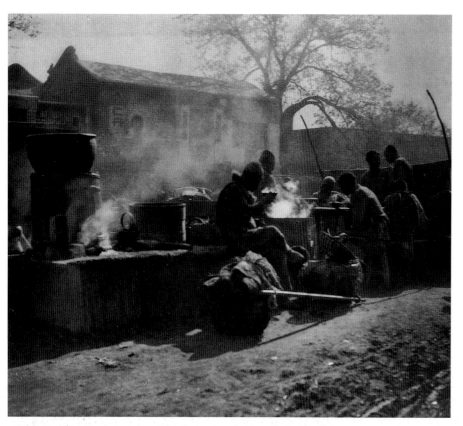

DONALD MENNIE

The Mid-Day Meal,

1920

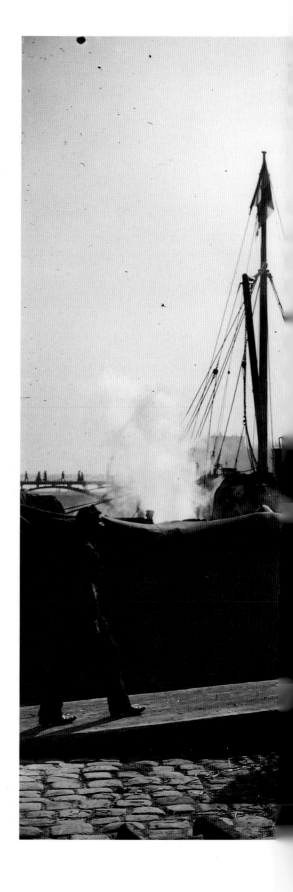

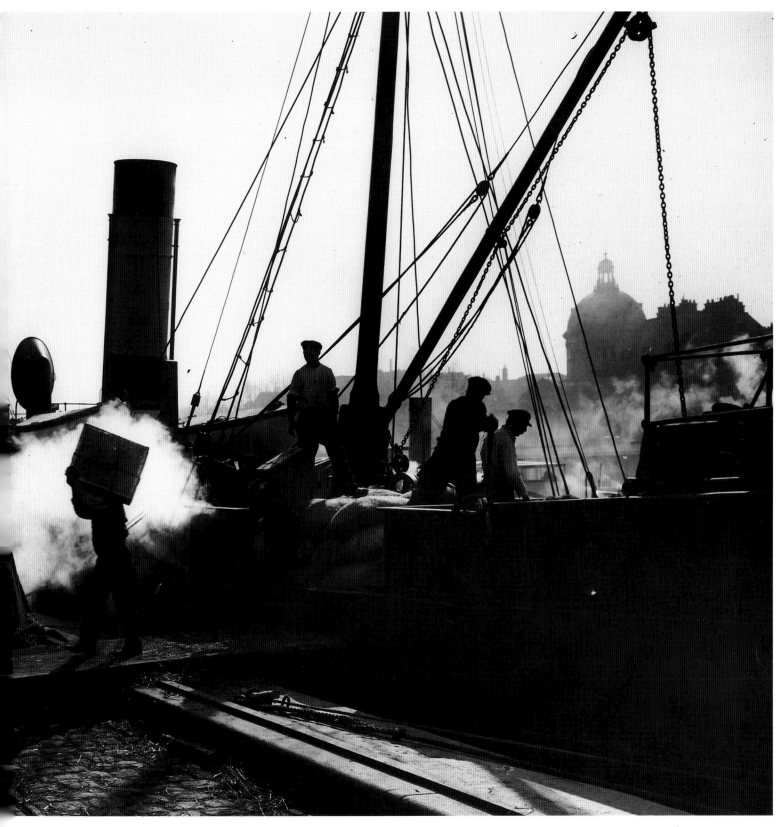

FRÈRES SEEBERGER
Boat Being Unloaded,
Quai de Louvre, n.d.

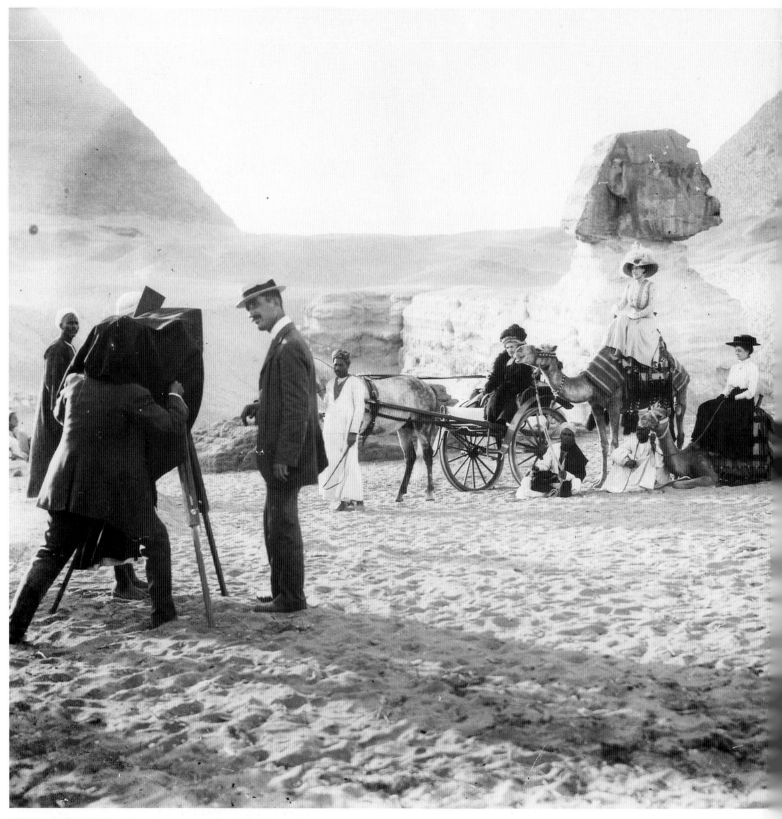

CHUSSEAU FLAVIENS
Untitled, n.d.

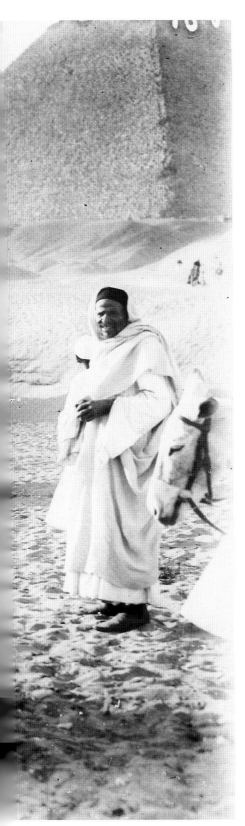

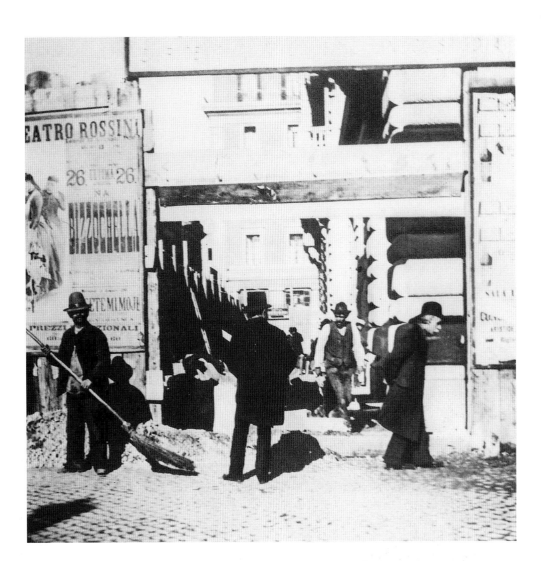

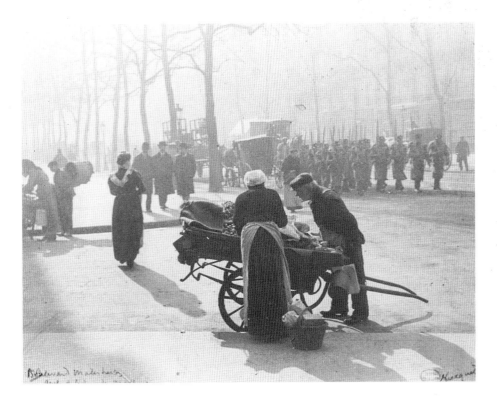

Above right: COUNT
GIUSEPPE PRIMOLI
Rome, 1890

Right: MAURICE
BUCQUET
Untitled, c. 1895

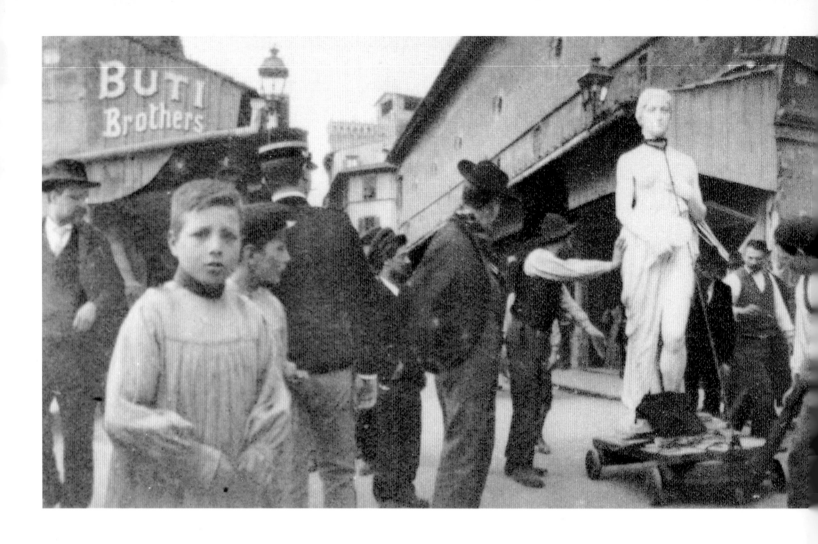

UNKNOWN
PHOTOGRAPHER
Untitled, n.d.

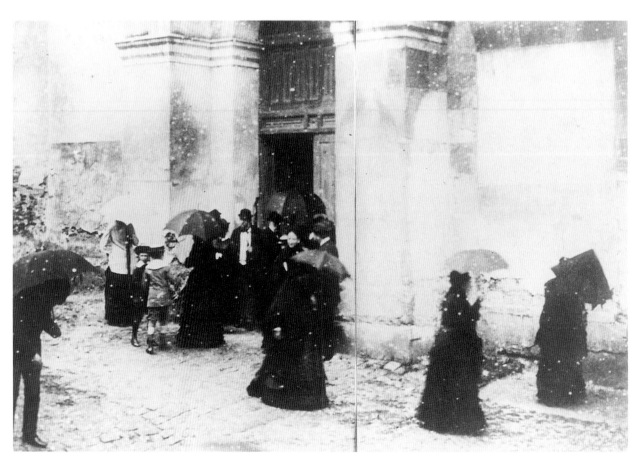

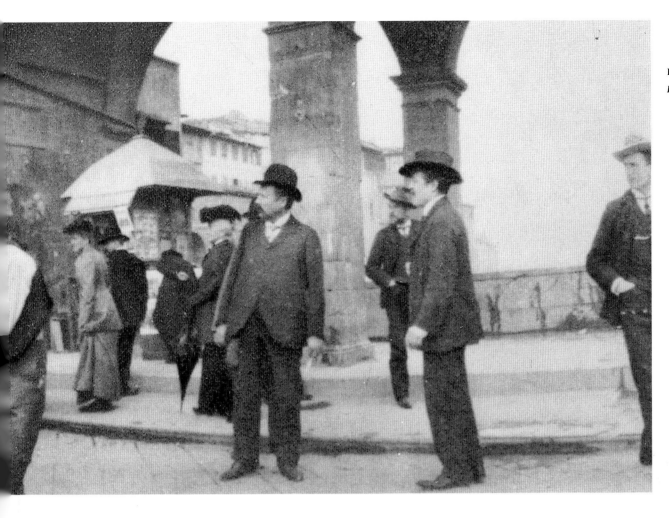

E. J. CONSTANT PUYO
Florence, 1920

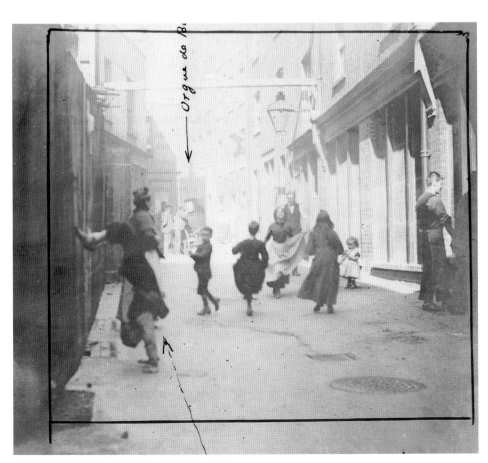

UNKNOWN
PHOTOGRAPHER
(French)
Street Scene, London,
c. 1890

57

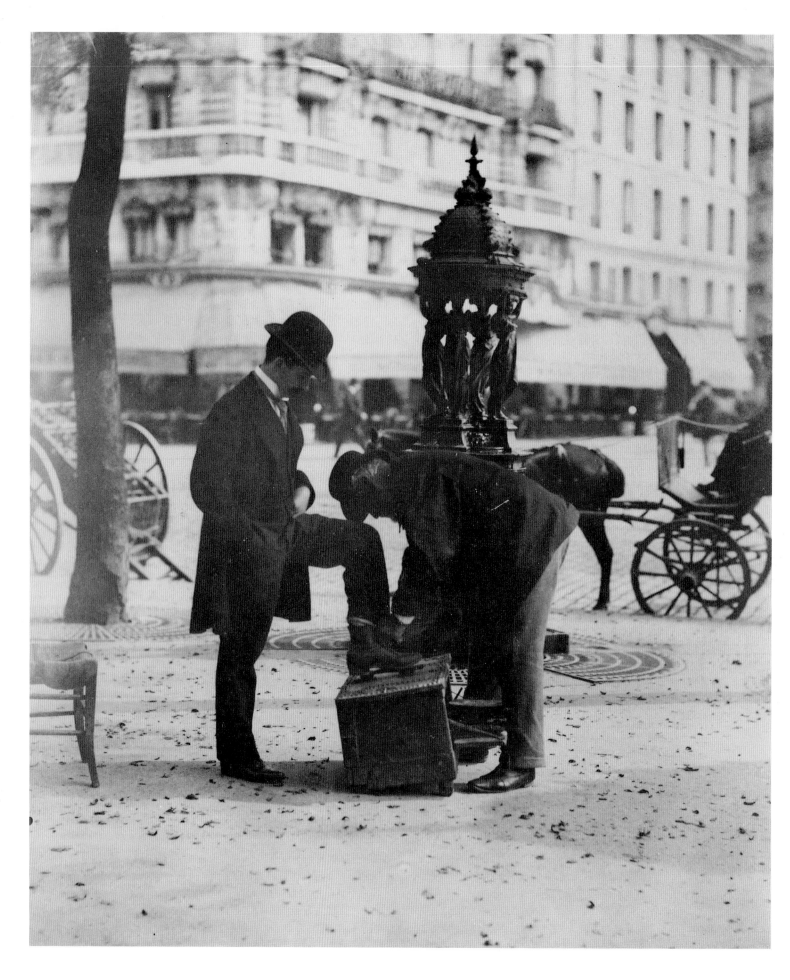

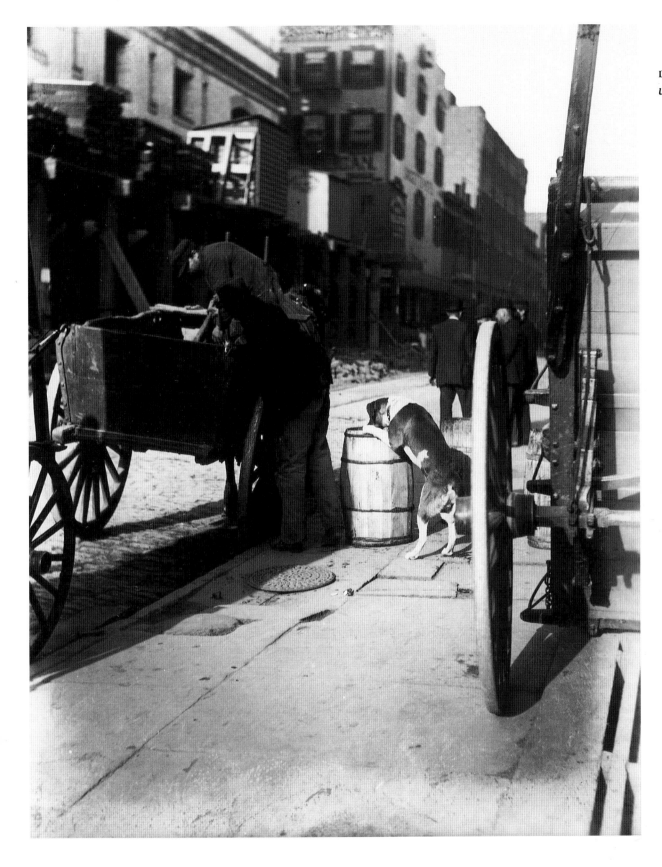

Left: EUGÈNE ATGET
Decroteur, 1899

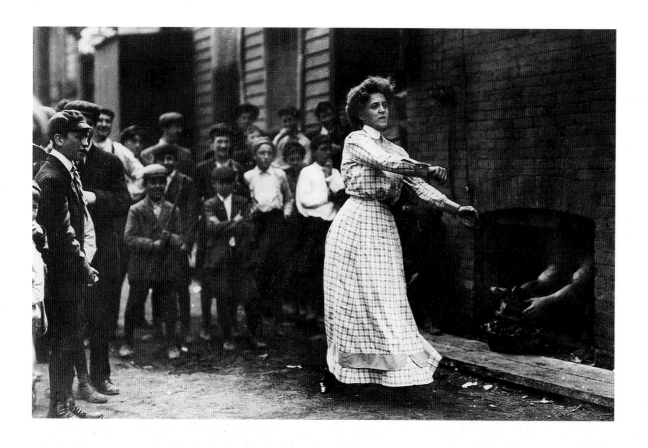

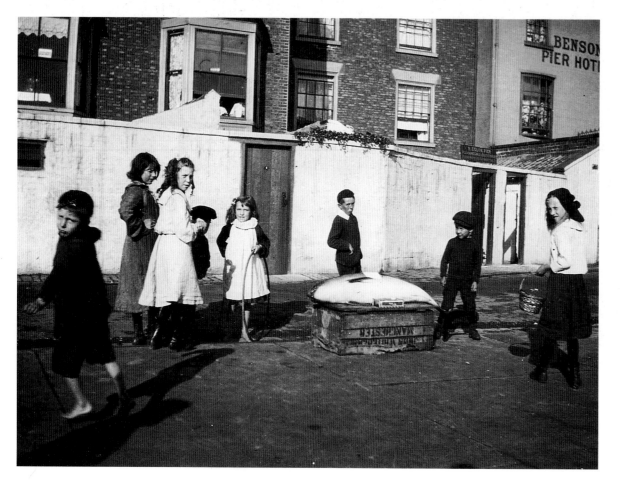

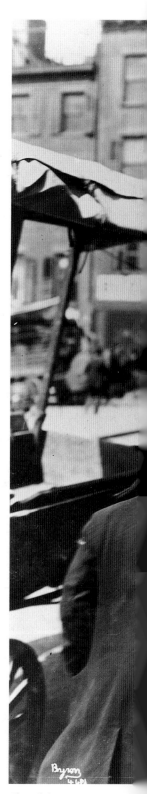

Above left:
J. R. TAYLOR
Milwaukee, c. 1909–10

Left: FRANK
SUTCLIFFE
Untitled, 1905

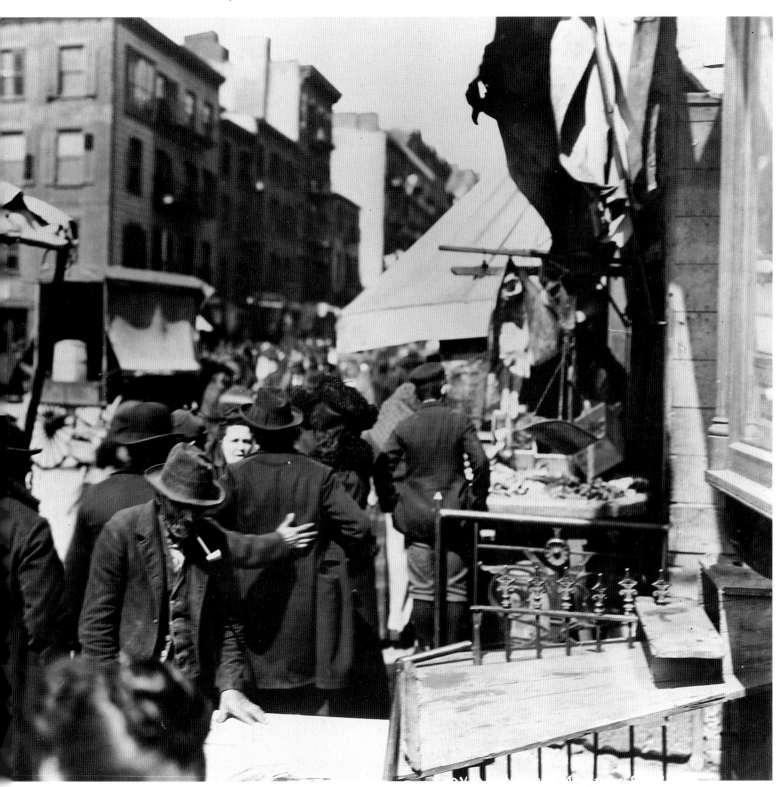

JOSEPH AND PERCY
BYRON
Mulberry Street, 1898

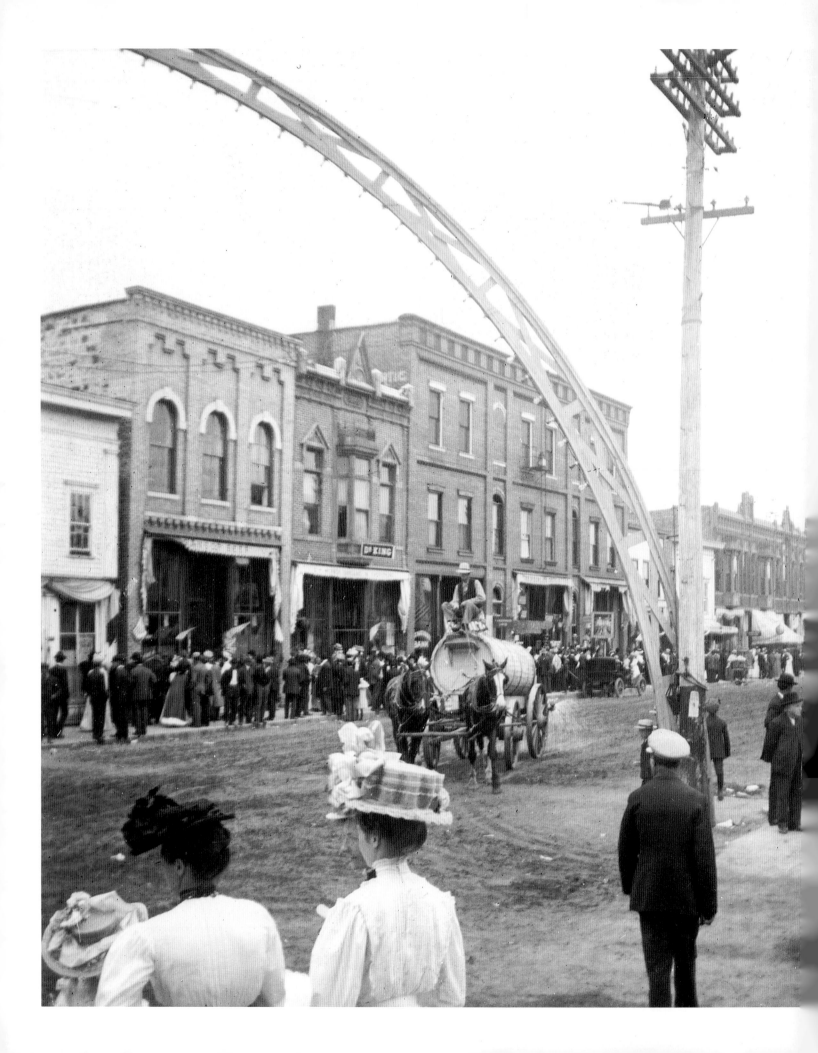

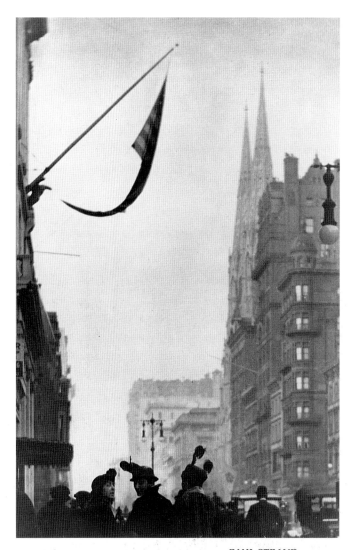

PAUL STRAND
Fifth Avenue, New York,
1915

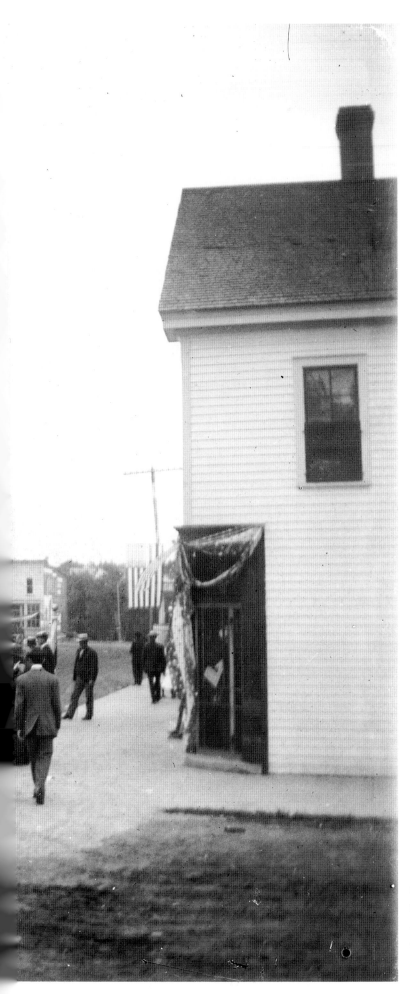

CHARLES J. VAN
SCHAICK
Parade, Black River
Falls, Wisconsin,
1890–1910

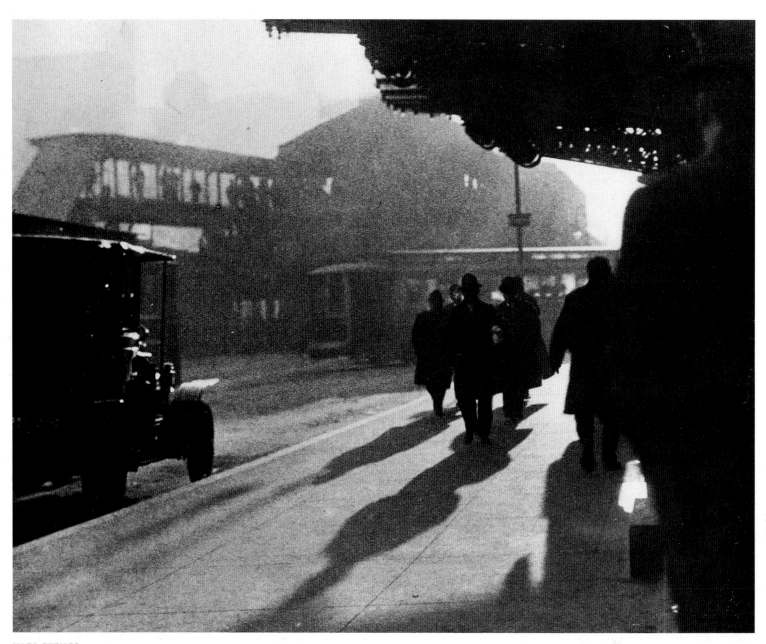

KARL STRUSS
Shadows, New York,
1912

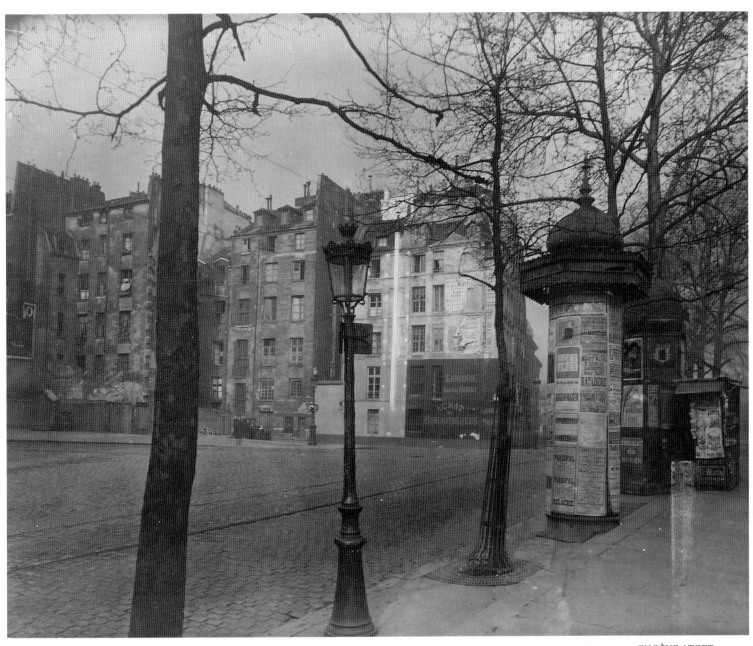

EUGÈNE ATGET
Coin du Quai Voltaire
et Rue de Nevers,
c. 1926

2: In the Beginning

In 1843, four years after announcing his invention of photography, William Henry Fox Talbot went to France to make views of cathedrals. Unlike the daguerreotype, Talbot's process, which was called the calotype, entailed a negative from which multiple prints could be made. An advantage, as he envisioned it, was that photographic sequences could be published as books, and he wanted to do one about French cathedrals in order to demonstrate. Unfortunately, he couldn't obtain some official permissions he needed and ended up trying to think of something else to photograph to make the trip worthwhile. From Orléans, he reported in a letter that he was "looking for views . . . rambling about the streets unknown to me."[1] Working under such circumstances didn't suit Talbot's temperament. When the cathedral project failed, he decided to base the book he had planned on views of his ancestral home, in Wiltshire, England. Thus did *The Pencil of Nature* come to be about life at Lacock Abbey.

In his commentary on the scenes done there, he explained the need for "artistically arranged" group shots. "If we proceed to the City, and attempt to take a picture of the moving multitude, we fail," he warned, "for in a single fraction of a second they change their positions so much, as to destroy the distinctness of the representation."[2] Other users of Talbot's invention proved less punctilious, however, including the one who made a view titled *Strada Levante* in some Mediterranean city during the 1840s (fig. 2.1). This image succeeds by virtue of the very imperfections Talbot abjured. Even the position its maker took at the foot of this stepped street crowded with pedestrians suggests that what appealed to him was the fluidity of the scene, the way that this stream of people would over-

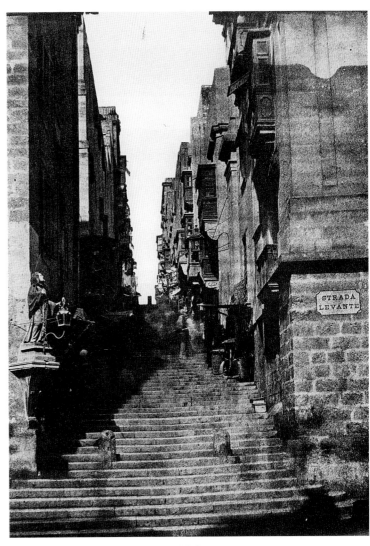

flow the negative's capacity to hold them in place.

The symmetry and balance Talbot looked for in a photographic composition are not lacking in this one; they have simply been reinvented out of unlikely, unstable materials. They exist in the two kinds of shadow the photograph juxtaposes — that which sunlight casts on the scene, and that which passersby cast on the calotype negative. Both are lucid, transparent. They are also reciprocal, like positive and

Fig. 2.1
UNKNOWN
PHOTOGRAPHER
(British School)
Strada Levante, 1840s

negative. In the sunshine the passersby are dark wisps against the light; in the shadow they are light against the dark. The only still, distinct figure is a statue of a monk who holds out a lamp as if in mockery of the photographer with his camera.

The identity of the calotypists who made such early images is often as ephemeral and uncertain as the prints themselves. The likelihood is that the maker of this one was somebody trained by Talbot. The picture was for years attributed to the Reverend Calvert Jones, a close personal friend of Talbot's who took one of the inventor's cameras with him on a tour of Italy and Malta three years after Talbot's own trip to France (pages 46–47). Another provocative calotype long thought to be by Jones is now suspected to be the work of Talbot's cousin Christopher, known in the family circle as Kit, who was traveling with Jones on his Mediterranean tour.

This is an image entitled *Villa Reale, Naples,* in which a little girl in a dark dress stands before the white pedestal of a statue (page 12). The statue is poised and powerful in its nudity, the little girl tentative in her loose, clumsy pinafore, her head enveloped in a great dark shock of hair. Just as she is overpowered by the statue, so is it overpowered by the amorphous, brilliant shape of the light bursting through the trees. This is an image that Henri Cartier-Bresson could have made.

The power that early street photographs like these have for us is of a very elemental type. It lies in the starkness of the contrast the calotype creates between dark and light. There was in the pure chiaroscuro of this process a simplicity that seems appropriate to the beginning of something. These first photographs were truly proto-images, pictures so basic that they made the enormous potential of the medium obvious right from the start. When we look at them today, part of the excitement we feel is that we can see in them the infinite possibilities the future held for photography.

These images aren't crude. They're fundamental, inchoate. They are a first, rough sketch of a picture that it would take time to realize fully.

Jones and Kit Talbot weren't the only practitioners in Talbot's own circle who were experimenting with the new medium. The Reverend George Bridges spent six years traveling around the Mediterranean and returned with seventeen hundred negatives. But the one other early photographer to see fully the potential of life on the street as a subject was a French painter, Charles Nègre, who took up the camera around 1850. Coming as he did at the very beginning of photography, Nègre had a career that seems to have prefigured everyone else's. He anticipated Eugène Atget by doing a series on street trades — the licorice-water vendor, chimney sweeps, musicians in Gypsy costume — and by devoting his energy to architectural photography. At the same time, he was much preoccupied with the photographic problem of stopping action, which was to be central to the work of successors like Cartier-Bresson.

As new a medium as photography was, there were already a great many conventions about how to use it by the time Nègre began. What made him prescient was his unorthodoxy. Then as later, for example, most of those working in the field of architectural photography tried to make each building sit among its shadows like a jewel being displayed on a black velvet cushion. In Nègre's pictures, as in Atget's later, the shadows tend to fall on the building rather than from it.

There was a standard procedure at the time for avoiding just the sort of shadow effects Nègre liked. It was spelled out in a how-to book by the Lille, France, photographic publisher Louis-Désiré Blanquart-Evrard. The idea was to homogenize the light and show up detail on the facade by alternating clouds with sunshine in a single exposure (the lens was to be capped while waiting for the one condition to replace the other). When Nègre photo-

Fig. 2.2
CHARLES NÈGRE
Chartres Cathedral,
1851

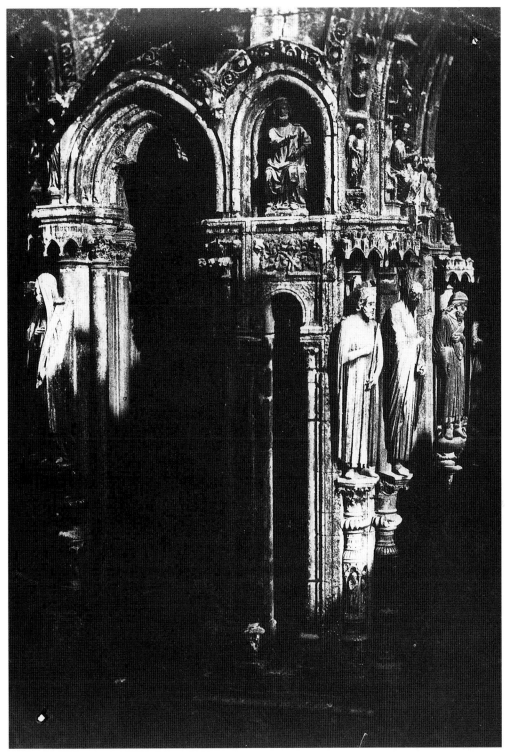

graphed a stock subject such as a porch on Chartres Cathedral, he ignored such advice in order to construct out of the shadows a cathedral all his own (fig. 2.2).

His attempts at action photography on the street were equally adventurous. Some of his calotypes do fail because, as Talbot predicted, motion blur made the negatives murky and unfathomable. But Nègre soon began devising ways to gain speed, first by designing a faster combination of lenses, then by experimenting with the new photographic technology of the stereograph. The latter enabled him to capture

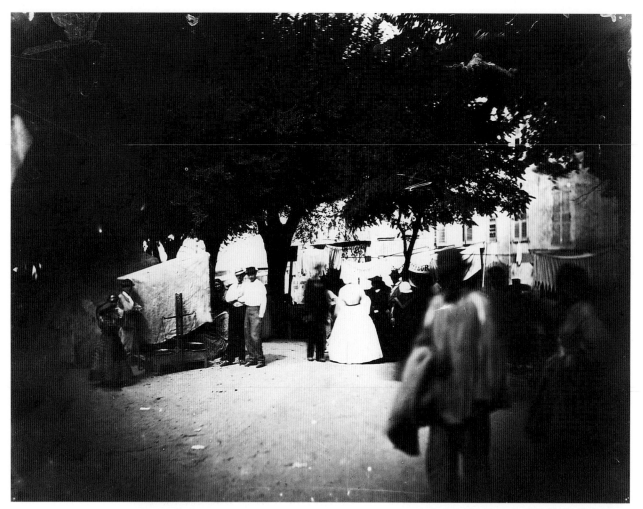

Fig. 2.3
CHARLES NÈGRE
Grasse, Place aux Aires,
c. 1852–53

spontaneous events, like a horse fallen in the street in front of his studio (page 48, bottom).

He tried the collodion wet-plate process too as soon as it was available, even though it was a step backward so far as speed was concerned. In a photograph of strollers in the Place aux Aires in Grasse, one of those accidents occurs — a shadowy man appears at the edge of a frame centered on a woman in white — that street photographers in every age have found instructive (fig. 2.3). The inclusion in the foreground of this hulking, poorly fixed figure, his dark mass offset by the brightness of the woman in the distance, makes the whole frame active and dynamic.

All of Nègre's experiments were prescient in some way or other, but none more so than one of the first photographic series he did, a set of calotypes of open-air markets along the Seine, in Paris (page 48, top). How inspiring he himself found them as an artist is obvious from the use to which he put some of them. The composition from one salt-paper print was rendered over as a sketch in oil, perhaps in preparation for a painting that he exhibited in the Salon of 1850. Other works that Nègre placed in subsequent Salons were actually painted *on* prints of his street photographs. The history of photography and the history of painting literally came into contact in his work.

One reason Talbot had gone to France in 1843 was that he thought his process would appeal to French artists. The use that Nègre was to make of it proved he was right, as did the success of the first volume issued by the calotype printing house Blanquart-Evrard set up in 1851. It was entitled *A Photo-*

graphic Album for the Artist and the Amateur.
As Talbot had correctly surmised, the calotype was to be useful to artists as a cheap, fast way to take visual notes, a mechanical étude, or study, from nature.

Its appeal was not only that it was a substitute for a sketch, however, but that it also looked like one. When Nègre painted directly on a photograph, he was using the print as another type of sketch, an *ebauche*, which was a preliminary rendering of the whole composition of a painting done in oils right on the canvas. This blocking out of the subject was a kind of underpainting executed in broad areas, often in monochrome. It therefore resembled paper negative photography, as the critic Francis Wey pointed out in an article about Nègre's work in 1851.

At that particular moment in the history of painting, the use of the *ebauche* was not just a technical matter. It posed an aesthetic problem that had been growing in painting since William Turner and the Romantics and was now influencing the use of the calotype as well. Nègre had studied at the studio of Paul Delaroche, into whose instruction certain Romantic precepts were incorporated. One of these was the "theory of sacrifices," the idea that detail should be suppressed in a painting. This resulted in a somewhat sketchy look that the calotype, fortuitously, imitated.

Another of Delaroche's students, Gustave Le Gray, published a work adapting this theory to photography, and Eugène Delacroix said that he preferred photography "in which the imperfection of the process itself . . . allows certain gaps, certain resting places for the eye."[3] Baudelaire was also, in his art criticism, an ardent champion of this kind of rendering. He offered a rationale for it in his essay about Constantin Guys, whose sketches of street life in Paris were done at the same time Nègre was making calotypes there. Baudelaire asserted that "in trivial life, in the daily metamorphosis of external things, there is a rapidity of movement which calls for an equal speed of execution from the artist."[4]

The need for a hasty working up of certain types of subjects was reinforced by the esteem in which such subjects were held in art, and this too rubbed off on the street photography of the time. Like Frank Sutcliffe, Alfred Stieglitz, and others later, photographers at the beginning of the medium's history sought mostly humble people as subjects. Talbot depicted various rustics who worked on his estate. Nègre photographed country millers, common laborers, itinerant peddlers, and musicians — colorful street types. The Scottish portraitists David Octavius Hill and Robert Adamson put out an 1846 album, *A Series of Calotype Views of St. Andrews*, that is a study of life in a fishing village. Like much contemporary work of this type, it is a collection of street portraits and group shots posed to look candid.

From Romanticism through Realism, in spite of whatever aesthetic conflicts may have existed between these movements, a taste for this kind of subject remained a constant of nineteenth-century art. Unlettered, uncomplicated people were felt to preserve an otherwise lost capacity for sincerity for which modern artists and intellectuals yearned. In his review of the Salon of 1846, Baudelaire argued that what makes an artist great is "the sincere expression of his temperament."[5] To this quality Baudelaire applied the term "naïveté," and he declared that the foremost artists of the day, such as Delacroix, were those who combined naïveté with Romanticism.

The supposed authenticity of the feelings of plain people made them an alter ego for Romantic poets and painters, who aimed at a comparable honesty in their art. The artist believed he must find new ways to use his medium so that it would enable him to have the sincerity of expression, the genuine life of passion and suffering, that his subjects represented to him. Their moral character had its equivalent, its affirmation, in the guilelessness with which he chose his words or laid down his pigments. In other words, there was in Romantic art a connection between the content and the style. Because the calotype's surface seemed to mirror the latter, it was inevitably made to reflect the former as well.

The quest for sincerity resulted in, among other things, a faith in spontaneity. Only spontaneous emotions free from second thoughts could be sincere. In his piece on the 1859 Salon, Baudelaire was still pursuing the ideas that had occurred to him more than a decade earlier. He was regretting the absence of naïveté in the public when he criticized its insensitivity to the new art. "The people are never . . . spontaneously artists," he said. "They feel, or rather they judge, in stages, analytically. Other more fortunate peoples feel immediately, all at once, synthetically." [6]

In paintings such as those by Gustave Courbet, the Realists, whom Baudelaire despised, demythicized the sort of subjects that the Romantics extolled. Nonetheless, according to art historian Linda Nochlin, the Realists also made sincerity their watchword and equated it with "spontaneous vision." [7] They pushed the sincere and the spontaneous, the immediate response, a step further by insisting on contemporaneity as well. Wishing to disabuse themselves of the sentimentality of nostalgia, the mooning over some golden past, into which they felt the Romantics fell, Realists like Courbet took for their motto Honoré Daumier's dictum about the need to be of one's own time.

And in the end this train of thought led to both Claude Monet's inspired, intuitive way of capturing light and Vincent van Gogh's impassioned Post-Impressionism, as well as to a conclusion that brings us back, once again, to the topic of street photography. For if sincerity led to spontaneity and contemporaneity in art, the latter led, in turn, to a desire for instantaneity. Nochlin summed up the case when she said that Monet's painting was " 'contemporaneity' taken to its ultimate limits." His attempts to render the most transient effects of light were "contemporaneity grasped on the wing as instantaneity." [8]

The promise of an instant image that even the earliest, slowest cameras held out invited photographers to use them in a spontaneous way, to react to certain subjects intuitively, as Monet did to light. The importance that the glimpsed truth suggested by such photographs had can be seen most clearly in the paintings of Edgar Degas or Gustave Caillebotte. Where Monet addressed the issue of instantaneity of vision in one way, through a painterly technique, Degas addressed it in another, through composition. His paintings exploit the illusion of a view that is simply given, like that in a photograph, rather than selected or constructed by the artist. Sir Kenneth Clark believed that Degas "found in snapshots . . . a new basis of style," [9] and Paul Valéry said, in a memoir of Degas, that in his work "the instantaneous [is] given enduring quality by the patience of intense meditation." [10]

Thus did street photography come into existence at a time when issues that it addressed by its very nature were among the most crucial facing the visual arts in general. No images are more rigorously bound to both the contemporary moment and instantaneous vision than photographs are, and street photographs most of all. As a consequence, such pictures had a kind of presence, or what might even be thought of as a valence, that allowed them both to contribute to and be influenced by some of the most important cultural developments of the period. Street photographs had in the earliest stages of photographic history a significance that reached beyond photography alone.

3: The View from Abroad

The little proto-cameras that William Henry Fox Talbot had constructed in the early days were referred to by his wife as "mouse-traps."[1] This wonderful name suggests not only the darting elusiveness of the photographic image itself and the trickiness of its capture, but the size and nature of the camera. It was an instrument of roughly the same dimensions as the Brownie, and not until the first Kodaks came onto the market in the late 1880s, or (in a more sophisticated vein) until the Leica did in the mid-1920s, would photography recover the easy portability that such early cameras seemed to promise.

The reason cameras quickly became larger and glass replaced paper as the base for negatives was that these changes improved the sharpness and resolution of photographs. A price that had to be paid for the gain, however, was in the spontaneity with which the medium could be used. For the collodion process that supplanted the paper negative in the 1850s was wet-plate photography, in which the glass plate had to be prepared just before the picture was taken, so that it could be placed in the camera wet, and then developed before it dried as soon as the exposure was made.

This procedure was so arduous and esoteric that photography became almost exclusively the province of professionals. This too was a change. As mentioned in the previous chapter, Blanquart-Evrard called his first publication *A Photographic Album for the Artist and the Amateur,* a title that indicates the extent to which the medium had at first been taken up as an avocation. But in this second phase of photography's history, the artists and amateurs were both superseded by a very different kind of practitioner, who, whether he worked out of a Paris or London studio or traveled in exotic foreign lands, made photography his business. Typical of the period would be Scot-tish photographer John Thomson, who published several travel books as well as, in 1877, *Street Life in London,* the first book ever devoted exclusively to street photography.

Because collodion emphasized sharpness at the expense of other qualities, such as the speed of both the preparations and the emulsion itself, it encouraged photographers like Thomson to pose human subjects meticulously and bring them to strict attention during long exposure times. That may seem a terrible limitation to us, but Thomson's pictures suggest that it was not an entirely un-

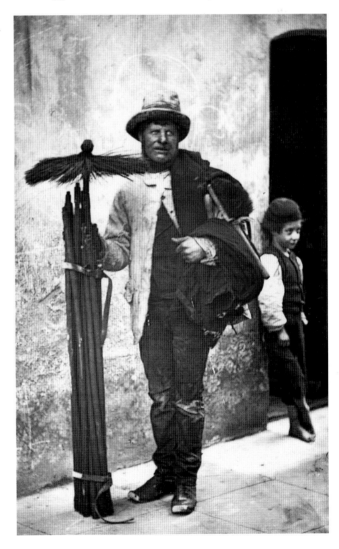

Fig. 3.1

JOHN THOMSON

Temperance Sweep,

1877–78

welcome one to him. Spontaneity was not a character trait highly prized by the Victorians, since theirs was an era when the pendulum swung back from the impetuousness of the Romantics. The ideal to which Thomson's street photography aspired was less the candid observation of life than the observance of proprieties.

A picture of a chimney sweep typifies the book (fig. 3.1). Before a social better like Thomson, the sweep may have felt uneasy. His discomfort can be seen in his posture and in the expression on his face. Both betray a tension to which the bristles on his broom give visible, almost comical form, like a fright wig. The cartoon halo graffitied on the wall behind him is another potentially comic detail; it beatifies the sweep, despite the infernal appearance that his sootiness gives him. Yet amusement was not what Thomson hoped to evoke from the viewer so much as piety before the simple innocence of this subject.

The audience for whom this photograph was made would have seen in the sweep's upright posture a moral rectitude. The image of the working poor as martyrs to their humble professions, sinners whose only road to salvation lay through hard work, was something to be viewed in deadly earnest. Photographs like this are a Victorian rhetoric for the eye, a mute homily. Elsewhere in *Street Life*, when Thomson involved more figures in the picture, he would work it up into a little scene. Now it became a vignette from a familiar melodrama, or a *tableau vivant*.

In the England of that time, in the parlors that picture books like Thomson's graced, tableaux were a popular home entertainment. These still scenes with live actors, often in costume, were a form of suspended animation like a photograph. The events depicted were as a rule moments from myth or history. Although the scenes in *Street Life* are just the opposite — nameless events without consequence — they take on the atmosphere of tableaux. It is as if everyday life also had great import and were charged with scarcely hidden meaning. Like a historic moment in a tableau, the street scenes in Thomson's book illustrate the moral order of the universe.

The formal self-consciousness with which his subjects stood for their portraits, the glowering earnestness with which they acted out the parts assigned to them, were common in the London photography of the day that dealt with ordinary life. The precedent that a book like Thomson's was following had been set a quarter of a century earlier by Henry Mayhew's *London Labour and the London Poor*. In the preface to *Street Life*, Thomson and his coauthor, Adolphe Smith, sought to identify their work with Mayhew's, which had been instrumental in the passage of the Second Reform Bill, in 1867. Mayhew had enhanced his text with illustrations based on daguerreotypes that portraitist Richard Beard made of street characters in his studio. In adapting these figures, the illustrator added whatever background he thought suitable.

Even O. G. Rejlander, a Pictorialist known for prints from multiple negatives, brought the street into the studio. To give a scene of urchins at play at least a semblance of instantaneity, he suspended a chestnut from a thread as if it had been tossed into the air. The enormous popularity of views such as these, the way in which they defined the genre of scenes from everyday life, made them examples that it would have been hard for Thomson to ignore even if he had wanted to.

Yet there were limits to the Victorian tolerance for staged reality, as the case of a man named Dr. Barnardo demonstrated. As advertisements for the East End Juvenile Mission, which he operated, Barnardo and his wife set up scenes for a photographer before a painted backdrop of the street. Sometimes the subject was an urchin in rags; at other times, before-and-after sequences were done to show how, under the mission's care, a child "once a little vagrant" was "now a little workman."[2]

The hitch was that the subject's real story was not always as represented. Barnardo had used one model, a girl who looked much younger than she was, in a variety of situations — first as a crossing sweeper, then a little match girl, et cetera. In 1876, he was accused of fraud and forced to submit to a public inquiry. His defense was that it was technically impossible to get photographs of the actual state in which his charges were found. This argument was disallowed by the tribunal, which held that his "artistic fictions" involved deception. The implications of the controversy could hardly have been lost on Thomson, since he was at the time taking the photographs for *Street Life*.

If you look back at Thomson's portrait of the chimney sweep once more, you'll notice that there is a second figure in it whose bearing and demeanor seem quite different from the sweep's: a little urchin who slouches against the doorjamb near the edge of the frame. Although he is a peripheral and gratuitous figure, his attitude is an arresting one. It has an insouciance, perhaps even a hint of insolence, that is very suggestive. His presence raises the question of whether Thomson didn't long for, or at least feel compelled to find, chances to make pictures that were more improvised and candid in nature.

He had actually had to do so, whether he at first liked it or not, during his travels overseas. The stay in London was sandwiched between two of these expeditions, each of which produced a book: the four-volume *Illustrations of China and Its People* (1873), whose publication he had returned home to supervise, and *Through Cyprus with the Camera*, done two years after *Street Life*. The London work was an extension of what he had done abroad, very much a part of the same career. The preconceptions, the social values, and the Victorian attitudes he brought to *Street Life* were all baggage he had carried with him to China and back. Yet in China, there had also been times when his travels to the far borders of the empire had taken him to the outer limits of his own Victorianism — times when he had gotten into unknown territory photographically as well as geographically.

In Asia, as in London, the custom was to stage the street photography in a studio. Sometimes a backdrop was employed with straw or dirt strewn on the floor to simulate a street. At other times a familiar sight — passengers being trotted along in a rickshaw, for instance — was acted out against bare walls. F. Saunders and L. F. Fisler, two photographers who worked independently in Shanghai from the mid-1860s until the mid-1880s, both did street scenes this way. So did Baron von Stillfried and his native protégé, Kusakabe Kimbei, in Japan. The most intricate facsimile of outdoor scenes was attempted by a member of the Bombay Civil Service named William Johnson. For an 1863 volume called *The Oriental Races and Tribes*, he photographed groups of figures in a studio and then inserted them into appropriate backgrounds by a crude form of photomontage.

Among the China hands, only two besides Thomson actually photographed in the streets. One was Emil Rusefeldt, who acquired Thomson's stock of negatives when he became proprietor of the Hong Kong Photographic Rooms in 1872. The other was Donald Mennie, who made his living in the import-export business and took pictures only for pleasure. Mennie didn't arrive until the end of the century, when the ambition and confidence that Thomson's generation had brought to China were beginning to fade. It was becoming apparent that the sun might set on the British Empire after all, a possibility that Mennie's photographs, frequently shot at twilight in an atmosphere saturated with smoke and dust, seem to reflect (page 52). These effects create in Mennie's 1920 *Pageant of Peking* a mood of fin de siècle weariness seen in a lot of contemporary Pictorialism.

But Mennie lived in an unquestionably different age from that of Thomson, who died in London, following a long retirement, the year after Mennie's book was published. As photographic historian Robert Sobieszek has pointed out, "The second half of the nineteenth century was a period of compendia, concordances, encyclopedia and taxonomic analyses. . . . Photography was a perfect adjunct tool for this Aristotelean materialism."[3] The new world order that imperial nations like England were trying to foster manifested itself in this compulsion for orderliness. It was one of the ways that Victorians hoped to keep up with their rapidly expanding world — by making lists of everything in it, on the theory that a well-kept inventory would help stave off confusion. This ceaseless cataloguing and classifying included the work done by travel photographers like Thomson.

It was to order the world the way his audience wanted that Thomson posed the street scenes he photographed. The same purpose can be heard in the tone that he and other British travel photographers took toward their adventures. The trick is to remain calm in the face of danger, their narratives keep saying, as Francis Frith did while crossing a treacherous breakwater into the mouth of the Nile. "Our Arab dragoman wrings his hands and weeps," Frith wrote, "but you and I and our English sailor are as cool and collected as if nothing were amiss."[4]

Like the fixed poses of the subjects in many photographs, this pose of unflappability made the world seem manageable. Thomson struck the same note in describing an incident in a village where his boat put in during his ascent of the Yangtze River. When he went ashore to make a photograph, the local Chinese, "who had never seen such devilry as manufacturing pictures without a pencil," greeted him with a hail of stones and blows. But he took it in stride: "we quietly secured the photograph, pocketed the insult and decamped," *Illustrations of China and Its People* reports.[5]

To our ears, the lack of concern Thomson and Frith showed is condescending. It borders on smugness. But to their original readers it displayed that most Victorian of all virtues, imperturbability. This was what was needed to keep the world in order, or to impose order on it, as a photograph of a carefully arranged street scene could do. But there were limits to this philosophy. In a sense, both the movement for reform of the franchise in England and the effort to learn about other cultures abroad, like that of China, had in them the same message, which was that everybody was now entitled to have his say. *Street Life* put this message into literal practice by including lengthy quotations from the photographs' subjects, "written down," a footnote informs us, "as they were uttered."[6] Genuine inquisitiveness, a desire truly to confront the newfound otherness and differences the world contained, always vied with the preconceptions to which Victorians made their experiences conform. This was the case where photography was concerned too.

That photographers sometimes wanted a more naturalistic effect in their photographs is apparent from the bitterness with which they complained about their inability to get it. "Only point a camera at a native," wrote an amateur in the *British Journal of Photography* in 1865, "and notwithstanding his natural grace, suppleness of limb and easy carriage and bearing when taken unawares . . . he becomes on seeing you as *rigid* as the camera-stand." Samuel Bourne echoed these remarks from India. Speaking of his own difficulties with native subjects, he lamented, "Their idea of giving life to a picture was to stand bolt upright, with their arms down stiff as pokers, their chins turned up as if they were standing to have their throats cut."[7] This self-sacrificial posture is found in street views ranging from those James Robertson made in Constantinople in the mid-1850s to the first plate of Thomson's *Illustrations*.

The exasperation that can be heard in these photographers' remarks resulted from the contradiction inherent in what they were trying to do, which was to bully or finagle their subjects into behaving naturally. The attempt to elicit authentic behavior by such manipulative means was, in part, the reason that the photographers couldn't get what they wanted. It

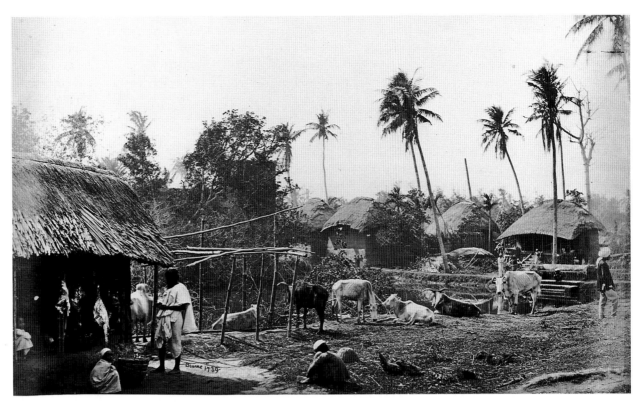

Fig. 3.2
SAMUEL BOURNE
Village in Lower Bengal,
c. 1865

was also a consequence of the conflict between their preconceptions about their subjects and their real curiosity about them. "By no amount of talking or acting," Bourne said of the Indians, "could I get them to stand or sit in an easy, natural attitude."[8] He took it for granted that the "obstinacy" preventing this was theirs, not his own.

The one time Bourne got away from the kind of stilted poses that angered him here, and that are indeed characteristic of his street photographs in such cities as Calcutta, was when he ventured to the very edges of the empire, on dusty roads past remote villages near Simla or in Kashmir. These photographs keep a respectful distance, one close enough to give us a glimpse into village life but far enough not to interfere (fig. 3.2). The space is just right. Perhaps the photographer was reluctant to come any nearer in areas whose isolation might make people suspicious of outsiders. Chances are his guides didn't understand the local dialect and couldn't have communicated his wishes anyway. Whatever the reason, we don't feel the photograph bearing in on its subjects, pressing them to perform. They watch Bourne idly to see what he's up to or go on about their business. As a con-

sequence, they appear here, there, and everywhere in the frame. The full frame *becomes* the subject.

Photographs that Felice Beato made on country roads in Japan have a fullness similar to Bourne's, and perhaps for the same reason (fig. 3.3). So do some of the photographs Thomson did on the Yangtze or for his book *Foochow and the River Min* (fig. 3.4). Shooting sometimes from a moving boat and working always under haphazard conditions may have forced Thomson to make some of these off-balance compositions. However it may have happened, he developed an occasional taste for a kind of improvised imagery. He readily improvised on the technical end of photography, as when he substituted lime juice and a local beer for chemicals he lacked in the tropics. The ability to be inventive on the aesthetic end was just as important when you were off in a backwater, thousands of miles from both your own civilization and the rules of composition it obeyed.

There were times when Thomson simply had to work extempore, and the proof of his enthusiasm for doing so is just that: the proof, the fact that he printed and published the re-

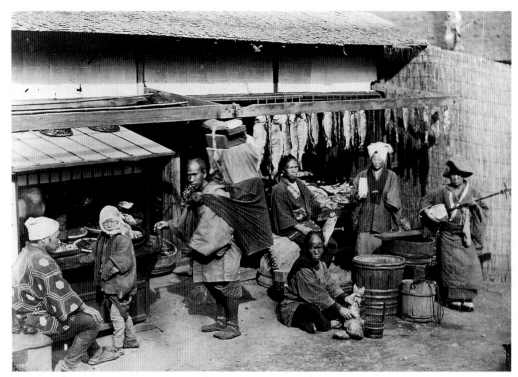

Fig. 3.3
FELICE BEATO
Fishmongers, c. 1867

sults. As he himself pointed out, "The [collodion] process had this advantage; as each plate was taken, it was at once developed, so that one could see and judge of its value."[9] Had Thomson disliked the unusual images he got under impromptu circumstances, he presumably would have remade or discarded them. Instead, he gave them prominent play in his books.

The photograph entitled *Physic Street, Canton* is particularly striking in this regard (page 51). In spite of its considerable formal properties, this image in which the light ripples with the motion of shopkeepers who ducked in and out during a prolonged exposure has a transient quality to it. As much as anything, what gives the picture its fascination is the old man in the foreground who turns his back on us with unconcern. He hunches his shoulders as if to shrug off the ceremony of the photograph and the watchful, apprehensive poses of the other men present. Facing away from us as he is, secreted in shadow, a wavering figure near invisibility, he keeps his own counsel. In him a stock character in the British melodrama of China — the inscrutable Oriental — comes unexpectedly to life. Just for a moment, we are able to fix in our minds both the cultural cliché and the human reality behind it.

Thomson clearly learned something he valued from a photograph like this. An area of motion blur showed where the ragged edge of the medium lay. It tested the boundaries. Collodion's great strength was its explicitness, but a photograph like *Physic Street* sacrificed that in the hopes of getting something perhaps even stronger. It gave up statement for suggestion. It toyed with the possibility that an image heading in the opposite direction, away from the stolid certainties to which collodion lent itself, toward more frail and equivocal effects, might be more powerful still.

A few other photographs Thomson made in China have these properties, and some done back in London for *Street Life*, such as *Hookey Alf*, continue the aesthetic experiment (fig. 3.5). Long exposures sometimes served to erase the blemish that passing figures might leave on the negative of collodion photographs. In pictures like *Physic Street* or *Hookey Alf*, such imperfection calls attention to itself. It is deliberately left in. It animates the scene. Most of the scenes in *Street Life* are not "decisive moments" so much as decided ones, illustrations of some foregone conclusion about how people should look and behave. But in *Hookey Alf*, Thomson made his exposure a moment too soon or too late to

Fig. 3.4
JOHN THOMSON
Part of the Lower Bridge
(from *Foochow and the River Min*)

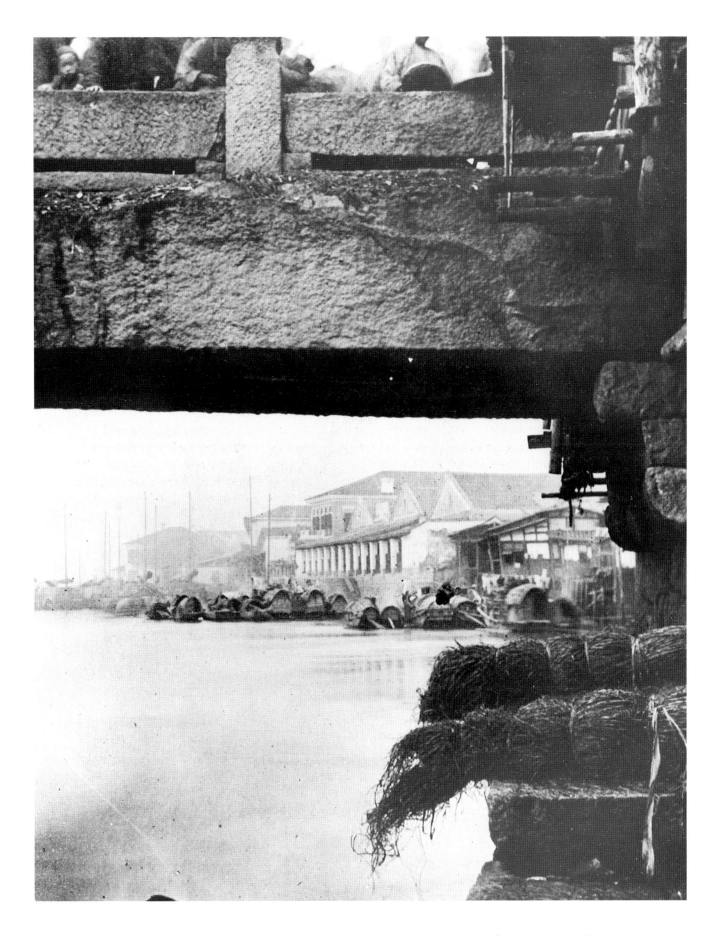

Fig. 3.5
JOHN THOMSON
Hookey Alf, 1881

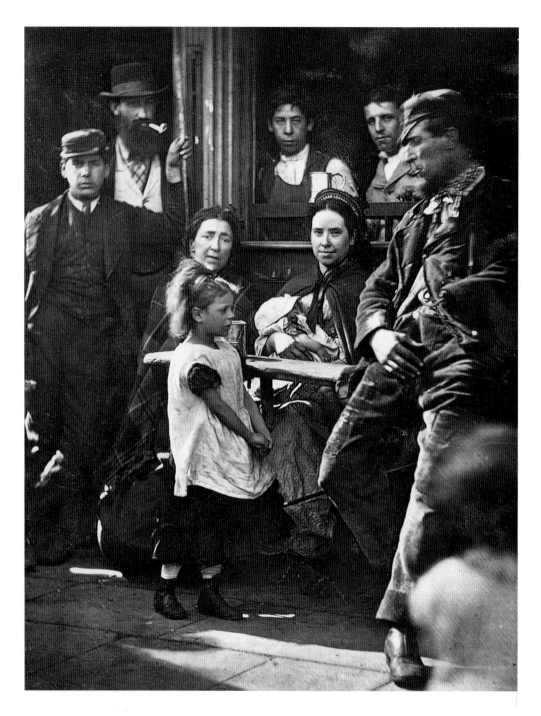

get that perfect equilibrium, that ideal stasis, to which most Victorian photography accustoms us.

The kind of effect that *Hookey Alf* courts literally crept into Thomson's street photography from the edges. It began in the hinterlands of the empire, where British photographers sometimes had to give up both the control and the certainty they'd enjoyed at home.

And it ended with peripheral figures like the little girl on the lower right in *Hookey Alf,* or the gawkers who have been allowed to intrude upon the frame in various other *Street Life* scenes. What we see on these bystanders' faces, as in a mirror, is Thomson's own, unabashed curiosity about life staring back at him.

4: Busmen's Holidays

Walter Bagehot, who was editor of the *Economist* in the 1860s and 1870s, once said that to succeed as a politician in his day a man needed to have "common opinions and uncommon abilities."[1] This was true of most commercial photographers as well. The sort of professionals who produced travel albums, landscapes, or urban views for a general clientele had to be capable of exercising their talents without surprising the expectations of their audience. For a photographer working in a country on the Grand Tour and selling his pictures to tourists as souvenirs, normative views were de rigueur. This was true not only for art treasures and ancient monuments, but also for genre scenes and, thus, street photography.

Sometimes this last was saved from monotony by sheer force of their subject matter. This is particularly true of photography from Italy, where so much of life was picturesque and was lived in the street. Naples photographer Giorgio Sommer needed to do little more than recognize that a pasta factory with racks of its product out front on the sidewalk was an engaging subject. Some street scenes made for sale by Robert MacPherson, a Scottish surgeon living in Rome, are similarly both unimaginative and irresistible. In other instances, a commercial archive contained interesting street photographs simply because an effort had been made to have it contain everything.

The Seeberger brothers covered Paris with this degree of thoroughness. They canvassed the city for every conceivable kind of client and therefore did every conceivable kind of photograph. The firm was started in 1899 by Jules Seeberger, and during the next three decades he and his brothers, Henri and Louis, were among the most prolific producers of views for postcards in France. They surveyed Paris from its fashionable women at the height of the social season to the victims of a historic Seine flood and the laborers along the river's banks. A major activity of the brothers Seeberger was doing production and publicity stills for the early movies, whose atmospherics their street photographs sometimes seem to imitate. In this way a porter silhouetted against a cloud of steam might be transformed into a demonic figure out of the *Fantomas* serials (pages 52–53). Such pictures invest common labor with the melodramatic allure of the silent screen.

Commercial photographers who catered to tourists and consumers of views, both at home and abroad, prospered so readily in the late nineteenth century that in many cases there was a division of labor. Two people were needed, one outside handling the camera and another inside handling the customers. This made such photography ideal for the kind of free enterprise that was the backbone of nineteenth-century capitalism, the family business.

The very model of this sort of photographic firm, and one of the first to go into business, was the Florentine concern of Alinari Fratelli. Having begun as a photographer in 1852, Leopoldo Alinari was doing well enough by 1854 to bring in his two brothers to run the office while he continued taking pictures. From portraiture and the depiction of Florence's art treasures, the firm branched out into three kinds of exterior photography — architecture and monuments, nature and the countryside (a series entitled "The Italian Countryside of the Divine Comedy" was the most popular the Alinaris ever issued), and what were called animated shots.[2] Under this last heading came a variety of posed street scenes. During the seventy years that the family retained control of Alinari Fratelli, the firm also built up a large stock of scenic views of the streets in Rome, Turin, and Genoa as well as Florence.

In this photography there is no virtuosity. What restrained any impulses of that nature at prominent firms like the Alinaris' was their own success. Even before Leopoldo's son inherited the company in the late 1860s, its volume had grown to the point where additional photographers had to be hired. To maintain quality control while increasing output, the Alinari brothers pioneered in the practice of training a firm's photographers so that procedures would be uniform. In effect, the craft of photography was turning into an industry, and the photograph into a standardized product.

As the century wore on, and the customers for commercial views became more and more of a mass market, these methods of mass production became ingrained in the operations of the biggest firms. The sort of training techniques employed by the Alinaris generated, for more aggressive companies, staffs of photographers supplying views from all over the world. The market for scenes expanded gradually from an elite clientele into a hoi polloi; album prints in limited editions were succeeded by cheap reproductions and mass distribution. A big breakthrough was the postcard. In 1894, the British Post Office permitted private cards to be sent through the mail for the first time. Within less than a decade, their volume had reached six hundred million per year in Britain alone, and seven billion worldwide.

The stereograph was the form of photography that was, because of its enormous commercial potential, the most convention-ridden. Stereography might have been the perfect instrument for street photographs, for the camera had a shorter focal length and higher speed than other types. This would have allowed the stereographer to get right into the thick of the crowd in the street and have a wide view of the action. But the camera's other, even more distinctive feature, the illusion of three dimensions it gave, drew him away again. It encouraged him to go in the opposite direction — up above the street, so that his picture would have a vanishing point.

This was the stereograph's great sales gimmick. To enhance its appeal, the major firms almost invariably had views of city streets taken from the elevation of a second-story window, a balcony, a platform, or even, as was the practice of Valentine Blanchard in London, the top of a hansom cab specially outfitted as a mobile darkroom. The relentless emphasis on perspective makes the stereograph a very hidebound kind of photography. A photograph done from a vantage point is completely different in mood from one made at street level. The former is official in some way that the latter isn't. The camera commands the view, which has, as a consequence, an impersonal authority.

Both the stereography and the photography done by the big firms — the most prosperous family partnerships, like Bisson Frères, Alinari, Underwood and Underwood, E. and H. T. Anthony, et al. — were shaped almost entirely by market forces. Those forces, the files of such companies reveal, discouraged individual initiative among staff photographers. But they also encouraged initiative, and sometimes a kind of wildcatting in photography, elsewhere. Even after the ascendancy of international firms, there was still room for many local ones. The market was like a giant furnace that photographers had to stoke. They threw into it every kind of image they could find to keep the industry going full blast. If the big firms had already covered the famous sights, smaller ones and free-lancers had to find more unusual subjects or make commonplace subjects interesting. Out to get pictures of yet another hometown parade, the local photographer aimed his camera at the spectators instead of the marchers, just for a change. He hoped to get a novelty item, something different in the line of what the department stores of the day called notions.

There were always small-time operators with harebrained photographic schemes, like J. R. Taylor in Milwaukee and Julius Wendt in Albany, New York. Taylor was the first staff photographer for the *Milwaukee Journal*. Since he was probably not able to support himself with that job alone, he may have eked out his living by having some of his less newsworthy but more entertaining street photographs made into postcards. These were the sort of pictures that appealed to the market for local color (page 60). Wendt was a newsdealer in Albany and a Kodak concessionaire. As a promotion, he set up a stereographic camera on the street outside his shop, from which he could see customers approaching a counter that opened onto the sidewalk. As they walked up, he took a stereo street portrait of them and the rest of the passing Albany scene. The casual nature of such imagery is a consequence of its having been, for the photographers who made it, a marginal business, a sideline.

As long as a firm remained the sort of collaboration in which only one person was responsible for the photography — a limited partnership in artistic terms, if not in financial ones — the pictures were not all likely to be routine. This was the case at the Dublin portrait studio of which William Lawrence was the proprietor. From the early 1880s until around World War I, Lawrence employed the photographer Robert French to travel and make views that could be offered through the studio, sold to other concerns for advertisements, or published as postcards.

A stickler for keeping his picture files current, Lawrence sent French back again and again to rephotograph the same subjects whenever something in the landscape changed. When electric trolleys replaced the horse-drawn variety in Dublin, Lawrence not only replaced his earlier views but had an intermediate set made recording the brief period when both kinds of public transportation were on the streets. When French traveled through Ireland's rural counties, Lawrence chose his destinations and set the itinerary. Yet he left the photography to French himself, whose assignment was simply to photograph Ireland.

Over the years French developed quite a feel for the Irish countryside, for the scale of it, and the incongruity of a certain human presence in it (pages 26–27). The people in his pictures sometimes seem out of place no matter where they stand. These subjects were often the customers who bought the photographs, tourists and vacationers who had recently begun flocking to the rural counties on their "hols." They don't fit among the Druid mounds, in this foreshortened landscape with a long history of elves, magic, and supernatural tricks.

The firm that covered New York the way that the Seebergers did Paris was another family business, the partnership of Joseph Byron and his son Percy. When Joseph immigrated to America in 1888, he already had a background in photography, his grandfather having founded a portrait firm in Nottingham, England, the year he was born. In New York he established himself as a society and magazine photographer, and within a year even his son Percy, though only eleven, had sold a picture to a newspaper. Each generation built up a specialty that became the mainstay of the firm's business. Joseph's was stage photography, and Percy's, developed after World War I, was to cover the ships and shipping in New York Harbor.

None of this extensive practice left a lot of opportunity for street photography. Yet in the decade around the turn of the century, somebody in the firm did quite a bit of it. It was probably Percy, although none of the photographs in the company's files was attributed. The street photographs were made before or between two periods when Percy was absent from New York, first to serve as a correspondent in the Spanish-American War, then to travel in the Far West. When he was home at all in those days, Percy was still very much the apprentice and a junior partner in the firm. His only chances to explore both the city and the medium on his own might well have come on Sunday excursions to the street markets on the Lower East Side, or when he

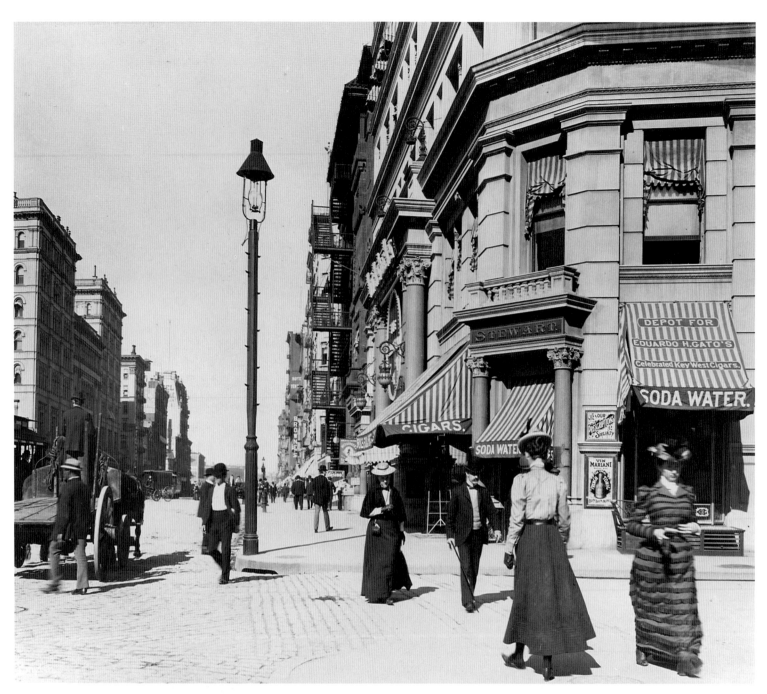

Fig. 4.1

JOSEPH AND PERCY
BYRON

*Broadway North from
Thirty-eighth Street*,
1898

could squeeze some personal work in between more humdrum assignments in the
theater district.

The Byron studio was at that time on Thirty-
fourth Street and Broadway, just south of the
theater district, where so much of the firm's
business was conducted. Young Percy often
had to run errands up to the theaters. Once in
1896 he brought a set of pictures to Sarah

Bernhardt. She was so pleased with them that
she kissed him. The delivery was made at the
Abbey Theater, just a few doors away from
the Knickerbocker, which appears in the
background of a number of the firm's street
photographs. Somebody who was going back
and forth to the theaters at the time was lug-
ging a camera along and stealing a few minutes en route to make pictures. Whoever it
was loved the diversion of a striped dress

Fig. 4.2
FRANK SUTCLIFFE
Saturday Afternoon,
c. 1889

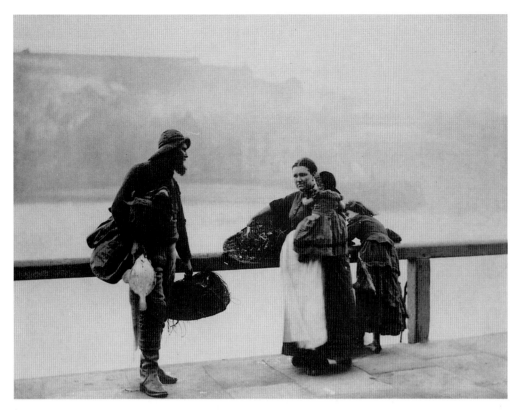

caught against striped awnings (fig. 4.1), or of a tête-à-tête on a street corner discreetly placed in the corner of the frame. He no doubt knew that some of these pictures would find their way onto postcards, thereby repaying the investment of time and materials put into them. Nonetheless, they were incidental to the firm's main business. They were a busman's holiday, which was their strength.

Other instances of work done in this way are not hard to find. Black River Falls, Wisconsin, was about as far as can be imagined from the Manhattan theater district. The town had only a couple of streets in it, and they weren't even paved. But that was no hindrance to the local photographer, Charles J. Van Schaick, who made street photographs every bit as good as those by Byron. Where Byron's pictures are poised and dapper, Van Schaick's are outlandish. Some of the subjects Van Schaick photographed in the street were clearly clients who had come to him for a portrait of their prize plow horse or of themselves in front of their store. The inherent homeliness of small-town glories makes even these photographs quaintly odd.

The subjects of Van Schaick pictures often stare out at us as if they were walleyed. They look touched in the head. This is why Michael Lesy could use Van Schaick's work as he did in his 1973 book *Wisconsin Death Trip*. But maybe Van Schaick himself was a little touched. He favored strangely unbalanced compositions wherein a figure was placed near the frame's edge, close up in the foreground, to emphasize the vastness of the street beyond (page 13). Like Robert French, Van Schaick was moved by the scale of the landscape in which he photographed. The main streets of midwestern towns like Black River Falls had been laid out with a nineteenth-century kind of optimism. They were wide enough to accommodate the congestion that the town fathers had been sure prosperity would soon bring. When we look at Van Schaick's pictures today, we can hear the wind whistling down these vacant streets and through the disappointed hopes they represent.

Who would have bought such photographs from Van Schaick is hard to imagine. But Frank Sutcliffe, the local photographer in Whitby, England, did find a market for his busman's holidays. Although he had already failed as a society photographer in the fashionable resort of Tunbridge Wells, Sutcliffe tried for a similar clientele with another portrait studio he opened in 1876 in Whitby, a shipping and fishing town in Yorkshire that had lately become a summer tourist attraction. During the season, Sutcliffe had to stay in the studio all day plying his trade. But in the evening, or early in the morning before the vacationers were up, he could wander the town while there was no one about except the locals, especially the fishermen coming back from having spent the night out in their dories. This was how Sutcliffe first came to make street photographs, and he discovered that the summer residents were a ready outlet for such pictures. Since the season was too short to support him year-round on portraits alone, he began selling the harborscapes, landscapes, and genre pictures as well.

Fig. 4.3
FRANK SUTCLIFFE
Everyday Scene in a
Fishing and Farm Town,
c. 1895

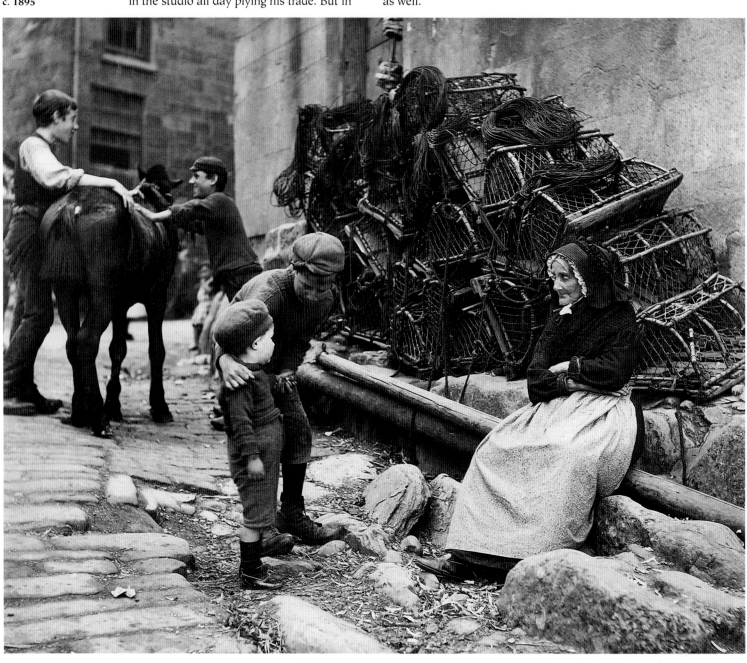

Street photographers often seem to love their subject for being everything that they are not. The street scene is a melee of extroversion and exhibitionism, a grand display of finery and emotion. The photographer, typically, is a rather introverted, reticent fellow. In Sutcliffe's case, the equation was reversed. It was the fishermen and other plain folk he photographed who were the taciturn ones. He was very outgoing, a man who enjoyed talking about photographs almost as much as taking them. In fact, in various essays and in a column on photography that he wrote for the *Yorkshire Weekly Post* for more than twenty years, he did talk about how he took them.

The basic account Sutcliffe gave is what we might expect from our look at Victorian street photography, beginning with John Thomson's. Early one morning, for example, Sutcliffe accosted a returning fisherman, who agreed to pose if it wouldn't delay too long his getting home to bed. The photographer hauled his subject out of the road and stood him and his wife against the rail by the harbor, to provide a background (fig. 4.2).

The only trouble was that, in Sutcliffe's own words,

> with one figure on one side and one on the other it looked as if they had been put there for the benefit of the camera. Then came a hasty look round among the small crowd that had gathered; a girl, not too big or too well dressed to look out of place, was pulled from among it, and placed behind the woman, leaning toward her, and told to look anywhere but in the direction of the camera. The man was asked to look towards the woman. After a hasty look on the ground glass . . . the shutter was touched. Then a handful of coppers was poured into the hands of the woman and the girl, the man thanked heartily for staying there, and up went the camera, and the photographer back to his day's work, trying to amuse restless babies, and copying faded daguerreotypes.[3]

The girl Sutcliffe pulled from the crowd certainly earned her tuppence, for she is the one who lends the most naturalism to the scene. While Sutcliffe's street photographs were as posed as Thomson's, Sutcliffe also learned, like Thomson, how to use bystanders in the background of the scene and on the edges to create the illusion of naturalness that wooden central figures might lack.

Notice how Sutcliffe's comments on a photograph he made around 1895 enlarge upon the possibilities seen in the picture discussed above, which was taken six or seven years earlier:

> The group of the two little boys and the old lady under the crab-pots is all wrong by all the canons of art, but that is the best of photography; no one expects a photograph to be perfect, and the photographer may do things in the way of composition which would be quite wrong for an artist to do. The two boys with the pony have no business to be where they are. The photographer had been taught so much, but for the life of him he could not find it in his heart to ask them to go away. I believe he asked them to stay, and emptied his pockets of all the money he had among the five[4] [*fig. 4.3*].

The mixture of self-mockery and self-indulgence heard here has about it much the same sense of humor seen in the photographs. Beginning as an apology for the imperfections of photography, Sutcliffe's remarks end up an endorsement of them. By the way he criticized the presence of the boys and pony in this picture, he was justifying their inclusion. In effect, his commentary makes these secondary figures the essence of what the photograph is about. Since they are in a part of the picture where the focus is soft anyway, Sutcliffe could permit them a greater animation than the principal figures. Because they play a more active role, and because they divide the viewer's attention a bit, just as life in the street does, they give the picture an authentic look that it would not otherwise have.

In a further effort to supplement his income, Sutcliffe did at-home portraits or pictures of clients' houses or businesses, and these increased his opportunities to photograph district life. Like Percy Byron on his rounds of the theater district, Sutcliffe would keep an eye out for a good photograph whenever he was on his way to one of these appointments. The byways around Whitby seldom offered more than a landscape with a flock of sheep in it; yet Sutcliffe wouldn't usually settle for less than a kind of country street photography.

As he explained in an essay entitled "Landscape with Figures,"

> When out with his camera the photographer *must* feel *whether he wishes figures in his landscape or not. He must say to himself, "This view wants a figure* exactly there, *and it must be a light figure or a grey figure or a black figure." For the life of him he may not be able to say* why *he wants a figure* there. *It is sufficient for him to know that its addition will make his photograph more satisfactory. If he has patience and waits long enough the figure will come. Then his friends will say "What a lucky snapshot; how well that figure comes there; an artist could not have put it in a better place."* [5]

These comments are interesting because they justify a found scene by talking as if it were contrived. They examine a candid picture as if it had been willed into existence. They offer as a rationale for such a picture the idea that it might look as composed as a painting. Whatever the reason given to make this kind of imagery acceptable, it was what photography like Thomson's or Sutcliffe's or Percy Byron's was headed toward from the beginning. It was a potential, a promise, that inhered in the camera itself. The strategy that Sutcliffe proposed — pinning yourself to an attractive place, then waiting for subjects to wander into it — was one that Cartier-Bresson was to use with great success.

5: Art for Art's Sake

Frank Sutcliffe was a mediating figure in the history of street photography in several respects. First, by being able to write about what he did, he bridged the gap between words and pictures that usually exists in this genre. Second, his own work struck a happy medium between the rigidly posed scenes of the collodion era and the truly candid ones that roll film and small, fast cameras were beginning to make possible by the end of the 1880s. And finally, as his most famous picture, *Water Rats,* demonstrates, he was a figure who straddled the two worlds of professional and amateur photography. This image of some truants stripped for a swim in Whitby Harbor got its first boost toward being one of his best-sellers when it won a medal at the 1886 exhibition sponsored by the London Photographic Society, which was among the more prominent of the many amateur organizations then active in England.

It's difficult to say where in the nineteenth century professional photography left off and amateur began. So many photographers crossed over from one to the other that the line between them became rather smudged. (Where Sutcliffe was a professional who got recognition from amateurs, for instance, his English contemporary Paul Martin was an amateur who eventually turned his hobby into a profession.) There was one person to whom the difference between the two was never vague, however: Alfred Stieglitz.

Amateurism went to the heart of Stieglitz's principles as a photographer. When his father once suggested he try selling his prints, Stieglitz was appalled. As curator and Stieglitz scholar Weston Naef has explained, " 'Amateur' was a word equal to 'artistic' " for Stieglitz and his circle.[1] In order to be an art, photography had to be practiced purely for the love of it. Yet Stieglitz himself was incon-sistent on this score, frequently publishing the work of people who made their living at photography in his journal *Camera Work.* Although the difference between amateurs and professionals remains fuzzy, one way to distinguish the photographers being discussed in this chapter from many of those in preceding chapters is by their interest in art. Professionals like Thomson or Van Schaick didn't care whether photography was regarded as an art form; the photographers under consideration here did. They were acutely aware of developments in the fine arts, particularly painting, and were influenced by them. This, more than anything else, was what set them apart.

In England, the history of amateur photography ran in tandem with that of the new painting being done in the late nineteenth century. Inspired by the Impressionists and wanting to do similar plein air painting themselves, some artists settled on the Cornwall coast at Newlyn, where they chose for subjects the same sort of fishermen and rustics Sutcliffe was using in Whitby. And just as such painters inevitably had a confrontation with the art establishment of the day, so did the photographers have one with the photographic establishment. In 1886, painters of the Newlyn group broke with the Royal Academy to found their own organization, the New English Art Club. In 1892, some photographers followed suit, leaving the Photographic Society of Great Britain to form a fellowship they called The Linked Ring. Sutcliffe was a founding member.

Like most who joined in this rebellion, Sutcliffe was aware of the most advanced art. His father, a watercolorist, raised him on *Modern Painters,* by John Ruskin, who later invited Sutcliffe to photograph his home and introduced him to Turner's painting. Sutcliffe did contre-jour harborscapes very Impressionistic in style. One, a study of a bucket dredger, looks like a direct allusion to *Impression, Sunrise,* the Monet painting from which Impressionism acquired its name. The fact is that Monet's painting was the crucial influence on all the young art photographers, or Pictorialists, of the day. His example was central in the period's most important tract, *Naturalistic Photography,* written by Peter Henry Emerson and published in 1889. Emerson argued that the new French painters like Monet were the first to understand nature truly. He wanted photographers to imitate Impressionist vision — by using differential focus, for instance — and he subsequently cited some Sutcliffe photographs as examples of what he meant.

Like the art from which it followed, the new Pictorialism caused controversy. The label that was most apt was the one Stieglitz put on his group — the Photo-Secession — for that's what the history of Pictorialism became: a series of secessions, the repeated splitting off of one faction from another as a consequence of aesthetic disputes. First Young Turks imbued with the values of modern painting would break away from an amateur society dominated by academic influences. Then those rebels advocating straight photography would differ from those in favor of manipulation, and those who believed in manipulating prints would disagree further with those who wanted to manipulate negatives.

There was something a little silly about the constant bickering. Having been one of the first Americans asked to join The Linked Ring, Stieglitz followed its example in 1902 when he withdrew his own rump group from the Camera Club in New York and formed the Photo-Secession. But within a few years new disputes compelled him to resign from The Linked Ring as well. Emerson had set a pattern for this kind of self-revision when he followed *Naturalistic Photography* a year later with *The Death of Naturalistic Photography.* By the time what he said in his first tract had resulted in the formation of The Linked Ring, his second tract had so alienated his disciples

that he wasn't invited to join. Such squabbles give this phase of Pictorialism's history a Gilbert-and-Sullivan quality.

Underlying all these conflicts were a couple of common elements, however. One was the all-pervasive influence of Impressionism. Another was the increasing interest in street photography. It was practiced not only by the Englishmen Sutcliffe and Martin but also by the American Stieglitz and many of the young photographers whose talents he fostered in *Camera Work.* A street photograph made in Italy brought Stieglitz early recognition in the form of a first prize, awarded by Emerson, in a London competition sponsored by the journal *Amateur Photographer,* in which Sutcliffe occasionally published articles. Stieglitz continued making street photographs in Paris and New York; and in Paris, Robert Demachy and Maurice Bucquet, two founders of the Photo-Club de Paris, did street photography too, as did Edward Steichen on Steeplechase Day at Longchamps racetrack. In New York, Karl Struss and Paul Strand, two younger photographers whom *Camera Work* published, took to the streets as well.

From J. Craig Annan in Glasgow to Arnold Genthe in San Francisco, Pictorialists of every persuasion concentrated on street photography at some point or other in their career. Most of these photographers combined the impulse to do street photography with a desire to make images that would look impressionistically sketchy. Annan didn't even consider himself a photographer. His medium was gravure, in which he reproduced all the photographs he took. The plates were often heavily embellished with a roulette so that they would have the appearance of artwork done by hand.

Other photographers reproduced their work by the gum-bichromate process. It was popular because it allowed the photographer to suppress detail and vary the effects considerably in the print, giving it the look of a charcoal or red chalk sketch. Demachy was the first to attract attention with gum prints, and thereafter Steichen and Genthe, among others, took advantage of the way the process enabled one to reproduce an image very large on fine drawing paper.

Steichen's pictures, both at the Paris races and in the New York streets, were printed this way, as was a series Genthe selected from the many candid snapshots he made in San Francisco's Chinatown. Each photographer followed the edict Robert Demachy laid down in *Camera Work* that "a straight print . . . cannot be a work of art."[2] Those who disagreed achieved similar effects, but by other means. Struss usually positioned himself so that the scenes he photographed would be strongly backlit. This reduced them to the kind of soft-edged graphics that the title he gave to one of his images, *Shadows,* suggests (page 64). Strand not only experimented with various kinds of manipulated printing, he made his negatives with a lens purposely designed to have a soft focus, one that, in his own words, "flattens and mushifies."[3]

Strand admitted that his reason for employing these devices was to make his work look "Impressionistic."[4] The heated debates about technique seemed superfluous, because this look was the goal for which everyone was striving. The technique that appeared to succeed the best — gum bichromate — was in fact the most questionable. Monet painted as he did in order to produce a more spontaneous image. Gum bichromate is a calculated effect, one achieved by drawing out the creative process rather than abbreviating it. An effect resulting from the search for greater truthfulness in painting becomes, in photography, an affectation.

Emerson had contempt for photographers who made gum prints — "paper stainers," he called them[5] — and Stieglitz, in turn, came to disapprove of the soft-focus technique Emerson advocated. The first advice Stieglitz gave Strand was to stop down his lens to eliminate its Emersonian softness, which was, he told his young protégé, "destroying the individual qualities of . . . life" in his photographs.[6]

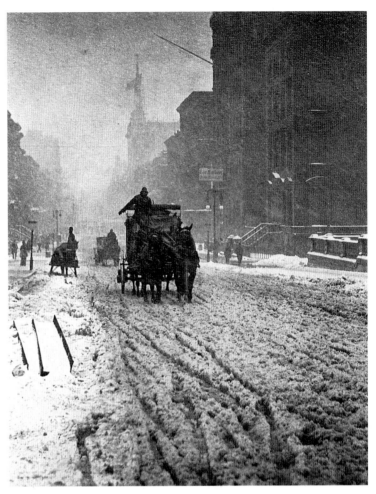

Nonetheless, Stieglitz published in *Camera Work* all of these photographers' pictures, no matter how manipulated; and his own street photography attempted in yet another way to achieve a look that was as Impressionistic as theirs.

The photograph that Edward Steichen claimed to be the most highly honored and widely published that Stieglitz ever did was *Winter — Fifth Avenue,* which he made during a blizzard in 1893 (fig. 5.1). He had never tried to make a photograph under such adverse conditions before; but, he reported to his biographer Dorothy Norman, "knowing that where there is light one can photograph, I decided to make an exposure." When he showed the negative at the New York Society of Amateur Photographers, the response was "For God's sake, Stieglitz, throw that damned thing away. It is all blurred and not sharp." His comeback was that it had turned out "ex-

Fig. 5.1
ALFRED STIEGLITZ
Winter — Fifth Avenue,
1893

actly as I want it to be." He told his incredulous listeners, "This is the beginning of a new era. Call it a new vision if you wish." [7]

Over the next decade, at least a half dozen of his best-known images — *The Terminal* (1893), *Icy Night* (1898), *From My Window* (1900–1902), *The Hand of Man* (1902), and *Flatiron* (1903) — were to rely on similar effects. Photographing "during a great storm," he said, left him "spellbound." What these pictures have in common with many more of his street photographs is that all achieve the softness seen in manipulated prints, but without the manipulation. Stieglitz waited until conditions in the street itself produced the effects that others were creating in the darkroom or in the camera. "I have always loved snow, mist, fog, rain, deserted streets," he declared. [8]

A 1909 issue of *Camera Work* carried an unsigned essay praising Impressionism, and recommending it as a model for photography, because it favors "blurred definition" as a way "to envelop figures and objects in space and atmosphere." [9] In Stieglitz's photography, the atmosphere in which the subject was originally wrapped became the subject itself in the end. The cloud studies of the 1920s and 1930s are an ultimate purification of the imagery he had begun developing in street photographs several decades earlier. The weather, which was used as a way to stylize the street photographs, turned into the sole subject of the later work.

Stieglitz called his cloud studies "equivalents," a title that suggests they are supposed to be thought of as visual metaphors. His titles often proposed a metaphorical interpretation for his pictures; thus was a close-up of the hindquarters of a gelding *Spiritual America* or a skyline belching steam and smoke a *City of Ambition*. What we see in the picture was intended as an objective correlative for something else that's invisible. Even in the New York street photography, the subjects that he chose were for him, as historian Jonathan Green has put it, "hieratic rather than ac-

tual." [10] The photographs are pictograms, thoughts or feelings written down with hieroglyphs.

Comments that Stieglitz made about having seen Eleonora Duse in *Camille* (a performance that left him in tears) reveal how a photograph could function for him as a metaphor for emotions felt elsewhere. Speaking of his experience making *The Terminal* a few days after attending the play, he said, "The steaming horses being watered on a cold winter day, the snow-covered streets and the stagecoach in *Winter — Fifth Avenue*, my sense of loneliness in my own country, all seemed closely related to my experience when seeing Duse." [11]

The reason he loved snow, mist, fog, rain, and deserted streets, he explained, was that "all seemed attuned to my feelings about life in the 1890s." [12] As both this remark and the anecdote about Duse indicate, his New York photographs represent feelings in search of an image. The emotions came first and compelled the photographer to go out looking for a subject that could express them. They weren't necessarily occasioned by that subject or by the situation in which it was found. This unique approach was what gave Stieglitz's street photography its particular character.

And yet there were times — if not in New York, then in Paris, a city that tended to lift his spirits as his hometown did not — when he did make photographs out of the sort of spontaneous, immediate reaction to street life that is more characteristic of the genre. In Paris, he could take a picture with a vaguely erotic side from which a teasing kind of artfulness seems to arise. "Paris is the only place I saw at the time," he said, "that had . . . women going through the streets without hats. The women were free, feminine." [13] The 1911 photograph entitled *A Snapshot, Paris* looks as if made to celebrate his observation (page 1).

In spite of the epithet "snapshot," it's an image with a great deal of formal control. The cross members of the railing on the lower left, functioning as a kind of schematic diagram of the picture beyond, direct our eye not only from front to back but also along an opposite diagonal, from the woman in the street to the one above her, behind the rail. The former, who is bareheaded, makes a stark silhouette against the pavement; the latter would blend unnoticed into the dark shapes behind were it not for the whiteness of her hat. The woman on the sidewalk, set off by her finery, is above the one on the street socially as well as physically. Yet the hatless woman has the more luminous presence. There is a hint of the physical liberation Stieglitz was talking about in the way that she strides through the drab, dank atmosphere of the street. The photograph implies a like sensation in the photographer, an agile gladness about being there.

During the century's first decade, when Stieglitz was giving Paul Cézanne, Henri Matisse, Pablo Picasso, and other modern masters exhibitions at his 291 Gallery — often their first exhibition in America — Lewis Hine sometimes took the students in his photography classes at the Ethical Culture School to see Stieglitz's shows. Among Hine's charges was Paul Strand. Fascinated by the modern art to which he was introduced in this way, Strand subsequently tried to make his own Cubist designs with the camera by photographing shadow patterns and groupings of pottery. He also wanted to turn the street photography that he was doing into a kind of abstract art.

To this end he made pictures intended to catch "the movement in New York — movement in the streets, the movement of traffic, the movement of people walking in the parks."[14] As he explained, "I wanted to see if I could organize a picture of that kind of movement in a way that was abstract and controlled."[15] The photograph he had in mind when he said this was one of the Morgan Guaranty Trust Building, on Wall Street. What made him think of it in these terms was its "huge, rectangular, rather sinister windows — blind shapes, actually"[16] (pages 116–117).

A comment Strand made about some of his other street photographs might also describe that done on Wall Street. He was after, he said, "physical movement expressed by the abstract spotting of people and shapes."[17]

The abstractness of the Morgan Guaranty photograph is enhanced by its elevated point of view because Strand went up the steps of the Subtreasury Building across the street to make his exposure. Other street photographs of his were made from atop a viaduct or the platform of a train station. *Fifth Avenue and Forty-second Street* was shot out of a window at the Modern Gallery, which overlooked the intersection; and still more views were made from windows in the Courts Building that opened onto a park or from various private houses. He also made use of strong linear forms to strengthen abstractness, deploying fences, for example, in a way that would block out large graphic designs in the frame. This line of development reached a peak with the 1917 photograph *Geometric Backyards*, which photo historian Naomi Rosenblum has called "a forerunner of an essentially American style of abstraction."[18]

Central as such pictures were to Strand's development, however, there was also an impulse toward a less patterned imagery, one that explored the medium instead of structuring it. This alternative kind of behavior with the camera is evident in a photograph that he made on Fifth Avenue in 1915 (page 63). It is literally the reverse of those in which he looks down at the street from above. Here he looks up from the street itself, and some of his other photographic priorities seem to get turned around as well. If there is any formalism at work in this image, perhaps seen in the way the flag looped up by one corner mimics the shapes of the steeples across the street, it is of a very tentative kind. This picture has more of a feeling of reflex to it than the ones discussed previously. Strand's reaction to the scene seems to have been all of a motion. He took a swipe at the street; the flag in the middle of the frame looks as if it *is* that swipe.

The result was precocious in a way that the more studied exercises in Cubism were not. The women's hats cribbed in along the bottom edge, the chunk of streetlight stuck on the side, and the flag placed just off center all seem to float free from the context that the background provides. Splattered about the frame in this manner, the various elements of the composition take on an irrelevance to one another that's provocative. The picture affects us the way a Surrealist collage might. Were this a painting, it would have the irregular, slathering, scumbling brushwork — the hats laid down in blotches, the flag with a slashing stroke, the lamp dribbled in — that belongs to an improvised technique.

Fig. 5.2
PAUL STRAND
Man, Five Points Square, New York, 1916

At the same time, though, the shapes with which we are confronted in this photograph compel us to seek some meaningful relationship among them, or else to invent one, precisely because they have been extracted as a group from the field of vision. As a view of the society in which Strand was living, the picture is radical politically as well as aesthetically. Hine's heritage emerges, along with that of Stieglitz, in the overt symbolism of the flag. It is a scimitar of a flag, a Sword of Damocles hanging over the heads of the people.

Politics was important to Strand, whose work was never shaped exclusively by art-historicizing influences like Cubism. "I'm a politically conscious person," he once explained. "I've always wanted to be aware of what's going on in the world around me, and I've wanted to use photography as an instrument of research into and reporting on the life of my own time." [19] Early stirrings of this desire can be seen in a 1916 series of candid street portraits done in New York, close-up studies of what he called "people involved in the daily process of living." [20] Affixing to an Ensign reflex camera a fake lens — a shiny brass mount that would draw attention away from the real one sticking out under his arm — Strand did studies of a sandwich-board man (fig. 5.2), a blind peddler, a wrinkled old woman, a derelict, and other street types.

These are photographs that have no precedent or counterpart in Stieglitz's work. They seem to crave direct human contact. They are completely without formalism and abstraction. Everything except a face or a figure is excluded from the frame, and in some instances where a whole figure was originally photographed — such as the image of the vacant-eyed derelict — Strand printed it as a portrait of the face alone as well. Here the influence of Strand's former teacher Hine is most noticeable. Strand's photographs search the faces on the street as if he hoped to discover in them some reason for the hopelessness and cunning, the alternations of hardness and despair, that they betray.

His social conscience would lead him to a deep involvement in left-wing politics during the 1930s, the decade when he would go to

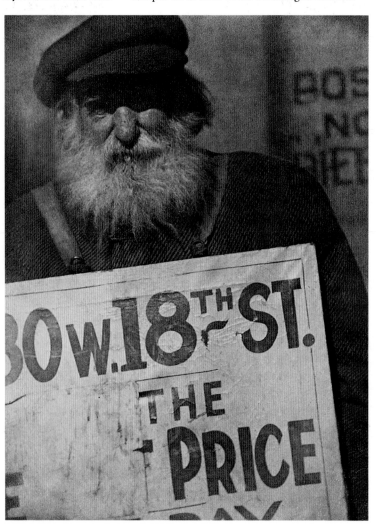

Moscow, work on the Pare Lorentz documentary *The Plow That Broke the Plains,* and become president of the agitprop movie unit Frontier Films. This was also the period of a sojourn to Mexico, during which the street portraits were to continue, and the studies of peasants and indigenous peoples done there merged with still more portraiture of the working poor later.

Yet most of this subsequent work idealizes Strand's subjects, perhaps because ideological tendencies were dictating the image in a way that his earliest street portraits do not. In a profile of Strand for the *New Yorker,* Calvin Tomkins admitted, "There is a certain ambiguity about human character in the early Strand — an ability to look unblinkingly on meanness and ugliness as well as on strength and dignity — which is rarely evident in his later work."[21]

The binocularity of Strand's view of human nature in the street portraits is seen nowhere more unmistakably than in the one of the blind woman (fig. 5.3). Her dead eye draws our compassion at the same time that the acquisitive gleam in her other eye, as it scans the street, makes us suspicious. This is a seminal image, one that a great many street photographers since Strand have acknowledged being guided by. Its power, like that of the other portraits in this series, comes from the fact that Strand got close enough to see all the inconsistency, the individuality and human paradox, that her features contain.

Sarah Greenough had a real insight into the significance of Strand's street portraits when she pointed out that their intention was not unlike that of Marcel Duchamp's Readymades, which were done at the same time. By exhibiting these purely documentary photographs of everyday people, just as Duchamp was exhibiting everyday objects, Strand was excising his subjects directly from reality and, Greenough wrote, "through his act of selection declaring them to be works of art."[22] Like Duchamp's, Strand's gesture was a way to

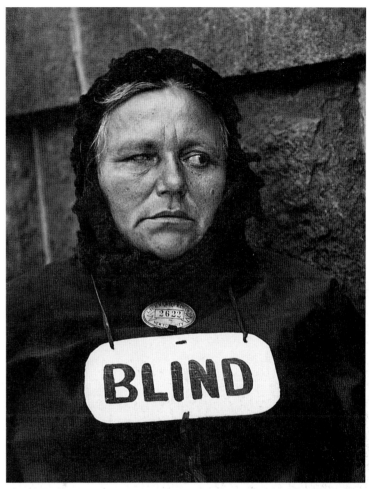

think about one's role as an artist in the modern world.

For Strand to have made these street portraits in the same year as his experiments with Cubism suggests that he was already trying to work out what was to become a long-term conflict in his work between Modernist art and social documentation. In certain pictures, such as the street photograph made on Lower Broadway in 1915, the two considerations seem to fuse into a single image; the intensity of the struggle between these alternatives is perhaps visible there in the explosive quality of a composition whose elements the photographic frame seems barely able to contain. Throughout the 1920s and 1930s, as long as this sort of tension continued to exist in Strand's work, he remained a vital force in American photography.

Fig. 5.3
PAUL STRAND
Blind Woman,
New York, 1916

Certain subjects, such as life at the beach, seem to have inspired candid pictures in all ages — even the Victorian age. Before the Romantics, no one in England had gone to the beaches. Even fishermen's huts turned their back on the sea. But Romanticism instilled a taste for wild nature, and Victorianism adapted this taste to theories of both health and morality that stressed the value of invigoration. On top of that, the Napoleonic Wars had transformed sleepy villages on England's south coast into important social centers. Then mass transportation in the form of railroads and steamships made ocean bathing accessible to the new holiday crowds created by, among other things, the Bank Holidays Act of 1871. In both England and America, the beach was one of the few places where Victorians could let down their hair and kick up their heels without being accused of impropriety.

The English amateur Paul Martin used a hidden camera to make photographs along the front at Yarmouth for just this reason, because there his subjects were, like the pictures he made of them, informal. And on the other side of the Atlantic, on the coast of Connecticut, an amateur named T. S. Bronson made nearly identical pictures at the beach using a view camera with dry-plate negatives. Bronson was a New Haven physician who was the official photographer for Yale University and an unofficial recorder of scenes of New England life from around the turn of the century until World War I. He was to New Haven what Robert French was to Dublin, Percy Byron to New York, or Van Schaick to Black River Falls, Wisconsin, except that Bronson's little plate camera was employed only for the amusement of himself and his friends at the New Haven Camera Club.

Candid photography was itself among the liberties that could be taken at the beach but were frowned upon elsewhere. Before World War I, there were many public places in which such photography was against the law. In London, you needed a permit to take pictures in the parks that Paul Martin frequented, and a photographer caught snapping the crowds instead of the scenery might be subject to arrest. In Paris, a ban on street photography was lifted by the prefect of police only in 1890. (This perhaps explains why there were no great Parisian careers in street photography between Nègre's and Atget's.)

Such prohibitions reflected the inhibitions of the Victorian era, which often required street photography to lead a secret life. Photographers working under these constraints in public places would resort to deceptions like Strand's fake lens, or else they would adopt the new "detective" cameras — models made to be either disguised or concealed — that manufacturers introduced onto the market toward the end of the century. Horace Engle used the Gray-Stirn Concealed Vest Camera, a flat, circular apparatus whose round negative rotated, like the cylinder in a revolver, behind a miniaturized lens that protruded through a buttonhole. A Pennsylvanian, Engle took street photographs as a hobby in the late 1880s, sometimes on trips to temperance conventions that he was attending at the time (fig. 5.4). He was a man whose need to be secretive affected other aspects of his life as well, including the diaries that he kept in hieroglyphics and code.

The brand of camera that Paul Martin used was the Facile, which came wrapped in brown paper as if it were a package. When Martin got caught in a rainstorm, the wrapping disintegrated, so he had a harness maker stitch a case that made the camera look like a satchel. This arrangement, with the lens sticking out through a porthole in the case, permitted Martin to get what he always said he wanted: "people and things as the man in the street sees them." [23] This remark echoes one Degas made about seeing the world as you do when "passing in the street" (see chapter 6, "Documents for Artists"). Other photographers devised their own disguises for their equipment. Samuel Coulthurst of Manchester, England, dressed himself as a rag-and-bone man and hid his camera under a pile of junk on his bar-

Fig. 5.4
HORACE ENGLE
Cora, 1888

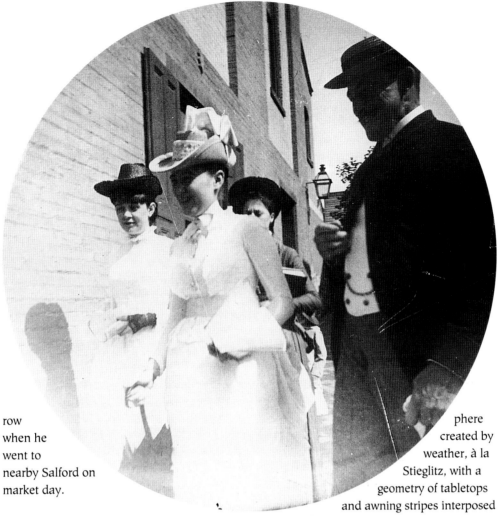

row
when he
went to
nearby Salford on
market day.

But even for photographers who didn't conceal their camera, street photography was still often a hidden activity, a covert part of the medium's history. If you look at the prints that Stieglitz owned by Paris photographer E. J. Constant Puyo, you find primarily misty landscapes reworked in gum bichromate or with oil pigment. Yet a little later in his life, on a trip to Italy, Puyo took along a panoramic camera with which he made snapshots of the street life there (pages 56–57, top). While he isolated figures and eliminated detail in his Pictorialist work, here he used the panorama as a wide net with which to pull detail in and combine separate scenes.

When a Pictorialist did publish a street photograph, the one he chose differed considerably from the sort he kept to himself. One of the most widely reproduced images by Puyo's fellow Photo-Club member Maurice Bucquet is a street scene entitled *Effet de Pluie*. As the title indicates, it's a photograph of an atmos-

phere
created by
weather, à la
Stieglitz, with a
geometry of tabletops
and awning stripes interposed
between the viewer and the subjects. Whereas Bucquet stood back out of the rain to get this composition, he could also plunge into a scene he was photographing to very different effect, as when he braved showers of confetti for a shot of a wedding or some other celebration included in his Paris miscellany (page 9).

The contrast between the Pictorialist work and the street photography done by Puyo or Bucquet can be found as well in the difference between the photography and the prose of Dallett Fuguet, or between the pictures Paul Martin took and the way he used them. A descriptive piece written for *Camera Work* by Fuguet, a wealthy New Yorker who was Stieglitz's associate editor, is a prose counterpart to much of the imagery the magazine published. It's the sort of fin de siècle pastoral that throws in archaisms like "forsooth." The languid tone that pervades this piece seems affected in light of the nimble, energetic street photography Fuguet was doing around the same time (page 59).

Paul Martin began making photographs while working as a wood engraver in London during the 1890s. He went out on his lunch hour to the fish and produce markets to take pictures of the porters. If he had a day off or a vacation, he went where the rest of the working class did — to a street fair, to Bank Holiday festivities on Hampstead Heath, or to the seaside resort of Yarmouth — and he toted his Facile hand camera with him. He sold some pictures from these excursions to his firm for conversion into engraved newspaper illustrations. But as he himself made clear in a memoir entitled *Victorian Snapshots,* recognition among amateurs was what he really craved. "My own great ambition . . . was to produce something new to show our society," he said, referring to the West Surrey Photographic Society, where he was a charter member.[24]

The very first pictures he did, the ones of the London markets, brought him the attention he wanted when he made them into lantern slides on which he painted out the backgrounds, thereby suppressing the atmosphere of hurly-burly in which his subjects were taken. He left only a small circle of pavement, like a base on a china figurine, for them to stand upon. Thus did he turn documents of London labor into Victorian bric-a-brac. This transformation by which a casual snapshot from the street became almost unrecognizable in the final work of art also occurred in the street photography of Arnold Genthe, who turned a series of tiny negatives shot in San Francisco's Chinatown into enormous manipulated prints on which backgrounds were held back and highlights brought out with a stylus.

Arriving in San Francisco from Germany in the mid-1890s, an accomplished linguist who had written a doctoral thesis at the University of Jena, Genthe was underemployed as a private tutor for a wealthy family. He filled his leisure time by exploring Chinatown, taking pictures of the street life there to teach himself

how to use the small Zeiss camera he had bought (pages 126–127). Will Irwin, a friend who accompanied Genthe on some of his outings, later recalled to him the way he worked "in the shadows and recesses of Chinatown, your little camera half-hidden under your coat, your considering eye and crafty hand . . . alert to take your shy and superstitious models unawares."[25] Lurking thus in a doorway, Genthe would wait until it was too late for his subjects to escape before bringing his camera into play.

Genthe's work demonstrates that it was not only the photographers who sometimes led a double life, but the photographs themselves. Made to be art, they survived as documentation. After the subject of his Chinatown pictures was destroyed in the earthquake and fire of 1906, the work itself took on a new significance. It alone among his possessions survived the disaster, because Irwin had prevailed upon his friend to store his record of Chinatown's street life in a bank vault. As the city was beginning to clear away the rubble and rebuild, Genthe was struck with an idea: to publish a book of his images. *Pictures of Old Chinatown* came out in 1908 with forty-seven reproductions and was reissued with about twice that number as *Old Chinatown* five years later.

For Genthe, the reconstructed community could never be as authentic as the original one he had known. After he had left San Francisco in 1911 for New York to establish himself as a celebrity portraitist, he added to *Old Chinatown* a "Postscript" in which he described a final visit he paid there amid "the glare of the blazing shop fronts [and] the noise of chugging automobiles carrying sightseers." This caused him to lament that "Old Chinatown, the city we loved so well, is no more."[26] Yet there is a certain irony to the tone of regret that creeps into Genthe's reminiscences here, for his own book, while commemorating the old Chinatown, had also contributed to making the new one into the tourist trap he was rejecting.

Every street photographer who has worked in a community in transition has probably had this kind of paradoxical effect on the process. Frank Sutcliffe looked upon the Whitby of his later years as having undergone no less a calamity than Chinatown. When shanties on Dock End were pulled down to make way for lodging houses and pubs to serve the summer residents, he complained that the fogs, mist, and dusk light he had employed in his photographs of the town were now necessary to hide the eyesores in it. At the arrival of these new residents each year, the fishermen who used to congregate around the harbor, in his own words, "melted away like the snow in summer." [27]

It probably didn't occur to Sutcliffe to what extent his own work was responsible. It was he who had earned Whitby the epithet of the Photographer's Mecca, thereby attracting the droves of vacationers who arrived each week on a packet boat from London aptly called *The Tourist*. After Sutcliffe retired from photography, he worked at a local historical society that was eventually to house a collection of his own photographs. The photographs themselves had helped to bring about this transformation of the present into the past and of the photographer into a curator. From Marville to Brassaï to the present day, street photography has often had about it an aura of self-fulfilled prophecy. The genre's ability to anticipate the subject's disappearance has at times been a way to precipitate the loss as well.

Nevertheless, such photography's value as documentation was acknowledged more and more as time went on, and this recognition was reinforced by the encouragement that Eastman Kodak gave to hobbyists to think of all aspects of everyday life as worthy subject matter for their Kodak snaps. These two developments gradually removed the stigma that was attached to taking photographs in the street. A key factor in this evolution was the use of the camera by the

preservationist movement in Great Britain, which developed in tandem with the rise of art photography. In fact, since an organization devoted to either kind of picture taking was likely to call itself a photographic society and commonly had members interested in both, the historic record and the art form tended to become conflated.

At first, professional photographers like Thomas Annan of Glasgow (the father of the Pictorialist J. Craig Annan) satisfied the need for a historical record of old quarters. The proprietor of a local studio, Annan was commissioned by the municipal government to photograph a slum district of ancient closes and wynds that was to be demolished under the Glasgow City-Improvements Act of 1866. Working from 1868 until 1877, he showed these cramped passageways to be places in which the stone and the pallid inhabitants were both nearly the same color as the pale,

Fig. 5.5
THOMAS ANNAN
High Street, Close No. 37,
1878–79

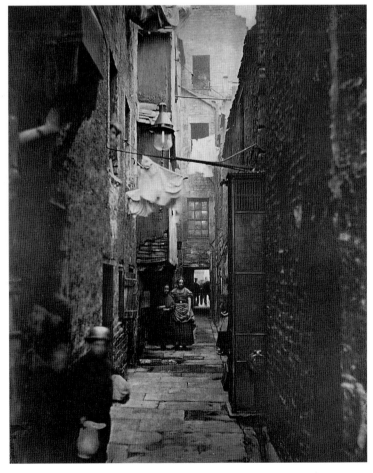

Fig. 5.6
SAMUEL
COULTHURST
At the Ale House Door,
1889–94

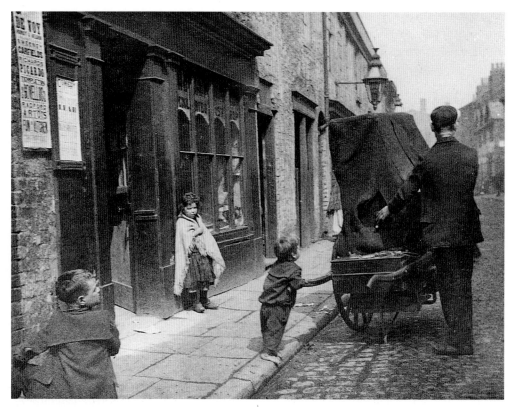

gray light (fig. 5.5). Like Genthe's work, Annan's led a double life — one as documentation, the other as art. The single difference is that Genthe's was appreciated as art first and only later for its documentary value, whereas with Annan's it was the other way around. The Glasgow pictures were published originally as documents by Annan himself in the 1870s, then given an artistic reincarnation in 1900 by his gravurist son, who retouched many of the photographs so that ghost figures were eliminated and details drawn into shadows.

The hiring of professionals like Thomas Annan continued for a while, but little by little amateurism took over all aspects of the preservationist movement in Great Britain. From 1874 until its dissolution in 1886, the Society for Photographing the Relics of Old London, a group of amateur historians of the city, employed professional photographers Henry Dixon and A. and J. Boole, whose carbon prints of ancient architecture soon to be razed were paid for by subscription. By the end of the 1880s the photography itself was being done by amateurs as well, the most notable being Sir Benjamin Stone.

Stone was the guiding light of the Birmingham Photographic Society and the founder, in 1897, of the National Photographic Record Association. An inveterate collector of British memorabilia, he did not limit his concerns to architecture alone. In 1889 he began taking a camera with him on his travels around the country, "always with the same object," he explained, "— to show those who will follow us, not only our buildings, but our everyday life, our manners and customs."[28] Stone's success in achieving these new aims through the Record Association was not as great as it might have been, because he restricted submissions to permanent prints, carbon or platinotype, of a fixed, full-plate size. Still, in having expanded his aims thus, he led the way for other amateur societies that also became more ambitious during that period.

One of these, the Manchester Amateur Photographic Society, was organized around the same time as Stone's Birmingham group and originally with the same purpose — to accumulate a systematic record of condemned buildings. In 1889 a "Record and Survey" section was formed by the society for this purpose, but within a year the objectives were extended from architecture to "any views of present-day Manchester that members might contribute" and then to the "business life, habits of the people, and how the poor live." These areas of consideration were to include snapshots "at crowded thoroughfares, busy markets and railway stations." [29] The Record and Survey didn't really get going, though, until 1892, when it was taken over by Samuel Coulthurst, the member who photographed the Salford market disguised as a rag-and-bone man. During his decade-long tenure, he built up a collection of more than two hundred views, about a quarter of which he made himself (fig. 5.6).

His appetite for street photography still unsated, Coulthurst also indulged it on trips around Britain and to the Continent. He was very aware that he was recording something "for future reference." Writing in 1895, he took the position that "our street trades, such as the organ grinder, street artist, hawker, scissor grinder, etc., will soon be objects of the past, and pictures of them will be of as much value . . . as pictures of old houses." [30] This attitude was increasingly widespread in photographic circles as the century drew to a close and the rate of change in British society accelerated.

Five years before Coulthurst issued his own call for greater emphasis on street photography, a writer in the Photographic Reporter had urged amateurs everywhere to "endeavour to secure street life in your own town. All things change in the course of time, and someday such pictures may become valuable." [31] In 1900, five years after Coulthurst wrote, an American named Osborne I. Yellott wrote a piece entitled "Street Photography," in which he argued that "the everyday life of the streets" is a subject "far more interesting than deserted mills or rustic bridges." He wanted to see more photography that strove not just to display technique, but rather "to depict the humor and pathos of life as we see it in our city streets." [32]

The growth in the popularity of photography was often dependent on the medium's alliance with some other pastime or cause, like preservationism. Many amateurs, such as the young Paul Martin, went on expeditions that were devoted to hiking as much as camera craft. Bicycling was another prominent hobby that got mixed up with photography. Walter D. Welford, a prolific author of photographic handbooks, was originally editor of a weekly journal entitled Cycling. In the late 1880s it began reproducing photographs, and by the decade's end Welford had switched his primary concentration to the camera, which should be used, he wrote, to "preserve for us the dress and fashion, the characters and incidents, the everyday life and bustle of the street." [33] Stieglitz despised mixed enthusiasms like Welford's because they made photography look like just another "fad." [34] He always believed that such divided allegiance was a distraction from photography's true calling, which was to serve itself rather than some other interest.

One reason for this proliferation of photo societies of every stripe in England was no doubt the chronic clubbiness of the British in all walks of life. This is in part a result of the long-standing British tradition of amateurism, the conviction that anything worth doing can be done best in one's spare time, and in part because the English find it impossible to be gregarious except in situations where all the social rules are spelled out, as in the bylaws of a club.

Sometime in the 1920s, a British camera buff wrote to one of the amateur magazines published by Eastman Kodak Ltd. commenting on how often he saw others photographing with Kodak equipment, but also lamenting, in true English fashion, that he felt diffident about introducing himself lest he be thought too forward. He suggested the company find a way to help hobbyists overcome their natural reserve. The company began issuing lapel buttons that said "The Kodak Fellowship," and without any further ado, this promotion led to a nationwide amateur union.

William Irwin lauded Arnold Genthe on the grounds that "you — more than any other man alive — have made art out of the play-time snap-shot."[35] A 1904 article for *Camera Work* praised Stieglitz's friend J. Craig Annan in like manner, for having "materially helped to popularize" the hand camera's "serious use."[36] Stieglitz liked the new small-format cameras himself, although he disapproved of detective models. (He found "distasteful," he said, the idea of "sneaking up on somebody and photographing him unawares."[37])

In the late 1890s, Stieglitz authored a piece entitled "The Hand Camera — Its Present Importance," wherein he told photographers how to get good results. His advice was essentially the same that Sutcliffe offered: frame the scene and then wait for passersby to come into it where they're needed to complete the composition. That was how Stieglitz had made *Winter — Fifth Avenue*, his first picture using a hand-held camera with a 4 x 5" format, which he bought when he returned to

Fig. 5.7
PAUL MARTIN
Bank Holiday on Hampstead Heath, 1896

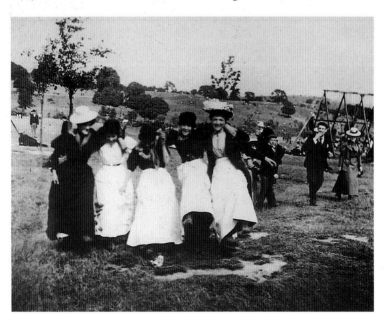

New York from Europe. Hand cameras were creating a surge of interest in street photography, as Maurice Bucquet explained in an essay he contributed to the 1893 volume *Esthétique de la photographie,* published by the Photo-Club de Paris. The great advantage of such equipment lay, he said, in its ability "to seize to the quick the scenes in the street and to render truly the attitude of the human being who is giving in to the passion of the moment."[38]

Since Kodak had pioneered the manufacture of the do-it-yourself camera in 1888, no consideration of amateur photography could be complete without taking the company's influence into account. What the articles by art photographers like Bucquet and Stieglitz cited above share is that they are essentially how-to pieces aimed at the camera buffs who were Kodak's primary market. The international leaders of the amateur movement were always mindful that photography — unlike painting, with its centuries of tradition — needed to have a high culture and aesthetic standards created for it. They therefore took care not to lose touch with followers who were less sophisticated than they.

In England, Eastman Kodak gladly provided everyone with a common ground on which to meet and thereby provided itself with an opportunity to connect the company's name with those of noted photographers. Kodak's vested interest in boosting amateurism led it to become an important benefactor of photo societies like The Linked Ring. It was no coincidence that one of that group's founders, George Davison, was picked by George Eastman to be the managing director of Kodak's English branch. In exchange for its services to the amateur movement, Kodak was able to exact from prominent art photographers cooperation ranging from a general encouragement of the use of the hand camera to endorsements of the company's products.

One way that Davison solicited the support of name photographers was to send them new camera models to test. Since he was a charter member of the West Surrey Photographic Society, for instance, he knew Paul Martin and gave him a Kodak Falcon Number 2 camera when it came on the market. Although Martin didn't like this equipment as well as his Facile camera (he recommended slower film and a faster shutter, modifications that Davison adopted), he did produce a set of pictures for Kodak.

Martin remembered later that the company exhibited snaps by a number of known amateurs at a gallery where a banner outside read "Come In and See What Can Be Done with a 'Kodak' "; and one day in Cheapside he came upon a crowd in front of a shop window in which there had been placed, he found on further investigation, an oversize enlargement of his own picture of girls capering on Hampstead Heath (fig. 5.7). A traveling salesman for Kodak subsequently told him the picture attracted such a throng that it had to be removed from the window — the police threatened to bring a charge of creating an obstruction.

Around 1900, Kodak was bringing out a lot of new models, and the practice of distributing them free to name photographers was at its peak. Frank Sutcliffe, who was more receptive to Kodak's overtures than Martin, probably received a succession of cameras at the time. He sent back to the company enough snapshots to fill three albums, which read like notebooks done in preparation for the views of Whitby he sold and published. He was referring to Kodak pictures when he wrote that "certain things . . . have a delightful precision or snap about them, which may be seen any day or every day — combinations of natural forms which arrange themselves in a certain way for an instant or two, and then alter entirely."[39]

Many of the pictures in Kodak's Sutcliffe albums are attempts to preserve these momentary combinations. On one occasion, at the dedication of the Caedmon Cross in Whitby Parish Churchyard in 1898, Sutcliffe used both the view camera and a Kodak. With the

former, he photographed the ceremony from the church tower; with the latter, he ran down in between time to work in the crowd.

Known photographers like Martin and Sutcliffe weren't the only ones whose pictures Kodak solicited. The company's advertising department ran contests in which snapshooters of every description were invited to submit their work. The winning entries were usually published in the official Kodak magazine and were saved by the company (fig. 5.8). In some cases, employees were given new models of Kodak cameras and told to experiment with them. This was in all likelihood how a series of panoramas in the albums that the company maintained came to be produced. At least, the similarity of composition suggests that they were done by the same photographer. But no record was kept of who did these or any other photographs, unless it was a name like Martin's or Sutcliffe's that Kodak

Fig. 5.8
UNKNOWN PHOTOGRAPHER
From a Kodak Amateur Photo Competition Album, c. 1895

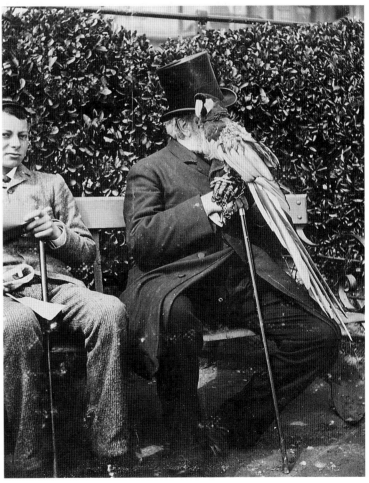

might exploit for its testimonial value in advertisements.

Ultimately consideration of this amateur work leads from photographers whose names are legend to those whose names have now been completely forgotten. Having begun with the work of Sutcliffe, Stieglitz, and Strand, the discussion arrives in the end at artifacts like an album of street photographs of London left behind by an unidentified Frenchman around the turn of the century. Was whoever made these snapshots a civil engineer studying the British capital from a professional point of view? That might explain why a number of pictures have an arrow drawn to indicate the location of the public convenience in a square or congested street. Lines drawn on many prints, like cropping instructions for a printer, suggest that the photographer planned to publish the work. Whatever the intentions or occasion may have been here, however, the salient fact that comes through from the pictures themselves is the prankish fun had in the making of them (page 57, bottom).

The impact that such images had on the history of photography was appreciated best in an essay that appeared in *Camera Work* in 1910. Entitled "On the Possibility of New Laws of Composition," this article by the critic Sadakichi Hartmann summed up the influence of the anonymous amateur:

> The main thoroughfare of a large city at night, near the amusement center, with its bewildering illumination of electric signs, must produce something to which the accepted laws of composition can be applied only with difficulty. Scenes of traffic, or crowds in a street, in a public building, or on the seashore, dock and canal, bridge and tunnel, steam engine and trolley, will throw up new problems. . . . As we examine amateur photographs as they are sent into the editorial offices of photographic magazines, we now and then will experience a novel impression. We do not remember of ever having seen it done just that way, and yet the

> objects are well represented and the general effect is a pleasing one. . . .

> If new laws are really to be discovered, an acquaintance with the various styles is prejudicial rather than advantageous, since the necessary impartiality of ideas is almost impossible. . . . Much will depend on the amateur who by sheer necessity will work unconsciously in the right direction. His knowledge will increase and his ambitions soar higher. And as he grows into esthetic perception, it will react upon the artist and urge him to attain a new and more varied, subtle and modern (though not necessarily more perfect) state of development.[40]

6: Documents for Artists

When Eugène Atget died in Paris in 1927, Berenice Abbott was afraid that his entire photographic archive might be destroyed because no one wanted it. She therefore sent a cable to Julien Levy seeking help, and he at once wired her a thousand dollars. In fact, the Atget estate was to be housed, exhibited, and represented for many years by the gallery Levy would soon open in New York. To Levy, as to many others in the art worlds of both New York and Paris, Atget was one of the great photographers of all time. Yet when Levy had first gone to see him at his tiny Paris apartment only a few months before his death, Atget had demurred at even being called an "artist." He was only an "amateur," he told Levy.[1]

Similar praise from Man Ray had brought from Atget a similar protest. Atget told the painter that he only made "documents for artists," as the sign outside his atelier said. When Man Ray wanted to publish Atget's work in the periodical *La révolution surréaliste,* Atget at first refused. Man persisted until the old photographer gave in. "But don't use my name," he stipulated.[2] Atget was a man of such reserve and modesty that one might wonder whether what he meant by "amateur" didn't include the idea of *un anonyme,* somebody who expected no recognition for his work. There was in his career an identification with ordinary, unknown people that began with his socialist tendencies and extended to his photographs, whose point of view is, even when nobody else is around, that of the man in the crowd.

Atget is the summary figure of nineteenth-century street photography in many ways, not the least being his resignation to an elusive anonymity of the sort into which the art photography examined in the previous chapter ultimately fades. Since he eked out a living at what he did, he should be regarded as a professional despite his disclaimers; yet insofar as he photographed only what he pleased, without much concern for what clients preferred, he can legitimately be considered an amateur too. It is because Atget managed to be both at once that he sums up the possibilities for street photography in his time. He worked in lonely obscurity most of his life, yet he was a seminal influence on those who came later. He used a view camera, yet he made imagery that was an inspiration to twentieth-century aficionados of the hand camera, who were among the first to discover and share his influence.

Perhaps it is this use of the view camera that ties him most decisively to the nineteenth-century tradition. Even after the invention of the dry plate, in the early 1870s, such a camera remained a fairly intractable apparatus. The only scene that was readily approachable with it was the mise-en-scène. Working often in streets that were deserted, but courting the kind of surprise compositions and curiosities of framing that would become common later, the best photographers of the time set the stage for the drama that would unfold in the street photography of Cartier-Bresson, Walker Evans, or Robert Frank.

Atget was chief among photography's scenic designers of this type. Even when he was functioning as a documenter of architecture, which was much of the time, he was capable of making images that would be inspiring to other street photographers later. The difference between his pictures of buildings and the conventional ones done by his contemporaries and predecessors in the field is that theirs idealize the architecture, removing it as much as possible from any particular time and place, while his always insinuate the actual streets of Paris where his subjects were found.

To appreciate Atget's achievement fully, it might be useful to consider first that of another documenter of Paris, Charles Marville. Marville can be thought of as a photographic twin — though hardly a kindred spirit — of Atget. While Atget operated at a remove from the sources of power in the France of his day, Marville worked close to them. Whereas Atget's imagery was the expression of no point of view other than his own, Marville's was supposed to be the official representation of a government policy. Nevertheless, the photography these two men created overlaps in certain regards. It suggests at times a common vision. It recalls us to a proposition we have already found implicit in other nineteenth-century careers: that the street has an inherent aesthetic to whose discovery the camera is drawn like a divining rod.

The document that Marville was to make of Paris had its sources in the coup d'état that Napoléon III staged in 1852. The regime that this self-proclaimed monarch established was the Second Empire, which lasted until 1870 — a period during which France enjoyed prosperity because of the centralized planning and massive economic development, in the form of public works projects, that the emperor introduced. His most ambitious project was to transform Paris into a modern city, the capital of the nineteenth century, and in 1853 he appointed Baron Georges-Eugène Haussmann to oversee the city's renovation.

Haussmann tore down vast districts of old housing, replacing them with a system of ring roads, wide, straight boulevards, and new streets on which proportions of building facades were regulated. The work Haussmann undertook was so extensive that he directed some members of his staff to cooperate with city officials in order to make a full record of the changes. This ad hoc group eventually became the city council's Permanent Subcom-

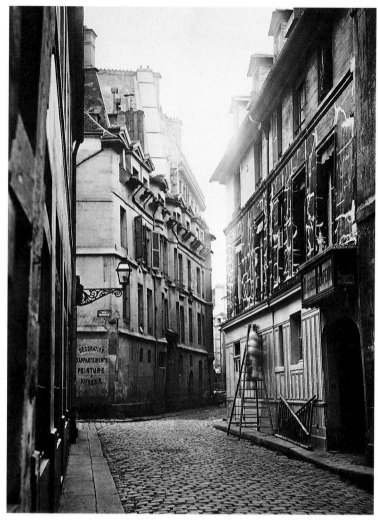

Fig. 6.1
CHARLES MARVILLE
Rue de Hautefeuille,
1862–66

mittee on Historic Works, whose main job was to compile the official *Histoire générale de Paris.*

One of the responsibilities the subcommittee took on was advising the photographer Marville, who had been commissioned to document the rebuilding of the city. Having begun this work sometime in the late 1850s, Marville was by 1862 entitled to call himself, according to the sign over the gate to his atelier in the Boulevard Saint-Jacques, *"Photographe de la ville de Paris."* Marville's documentation of the city was as comprehensive as Haussmann's plan.

When the first volume of the *Histoire générale* appeared, in 1866, Haussmann wrote for the preface an open letter to Napoléon III in which he praised the emperor's desire "to

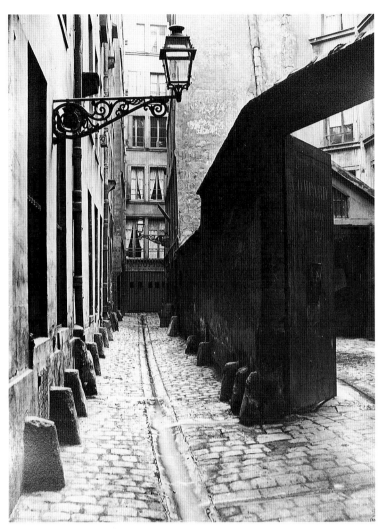

Fig. 6.2
CHARLES MARVILLE
Impasse de la Bouteille,
1862–71

seek in the past the explanation for the present and the preparation for the future."[3] The Janus-like rhetoric of this phrase might describe the program that Marville followed with his camera as well. He photographed each of the condemned districts before demolition began, while it was in progress, and after it was completed. He aimed his camera up the street in one direction and down it in the other. Where two streets crossed, he might make exposures from all four sides of the monument in the intersection.

Marville was an unlikely choice for this work. As an illustrator in the 1830s and 1840s, and then as a maker of calotypes when he first switched to photography in the early 1850s, he hadn't associated himself with such forward-looking projects as Haussmannization. One text to which he contributed engravings,

for instance, was about the France of Louis XIV and Louis XV. It was entitled *Yesteryear, or the Good Old Days,* and appealed to a taste for nostalgia rather than progress. The calotypes that Marville did for the Lille publishing firm of Blanquart-Evrard were similarly romantic — pastoral scenes like a deserted mill or blasted oak, travelogues to Algeria and the Rhine Valley. This conventional art photography was utterly different from the Paris documentation not only in spirit, but in look.

In Paris, Marville became an engineer of the camera as Haussmann was of the city. His photographs were attempts to clear the sight lines of ancient, twisted streets much as Haussmann's pickax crews would clear away the buildings soon after Marville's initial visit. Marville handled his camera the way a surveyor uses a sight gun. If he placed the camera just so, choosing the one standpoint from which none of the jutting edges of the buildings overlapped, he could see straight to the end of even the most narrow, winding street (fig. 6.1).

He spoke of the demolitions as *"percements,"*[4] and his photographs were comparable efforts to pierce the old quarters of the city, to drive a needle of vision through the crevice of the streets. The problem of visual leverage that he posed for himself was how to get the maximum amount of information into each picture. Sometimes he needed to make the frame bridge a gap between two subjects that were spread apart (page 49). More typically, the problem was the opposite — to excavate the deepest possible well of light in the center, letting the sides of the frame fall where they might.

Although shaped by the purely logistical problem of how to get at the subject and by Marville's struggle with the restrictions that cramped spaces imposed, the photographs done before renovation began are the ones that seem most artful today. Their appeal is not just that they depict a quaint Paris now gone, but also that they have a certain look, a recognizable style. Since this photographic record was being kept to justify tearing down most of the subjects, it was not to Marville's advantage to have them look conventionally picturesque. But this does not mean that his images strike us as being without any conventions at all. They are architectural studies in which form follows function. The alignment of the central axis in picture after picture comes to be a convention in its own right. So does the chance framing that results from this photographic practice.

A recurrent imagery in Marville's work is of scenes where we look directly down the street in front of us, but also obliquely through a gate and into a yard on one side (fig. 6.2). It is as if the photographer, seeing that the view straight ahead led his picture into a cul-de-sac, had allowed his imagination to fork off toward the edge of the frame. In many cases, an unexpected detail along the border of a print — a partly demolished wall that runs down the side of the image and seems to give the image itself a jagged, broken-off edge, a heap of rugs slumped against a fence like a human form, a side of meat hanging on the corner of a butcher shop — becomes the focus of attention. No matter how incidental their inclusion may have been, peripheral visions such as these are what differentiate the photographs from one another, bringing each alive.

By the time Eugène Atget was photographing in the old sections of Paris several decades after Marville, a reaction against Haussmannization had set in. Decrepit districts were now thought so picturesque that a curator at the Musée Carnavalet entertained friends in the early 1900s by taking them to see the Zone, a band of makeshift huts beyond the city's fortifications. This man was Georges Cain, who was to buy many prints from Atget for his collection. It's conceivable that Atget met Cain at the Zone, for Atget was photographing there at the time of the curator's visits.

By the late 1890s, concern over the fate of historic districts had led to the establishment of the Commission Municipale du Vieux Paris, which gave official encouragement to preservationist groups ranging from neighborhood committees to the Bibliothèque Historique de la Ville de Paris. It was from the ranks of this movement that Atget's clients were drawn. This revival of interest in old Paris and its preservation was in effect a Romantic revival. That was the prevailing mood to which Atget's pictures appealed.

Atget's work and Marville's were, then, done at cross purposes. And yet, just to look at them, the two men's pictures of Paris don't seem contradictory. In each photographer's work, the city has a kind of ungainliness that's very beautiful. The fact is that Atget knew Marville's pictures and was influenced by them. In 1899 the chief librarian at the Bibliothèque Historique hired a commercial photographer to restore and print the roughly four hundred Marville negatives in the library's collection. In 1907 Atget was commissioned to expand the archive into which the Marville material had finally been incorporated a couple of years before. By then Atget was already well aware of Marville's work, for he had sold more than twenty-five hundred of his own images to the library. This volume of business required a great deal of coming and going during the period when the freshly reprinted Marville material was often laid out on the library's tables.

Since Atget photographed in the same sort of constricted locations as Marville, it is not surprising that their images should look alike in some respects. But perhaps certain similarities, especially a somewhat elegiac mood that seems to pervade both men's work, are also a result of their having been artists with Romantic inclinations in their youth. Each subsequently went through a period of failure and possibly disillusionment when he developed an interest in socialism; and in the end, each took up a career as a documenter in which earlier aesthetic passions were, it seems, suppressed.

Atget's Romanticism took the form of a career as an itinerant actor that lasted until he was forty. Performing in third-rate provincial touring companies, he preferred Romantic plays like *Ruy Blas* and roles like that of the legendary rogue hero Robert Macaire. Atget was part of the generation in Europe to which his contemporary William Butler Yeats referred as "the last Romantics."[5] A great deal of modern art has been the result of a fallen Romanticism, a disillusionment after which the artist assumes a less vulnerable and more stoic, impassive attitude toward the world. It may be that Atget's late career reflects such a development as well.

The Atget who lived in Paris from the mid-1890s until the mid-1920s was, at any rate, a very enigmatic figure. He kept no diaries or daybooks. His only testament, aside from the pictures, is in the form of business ledgers, albums that he either hoped to sell or used for showing his wares, and correspondence regarding transactions with the *bibliothèques*. The poet Robert Desnos, who knew Atget, eulogized him in an article entitled *"Les spectacles de la rue,"* in which he said that the photographer's albums were "the visions of a poet handed down to poets."[6] If poetry, however, these albums are poems of a singularly mute kind. While telling us a great deal about Atget's predilections where Paris is concerned, they are a less certain testament on photography itself. In the final analysis, we just don't know whether he liked one picture more than another, or even whether he was capable of telling his great pictures from the many mediocrities he also kept in stock.

It is clear that with certain types of subjects — especially ironwork, carved stonework, shop signs, and other Parisian street decor — he tried to make as comprehensive a survey as he could. This meant finding the unusual and whimsical as well as the typical. If he did a series of lion's-head door panels, for instance,

he would include the one where the smiling beast's forelegs are tied in a knot like a drape sash.

In many cases, however, it is not the subject matter — or not only that, anyway — that makes the image arresting. It is the way the subject is treated, the attitude that the photograph takes toward it. To seek out among the many ordinary pictures the ones that are remarkable for this reason seems an appropriate homage to pay Atget, since the discovery of what is remarkable in them often requires a similar searching of the image itself. Consider the photograph (circa 1908) of the work yard of a coppersmith (page 50). Because the camera stares straight ahead inexpressively, its central focus fixed on a blank wall, we don't immediately spot the woman looming in the window of the low-ceilinged room above. Once we do, we are taken aback by her freakish presence, because it is so unexpected in an otherwise routine scene.

There is a kind of discretion in the image — it doesn't gawk at its subject — and this suggests an impassivity in Atget himself, who doesn't give away his reaction to the things he photographs. This is the quality in the work of which Walter Benjamin was speaking when he said that Atget photographed Paris as if it were "the scene of a crime."[7] An understated point of view like this is seen in a great deal of street photography. It is also seen in the way that Atget left his life's work for us to make of it what we would. Perhaps the sense he had of his collection as a whole was the same that the individual pictures in it often seem to make. In them, too, he refrained from pointing out what was exceptional or mysterious.

Curiosities like the knotted lion's paws or the coppersmith's yard can be found throughout Atget's work. In one image, a crowd watches an eclipse through bits of smoked glass; in another a fountain has been emptied of its water and filled with workers who are cleaning it; in yet another the face of a street peddler posing

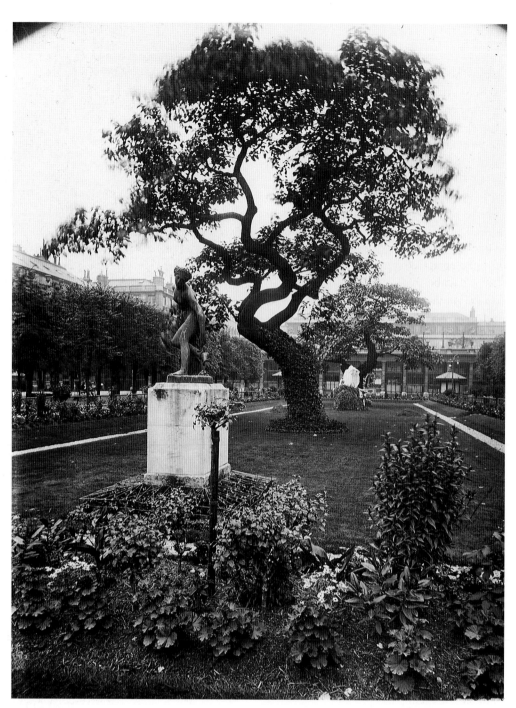

Fig. 6.3
EUGÈNE ATGET
Paris, Palais Royal, n.d.

for his portrait is hidden behind a puff of smoke that he exhaled just as the picture was taken.

Another kind of oddity that turns up in files of Atget's work is the slight blurring of human subjects who moved during the long exposures his view camera required. (The shudder we feel at the sight of the coppersmith's wife began with a trembling of her own.) There is in such pictures a disparity between the slow time of the city — the ancient buildings, the streets, the stones themselves — and the brief

time of its inhabitants. This often seems to be the point that, intentionally or not, these flawed images are making.

Old Paris was for Atget a necropolis, a city from the past inhabited by ghosts. They flit across the pictures in the shadows, avoiding the light. Because he was a master of the balanced exposure, his negatives frequently read the exterior of a building while also penetrating the interior, even if there is a closed window separating them. The figures on the other side swim into sight, watery apparitions in the glass. In other pictures, subjects are equally insubstantial. They are half-dissolved in gloom beneath a passageway or beyond a casement that's ajar. All these figures are seen in passing in a couple of senses. We feel as if we are only passing by, catching just a glimpse of them as we go. And at the same time they themselves seem to be passing away, fading from sight even as we look at them.

Little by little over the years, Atget emptied his photographs of people altogether. What finally absorbed his interest was not life on the street, but the life *of* the street: the spirit of the place itself, the movement of the spirit in the stones. The most animated pictures he took were, paradoxically, those of statues. A bust at Versailles appears physically smitten by a shaft of sunshine; it cries out in pain. At the Palais Royal, another statue ducks under the lash of a tree, gnarled and writhing in the background (fig. 6.3). Atget's penchant for formalism — for corresponding shapes deftly fitted together to provide the structure of a picture — found a perfect outlet in images like these. The shapes do not just interlock. They interact. They quicken an otherwise desolate scene.

The best of the studies of statuary, as indeed of Atget's work in general, were made in the parks at Sceaux and Versailles during the 1920s. This was the period at the end of his life, after he had created a small retirement fund by selling off the bulk of his archive, when he worked with complete independence. The only person present when most of these pictures were made was Atget himself. If they seem to represent the essence of his career, it is because they make us realize that his presence is the one that we have been sensing all along in his work. The everyday life in the street that his photographs reveal is his own. The human experience to which they make us privy is the one that he himself had while wandering Paris and the surrounding countryside, looking for pictures.

A decade or so before Atget came to Paris, Edgar Degas had observed, "Never yet have

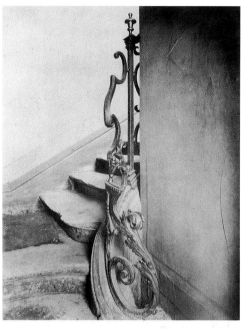

Fig. 6.4
EUGÈNE ATGET
91, Rue de Turenne,
1911

monuments or houses been done from below, from close to, as one sees them passing in the street."[8] Atget's photographs were made as if to answer the complaint. From the city to the outlying parks, there are a number of series that he did where, by tracing consecutive negative numbers, we can literally follow his path as he reconnoitered a subject. But even a lone study of a subject often conveys an impression of the circling, probing approach Atget must have taken to find just the right point of view.

The picture of the statue and tree at the Palais Royal is such an image, and so is an interior he made of a stairwell in 1911 (fig. 6.4). We can feel him entering the building and passing through the courtyard into the darkened corridor where this subject suddenly confronts him. As he begins to ascend the steps, the handrail gleams with malevolence. It writhes like a scotched serpent, as if recoiling from his imminent touch. The French curve it describes loses all the grace and harmony that classical design is supposed to have. It ceases to be inert iron cool to the touch and becomes something organic, convulsed. Atget is showing this subject to us through the eyes of a thousand Parisians who have trudged up such stairs a thousand times. We are seeing it from the point of view of a man who is one of those people himself. Having left early this morning, before anybody else was afoot, he returns now with his camera. He climbs with it to his

Fig. 6.5
EUGÈNE ATGET
*Coin de la Rue Valette et
Pantheon*, 1925

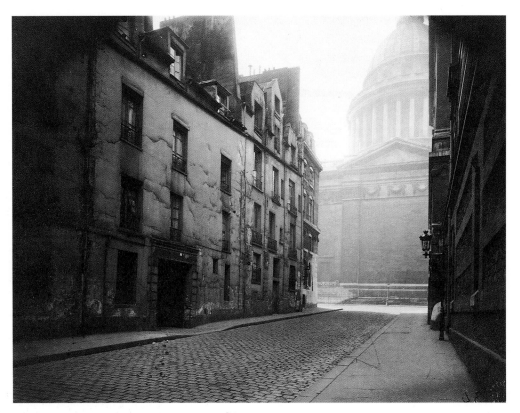

own apartment on the fifth floor at 17 *bis* Rue
Campagne-Premiere.

When art dealer Julien Levy saw the photograph of the serpentine handrail in the early
1920s, he was reminded of Pierre Roy's Surrealist painting *Danger on the Stairs*, in which a
snake slithers down a staircase. This Atget
image was also one of a number reproduced
in the journal *La révolution surréaliste* during
the two years before Atget died. Atget's photography was admired by these representatives of the avant-garde partly because it had
one of the essential qualities prized in modern
art: originality. His street photographer's vision was something distinct not only from the
Romantic clichés of his day, but from the
classic photography of architecture as well.
To appreciate how radical his vision of Paris
was, we need only compare it to what went
before.

At the time Atget began photographing in the
1890s, a study of old Paris that had been a
standard reference and guide for more than
half a century was the three-volume *Paris his-

torique, promenade dans les rues de Paris*. This
book was a survivor of that earlier stage of
French Romanticism of which Atget's own period saw a revival. Atget almost certainly
knew the book, as had Marville, who did illustrations in the mid-1830s for another work
by *Paris historique*'s primary author, Charles
Nodier. The enclosed atmosphere of old
streets becomes, in the book's lithographs, an
artistic effect. The obstructions to the view
found in real streets have been converted here
into decorative borders. Thus does an arch or
the edge of an adjacent building serve to
frame a composition at the top and sides. The
light becomes a form of highlight around
which everything except the central building
is in deep shadow. With the help of such artwork, the veil of history is repeatedly pulled
aside to reveal whatever house or hall Nodier
is discussing at the moment.

Atget sometimes approximated this kind of illustration with his camera, but deference to
the picturesque, to received opinion of how
old Paris should look, is relatively rare in his
work. He soon realized, as had Marville be-

fore him, that he had to accept the inescapable welter of detail and the indifference of the light to his wishes as stage manager of his photograph. Out of these hindrances, out of the obduracy of the real world, the street photographer must make his art if he is to have one at all. Nor was the popular Romanticism of *Paris historique* the only inherited convention that Atget shunned. As Molly Nesbit has pointed out, even his presentation albums "provided . . . concrete evidence of Atget's defects, evidence of how habitually he had come to fidget within the regulation forms of the document" set down by the official archives.[9] He broke most of the accepted rules for rendering architecture, from those observed in *Paris historique*'s lithographs to those practiced at the Ecole des Beaux-Arts. In the process, he contradicted what was thought correct by more illustrious predecessors in photography, such as Edouard Baldus.

In the most successful Paris pictures by this midnineteenth-century architectural photographer, the camera appears to hover before the facade head-on, dead center. This is an unearthly point of view, higher than a man stands yet not superior to the building it studies. It would be a God's-eye view, if God were an architect. It is also the point of view found in contemporary elevations and presentation drawings done at the Ecole des Beaux-Arts, where the ideal way of representing buildings was taught. If an officially sanctioned view of architecture existed, that was it.

The centrality of this point of view, in both optical and social terms, made it a limited one for photography, however. Baldus could make it work only with monumental structures important enough to sit on open ground and afford him the advantage he needed. The results are exactly the opposite of those sought by Atget. On the occasions when Atget did photograph monumental public buildings, he never took the privileged point of view found in Baldus's work. He kept his distance from a subject like the Pantheon, which, in his best shot of it, looms hazily at the end of the Rue

Valette (fig. 6.5). The photograph invests the building with the remoteness and insubstantiality that grand institutions have in the lives of ordinary people.

Atget and Marville both celebrated a kind of uncouthness of old Paris that seems to inhere in the subject. Each discovered in the streets themselves, and in his camera, an aesthetic to which neither would have laid sole claim. The distinct character that their work has is but a part of the larger personality that belongs to street photography as a whole. Atget had a genius for photography. He *was* an artist. Yet his work makes sense not in the context of art photography — of pictures done by those who were self-consciously calling themselves artists, as he was not — but in the company of other photographers who were anonymous. The history of street photography is full of them, slogging professionals and eccentric

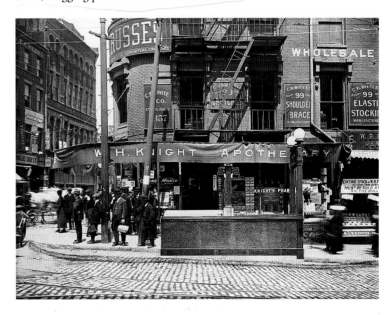

amateurs about whom little is known, not even their names, but in whose images the imprint of the street itself unmistakably appears.

Such pictures can be found in the archives of historical societies and the files left behind by local documenters almost anywhere. An architect's album prepared during the construction of the Boston subway system is a very

Fig. 6.6
UNKNOWN PHOTOGRAPHER
Untitled, n.d.

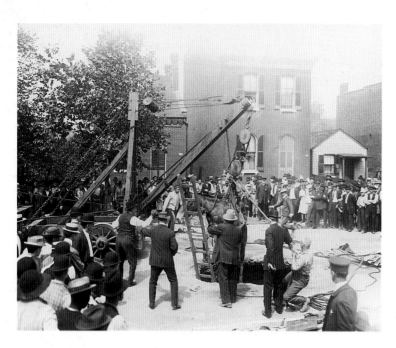

Fig. 6.7
UNKNOWN
PHOTOGRAPHER
Untitled, c. 1900

suggestive artifact in this regard. The first page is a photograph of a street corner on which a street-level entrance to one of the stations has been constructed, or so it appears (fig. 6.6). In fact, the image of the entrance has been cut from a second photograph and pasted on the one of the street corner. On subsequent pages, hand-drawn alternate designs for entrances have been pasted on the same background photograph.

These experiments are very different in feel from a group of drawings in the back of the same album, where, without prints of the photograph as background, entrance kiosks sit in blank space occupied only by a single, posed figure sketched in for scale. As the drawings pasted on the photographic prints in the front progress, the design becomes less boxy and sarcophaguslike in a way that allows it to blend in better with all the extraneous but stimulating information — the zigzag of a fire escape, a utility pole that's out of kilter, the patchwork of advertising signs on a building, the unsightly throng of the crowd on the sidewalk — that the photograph provides. Perhaps through photographs of city streets like this one, twentieth-century urbanites were already "learning from Las Vegas" long before the Post-Modernist architect and theoretician Robert Venturi coined the phrase.

Another example of the street's sheer presence as subject matter is apparent in the work of a man who seems to have held a post in Atget's time as an evidentiary photographer for the Department of Streets of the city of St. Louis. This photographer — perhaps a man named Kuhn, who appears on the directory of municipal employees during the period — spent his time documenting the construction of roadways, the laying of sewer lines, the opening of new parks and trolley routes, and the need for street repairs or the removal of obstructions to the flow of traffic.

Although such assignments would have had a skull-flattening monotony to them, he doesn't seem to have done the work with indifference. The pristine whiteness of freshly laid concrete is set off by the dirty urchins who are permitted to lounge on it as the picture is taken. In the middle of a street where a crowd has gathered, a horse is being winched either into or out of a gaping hole in the ground (fig. 6.7). With this photographer's work, as with Marville's, there are simply too many of these wonderful little anomalies in the pictures for us to dismiss them as mere flukes. This is not to suggest that this practitioner had a talent like Atget's or a comparable ability to learn from what he saw when he peered into the ground glass. But even in his pictures, the everyday life *of* the street — the inherent beauty and fascination that public spaces have in modern times — possesses an undeniable power.

PART TWO

Cartier-Bresson
& Europe in the Twentieth Century

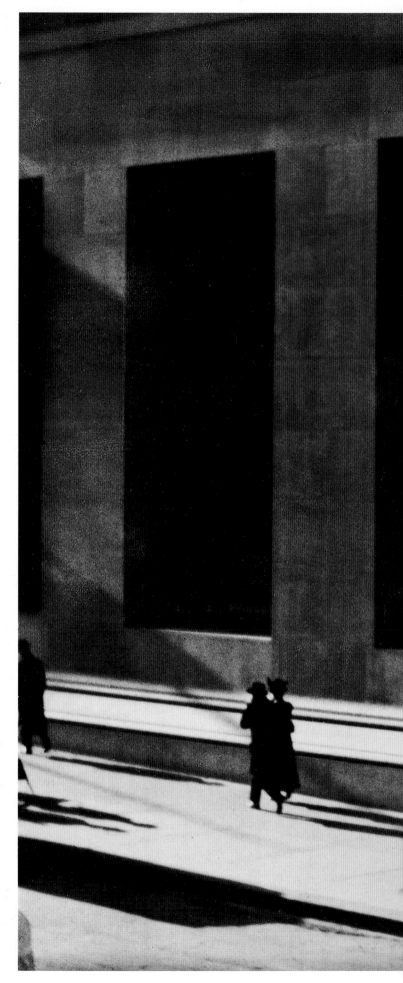

PAUL STRAND
Wall Street, New York,
1915

116

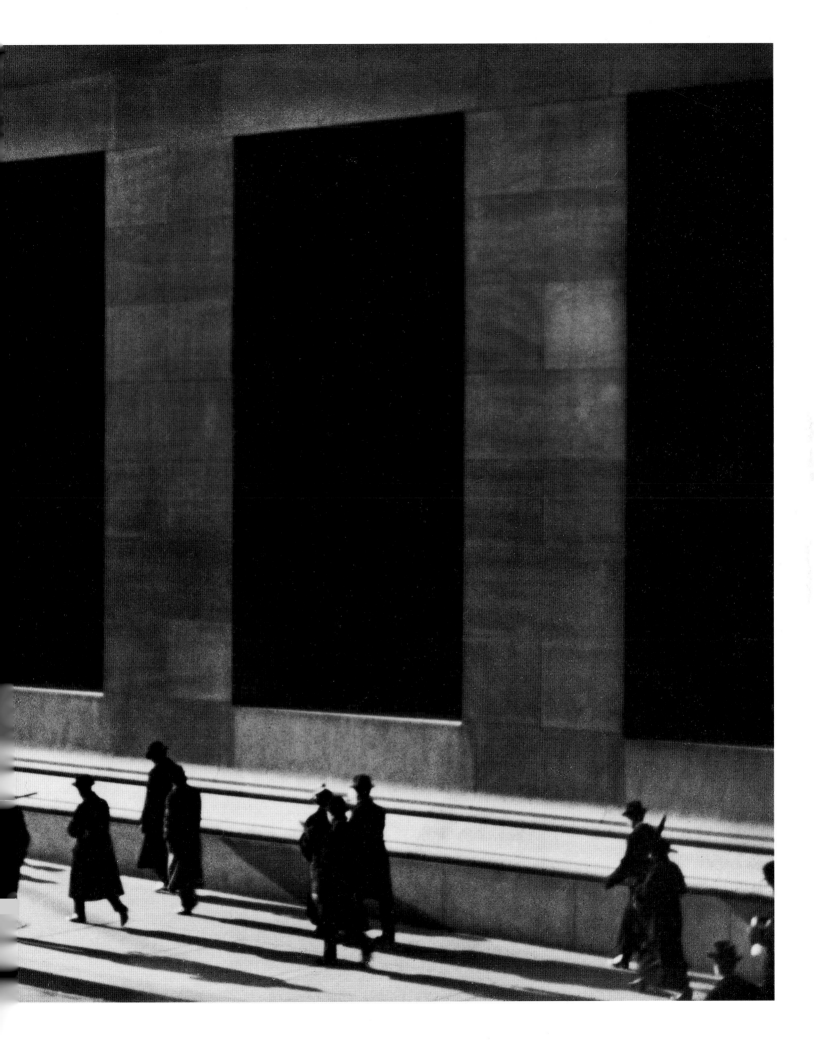

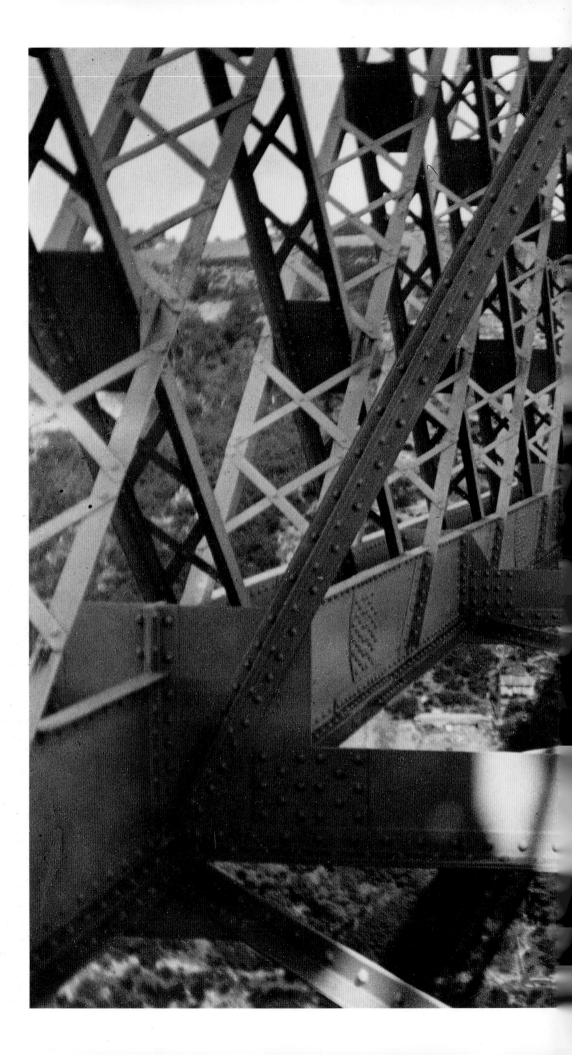

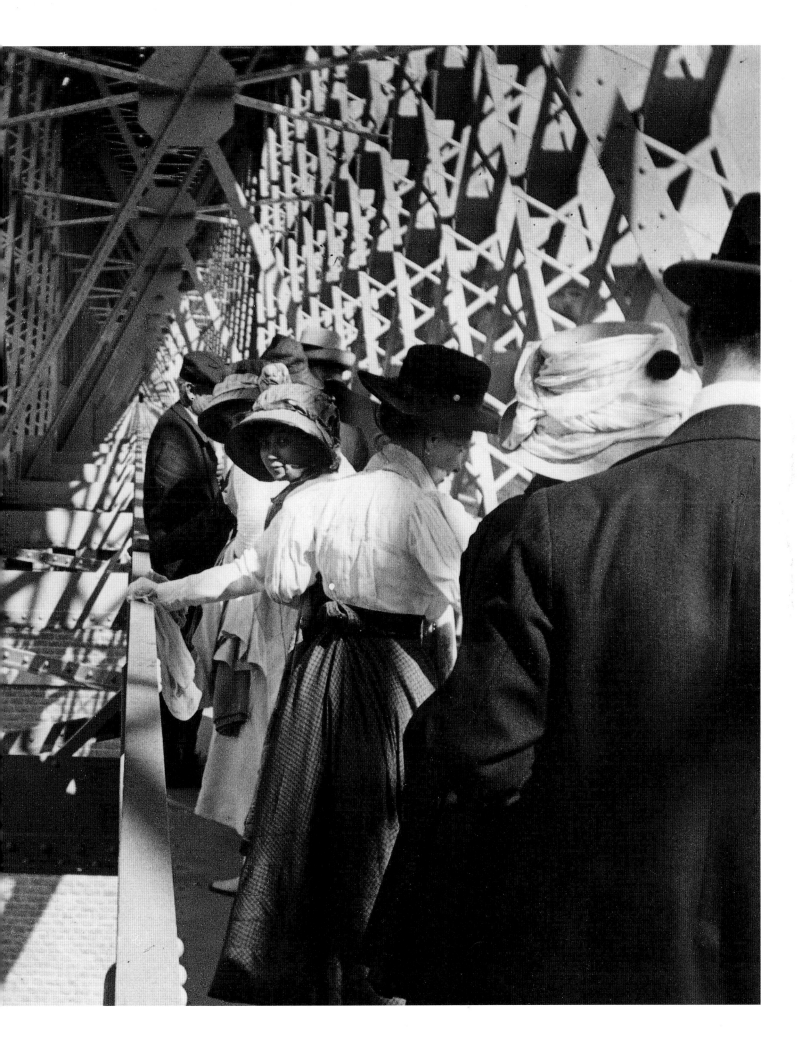

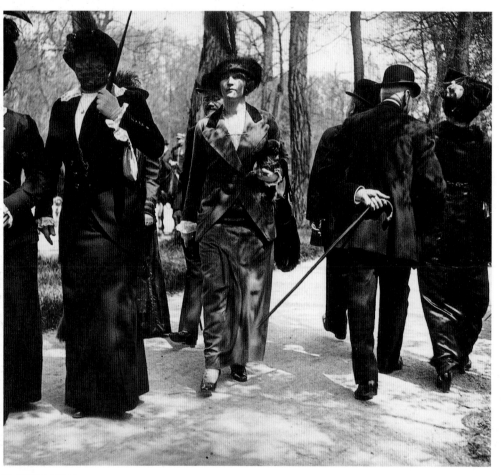

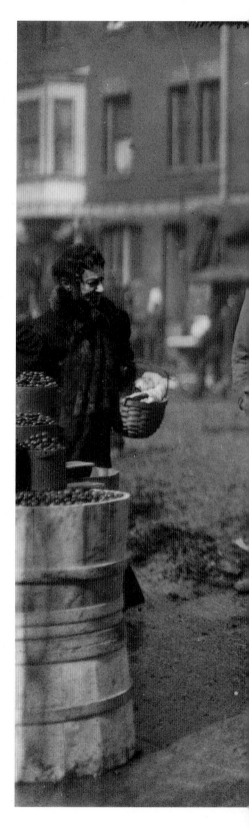

JACQUES-HENRI
LARTIGUE
Au Sentier de la Vertu,
1912

120

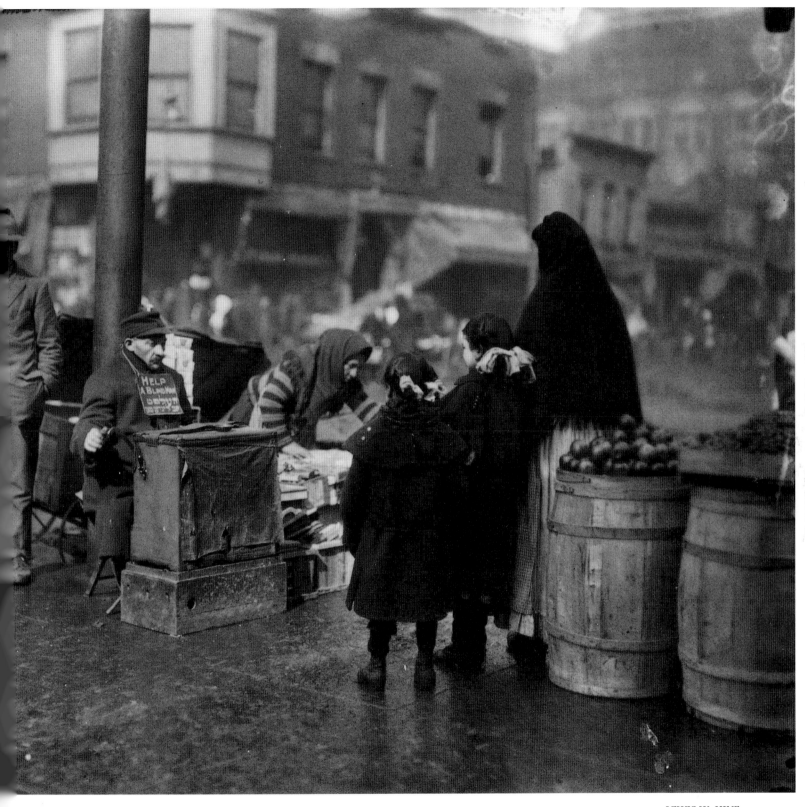

LEWIS W. HINE
Blind Beggar in Italian
Market District,
1911

121

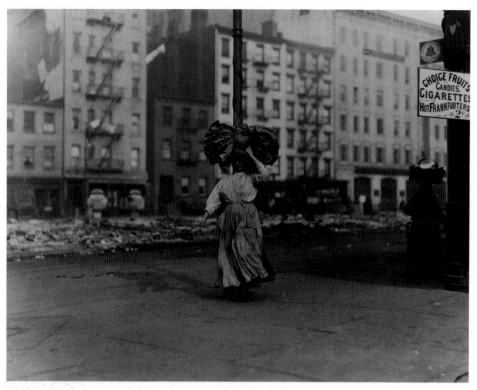

LEWIS W. HINE

Italian Immigrant, East
Side, New York, 1910

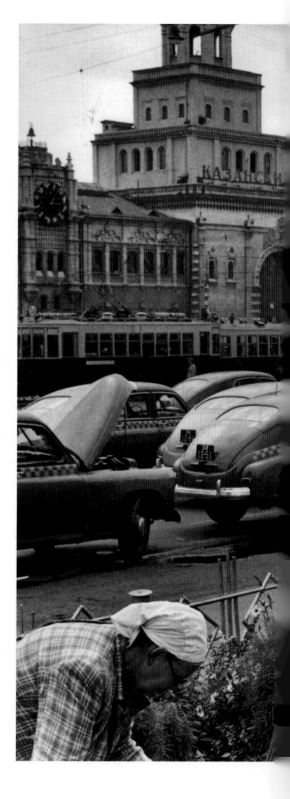

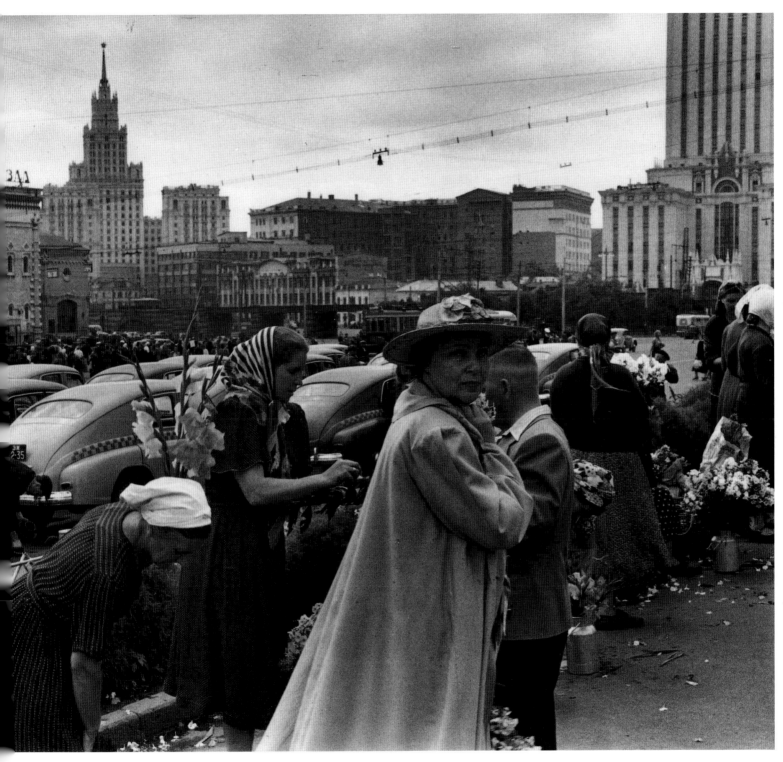

HENRI CARTIER-
BRESSON
U.S.S.R., 1954

123

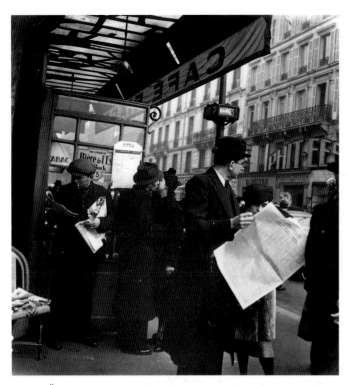

BRASSAÏ

Lovers, Paris, 1937

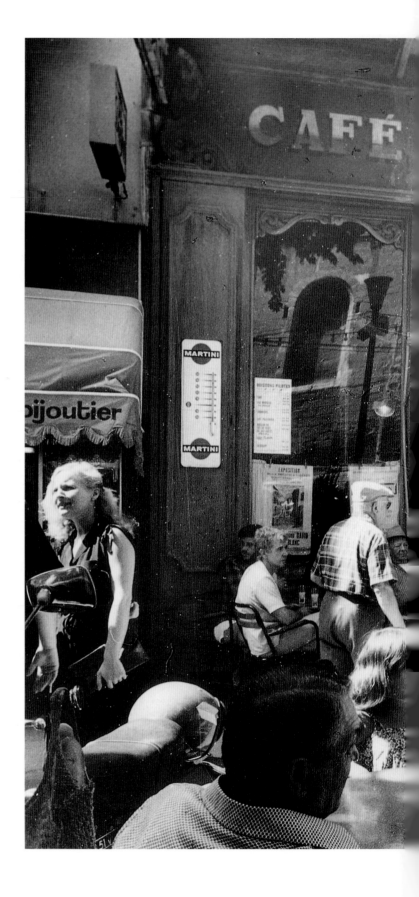

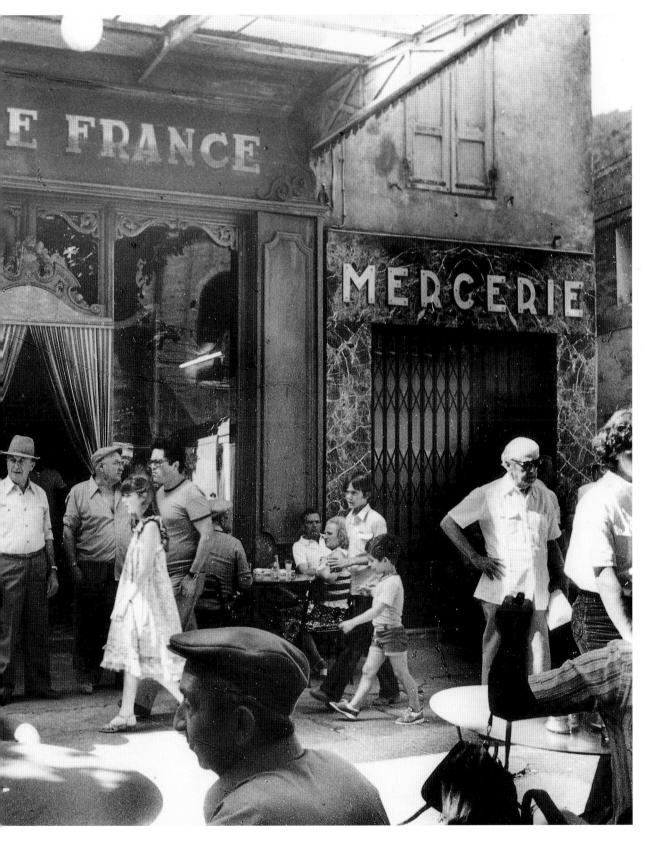

WILLY RONIS
L'Isle-sur-la Sorgue,
1979

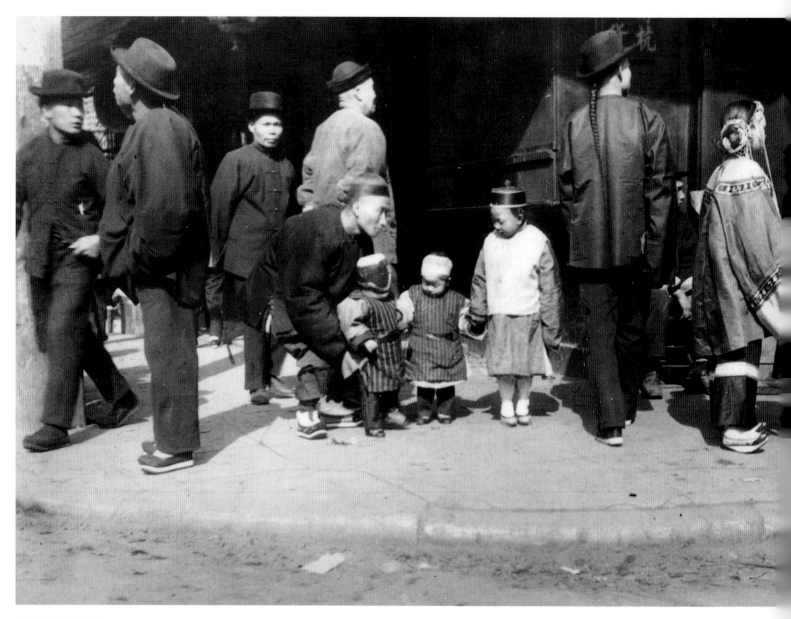

ARNOLD GENTHE
The Children's Hour,
No. 4, 1895–1906

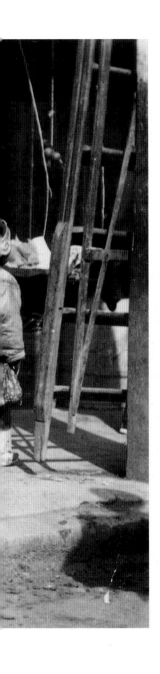

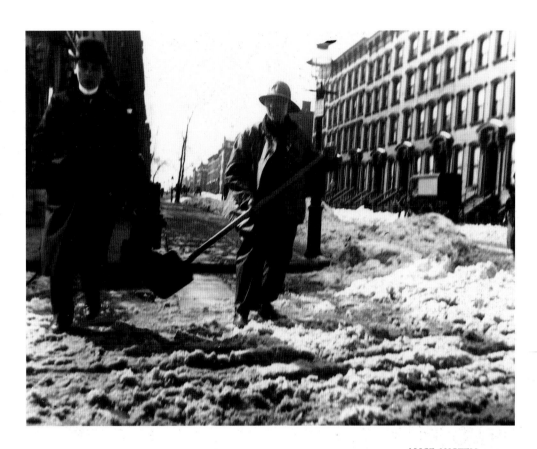

ALICE AUSTEN
Street Cleaner in Oilers
with Shovel, New York,
1896

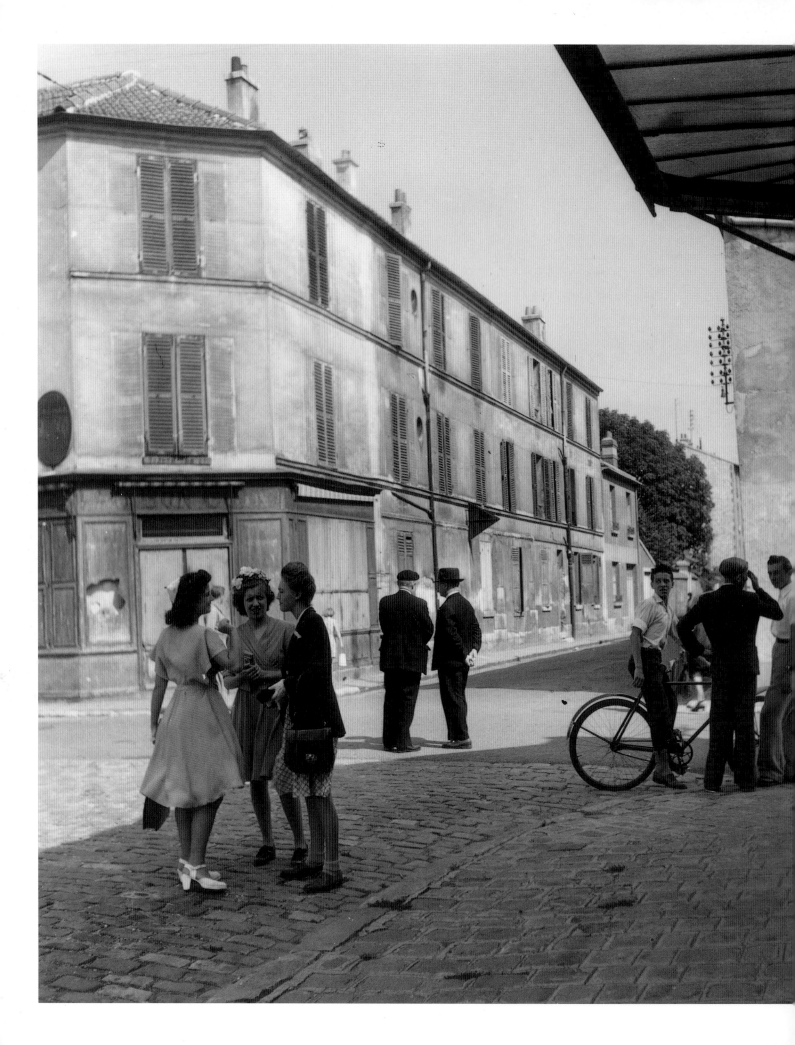

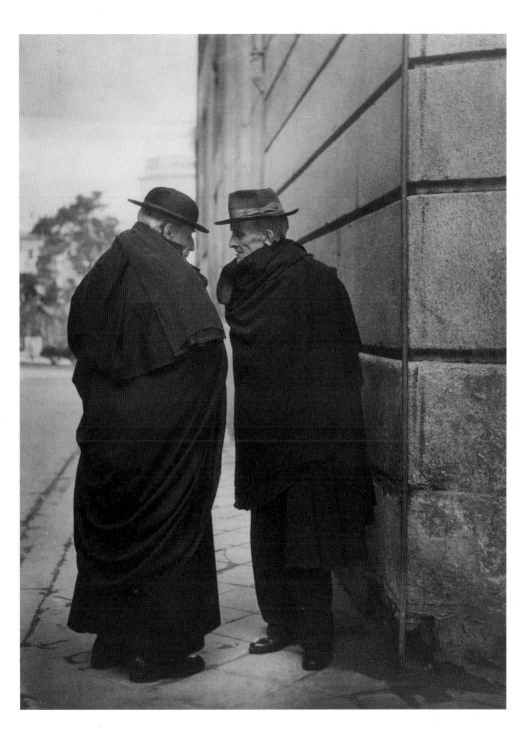

BRASSAÏ
Seville, 1952–53

ROBERT DOISNEAU
*Sunday Morning in
Arcueil, 1945*

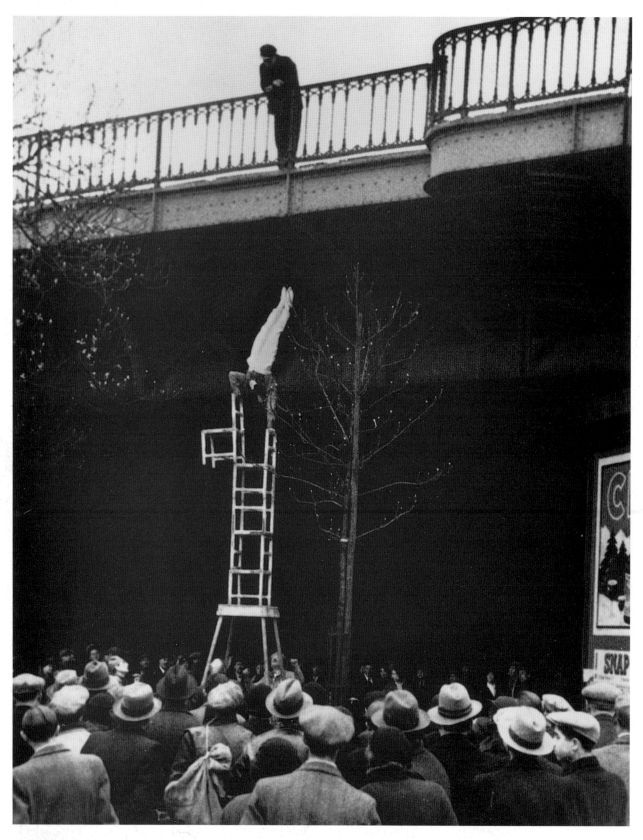

ANDRÉ KERTÉSZ
"Fête Foraine," Paris,
1931

Right:
ANDRÉ KERTÉSZ
Poughkeepsie, New
York, 1937

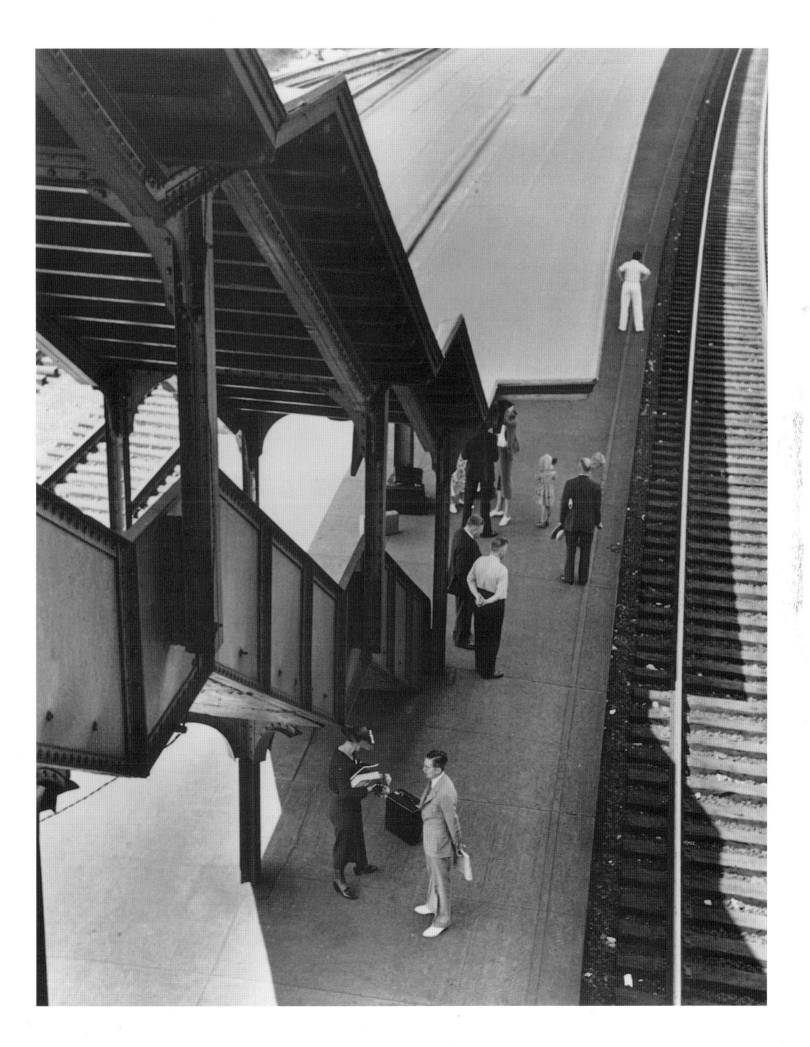

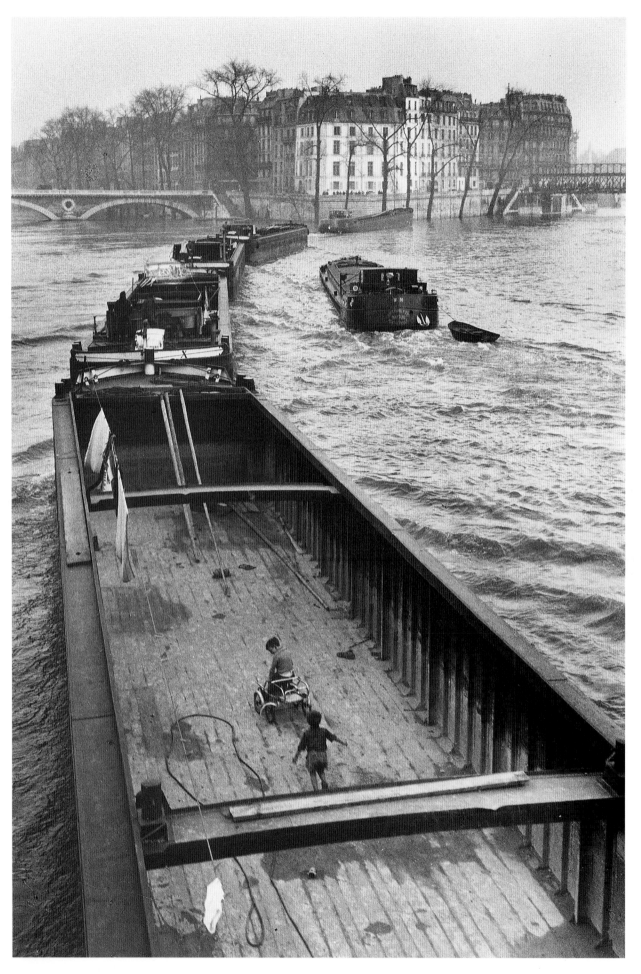

WILLY RONIS
Barge with Children,
1959

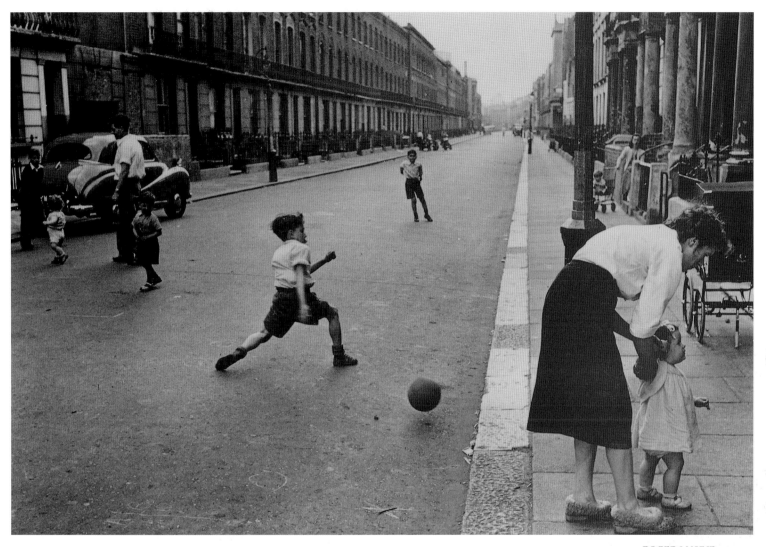

ROGER MAYNE
Untitled, 1956–61

MANUEL ALVAREZ
BRAVO
*Conversation near the
Statue, Mexico City,
1934*

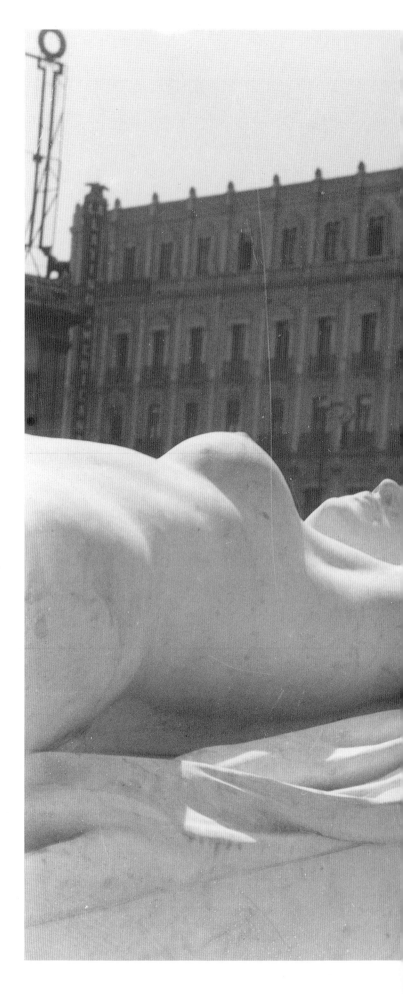

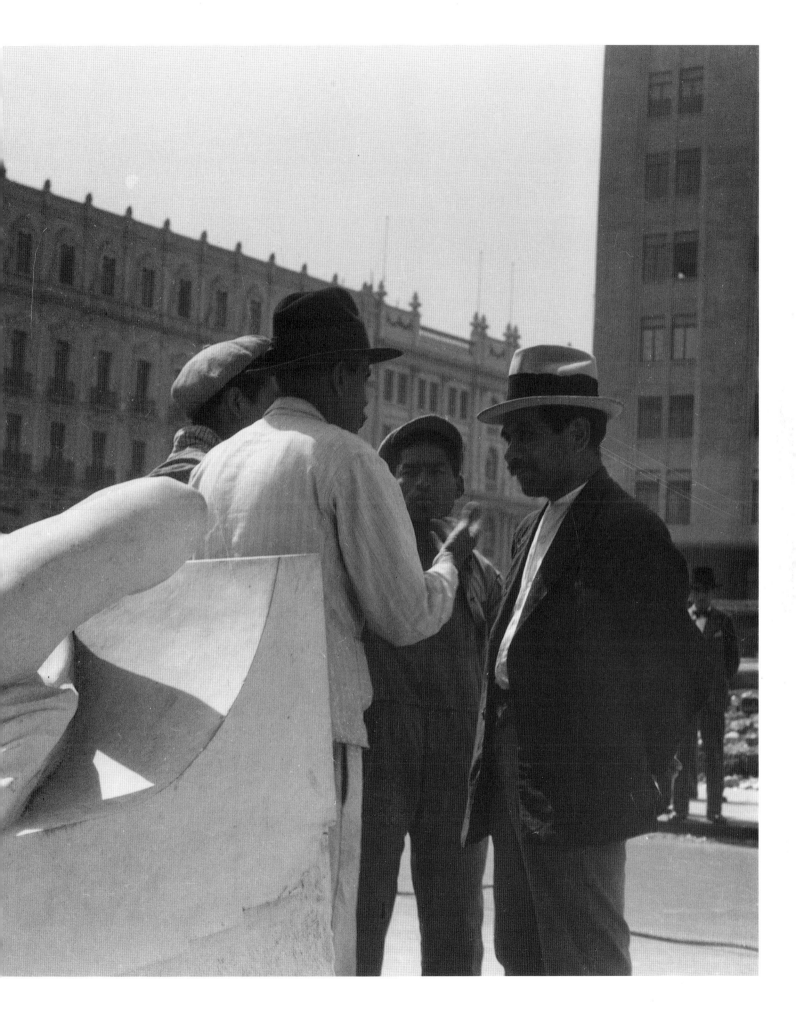

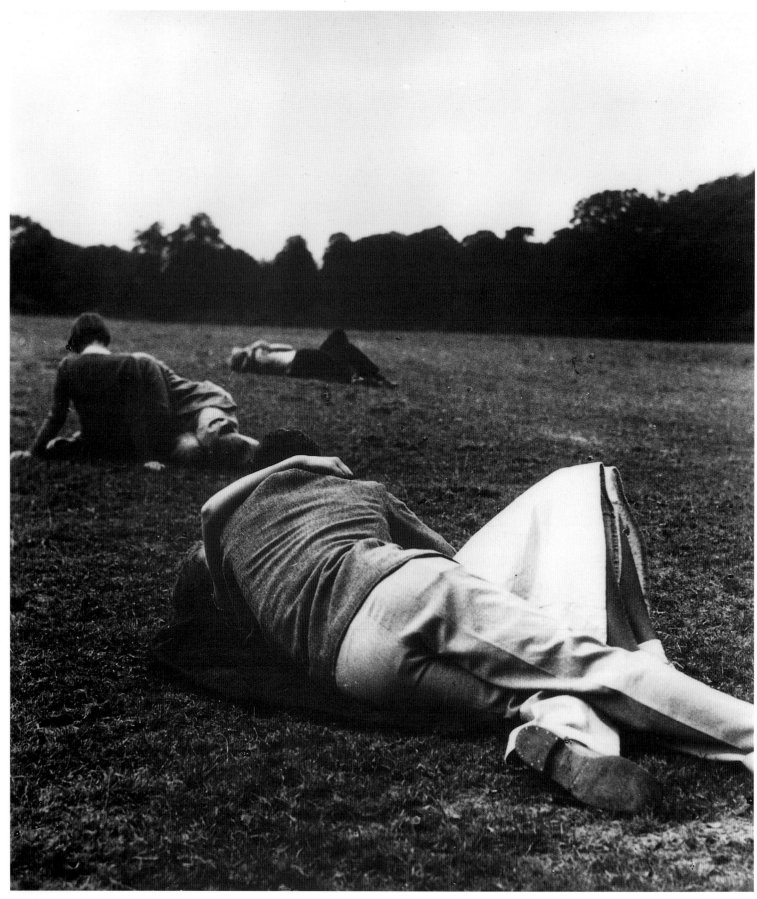

BILL BRANDT
Evening in Kenwood,
1931–35

136

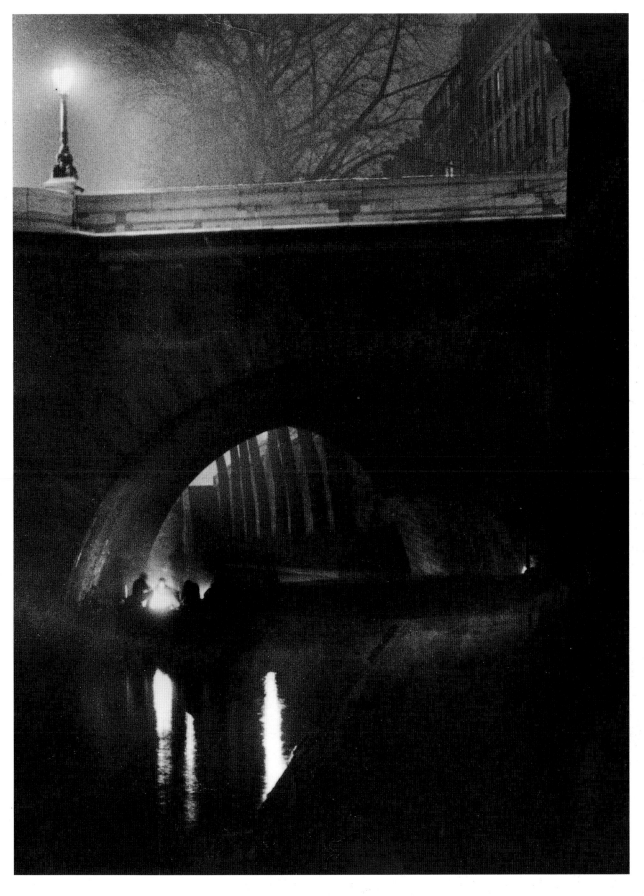

BRASSAÏ
Clochards Under the
Pont Neuf, 1932

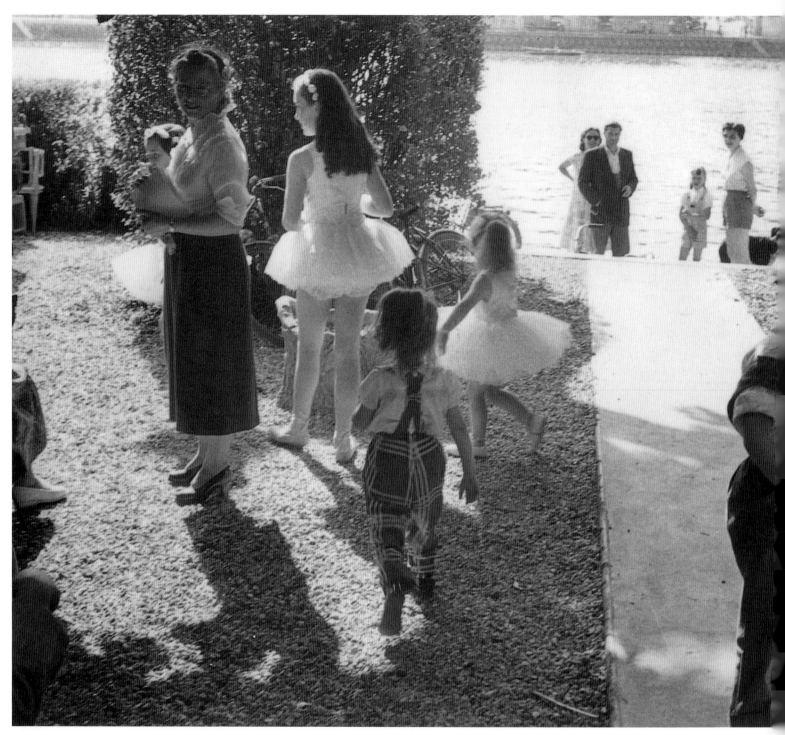

HENRI CARTIER-
BRESSON
*Children's Party Along
the Seine,* 1956

138

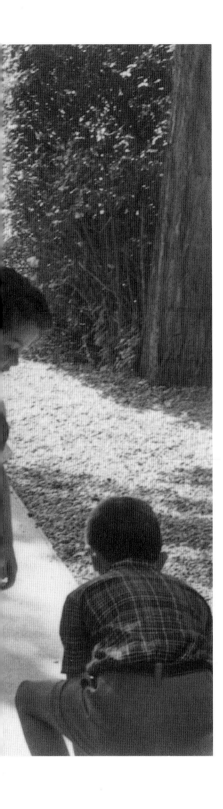

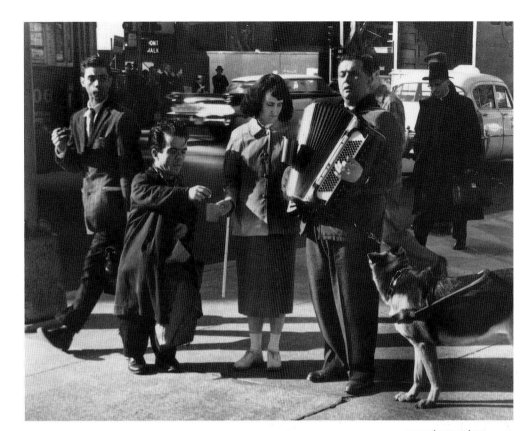

ANDRÉ KERTÉSZ
Sixth Avenue, New York, 1959

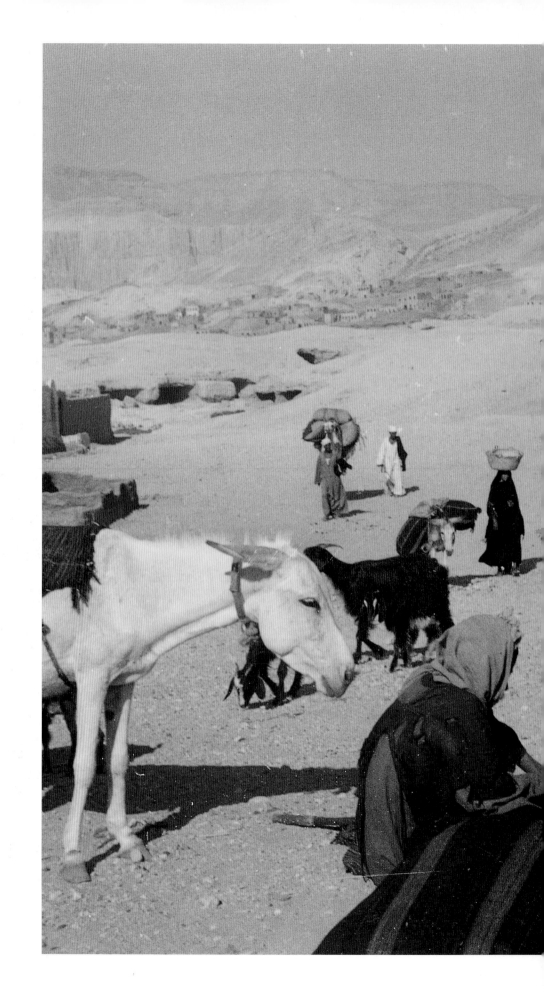

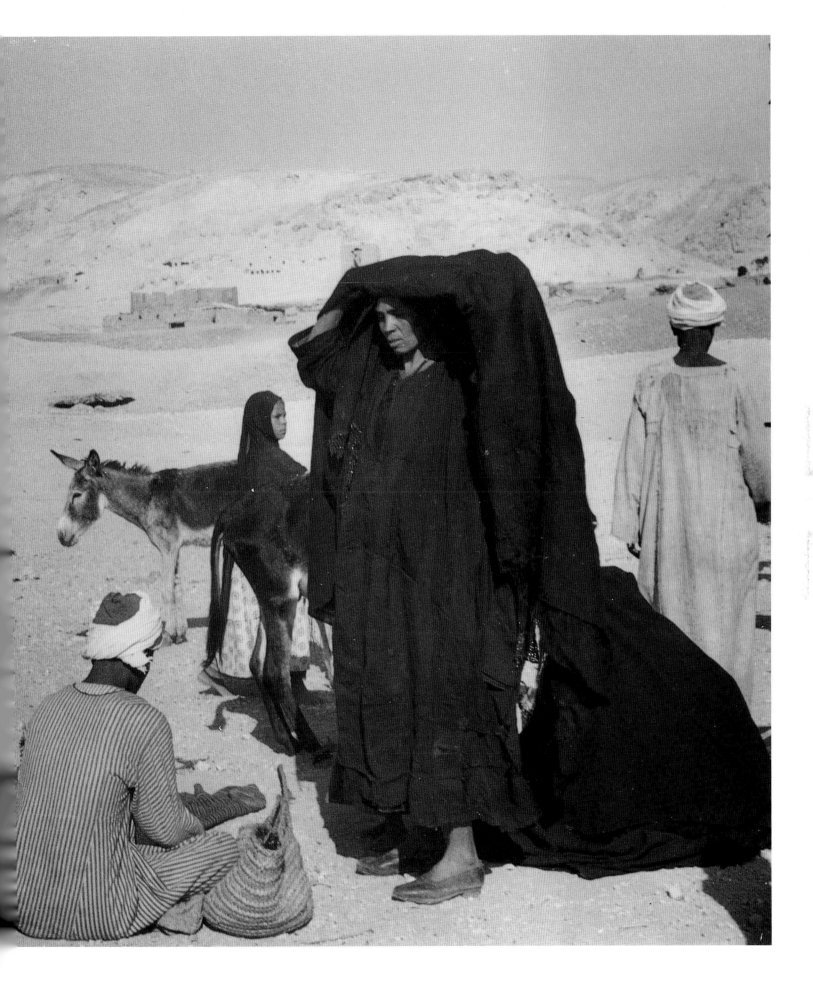

7: Children of the Century

For certain people who were young and privileged around the turn of the century, the camera had a special fascination. The world was theirs. It seemed more secure and enjoyable than it ever would again. "To be young was very heaven," as the title of an American memoir of the period put it.[1] These people were giddy and silly and ready for nonsense all the time, and the photographs that some of them made have a sense of sport not found anywhere else in the medium's history. From the midnineteenth century until World War I, many rich hobbyists of this sort were to be found in both Europe and America. None were more typical of the breed, nor better photographers, than Count Giuseppe Primoli in Italy, Alice Austen in New York, and Jacques-Henri Lartigue in France.

Most of these amateurs began by taking pictures of their family and friends, and that was as far as they got. But some were either sufficiently driven or sufficiently talented to carry their cameras beyond their home into the world at large. They went to such exciting social events and met so many famous people that they wanted pictures of them all. They felt their own special, private world to be connected to a much bigger public one that was equally enchanted. Thus did Count Primoli photograph the comings and goings of Eleonora Duse, Sarah Bernhardt, Guy de Maupassant, Edgar Degas, Prince Victor Emmanuel, and even Buffalo Bill and Annie Oakley.

So too did Lartigue make snapshots of the notables of his day in Paris. He photographed the president of the Republic riding in his carriage in 1904, and Ingrid Bergman almost half a century later vacationing at Cap d'Antibes in the company of the young American senator Jack Kennedy. He watched Maurice Chevalier do handstands on the beach and attended a dinner party at the playwright Sacha Guitry's, and he recorded it all with his camera. These socially elite photographers who carried their cameras to state occasions, exclusive resorts, and world capitals inevitably took them into the streets as well to make pictures of the everyday lives of ordinary people.

Lartigue began photographing and keeping a journal in 1902, when he was eight. In 1970, excerpts of both the writing and the pictures appeared under the title *Diary of a Century,* which became one of the most popular photography books of the day. But it was also a work of popular mythology laid out by a prominent New York magazine designer, and it misrepresents the original material. Although the selections from the journal are used in a fairly straightforward way, the photography has been manipulated not only by the sequencing, but through enlargement.

The book tries to bring the past near and give it dramatic impact by zeroing in on small sections of the negatives, so that the subject is reproduced big, grainy, and close up. The full frame shows the incidents recorded, which range from a spectacular crash at an air show to people walking on fashionable promenades, at a much greater distance. In the original photographs as Lartigue put them in his boyhood albums — tiny contact prints of often distant, almost illusory events — there is a much more powerful myth, one truer to both the photographer who took the pictures and the historical moment that is depicted in them.

The album pictures describe a rite de passage from the private world of home and family to a social one of public events, a journey on which Lartigue traveled by automobile, airplane, and camera. Around age ten, he com-

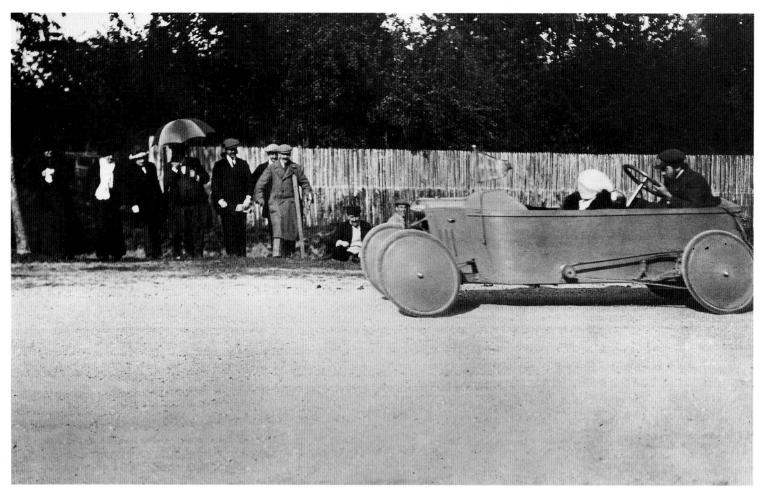

plains to his journal that he and his older brother Zissou are considered too young to have their own automobile. They make up for the deprivation with their bicycles and a variety of coasters of their own design. The latter all have two bucket seats, and cousins and friends are endlessly enticed — because the added weight increases the velocity — to come along for the ride. In the photographs, people in the absurdly formal clothes of the Belle Epoque hurtle along manicured driveways; they lean into the turns, faces scrunched against the flying gravel. It is as if, having gotten dressed that morning in the nineteenth century, they are racing now out of control into the twentieth.

Some of little Jacques's early adventures out in the big world beyond the gates of the family estate at Rouzat are taken from the passenger seat of an automobile beside Papa, whom he photographs in his driving goggles at an as-

tounding eighty kilometers per hour. The sense of power that acceleration in the family's Hispano-Suiza gives to Lartigue is translated into social terms. On passing another car he exults, "Oh, what a fantastic moment. . . . I feel cut off from the rest of the world, wonderfully superior to everybody else; I wish we would *never* stop."[2] When he attends his first race, in 1905, he wants to photograph the cars as they barrel down the straightaway wide open. "I am going to use 300/second," he announces in the diary, "because of the cars' speed."[3]

The appeal of the camera is that it too is a kind of machine, an instrument of speed. The distortions that motion creates in the photographs make them look like Futurist art — Giacomo Balla's *Speeding Automobile*, perhaps, or Umberto Boccioni's *Unique Forms of Continuity in Space* (fig. 7.1). These artists, whose work was contemporary with

Lartigue's, were searching for ways to represent the sensation of going fast that his photographs capture by chance.

Lartigue's photography focuses on airplanes, of course, as much as automobiles. In the pictures, the reality of flight emerges from mere aspiration with all the ungainliness of an insect struggling out of its chrysalis. What begins with Zissou jumping off a wall holding an open umbrella ends with air shows at new suburban aerodromes. In the albums, the contact prints of the negatives Lartigue made at these events suggest by their tininess how uncertain and tentative flight seemed at first. The planes are nothing but a fretwork in the sky, a cross-hatching of lines drawn with an unsteady hand on a blank sheet of paper. They are spindly, sputtering shapes that hover above looming demon heads in the foreground as if flying were still nothing more than a bright idea in the spectators' minds (fig. 7.2).

These new flying machines were but the most exalted creations in a paradise that also included little Jacques himself, his brother, his cousins, and everyone else he knew. The albums are full of imagery of people running, leaping, diving, turning somersaults. His nanny butts a giant ball into the air with her head. His father's secretary hurls his dog across a stream. A cousin clears four lawn chairs at a single bound. In the street, Zissou makes a rush at a flock of pigeons, which ascend from the pavement in a cloud (fig. 7.3). And in a picture of one of Zissou's test flights, Lartigue includes a member of the ground crew running with a towrope, straining with all his might to get the glider airborne.

There are no discontinuities in this world. The ability to fly grows directly out of one's own muscles and brain. It's as if all the automobiles and airplanes were being powered by the sheer exuberance of Lartigue's family and friends. These people have a boundless, heedless enthusiasm for life. Everybody is going flat out. The result is that the runners and leapers look as preposterous in midair as the

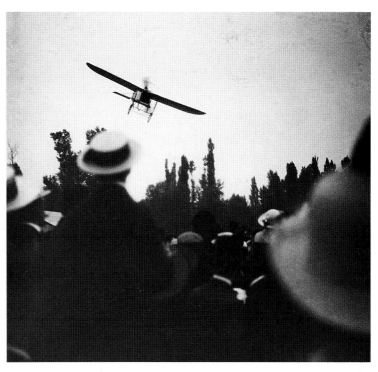

Fig. 7.2
JACQUES-HENRI LARTIGUE
Edmond Audemars in a Bleriot X1, **1912**

airplanes do. Among Lartigue's earliest pictures are some candid shots at the beach. He loves to go there, he says in the journal, because it "must be the most open and vast place on the whole earth. You can run and run . . . there are no limits, and no one cries out to you 'Be *careful*, now.' "[4] No limits: this is the feeling that all Lartigue's pictures have.

The unlimited horizon was one where there was no line between fantasy and reality. When he says in his journal in 1906 "In my sleep I can fly,"[5] he is only repeating a common boyhood dream. Yet for him it had an unprecedented power because grown men all over France and America were making it come true for the first time. The eternal fantasy that children have had in every age, the myth of Daedalus, was about to turn into reality. Boys have always had dreams of omnipotence in which they lead grand armies into battle or soar above the earth. But this boy's brother actually can fly, and the boy has the pictures to prove it! The camera's importance was that it gave him his way to participate in the euphoria. "Robert, Zissou and Louis are too big and I am too small," an early entry in Lartigue's journal laments. "Most of the time they

Fig. 7.3
JACQUES-HENRI
LARTIGUE
February, Monte Carlo,
1908

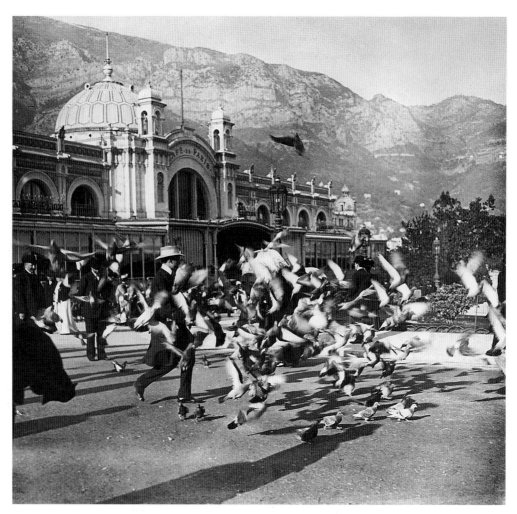

won't let me play with them; I have to be a spectator."[6] But taking photographs soon turned him into a participant too.

That taking pictures is his way to take part becomes apparent when the camera breaks. In his own mind, this banishes him to the sidelines once again. Since he immediately invents an imaginary camera as a replacement, his distress doesn't last very long. Nonetheless, the experience is notable for the sharpness of the loss Lartigue feels. The effect is the same as when he comes down with the flu a little later. Both incidents put him out of action briefly, and he talks of the inability to photograph as if it too were a physical affliction. It is in a sense. It's a kind of amputation, for like other inventions that seem to grow out of his own mind and body, the camera is but an extension of the self.

How sentient an instrument the camera has become is obvious when, at the height of Lartigue's fascination with cars, planes, and speed, a new subject suddenly distracts him: women. In a caption in an album dated June-July 1907, under a picture of his cousin in her bedroom all dressed up to go out for a walk, Lartigue writes, "A new idea: that I should go to the park to photograph those women who have the most eccentric or beautiful hats."[7] Within a year he writes in his journal, where he has always made sketches as well as verbal entries (just in case a photograph should not turn out), "Instead of drawing racing autos, lions or palm trees, I now draw women. Women . . . everything about them fascinates me — their dresses, their scent, the way they walk, the make up on their faces, their hands full of rings and, above all, their hats."[8] The park he goes to is the Bois de Boulogne, where he situates himself on an iron chair beside the Avenue des Acacias in a promenade known as the Path of Virtue (page 120). He is, he says, "ready for action the moment I see someone really elegant coming along."

Yet the action is of a (for him) significantly hesitant kind. This is a crucial moment in Lartigue's young life; photographically, we might say, his voice is changing:

> She: *the well-dressed, eccentric, elegant, ridiculous or beautiful woman I'm waiting for. . . . There she comes! I am timid . . . I tremble a little. Twenty meters . . . ten meters . . . five meters . . . click! My camera makes such a noise that the lady jumps . . . almost as much as I do. That doesn't matter, except when she is in the company of a big man who is furious and starts to scold me as if I were a naughty child. That really makes me very angry, but I try to smile. The pleasure of having taken another photograph makes up for everything! The gentleman I'll forget. The picture I will keep.*

While a glowering man appears in a number of his photographs, it is really the women who terrify him more. Still, he persists: "There comes a very, *very* beautiful one, with a little girl and another lady. She comes closer. I focus . . . and *click!* I hope the photo will be sharp, it was all so fast."[9]

When his camera broke, Lartigue felt it almost physically, as an injury. Here we see more explicitly the conversion of the camera's springs, bolts, and levers into pure physiology. What was an engine of speed for him now becomes an organ of puberty. It becomes what Freud says the camera is, a prosthetic device, a contraption that extends bodily function or that serves as a replacement for a lost member. The loss Lartigue has suffered is in temerity. He has lost his child's freedom from self-consciousness. Whereas before he could photograph a racing car with a sure hand, now he is afraid that a woman simply walking down the street has moved too fast for him.

In his photographs of the *grandes dames* and *damoiselles* of the Bois, so much an imagery of the Belle Epoque, Lartigue is no longer the harbinger of things to come that he is in the pictures of cars and planes, but rather the preserver of a "remembrance of things past." He turns from a proto-Futurist into a proto-Proust. (It was as a prosthesis of the memory, one of technology's "materializations of the power . . . of recollection," that Freud saw the camera.[10]) As different as little Jacques-Henri and little Marcel seem — the one a dashing boy who negotiates life with his camera as if he were negotiating the turns at a Grand Prix, the other an asthmatic shut-in who contemplates the world from his bed like Descartes — their personalities seem to merge with the onset of puberty.

Like Proust in *Swann's Way*, Lartigue haunts the Avenue des Acacias to catch a glimpse of certain women by whom he is both threatened and irresistibly attracted. He wants to go right up to them yet to remain unnoticed, to observe them from afar. Again, he is not as close when he takes the pictures as later reproductions have at times led us to believe; his subjects in original prints seem more remote and inaccessible.

The two child Lartigues, the innocent speed demon and the edgy, embarrassed pubescent, are of course both there from the beginning. The latter grows out of the former, for among the running, leaping cousins at home are a variety of girls whose picture Lartigue always seems to snap just as their skirts have flown up around their knees. Like his pursuit of fast planes and cars, his pursuit of women leads him from a protected life on his own lawn into a larger, uncertain world beyond. It is another rite de passage between the security of boyhood and the perils of manhood, between private friends and public strangers.

In his photographs, the women that he sees look enigmatic, remote, even forbidden. It is the hats and veils that do it, as he himself notes repeatedly in the journal. No wonder he

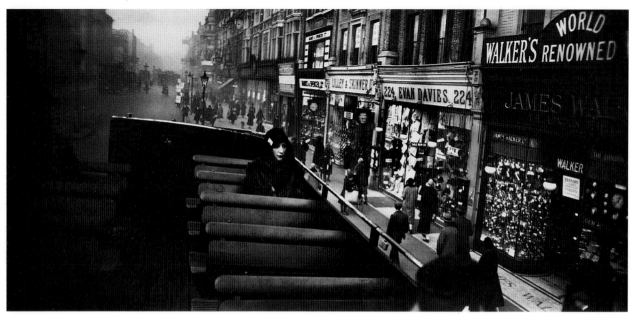

Fig. 7.4
JACQUES-HENRI
LARTIGUE
Bibi, October, London,
1926

is so taken with them. Under the brim of a hat, the light can play funny tricks. It sometimes diffuses around a woman's head in such a way that her serene expression appears to float above her body. The hats and veils become a sanctuary, like a boudoir, into which the women retreat, only partly drawing the curtain behind them. By their sheerness the veils make their wearers look seductive and untouchable at the same time.

These women encountered in the Bois have a street presence based on anonymity, on near facelessness. This makes them appropriately obscure objects of desire for young Jacques, who is at an age when sex is a kind of general yearning, a baffling attraction to all women rather than the one woman upon which a lover, at a later stage of development, will fixate. Unfortunately, when that later stage does come in Lartigue's life, however fulfilling he may have found his experiences personally, his photographic record of them falls off sharply. There is a wife, named Bibi, of whom many photographs are taken. But the earlier feeling that there are "no limits" is definitely gone after the war.

Once he marries, in 1919, he withdraws into a world far more private and much smaller than that which he knew at home as a boy. As an adult, he continues to photograph famous people, racing cars, and sporting events. Yet his sphere of action seems now restricted to family and a few friends. He becomes a shut-in not so much physically, like Proust, but mentally. The occasional street photograph that he takes usually contains himself or Bibi standing alone on the pavement somewhere. Certain pictures have a peculiarly forlorn quality (figs. 7.4, 7.5.). The subject standing still amid the moving cars and people looks as if invisible to everyone except the photographer. Each looks, literally, like someone whom the world is passing by.

Like Lartigue, other rich youngsters with cameras, full of themselves and pleased with the world, often ventured out into the streets after having begun photographing at home. The house in which Alice Austen grew up during the last part of the Victorian era was Clear Comfort, a seventeenth-century homestead on Staten Island, New York. Also living there at the time was a colorful uncle who was a sea captain and who gave Alice her first camera when she was about ten or twelve. Her earliest surviving pictures are from 1884, when she was eighteen.

Austen tends, more than Lartigue, to appear in her own photographs. The ones made before the turn of the century show her to be a

Fig. 7.5
JACQUES-HENRI
LARTIGUE
Bibi, October, London,
1926

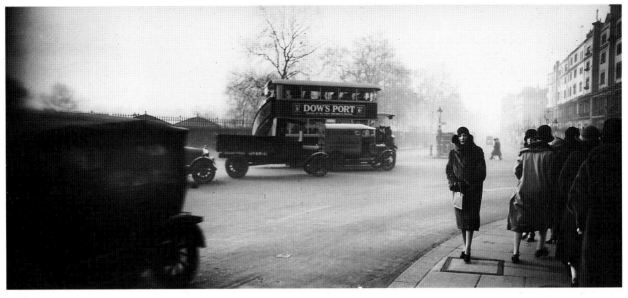

plain and solemn young woman — or maybe just deadpan would be a more accurate description, for it's clear that she too had a mischievous sense of fun. She sometimes spent an hour carefully posing pictures for comic effect, as parodies of conventional group portraits of the day: a tea party gone slightly awry, or a fellowship of young men, gay blades posturing manfully for the camera, who are in fact Alice and some girlfriends wearing long pants and sporting painted-on mustaches.

Although staid and self-conscious compared with Lartigue's, these pictures share with his a certain intention to be naughty. They are a send-up of old proprieties. And when she went outdoors with her camera, the imagery even begins to look like his. On the extensive grounds of Clear Comfort, which ran right out to the Verrazano Narrows at the entrance to New York Harbor, she photographed the same fleeting kind of subject that Lartigue would two decades later. A boy leaps over a box. A young woman whizzes by on a bicycle. A pony cart moving at a crisp pace makes a soft, motion-blurred image on the negative.

Like Lartigue, she had among her friends tennis players of national standing whose matches she photographed. Austen played tennis herself, and another sport in which she took a keen interest was automobile racing.

She recorded the auto speed trials at a racetrack in 1903, perched on a fence post by the rail. An avid reader of *Popular Mechanics,* she speculated later that she'd never married because she put off boys by being good at sports and handy with machinery, such as cameras. Lartigue's pictures of engines being tuned, tires being changed, and touring cars undergoing roadside repairs all have forerunners among the ones Austen took.

When she first set out for Manhattan, across the harbor, her purpose appears to have been to make a compendium of street types. *Street Types* was in fact a portfolio she deposited for copyright at the Library of Congress. The subjects represented include postmen, cops, and street sweepers, bootblacks, newsies, and ragpickers. Like some of the pictures from Clear Comfort, many of these are posed. The postman, for instance, demonstrates through a sequence of shots how he collects the letters from a mailbox on his route. It is likely that Austen had some thought of illustrating a social studies text for schoolchildren or possibly for the immigrants who are so often the subjects of the other street photography she did.

Not all the pictures are as didactic as this, however. Some of the tomfoolery she enjoyed at home also sneaks in. She photographed a girl plying her trade as a newsy in an outrageous flowered hat, and framed to one side to

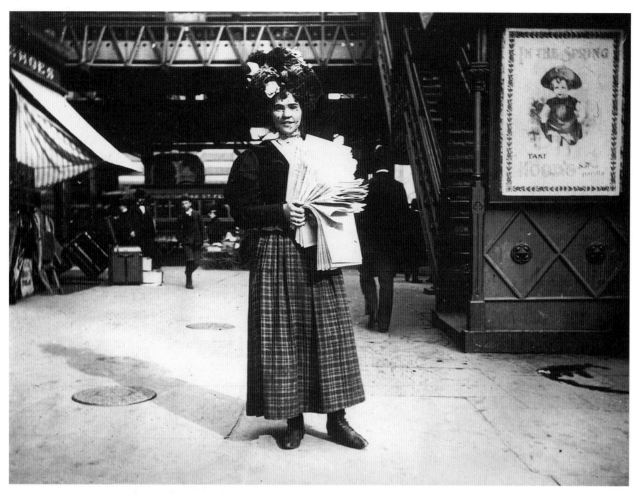

pit this image against that of another child on a poster (fig. 7.6). Perhaps the girlish ebullience she felt on these trips into the city is recorded best in a series of photographs of parades she made beginning in the 1890s. One taken from a high window or rooftop is of Bowling Green, in Lower Manhattan, full of tiny marching figures under a confetti-filled sky (fig. 7.7). It's the perfect image of the chaotic feelings of joy and relief that accompany a war's end.

On another occasion she went down to street level to get shots of cavalry passing through masses of wavering civilians. Indeed, the last street photographs she seems to have taken are some of this type made during the victory celebration following the armistice of 1918. In them the commotion in the street is sometimes so great that the image is all but unreadable. These last, wobbly negatives have an unsettling aptness rather like Lartigue's from

the period of World War I and after. The truth was that the ground on which Austen had stood, the stable, genteel world of her youth, was beginning to crumble under her at this moment. The frenetic period of the 1920s was to end in the ruination of the family fortune and of Austen's life at Clear Comfort, with the consequence that she was to spend her final days in the poorhouse.

Between Austen's photographs and Count Primoli's, as between Lartigue's and both of theirs, there are uncanny parallels. One is that Austen and Primoli made sequences in which their friends act out, as if in a little silent movie, a Victorian romance of male supplication and female refusal followed by acquiescence. Primoli came earlier than Austen or Lartigue, took up photography later in his life, and was generally wealthier, more privileged, and more cosmopolitan. His work seems the very quintessence of photography by a man of means.

Born in 1851, Primoli was related to the Bonaparte line, inherited a palazzo in Rome and an independent income, knew everyone, went everywhere, did everything. He divided

melodrama is la Rejane, who really is a stage star of the day. Everyone in the street seems to be a member of Primoli's entourage.

It's easy to see how his eye wandered from friends and acquaintances observed on the street to strangers in an exclusive setting, like

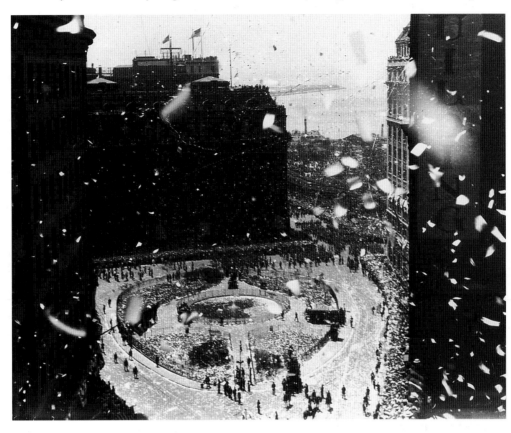

Fig. 7.7
ALICE AUSTEN
Victory Parade
Following World War I,
Bowling Green,
New York, 1918

his time among Rome, Venice, Paris, and the Italian countryside. He attended royal weddings and state occasions, went out on fox hunts and military maneuvers, watched public processions and market festivals. And he took pictures of it all. He was the ultimate photographer of the Belle Epoque.

Where his street photography fits in is suggested by a picture he made in Paris in 1889, an exquisitely timed grab shot that works as both a parable and a parody of the figure of the hussy (fig. 7.8). It is a little photo-proverb on the theme of the brazen woman. Yet the stereotyped characters who have obligingly provided the scene are not just a bunch of nobodies. The man emerging from the doorway is Edgar Degas, and the leading lady in this

Longchamps on the day of the Grand Prix. It was all the same to him. While riding in the wedding procession of Victor Emmanuel, the prince of Naples, he got a shot of the masses perched on lamp standards and windowsills to watch. Although the street photographer often focuses on the crowd while letting the parade pass by, he seldom gets to do so because he is *in* the parade. The privileged point of view in Primoli's work reflects, nonetheless, an attitude implicit to some degree in all street photography.

When we look at his pictures of ragged beggars, glassy-eyed madonnas, or other characters of the Roman streets (page 55, top), we don't assume that the relationships suggested or the emotions expressed are necessarily in-

Fig. 7.8
**COUNT GIUSEPPE
PRIMOLI**
*The Admirer of la
Rejane,* 1889

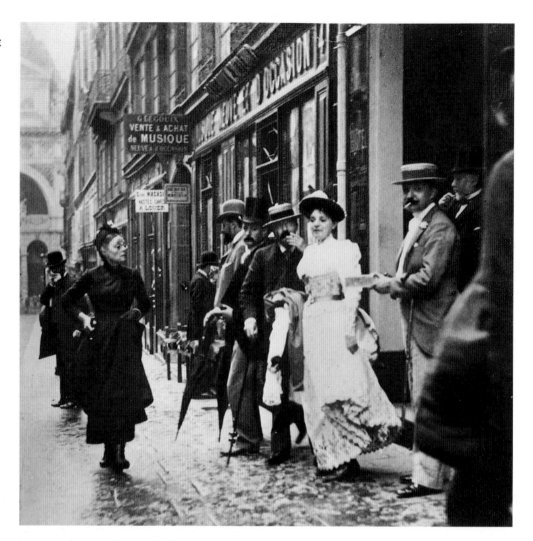

trinsic to the situation itself. They may be a
purely fictitious drama that Primoli has manipulated either the camera or the scene to
create. What might actually have been happening at the moment the photograph was
taken is irrelevant to its charms, which depend upon a certain indifference to reality as
such. The photographer is unconcerned with
the real lives of his subjects. He cares only
about the symbolic life he gives to them.
Street photography cannot help being ex-
ploitative in this way. It is an act of appropria-
tion. It always requires in some measure the
kind of *rite du seigneur,* the sense of one's personal powers of eminent domain, that comes
naturally to a man like Primoli.

8: The Decisive Photographer

Henri Cartier-Bresson once told *Newsweek* magazine that of all photographers, he admired Lartigue most. He might have *been* Lartigue, had he been born a little earlier. Like Lartigue, he grew up amid a wealthy, protective family and acquired his first camera, a Box Brownie, as a child. He too was a natural who produced some of his best pictures the minute he began to work in earnest. But that was not until he was a bit older than Lartigue had been. By the age at which the latter had taken most of his great pictures — his early twenties — Cartier-Bresson was just starting out. At the point in life when Lartigue was withdrawing into the familiar, exclusive world of family and friends, Cartier-Bresson was striking out on his own on travels with his camera that were to last more than thirty years.

Why Cartier-Bresson did not turn out to be another Lartigue is difficult to say. It was a matter of temperament, no doubt, and of the degree of genius for photography. But it was also a question of the world outlook that each man developed. Historians of modern Europe with very different approaches have agreed that 1905 was a "watershed" between generations in France that looked in two opposite directions — the one toward the past, the other to the future.[1] Perhaps the difference between Lartigue and Cartier-Bresson lies partly in having been born on opposite sides of that watershed year. The former, born in 1894, inherited a view of the world to which the latter, born in 1908, could never lay claim. Lartigue continued to cling to that view, even when the world itself changed. His photography helped him to preserve and prolong the past. Photography helped Cartier-Bresson to liberate himself from the sort of family history that Lartigue had hoped would go on forever.

In the summer of 1932, the young American Julien Levy, who was in Paris scouting for the New York gallery he'd just opened, was invited for a Sunday afternoon at the country home of Caresse Crosby, the founder, with her late husband, Harry, of the Black Sun Press. It was on this occasion that, as the dealer recalled in a memoir, "Peter and Gretchen Powell arrived with their latest protege, a baby-faced photographer damp with shyness and fussily mothered by Gretchen. I was urged to interest myself in his unusual photography. . . . His name was Henri Cartier-Bresson."[2]

Levy was to give Cartier-Bresson his first show a little more than a year later. By then, the photographer had already taken quite a few of the pictures that, reproduced again and again, were to make him famous. With him more than any other photographer, it's appropriate to go right to the pictures, to begin there, because he himself did. "The best pictures in *The Decisive Moment*," he has said, speaking of the 1952 book of his work, "were taken immediately, after a fortnight."[3] Growth, he has stated, is a "false concept" in photography.

There's no question that Cartier-Bresson established a new look in photographs right away. Levy felt the work was so unusual that the American public would need some preparation for it. Under the pseudonym Peter Lloyd, he wrote himself a letter about Cartier-Bresson that he published as the catalogue essay for that first show. "Call the exhibition amoral photography, equivocal, ambivalent, anti-plastic, accidental photography," the letter declared: "Call it anti-graphic photography."[4] This last term was the one that stuck and has been repeated most often in connection with Cartier-Bresson's work. It catches the spirit of the imagery in a couple of ways.

First, literally, the pictures are without the contrasts of bright light and deep shadow with which much art photography of the day created bold graphic patterns in the prints. If there is sunlight in a Cartier-Bresson photograph, it usually falls on the background, while the foreground subjects are in shade. Preferably, there is no sun. Cartier-Bresson would rather photograph on a gray day (page 15). "The sun," he has explained, "is very troublesome: it forces, it imposes. Slightly overcast conditions allow you to move freely around your subject."[5] Moreover, he has always liked the print itself to be gray and even in tone. He has wanted it to be, as John Szarkowski once put it, "a tapestry."[6]

Another sense in which a Cartier-Bresson photograph is antigraphic is that it is not what a newspaper editor would call "graphic illustration." Levy might have thrown in *antidramatic*, even *anticlimactic*, along with his other adjectives. The image doesn't seem to have a specific story to tell, or if it does, the story has no particular point to make, no obvious moral. The photograph is, as Levy said, "amoral." Like the print, the content of the picture is strangely neutral in tone. Lincoln Kirstein has pointed out that Cartier-Bresson "is not even an ironist, for irony . . . presupposes a partial judgement."[7] This photographer's observations on human nature are neither misanthropic nor philanthropic. His ability to walk down a street in Paris or Seville or Shanghai, and respond with such equanimity to whatever he finds there, results from his openness to human experience in all its forms.

Although a typical Cartier-Bresson photograph doesn't contain a clear incident, there is still usually a lot going on in it. Like Lartigue, Cartier-Bresson has always seized upon action. The bicycle streaks past. The fat man leaps in the air. The arm emerges from the crowd holding a photograph (fig. 8.1). The child reels back in pain or ecstasy; we can't

Fig. 8.1
HENRI CARTIER-BRESSON
Moscow, 1954

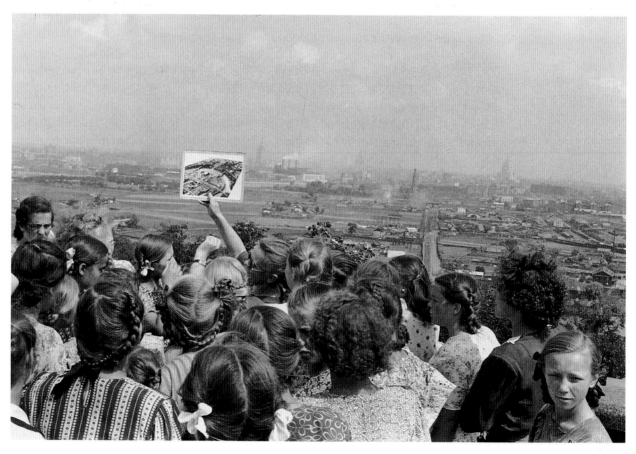

tell which. Cartier-Bresson is also fascinated by where he is as much as by what happens there. In much of his work, the place is sharp-edged and timeless, the human presence motion-blurred and evanescent. The image is balanced precisely halfway between a meticulous composition and a knee-jerk reaction. The two elements are contradictory yet mutually dependent. Each is poised against the other like the tightrope walker against the rope.

Looking back over his photographs from the vantage point of the mid-1970s, Cartier-Bresson told an interviewer from *Le Monde*, "What counts are the little differences. 'General ideas' mean nothing. Long live . . . the details! A millimeter makes all the difference."[8] When you look at even very early pictures, it's easy to see what he's talking about. A few flyspecks on the negative are the linchpins holding the composition together. Details provide the formal structure, as when the symmetry of the jumping man about to land and his own reflection coming up to meet him in the puddle below is repeated, and mocked, by little figures on identical dance posters in the background (page 28).

If the details of a poster behind the subject are to count in the print, the focus must be accurate enough to reveal them. As Cartier-Bresson told Beaumont Newhall at the time of his first exhibition at the Museum of Modern Art, he likes an image that is *"aigu"* — sharp.[9] Even so, when you see large exhibition prints, you are often struck by how approximate the focus is. Because in many instances he would have lost the picture had he stopped to fiddle with the camera, he shot with the focus at a preset distance. As Newhall explained, *aigu* refers "not so much to the quality of the optical image as to the precision of the plastic organization and the intensity of the content." The detail crucial to such precision might be the very one that isn't sharp: the speeding bicycle, the figure springing up in the foreground, the gesture or face on the edge of the frame, where the centered view of the focus scope is least effective. The sharpness comes from the accuracy of the placement rather than the crispness of the edges.

The photographer taking pictures with a Leica camera squints through its parallax viewfinder with just one eye. Cartier-Bresson has always felt that he needed only one anyway because the image finally depends more upon a certain inner vision. "As I photograph with my little Leica," he told Dorothy Norman at the time of that first show at the Modern, "I have the feeling that there is something so right about it: with one eye that is closed one looks within. With the other eye that is open one looks without."[10] The photograph shows us, in other words, the photographer as well as his subject.

Cartier-Bresson has said that the photographer himself is revealed more clearly by his contact sheets than by prints. On his own sheets, you can see the sequence of shots building toward the best picture. When he goes over them, he marks the best negatives with one to four sidebars that rate each from "maybe" to "perfect." And when younger photographers ask to show him their work, it is only the contacts he wants to see. "I prefer to look at contact sheets," he told *Le Monde*, "[because] there one can see the individual."[11]

That this is what he hopes to see in other people's photographs confirms Lincoln Kirstein's observation that Cartier-Bresson's vision is "the lyric, rather than the tragic or the comic."[12] As opposed to the tragic poet, who tries to read in other men's fates the moral laws of the universe, the lyric poet tells us what is in himself. Singing his song in the first-person singular, he reveals primarily his own emotions and character.

In Cartier-Bresson's most powerful photographs, we sense clearly the binary nature of this vision that looks in as well as out. The world before us is both the public one of the street where the photograph was taken, and the private one of the subconscious where the composition was formed. The prime example of such imagery is a picture he made in Seville in 1932 (pages 4–5). The setting is all lines — scored concrete paving, shutter slats, the whitewashed corners of buildings, and hard, slantwise shadows. It is an unmistakably Spanish *calle*, yet a completely abstract, imaginary space. While the street has this harsh geometry, the two boys at opposite edges of the foreground are a soft, uncertain presence. They are inside the camera's focal range, in motion, in enveloping shadow save for a highlight here or there. Visually they are out of place, a pure contrast to the street.

Nonetheless, they complete the scene in which they stand. The blankness of the architecture and the vacuousness of the boy's expression on the right are of a piece. It is as if these children had been slammed against the outer walls of the picture by the intensity of the sun in the center. They appear as prisoners of this severe setting, this unforgiving light. Although the situation is innocuous, the image itself is ambiguous in an unsettling way. Emotions this paradoxical are glimpsed only deep within the self, where the landscape is symbolic rather than actual. It is the psyche, as much as the street, that speaks to us here.

In the letter Julien Levy wrote to himself, the most astute words he applied to Cartier-Bresson's work were "equivocal" and "ambivalent." These are the qualities that the picture from Seville has, and the ones hinted at in the French title for Cartier-Bresson's 1952 book, *Images à la sauvette. The Decisive Moment* is misleading as a translation, for the moment referred to is that just before a decision is made, the moment of anticipation rather than conclusion.

A la sauvette is a colloquialism roughly equivalent to "on the run," but, according to a gloss on the phrase that Françoise Boas gave to Grace Mayer at the Modern, there is also an untranslatable future element involved. The instant being described is the one when you are just about to take off, the point at which the shortstop is ready to dash in any direction as he watches the batter step into the ball, or when the pickpocket waits for his victim to be distracted so that he can strike. *Images à la sauvette* is the right title because it characterizes the photographer's actions as well as his subject's — it looks both out and in.

The moment truly typical of street photography, from John Thomson's work in the 1870s through Cartier-Bresson's more than a half century later, is the indecisive moment. Ernst Haas came close to the mark when he described Cartier-Bresson's work as "off-compositions." Haas said that they were "perfect in their imperfection." [13] The self-contradictory phrase emphasizes the paradoxical nature of those compositions. Cartier-Bresson's photographs *à la sauvette* are of actions that are yet to be resolved. They are of events that are inchoate. Stopped at just this point by the photograph, they remain forever irresolvable, equivocal, ambivalent.

The Cartier-Bresson whom we encounter in his pictures is, first of all, Cartier-Bresson the photographer. The tautness of the image gives us a strong impression of a sinewy, sudden man as its maker. We can literally see him at work. His motions seem as abrupt as an arc of electricity, as fluid as coursing water. He elongates himself "like a rubber band," as one observer put it, in order to stretch over the heads of a crowd for a picture. [14] He insinuates himself into every crowd as softly as a wisp of smoke works its way through the chinks in a wall.

Since he is himself a lyric poet with a camera, the most poetic descriptions of his behavior seem the most satisfying, the truest to the pictures. Perhaps the best is one Truman Capote wrote: "I remember once watching Cartier-Bresson at work on a street in New Orleans — dancing along the pavement like an agitated dragonfly, three Leicas swinging from straps around his neck, a fourth hugged to his eye: click-click-click (the camera seems to be part of his own body), clicking away with a joyous intensity, a religious absorption." [15] How fiercely busy a figure Cartier-Bresson cut on the street is apparent from the number of cameras Capote remembered having seen in action, since Cartier-Bresson himself claims never to have carried more than two. The animation with which this photographer impresses witnesses is the sort that only characters in cartoons are capable of.

Cartier-Bresson is a dragonfly, a gadfly, the fly on the wall of the modern world. He can flit unnoticed through every situation because his reflexes are so quick that he seems to anticipate the course of events. The writer John Malcolm Brinnin hit upon the same metaphor when he observed that Cartier-Bresson's "eye is polyhedral, like a fly's. Focusing on one thing, he quivers in the imminence of ten others. . . . When there's nothing in view, he's mute, unapproachable, humming-bird tense."[16] Brinnin's description also suggests that however deft and precise the photographer's movements may be, there is something out of control about him. The act of photographing is a compulsive and involuntary one. Capote was aware of this as well, calling the photographer "a bit of a fanatic."[17]

Cartier-Bresson has freely admitted on numerous occasions that he is a bundle of nerves. But, he explains, "one must seize the moment before it passes, the fleeting gesture, the evanescent smile. . . . That's why I'm so nervous — it's horrible for my friends — but it's only by maintaining a permanent tension that I can stick to reality."[18] This permanent tension is what makes him equal to all the unresolved ambiguities of which reality, truly seen, consists.

To understand Cartier-Bresson's relationship to the medium, we must ultimately recognize that the ambivalence upon which he depends most is the one he has toward photography itself. His compulsive need to take pictures is matched by a sublime contempt for them. Photography is, he now says, just a brief and minor chapter in the history of visual representation, "like stained glass windows."[19] This is the attitude he has had from the first, for despite the intensity with which he has prac-

ticed it, he took up photography with a casualness bordering on indifference. When Julien Levy met him that Sunday at Caresse Crosby's, Cartier-Bresson was about to embark on a series of travels and adventures in which picture taking played only a part. At most it was a way for this restless, keyed-up young man to try to focus his energies.

By his midteens, the nervy and impulsive Cartier-Bresson was already superbly unsuited to be the heir apparent of the wealthy family of thread merchants into which he was born. When he failed his baccalaureate for the third time, his father gave up hopes of bringing him into the family firm. Instead, Cartier-Bresson set off in 1931 on a voyage around Africa, during which he jumped ship in the Ivory Coast. There he spent a year in the bush hunting by the light of acetylene torches and photographing with a secondhand Krauss miniature camera.

When he developed the film upon his return to France, it turned out that all of it had been ruined by moisture. That the first of a lifetime of far-flung adventures should have resulted in no photographs was prophetic in a way. At times, it seems, the pictures would be almost expendable. A few years later, during a year in New York, he studied filmmaking with Paul Strand, never left Manhattan, and took no pictures at all. You have to conclude that one reason his photographs were so good, when he did make them, was that they were a somewhat incidental part of his experience. He regarded the medium with a certain neutrality that translated into objectivity in the pictures themselves. Although he might have been nervous by nature, he wasn't anxious, not about taking photographs, anyway. This was a source of the disinterested quality apparent in his best work.

Cartier-Bresson might have been born with the personality he has as a photographer. He might not have needed to develop. But he was still susceptible to powerful influences that refined his talent for him. The Surrealists, especially, were part of a process whereby the

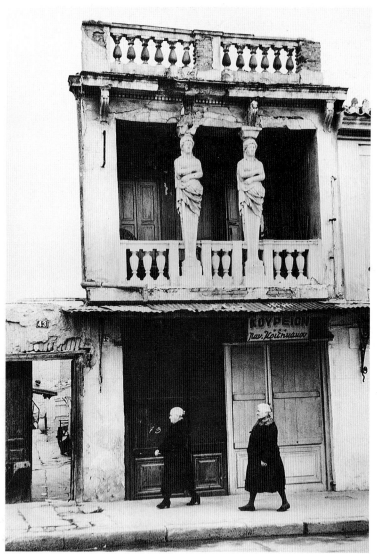

Fig. 8.2
HENRI CARTIER-
BRESSON
Athens, 1953

Readymades, the Surrealists picked up materials for their art in the street. Seen in the perspective of their work, a street photograph becomes yet another form of found object. Their international exposition in 1938 turned an art gallery into a Surrealist street crowded with mannequins wearing cast-off clothes, a bird cage, and other mass-produced goods. The street led to an installation by Salvador Dalí in which rain poured down inside a Paris taxicab.

Although Dalí and his wife were also at Caresse Crosby's the afternoon that Cartier-Bresson met Julien Levy, it was from Breton, the oracular poet of Surrealism, who was present as well, that the young photographer got the most stimulation. Breton's ideas about art followed from his experiences in World War I, when he had used some of Freud's techniques to treat victims of shell shock and battle fatigue. "I resolved to obtain from myself what we were trying to obtain from them," he explained in the 1924 *Manifesto of Surrealism*, "namely, a monologue spoken as rapidly as possible without any intervention on the part of the critical faculties, a monologue consequently unencumbered by the slightest inhibition and which was, as closely as possible, akin to spoken thought." [22]

personality was turned into a sensibility. They helped to channel the young man's craving for excitement and danger into the pursuit of a rather different kind of risk, the aesthetic kind that André Breton called, according to Cartier-Bresson, *le hasard objectif.* Cartier-Bresson has spoken more than once of his "search" for what Breton was describing. [20] "The camera is a marvellous instrument," he told one interviewer, "for seizing this 'hasard objectif.' " [21]

Surrealism provides a context in which Cartier-Bresson's photographs make sense, or rather, in which the nonsense they make seems appropriate. It proposes a new way to think about photography, as a kind of found art. Taking their inspiration from Duchamp's

Breton wanted to write, in other words, in the same pell-mell state in which Cartier-Bresson was shooting. "If such and such a sentence of mine turns out to be disappointing, at least momentarily," he said, "I place my trust in the following sentence . . . I carefully refrain from starting it over again or polishing it. The only thing that might prove fatal to me would be the slightest loss of impetus." [23] The progression of words must build, like the sequence of frames on the contact sheet, toward the best image.

In addition to describing the photographer as he advances down the street, camera in hand, Breton's manifesto seems to account for the pictures that he takes along the way. The poet Isidore Ducasse, a forerunner of Breton's known as the comte de Lautréamont, gave the classic formulation of the Surrealist image as "the chance encounter of a sewing machine and an umbrella on a dissection table."[24] An image of this type is, Breton explained (quoting the writer Pierre Reverdy), " *'a pure creation of the mind . . . born from . . . a juxtaposition of two more or less distant realities* [Breton's italics].' "[25]

Every Cartier-Bresson photograph is about realities juxtaposed thus — the bicycle pedaled furiously through the labyrinth of iron banisters and stone steps in which it is trapped, a cluster of faces in the foreground against a smattering of high, tiny windows in the background (pages 10–11), the old women in black beneath the caryatids (fig. 8.2). "Poetry includes two elements which are suddenly in conflict," Cartier-Bresson has said, speaking of photography, "— a spark between two elements."[26] His poetry sounds exactly like that which Breton described as "the fortuitous juxtaposition of . . . two terms [from which] a particular light has sprung, *the light of the image* [Breton's italics]."[27]

Even the influences that affected Cartier-Bresson seem to have needed to generate a certain tension in him to take hold. What made Surrealism attractive as a philosophy of life was that it offset to some degree the art education he had already received from André Lhôte. Part of the reason he has had disdain for photography is that he always wanted to be a painter more. To this end in 1928 he entered the atelier run by Lhôte, one of the foremost painting teachers of the day, and he has said that Lhôte's two *Treatises* on landscape and the figure were for him "fundamental books."[28] What he learned from Lhôte was not the kind of improvisatory technique emphasized in Breton's writings, but rather the opposite — the careful construction of a visual space.

Lhôte's ideas were derived from the analytic side of Cézanne and the Cubists. He mistrusted the "disorder of execution . . . inherent in fixing a perishable scene, or one in which changes are rapid and manifold."[29] He had

contempt for the kind of artist that he characterized as "a wild snarer of images."[30] (No wonder Cartier-Bresson came to disparage his own activities as a photographer.) At the time Cartier-Bresson studied under him, Lhôte was working out a system, which he would publish later in his two books, for analyzing masterpieces with mathematical rigor. His method was based on the "golden section," a progression of numbers in which each is the sum of the two preceding figures and the mean of the two on either side.[31]

This geometrical sense of space can be seen in the background, literally, of Cartier-Bresson's photographs. "Just as one can analyze the structure of a painting," he has said, "so in a good photograph one can discover the same rules, the proportional mean, the square within the rectangle, the Golden Rule, etc. That's why I like the rectangular dimension of the Leica negative, 24 by 36 mm. I have a passion for geometry."[32] The "two elements . . . in conflict" in his photographs might be said to include, then, the contrary influences of Lhôte and the Surrealists. Being pulled in these two different directions as an artist has created the tension that exists in his work between background and foreground, the elegantly composed scene and the vanishing figure in it, the eternality of forms and the immediacy of action.

It was not only by suggesting an alternative to the formalist visions of Lhôte that the Surrealists enlarged Cartier-Bresson's sense of his art. They also encouraged him to see photography as an aspect of public life, a medium whose social and political implications are inextricably bound up with the aesthetic ones. This side of their influence was especially important in the late thirties, when he was working on a regular basis for both the Communist-backed weekly *Regards* and the Communist daily *Ce Soir,* which was edited by Louis Aragon.

Having met Breton during World War I, Aragon, who was also a poet, became a co-

Fig. 8.3
HENRI CARTIER-
BRESSON
*Trafalgar Square on the
Day of Coronation of
George VI, London,
1937*

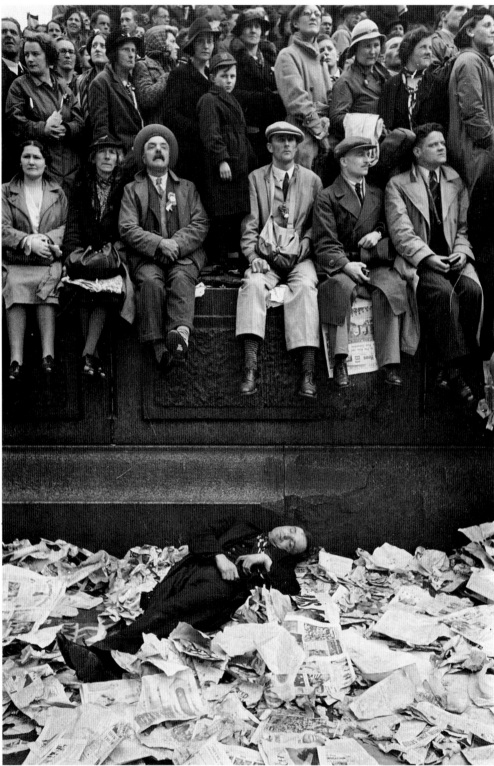

founder of the Surrealist movement and its early journal, *Littérature*. As editor of *Ce Soir* he put into action the second half of the program that Breton had set for Surrealism in his second manifesto. It decreed that while relying on "Freudian doctrine as it applies to the evaluation of ideas," Surrealism must "deliberately opt for the Marxist doctrine in the realm of social problems."[33]

It was Aragon who made the most fervent commitment to Marxism and, by the 1930s, to

Russian communism. He was traveling extensively in the Soviet Union at the time, often in the company of another former Surrealist, the journalist and film critic Georges Sadoul, who was married to Cartier-Bresson's sister. Cartier-Bresson found a lot to stimulate him in Aragon's 1926 book *Paris Peasant*, an itinerant's account of the streets of the city and the inherent Surrealism of the sights and incidents found there. Although Cartier-Bresson covered similar scenes for *Ce Soir*, his standing assignment appears to have been not just the man in the street, but man in the mass. The pictures that he took for the newspaper were primarily of crowds, parades, and other public manifestations.

Among the staffers at *Ce Soir* was another photographer, David Syzmin (later known as David Seymour), whose photo credit was Chim. Earlier, when he had been at the rotogravure weekly *Regards,* he had sponsored careers not only for Cartier-Bresson, but for a young Hungarian photojournalist working under the pseudonym Robert Capa. All three would go to *Ce Soir* together when it started up.

The take from one of the public events Cartier-Bresson covered for *Regards,* the coronation of George VI as king of England, included a picture that typifies his work for these Communist publications: a photograph in which a spectator in Trafalgar Square has slipped from his perch on a wall (fig. 8.3). He lies in cozy oblivion amid the trash while the royal procession in which everyone else is absorbed passes him by. One of the niceties being observed on this ceremonial occasion is that nobody has taken the man's seat. To do so would be to acknowledge his indiscretion. This is such a lovely English touch — to ignore someone by being mindful of his proprietary rights. No political cartoon could have satirized British social attitudes more effectively.

The early 1930s through the late 1940s was the period when Cartier-Bresson's political consciousness was formed. Like many of his countrymen, he was deeply affected by the fate of Spain, whose civil war was the most serious crisis to face the French government of Léon Blum during the Popular Front. Cartier-Bresson began working for *Ce Soir* the summer that Blum's left-wing coalition collapsed. Robert Capa's coverage of the fighting in Spain made him famous, and the Paris funeral of his photojournalist girlfriend, Gerda Taro, killed in Spain while on assignment for *Ce Soir,* became the occasion for a massive outpouring of support for the Spanish Loyalists.

When Britain and France declared war on Germany in the fall of 1939, Cartier-Bresson enlisted and was made a corporal in a film and photo unit. In the early summer of the following year, he was captured in the Vosges Mountains on the day that the armistice with the Germans was signed. One of the articles of the armistice agreed to leave the French POWs, most of whom were taken in the last days of the fighting, in German custody until peace was concluded on all fronts. The French general staff was convinced that if the Nazis could roll over them so easily, England would be defeated as well in a few weeks. This final miscalculation on the part of the military consigned a million and a half Frenchmen to German prison camps for the next four years.

Cartier-Bresson was not to be one of them, however. Constitutionally incapable of sitting still, he succeeded in escaping on his third attempt within three years. He got back to Paris with the aid of false papers and soon landed a contract for a book about French artists, an unrealized project that nonetheless produced some of his greatest portraits, including ones of Matisse, Pierre Bonnard, Henri Rousseau, and Georges Braque (who has a grave expression in the picture because he was listening to a clandestine radio report of the D-day invasion). Cartier-Bresson, along with Robert Doisneau, was also part of an organization of professional photographers working with the underground to document the German occupation and the impending liberation of Paris.

After the Allied victory, Cartier-Bresson had an opportunity to return to something he had been doing just before the war — not photography, but filmmaking. In the late 1930s, after he had studied filmmaking with Paul Strand in New York, he had made a documentary

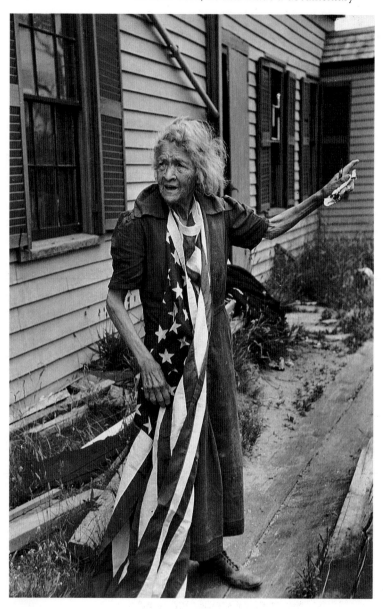

Fig. 8.4
HENRI CARTIER-
BRESSON
Cape Cod,
Massachusetts, 1947

about medical aid to the Loyalists in Spain and had worked with Jean Renoir on a propaganda film sponsored by the French Communist party. Then he had gone on to assist Renoir on two features, *A Day in the Country* and *The Rules of the Game,* whose very personal kind of humanism affected him as deeply as the aspirations of communism had a few years earlier. Now he was asked to do a

film that was being sponsored by the U.S. Office of War Information, a documentary called *Le retour,* about displaced persons and POWs finding their way home again.

Professionally this project proved to be a decisive moment for Cartier-Bresson himself, a turning point at which his postwar career was, ironically, refocused on photography. The frustration he experienced because interference prevented him from doing much of the actual shooting of *Le retour,* plus the cutting of the release prints from three reels to two, reinforced the dislike he had always had for the collaborative aspects of filmmaking.

Furthermore, something that happened during the shooting made him realize that, at least in his hands, still photography was a more powerful medium anyway. One scene, showing a Gestapo informer being denounced by a woman at a deportation camp, was revealing because Cartier-Bresson captured it in a photograph as well as on movie film. In the film, as Cartier-Bresson himself recognized at once, this image gets buried in the flow of the action. The moment is unremarkable. But the photograph seems to contain the entire drama of Europe at the war's end in a single scene. The abstract horror of Nazism is here brought down to a human scale. It is given the classical proportions of tragedy, a tale of cruelty and revenge. From the partitioning of India to the Communist revolution in China, Cartier-Bresson's postwar photographs would often make vivid in this way events otherwise dimmed by their own complexity and vastness.

This still from *Le retour* was but one of many signs he had that photography was his real métier, and fortunately an opportunity presented itself to reestablish his career in that field. A rumor of his death had spread in the United States while he was a POW in Germany, and Beaumont Newhall, then curator of photography at the Modern, began working with his wife, Nancy, on a posthumous exhibition. When word got through that the rumor was false, the exhibition was converted from a memorial into a midcareer retrospective, and new plans were made to bring Cartier-Bresson himself to New York for the occasion. He was ready. He saw both the exhibition and the stay in America as chances to pick up where he had left off as a photographer in the late thirties.

At the time of the exhibition, Robert Capa had cautioned him, "You must not have a label of a Surrealist photographer. If you do, you won't have an assignment and you'll be like a hothouse plant. . . . The label should be photojournalist." [34] Cartier-Bresson scrupulously followed this advice in interviews, and soon one American editor, Carmel Snow at *Harper's Bazaar,* was giving him a fair amount of work. Nevertheless, this was an unsettling period. Turning his vocation for taking pictures into a daily profession, however necessary in order to make a living, was not an entirely happy prospect.

He had met Snow in New York in the 1930s and then again in Europe just after the war, when she came to recruit photographers for her magazine. When he returned to New York in 1946, she gave him several assignments. One was for a piece on the Brooklyn Bridge to be written by Alfred Kazin, who was at the time working on a reminiscence of growing up in New York called *A Walker in the City.* Kazin was another restless pacer of pavements, someone with an intuitive sympathy for Cartier-Bresson's habits. After covering Lower Manhattan and parts of Brooklyn with him, Kazin concluded that for Cartier-Bresson,

> what counted was the city man in the city setting, the man and the street as one. He started with the human passer-by in a social world that was the other side of himself, Cartier-Bresson. This passer-by, this stranger, was what I lived with every day of my life without always seeing him. Cartier-Bresson was teaching us to see him.[35]

A second assignment from Snow that year was to go to New Orleans with literary wun-derkind Truman Capote, through whom he met yet another writer, John Malcolm Brinnin. Cartier-Bresson soon interested him in collaborating on a book about the whole country. He took to referring to himself and Brinnin as *"les flâneurs des deux oceans."* [36] *Harper's Bazaar* agreed to do features on celebrities in the arts — William Faulkner, Robert Flaherty, Frank Lloyd Wright — who would be photographed along the way, and the two men set out in a car Brinnin had bought for the journey. But by the time they returned to New York more than two months later, according to Brinnin's memoirs, "we'd driven more than sixteen thousand miles, worn out eleven tires, four windshield wipers, three batteries, and each other." [37]

Before they departed on the trip, Max Ernst had suggested that Brinnin look up the French term *brise-cou,* which means "break-neck pace" or "roughrider." [38] The long string of insults, slights, evasions, and abuses that Brinnin suffered reached its denouement when Cartier-Bresson literally rode roughshod over his hapless traveling companion at a Fourth of July parade on Cape Cod. Having been stiff-armed out of the way of a shot Cartier-Bresson wanted, Brinnin picked himself up off the sidewalk determined to throw the photographer under the wheels of a passing fire engine. The only thing that saved Cartier-Bresson was that Brinnin first came upon a demented old woman wrapped in the American flag (fig. 8.4). He was so thrilled with his discovery that instead of killing Cartier-Bresson when he found him, he guided the photographer to the subject of one of his best American pictures.

By the time this photograph was taken, near the end of the trip, waving the flag had roughly the same effect on Cartier-Bresson that the muleta has on the bull. It had become one of his favorite subjects, as it would for another European photographer, Robert Frank, who came to America in 1947. "I have no need to kiss the stars and stripes," Cartier-Bresson had declared at the beginning of the trip. "This country makes welcome only those

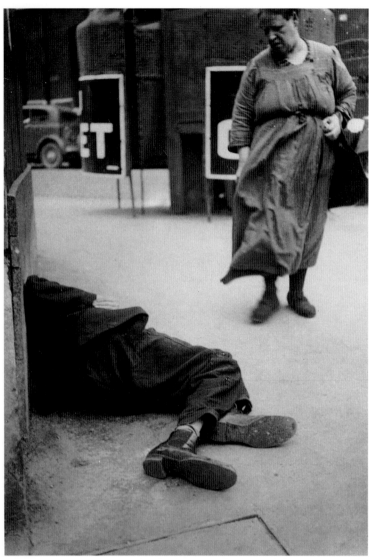

Fig. 8.5
HENRI CARTIER-
BRESSON
La Villette, Paris, 1929

comparable subject in Paris in 1929 (fig. 8.5). The glance that this earlier photograph gives to the scene it records is as quick and discreet as the one that the woman in it gives to the derelict. Like her, Cartier-Bresson doesn't look too closely. He leaves the derelict his shred of privacy. By showing him to us only as he is reflected in the expression on her face, Cartier-Bresson preserves the humanity in a scene that might have been merely revolting.

Cartier-Bresson told Brinnin that he would never photograph anyone "in distress. . . . You must honor all persons." [40] In certain pictures unique to the American trip, he violated this principle. It is not surprising that the book he had planned with Brinnin never materialized. It was impossible, Cartier-Bresson says, because "America was too vast." [41] The photographs he made give the impression that in America he had to resort to a 35mm lens, instead of his 50mm, far more often than in Europe, as if he couldn't get America to fit into the normal frame of things. He had to bend the space, to push it away, in order to take it all in.

Yet the problem was not just America. It was the prospect of turning photojournalism into a full-time career. It put him out of sorts, for he remained as conflicted as ever about the medium. Painting was what he preferred, but photography was what he had the talent for. Out of his irresolute attitude came the irresolvability that made his pictures great. Still, to contemplate a life's work based on such tensions must have been distressing. And even more distressing was the likelihood that under the regimen of constant work, the tensions would disappear. The paradox was that to retain the disinterested quality that made it good, his photography had to continue to be something he could take or leave. It was a reflex that could never be forced, no matter how involuntary it may have been. The same ambivalence that made photography difficult also made it worthwhile. How could the Surrealist elements of surprise and accident be kept alive in a daily profession?

who do. America the beautiful. O say can you see. Beggars in the subway? Fat women in furs? . . . Capitalism, the American century, it is an arrogance." [39] Part of the difficulty Brinnin had with Cartier-Bresson was that, in addition to carrying his camera bag much of the time, Brinnin had to bear the brunt of the foul humor into which America put the always edgy, mercurial photographer.

A New York picture from 1947 of a man lying at the head of (it seems) a stream of his own vomit has about it a pure nastiness characteristic of the American work. The photograph reduces its subject to a crude symbol, like the flag. How America differed from Europe in Cartier-Bresson's perceptions can be seen from the very different treatment he gave to a

One answer, as paradoxical as the problem and as conflictual as everything else in Cartier-Bresson's life, lay in the photo cooperative Magnum, which he, Capa, and Chim founded in 1947. This agency offered great advantages to him, the chief being that, like his camera, it functioned as an extension of himself. When he took pictures, he concentrated on the subject; he didn't have to think about the Leica with which he was shooting. Magnum was the same kind of tool because it removed the need to worry about how or where he could sell his imagery.

Ideally, Magnum would make photojournalism as automatic as a camera, thereby allowing him to take the detached attitude crucial to the pictures. Yet because the cooperative permitted him continuous employment, it also compounded the problem of being a workaday photographer. His thoughts about the need to turn photography into a disciplined routine can be traced, in a sense, by tracing the route over which his travels for Magnum were to take him during the next twenty years.

Magnum was the concrete, practical form that the political and social insight Cartier-Bresson had gained from the experiences of the previous decade took. He was able to act on his ideas at the time because his two like-minded colleagues from *Ce Soir* also happened to be in New York. "After World War II, I had a feeling with Bob Capa and Chim," he has explained, ". . . that going to colonial countries was important. What changes were going to take place there? That's why I spent three years in the Far East. It was to be present when a situation was pregnant, when there was the most tension."[42] He believed that there existed at the time what he has called elsewhere a "thirst for the world,"[43] and his internal divining rod guided him to Asia as the place to slake this thirst. It was there, the political analysis with which he had emerged from the war told him, that the most important postwar history would be made.

As soon as Magnum had been founded, shortly after the trip with Brinnin, Cartier-Bresson rushed to India to cover the partition, the final days of British rule, and, as it turned out, the assassination of Mohandas Gandhi. From there he went to Burma and while in Rangoon received an assignment from *Life* to go to China. After staying there nearly a year — half during the last days of the Kuomintang, the rest of the time under the new, Communist regime — he went to Indonesia when its independence was declared. A decade later he would be in China once more, and later still he would come back to Asia again for a three-month residence in Japan. With this journey of twenty years, he was retracing the route by which Dhyāna Buddhism migrated from the Indian subcontinent to the Japanese islands, where it became known as Zen.

"I was born in the West and raised in the Christian tradition," he says, "so it's impossible to speak of myself as a Buddhist." Yet at the same time, he adds, "I would be one if I could."[44] That respect was crystallized for him by his reading of Eugen Herrigel's *Zen in the Art of Archery,* which he has characterized as his favorite book. Like other key texts in his life, such as Lhôte's treatises, this one didn't influence him so much as illuminate behavior he had already adopted. In the interview published in *Le Monde,* he explained,

> *That book of Herrigel's, which I discovered many years ago, seems to me to be the basis of our craft of photography. Matisse wrote similarly about drawing — that it was the practicing of a discipline, imposing a rigorousness on oneself and thereby forgetting oneself completely. In photography, the attitude should be the same. . . . My sense of freedom is like this: a regimen that allows for infinite variations. This is the basis of Zen Buddhism.*[45]

Herrigel's book gave Cartier-Bresson a new and useful way to think about his work. On the one hand, Zen is, in the form of Bushido, the way of the samurai swordsman. It is a philosophy sufficient to matters of life and death; it is capable of refining mere love of danger into a disregard for it, a vocation of disinterestedness. On the other hand, Zen is also the art of the tea ceremony and of flower arrangement. There are no high or low arts in Zen. The meditation of the master, his self-abnegating self-possession, is equally valid whether the instrument with which he expresses it is a spray of blossoms or a sword of war, a calligrapher's brush or a camera. The mental state that the Zen disciple achieves is the same reflexive one in which Cartier-Bresson works. He could have been quoting a passage from Herrigel when he said, "Thinking should be done beforehand and afterwards — never while actually taking a photograph. Success depends on the extent of one's general culture, on one's set of values, one's clarity of mind and vivacity." [46]

Over the years, Cartier-Bresson had had to make photography a Zen exercise in order to turn his vocation for the medium into the profession of photojournalism. For only by making the daily chore of photographing into a form of practice for perfection — the ceaseless ritual practice that Zen requires — could he reconcile himself to a career in photography. Every composition that the Zen painter creates is in effect preparation for the next attempt he will make to paint. On that occasion all his past experience with the brush culminates in the moment when he lapses, as Herrigel said, "into profound concentration, in which he sits like one inviolable." Then, suddenly, "he produces with rapid, absolutely sure strokes a picture . . . capable of no further correction and needing none." [47] His discipline combines the spontaneity of Surrealism with the exactness of Lhôte.

After the war the quality Julien Levy termed ambivalence became a kind of absolute in Cartier-Bresson's work. He came to prize a multifariousness, a feeling almost of enigma, above all else in his photographs (pages 140–141). One day in the mid-1960s, Romeo Martinez found Cartier-Bresson at Magnum going through his life's work, intending to destroy the bulk of it. Martinez prevailed upon his friend not to do so; instead Martinez,

Cartier-Bresson's editor and publisher Robert Delpire, and Magnum's printer Pierre Gassman were each permitted to edit the work. When they had finished, the photographer was still dissatisfied, however, rejecting any pictures they had included that he felt had, as Martinez put it, "a closed form." He could no longer accept compositions that relied on formal control. The reason he gave, according to Martinez, was that such images were "too perfect — they don't have enough ambiguity." [48]

The cultivation of the ambiguous as an end in itself is what sets Cartier-Bresson's late work apart from that of the 1930s. Although the nature of his talents may not have changed, his temperament did, and this subtly altered the work. *The Decisive Moment* accurately reflects Cartier-Bresson's career in this respect. The book can be divided exactly in half. The first part contains pictures from Europe and America, most of them made before the war. The second half is of pictures made (with only one exception) in emerging nations after the war. And those later pictures are very different in character.

Most are not focused on any central incident — a leap, a fall, a glance, a shrug, as so many early pictures are — or on any single individual. They are human panoramas of crowds, gatherings, mass actions, and demonstrations (fig. 8.6). Their effect is at once intimate and impersonal. On the one hand, we are overwhelmed by a dozen different emotions pressing in on the lens, and on the photographer. On the other, we are aware of his self-restraint in not choosing among them.

While Cartier-Bresson's later work may take a somewhat less athletic, more serene view of humankind, one thing it preserves from the early period is a certain neutrality. We still sense the bemusement at human nature, and the detachment, the ability to remain, like the Zen painter, "inviolable" even as the picture is being shaped by one's own hand. Lincoln Kirstein has observed of Cartier-Bresson that "he is not interested in the propriety of an

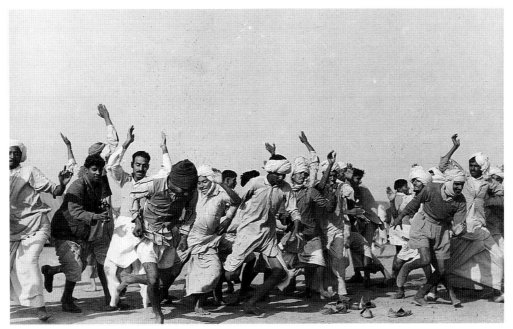

ethic, but in *les moeurs*, the actual, essential behavior of men."[49] Ernst Haas also noticed this nonjudgmental quality. But to Haas, who was a more eloquent and perceptive observer of his colleague than anyone else, this character trait had a distinctly Asian tinge. "There is a Chinese way of thinking in him," Haas said, "which makes him equalize contrasts to a total whole — an agnostic accepting metaphysics without questioning them; a man in proportion accepting good and bad as human — all too human."[50]

This is a description of the pictures, the photographic surface, as much as of the man. ("HCB is like his photography," Haas added a sentence later.) Those even-toned Zone 5 prints Cartier-Bresson likes reflect the spiritual equanimity of the pictures' making, the photographer's capacity for accepting both good and bad as human. In the photographs of masses of people, moreover, this visual style finds its perfect subject. The diffused human presence becomes a counterpart to the diffused light in which Cartier-Bresson shoots. Both the content and the look of the image, as Haas said, equalize contrasts to a total whole.

Critic Arthur Goldsmith is only one of a number of commentators on Cartier-Bresson's photography who have seen it as "self-effacing,"[51] which is also a term prominent in Herrigel's account of Zen. It is but another name for what Herrigel calls "purposeless-

ness" or "egolessness" or "self-abandonment,"[52] and it is a prerequisite state for the attainment of the bottomless ground of Being. To make the sort of street photographs Cartier-Bresson does, one's presence must be turned into an absence this way.

Speaking of this "tendency to self-effacement" in Cartier-Bresson, John Malcolm Brinnin elaborated, "The extraordinary effect of it was to render him temperamentally neutral and, physically, all but anonymous."[53] Cartier-Bresson himself sees the street photographer as being, of necessity, an invisible man. Were this not his profession, he has said, he might be a cab driver, "an anonymous someone to whom people reveal their inner selves. . . . Though remaining faceless to his passengers, the driver can see their faces in the mirror. The photographer should be like that — unobtrusive, detached, yet close to people."[54]

Whatever the best picture by Cartier-Bresson may be, the best picture *of* him is one Beaumont Newhall took. It's an image of an empty room through whose doorway we just catch sight of the backside of a man departing. This portrait is a good likeness because everybody who has ever taken a walk with Cartier-Bresson agrees that the man can literally vanish. In Newhall's own version he disappears right out of the midst of a group of friends, then turns up again at the next corner, "waiting patiently," the frame counter on his Leica having advanced several numbers.[55] Newhall's snapshot is telling because its subject really is as evanescent as this, not only as a photographer taking his own pictures, but as a public figure forever dodging other people's cameras aimed at him.

An incident at a reception for Cartier-Bresson in what was then the Soviet Union is typical. Expecting a few dozen photographers to be present, he arrived to find that three hundred were there. "They started taking pictures of me, and I got frantic, . . . hysterical," he has confessed.[56] The self-consciousness he feels on such occasions is intolerable to him not because he's ungracious, but because it is a contradiction of the self-forgetfulness in which his own pictures had to be made. "I've spent all my life disappearing," he laments, "and now people want to treat me as a celebrity."[57] He feels that for him to get a lot of personal attention belies the very work for which he is being honored. As a result, he tries to refuse all recognition except that being accorded to the medium as a whole rather than to him alone.

What he rejects is not just the award itself, but the whole ideal of individual achievement on which so much of French culture has been based. He would almost certainly concur with an observation historian William Shirer made about the epoch in which he, Cartier-Bresson, came of age. Writing of the period 1870 to 1940, Shirer asked, "Did not [the] cult of the individual, so strong and so extensively cultivated in France in these years, contribute to the weaknesses of the nation and its society? . . . Did it not make for an undue selfishness of persons and closely knit families?"[58] Cartier-Bresson came from such a family, and he too saw the weaknesses inherent in French society and politics in the years before World War II.

Photography helped him to see through the bourgeois self-importance of the French, including himself, because it demanded something quite the contrary — anonymity. This was not just a physical attitude with which

the photographer has to approach his subjects, but a characteristic of the medium itself to which he must remain faithful. Even the contempt Cartier-Bresson sometimes seems to have for photography is really more a commitment to an unadorned truth, a refusal to heroicize the medium. He has repeatedly stressed photography's nature as a collective rather than a personal vision. To one interviewer he said,

> It seems to me . . . important that in our day — when the trend is toward an exaggerated individualism — a large number of photographers should have the same kind of attitude toward their profession. The anonymous side of photography is very much like the sculpture of the Middle Ages: it is based on a common principle and attitudes, and it differs only in degrees of sensitivity.[59]

When you consider that Cartier-Bresson was at one time the most famous photographer in the world, it is ironic, and instructive, that he should often sound so much like one of the most obscure, Atget. Cartier-Bresson also speaks of himself as an "amateur"[60] and partly means by this what Atget did: *un anonyme*. He doesn't take a proprietary attitude toward his own vision, even though he has zealously guarded the right to his pictures, just as Atget did. He too recognizes that his work belongs to a larger sensibility that is photography itself. Like Atget as well, he was a discovery of the Surrealists. Through them he was introduced to Atget's work, which inspired him to experiment with a view camera at one point early in his career. In fact, when he was first starting out, Surrealist Eugene Berman sometimes accompanied him on photographic excursions to Saint-Cloud, the park of which Atget had made the definitive document a decade earlier. The idea that Cartier-Bresson was somehow following in Atget's footsteps is a very compelling one. As different as both their cameras and their pictures are, their wisdom about photography seems in the end much the same.

9: Hungarian Rhapsody

"It was not enough to be a genius, you also had to be a Hungarian," Stefan Lorant once said.[1] He was referring to the period in the late 1920s when Hungarian-born pioneers like him and László Moholy-Nagy were working in Germany, developing new applications for photography in the fields of journalism and design. Moholy-Nagy had incorporated photography into the curriculum at the Bauhaus because he was convinced that "a knowledge of photography is just as important as that of the alphabet."[2] And Lorant was the Berlin editor of the *Münchner Illustrierte Presse*, where he was refining the idea of the photo essay, on which magazines like *Life* and *Look* would thrive later.

This is not to minimize the contribution of the Germans themselves in this period. The new uses for photography created then relied heavily on Germany's own innovators, from Dr. Erich Salomon and Wolfgang Weber, urbane, highly educated men who were the first candid photojournalists, to August Sander, Karl Blossfeldt, Albert Renger-Patzsch, and Franz Roh, all of whom shaped the New Photography that was a counterpart to the New Objectivity in painting. (Even the small camera that made many of the stylistic innovations possible was the invention of a German, Dr. Oskar Barnack of Leitz Optical, who had brought out the prototype for the 35mm Leica before World War I.) Still, in both Germany and France, it was often Hungarian émigrés who showed the way, especially in photojournalism.

The remark about needing to be a Hungarian in addition to being a genius has been attributed to Robert Capa as well as Lorant. Capa, Martin Munkacsi, Tim Gidal, André Kertész, Brassaï, and Lucien Aigner were all young Hungarian photographers whose work in the twenties and thirties gave the new photojour-

nalism, based in magazines rather than newspapers, its distinctive look.

Aigner's career might typify that of the Hungarian picture professionals of the day. He arrived in Paris in the mid-1920s as the correspondent for a Budapest newspaper, which was unable to pay him enough to live on. Since he was not sufficiently fluent in French to get free-lance work as a reporter, he turned to photography to make himself more marketable. By flashing his reporter's credentials while hiding his Leica in his hip pocket, Aigner could get much closer to statesmen and politicians than the newspaper photographers with their bulky cameras, who were re-

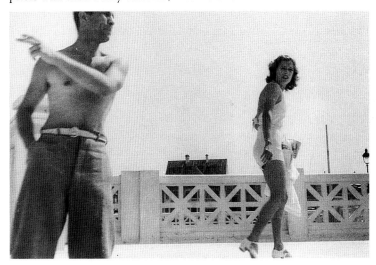

Fig. 9.1
LUCIEN AIGNER
Damita, Le Touquet,
Normandy, 1933

stricted to the press gallery. "The results," he has commented, "were generally caricatures: the grimace, the unaware moment, the pratfall, showing the mighty made human, 'in pajamas,' if possible."[3]

Photojournalism in France had to be smart, like fashion. At publications such as *Vu*, the French equivalent of the early German picture magazines, the photography was often smart in the sense of being not only bright and observant, but also stinging — smart-alecky. This was the market that Aigner quickly

169

learned to supply, although he found that both the official press photographers and his subjects were unhappy with his successes. His colleagues sabotaged his work by jostling him at just the moment he needed to hold still, and the dignitaries he approached learned how to take evasive action. "The politicians and their aides," he says, "grew wise to the political damage in these innocent-looking little instruments." Consequently, "controls were tightened." He realized that "the marauding days of the candid camera were numbered."[4]

One solution was to put emphasis on more accessible, less suspecting subjects, even though this required a fundamentally different approach. When focusing on public figures, Aigner always went for "the 'grab shot,' the sneaky indiscretion," as he himself has characterized it. He says that "in those days, what interested me was human pettiness."[5] But when doing candid photographs of ordinary people, it was pointless to take advantage of your subjects, since they had no public image to strip away. Aggressive photographs of them did not appear smart, but only heartless.

In addition, since the subject was less inherently interesting, the picture itself had to be more so. Work like his, with approximate focus or motion blur, usually became an indecipherable mess in a newspaper. But *Vu* permitted Aigner the latitude to experiment because the photographs held together on the page when reproduced in the sepia rotogravure process that the magazine used. He began frequenting places where revealing little human dramas were likely to occur — railroad stations, cafés, the beach at Le Touquet (fig. 9.1). Having begun as a news photographer, he became a street photographer.

One of the biggest assignments Aigner got from *Vu* was for a three-part article about the Latin Quarter, for which he shared the photo credit with André Kertész. They had met at the Café du Dôme, where Kertész socialized and kept up with the network of contacts —

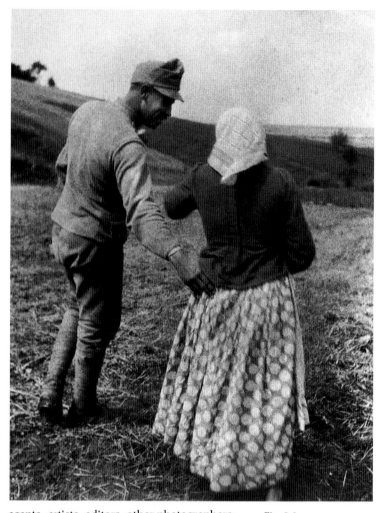

Fig. 9.2
ANDRÉ KERTÉSZ
The Tender Touch, Bilinski, 1915

agents, artists, editors, other photographers — on which he depended for his livelihood as a free-lance photojournalist. The two men's careers ran parallel not only on account of a Hungarian past, Parisian present, and American future, but because of a mythic incident that their life stories, as recounted by them, had in common. This was the loss and eventual recovery of a suitcase full of negatives.

Aigner's was left behind with his sister when he emigrated from France to America in the late 1930s. When she fled south during the war, she put it in the bathtub of her apartment, which was requisitioned by the Nazis. After the war the suitcase was, miraculously, right where she had left it, so she forwarded it to her brother. But he then stashed it in his darkroom and forgot all about it until twenty-five years later, when he opened it to rediscover his entire prewar production.

Kertész also claimed later to have left a suitcase of work behind in Paris, in the care of a woman who ran a picture agency, when he came to America in 1936. After the war, he said, he could find no trace of her and assumed his material was gone forever, until she contacted him from her home in the south of France when he had a retrospective in Paris in 1963. He recovered his negatives at that time and often told thereafter how she had lugged them with her in her flight from the Germans, then stored them in an attic where they had remained forgotten until an article about his new exhibition reminded her.

The truth, at least in Kertész's case, appears to have been somewhat different, for a sequence of photographs made after the war shows Kertész himself removing from a cave some crates in which the negatives in question had actually been stored for safekeeping. The motive for his bit of mythopoesis seems obvious, however. For one thing, the legendary incident repeated an earlier one, at the end of World War I, when Kertész left a cache of his best negatives in a village where he had been recuperating from a wound. He planned to return as soon as his recall to active duty at the front permitted. But the war ended before he could get back, unexpectedly cutting off any chance of return because of the way the area's map was redrawn, and this time there was no happy ending years later. Moreover, the long-lost suitcase imparts to his career, as it does (more authentically, perhaps) to Aigner's, an atmosphere of vagabond romance. True or not, each man's story has about it the distinctly Hungarian flavor of a life both charmed and cursed at the same time.

Kertész's career fell into three distinct periods in three different countries: Hungary up until the end of World War I, France between the wars, and America after World War II. The photography in each phase has its own character as well. The pictures from Hungary have a pure exuberance that later work,

no matter how wonderful in its own right, would never quite match. They possess the unformed energy of youth also seen in Lartigue's early photographs. Although nowhere near as privileged when he was growing up, little André might be thought of as a country cousin of Jacques-Henri. Kertész said that he wanted to photograph only "the little happenings . . . what I see around me."[6] He sounded just like Lartigue.

Indeed, they sounded even more alike when Kertész talked about how he took up photography. As a small child on vacation at his uncle's estate outside Budapest, he happened one day to look through an illustrated magazine. "That set me off," he recalled. "For years before I even got a camera — and also after — I took imaginary pictures in my mind. I made photographs without the camera, visualizing exactly what I wanted to do"[7] — and doing exactly what Lartigue, who was born in

Fig. 9.3
ANDRÉ KERTÉSZ
Wandering Violinist,
Abony, Hungary, 1921

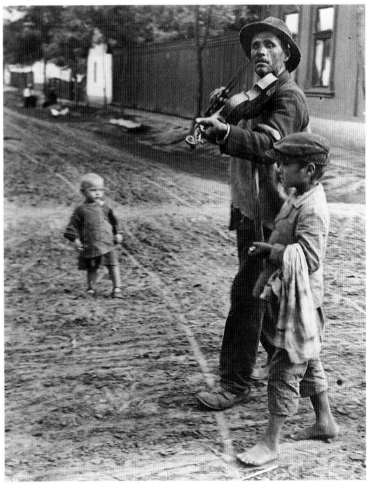

Fig. 9.4
ANDRÉ KERTÉSZ
Displaced People,
Budapest, 1916

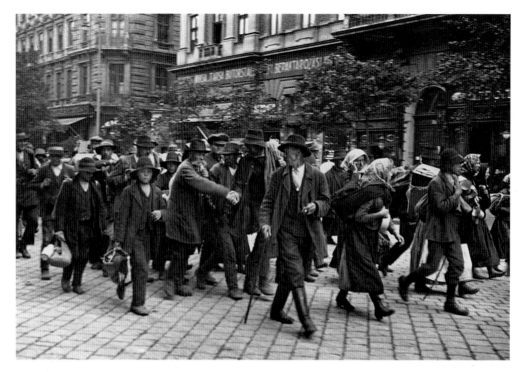

the same year, often did as well. Kertész didn't actually own a camera until 1912, when he was eighteen. Between then and the early 1920s, he made photographs that preserve the sensuous appreciation for life of someone young, a mere boy, growing up in the Hungarian countryside.

The pictures all look as if they are the flowering into imagery of the subjects they contain. An earthiness in Kertész clings to them much as the earth itself clings to the stubby fingers, peasant faces, and clumsy clothes of the subjects. The sheer sweetness of life is what these pictures are about (page 8). From the presence of nature all around the photographer there sprang a human sexuality in his pictures. Even when he went off to World War I in the Hungarian army, the physical humor he had always found in life sustained him.

A photograph of a soldier reaching to caress the buttock of a peasant girl was done in this spirit; so was one of some members of his unit sitting on a latrine. Both photographs take a delight in bodily functions. Both involve the erotic nature of life. The former, among Kertész's favorites from that period, he entitled *The Tender Touch* (fig. 9.2). Even in the midst of the war, the belief that life could be pleasurable and nature gentle was not completely lost.

Yet there is also a sadness in the Hungarian work. The music that it plays is not just sweet, but bittersweet. It has the sounds of Hungarian violins in it, particularly in a 1921 image from Abony of a blind street musician whose only audience is a distracted child (fig. 9.3). The beauty of such pictures lies in a kind of desolateness they contain that was a property of the countryside itself, the central plain of Hungary known as the *puszta.*

Kertész always said that certain photographs he had made took on special personal meaning for him. He seems to have read them almost like tea leaves. One of the negatives from the long-lost World War II suitcase took on this status when it emerged broken in a way that made it look as if it had a bullet hole in it. (Kertész often reproduced it afterward, hole and all.) And an image from the early period that probably had this power for him is one he made in 1916 of a group of displaced persons passing through the area where he was stationed (fig. 9.4).

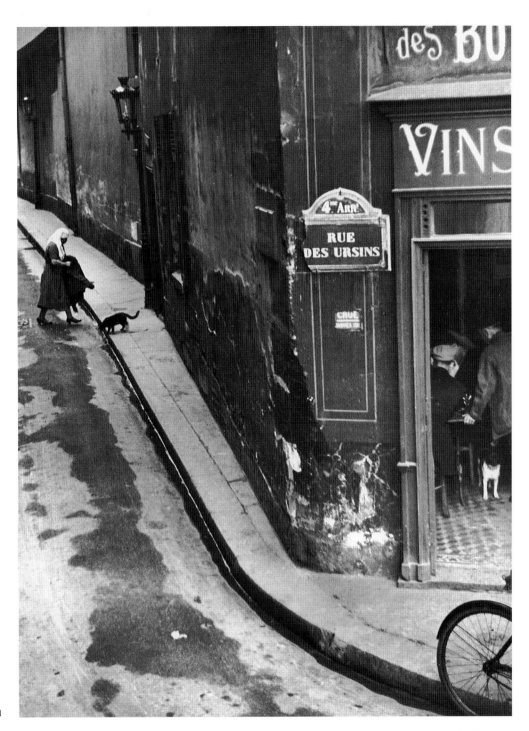

Fig. 9.5
ANDRÉ KERTÉSZ
Rue des Ursins, 1931

By Kertész's own account, the man in the middle of the picture had turned to shake hands with another man whom he recognized from his home district. Yet in the picture it's obvious that the two men did not even stop moving to greet each other. The furtive handshake must have been made, literally, on the run. The photograph's effect is to make us feel the tragedy of peasants turned into refugees, a

consequence of the war that compelled Kertész to think about his own situation at the time as well. He realized that for him too a return to the stable, traditional life of before the war was unlikely.

Although after the war Kertész at first stayed in Budapest and worked at the stock exchange to please his mother, she eventually

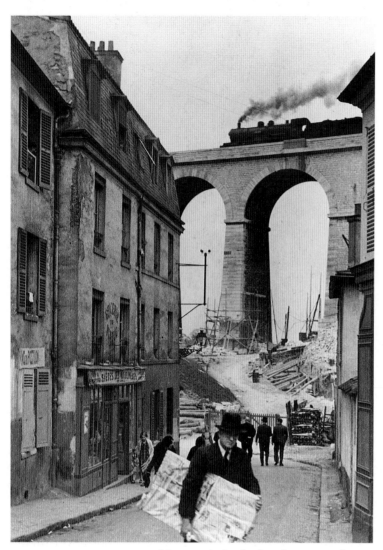

Fig. 9.6
ANDRÉ KERTÉSZ
Meudon, Paris, 1928

take a break to dance with some of them. Kertész took a picture of that too. He himself seems to have found a similar niche in Parisian life, both working and joining in at the same time. The photographs from those days found their way into two of his early books, *Paris Vu par André Kertész,* which came out in 1934, and *Day of Paris,* published in America in 1945. The second one, especially, gives to the city the feeling of sociability that life in a village has. The bohemian community in Paris in the 1920s *was* a little village.

When Kertész first arrived and could not speak French very well, he stuck close to a tiny enclave of Hungarian artists; but even after his circle of acquaintances expanded to include many Frenchmen, the scale of life in Paris in the districts where he and his friends lived remained intimate. Between Kertész's Hungarian pictures and the Parisian ones is an overlap similar to that which occurs when a photographer repeats at the beginning of a new roll of film the last shot on the previous roll, just to remind himself of the sequence of events that might otherwise become jumbled in his mind.

Yet another Kertész photograph from this period that was to take on special significance is the one made in the Paris suburb of Meudon in 1928 (fig. 9.6). Many years later, long after he had moved to America, he showed this picture to a European curator with whom he was planning an exhibition, and she exclaimed that the man in it carrying a painting wrapped in newspaper was her father. Here we are once more back on that village street where two displaced persons hurrying along suddenly recognize each other. Touched as it was by one of those Hungarian coincidences, the photograph places the photographer yet again in the kind of small world he knew as a boy.

At the same time, though, there is a quality to this photograph that's not merely anecdotal in the manner of earlier work. With its busy edges and empty middle and its symmetry between art and industry, the one being carried

gave him permission both to become a photographer and to go to Paris. He arrived in 1925 and at once began exploring the city with his camera. The striking thing about the early results is how closely they follow from what he had done back home. A sad-faced boy with his puppy in a Paris photograph could easily be part of the series of children cuddling animals in Hungary, just as a shot of men gathered inside a Paris café while women go about their business outside might have been done in Estzergom or Abony (fig. 9.5). The blind musician from Abony even has his counterpart in a blind beggar called the Gondolier because he navigated the Paris streets with an oarlike staff.

One café that Kertész frequented had a waiter who would serve the customers awhile, then

in one direction along the bottom while the other, in the form of a train, goes the opposite way at the top, it is a more self-conscious, modern, and Modernist image than those from Hungary.

In 1927 Paul Dermee wrote a poem about Kertész's photography whose first line declares that he has "child's eyes for which each look is the first."[8] In Paris he remained initially the child photographer he had been in Hungary. Yet ironically, the occasion for which Dermee composed his tribute — Kertész's first exhibition, which was held at the gallery Au Sacre du Printemps — was his coming-out party in the world of avant-garde art. Among those who attended was his new friend Piet Mondrian, whose studio had been the subject of a photographic study by Kertész the year before.

His contact with the leading abstract painter explains in part a new formalism that was emerging in Kertész's work. This can be seen in the contrast between two pictures whose comparison Kertész himself proposed when he placed them opposite each other in his book *Day of Paris*. Both are of boskers doing stunts in the street. The first is just a front-row shot of two little girls performing an acrobatic feat (fig. 9.7). It's a human-interest shot. But in the second picture, Kertész took a more detached view (page 130). He stood well to the back of the crowd on some vantage point that raised him well above everyone else's head. And the picture he took has a more abstract interest in the scene. It's a response to the way the acrobat doing a handstand inverts and reverses the posture of a lone passerby, pausing on a bridge above, who bends over a rail to watch. The visual acrobatics of the photograph balance dark against light. A formalistic approach to the subject has replaced the kind of informality that the other picture represents.

Some experiments Kertész began to make with different lenses were also a sign of his increasing concern with formal issues around this time. In 1927, for a view looking down a public stair in Montmartre, he removed the front element from the lens assembly on his

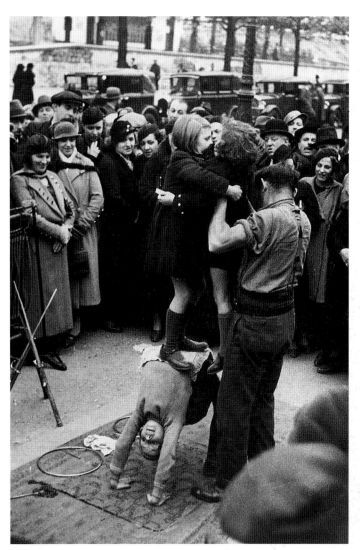

Fig. 9.7
ANDRÉ KERTÉSZ
Paris, 1929

Voigtlander camera. The result was a slight telephoto effect that flattened the scene and thereby made the picture function more as a two-dimensional surface. This pleased him, so he developed various ways to enhance it, eventually acquiring custom-made lenses ranging from 90mm to 260mm.

These new modes of perception Kertész was trying made his work highly compatible with the New Photography coming out of Germany. Lorant began using his material in the *Münchner Illustrierte*, as did Kurt Korff, the editor of the rival magazine in Berlin, and Moholy-Nagy gave him a prominent place in his "Film und Foto" exhibition of 1929. It's hardly a coincidence that the view from above so characteristic of the Bauhaus photography of Moholy-Nagy, and which the abbreviated perspective of the telephoto lens also encouraged, began to become increasingly important in Kertész's own pictures during this time.

The gallery show that Kertész had in 1927 also brought his pictures to the attention of Lucien Vogel, the founder of *Vu,* and led to his frequent appearance in that magazine when it commenced publication soon afterward. This venue for his work, coming on top of the prominence it was achieving in German publications, made him one of the preeminent photographers of the day. The extent of his reputation is apparent from some overtures he received in 1936 from an American picture agency called Keystone to join its staff. His wife, Elizabeth, joked that she would divorce him if he accepted the job offer in New York, and his decision was made doubly difficult by the fact that the French government at this time offered him citizenship, which he coveted, in recognition of his artistic achievements.

Despite these reasons for staying, he decided to go. Thinking he would be away a year at most, he asked the French government to defer his acceptance until his return. But when he arrived in New York, he discovered that Keystone's director, a fellow Hungarian whom he had trusted, was actually bankrupt. He stayed on in New York for two years, partly for lack of money, and by the time he was ready to return to France it was too late — the war had broken out.

Thinking back to that fateful Atlantic crossing, Kertész said later, "All the experiences that happened after with me . . . better forget it."[9] As an enemy alien in the United States, he was forbidden to photograph outdoors, a prohibition that again put him in financial difficulties. In 1944, just so he would be permitted to work as a photographer, he became an American citizen. By the time the war was over, the French economy was in such disarray that he could hardly have made a living if he had returned. So he lingered in America, accepting in 1946 a contract with *House and Garden,* one of the group of Condé Nast magazines for which his friend Alexander Liber-

man, picture editor at *Vu* when he was in Paris, was now art director.

Although that contract lasted until 1962, it was for Kertész a bleak period. None of the American magazines was ever as receptive to his work as the French had been, nor did the publishing houses appreciate his pictures. In 1939, an editor at *Life* told him bluntly, "You are talking too much in your pictures,"[10] and a book editor to whom he proposed a project on New York the same year said, "You are too human, Kertész, sorry . . . make it brutal."[11]

In 1937 he had taken a photograph of a small, lone puff of a cloud drifting before the limitless facade of a New York office building — a picture that he entitled *Lost Cloud.* He probably felt rather that way himself after the war. In a later series, on pigeons, the subject often seems similar to that cloud, a forlorn, vulnerable being amid the monolith of the city, a creature with whom Kertész could identify. He didn't want to make his own work brutal, but he did find himself recording in it the brutality that he saw around him.

In one picture, a man on the sidewalk cleaning an antique statue of the Buddha seems to be gouging its eye with his knife. In another, a game of ball some boys are playing in the sunken concrete court behind an apartment building looks more like a melee (fig. 9.8). A couple of them are obscured from view by the stake iron fence behind which their game is confined. The image is one of faceless violence. Such photographs are typical of his American street work. Kertész saw gentleness only in the flights of the pigeons.

While his standing as a photojournalist was diminished by the move to America, his career as an exhibiting artist was all but ended. In 1946 Hugh Edwards, the curator at the Art Institute of Chicago, gave him his first one-man show in his new country; but he would not have another museum retrospective of significance until almost twenty years later,

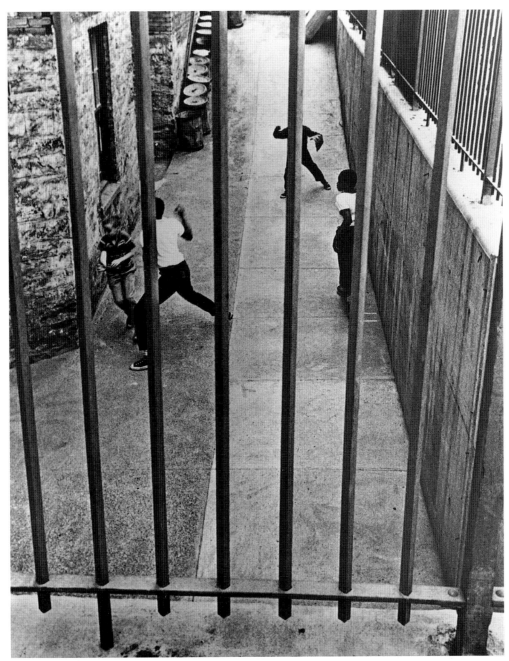

Fig. 9.8
ANDRÉ KERTÉSZ
New York, 1966

when John Szarkowski restored his reputation with an exhibition at the Modern.

When the Kertészes finally settled down with resignation to a permanent life in New York, it was in an apartment that was for André, as a photographer, just such a refuge from the streets below. He and his wife were among the first tenants to occupy a new high-rise building a block or two north of Washington Square, in Greenwich Village. The apartment had a balcony that commanded panoramic views in two directions, and after he moved there in the early 1950s, photographs looking down from above, which had already been growing in prominence in his work in Paris, came truly to dominate it.

The imagery that resulted is almost wholly preoccupied with compositional effects of the type that would interest a painter or graphic artist. The pattern that tracks make in snow or the power of singular details to hold the picture space — a couple lying on the grass, a spoked wheel glimpsed through the impasto of the foliage — becomes a form of abstract design. The exceptions to this tendency are often photographs in which the eroticism of the European work seems to degenerate into voyeurism, pictures where women are spied on from afar behind the windows of their apartment, sunbathing bare-breasted in a rooftop garden, or catching what they thought was a few moments to themselves.

In 1962 a serious illness brought to a crisis Kertész's discontent, both professional and personal, with his life in America. He felt

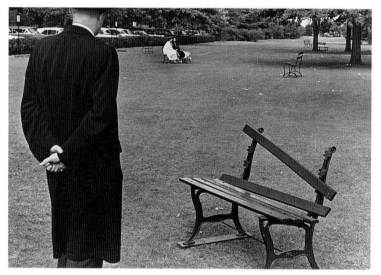

Fig. 9.9
ANDRÉ KERTÉSZ
Broken Bench,
New York, 1962

later that a photograph he made that year — one of an old man contemplating a broken park bench — symbolized eloquently the dilemma he faced at the time (fig. 9.9). Lobotomized by the edge of the frame, his face turned away so that he has no identity for us, the man stares at the empty, useless bench as if he saw in it his own image, which was what Kertész saw in the photograph itself.

During his recuperation, Kertész resolved to leave Condé Nast to devote himself to his personal work. Shortly thereafter, the series of retrospectives and books began that was to revive his reputation. In that regard, he made the right decision. But he was a considerably older man now, both physically and emotionally, and his work could never recapture its former vivacity. *Malheureusement* — "unfortu-

nately" — was the expletive that most often punctuated his remarks near the end of his life. He himself summarized his situation best when he said, looking back, "I am a sentimentalist — born that way, happy that way. Maybe out of place in today's reality." [12]

More than a sentimentalist, Kertész was what might be called a nostalgist. He had begun to photograph seriously during World War I to recapture scenes from boyhood that, he realized, might disappear in the war's aftermath. It was the threat of imminent loss that compelled him and gave the pictures their poignancy. In like manner, his book *Day of Paris*, which he compiled and published after coming to America, is his most tender portrait of the city he loved so much. Perhaps only in a mood of yearning and regret could he understand fully what these places meant to him.

In 1962, around the time of the crisis that the photograph of the broken bench summed up for him, he made another image that seems to epitomize the whole predicament of his life in America. This is one of a carousel horse in a garden beyond whose wall a dog is being walked in the street (fig. 9.10). It is a characteristic view from above in which the intersecting lines of walls, roof, and curb compartmentalize the space on a diagonal the way certain Mondrian paintings do. Although the dog is an ordinary boxer, its hunched gait and long shadow give it the ominous look of a mastiff on the prowl. Behind the wall the carousel horse seems frozen in fear. Such horses are mythical beasts, creatures out of childhood, out of memory. The lost landscape of Hungary, or of Kertész's youth both there and in Paris, is what this little corner of a garden evokes.

The horse is also a companion piece to a group of figurines of animals and gods that Kertész was occasionally photographing on the windowsill in his apartment. In the end, he incorporated some of these statuettes into still lifes that contain as well reproductions of

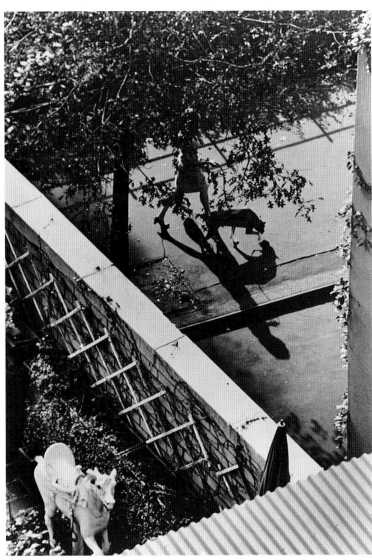

Fig. 9.10
ANDRÉ KERTÉSZ
The White Horse,
New York, 1962

a problem. He had spent the last two years perfecting his ability to photograph in the dark.

It had been almost a decade since Brassaï had left Brassov, the little town in Transylvania from which he took the name he was known by in Paris. During that time, he had explored the French capital as few of the natives ever did. The photographs he made that night atop Notre Dame give the impression that now he was poised on the brink of the city, ready to swoop down on it like one of the odd, winged creatures on the parapet next to him.

The imagery suggests that going down into the streets below would be a kind of descent into hell. Light suffused by the photographs' long exposures drifts up as if borne aloft on sulfurous clouds from brimstone pavements. The gargoyle silhouetted in the foreground of one of the views is all the more evil because lit from underneath; yet the languid way the demon cups his head in his hands is also rather comical. If this is a vision of hell, it is a very attractive and tempting one. It's the sort of vision we might expect from a countryman of Count Dracula.

The history of street photography often seems to have paired off the major figures in it: Riis and Hine, Lartigue and Primoli, William Klein and Robert Frank, are all Gemini of this sort, linked either by circumstance or similarity. So are Brassaï and Kertész. Brassaï was born a few years after Kertész but arrived in Paris a year ahead of his friend. Since both spoke Hungarian as their native language, they inevitably traveled in the same circles. When Brassaï began taking pictures, it was Kertész who taught him how to do night photography; when he published the first fruit of his labors in a 1933 book called *Paris de nuit,* he set an example from which Kertész's *Day of Paris* would follow. Brassaï also had a long, prosperous period in the postwar era when he was associated with an American fashion magazine, *Harper's Bazaar.*

his own photographs from Hungary. Like the figure of the horse in the garden, these early images within late ones suggest the way in which the circle of Kertész's life eventually closed around him.

One night early in 1933, Brassaï bribed the concierge of Notre Dame to permit him to go up on the cathedral's towers after closing. An enormous woman with heart trouble who seemed about to expire with each of the two hundred steps she had to climb every day, she let the young photographer ascend alone with his camera. Her one condition — that he not show any lights, lest the police spot him from the prefecture across the way — was not

In the crisscrossed careers that the two photographers had, each man underwent a development that reversed the other's. Having attended the art academy in Budapest and come to Paris to be either a painter or sculptor, Brassaï was more advanced in his ideas than Kertész when he arrived. The interest in formal problems that Kertész gradually acquired Brassaï had right at the start and gradually shed as the years passed.

The formalism of *Paris de nuit* is apparent on every page. A spiral-bound book of sixty pictures, its images are reproduced without borders. This permitted Brassaï to match pictures so that the lines in one would seem to continue in that opposite — a circus ring on one page completing the partial circle formed by the arch of a bridge on the facing page, a catwalk on which a corps de ballet performs, extending a promenade at the Paris Opera, et cetera. Deep shadow and halated light create abstract patterns in almost every picture. Because Brassaï worked late at night, Paris is a largely deserted city in this book. When people do appear, they are subordinated to the graphic elements in the photograph, or at least incorporated into them. Thus cancan dancers doing their high kicks are viewed from above so that the design their legs make will blend into the herringbone pattern of the dance floor.

Strong though his compositions are as forms, however, Brassaï was not without a sense of content as well. Implicit in the visual associations on which the book relies is a social perception. Pairings of shapes are made a basis for comparisons between the haut monde and the demimonde. This can be seen in two juxtaposed images where the shape of a fountain in the Place de la Concorde is repeated in that of a bridge under which some clochards are huddled around a fire (page 137). Memorial Paris here contrasts with that which is furtive and fugitive. The comparison between the pictures is echoed within the second one by the way an ornate street lamp on top of the bridge glows in counterpoint to the fire below. Paris is both the City of Light and a city of the night — both the world capital for public elegance and glittering beauty, and a shadowy underworld punctuated here and there by the watch fires of vagrants.

Shortly after shooting the pictures that make up *Paris de nuit,* Brassaï moved his camera from the streets themselves into the cafés and dance halls that lined them to begin the series he called *Paris plaisir.* "The dance halls were full of poetry and dreams," he wrote many years later, "but they were also full of pitfalls: there love came close to prostitution. In these dance halls, young pickups seduced girls and recruited the labor force for the streets and the whorehouses." [13] As the screenwriter Jacques Prévert, who sometimes accompanied the photographer on his nocturnal rambles through Paris, aptly observed, Brassaï was drawn to this subject matter by "the beauty of sinister things." [14]

Brassaï's recognition of the relationship between romance and degradation became a social message implicit in the work. A photograph taken at the Bal Musette in 1936 illustrates (fig. 9.11). In it, a young woman basks in the attention that the man at her side gives her. But somewhat uncertainly above their heads, reflected in or through a plate glass window, appears another, more sullen couple who are dancing. It is as if this unfocused and partly obscured reflection were anticipating with its dancers' embrace both the seduction about to occur in the foreground and the disillusionment to which it will lead.

In the course of the *Paris plaisir* series, Brassaï worked his way from the streets and parks into the inner sanctums of Parisian vice, the bars where men danced with other men, women with women, and blacks with whites; the cheap bistros where street toughs, pimps, and petty criminals huddled with their girlfriends; the common brothels, "houses of illusion," and opium parlors. The streets that had attracted his attention in the first place were the ones that these people appropriated as their own each night. In his work more than any other photographer's, the idea of the street — of a common ground on which a society meets both to conduct its business and take its pleasure — is extended from the pavement itself into adjacent venues.

The cafés, bistros, and dance halls were an attractive mise-en-scène because they were richly ambiguous places, a human buffer zone between the public world of the streets outside and the private dens of iniquity where tastes for sex or drugs were satisfied. On the one hand, they were open to the public; anyone with the price of a glass of wine was free to walk in, take a seat, have a turn on the dance floor. On the other hand, if you weren't known there, a regular, all eyes would turn your way and all conversation cease when you arrived.

As a consequence, Brassaï had to cultivate his subjects for the café pictures with a cautiousness that might raise questions in our minds about how candid the pictures could possibly be. He functioned as if he were a movie director to get some of them, such as one street shot in which two men are forcing a third into a car in a gangland-style abduction. This was published in the pulp magazine *La scandale*, which lived up to its title. Brassaï could get cooperation in making little photo-*policiers* for the magazine because, although some of the petty criminals he knew may have been leery of his camera, others were flattered to read fictionalized tales of their exploits.

If secretiveness could be an impediment to a spontaneous, candid, naturalistic picture, so too could the cumbersomeness of Brassaï's equipment. In the dark streets and dim interiors where he worked, his Bergheil Voigtlander usually required exposures of three or four seconds or more, sometimes much more. When long exposures were not needed, it was only because his assistant, Robert, fired a magnesium-powder flash. This means that Brassaï's subjects were either asked to hold their pose during a prolonged exposure or else alerted by his signals to Robert synchronizing the flash. How complicated such techniques

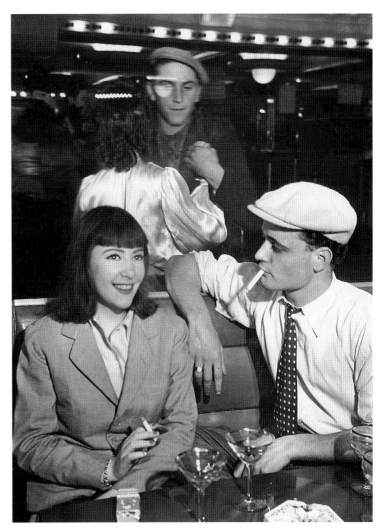

could be is apparent from an image made in a brothel where Robert's arm holding the apparatus can be seen as he reaches around a doorjamb from the next room in a contorted effort to illuminate the scene while concealing himself.

Fig. 9.11
BRASSAÏ
Couple at Bal Musette,
Rue de Laffe, 1936

Despite the careful staging necessitated by the slowness of his equipment and the initial wariness of his subjects, however, the photographs somehow convince us of their authenticity. The contrivance we can detect in them doesn't bother us, because it's uniquely suited to the people he's depicting. There is a degree of collusion between them and the photographer in which we are accomplices. The world Brassaï photographed was, after all, that of the apache dancer, a world of poseurs and studied toughness in which the inhabitants wore their emotions on their rolled-up sleeves. We take it for granted that the natural behavior of these café and dance-hall types was full of artifice, and the photographs themselves trade on our belief in their subjects' paradoxical behavior.

What is more, Brassaï had his ways of distracting such subjects and outsmarting their resistance. His method might be thought of as the opposite of Cartier-Bresson's. The latter relied upon his invisibility to make his pictures, the former upon his presence. Brassaï's natural gregariousness and charm made even the most reluctant habitué of the bistros he frequented forgetful of the camera. Having drawn attention away from Robert and the equipment, he could then use his exceptional peripheral vision to scan the activity around him. He was aided in this ability by prominent, almost protruding eyes that inspired Henry Miller to call him, in the introduction to a memoir Brassaï wrote of Picasso, "The Eye of Paris." Miller elaborated, "It was his eyes which I noticed upon first being introduced to him. . . . His eyes were unusual not only in a physical sense, but for the impression they conveyed of an uncanny ability to take in everything at once." [15]

Just as there is a found Surrealism in Cartier-Bresson's pictures, there is in Brassaï's a kind of found Cubism initially inspired, perhaps, by the influence of his friend Picasso. This element is especially noticeable in the café pictures where mirrors are involved. They break up the composition into multiple perspectives and cause one picture plane to intersect another in the oblique, controlled geometry typical of Cubism's analytic phase. Thus are the café pictures an extension of the formal concerns seen in the night pictures reproduced in Brassaï's first book. In the best of these photographs, the aesthetics and the emotion are like crosscurrents that travel along the frame's diagonals, holding each other in suspension.

A comparable intersection of form and content is found in all Brassaï's work of the period. Out on the street, where he usually placed himself at forty-five degrees to the wall whose edge masked his light source, the illumination moves along one of the picture's diagonals while the action — a solicitation, a kiss, a threat — takes place at right angles to it. Right up until the end of his life he continued to defend this almost schematic approach to picture making because, he said, "I don't like snapshots. I like to seize hold of things, and the form is very important for this. . . . Only through form can the image enter into our memory. It's like the aerodynamics of a car, don't you see? For me, form is the only criterion of a good photograph. One doesn't forget such a photograph and wants to see it again." [16]

10: Foreign Correspondents

By the 1930s in Europe, street photography was becoming for the first time what an art historian might legitimately call a tradition. Demonstrable lines of influence were developing, and what began with a few innovative photographers as a personal style or new idea about how to use the medium became precedents within which many others tried to work. Photography from the Continent had a tremendous impact on the medium's history in England, for instance, partly because key figures from Germany fled to England when the Nazis came to power. Among these were László Moholy-Nagy and Stefan Lorant. Moholy-Nagy brought a Bauhaus sensibility to England, even though the point of view in the photographic book he did there, *The Street Markets of London,* was much more down-to-earth than his work in Germany had been. Lorant started up two new magazines, *Lilliput* and *Picture Post,* that firmly established in Britain the sort of editorial treatment of photography he had pioneered in Germany.

Lilliput, a little satirical journal featuring work by Moholy-Nagy, Kertész, Capa, and Munkacsi, proved so successful that press lord Edward Hulton made Lorant editor of *Picture Post,* which was to be an English counterpart to *Life,* when it was introduced in 1938. Lorant promptly put on staff other refugees such as photographers Kurt Hubschmann, who worked under the name Hutton, and Felix Man.

The same sort of human-interest stories Hutton had done in Germany he did again for *Picture Post* — pieces like *Unemployed,* about the daily routine of a man out of work during the Depression (fig. 10.1), or *And Again: Back to School,* in which dozens of families bid farewell at a train station to sons returning to boarding school after vacation. For this second feature, Hutton frequently stood back

from his subjects so that there would be a number of tender partings visible in the picture. To close in on any one of them would be to turn the piece toward pathos, whereas to take in several at once, as examples of class behavior, was to mock gently this British ritual.

Fig. 10.1
KURT HUTTON
Unemployed Man and Dog, 1939

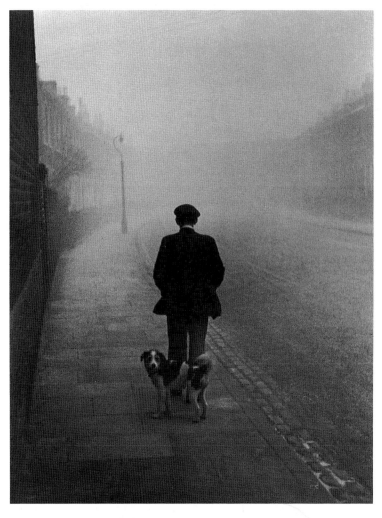

Although the photography itself might run to mild social satire, Lord Hulton wanted his magazine to be very "up England," so the names of these foreign photographers had to be Anglicized. That's why Hubschmann became Hutton. (Hans Baumann had already obliged by changing his name to Felix Man

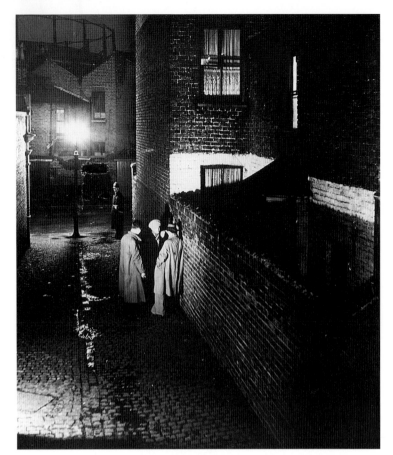

Fig. 10.2
BILL BRANDT
Off India Docks Road,
1931–35

graphic apprenticeship in Paris in 1929 as an assistant to Man Ray, to whom he had been introduced by Ezra Pound, a family friend. His photojournalism was published in France first, before he settled in London in 1931, and it continued to appear in various Parisian magazines, including *La scandale*, the pulp *policier* that also carried Brassaï's work. Moreover, *A Night in London* was brought out by a French firm, which titled the version done for the home market *Londres de nuit*.

Brandt's subjects are often love, carousing, and vice, like Brassaï's. Chorus girls dance in a music hall. A couple snuggles on a park bench under cover of darkness. A woman meets clandestinely with some men in a street door. In a room with a rumpled bed, a man and woman whose faces are concealed from view are locked in a passionate embrace. Is this a romance or, as in Brassaï, a prostitute turning a trick? Outside, three hooligans huddle conspiratorially under a street lamp or in an alley, where a bobby watches them with suspicion (fig. 10.2).

As this last picture demonstrates, Brandt's scenes mix spontaneity with theatrical poses to an even greater degree than Brassaï's. The three hooligans were actually Brandt's younger brother Rolf and some friends, who were giving a performance so convincing that a real bobby on patrol paused to look them over. Rolf also appeared as the man importuning a woman, played by his wife, Esther, in a photograph entitled *Street Scene*. Elsewhere in the book, Bill Brandt's own wife and his mother, Lilli, play parts as well. Even more than Brassaï's street photography, Brandt's is of the sort that mingles documentation with pulp fiction.

Like Brassaï's book of 1933, Brandt's in 1938 was only the tip of an iceberg, a small selection of a much larger body of work — his own London pleasures, as it were — that he was doing at the time. Even more striking parallels to Brassaï are seen in some of the pictures that didn't appear in the book, such as a se-

before leaving Germany.) But there were British photographers who readily got into the swing of the new style as well. Humphrey Spender, a brother of poet Stephen Spender, had an advantage because another brother who worked for Leitz Optical in the 1920s had introduced him to the Leica, and he himself had studied in Berlin at the end of the decade, when the new German magazines were coming into being. Spender worked first for a London newspaper and then later for *Picture Post*. Another talented young Englishman, who had linked up with Lorant already when the editor was at *Lilliput* and would do feature work for him at *Picture Post* too, was Bill Brandt.

The most important English street photographer of his generation, Brandt also owed a debt to influences from the Continent. But for him the greatest of these came from Paris, rather than Berlin or Munich, as was apparent even before one opened to the pictures in the book he published in 1938. Its title, *A Night in London*, was a direct allusion to Brassaï's *Paris de nuit*. Brandt had served his photo-

quence shot in a seedy pub in Limehouse where right Cockney lasses wearing sheer black stockings or slacks drink moodily and neck openly with their boyfriends. Some of this material Brandt didn't release at all until later, maybe because he was concerned that too great a similarity to Brassaï's work would make his look derivative. He needn't have worried, for even if he did copy Brassaï's project, what finally impresses us more is

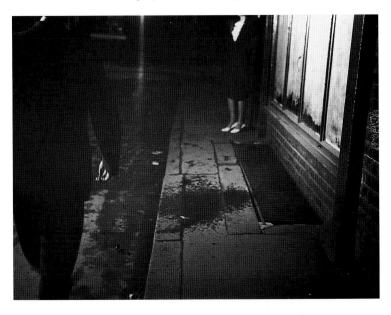

Fig. 10.3
BILL BRANDT
Footsteps Coming Nearer, 1936–37

the extent to which he made it his own. He established in his pictures a uniquely English atmosphere.

There's a chill in the air in Brandt's London, a drop in the emotional temperature of life on the street. Fear breaks out like a cold sweat in certain pictures, particularly one entitled *Footsteps Coming Nearer,* which shows a man walking along a curb toward a woman who waits with her back to a wall on a deserted sidewalk (fig. 10.3). This is an image whose morals are as murky as its optics. The way Brandt printed the picture for reproduction in his book, the woman's shoes and blouse have an unnatural whiteness that seems to give off mixed signals. Does it represent a flag of surrender or a badge of defiant virtue? Is the approaching sexual encounter implicit in the situation to be voluntary or forced?

Either way, it has been rendered faceless and nameless by Brandt's framing, which places both subjects' heads outside the picture. This makes the scene feel like illustration for the kind of article that might be called "London Confidential," in which editors put black bars across the subjects' eyes. Or perhaps the framing is a more menacing gesture than that, an act of decapitation carried out in one of the Whitechapel side streets where Jack the Ripper once lurked.

The atmosphere in Brandt's pictures is not always as ominous as this, but it's usually a lot grimmer than in Brassaï's. Whereas Brassaï used the mirrors lining Paris cafés both to create photographic illusions and betray the romantic ones of his subjects, the London pubs as seen by Brandt are a world without illusions. It's the glumness of the women that you notice first. A certain look comes into their eyes again and again. In the picture *Street Scene*, the woman, who literally has her back to the wall, glances away just as the man she is with leans toward her imploringly. Her averted gaze is the same as that of various other women in Brandt photographs eating in grills with male companions.

The mood in each of these pictures is the opposite of that in Brassaï's. His women are fun-loving and brazen. Brandt's are fallen. They are morose and withdrawn. They are not bohemians, but Victorians. "It's man's place to try, and woman's to deny," we can hear their consciences whispering in every picture. The men must believe it too, judging by the miserable looks they give to these women who steadfastly resist them. The pleasures these people experience are mostly guilty ones. Their sins never become "innocent," as Brassaï said those committed by the Parisians were. That bedroom into which Brandt sneaks us isn't necessarily in a brothel. Still, the room is sordid, the sex tawdry, and love compromised.

As soon as they became available, Brandt began using the Rolleiflex camera and the brighter, safer flashbulbs that were replacing flash powder. Although this means his equipment was much faster than Brassaï's, his pictures frequently look stiffer. The reason is that the Latin qualities of passion and impulsiveness Brassaï intimated in his subjects were simply not part of the English character as Brandt saw it. The people in his photographs frequently look as stricken as those in John Thomson's work some fifty years earlier. Brandt's pictures seem tightly controlled, like Thomson's, not because he couldn't make them otherwise, but because that's the way his fellow countrymen seemed to him. His subjects appear less candid than Brassaï's not only with the camera, but with each other.

The difference in Brandt's point of view is summed up by the last picture in his book, which is of milk bottles and newspapers on a front porch. At the end of the night we have emerged once more into the daylight, into the normal, middle-class world of milk deliveries and the morning papers. In Brassaï's photographs, the night is an exotic world all to itself; the people in it are, like Brassaï, noctambulants who sleep during the day and go out only after dark. But in Brandt's England the night has a continuity with the everyday that's never completely lost.

In fact, *A Night in London* is in many respects a sequel to the book Brandt had published two years earlier, *The English at Home*. That title indicates the real center of Brandt's interest in all the photography he was doing in the 1930s — the domestic life of the English, whose nightlife was for him just one aspect of this larger topic. He brought out the difference in emphasis himself in some of the pictures in *A Night in London* that most resemble Brassaï's, such as the one in a bedroom with a woman in her dressing gown and a man pulling off his shirt behind her. This copies almost exactly the disposition of the figures in some Brassaï pictures, except that here the man isn't being serviced by a prostitute but retiring for the night with his wife. The woman isn't squatting on a bidet or getting dressed to

go back out on the street, she's brushing her teeth. Brandt meant the title of this first book quite literally. It was intended as a study of the English "at home."

If Brandt photographed a building facade, it was not the café or brothel that Brassaï would have chosen. It was a residence, shop front, or flat, or else a redoubtable private

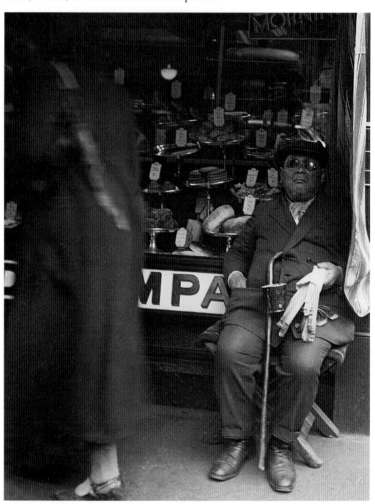

club like the Reform Club in Pall Mall. The facade of respectability was the one he wanted to get behind. The blankness of the face that English architecture turns to the world — the drawn shades, the darkened windows, the glass reflecting the street back on itself — is duly noted again and again in his photographs.

Still, Brandt had his ways to get inside. Examples may be drawn from either book. In one instance, which happens to be from *A Night*

Fig. 10.4
BILL BRANDT
A Whitechapel Blind Beggar, 1931–35

in London, a glimpse through one of these windows yields an insight into the reticence that English couples practice with each other. Looking into a middle-class parlor from outside, we find a husband reading his paper while his wife plays solitaire. These people are as distant as the lovers who never seem able to look each other in the eye. Brandt's last book returned, like Brassaï's, to his photography from the thirties, and at the beginning of one of the book's sections he placed a picture of a maid raising a window to air out a stuffy room. He thought of his photographs as windows opened onto English life for the same reason.

In *The English at Home*, there's a photograph of a blind man with his cup and cane sitting before the window of a bakery whose awning hangs down beside him, flapping gently in the breeze (fig. 10.4). Behind his dark glasses, his face is as set and inexpressive as any facade Brandt ever photographed. The picture reflects the sightless world in which its subject lives. Only those things that a blind man might sense, like the cakes and loaves behind him with their warm, sweet aroma, are in pin-sharp focus. The awning and a woman passing are, by contrast, indistinct. Her shoe is clear upon the pavement, like a footfall; but the upper part of her body disappears in a dark haze amid the shadows on the glass. She becomes for us what she is for him: a rustling and scraping along the street, a maddening blur that he strains to make out.

The blind man becomes, ironically, like the photographer, someone who tucks himself into a corner of the street and waits, taking it all in, trying not to miss a thing. At the same time, he might also be a stand-in for other Brandt subjects, a figure of blind propriety of the sort that appears to see nothing. That's what the spectators at the coronation of George VI did when they studiously ignored, in Cartier-Bresson's photograph, the man who lay stretched out in the trash. Brandt photographed similar indiscretions being overlooked at Ascot, and even in that rough-

looking pub in Limehouse, such niceties were observed. In one of the pictures that he made there, while a woman sits on a man's lap kissing him hungrily, another man right across the table seems not even to notice the wanton display (fig. 10.5).

Like *A Night in London*, *The English at Home* is modeled on *Paris de nuit*, although in a different way. The similarity here lies in the way the pictures are paired to create formal effects and editorial comments. The social message Brandt sent through such montage is very similar to Brassaï's, as when Brandt placed customers in a workmen's restaurant opposite members in the lounge of a posh private club, or an image of children playing in the street of an East End slum next to one of a birthday party in a Kensington drawing room.

The strongest two-page spread in either man's book is the one that pairs a picture of miners emerging from a coal shaft with an image of three children hanging out of a basement win-

Fig. 10.5
BILL BRANDT
Corner Table at Charlie Brown's, 1931–35

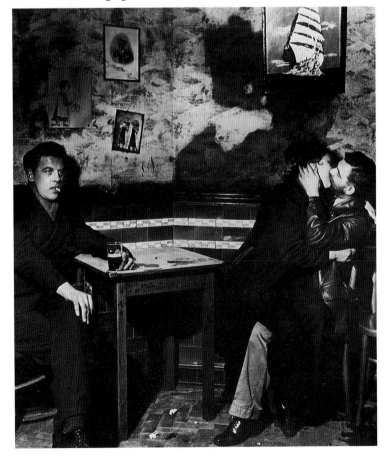

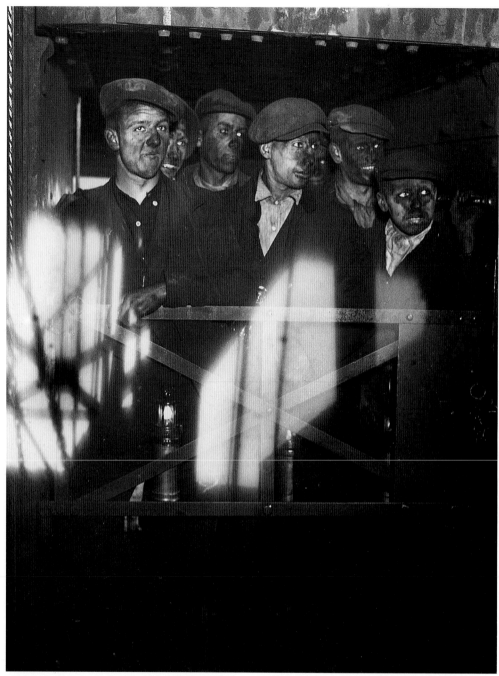

dow (figs. 10.6, 10.7). A beam of sunlight falling on the miners' chests and the cross-braced gate of the elevator they stand in make it seem as if they're trapped in the cogs of giant gears. Over the children's heads is some chalk graffiti that bears a queer resemblance to the pattern of the light on the miners; thus does the unexpected burst of sunshine they're bathed in make us aware that even the children here live in a subterranean world the sun seldom penetrates. In each of these pictures,

the mysterious shape through which they are linked looks like a crushed and mangled Union Jack.

Whatever political commitment Brandt had in the 1930s came to a peak on a trip he made in 1937, without commission, to the coal towns of the north of England. Yet even in these photographs, we can see a broader kind of social consciousness prevailing over social conscience. Dismayed though he was

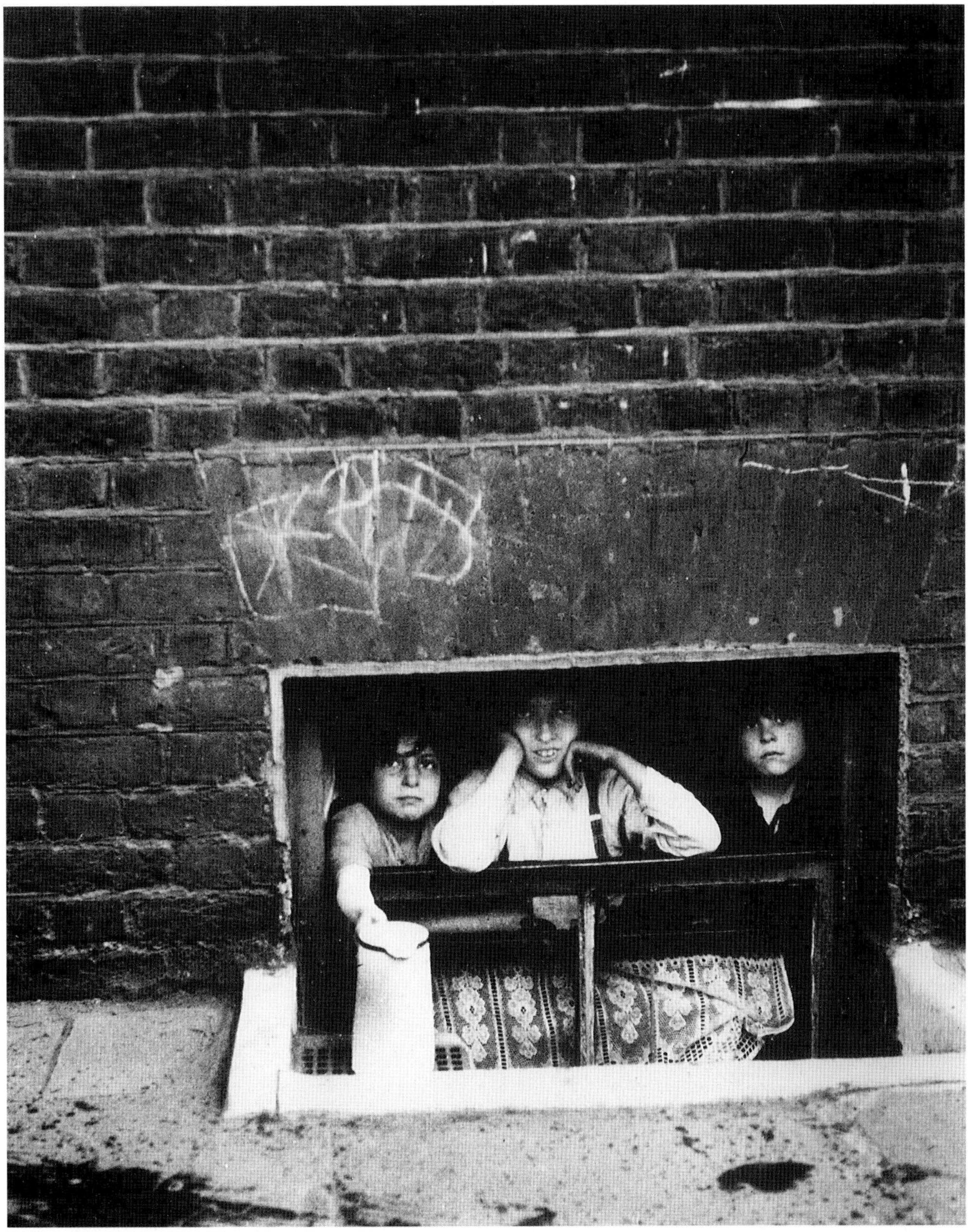

Fig. 10.7
BILL BRANDT
Window in Osborn Street, 1931–35

with the poverty he witnessed, he couldn't help being fascinated as well by the cultural habits and tacit social attitudes he found. In a picture of a begrimed miner having his afternoon cup of tea by the fender or sitting at a table eating his supper while his wife looks on attentively, what comes across is how the British need for decorum transcends class differences.

On a similar note, when Brandt photographed Halifax miners' houses whose street side was nothing but a brick wall with a door let into it,

he was not expressing concern for the living conditions of the proletariat so much as wonderment at the English as a race. Only in Great Britain could a coal company mask its exploitation of miners as benevolence by building them row houses without windows. The subject here is the ultimate example of the impenetrable English facade, a perverse symbol of the obsession with privacy, with keeping up a front.

With behavior as with architecture, what caught Brandt's eye was an underlying Englishness that cut across class distinctions. The significance of that stony, faraway look women have in his photographs is that it can be found from a side street in Wapping to one in Peckham, from an East End pub to a Chelsea grill to the Café Royal. In Brandt's photography, a social malaise settles over everyone in England. Consider once more that photograph in a Limehouse pub where a couple is necking on one side of a table while a lone man across from them stares into space (fig. 10.5). His obliviousness is only part discretion, the rest being sheer indifference. His glazed eyes remind us of the looks on the women's faces in other Brandt photographs — looks in which we now see, along with aversion, a kind of paralysis.

As Brandt saw it, English life is, above all else, a game played by the rules. A number of his pictures are set at sporting halls, fight rings, dog tracks, cricket fields, or Ascot on the day of the Royal Hunt Cup. On a pitch where a rugger match might have been held in the afternoon, couples lie intertwined at dusk (page 136). Love is also a contest in which rules are strictly observed. The quintessential Brandt street scene of a lower-class district is a picture in which two boys dressed in jackets and knee britches — which is to say, wearing their Sunday best — are giving one another a proper bashing (fig. 10.8). It's all by the Marquess of Queensberry rules, to be sure, both little pugilists having the gloves on, while a group of spectators, mostly girls, defines a neat perimeter. This is a society in which brutality is confined behind a facade of civility.

In one regard, *The English at Home* was a very mundane exercise in journalism. The pictures had to provide a lot of raw information about everyday life in England since the book was intended for the French market, where such pedestrian detail would be of interest. Like so many street photographers before him, Brandt felt a need to make the pictures themselves exciting precisely because the subject matter wasn't. But as time went on, he moved steadily away from the sort of pure documentary topic that his first book represented. After the 1930s, the nature of his photography changed considerably; only the theme of it — the essential Englishness of English life — remained constant.

His main project of the 1940s, the series done during the London Blitz, extended his study of the English character. In these pictures of the city with its lights out and people sleeping in Anderson shelters or tube stations, the English are no longer literally at home. But this provided Brandt with a new opportunity to peek behind the shades. Now people were forced to set up housekeeping overnight in public, and the hard choices they made about what to bring with them — because they might awake in the morning to find that these few, prized possessions were all they had left — were as revealing to Brandt as their habits might be when observed in private. Meanwhile, left behind in the blackout above were the darkest, most forbidding facades,

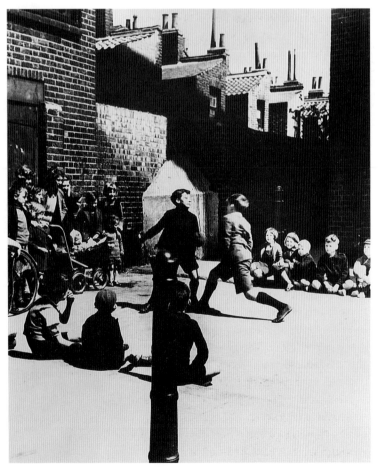

the purest symbol of the stiff upper lip, that Brandt had ever had the chance to photograph.

On the one hand, this project was a straight news assignment (it came through the Ministry of Information). On the other, the silhouetted buildings and makeshift domesticity in the underground were fabulous exaggerations of the themes in Brandt's earlier work. The Blitz series was at once the most strictly reportorial he had ever done and the most metaphorical. It became a watershed beyond which Brandt, according to Cyril Connolly, "decided definitely to remain a poet rather than a reporter." [1]

In the 1950s Brandt began to reprint earlier work on a hard, high-contrast paper that gave everything he did, old and new alike, a uniformly grainy, gritty look. Various reasons have been advanced for why he did so — because he was developing glaucoma and couldn't appreciate subtle gradations anymore, because he had been influenced by William Klein, or because he was under the sway of Orson Welles, American film noir, and British filmmaker Lindsay Anderson. Whatever the explanation, the effect was to increase both the look of realism and an air of unreality in his work. The degree of personal interpretation was obviously greater in images printed in such harsh black-and-white terms. At the same time, the actual grimness of the 1930s in England came through all the stronger in the new prints.

Even the nudes, which were his major postwar series, seem an extension of the concerns of the thirties. This is particularly true of the early studies in which women in dim, sinister Victorian interiors stare at us with the same dead eyes as the women in the pubs and the streets of London a decade earlier. Perhaps it takes another English photographer of Brandt's own time to understand fully what he hoped to get his fellow countrymen to see about themselves. Nigel Henderson, an artist who took up photography in London after the war and knew Brandt, came very close to the

mark when he characterized Brandt's work as an attempt to expose the "portentous view of the Baldwinian era — wooden faces, iron closures — the uncompromising severity of the social caste system." The photographs mirrored, Henderson said, "the terrible rectitude of learned attitudes." [2]

Brandt's imitation of Brassaï notwithstanding, he was someone who, as John Szarkowski said of him, "might have invented photography in secret and practiced it in isolation." [3] The same could have been said of many English street photographers both before and after the war. Although they were part of an emergent tradition through which their careers paralleled those of photographers elsewhere, they were also continually creating the aesthetics of street photography for themselves, out of the situations into which they took their cameras, just as their nineteenth-century predecessors had when working in true isolation.

Nigel Henderson has described his own experience with the medium much as Szarkowski did Brandt's, noting that "if you encounter photography for yourself and if you're restless, you're going to reinvent photography for a while." [4] Like Brandt, Henderson was trying to get at what was essentially English. He had been a pilot during the war, and photography may have worked for him as a way to come back to earth again. It helped him to remember what it was about ordinary life that had been worth fighting for.

He became interested in the medium around the time that he came to London to study painting. "Walking around, always taking streets unfamiliar to me, had become a soothing experience," he remarked in an interview.

> Living in Bethnal Green I was often aware of how beautiful it was — the rhythm of the streets and the sound of the kids — it had a brilliance. . . . I was looking for bits of typification of Englishness — the British Oak or the Player's cigarette advert. It meant something to me. I think the steadiness of the

English character and the war brought it out and I found it very impressive.[5]

Where Henderson's career differed from Brandt's, but was unfortunately much like those of other English street photographers, was in its brevity and the faintness of the trace it left on the medium's history. (He began photographing in the late 1940s when he entered the Slade School of Art, and he quit in 1952 when he moved out of London.) English street photography might be comparable to American in importance were it not for the transience of the photographers' careers and the limited circulation of their work. In addition to having in Brandt a towering figure like Walker Evans, England had in the 1930s a documentary project, Mass Observation, similar in intent to New York's Photo League or the U.S. Farm Security Administration. In the fifties there was even a photographer, Roger Mayne, who might be thought of as England's Robert Frank.

Whereas the documentary photo units formed in America during the Depression fostered the careers of numerous street photographers, Mass Observation had only one photographer associated with it, Humphrey Spender. The purpose of this cooperative organization, according to one of its own publications, was to document "what happens from day to day" in English life.[6] The focus of the primary study undertaken by the group was Bolton, one of the "black towns" in the part of the country depicted by George Orwell's *Road to Wigan Pier*, an industrial region of smoggy skies, grinding poverty, and a bleak landscape dotted with factories and collieries. There, in 1937–38, Spender photographed political campaigns, funerals, women coming away from their jobs in the mills at quitting time, men whiling away their time in dim, drab pubs.

Unlike American counterparts, which were initiated and subsidized by the government, Mass Observation was a typically British combination of volunteerism, amateurism, and improvisation. Funded by a book contract or

two, Tom Harrison, the anthropologist who organized the research, set up the Bolton study as a much more serious endeavor at data gathering and social-scientific investigation than the FSA ever undertook. Overheard conversations were written down, patterns of behavior described, and all the information sifted and analyzed in various publications.

But Spender was working alone and, to make matters worse, doing so only in his spare time when he could get away from the London newspaper at which he was employed. Moreover, it wasn't until long after the war that the importance of his photographs was recognized and books on Mass Observation's activities began to include them. The organization had been, for the most part, too poor to publish at the time, and as a result the work never had the impact, even on Spender's own subsequent career, that the far larger, more widely distributed, and celebrated FSA archive did in America.

A fate not dissimilar befell the work of Roger Mayne two decades later. A photojournalist who did a personal project studying street life in a London neighborhood in the midfifties, Mayne managed to publish some of the results in the *Observer* as early as 1956 and still more of them in a magazine called *Uppercase* in the early sixties (page 133). He invites comparison with Robert Frank because of a handmade album he did as, apparently, a maquette for a book. This dummy is like ones that Frank had made earlier, and for certain British photographers — Bryn Campbell, Ian Berry — Mayne served as an example comparable to Frank's in America. But Mayne's book didn't materialize at the time, while the imagery had that urgency of newness that can never be recovered later. As a result, his work never achieved the historical importance that it might have deserved.

There is no evidence that Mayne did another personal project like this, and Spender gave up photography altogether after the war. Because there is this fleeting quality to the history of street photography in England, the figure who might serve to epitomize the genre there is Richard Darwell. A staff photographer at *Picture Post* in the late thirties, he gets a credit line on occasional sidewalks-of-London features with titles like "Some Flowers and Some Faces" or "Bond Street." In 1939, he filed at least one picture story from Germany, "Berlin on a Sunny Day," but then he completely dropped from view. The harder one looks at photojournalism in England at that time, the more illusory it becomes. Many once active as street photographers disappeared from the field with hardly a trace.

M anuel Alvarez Bravo, while working at a greater remove from French influences, nonetheless availed himself of them even more fully than Brandt did. He began taking pictures in his native Mexico in the early 1920s and remained an amateur, supporting himself as an accountant or typist in government bureaucracies, until the early 1930s. But he had already had an extensive art education and would shortly come into direct contact with some key European artists. His grandfather and father, the latter a high school teacher, had both been painters. At age sixteen he had enrolled in art courses himself; by eighteen his tastes were sophisticated enough for him to prize owning a copy of Maurice Raynal's *Picasso*, an important early monograph about the painter.

By the mid-1920s he was doing photographic abstractions — white-on-white images of folded paper, for instance — not unlike those done earlier by Paul Strand, whom Alvarez Bravo met for the first time in 1933. The following year he met Cartier-Bresson, with whom he planned an exhibition that would open at Julien Levy's gallery in New York and

Fig. 10.9
MANUEL ALVAREZ BRAVO
Girl and Dogs, 1966
(original in color)

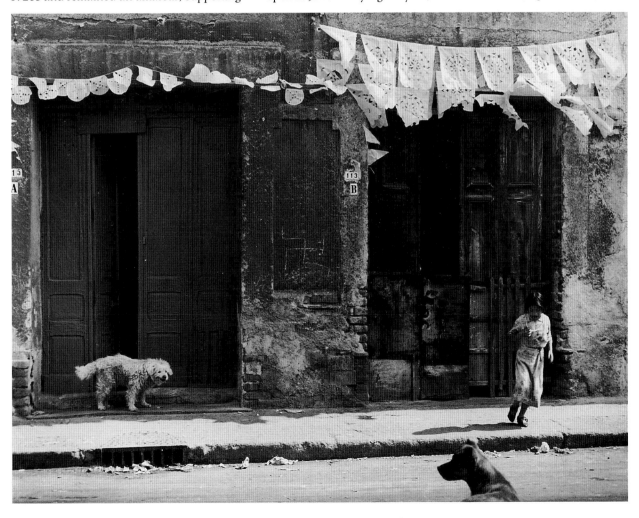

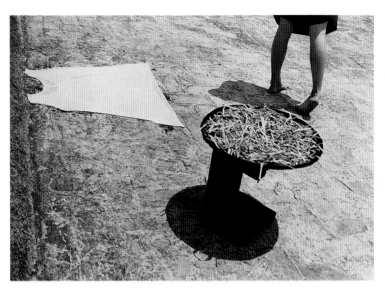

Fig. 10.10
MANUEL ALVAREZ
BRAVO
*Somewhat Gay and
Graceful*, 1942

Dogs are seen here, there, and everywhere in his pictures, much as they are on the streets and in the villages of Mexico itself. His pictures make us aware of the privileged position dogs occupy there. They find some cool shade to sleep in during the heat of the day, showing their masters how to live in such a climate. They live off the fat of a land in which the people often have a lean and hungry look. They have the run of the streets, like cows in India. But their sacredness is of a secular and rather demonic kind. In Alvarez Bravo's photographs, they sometimes look like mad dogs. Whether lounging in doorways or prowling in gutters, they have an imperious and demented air (fig. 10.9).

The motif of death in Alvarez Bravo's photographs is even more pervasive and, of course, more serious. Yet it is not solemn in the way we might expect. Its special quality was noticed as long ago as 1945, when Mexican author Xavier Villaurrutia, writing for the catalogue of a Mexico City exhibition, observed that "the presence of death in the photographs of this poet of the image has no . . . accent of the macabre . . . nor a dramatic sense of horror."[8]

In his pictures of a coffin shop, a dead bird hung by its neck from a dead branch, a cow being butchered, or a striking worker who has been assassinated, curiosity overrides revulsion so that death itself can be honored by the photograph. There is an undisguised feeling for the sensuousness of death. The response is not disgust, as we might expect, but rather a fascination to which we are not accustomed. As Alex Castro has pointed out, "Here death is not the negative death assumed by most of Western culture, but, rather, a positive element which is especially Mexican and particularly Indian."[9]

Alvarez Bravo's attitude toward death is, if not culturally conditioned, at least the result of a life story that could only have been lived in Mexico. As a boy growing up during the revolution of 1910 (he was born in 1902) he heard cannon fire in the distance while he was on

travel to Mexico in 1935. In 1938 he was introduced to André Breton, who invited him to contribute to a Surrealist show in Mexico that year.

Alvarez Bravo borrowed inspiration freely from a variety of Modernist sources in Europe. On the one hand, he had a feel for the found Surrealism of signs and advertisements, like the front of the optician's shop covered with pairs of eyes that he photographed in 1931. On the other hand, he also had a penchant for a kind of formalism more typical of Cubist and abstract art. His color photographs, especially, have this dual nature. He has an ability to use color itself as a formal element, almost as a kind of abstraction. His own awareness of this in his color work is indicated by the title he has given to a photograph he took of a rust-colored boy sweeping a rust-colored sidewalk: *El Color* (page 400).

As open as Alvarez Bravo was to the influences of French painting and Modernist art photography, however, they do not really account for the way his work looks. He himself has said he thinks that "my work is more related to Mexican art and Mexican life than to photographic traditions."[7] Foreign influences have been assimilated to native ones in his photography. What gives Alvarez Bravo's work its character is not a style either formal or fantastical, but rather certain themes that are distinctly Mexican, like dogs and death.

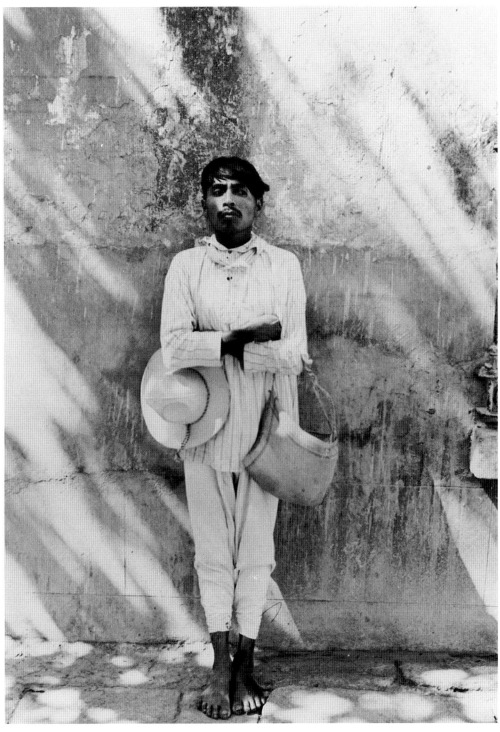

his way to school. Sometimes street battles would force the cancellation of classes, and at other times he and his friends would come upon the bodies of those killed. The revolution instilled a sense of wonderment not only at death, but at the Mexican peasantry, by whom, and in whose name, the fighting was done. The Mexican artists who came after, such as Diego Rivera and José Clemente Orozco, were preoccupied with the peasants.

Alvarez Bravo has claimed that these painters, who were his friends, affected him "not through their works but through their ideas."[10] His own work manages to be both about the peasants and of them. He saw the world through their eyes. He tried to be in touch with the ancient history of Mexico in an instinctual and hereditary way instead of just an intellectual one. In a letter to Nancy Newhall written in 1943, he explained his life by saying, "I was born in the city of Mexico, behind the Cathedral, in the place where the temples of the ancient Mexican gods must have been built."[11]

This was his way of claiming as his heritage the native culture of his nation, as opposed to the colonial culture. In 1930 his friend Tina Modotti, who was being deported for her political activities, passed on to Alvarez Bravo her job as photographer of art for the journal *Mexican Folkways*. His assignments there permitted him to explore more deeply than ever the peasant imagination on top of which Catholicism had been built like a new facade over prehistoric ruins.

There is a distinct group of his photographs whose subjects — bits of paper or ribbon tied to a dead branch, the abandoned animal remains of a folk ritual — seem frail with age and vestigial by nature. They are the tattered fabric of a high civilization that has reverted to a primitive state. A little corpse of a bird dangling from a tree limb in one of these pictures is an obscure fetish, a cult object, and Alvarez Bravo no doubt wished his photograph of it to be something similar. He has wanted his pictures to transmit the superstitious power of their subjects, to preserve that power, or even to inherit it themselves. He has tried to make photographs that can be used like scraps of tablets recovered from time immemorial, pictograms in which are inscribed the secrets of a primordial past.

This is the true significance of what seem his most Modernist images. In *Somewhat Gay and Graceful,* for instance, he caught in a single frame a freshly laundered chemise stretched on the ground to dry, a tray of some kind of vegetables or twigs set out on a stand, presumably for the same purpose, and a pair of fleeing legs (fig. 10.10). The conjunction of elements is Surrealistic, like de Lautréamont's

meeting of a sewing machine and an umbrella on a dissection table. At the same time, the trapezoid of cloth and the ellipse of the tray are a pure geometric abstraction. The image could easily have been made by Cartier-Bresson.

Yet the mix of subjects in it likely struck Alvarez Bravo more as a kind of talisman in picture form, an image that, having just the right combination of charms — a girl's legs, a strange herb, a patch of cloth — might fend off evil in modern times the way an amulet worn around the neck was once believed to do. Most of his street photographs seem like attempts to touch today's viewer with the healing power of the peasant world.

The world in which Alvarez Bravo himself has lived is an animistic one. He sees everything from statues to old newspapers blowing in the wind as if they were alive. In one of his most famous pictures, laundry flutters above passersby on the street the way a host of awkward angels might hover protectively over people unaware of their presence in a primitive painting. In a second image, a nude carved in stone appears to eavesdrop on a conversation nearby (pages 134–135). In still others, a merry-go-round horse hides behind a curtain in fear, or an empty dress sits in a chair as though someone were in it. There are signs of life everywhere, if only one knows how to read them.

The impulse in Alvarez Bravo's work is not ultimately toward formalism so much as a kind of native formality. Mexico is a culture in which decorum compensates for poverty. The dignity with which the peasants present themselves to both the world and his camera he takes as a courtesy that he feels obligated to repay. In a street portrait called *Man from Papantla,* the barefoot subject has been given time to collect himself before the picture was taken (fig. 10.11). He stands ramrod straight with arms folded, a skeptical look on his face as he glances to one side. He is polite but watchful, a mirror image of the photographer.

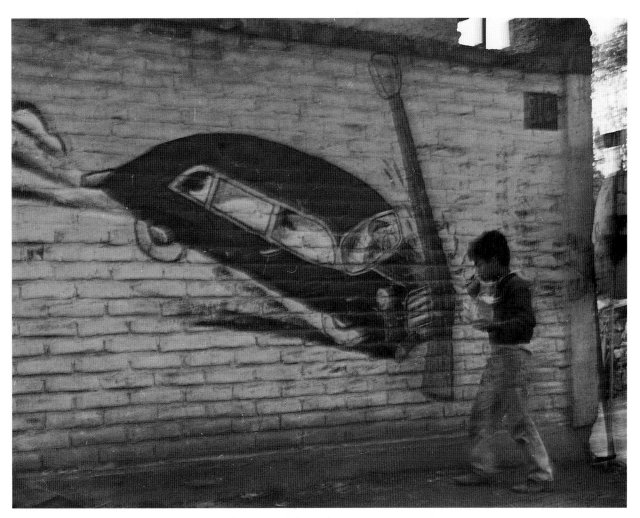

Fig. 10.12
MANUEL ALVAREZ
BRAVO
The Collision, 1967

Alvarez Bravo's work has the character it does because he feels no superiority to a subject like this, no distance from him. The photographer sees himself as a peasant of the camera. He becomes a nameless artist like the ones he celebrated in a 1966 monograph entitled *Painted Walls of Mexico: From Prehistoric Times Until Today*. Done in collaboration with Emily Edwards, the book was a scholarly culmination to Alvarez Bravo's lifelong interest in this subject.

Primitive art often seems the model on which his own imagery is based. Some of the photographs he has taken of contemporary wall paintings reveal the continuity that exists in his mind not only between their art and his, but between folk art and life in general. These photographs typically give the illusion of some interaction between the wall painting and the real street scene around it. An imaginary horse runs under a real tree planted a few feet away; the car in a painting of an accident seems to hit a boy passing on the sidewalk (fig. 10.12). These relationships set up a kind of reverberation between photograph and wall. The former becomes but an enlargement upon the latter.

In fact, a statement of Alvarez Bravo's in *Painted Walls* probably comes as close as any he has ever made to being his explanation for his own life in photography:

> *A popular painter is an artisan who, as in the Middle Ages, remains anonymous. His work needs no advertisement, as it is done for the people around him. . . . Before the Conquest all art was of the people, and popular art has never ceased to exist in Mexico.*

The art called popular is fugitive in character, with less of the impersonal and intellectual characteristics of the schools. It is the work of talent nourished by personal experience and by that of the community — rather than being taken from the experiences of painters in other times and other cultures.[12]

The farther away from Paris in the twenties and thirties you go, the more obtuse the question of lines of influence in street photography becomes. That Brandt's work was given a strong sense of direction at first by Brassaï's cannot be disputed. But Alvarez Bravo's seems to have been shaped only in a general way by his exposure to the art of the School of Paris or even by his early personal contact with Cartier-Bresson. And what are we to make of the work of Kuwabara Kineo, who began in 1932, in his own words, "photographing the city where I was born with my Leica"?[13] That city was Tokyo, and the delight that he took in it seems identical to that which the young Cartier-Bresson was taking in Paris or Seville at virtually the same time.

Kuwabara recognized from the first that his main chances as a street photographer lay in incongruities, particularly those between ancient, traditional Japan and the Westernized, modern nation that was already beginning to emerge. Thus does he catch the clash of styles and modes — indeed, of centuries and civilizations — in a line of people waiting to board a streetcar, or a woman in traditional costume, her face demurely concealed under a parasol, passing by a newsdealer in a straw boater with a cigarette dangling from his lips. He photographed men in business suits and fedoras, department-store mannequins in the straight-hipped skirts typical of the thirties, and bathing beauties at the beach in knit tank suits (one has wrapped herself in some diaphanous material like a Kewpie doll packaged in cellophane, as if she were a prize somebody had won at an amusement park). Kuwabara enjoyed as much as did Cartier-Bresson, and dozens of other French street photographers since, the disproportion be-

tween the figures blown up on a movie poster or a mural and the actual human scale of people passing on the sidewalk or sitting in a restaurant.

But did he actually need to know Cartier-Bresson's imagery in order to take such pictures? Tokyo looks as if it has been opened up to the influence of the West to a surprising degree in these photographs he made during the decade before the war and the American occupation. It is not inconceivable that he might have obtained some copies of *Vu* or seen elsewhere a couple of key images by Cartier-Bresson or Kertész or whomever, just as Cartier-Bresson himself had picked up the few clues he needed from a scant handful of examples of Munkacsi and Salomon. Just the fact that Kuwabara was knowledgeable enough to get a Leica when only a year out of high school suggests he was well aware of photography in Western Europe.

But precisely because Tokyo was already in many ways a typical city of the twentieth century, he really had right there everything he needed to become the street photographer he did. As we have seen before in numerous instances, all that's required is a camera and the street itself. Beyond that, what matters more than assimilating international influences is, as the careers of Brandt and Alvarez Bravo demonstrate, an ability to preserve local ones. It is the capacity to make your work both a reflection and an expression of your own culture, rather than an extension of someone else's Modernism, that makes a street photographer great.

11: The Fourth Estate

There was a brief moment just after World War II when Robert Doisneau and Henri Cartier-Bresson joined the same photo agency, a newly formed cooperative called Adet. The venture proved short-lived, however, and afterward the two photographers' careers took different turns. Cartier-Bresson went on to found Magnum, and Doisneau went back to Rapho, the agency he had been with before the war. Later Cartier-Bresson invited Doisneau to join Magnum, but Doisneau declined. "Rapho suited me better than Magnum," he explained, "so I said no thank you. Magnum was an agency that took big trips. . . . I wasn't really made for that kind of travel work." [1]

Although viewers may sometimes confuse Doisneau with Cartier-Bresson stylistically, the former's decision to remain in Paris, which was what sticking with Rapho amounted to, makes Brandt or Alvarez Bravo a better analogy. Like them, or even like Atget, whom he met when he was young, Doisneau was a photographer who stayed at home and made his reputation out of a single subject, a particular place with which he became completely identified.

Cartier-Bresson, although born to wealth, rebelled against his background; Doisneau liked his just fine, despite the fact that he was poor. "I was born," he told Walter Rosenblum,

in a banlieue of Paris in 1912, in the suburbs, which is not, as in New York, where the rich and the middle class live. In Paris the suburbs are for the working class. When I was very young, I lived with my aunt, my mother was dead. We lived in a small apartment where I would sit behind the window, looking out onto the street and try to draw what I saw. I could see that the environment was very inhuman, but it nevertheless had a kind of charm. . . . There were all kinds of people living there. . . . The banlieues of Paris have always been a most important part of my life. I was born here, I was married here, and I still live here. [2]

The variety that life offered was what he liked: the different kinds of people, the many shops, each with its own special merchandise, the seasonal patterns by which everything from people's habits in the street to the nature of the light would change. When he went to art school as a young man, he was made to sit copying Greco-Roman busts in a studio whose windows were covered with vellum shades that made the light as uniform and dull as the subject matter. This made him want to escape back into the streets again, where both the life and the light were varied.

As he went to and from home in the suburbs, he started carrying a camera with which to record those things that were more familiar and pleasant to him. Little by little he began to know the entire city the way he knew his own neighborhood. "I think of Paris as a kind of crazy-paving footpath," he said,

the sort that lets you cross a lawn by stepping from one paving stone to the next without ever touching the grass. I can go from Montrouge in the south [his home] to the porte de Clignancourt in the north following a sort of dotted line. Every few hundred yards I come across someone I know — a bistro owner, a cabinetmaker, a printer, a secondhand-book dealer, a painter, or just someone I once met in the street. [3]

He spoke of looking at his photographs in similar terms, as a "walk along [a] visual path," [4] and often the subjects in them also form a kind of crazy paving. The eye moves

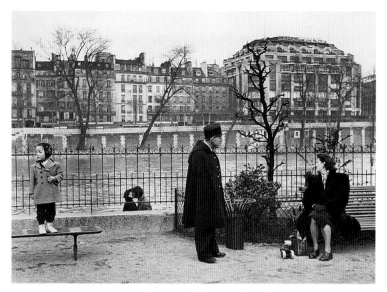

Fig. 11.1
ROBERT DOISNEAU
Square du Vert-Galant,
Paris, 1950

cityscape where "every small store was in its place, the people seemed to fit into their environment."[5]

Doisneau apparently internalized the social conditions and spatial relations that prevailed in this Paris of his. Its "nooks and crannies,"[6] as he called them, shaped his personality. "When we live, we occupy a certain space," he said, "and I try to make my space as small as possible. I weigh 110 pounds, am five foot four, and I have a small car. I like people who are 'concentrated.' "[7]

A habituation to living in tight quarters created in him the ideal mentality for the street photographer, who must also make himself compact and unobtrusive to take his subjects unawares. An aesthetic opportunity arises from a social disadvantage, from a kind of psychology of poverty that Doisneau himself described. "I'm afraid of taking too much of people's time, too much space, by imposing myself with solemnity," he told Paul Hill and Thomas Cooper. "I'm a little like the poor Martin who dug his own grave in order not to

from one figure to the next at the same varied but leisurely pace with which Doisneau himself moved through Paris. In a picture of a woman and a gendarme in a park by the Seine, our glance follows a zigzag route across the frame of a picture. Our gaze enters the scene in the middle, where the gendarme is, and is then deflected from him to the woman to the couple to the child, who passes it back out of the frame again (fig. 11.1). A similar path across the picture space is described by the subjects of dozens of other Doisneau photographs.

The placement of the figures in these images has a certain justice to it. The visual symmetry suggests a social balance. The discreet spaces between subjects reflect a society where there is a place for everyone and everyone is in his place. Doisneau's neighborhoods are like the facade of Notre Dame: each creature, from the devils to the angels, fits perfectly into his niche as if ordained to be there.

Sometimes, the boundaries of the world the subject occupies are actually visible. The composition relies on a kind of frame within the frame created by the shelter at a bus stop inside which people wait, or by the shop doors out of which a grocer leans to greet a pretty woman who smiles back at him from the next shop (fig. 11.2). The picture seems a transliteration of Doisneau's remembrance of the *banlieue* in which he grew up as a

Fig. 11.2
ROBERT DOISNEAU
Neighborliness Among
Shopkeepers, Place du
Marche, Saint-Honoré,
n.d.

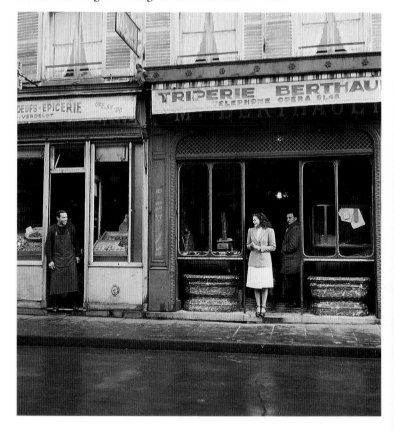

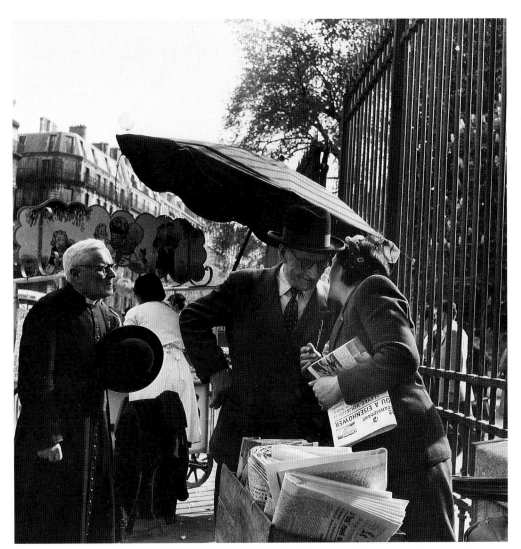

bother the gravedigger. It is a little bit like my grandfather. He would excuse himself all the time. He always sat on the edge of a chair."[8]

If this sort of timidity compelled Doisneau to be surreptitious about taking pictures at certain moments, at others it prevented him from taking them at all. This is why he staged some of his most famous shots instead — images such as his 1950 *Kiss at the Hôtel de Ville*. These photographs blend in seamlessly with the truly candid work in his oeuvre because they were the result not only of the same capacity for acute observation, but of the same, thorough familiarity with the lives, natures, and habits of his subjects. He knew these people so well (since he knew many of them personally) that at times he couldn't bring himself to pounce on their foibles or their in-

discretions with that *brise-cou* abruptness of which Cartier-Bresson, working more anonymously, was capable. It would have been too rude a breach of decorum. The alternative was to approach these moments obliquely, by recreating them, or even creating completely fictitious situations that would illustrate what he had come to understand about his subjects from living among them.

It was for the sake of his own dignity, as well as that of his subjects, that he didn't like to be caught looking. The self-denigrating note heard above returns in Doisneau's description of his habits as a street photographer. He tried not to let his subjects observe him as he was taking their picture because he would have been mortified if they did. Fear of being noticed provided a motive for achieving the in-

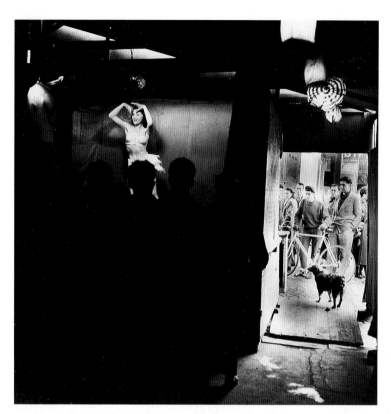

Fig. 11.4
ROBERT DOISNEAU
*Wanda Wiggles Her
Hips*, 1953

ferent photographs that are, nonetheless, very similar.

In the first, a woman at a newsstand whispers something into the ear of a rather grand man in a homburg (fig. 11.3). Next to them a curé with hat in hand, anxious not to miss anything, leans forward as if he were eavesdropping. In the second photograph, a carnival dancer does her stuff in her tent, while men outside are queuing up for the next show (fig. 11.4). The intensity with which they listen to her unseen pitchman makes it seem as though their eyes are boring a hole right through the tent wall to get a look at her. The third photograph is of a Sunday painter on one of the Seine bridges doing a study of a woman sitting on a bench (fig. 11.5). He blocks our view of his model, but we can see that on the canvas she is nude. A man walking his dog has noticed this too and cranes his neck to get a better look.

visibility necessary to the work. "I'm a little ashamed of my illogical steps, my gesticulations," he said. "I take three steps to this side, four to that side, I come back, I leave again. . . . People would think me insane. The way I work is so illogical, and my movements are so unfunctional."[9] This is the kind of excess of modesty we might hear from a craftsman who suspects that the ingenuity with which he practices his trade will be seen as clumsiness by other people.

The awkwardness Doisneau felt as a photographer was very like what his grandfather felt sitting on the edge of his chair. It was a self-consciousness of the sort one gets from years of living with too little privacy in surroundings that are too cramped. Such embarrassment could be relieved only through laughter, through having the sense of humor Doisneau displayed so often in his photography. Whenever he photographed an "intimate sight," he said, he took "refuge . . . in humor" in order "to excuse myself for having been witness and voyeur."[10] This sense of humor was the most valuable legacy he had from his working-class background. Look at how it shaped three dif-

So there they all are in a row: the painter, the bystander, and the photographer. All three are, like the little curé straining his ears or the suckers lining up for the burly show, a kind of street character that we have encountered before, in the nineteenth century. He is the *badaud*, the gawker who is overcome with curiosity and stops to see what's going on. Doisneau's photographs gently mock these people in the crowd, and yet, we are always aware, he is one of them himself. Taking photographs was for him a way to join in the fun, just as it was for Lartigue. That their social backgrounds were poles apart doesn't matter. What does is that each loved the world into which he was born.

The sense of humor that Doisneau had is the one you need to get on well with everybody at a neighborhood bistro where all the customers know one another. He had an infectious way of hugging himself with mirth when he talked. Life was so silly, he would just crack up. "I can't take myself seriously. . . . One just can't," he protested.[11] He was a lot like Brassaï in the sense that he took his pictures with his personality as much as his camera. He was as inspired as Brandt was by Brassaï's *Paris de nuit,* which he said showed him that "my need to be filled with wonder could find stimulation in the photographing of everyday life in Paris." [12]

He was also like Brassaï in the amiable patience with which he cultivated the subjects he wanted to photograph, especially around Les Halles, where he spent many evenings drinking with the customers in the cafés and getting to know them before he brought out his camera. "I worked at Les Halles," he explained, "because I like places that are all curved, that are all huddled together." [13] The old market provided surroundings, in other words, into which he could fit snugly. It was for him the ultimate Paris neighborhood.

The photographs that Doisneau took in the places he frequented deal mostly in truisms and stereotypes. All have in them the kind of popular wisdom that the picture of the carnival dancer contains, suggesting as it does that her charms are greatest before you enter her tent. To be able to take and give pleasure by repeating what everybody already knows, the way Doisneau's photographs do, is also part of the atmosphere of a working-class bistro. This is a form of social discourse to which photography is supremely well suited. It is not mere coincidence that the French word for a photographic negative is *cliché.* Photography does, by its nature as a medium, trade in clichés. But then, certain views of life become clichés only because they seem so true that nobody can deny them. If only one could see past the excessive familiarity that has deadened them, the human truth they represent would become apparent once again. At their best, this is what photographs like Doisneau's accomplish.

Because photography relies thus on shared insights and perceptions, its vision is, as it were, in the public domain. No photographer can really own the copyright on a subject or even a style. Thus is a point of view sometimes possessed jointly by a group of photog-

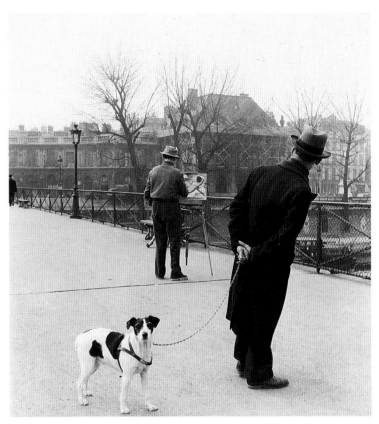

raphers, the way a trade secret might be by the members of a guild. (This is the aspect of the medium that Susan Sontag has referred to as "corporate." [14]) In France in the period since World War II, there have certainly been many other photographers doing work comparable to, and in cases indistinguishable from, that by Doisneau. To this fraternity of Parisian photographers belong — besides Kertész and Cartier-Bresson or Brassaï — Willy Ronis, Edouard Boubat, Guy Le Querrec, Marc Riboud, Inge Morath, Richard Kalvar, Rene Maltet, Izis, Leonard Freed, Gilles Peress, and many, many more.

How different photographers ultimately conform to the same vision can by seen from even a cursory look at the work of Ronis, who has, after Doisneau, the most practiced and sensitive touch where Paris is concerned. He sees the city's neighborhoods in exactly the same terms that Doisneau did. In his work too the people fit into their environment the way Doisneau said they should. The social order of French life is reflected by the orderliness of the compositions. This is why Ronis has also

Fig. 11.5
ROBERT DOISNEAU
Fox Terrier on the Pont des Arts, Paris, 1953

used the device of a frame within the frame to make some of his most charming pictures, such as the one in which children make a playground out of the empty cargo bay of their father's barge (page 132). Ronis's subjects are "huddled together" just as Doisneau said the denizens of Les Halles were.

The appropriateness of Doisneau's words to Ronis's photographs demonstrates how Doisneau, like Frank Sutcliffe before him, might have served as a spokesman for a whole generation of street photographers. Doisneau claimed he didn't like to talk too much about photography for fear it would ruin his ability to do it. "If I took apart my old alarm clock," he said, "I could find out how it works, but afterwards I might not have a way to get up in the morning." [15] The vividness of his metaphor shows that, despite his claim that he was reluctant to speak, he had a gift for talk as for photography, and he couldn't resist the pleasure he took in either.

If Doisneau's formulations about his own work apply to Ronis's as well, then they apply to that of any number of photographers whose pictures look similar. Moreover, that certain images by Ronis seem almost identical to ones by Aigner, or by Kertész in Day of Paris, doesn't mean that Ronis's work is derivative, but only that he shares in the consensus. Cross-references like this could be found among any of the photographers of Paris mentioned above. The city brings out the egalitarian and fraternal quality of the medium because so much of the work done there seems equally good. Paris has been, as a subject matter, an occasion to which photographers have risen. It is still the world capital for a kind of personal photojournalism whose practitioners include a great many Americans as well as Frenchmen.

The imagery that's indispensable in this collaborative study of Paris, however, is that done by residents of long standing, like Doisneau. For many of these French photojournalists, the only really solid ground on which their reputations rest is native ground. The more far-flung their travels as correspondents, the weaker the work is. Edouard Boubat, for instance, is another photographer whose pictures in and around Paris often vie with Doisneau's in excellence. But because he traveled as a staff photographer for the magazine Réalités from 1952 until 1965, he spent considerably more of his working life away on assignment than Doisneau did, producing a body of work whose scope is more international, yet more restricted. The subjects of Boubat's pictures are emotional needles plucked from topographical haystacks. His own emotions get generalized to the whole human race, which spreads them too thin.

Doisneau's photography has a more genuinely global reach, paradoxically, because he stayed at home. His wisdom, demonstrated when he declined the offer from Magnum, was to recognize that his talent was rooted in a particular subject on which it depended and by which it was sustained. Only rarely does someone like Cartier-Bresson come along who can use his photographic style as a kind of passport to all nations and all walks of life. To follow in his footsteps, you have to be the same sort of cosmopolite that he is — someone like Elliott Erwitt, who is the leading member of the photographic jet set that contains Cartier-Bresson's heirs apparent.

Although Wilfred Sheed once compared Erwitt with Doisneau as a master of "the Comic Casual," [16] their personalities as photographers seem very different. Consider the way that each treats dogs, which are a subject so dear to Erwitt's heart that he once devoted an entire book to them. Doisneau's dogs tend to be feisty little underdogs like himself, alert and perky creatures such as the one in his picture of the Sunday painter on the Seine bridge (fig. 11.5). Erwitt's dogs are rangy and mangy. They are hangdogs. Life has not treated them well, and Erwitt empathizes with them totally.

He understands how they feel so well that his photographs sometimes seem to have been made from their point of view, as if he too saw the world as an odd lot of details that don't quite make sense. Erwitt himself is not really confused in the least, of course. It's just a pose, this tendency he has not only to photograph lost strays but to prowl around as if he were one himself. Behaving this way allows him to disguise sophistication as puzzlement. He's like Woody Allen creating for himself the persona of a klutz.

The truth is that Erwitt is also a gadfly and a wit. A wag with an urbane sense of humor like that of the late publisher Bennett Cerf, Elliott interrogates the world the way Cerf used to question contestants on the television program *What's My Line?* He can make the most awful visual puns with a straight face. No photographer has used the ability of shapes to look alike, much as two words can sound alike, to more devastating effect than he has. The couple chatting in the catacomb and the withered corpses stacked against the walls strongly resemble each other, as do the child's wild, flying hair and the palm trees against which she is silhouetted (page 310, top). The turnips on the shelf appear to be the shriveled dugs of the woman sitting behind them. The splash of water on which the man has stepped becomes his misshapen shadow. These pictures were made from Poland to Mexico and from Nice to Nicaragua. Erwitt is a globetrotter with a truly international perspective. He finds people the same the world over.

He is still bouncing around much as he did while he was growing up, when he lived first in Milan, then New York, and finally Los Angeles. He never did have a home like Doisneau. Travel is all he knows. This is why his photography presents a sharp contrast to that of Doisneau, Ronis, or Boubat. The place of honor that these others often accord to children, who can be counted on to brighten up the gloomiest scene, he gives to dogs, because he finds them, like himself, doleful and unimpressed with human beings. The view he takes of mankind, while not exactly jaded — that puts the matter too strongly — is somewhat jaundiced. His photographs may not be nasty, but you wouldn't accuse them of being mushy, either. He plays both ends against the middle (especially the middle class).

Erwitt's work is very good — too good, perhaps. He makes his imagery look so effortless that it seems to lack substance, or at least not to have as much of it as Cartier-Bresson's does. But then, how could he be as important a photographer as Cartier-Bresson, having come after Cartier-Bresson himself? The honor roll of the postwar generation in France, the one to which Erwitt, even though he is an American, also belongs, is a list nearly as lengthy as that on which Doisneau and Ronis appear above. Among the names that should be on it are Bruno Barbey, René Burri, Jeanloup Sieff, François Hers, Serge Bois-Prévost, Martine Franck, Michel Delluc, Jacques Minassian, Hervé Gloaguen, Daniel Arnault, Patrick Bruchet, Jean Gaumy, Claude Raimond-Dityvon, Philippe Salaün, Jean-Philippe Charbonnier, and Harry Gruyaert.

The dilemma for all these photographers, including Erwitt, is that they are in the unenviable position of having to follow Cartier-Bresson's lead. The refinements that they have introduced into his vision are like the seconds that younger runners can always knock off a previous world record. Cartier-Bresson showed that the four-minute mile was possible; now each of his successors manages to better his time by a little bit more. It really is a matter of speed. With black-and-white films that allow them to shoot at 1/1000 of a second, these photographers have opened up new possibilities of imagery that were not even visible before. The faster and faster reflexes they have developed create ever-quirkier, more exotic pictures.

Doisneau once made the knowing observation that there is "a delicate line between facility and vulgarity."[17] How to be facile is what all the French street photographers since Cartier-Bresson have learned from his example. His insight into the medium was almost too lucid. It made certain tricks of the trade too available, so that they could be picked up

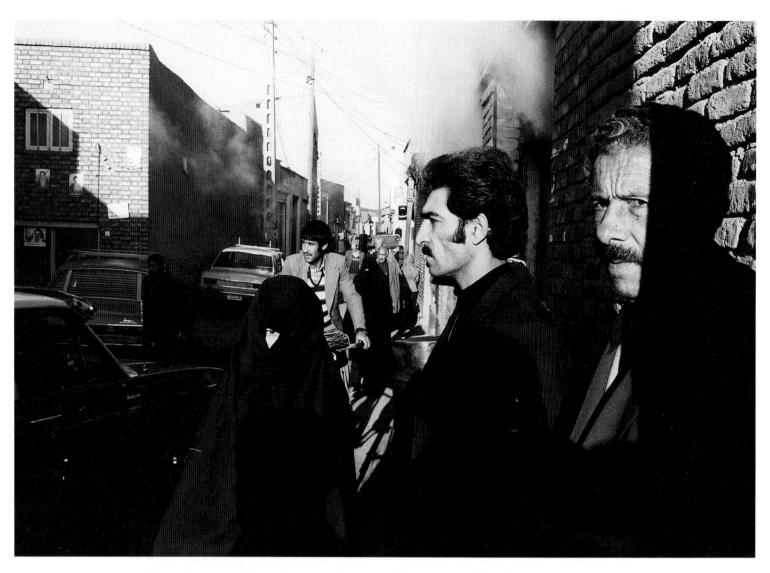

Fig. 11.6
GILLES PERESS
From *Telex: Iran,*
1979–80

without the prerequisite temperament he brought to photography. The result has been a photographic tradition that is fickle and even a bit unstable.

This trend is like a seduction in which an avowal of attachment, once it succeeds, gives way to contempt. One minute the imagery tends toward sentimentalism, and the next minute it veers toward cynicism. The latter set of emotions is really just a twin of the former. Having idealized subjects whom the camera makes both accessible and vulnerable, photography can just as easily become disenchanted with them. The timing and point of view need only change a little, like the curl of the lip when a smile turns into a sneer.

The virtuosity of Cartier-Bresson's pictures ultimately caused everyone who came after him a historical problem not unlike that to which other Modernist art, such as the architecture of Mies van der Rohe, also led. The utter simplicity that makes the style international makes it too easy to imitate as well. Once a dexterity can be turned on and off at will, it loses its specialness for the person who possesses it. When it gets to the point where it can no longer be turned off at all, respecting it becomes harder still. Now it is a Midas touch, a magic that turns into a curse on the magician, an ability that, being inescapable, becomes irksome. Surfeited on his own talent, the photographer sometimes begins to use it in perverse ways.

Until recently, the street photographer in general has been what screenwriter Jacques Prévert once said Boubat was: "a peace correspondent." [18] But during the past few decades, photographers working in this genre have often become de facto war correspondents instead. As more and more modern societies have slipped into a state where it is impossible to tell war and peace apart, the everyday life in the street that the photographer records has come to include acts of terrorism and guerrilla warfare.

Under these conditions — combat conditions — Don McCullin and Raymond Depardon are street photographers of a sort. So are Koen Wessing in Nicaragua and Susan Meiselas in El Salvador. In a black township on the outskirts of Johannesburg, Peter Magubane has worked in the same spirit as Doisneau in the suburbs of Paris, except that Magubane's take also has included coverage of riots, roundups, and constant police brutality. At times, as when an American free-lancer named P. Michael O'Sullivan went underground with the Irish Republican Army to do a book called *Patriot Graves,* the street photographer has turned into a cadre.

In circumstances such as these, the decisiveness, unobtrusiveness, and sheer stealth of which a street photographer is capable are no longer just a form of talent. They are survival skills, and the pictures that result from the photographers' use of these skills can at times remind us of the necessity of street photography itself. Photographers again become what they have often been in the past — culture heroes of a sort, urgent messengers.

Having gotten a premium ranging from a few hundred to a few thousand dollars for risking their life, these photographers see their work published in magazines with a shelf life of a week or a month. But sometimes the pictures live on in the form of a book. Scores of publications of this type have come out in the last few decades. Although they are remaindered once they lose their topicality and currency,

the best of them reveal the significance of the stories they report in a way that no other form of journalism can.

One example of the power such pictures can have in book form is to be found in *Telex: Iran — In the Name of Revolution,* the volume that Gilles Peress published of his coverage of the Iranian revolution, at the end of the 1970s. Like other modern revolutionary societies, this one was both forming and *in*forming itself through posters. In them and on the state television network, the entire nation's anger and recrimination were coming out in a paroxysm of images.

Yet as this book suggests with the placement of a photograph of a television screen next to one of detainees in a cell — the scan lines in the former picture dissolving (so to speak) into the cell's wire mesh in the latter — the Iranians were a people imprisoned within their own imagery. This new Islamic Republic, as it called itself, was obsessed with visual representations of its own pain and rage; yet it retained the traditional Muslim mistrust of cameras. While shunning images, it was also using all the media at its disposal to make an exhibition of itself, to parade its emotions before the world. The edginess apparent in most all of the street photographs Peress made there reflects the contradictions with which this society was living at the time (fig. 11.6).

In New York, where Peress has lived for a number of years, he is still thought of as a French photojournalist. But in Paris, where he was born, they now think of him as an American. The supreme example of a photographer who has become this sort of man without a country is a colleague of Peress's at Magnum, Josef Koudelka. For many years after fleeing his native Czechoslovakia in 1970, the only home Koudelka knew was Magnum's Paris office, where he would sleep on the floor in a sleeping bag.

Koudelka is in a privileged position at Magnum because he is allowed to remain a member without having to take the regular assignments through which the others contribute to the support of the cooperative. "Publishing photographs is not important to me," he says; "I like to concentrate on working and not to be disturbed."[19] The project that gained him the status to be able to work in this way was also the one that led him to become a man without a country — a study of the Gypsies that he did in Czechoslovakia between 1962 and 1968.

The discussion of Koudelka has been left for last in this section on European photography not only because he himself is in many respects a summary figure, but because the Gypsies are a subject in which are condensed all the romance, difficulty, and elusiveness of the other subjects we have seen street photographers pursuing in earlier chapters. Koudelka first tried to work with the Gypsies in his native state of Moravia, but it was in East Slovakia that the majority of his pictures were taken. Here the Gypsies had been made to live in "separated settlements,"[20] pastoral ghettos where the state put an end to their nomadic existence by confiscating their horses for slaughter and removing the wheels from their wagons. The result was a kind of mass house arrest.

The land on which they were settled is barren, an empty plain with mud and standing water everywhere, with frozen ruts and ice slicks in the winter, stubble, dust, and broken rock in summer. Deprived of their traditional ways, the Gypsies lead a perfectly eventless life in an absolutely featureless landscape. And yet it is a life filled with ceremony and occasion (page 19). It is, as Koudelka saw it, human existence so materially impoverished that only feeling and spirit are left — a culture stripped of profession, money, and comfort until pride, laughter, sorrow, love, murder, and passion are all that remain.

The isolation of this society is, in short, even greater than revolutionary Iran's. The atmosphere here is more rarefied than the Mexico of Alvarez Bravo's peasants and Indians. The al-

ternations of bravado and despair are a still more extreme version of what we encountered amid Brassaï's apache dancers, petty criminals, clochards, and bohemians. Because the Gypsies entered Western Europe by way of the Czech territory of Bohemia, the French term for them is *bohémien*. The artists, models, and nightclub performers Brassaï knew were a Parisian reincarnation of the Gypsies. So were the artists that Kertész portrayed. With Koudelka's documentation of the Eastern European Gypsies, a photographic tradition that Kertész had begun a half century earlier only a short distance away, in Hungary, comes full circle.

As much as anything else he had done before, what prepared Koudelka for photographing life among the Gypsies was having done production stills for the theater in Prague. His first exhibition as a photographer was at a theater, and by 1962, when he began working on the Gypsy project in earnest, he was also contributing pictures regularly to a drama magazine. One director in particular made a profound impression on him, Otomar Krejča, a prominent figure in the avant-garde who had his own theatrical company. When Koudelka's work on the Gypsies was published in Paris many years later, the photographer wrote an introduction in which he thanked Krejča for teaching him that, as he still says, "all of life is theater."[21]

It was in 1965 that Koudelka began working closely with Krejča, who permitted him to have the plays he photographed performed five times just for his camera, so that he could be on the stage moving among the actors as he took the pictures. This way of working was a paradigm for his photography among the Gypsies. With them too he had to take a part in the play in order to photograph it. He devoted an enormous amount of time to the Gypsy project with the aim of seeing his subjects' lives from the inside.

This psychological involvement had an optical counterpart in the wide-angle lens he used for much of the work, a 25mm that permitted

Fig. 11.7
JOSEF KOUDELKA
Utekac, Czechoslovakia,
1963

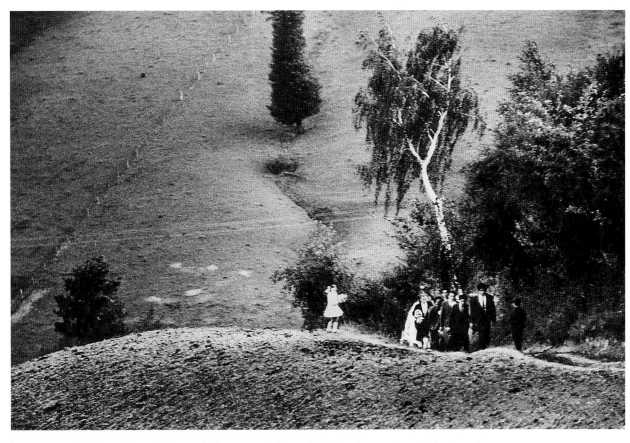

him to stand in the midst of the people he was photographing. With Gypsy subjects, who tended toward expansive moods and impetuous gestures, this lens produced pictures in which arms, legs, and even whole bodies fly in every direction. Kids sliding on the ice in the yard in winter veer toward the edge of the frame, threatening to puncture it with their sprawling limbs. A dog that refuses to sit still for a family portrait bolts from the picture plane as if about to leap right out of the photograph. There is a visual anarchy in the pictures to match the wildness and lawlessness of the Gypsies themselves.

More dramatically still, some of Koudelka's pictures look as if he were seeing the world through his subjects' eyes, as a place animated by ghosts and strange happenings. Certain pictures seem to be light-headed, like hallucinations brought on by hunger or drunkenness. Like Alvarez Bravo, he is given to visions when he looks through his camera. The way he uses his wide-angle lens, the verticals and the horizontals — walls and floors,

hills and plains, the streets and the buildings — sometimes swim together in our sight.

At other times, a subject seems to float free from both axes. As a band of people ascends a path, one little girl in white breaks away not only from them, but from the hillside and even from the light by which the rest are firmly anchored in the landscape (fig. 11.7). Her white dress glowing luminously, she levitates. This photograph is of one of those occasions that inexplicably break through the listless monotony of Gypsy life. It might be a wedding or a First Communion; it is definitely a movable feast, a ceremony that has struck out cross-country on its own.

Like Alvarez Bravo's subjects in Mexico and other primitive peoples, including his own Gypsies — indeed, like Alvarez Bravo himself and all other street photographers — Koudelka sees the world in terms of symbolism, not actualities. He is more interested in what an image portends than what it contains. Some of the photography in the Gypsies

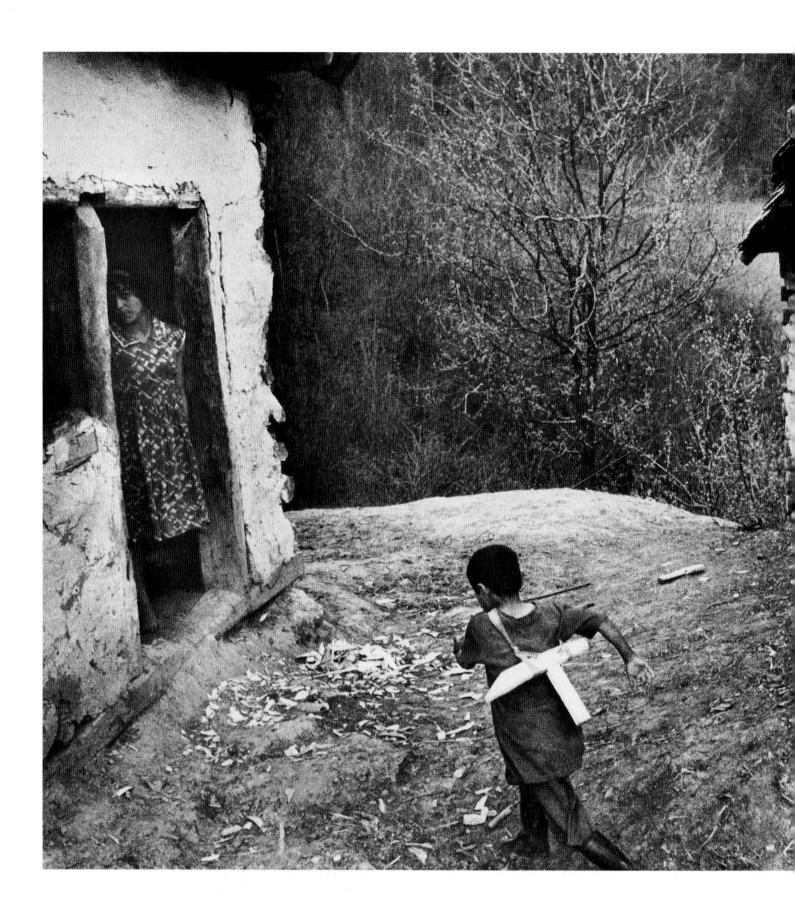

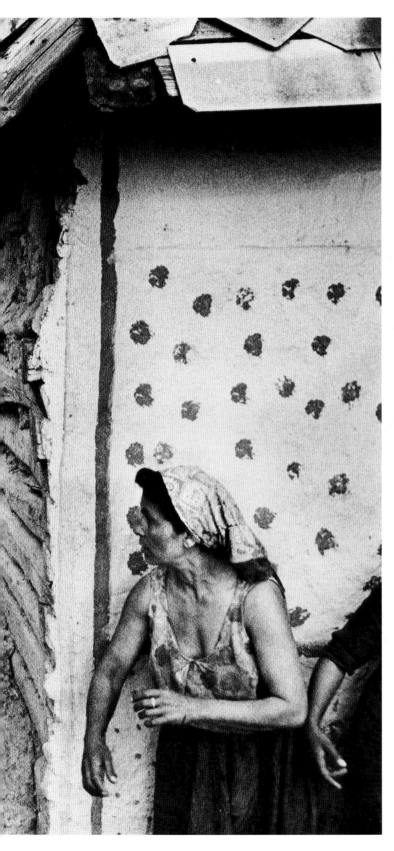

Fig. 11.8
JOSEF KOUDELKA
Spisske Bystre,
Czechoslovakia, 1966

series seems to abstract from the situation a larger truth about oppressed minorities and dispossessed cultures everywhere. One such image is of a boy sprinting across a narrow patch of yard between two houses, a toy submachine gun slung across his back (fig. 11.8). The image is on one level a dash toward manhood, a rité de passage between a mother and a lover or a bride. But in another way it also seems a premonition of a kind of news picture that would become familiar later from Beirut or Belfast.

By the time Koudelka's book entitled *The Gypsies* came out in Paris, in the mid-1970s, an ironic parallel existed between its depiction of the Gypsies' fate at the hands of the Czechs and the fate that the Czechs themselves had suffered at the hands of the Soviets. Koudelka's own involvement in the events of 1968 came about as coincidentally as other critical episodes in his life. His pictures from Krejča's theater in Prague were on display in the lobby there, and he was working on a new series, when a girlfriend came to tell him that people were rioting in the streets. He went out to see what was happening and found students in Wenceslas Square trying to hold back Russian tanks with their hands, so he began to take photographs.

In the aftermath of the invasion, the exhibition in the theater lobby was lost. In effect Koudelka traded one set of photographs, of a sort to which he would not return, for another set, which were to change the course of his life. The pictures that he made of the invasion were smuggled out of the country and published in *Life* anonymously to prevent reprisals against his family. The magazine later gave the pictures an award, again without naming their author. Koudelka stayed in Czechoslovakia until 1970, managing to carry out with him the maquette he had made for a book of his Gypsy pictures.

It took a number of years for him and Paris publisher Robert Delpire to agree on the form in which the book should be published. In the meantime, Elliott Erwitt, as president of Mag-

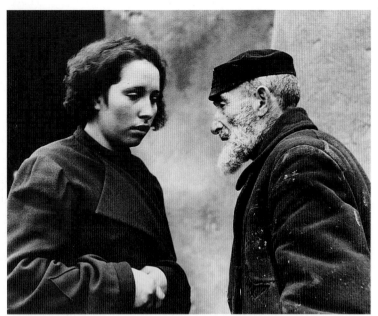

preserving at least the image of a culture when little else has survived. The photographer who performed this service to history perhaps more bravely and selflessly than any other was Roman Vishniac, who traipsed across Poland from the Baltic to the Carpathians in the late 1930s, surreptitiously getting the last glimpse of life in the shtetls there that anyone was to have. He knew that this would be true. A Russian Jew who was living then in Berlin, he considered it his religious duty to go.

The furtiveness with which the work had to be done was but a mirror image of that which we see in the photographs themselves in chance encounters between Jews on ghetto streets (fig. 11.9). Like Koudelka, Vishniac made himself a part of the world he was photographing to be sure he got it right. Like Kertész at home in Hungary, he was motivated by a sense of impending doom. He wanted to make a record before it was too late. It seems that in every generation there has been a street photographer in Eastern Europe who took on this responsibility.

num, had proposed Koudelka for membership, and he continued to work throughout Europe as he had in his homeland. If the specific subject of the Gypsies has been replaced in his wider travels by any one imagery, it is that of dwarfs, hunchbacks, cripples, idiots, and cretins — people who are marginalized in some way by their own humanity, as the Gypsies were.

When Koudelka left Czechoslovakia, he sought asylum in England as a "stateless" resident, and he retained that status until the 1989 Velvet Revolution in his homeland permitted him to return once more. (At present, he divides his time between the Czech Republic and Western Europe.) Nonetheless, even though history has at last permitted him a repatriation of sorts, his work may be thought of as completing a historical cycle that began with that Kertész photograph, discussed earlier, in which two displaced persons tramping along recognize each other and exchange a handshake in the midst of their flight. After the 1968 invasion, Koudelka became a displaced person too. He decided to remain a man not only without a country, but without a profession. He refused to be anything more than a street photographer.

Koudelka's documentation of the Gypsies is part of street photography's long tradition of

PART THREE

Walker Evans
& America Before the War

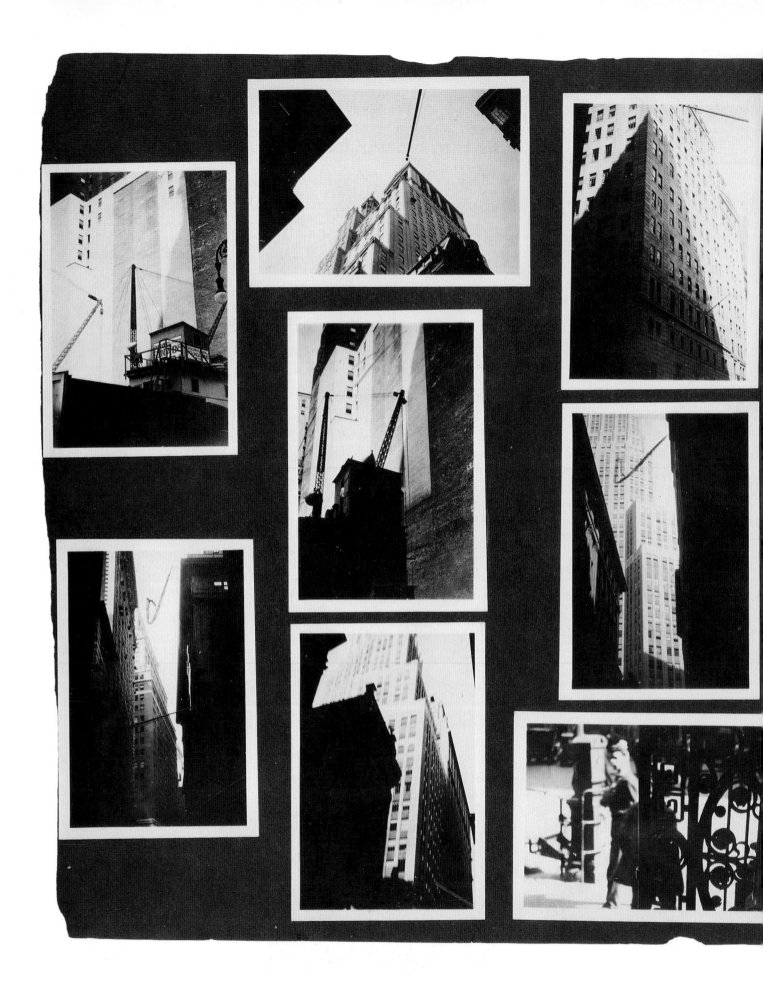

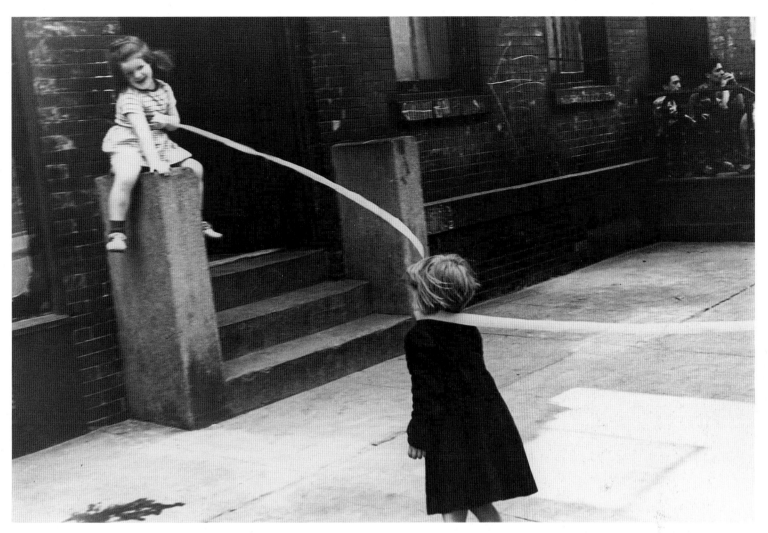

HELEN LEVITT
New York, c. 1942

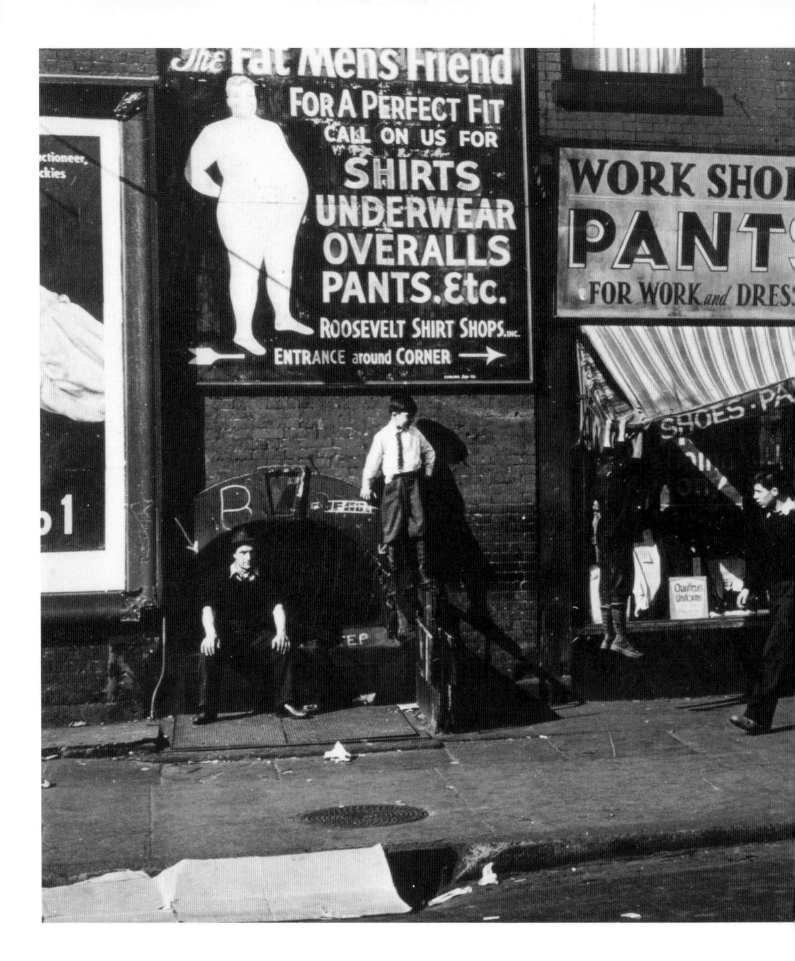

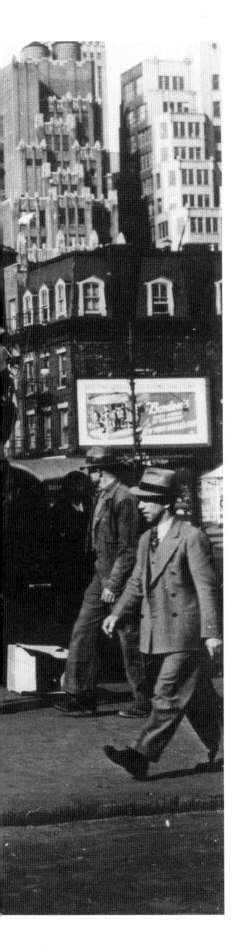

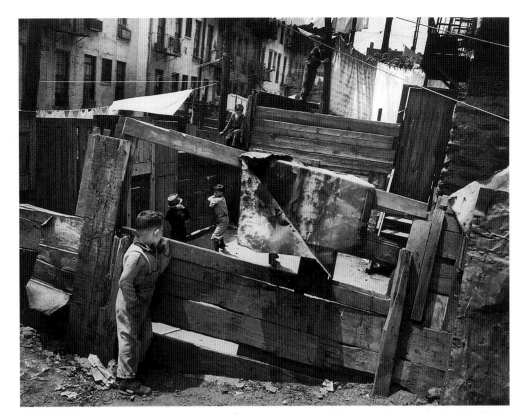

MAX YAVNO
Backyard Baseball,
c. 1939

SID GROSSMAN
Pants Store, from
Chelsea Series, 1938–39

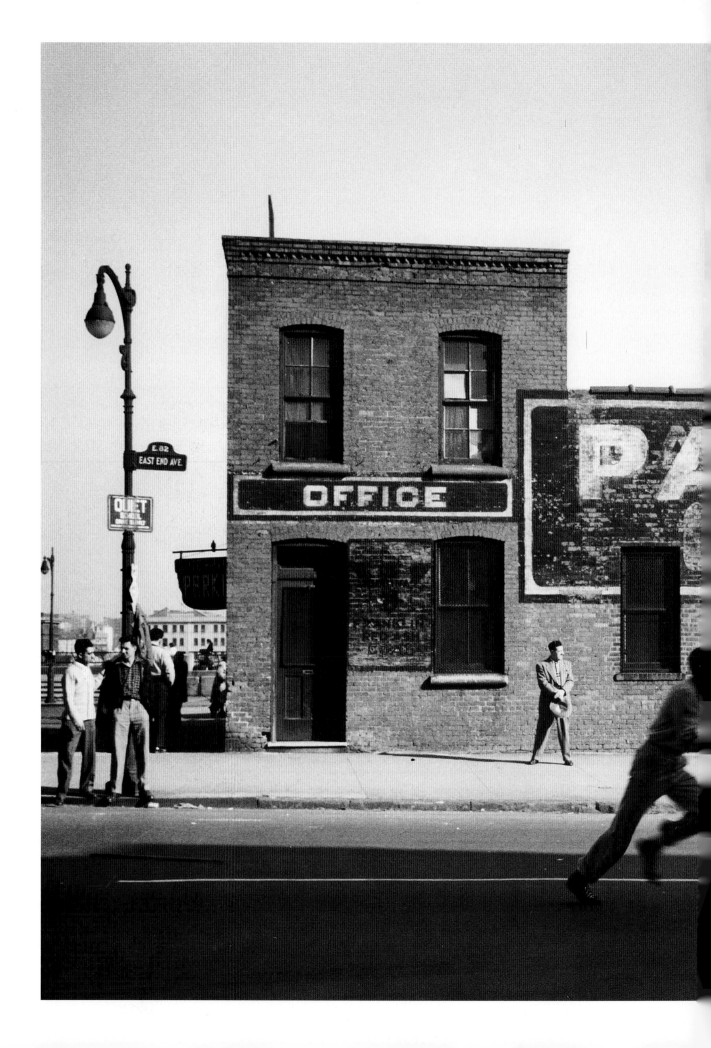

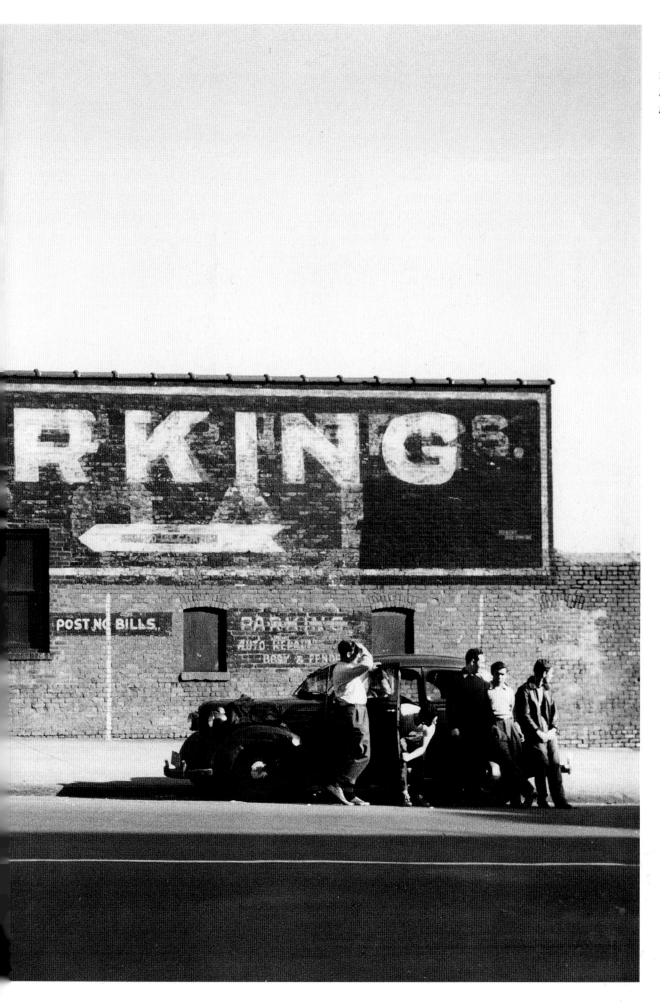

DAN WEINER
East End Avenue,
New York, 1950

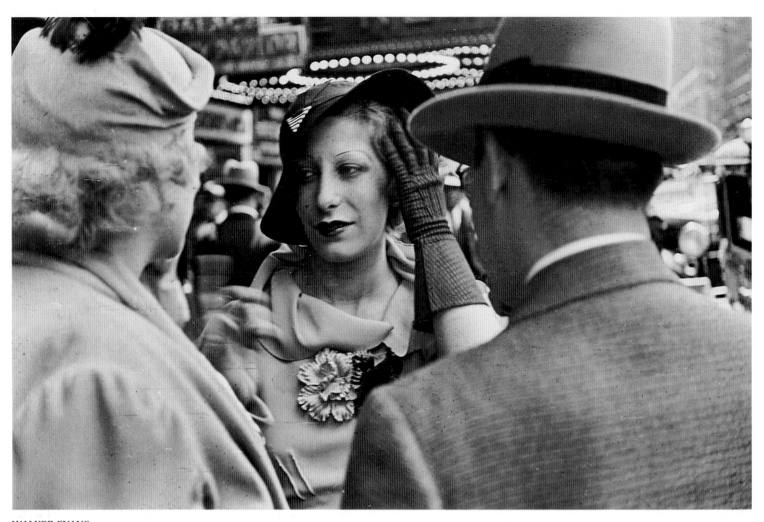

WALKER EVANS
New York, c. 1930

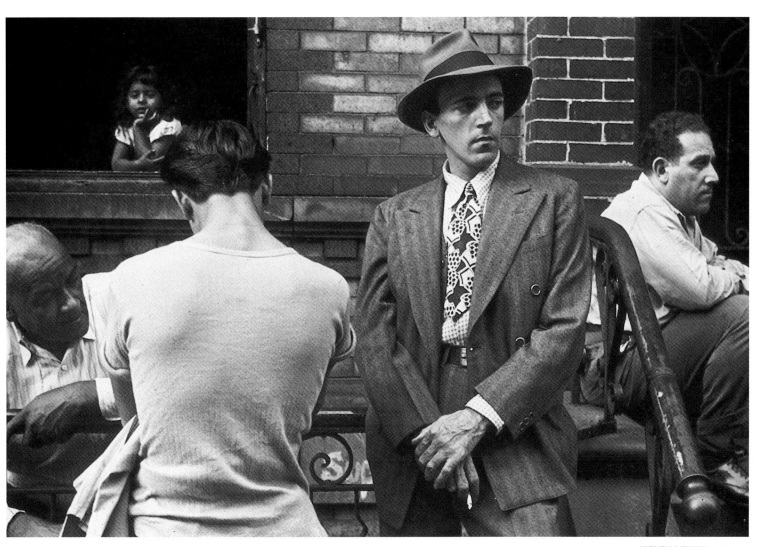

HELEN LEVITT
New York, c. 1945

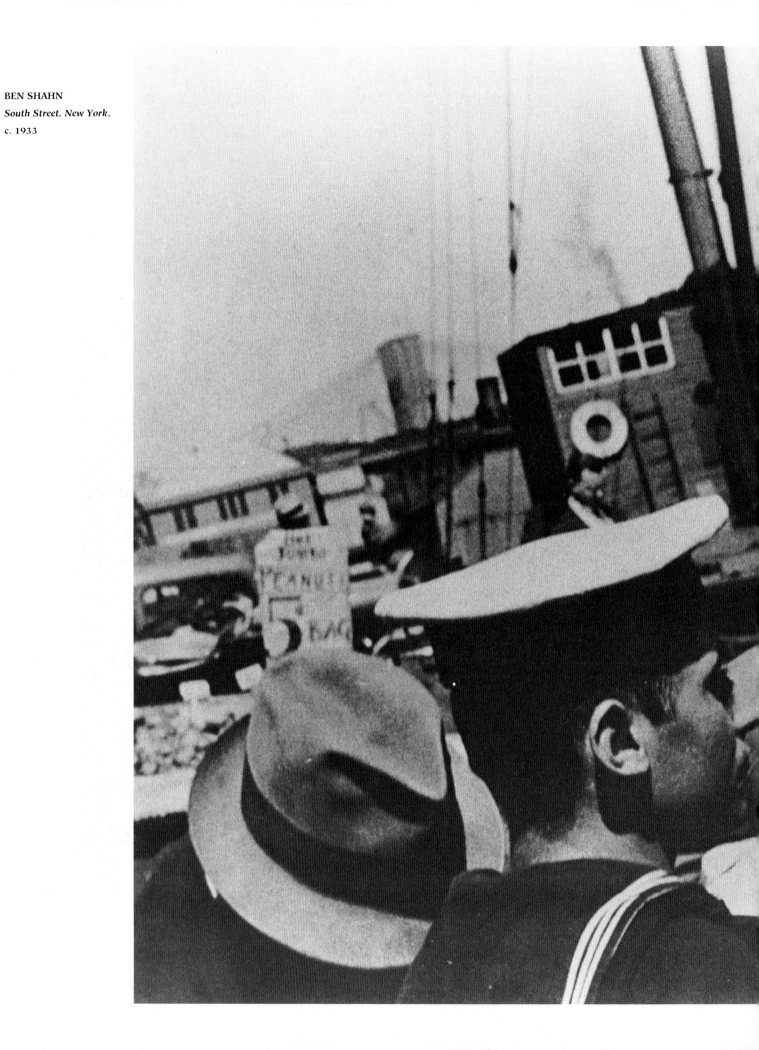

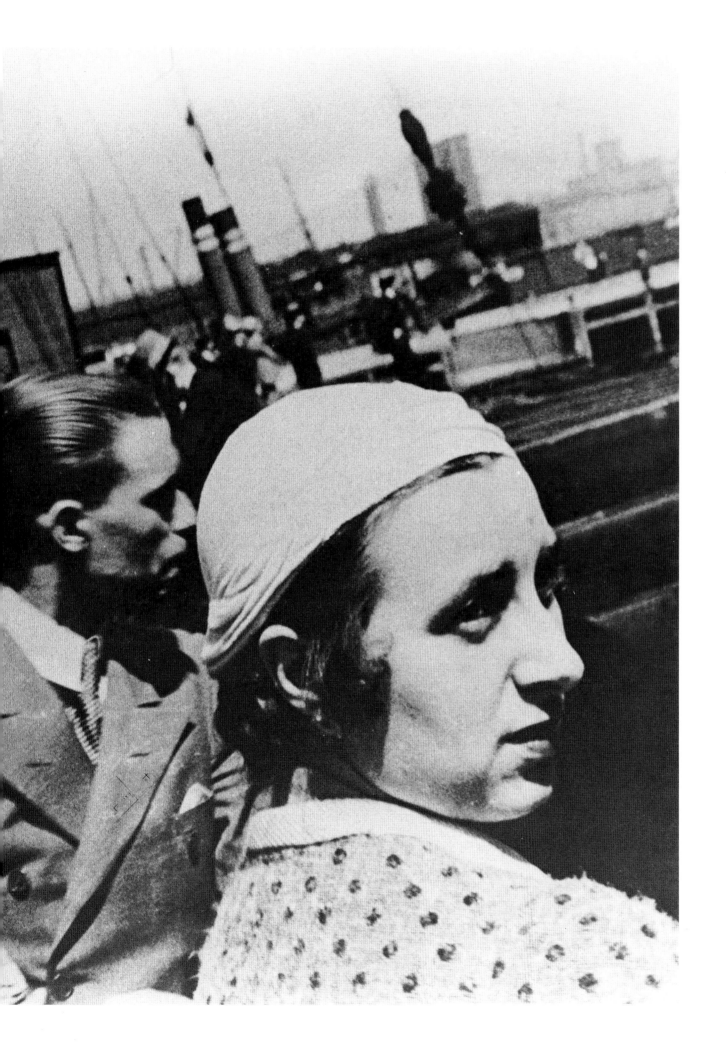

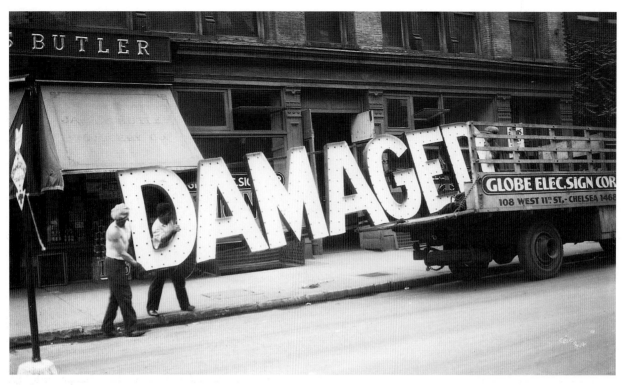

WALKER EVANS

Truck and Sign, 1930

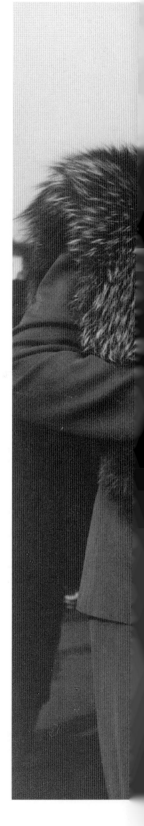

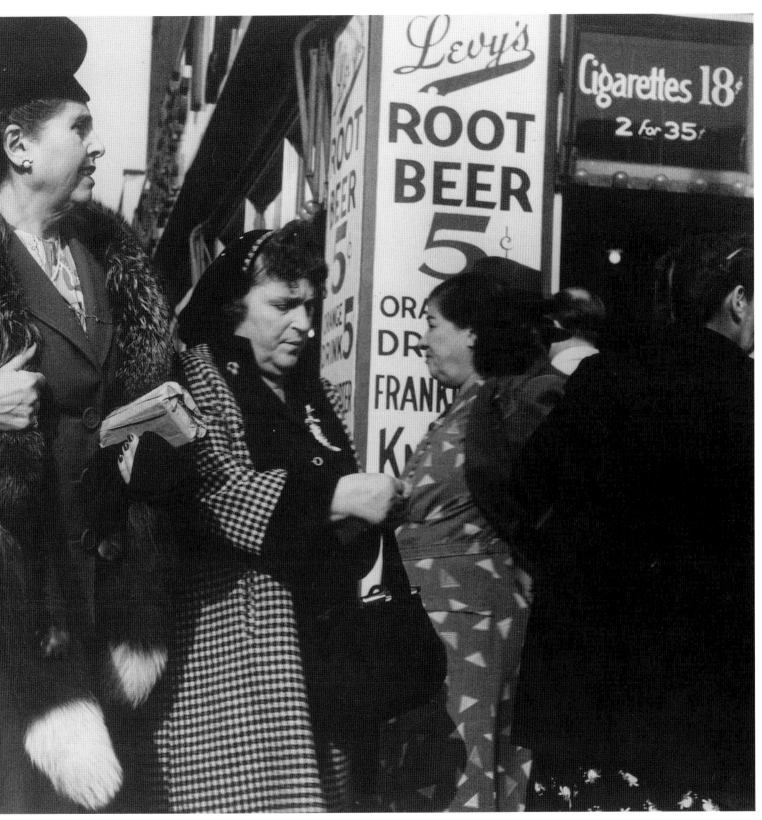

REBECCA LEPKOFF
Delancey Street,
New York, 1947

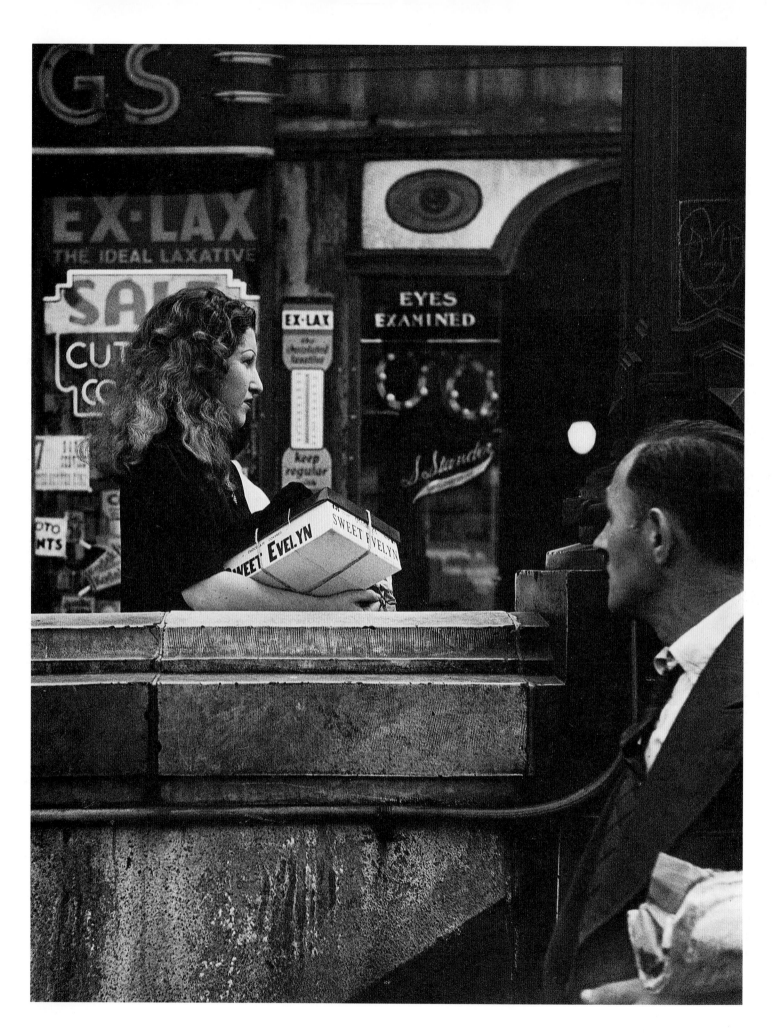

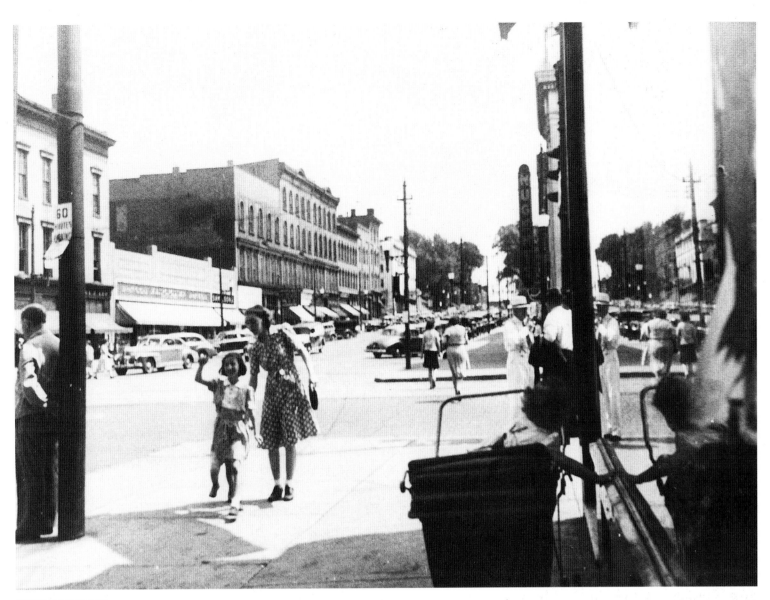

MARJORY COLLINS
Oswego, New York,
c. 1940

MORRIS ENGEL
Sweet Evelyn, East Side,
New York, 1937

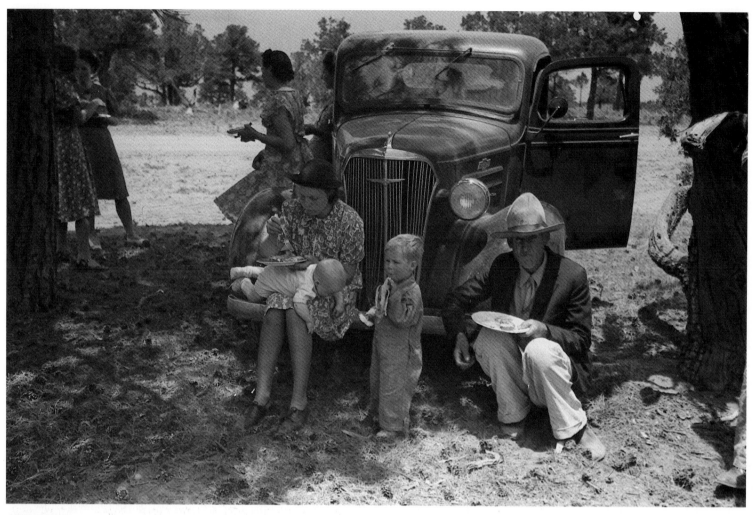

RUSSELL LEE

Pie Town, New Mexico,

1940

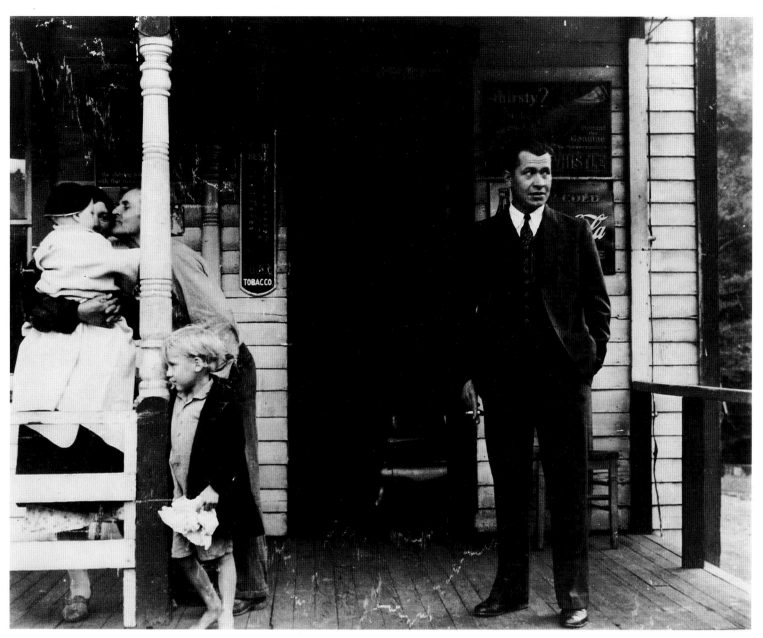

BEN SHAHN
*Front Porch, Country
Store, Scott's Run,
West Virginia,* 1935

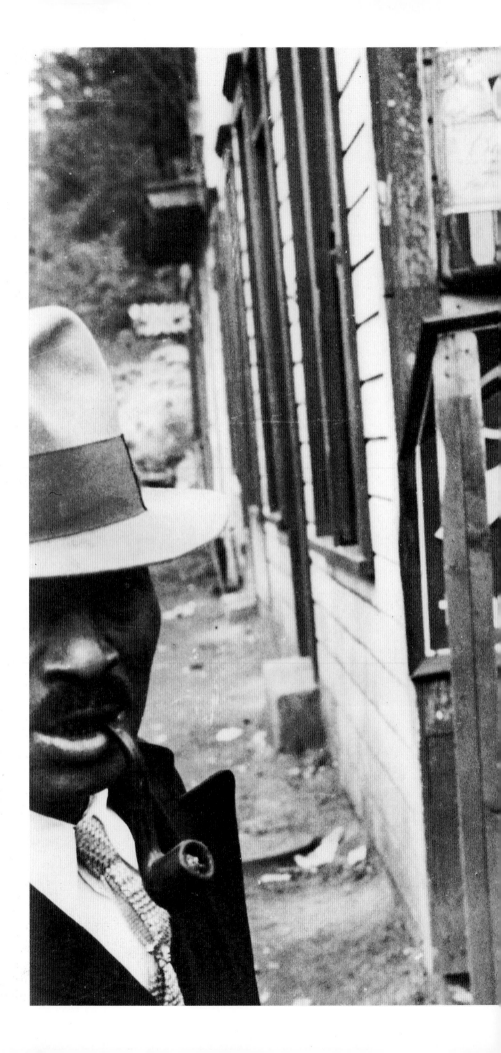

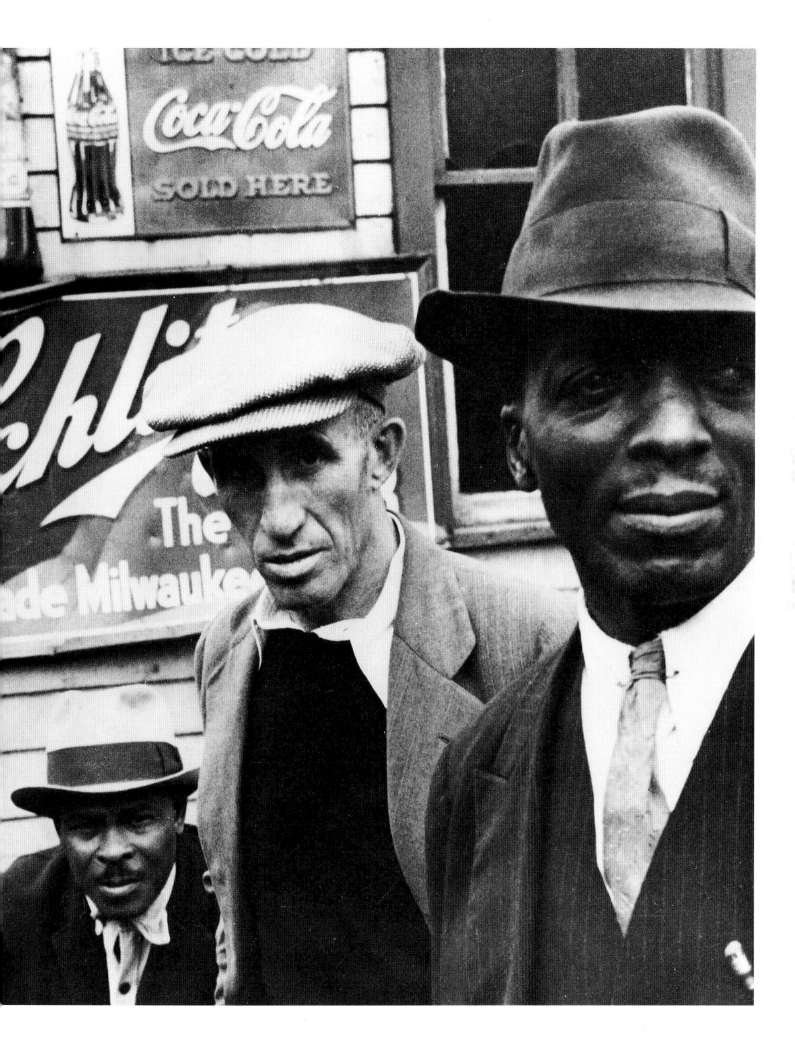

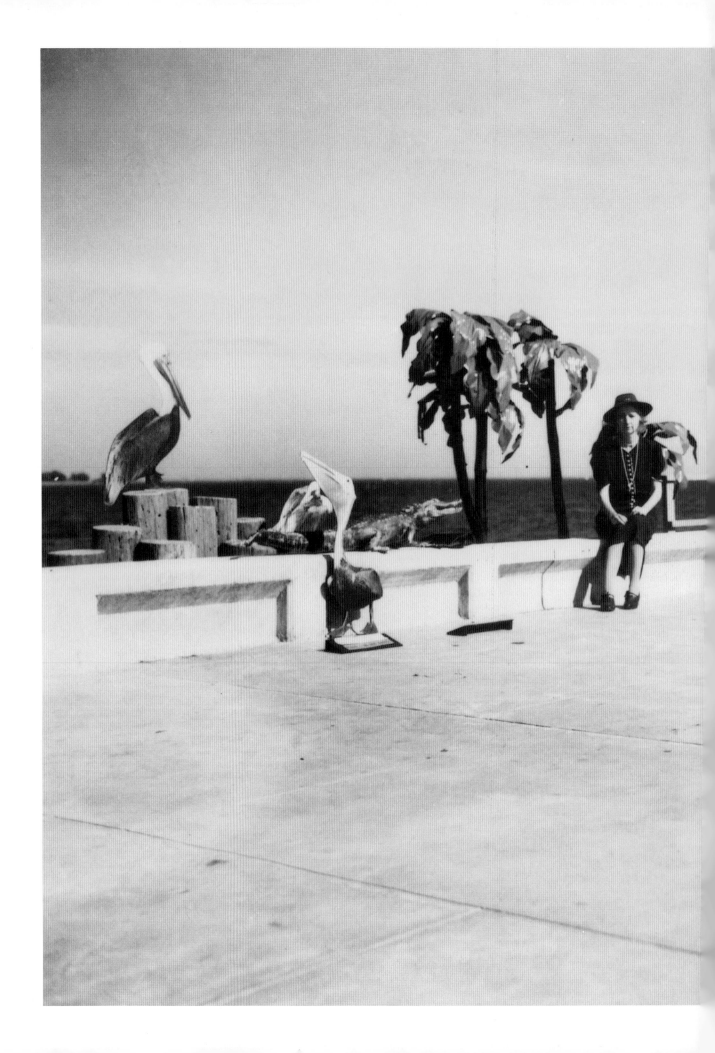

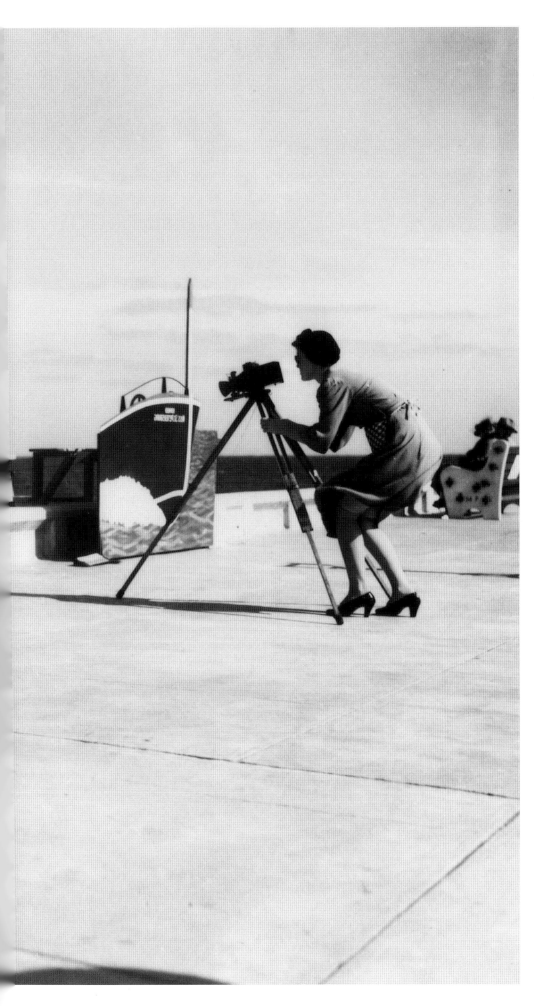

WALKER EVANS
Photographer, Florida,
1941

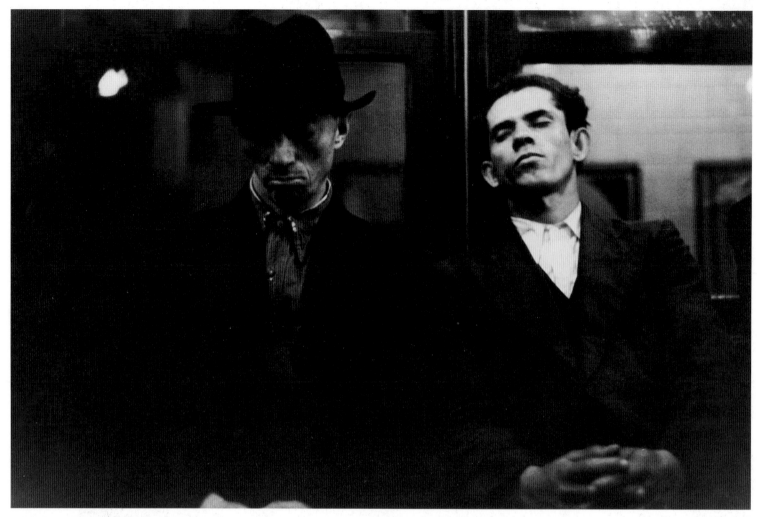

WALKER EVANS
New York Subway
Portraits, 1938–41

WALKER EVANS
New York Subway
Portraits, 1938–41

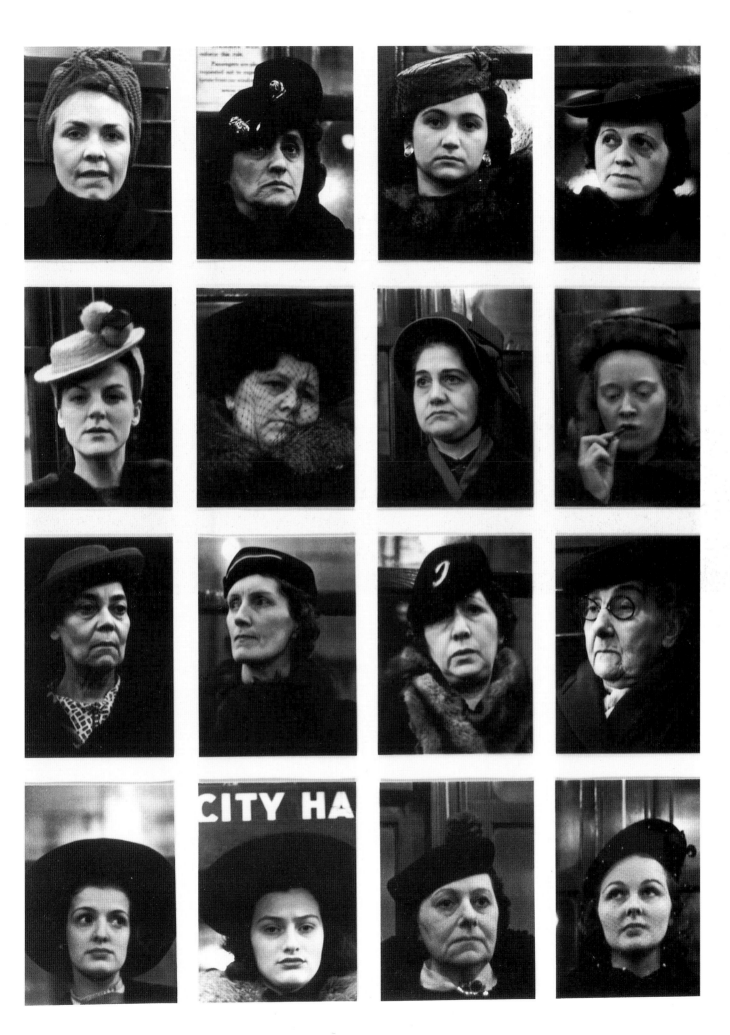

12: Social Uplift

Jacob Riis was not a photographer. He was a yellow-press journalist turned crusader and reformer who took up photography only as a visual aid for his lectures and publications. Because he had been destitute on the New York streets himself after his arrival from Denmark as a penniless immigrant in 1870, he came to feel that he had a special insight into the causes of the crime that he covered, during his twenty-two-year career as a police reporter, among the Irish, Italian, Jewish, and even Iroquois populations of the Lower East Side. It was to document the congestion and exploitation there that he first turned to photography, which he used to supply himself with both lantern slides for the lectures and illustration for his 1890 book *How the Other Half Lives.*

But even after he had realized the value that photographs might have for him, he had not wanted to take the pictures himself. At first, he solicited amateur volunteers; then later, when they began to lose heart for his late-night crawls through the slums, he hired a professional, who cheated him. Finally, out of sheer exasperation, he decided to learn how to make his own photographs. He practiced the medium for only ten years and made perhaps as few as 250 exposures. In fact, it's likely that some of the best-known images attributed to him were done by one of the amateurs, Richard Hoe Lawrence, who was recruited with the help of a doctor Riis knew at the Health Department.

When you look at the results Riis got, whether by his own hand or someone else's, you can see how indifferent he was to photography for its own sake or to any rules of composition as they were then understood. For instance, in attempting to make a candid street photo-

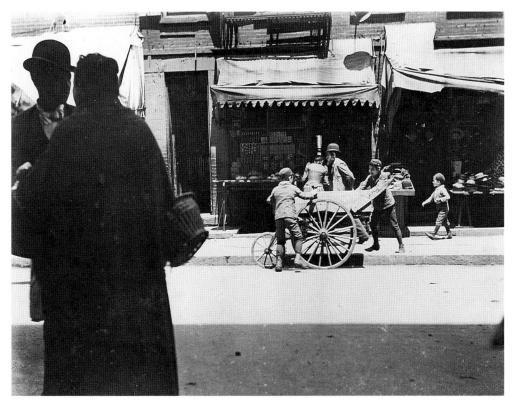

Fig. 12.1
JACOB RIIS
What the Boys Learn on
Their Street Playground,
c. 1890

graph of some boys at play (fig. 12.1), he allowed two adults to remain in the shadows in the foreground, where they largely overwhelm the central subjects. The reason he didn't bother to make his work better was that, as he recognized from the very beginning, a picture made ineptly was more effective for his purposes.

He admitted that the first plate he ever made, of a mass grave for paupers in Potter's Field, had been overexposed to the point where it was "so dark . . . as to be almost hopeless." But, he continued, "the very blackness of my picture proved later on, when I came to use it with a magic lantern, the taking feature of it. It added a gloom to the show more realistic than any the utmost art of professional skill might attain."[1] A similar comment might be made in praise of the street photograph mentioned above. The dark, intrusive presence of the adults at the edge of the frame introduces an aptly foreboding note. They overshadow the brief moment in the sunshine that the boys are enjoying.

In another Riis picture, one made in a crawl space under a pier, the focus has been put in the wrong place. Refuse is clear in the foreground, while the band of petty criminals who are supposed to be the subject squat hazily beyond. Yet the photographic mistake puts the social emphasis where it belongs, on the vermin-breeding conditions in which these men live. "It is a bad picture," Riis admitted, "but it is not nearly so bad as the place."[2] The remark raises the possibility that an even worse photograph might have done the place more justice still.

Riis wanted his photographs to be equal to the ugliness he saw in poverty. Art couldn't help, because it required artifice, which would make people think that he was falsifying the evils of the tenement and the sweatshop. If the photographs were to convince the viewers, thereby moving them to action, they had to look absolutely guileless and authentic. They should look as raw and awful as the conditions they documented. Despite some lip ser-

vice he later paid to photographic art in his autobiography, the only aesthetic Riis had was this anti-aesthetic.

His involvement with photography began in 1887, when he first read about the invention of flash powder, or *Blitzlichtpulver,* as it was called. He realized at once that it would permit him to record directly the conditions in the airless halls and windowless rooms of tenements. When *The Other Half* appeared, it reproduced more than a dozen line drawings based on photographs and as many halftone

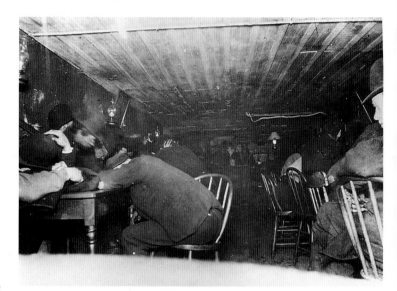

Fig. 12.2
JACOB RIIS
An All-Night Two-Cent Restaurant in "The Bend," c. 1890

plates of the photographs themselves. To obtain the flash shots, he often sneaked into a tenement or a dive, set up his equipment under cover of the semidark, fired off one exposure, and beat a hasty retreat before the blinded subjects could recover their senses.

It is partly as a consequence of this working method that his negatives abound in chance effects. Riis never knew what he would get. A lurching face might appear at the side of the frame like a death mask hung on a wall, as in a picture of a "two-cent" restaurant where the price of the meal entitled you to sleep all night with your head on a table (fig. 12.2). There is an aesthetic violence in this picture that suggests an atmosphere of physical violence in the place depicted. The lip of one of the tables has obscured the lower quarter of the image, cutting into the field of vision like a knife blade wielded by someone trying to slash the photographer's throat. The magnesium flash has created a flare in the middle of the picture, as if you could see the cholera hanging in the air of the unventilated room.

Riis's efforts (including, especially, *The Other Half*) put him in the good graces of New York's young police commissioner, Teddy Roosevelt, who was able to accomplish by executive order one of the reforms Riis had ardently sought — the abolition of the infamous police lodging houses to which the most destitute of the city's homeless were consigned. By 1900, Mulberry Bend in the Five Points area, whose infestations of criminals and disease Riis had railed against incessantly, was razed and replaced with a park. Yet as the battles he fought have receded into the past, his reputation as a reformer has tarnished. His relationship with Roosevelt, for whom he eventually wrote a kind of campaign biography, has of late been attacked as little more than social climbing done over the backs of the poor.

Unlike his motives as a reformer, however, his ambitions in photography can't be impugned, since he had none. In part because even he did not think of himself as a photographer, no one else did either, until fifty years after he had done his work. The odd effects and chance juxtapositions that the *Blitzlichtpulver* created indoors are similar to the results he got outdoors, as a street photographer. His work has a definite and consistent look, a style. But nobody thought of it in those terms until other developments later had, as it were, made room for Riis in the medium's history. To see his full significance, therefore, we shall have to return to the subject of his work in a few chapters.

Riis and Lewis Wickes Hine have both had reputations with two distinct phases: the first as a crusading journalist, the second as an honored photographer. The impact of each man on American social history was immedi-

ate, while that which they had on the history of photography occurred many years later. There was even an overlap between their careers, since Riis was still contributing an occasional article to the reform journal *Charities and the Commons* in 1907 when the editors began publishing pictures by Hine, who had until then been teaching photography at New York's Ethical Culture School. The links and parallels between the two men's careers have made it natural for historians to equate them.

Hine began as Riis had, with *Blitzlichtpulver*. Hine's first project was photographing the immigrants on Ellis Island; and after mastering the use of flash in the dark, cavernous buildings there, he took it into the same sweatshop environment on the Lower East Side where Riis had done much of his photographing a decade earlier. Whereas Riis's objective had primarily been to expose the living conditions of the poor, Hine's was to expose their working conditions. Riis had gone from sweatshops to tenements, doss houses, and police lodgings, while Hine went to the mines, factories, and mills. But in each case the idea was to penetrate the inner sanctums of squalor and exploitation in America, to uncover something that was purposely being concealed from view.

Because this was the goal, neither man could have been content with street photography alone. Each needed to get *inside,* off the street, to get at the truth. To gain access to a factory, Hine would claim that he worked for a machinery company and wanted to photograph the installation in the plant, or that he was selling workmen's compensation or life insurance and needed to have pictures by which his policyholders could be identified if they had a claim. Only when a ruse like this wasn't possible did he photograph workers on the street. He caught them either as they departed for the factory each morning at dawn or after their return in the evening, when they loitered outside the boardinghouses and clapboard shanties where they lived. The street was the most advantageous setting for him, as for Riis, only when he photographed the peddlers, vendors, and newsies for whom the street was the workplace itself.

Thus might it be said that some of Hine's techniques, and even his goals, were not unlike Riis's. Yet in spite of a mutual association

raphy might be applied to his cause. Hine was in essence a researcher who published his findings in sociological journals. His ideas had more complexity — or at least a duality — which made taking photographs a greater challenge. As he himself put it in his charac-

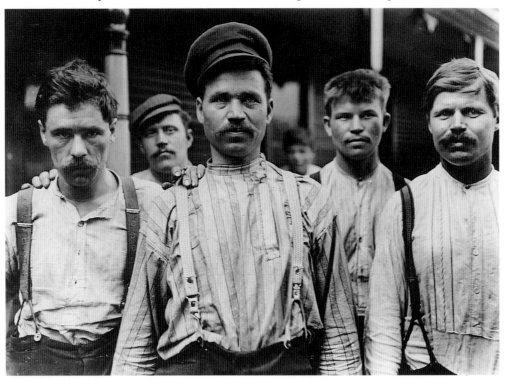

Fig. 12.3
LEWIS W. HINE
Russian Steelworkers,
Homestead,
Pennsylvania, 1907

with *Charities and the Commons* and other points of contact between their careers, there is no record of Hine's ever having acknowledged Riis's work as a precedent for his own. Indeed, the attitude that these men brought to their photography was entirely different. Whereas for Riis the separation of photography and reform was almost total, for Hine the two were all bound up together, at least in his own mind.

Riis was a muckraker whose background was in police reporting. He had the greatest faith in the images that were most sensational. This was the real reason that a photograph made out in the open, in a public place like the street, seldom pleased him as much as a flash-powder assault on a lodging house cellar. He had but one idea, to show the degradation poverty caused, and this single-mindedness limited his sense of how photog-

teristically terse, unornamented fashion, "I wanted to show the things that had to be corrected. I wanted to show the things that had to be appreciated." [3]

The second of these two aspirations sounds a positive note that made Hine, more than Riis, the photographer of record for the Reform movement in America before World War I. The official position that he held at the time was as photographer for the National Child Labor Committee. In this capacity he traveled throughout the industrial regions of New England, the midwest, and the south between 1908 and 1918. His job was to produce documentation that would support a campaign against child labor practices. His photographs were used to illustrate books and lectures as well as articles, but it was the last of these, especially the ones that appeared in the magazines published by social welfare advocate

Paul Kellogg, that made the greatest contribution. The passage of the Keating-Owen Act in 1916 finally incorporated into law reforms the NCLC had been proposing, with the crucial aid of Hine's photography, for nearly a decade.

When he worked on the street, Hine had two or three different approaches. The simplest was to do loosely posed group portraits like the one of immigrant Russian steelworkers made in 1907 for a Kellogg study entitled *The Pittsburgh Survey* (fig. 12.3). Since the relatively new Graflex camera Hine used was a top-viewer, it was held at waist level. The closer Hine moved, the more the camera had to look up to its subject. This gave the figures in the street portraits a rather heroic prospect. The Russian immigrants were photographed in the Pittsburgh suburb of Homestead, where steelworkers like them had been shot in the streets during the Homestead Strike of 1892. The breaking of the strike with scabs, troops, and Pinkerton agents had crushed the first effort to organize steelworkers into a union. But now, massed in the frame and photographed from below, the men in Hine's picture seem to present a new image of solidarity. They have the dignity and presence, the human spirit, that Hine wanted us to admire.

A core of portraiture like this ran through every photographic project Hine undertook, from the Ellis Island studies to *Men at Work*, the children's book he published in 1932. Such pictures were his articles of faith as a photographer. Alan Trachtenberg has said of Hine, "He went to Ellis Island a school photographer; he left it a master. He learned his work there not only technically . . . but aesthetically."[4] The aesthetic Hine learned there, making flash-lit pictures amid gloomy, nondescript surroundings, is one in which the only focus is on the human subject. The background becomes a backdrop, an indistinct area against which the subject is thrown into relief. What gives Hine's street photography its character is the ability he had to adapt that portrait aesthetic to the street. Even when he

photographed candidly, stepping back to get the full figure in the frame and trying to catch the action of a scene, he still made the pictures serve the pledge that he had taken as a photographer: "Ever — the Human Document to keep the present and future in touch with the past."[5]

It is clear in the pictures themselves how Hine favored settings that would allow him to separate his subjects from their background, whether that was a dusty, shack-lined road in Mississippi or an Italian street market in Chicago (pages 120–121). Since the Graflex had a long lens and, consequently, shallow depth of field, it worked best at short range as a portrait camera that let him focus on the human face or figure while everything in the distance slipped into a suffused haze. Such compositions established the distinction he wanted to make between the people and the conditions in which they lived.

Even when Hine was at a distance from his subjects, as in a picture (circa 1909) of a squad of children picking over the refuse at a

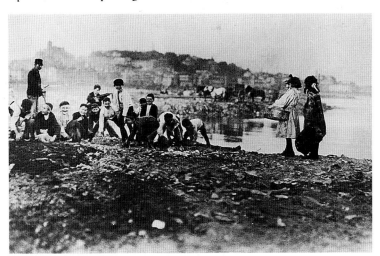

Boston dump, he still kept them in a single focal plane (fig. 12.4). Seen from the prospect of this unrelieved bleakness, the city on the hill looms vaguely behind the boys as if it were just a slag heap itself. The contrast that the boys make, grinning and capering for the camera, is what Hine's photography is all about.

Fig. 12.4
LEWIS W. HINE
Children at the Dump,
Boston, c. 1909

His most widely reproduced photograph is one that distinguishes subject from background in the same way. It was done on the Lower East Side, in New York, on a corner of a street with an island divider down the middle (Allen Street, perhaps) strewn with rubble and garbage (page 122). Having chosen his

a thinness that makes the social conditions it contains seem wavering and, therefore, eradicable. Only the woman herself has substance. As an image of exploitation, the photograph reveals something that "had to be corrected," as Hine said; but in the figure of this woman with her erect carriage and purposeful walk,

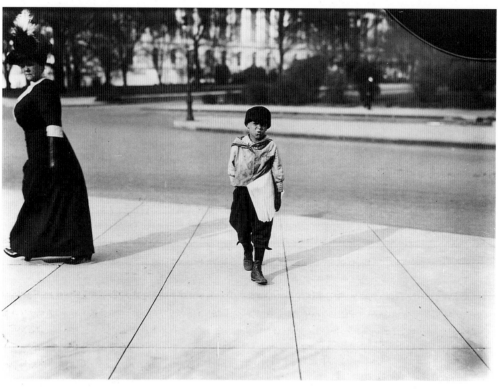

Fig. 12.5
LEWIS W. HINE
Dannie Mercurio,
Washington, D.C., 1912

spot so that the background across the street would be far away, he probably fixed his focus on the foreground and waited for someone to walk into the picture. The woman who came around the corner with a bundle of clothes on her head gave him a photograph later used so extensively by the International Ladies' Garment Workers' Union that it practically became its logo.

It is understandable that this picture, like so many others Hine made, should have meant a great deal to people in the labor movement. Its effect is of the human form rising phoenix-like from the desolation and squalor of the social environment. Between the soft focus beyond the subject and the fact that Hine's lens fell off rapidly with distance, the background is seen as through a veil of dust. It has

it also reveals something that "had to be appreciated."

To see Hine's intentions in this image fully, however, we have to look at the entire frame as he made it. The version that became an icon for the labor movement has been cropped to remove a second figure, silhouetted on the right, who is about to disappear behind the edge of a building. Because she too has something balanced on her head — a basket — she appears as a doppelgänger of the pieceworker who is the photograph's central subject. Dark where the primary subject is light, turned away from rather than toward us, she is a baleful presence who haunts the other woman's steps. She is also the sort of figure whose inclusion requires the luck, pluck, and timing of a Cartier-Bresson. She makes the image into a street photograph of the elemental type in which two figures are played against each other for symbolic effect.

Another picture of this sort is the 1912 one of Washington newsboy Dannie Mercurio (fig. 12.5). It's a typical Hine composition with a single plane of focus in front of an uncluttered background. But the presence of the dowager who exits the frame at the left edge adds another dimension, that of irony. At the same time that the social comment the picture makes has a serious intent worthy of Hine, it also has a sense of humor like Cartier-Bresson's. As Hine's facility with his equipment reached its peak near the end of his decade-long stint with the NCLC, his taste for idiosyncratic compositions seems to have increased. Where clusters of his work appear, as in the book *Street Land,* published in 1914, or *Boyhood and Lawlessness,* which came out the following year, there are often a number of classic street shots like this.

There were, then, two aspects to Hine's photography. It was a work of social conscience that had an impact on the Reform movement in the United States, and it represented a pioneering contribution to the aesthetics of street photography. The mediating position he held was symbolized by the Graflex he used, which was half view camera and half hand camera. It made possible those portraits that gave such dignity to the working-class people of his day, but at the same time it gave him a certain latitude and agility as a photographer that view cameras didn't permit.

Its great innovation was a hinged mirror that could be set at an angle inside the chamber between the lens and the back, thereby reflecting the image onto a viewing glass in the top. At the moment the picture was to be taken, the mirror would be flipped up out of the way again so the exposure could be made. A prototype for the single-lens-reflex models that would be developed a half century later, this design allowed Hine to anticipate in some of his compositions the sort of quick-

wittedness that we associate with 35mm street photographers.

Because they express an idea that people can transcend their environment and rise above social adversity, Hine pictures like the one of the pieceworker taking home a bundle of clothes on her head had great appeal during the Depression. It was an appeal to the spirit of progressivism, a social philosophy that had its origins in the Reform politics of the turn of the century and of which the New Deal was in many ways an extension. The revival of this social philosophy during the thirties brought with it the revival of Hine's reputation, which had to some extent been eclipsed during the prosperity of the 1920s. At the heart of the Progressive view was an optimism, a belief that human nature was basically decent and that America could solve through either education or legislation all the problems it faced.

The school run by the Ethical Culture Society, where Hine first came to New York to teach in 1901, attempted to put into practice educational reforms that the Progressives advocated. The magazines edited by Paul Kellogg, who published Hine's photographs from 1907 until the year before his death, in 1940, attempted to bring about the social reforms Progressives proposed. Both the teaching and the journalism fed Hine's idea that "The Camera May Help in the Social Uplift," as the title of a lecture he delivered at the 1909 National Conference of Charities and Corrections put it. The phrase "social uplift" is progressivism in a nutshell.

In the same year that Hine gave his lecture, Paul Kellogg changed his magazine's name from *Charities and the Commons* to *The Survey,* thereby indicating a change of emphasis from philanthropy to reform carried out on a scientific basis. After that, Hine's photographic activity for Kellogg stepped up. When Kellogg began a monthly supplement called *Survey Graphic* in 1921, Hine switched over to it, and he continued to supply the new magazine with pictures throughout the rest of his career.

Survey Graphic provided a crucial link between the progressivism of the prewar era and the New Deal. Not the least of the ways in which it did so was by introducing Roy Stryker to Hine's work when Stryker was still an economics student at Columbia University. In 1925, one of Stryker's Columbia professors, Rexford Tugwell, was at work on a textbook entitled *American Economic Life and the Means of Its Improvement,* for which he asked Stryker to research the illustration. Unable to find suitable material, the young graduate assistant got in touch with Hine, who brought him boxloads of work done more than a decade before. From these Stryker selected more than a third of the two hundred photographs used in the book.

Hine's contribution to the history of photography lies not only in the importance of his work in its own time, in fact, but in the effect it had during the 1930s on a variety of factions ranging from the members of the Photo League to Roy Stryker's staff at the Farm Security Administration. The former were the disciples who mattered most to Hine, because he knew many of them personally, and the discussion will return to the subject of the Photo League in a moment. But first, even though the next chapter deals with the FSA at length, Hine's influence on that organization should be considered while his work and career are fresh in the reader's mind.

As Tugwell later acknowledged, the New Deal was built in part upon the Progressive point of view implicit in his textbook's title. And as Stryker was later to acknowledge, it was through his contact with Hine that he learned how to translate that point of view into visual terms. Speaking of Hine's "impact," Stryker said, "I never realized how great it was going to be on me."[6] How great it was can be seen from the kind of picture Stryker chose to emphasize in building up the FSA's photo file. The photographers he favored — Arthur

Rothstein, Carl Mydans, Russell Lee, Dorothea Lange — were those who kept him supplied with the sort of portraiture Hine had done. What Stryker wanted, he said, were pictures of "men with guts still showing in their faces."[7] This phrase echoes the Progressive's faith in the American character to which Hine's pictures had given image.

Elaborating on the phrase on another occasion, Stryker made the debt owed to Hine more evident still:

> *The faces to me were the most important part of the file. . . . I have always believed that the American people have the ability to endure. And that is in those faces. . . . Experts said to me, oh no, that's a face of despair. And I say, look again, you see the set of that chin. You see the way that mother stands. You see the straight line of that man's shoulders. You see something in those faces that transcends misery.*[8]

Stryker saw in those faces what New Dealers had to believe was there. If what one saw was anger, bewilderment, or "despair," then the Communist party's critiques of American society were valid and revolution might be inevitable, as the party claimed. But if American faces had in them the dauntlessness, Emersonian self-reliance, and "transcendence" that Hine had taught Stryker to look for, the alternative to revolution that the New Deal was trying to offer, the old Progressive ideal of reform, might still have a chance.

Despite the debt he owed to Hine, Stryker was not grateful enough to offer the photographer a job when he applied for one with the FSA in the 1930s. It was only at the Photo League that Hine found the place of honor he deserved among Depression photographers. His quiet, unassuming visits to the league headquarters on East Twenty-first Street are among the most vivid memories of the period for Walter Rosenblum, who was one of the mainstays of this documentary organization run by volunteers. "I knew him as 'Lewhine,' "

Rosenblum has recalled, "and I was completely under his spell. . . . I felt embraced by his presence."[9]

Hine's influence on the league in the years just before World War II was actually a moderating one. The organization had originally been founded in 1930 as the Film and Photo League, an agitprop unit sponsored by the Berlin-based International Workers' Relief for the purpose of making films about class struggle in America. In 1936 a faction calling itself Nykino, led by Leo Hurwitz, split off and became Frontier Films; joining Hurwitz in the

the Feature Group, a photographic elite corps directed by Aaron Siskind. Lesser projects were devoted to, among other subjects, Chelsea, Park Avenue North and South, the Bowery, and Pitt Street, which Walter Rosenblum chose as a focus because he lived nearby.

Since the education program was the backbone of the league, the key figure was the man who ran it, Sid Grossman. He was also Hine's staunchest supporter among the members. When the coming of the war depleted the enrollment in his courses, Grossman used

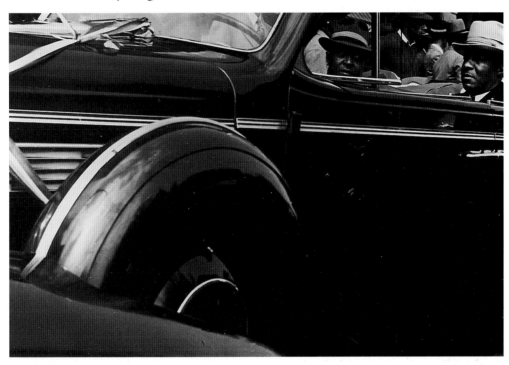

Fig. 12.6
AARON SISKIND
A. Philip Randolph,
New York, c. 1932–36

new production company were Ralph Steiner, Paul Strand, and Ben Maddow. At the same time, two other members from the early days, Sid Grossman and Sol Libsohn, made the Photo League into an independent entity.

The Photo League ran a series of projects documenting life in New York and had an education program offering monthly guest lectures as well as photography courses. The courses supplied the member-volunteers to man the projects, which were, nonetheless, very uneven in terms of their quality and the dedication of the participants. The most elaborate of them was the Harlem Project undertaken by

the free time he had as a result to print a series of portfolios of Hine's work from the negatives given to the league by his son after the photographer's death, in 1940.

Among the Hine admirers who were drawn into the league's orbit was Berenice Abbott. Hine had an appeal that ranged from politically uncommitted view-camera photographers like her to ideologues with 35mm equipment. Grossman, for one, was wild about 35mm cameras. Although he at first used the old Graflex that the league made available for members to sign out on loan, he preferred the smaller format. After the war he used a twin-lens reflex held at eye level, the way a Leica would be, to shoot a series at Coney Island as well as other pictures; and until he could afford a 35mm of his own (bought with the fee for a photomural commission), he borrowed them. Predictably, much of his work reflects the street shooter's love of chance formalism and surreal moments (pages 220–221).

The presence of such qualities not only in Grossman's work, but in that of many others associated with the league, makes it clear that Hine's love of street photography for its own sake was as important a component of his influence there as his political idealism. Helen Levitt, as a young girl just starting out, was pleased by the attention she attracted from the league, which at one point offered her a show. She felt that she learned a lot from the exchange of views about the medium that went on at the league's headquarters. But when some of the members praised her work for its political content, although she smiled

Fig. 12.7
DAN WEINER
Fifty-seventh Street,
New York, 1950

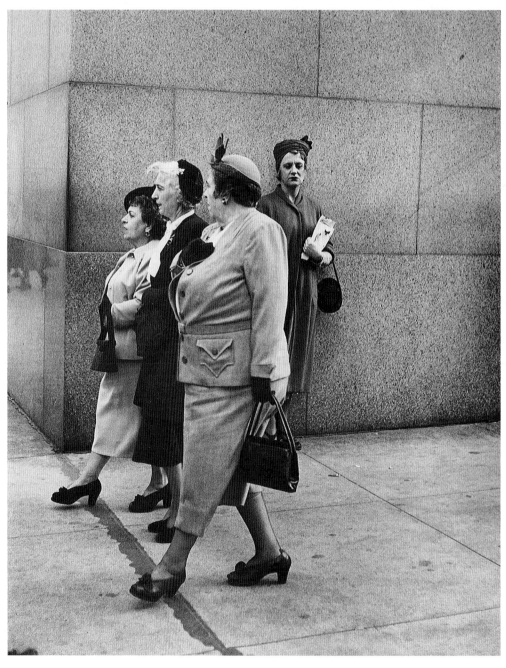

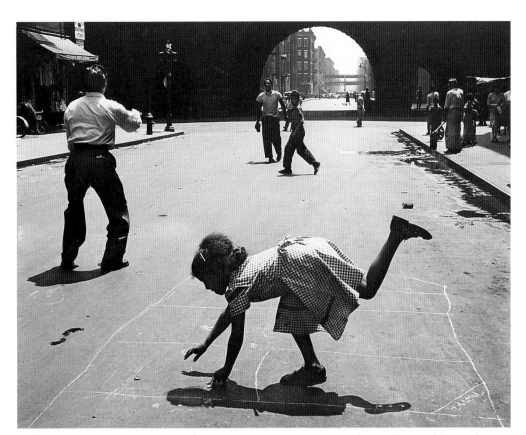

Fig. 12.8
WALTER ROSENBLUM
Hopscotch, New York,
1952

politely because she didn't want to offend anyone, she could never understand what they were talking about.

Even in the inner circle of the league's leadership, there were those who mistrusted political uses of the medium and who held their own work aloof from what they considered to be its manipulation or exploitation. When Grossman invited Siskind to come into the newly reorganized league in 1936, Siskind did so only on the condition that he be allowed to concentrate on production and not have to perform any duties as a league functionary. This hands-off agreement was what enabled Siskind to put together in the Feature Group the most prolific team of photographers the league had.

What political implications there are in Siskind's own Harlem work often seem inadvertent, or even inappropriate. For instance, in a photograph made as part of his first series there, which was devoted to A. Philip Randolph's Brotherhood of Sleeping Car Porters, the black union leader appears in an open touring car shot from a low angle in such a claustrophobic way as to make the subject look almost like a gangster (fig. 12.6). The photograph is effective at the expense of a subject who was, as Siskind himself readily admitted, one of the most principled, selfless leaders of any color that the labor movement had. Already typical of Siskind's work were photographs more concerned with graphic patterns than social ones. These pictures of building facades or laundry suspended over a tenement yard strewn with trash anticipate the pure abstractions to which the photographer would turn in the 1940s.

Certainly there were signs that the social conscience developed early in some league members continued to influence their work when they went on to professional careers in photography. A case in point would be Dan Weiner in his sensitive, astute coverage of the Montgomery, Alabama, bus boycott in 1956 for *Collier's* magazine. He seems to have photographed wealth and power as much as poverty, and within his work as a whole, the one plays off against the other in much the same way two figures might in a single street photograph. Each subject provides a certain comic relief from the other. Weiner loved both to deflate the pomposity of the upper classes and to celebrate the pleasures of the lower ones (fig. 12.7). Whatever political bias may have survived from his youth was finally less important, though, than his love of the sheer energy of life on the streets, particularly the streets of New York (pages 222–223).

After the war, Max Yavno, who had collaborated with Siskind on a Harlem series entitled "The Most Crowded Block in the World," took the photographic education he had gotten at the league to Southern California, where any New York seriousness the league may have instilled in his photography promptly melted. What was left was a residue of bemusement at the antics on Muscle Beach and the incorrigibility of poverty that could bask year-round in sunshine and cheap wine. There is almost no trace in his work of the kind of political or social doctrine that, after the war, the league would be accused of representing. The same might be said of the work of any number of other onetime members — Rudy Burckhardt, Morris Engel, Sol Libsohn, Jack Manning, Lou Stoumen, Walter Rosenblum (fig. 12.8) — who learned how to do street photography under the league's aegis.

For more than one of these photographers, the love of the medium that the league had fostered ended in a tragic irony. Grossman, who was the organization's exemplary member in so many ways, had unfortunately put himself in a position to be the leading example of its victimization in the postwar era as well. In 1947, the U.S. attorney general accused the Photo League of being a Communist front, the FBI began trying to link all the current members with the old days at the league, and a witness at a conspiracy hearing conducted by the House Un-American Activities Committee named Grossman as a Red. The consequence was that the other league members ousted him, hoping, perhaps, to save themselves by this panicky gesture.

Combined with his isolation from his former friends, Grossman's persecution by the government finally made him so paranoid that he locked his students in his apartment for their classes and was afraid to go out into the streets himself anymore to photograph. The strain of it all unquestionably contributed to his early death from a coronary, in 1955. The irony is that his images never did illustrate any political philosophy, nor could they have been made to serve a political program even in the way that Hine's did.

Among American artists and intellectuals of the 1930s, the more radical you were politically, the more radical your aesthetics tended to be. Yet since the relationship of Marxism to Modernism was also one of the great quandaries of the period that was never resolved, even in advanced cultural circles like that around the *Partisan Review,* it is not surprising that the issue was never satisfactorily worked out at the league either.

Perhaps the best answer was a mute one suggested by Cartier-Bresson when he was asked to give a talk at the league after the war. The reason he was invited was not that he had joined the Communist party or worked for *Ce Soir* in the 1930s, for all that most members knew about him was the photography itself (Jay Leyda had lent the league a show of his work in 1939). His lecture was among the best-attended evenings the league ever had, and the high point came when the photographer was asked to explain how he got such extraordinary pictures. Without saying a word, he crouched low to the floor and began darting and wheeling around the room, camera in hand. The audience was electrified.

13: Collective Vision

In France, street photography was first personified and then institutionalized. It was the creation of a few individuals — primarily Cartier-Bresson and Kertész — working independently of one another in the 1930s, and it took the form of a cooperative only later, after the war, with the founding of Magnum. In America, the institutions came first, and the individuals who made their mark as street photographers emerged from them. The most important organizations to foster street photography during the thirties, besides the Photo League, were the Federal Art Project sponsored by the New Deal's Works Progress Administration and Roy Stryker's Historical Section at the Farm Security Administration. None of these was started specifically to promote street photography. Their real purpose was not photography per se so much as to study the life of the common man in America. Street photography just came along as a natural consequence of that purpose.

Although the culture of a democracy always focuses special attention on the common man, in the America of the thirties he became a national obsession. Photographic projects like the league and the FSA were but part of a vast effort to learn more about him. Such innovations of the 1930s as the Gallup Poll were part of that effort too. So were many sociological studies that followed the pattern set by Robert and Helen Lynd's *Middletown,* and the reports from the hinterlands filed by innumerable writers who abandoned their usual research or sources to take to the road.

Along with these efforts to find out how "the people" felt came, predictably, efforts to tell average Americans how they ought to feel. The latter ranged from Dale Carnegie's *How to Win Friends and Influence People,* which was near the top of the decade's best-seller list, to the Communist party's "Popular Front." Each

of these was an endeavor to *Meet John Doe,* as Frank Capra titled the 1941 movie in which he tried to sum up the experience of the preceding decade. Perhaps the 1930s innovation that tells us most about the times was the new soap opera on radio. Like the Gallup Poll, the soaps were an attempt to get at the everyday feelings of ordinary people.

This common man whom everybody from George Gallup to Ma Perkins was trying to second-guess was the man literally in the street. With a median figure of around ten million unemployed throughout the decade, he was the man who had been put out on the street. (The reason he wanted to learn how to win friends and influence people was to get his job back.) Conditions being what they were, the street became the setting for the drama of the times. It was the only set for Elmer Rice's *Street Scene,* the 1929 play whose Everyman characters and common desperations made it a powerful influence on the theater of the following decade. So much real-life drama was being played out in the streets — as when General Douglas MacArthur routed the Bonus Marchers from the nation's capital in 1932 — that photojournalists like Joe Costa of the *New York Daily News* became de facto street photographers. Street photography flourished in the 1930s because the common man, about whom everyone was curious, presented himself before the camera.

Early in the decade, Dorothea Lange noticed how the flow of people along the street had changed outside the windows of her portrait studio in San Francisco. Less hurried and purposeful, the pedestrian traffic had also become, in its aimlessness, more interesting to look at. "One morning as I was making a proof at the south window," Lange recalled, "I watched an unemployed young workman

253

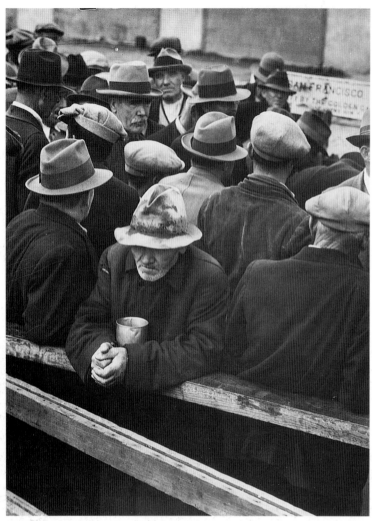

Roy Stryker during the latter's first few weeks on the job at the FSA.

Stryker had come to Washington when his mentor, Rexford Tugwell, was called there as a member of Franklin Roosevelt's brain trust. Impressed with his former student's work illustrating the economics text he had done in the twenties, Tugwell had installed Stryker as head of a unit doing photo documentation at the Resettlement Administration, which was later to be the Farm Security Administration. Thus did Roy Stryker become perhaps the most powerful arbiter of American documentary photography of the Depression era.

By the time Stryker arrived in Washington, his association with Tugwell had refined the agrarian populism of his youth in Colorado into a progressivism with the more national outlook that working in the service of the New Deal demanded. The photographic file that Stryker was to assemble at the FSA had an enormous effect on the way people saw the times in which they were living. Even today, the image we have of that period in American history is largely the creation of photographs that organizations like the FSA, the WPA, or the Photo League produced. None of these photography units was well known to the public at the time. Yet in later years Ben Shahn, who did assignments for Stryker from 1935 until 1938, claimed that FSA photographs were widely reproduced and even played a role in Roosevelt's 1936 landslide.

Although officially intended only for government use, the FSA file was made available free to any publication that wanted to borrow from it. Stryker's own recollection was that it never reached as wide an audience as he had hoped it would; yet the fact is that the pictures appeared in *Fortune, Look, Time,* the *New York Times, Life,* many lesser magazines, and a variety of books. Perhaps even more crucial to the political impact that Shahn claimed for the FSA photographs were certain exhibitions. Their chance to affect the 1936

coming up the street. He came to the corner, stopped, and stood there a little while. . . . What was he to do? Which way was he to go?"[1] After Lange observed him for a few minutes more, her thoughts returned to photography. She said to herself, "I'd better make this happen," and decided to leave the studio for the streets.

The first time out she ventured only a short distance, to a neighborhood storefront where a philanthropist was distributing food. This operation was known locally as the White Angel Breadline, and Lange's picture of it, one of her first on the street, became one of the Depression's most famous images (fig. 13.1). A short time later she included it in a portfolio of her work that her economist husband Paul Taylor carried to Washington and showed to

election came at the Democratic convention, for which Shahn himself designed an FSA display. Stryker's biographer wrote that similar exhibitions in such urban centers as Boston and Los Angeles attracted special interest groups, like intellectuals, who had crucial influence on national policy.

While the influence the exhibitions had on the body politic is hard to gauge, that which the FSA itself had on American photography is not. Stryker liked to point out that his unit was formed a year before the founding of *Life*. In fact, the FSA became a feeder of talent to it and other mass-circulation picture magazines. Half of Stryker's staff went on to careers as photographers or editors at *Time, Life,* and *Look*. But beyond that direct effect, there was a more pervasive one, which resulted from the notice photographers in general took of work by organizations like the FSA. Here Shahn was probably a more reliable judge than Stryker. His sense of visual style in magazines and the arts was much more acute than Stryker's. And Shahn felt that the FSA's influence "revolutionized" photography at the time.[2]

Exhibitions of FSA photographs were mounted for the College Art Association meeting in 1936, by *U.S. Camera* and the Carl Zeiss Company in 1937, and by Willard Morgan representing the manufacturers of the Leica camera in 1938. The last of these, originally seen at the Grand Central Palace in New York, was later sent on tour all over the country by the Museum of Modern Art. It was one of the decade's seminal exhibitions, and two other New York shows seen within a year of it were equally important: Berenice Abbott's "Changing New York" and Walker Evans's "American Photographs," both of which were accompanied by books that extended their influence beyond the exhibition itself. All three of these exhibitions were composed primarily of street photographs and contained *the* image of Depression America that made itself felt in photography everywhere.

In Paris, with its magnificent squares and promenades like the Bois de Boulogne, its sidewalk cafés and boulevardiers, there had always been a life on the street waiting to be photographed. In the United States, nothing comparable in its appeal to photographers existed until the 1930s. Here public idling of the

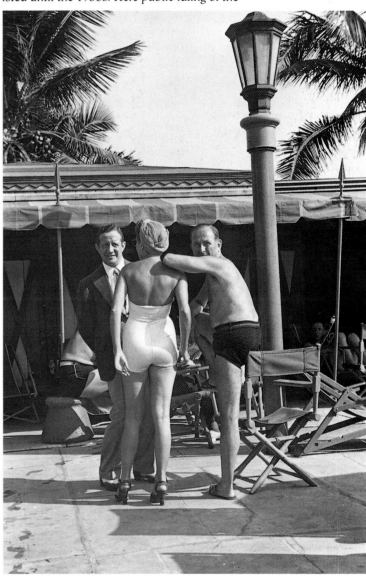

sort the French enjoyed had always been frowned upon. Yet once a street life did come into existence in America, as different as it was from the European version in its origins and character, it inspired a street photography often very similar. In the archives of the FSA, particularly, there is often a Surrealistic edge to the pictures and a playfulness characteristic of Cartier-Bresson's work.

Fig. 13.2
MARION POST WOLCOTT
Miami Beach, 1939

Among the photographs of this type that Walker Evans made while traveling for the FSA is one taken in front of a New Orleans barbershop in 1935 (page 22). The woman's zebra-pattern blouse against the stripes painted on the shop facade and the contrast she makes with the seductive face in a cosmetics ad next door are the sort of pairings to which Cartier-Bresson would have responded. Many of the best FSA photographs of this type were made late in the photo unit's brief history, in 1940 or after, by photographers who were in effect the FSA's second generation. They were the ones who learned photography from the FSA's own file and whose pictures are the kind that result from a medium's influence upon itself.

Maybe Marion Post Wolcott's photographs of Florida beginning in 1939 poke more fun at their subjects than is typical in FSA work because this was the one time an FSA photographer dealt with the idle rich instead of the common man (figs. 13.2, 13.3). But John Vachon's pictures from the same period, although of people who really were just the man in the street, have the same tongue-in-cheek quality. Like Cartier-Bresson, Vachon had a feel for the street as a place of constant metamorphosis, a production line for symbolism.

In a Vachon photograph of this sort, for instance, just as a man dressed all in black strides along a dazzling white fence, around the corner a woman in white is disappearing amid dark shadows (pages 216–217). A photograph like this is a lottery ticket, a combination that is played as a hunch at the moment the negative is made and pays off later in the print. The same winning combination Vachon had in this 1940 picture made in Chicago was played two years later in New York by another FSA photographer, Marjory Collins (fig. 13.4). In this photograph of a woman sweeping a front stoop, the whiteness of the subject's shoes and socks, especially, are a reproach to the dingy old man whom it seems she might sweep into the gutter at any moment. Collins's name has never been associated with the FSA, because she didn't join the photographic staff until very late, when everyone was being transferred to the Office of War Information. Nonetheless, her pictures have a fullness characteristic of street photography that earlier FSA work also has.

Fig. 13.3
MARION POST WOLCOTT
Winter Tourists Picnicking near Trailer Park, Sarasota, Florida, 1941

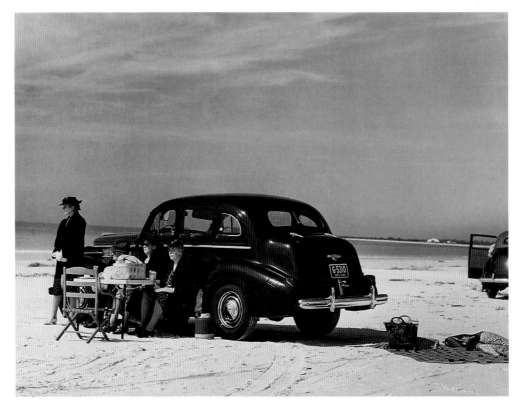

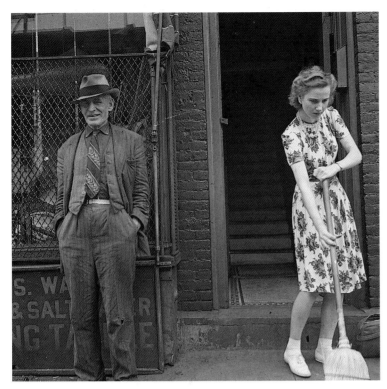

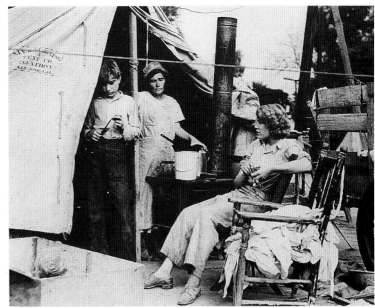

FIg. 13.4
MARJORY COLLINS
Fourteenth Street under the Third Avenue Elevated, New York, 1942

FSA staffers more familiar today are known for work of a different type, but several of them were doing street photographs as well. An example is a picture made by Russell Lee at a picnic in Pie Town, New Mexico, in 1940 (page 232). Lee and his wife, Jean, were drawn to Pie Town because of its name. The whole visit was in the spirit of a lark, and the pictures reflect this. Because of the old codger's scowl and the woman's casual use of her baby as a dinner table, this particular picture has in it, despite the town's name, less of apple-pie America than is usual in Lee's work. A number of other pictures Lee made on that trip through the southwest are equally amused. Something about that part of the country affected Lee's sense of proportion in novel ways.

Even Dorothea Lange's work contains moments of dry laughter. The listless, uprooted life in the Okie and Arkie camps she frequented abounded in street theater of the absurd, in dispossessed drawing room comedies staged before an audience of passersby. A picture made in Exeter, California, in 1936 looks like a production still from one of these plays (fig. 13.5). How enduring and irrepressible the urge to make street photographs was for Lange can be seen from the fact that she was still doing it back home in Berkeley a decade and a half later. One of her best dates from then (page 218). The woman in this picture is making a fashion statement. She doesn't realize that her son, who tags along behind, is simultaneously issuing a retraction.

Where this kind of photography at the FSA diverged from its European counterpart was in the direction of a certain American wildness. There were times when it was not any visual correspondence or specific incident that the photographer was after — not the zebra blouse against the barbershop facade or the black figure by the white fence. It was not the arrangement in the scene, but its disarrangement that appealed to the photographer. These images have little of the balanced control or formalism of classic French work. They are the sort of picture that John Vachon made in 1941 of some jaywalkers in Chicago; here it is purely the jumble of people and cars that we are being asked to take an interest in (fig. 13.6).

Like a mimic with an ear for gibberish, FSA photographer Jack Delano had an eye for this kind of image. A picture he made at a "World's Fair" in Tunbridge, Vermont, in 1941 demonstrates (fig. 13.7). He took the

Fig. 13.5
DOROTHEA LANGE
Drought Refugees from Texas Encamped in California near Exeter, 1936

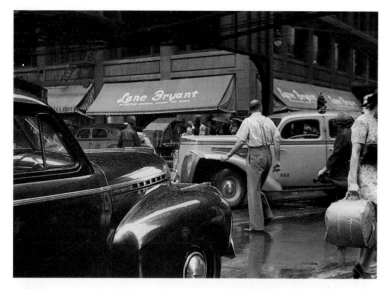

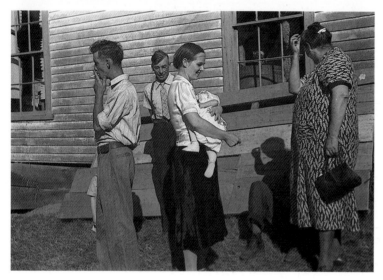

Fig. 13.6
JOHN VACHON
Jaywalkers, Chicago,
1941

Fig. 13.7
JACK DELANO
At the "World's Fair,"
Tunbridge, Vermont,
1941

picture at a moment when none of its seven subjects were actually looking at each other. Even we do not at first notice the presence of two of them. Street photographs often revive the pleasure one could get as a child from puzzle pictures, the kind whose object was to find the little animals or dwarfs drawn into a seemingly empty landscape. Delano's picture has some of the same fun of the treasure hunt. It coaxes the viewer's eye to move around in a fashion as delightfully disorganized as that of the fairgoers who are in it. The photograph gives us that vicarious sense of reality which documentation ought to provide. It invites us to roam over its surface with the same Saturday-afternoon lack of purpose that they enjoy.

The photographer who went further in the direction of such wildness than anyone else was Ben Shahn. Shahn was one of the early photographers to come with the FSA, being loaned to Stryker in the fall of 1935 by the Special Skills Division at the Resettlement Administration, where he had been doing poster design. Already an established painter who had been working on mural projects under the sponsorship of several different federal programs, Shahn had begun doing street photography on his own back in New York.

Shahn didn't paint whenever he was photographing for the FSA during the period 1935–38; and he said later that when he was working intensely at anything like that, he thought of it as his life's work, something he'd go on doing forever. Since he made in those three years between five thousand and six thousand photographs, he couldn't have had time to do much else. In 1938 he actually transferred into the FSA at half the salary he had been making so he could go on photographing. But later that year, to the amazement of many people in an era when job security meant everything, Shahn abruptly resigned his position with the FSA and completely gave up photography. It would be more than two decades before he picked up a camera again, and then only as a tourist in Asia.

Shahn originally turned to the camera as an aid in painting, a more efficient means than the sketch pad to take certain kinds of visual notes. "What the photographer can do that the painter can't," he said, "is to arrest that split second of action in a guy stepping onto a bus, or eating at a lunch counter."[3] It was the painter's "love of exactitude," critic James Thrall Soby claimed, that made Shahn take up photography.[4] Shahn himself later explained that "I was particularly interested in the fold of a coat, you know. I said to myself, 'A coat one pays fifty dollars for has a different kind of fold than one you pay twelve dollars for' and I was very keen on getting the detail and I found that sketching alone, there was neither the time nor could I get people to stand still long enough, so that I needed an adjunct."[5] The place where you found a cheap coat like that was, of course, on the man in the street.

At one point in 1931 or 1932 Shahn was trying to sketch some blind musicians who worked Fourteenth Street every day. He went there repeatedly, walking backward in front of them and attempting to draw as he went. Finding situations like this impossible, he persuaded his more prosperous brother to buy him a used Leica for twenty-five dollars on a bet that he could get something off his first roll of film published. He did, selling to the *Century* magazine a little series he called "The Sidewalks of New York." By the time he was working on a mural project for the new prison being built on Rikers Island in 1934, he was photographing on the streets constantly. In those days fellow muralist Lou Block was sharing Shahn's studio on Third Street, his Rikers Island commission, and his enthusiasm for photography. Recalling the last of these, Block said that he and Shahn would go out on the Lower East Side and "work both sides of the street like a couple of peddlers, snapping everything."[6]

Shahn's photographs did indeed turn up in his paintings, and not just in the rendering of details. One of those musicians from Fourteenth Street became the subject of the painting *The Blind Accordion Player;* and *Handball, Vacant Lot, East Twelfth Street,* and others were based on photographs as well. Like Russell Lee and his reaction to the southwest, Shahn had his whole sense of proportion altered by photography. The medium changed his feel for scale in a picture; it made permissible certain jumps in the relative size of subjects and their background and in the range at which each was viewed. One recurring motif of Shahn's painting deriving from photographs was the isolation of a small, distant figure in an undifferentiated landscape. James Thrall Soby observed that such "easel subjects are often presented as if viewed through

one end of a telescope or another."[7] But actually Shahn discovered both these exaggerations in perspective by looking through a wide-angle lens on a Leica.

Despite Shahn's claim that when he photographed he thought of himself as nothing but a photographer, really he never stopped being a painter. He admitted as much on numerous occasions. That photography was always secondary with him was probably what made his work in the medium so original. It liberated him. He would try anything with the camera, because his opinion of himself didn't depend upon his ability to photograph. He wasn't afraid to fail, and he often did. He once shot an entire roll at a barn dance in available light at shutter speeds so slow that not one picture turned out. He didn't care. Not having his ego involved was what allowed him to make such an enormous number of negatives in a short time and, therefore, to learn more quickly than other photographers.

He used a German film that was very fine-grained. Although its slowness cost him many pictures, the ones that turned out gave him back the full description that mattered to him. He wanted to make images, not photographs, so he cared little about print quality. He needed *not* to have standards. Shahn was as ready to hand-hold a ten-second exposure as to whip out the camera and shoot from a moving car. To make it handy for anything that came his way, he used a Leica that had a fixed lens (as opposed to interchangeable ones), because that made it flat enough to be carried in his hip pocket.

If there was any one unorthodoxy that was crucial to making his pictures look different, it was his willingness to use the right-angle viewfinder, which he adopted from the start. This device allows a street photographer to sight along the camera body while standing sideways to his subject, who consequently fails to realize that he *is* the subject. The sort of photographers who are real purists

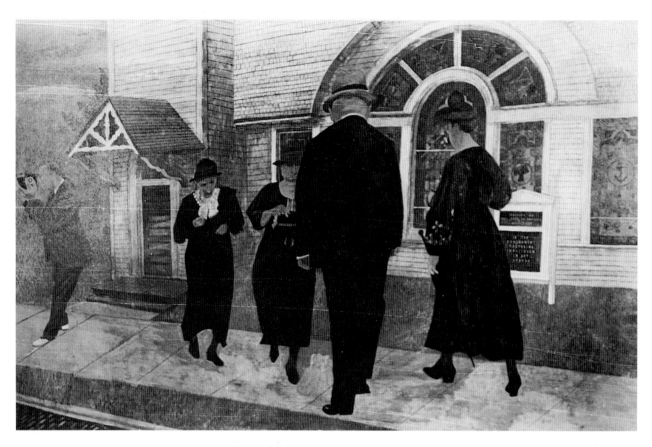

Fig. 13.8
BEN SHAHN
Myself Among the
Churchgoers

about the medium can't use the angle viewer without being a little ashamed. Resorting to this device makes them feel their art is based on gimmicks. It's a breach of professional ethics, as if the matador were to sneak up on the bull from behind. But not being a professional, Shahn didn't have these compunctions.

There were things he was reluctant to do, such as use the flash, but that was because the flash interfered with reality, not with his photographic principles. (Actually, Shahn was once persuaded to try the flash. He put it and the angle viewer on his camera together, with the result that the bulb went off in his face.) To complete the charade that the angle viewer entailed, Shahn needed a fake subject to stand in front of him. This was a role often played by his wife, Bernarda, who accompanied him on his FSA field trips to the south and midwest. As obvious a trick as the angle viewer seems today, it worked then because small hand cameras were new and people were naive about them. According to Helen

Levitt, only the children caught on. The great advantage the angle viewer afforded Shahn was that it made possible some of the experiments with extreme composition and framing that typify his work.

At the same time that a wide-angle lens gives the illusion that the background is farther away than it seems to the eye, the two-dimensionality of the photographic print collapses the distance between background and foreground. Shahn liked that. He especially liked the disparity in the sizes of figures near and far who, in the photograph, stand on top of each other. The angle viewer allowed Shahn to accentuate this disparity by getting very close to the foreground figures. It also allowed him to expand the number of subjects in each photograph because none was scared off by his approach. He could lever complex groupings into position in the frame while no one felt a thing in reality. As a consequence there is a feeling of disparity in his photographs, not only between foreground and background, but from edge to edge.

The influence on Shahn's painting of such straining, precarious compositions in the photographs is revealed by *Myself Among the Churchgoers* (fig. 13.8). Shahn isn't really "among" the picture's subjects at all; he appears in a detached position, standing on the extreme left and photographing members of the congregation with his Leica and angle viewer. This dislocation of one figure from the group reads as a form of dissociation between them as well. The same effect is found in a Shahn photograph of the front porch of a country store (page 233). The darkened doorway is a fulcrum balancing the family that embraces on one side of the frame against the bystander who looks away casually on the other. The doorway gives image to the gap we perceive between the bystander's indifference and the family's emotion. He is so nonchalant compared with them and so much better dressed that he seems to live in a different world. At the very least, he seems to be standing in a different picture.

Figures that seem to stand in different pictures are the effect of a certain kind of painting too: mural painting, which was the kind Shahn was usually doing in the 1930s when he wasn't photographing. It is there, rather than in the easel pictures, that Shahn's photography and painting come to bear on each other most closely. As executed by Shahn, a mural is a series of realistic scenes coexisting in an abstract space. Each event or set of figures has its feet firmly planted on the ground, but all the scenes together float over, under, and around each other in a free-form design. This makes the transitions between scenes the most difficult area aesthetically. Here is where realism and abstraction must meet. And Shahn's photographs abound in clues as to how he solved this problem in the painting.

If there was a subject matter he was actually trying to document in his photographs, it was how reality itself makes these transitions from one place or occurrence to another. The photographs are full of ambiguous spaces like the doorway described above, areas where a non sequitur occurs. Shahn particularly liked to position himself at the point where two storefronts of different design abutted each other, or before a shadowy passage or entranceway from which people walking toward the camera emerged into a sunny street where the flow was back and forth in front of him. In some of these photographs we at first think the camera has malfunctioned so that two separate negatives were run together. It's as if Shahn were teaching himself how to make convincing transitions in the murals by studying how abrupt the disjunctions could be in reality.

The similarity of the photographs to the murals exists not only in the juxtapositions of scenes, but in the way Shahn created changes of scale and overlaps from one mural scene to the next, just as he did from foreground to background in the photographs. Loving photographs for their endless description of detail, he came to realize how much strength a detail could have. In the murals he used seemingly incidental details as a form of spot weld with which he could fasten the different scenes together once they were assembled on the wall. He would allow the handle of a hoe or cuff of a shirt in one scene to jut over the edge of a door frame in the next scene, thus fixing our sense of the relationships among the spaces depicted. Shahn's fascination with slight impingements like these is unmistakable in the photographs.

By working out relationships between abstract and realistic spaces in the murals of the thirties, Shahn was working toward the more fantastical easel paintings of the forties, and the street photography he did in the thirties was a part of that development. In an essay done for a WPA anthology entitled *Art for the Millions*, Walter Quirt, Shahn's fellow muralist from the New York Project, spoke of art as "a language of emotions" and said that the artist must "release his own fantasies, . . . free from self-censorship and intellectualization."[8] This was a goal toward which Shahn had been striving since the late 1920s, when he began to turn away from the influence of the European painting he had studied and to get back to his own early life as a source of inspiration. Tak-

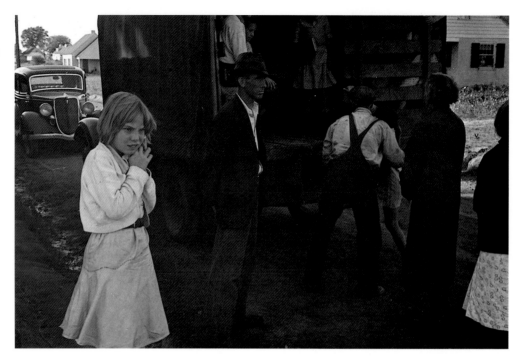

ing pictures by reflex and being ready to try for every conceivable kind of shot, he even made his street photography into an exercise in the sort of uninhibited response Quirt was talking about. Photography became a way to learn the language of emotion that art needed. The inescapable actuality of the photographic document served as a springboard to the artistic fantasy of his later work.

The atmosphere of a disturbed dream that we often sense in the paintings is in Shahn's greatest photographs as well, nowhere more forcefully than in one he took in Red House, West Virginia, in October 1935, at the beginning of his first trip for the FSA (fig. 13.9). Its composition is not unlike that of the picture on the porch of the general store discussed above. Here as there, a single figure stands opposite a group. Although separate and apparently unrelated, or at least unattentive, the lone figure again seems to comment on the activity in which the group is engaged. In the porch picture, a doorway functions as a dead space sealing off the two sides of the frame. In the Red House picture this function is served by the man who stands in the middle, his face blank and his eyes fixed on nothing in particular. The picture makes apparent a mood of

menace and distress that is implicit in more than one of the many photographs Shahn took in which the figures are similarly disposed.

There are moments in street photography when images of children seem to turn into images from the photographer's own childhood. What he sees in the viewfinder revives half-lost memories, old phobias, bad dreams. Shahn's picture from Red House impresses one as this kind of déjà vu. It suggests a racial memory taken personally, a moment when some memory Shahn had inherited was tinged with anxieties of his own. Although the photograph documents a rehabilitation project run by the Resettlement Administration, it looks more like a scene from a deportation.

For a Lithuanian Jew whose parents had fled Eastern Europe at the time of the pogroms and who was now witnessing the consolidation of Stalinism in the Soviet Union and of Nazism in Germany, the scene that presented itself here must have aroused terribly mixed feelings. Perhaps what we see exposed in this photograph is the roots of Shahn's radicalism — his refusal to be the grateful, trusting immigrant, his lifelong suspicion that the terror in which his ancestors had lived could happen here, in America, too.

Approximately four years before this photograph was made, Shahn had done the Sacco-Vanzetti gouaches that established both his style and his career, and he had remained aware of America's capacity for political repression. Four years after this photograph he would move his family out of New York because of the constant activity of the pro-Nazi Bund in the Yorkville section of Manhattan, where he was living. At times Shahn has to have had very conflicted emotions about the government programs for which he was working throughout the 1930s. Their potential for political abuse could never have been hard to imagine. This photograph from West Virginia does imagine it.

The one other government agency that stimulated a lot of photographic activity was the Works Progress Administration, whose roster of creative photographers was as distinguished as the FSA's. It included Edward Weston, Minor White, Clarence John Laughlin, Berenice Abbott, and Helen Levitt. Moreover, the street photography sponsored by this agency tended to be concentrated in big cities to a greater extent than that done for the FSA. In New York alone, there were more than a half dozen street photographers getting at least some WPA funding. David Robbins did a series entitled "Along the Waterfront," and he and Arnold Eagle collaborated on another one, called "One Third of a Nation." Andrew Herman worked on "East Side Market Scenes," and Sol Libsohn did "Food for New York City," among others.

Yet Abbott's was the only street photography of great merit that was truly supported by the WPA. Other projects were either too short-lived to be more than an exercise in photojournalism, or they were done by photographers who, with the exception of Levitt, were considerably less inventive than those Stryker gathered around him. Levitt was the sole 35mm street photographer of more than

local interest to whom the WPA gave even minimal assistance, and the agency's funding of her efforts was so fleeting and intermittent that she can scarcely be said to have been part of its program at all.

In fact, Levitt is the one American photographer in the thirties who can truly be said to have gone it alone like Cartier-Bresson. She is also the American photographer whose work comes closest to his. She had a knack for his kind of street photography from the very beginning; and although she neither went to France to get an art education nor joined photographic organizations like the Photo League and the FSA, she had the advantage of being younger than the other thirties photographers by just enough to be able to benefit from the examples they set. She never met Shahn, but she did see a handful of his pictures, the memory of which stayed with her over the years. She saw some work by Evans too and liked it so much that she called him up to see whether he would look at her photographs. The day she visited his apartment, James Agee dropped in, and thus began her lifelong friendship with him. Evans encouraged her, so they spent more time together, including occasions when she accompanied him on his own photographic junkets through New York.

Each of these men helped form Levitt's intelligence as a photographer, but the one whose work lodged in her mind most decisively was Cartier-Bresson. In 1935 or 1936, during the period that Cartier-Bresson was in New York, Levitt used to go with her friend Sidney Meyers to Willard Van Dyke's studio on Ninth Street, where a group of people gathered who were trying to form an independent motion picture production company. One of them was Cartier-Bresson, who showed Levitt a good deal more of his work than she had been able to see before. His pictures made her feel that photography was, as she later put it, "limitless." They completely altered her sense of the medium, so that, she said, "the boundaries fell away."[9] Although she wasn't exposed to either Cartier-Bresson or his work enough to be considered his protégée, her intuitive grasp of what he was trying to do was greater than any other American photographer's.

One trait that Levitt shared with Cartier-Bresson was a certain shyness. This disposition coupled with an insatiable curiosity about life led both photographers to a need for self-effacement — in fact, for invisibility — and for the power to see without being seen. Certain photographers' emotions seem to secrete this need, like adrenaline, and with comparable effects on their behavior. A camera provides what military strategists refer to as preemptive-strike capability. It makes it possible to take the world by surprise before the world has a chance to notice you. Failing that, the photographer needs an effective subterfuge, which Levitt found in the angle viewer, or, as she calls it, *Winkelsucher*. (The English-language term is a literal translation of this German word, by which she first knew the device.)

Her shyness is apparent as well in the subjects she chose when she first took up photography. The series she did for the WPA is all of children in the street and of the chalk graffiti they draw there. Photographing graffiti is a way to pursue human beings on the street without having to confront them directly. Like the little mirror in the elbow of the *Winkelsucher,* the drawings reflect their creators obliquely. The children themselves, for that matter, offer an oblique view of human nature.

The shyness of the photographer who chooses children as her subject is obvious. Children are much less intimidating than adults, much more approachable. For just this reason, street photographers who concentrate on children often slip into triteness. It's one thing for a chance image of a child to strip away the photographer's inhibitions, as Shahn's picture from West Virginia (fig. 13.9) or Cartier-Bresson's 1932 picture from Seville (pages 4–5) seems to have done. But it's another matter when the photographer sticks to chil-

dren out of a dependency on *their* lack of inhibition. Street photographers who specialize in children produce too many pictures that are cute, like photographers who specialize in cats. To be any good, the pictures have to transcend their subject. We never take novels about children seriously unless we can take them as allegories of an adult world. The same strictures apply to street photographs of children.

Levitt's pictures give the impression that she doesn't particularly like children. That's why the pictures are good. Children in her photographs are never lovable; they are often vaguely sinister or dangerous. The aura of adulthood shows in their play the way the humidity of an approaching storm hangs in the air of a summer day. Like Diane Arbus and Yasuhiro Ishimoto after her, Levitt was taken with those moments when children anticipate the self-consciousness of adults by putting on masks. In one of Levitt's most widely known images, children step out onto a stoop wearing masks (fig. 13.10). Dressed in their Sunday best, they are crossing a threshold into the adult world, taking on grown-up ways. Their postures are tentative, yet studied.

Even when there was none of this adult self-possession in a child's behavior, Levitt saw in him the image of the man. In an application she wrote in 1946 for a fellowship offered by the Modern, she observed that "the games of children [have] . . . sudden nuances that reveal the deep repressions of the unyoung." [10] One picture taken around that time makes a good illustration of the remark. In it a small boy inside the back of an empty truck leaps with all his might (pages 6–7). Against the uneventful, workaday street outside, his leap in the shadows has a blurry, astonishing violence. He becomes an image of hidden impulses, a glimpse into the libido. Although its subject is a child, the photograph stays on edge, alert to the full complexity of human nature.

Throughout the forties, Levitt was photographing "the nabes" of New York. She

Fig. 13.10
HELEN LEVITT
Untitled, New York,
c. 1942

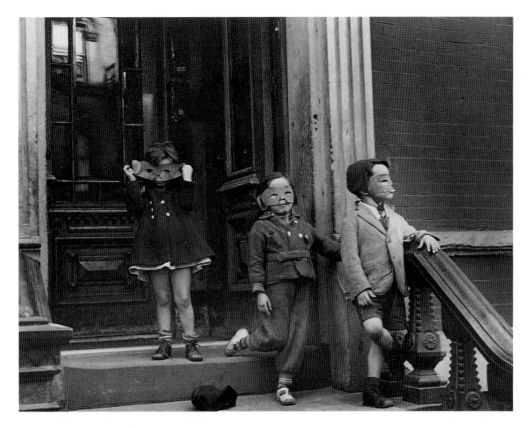

went to Spanish Harlem, to the Lower East Side, wherever she found life on the street. She used her Leica, outfitted with the *Winkelsucher*, rather differently from Shahn. Instead of taking advantage of the closeness the angle viewer permitted as he did, to make an unbalanced, often unfocused image, she made a classical frieze of figures (page 225). Her pictures retain more of the order and control characteristic of Cartier-Bresson. The human attitudes range across the frame in her pictures from pathos to exuberance, from inquisitiveness to cretinism. Nothing human was foreign to her. Having begun by concentrating on children, she now expanded her repertoire of street types to include Gypsies and sharpies and shopkeepers and old people. The sharpies posed fatally in zoot suits and big fedoras.

In 1941 Levitt took a trip with James Agee's wife, Alma, to Mexico City, where she went right on photographing in the suburb of Tacubaya much as she had in New York. Since Cartier-Bresson had come straight to New York from Mexico in the late thirties, it's possible that a lot of Mexican pictures he showed to Levitt encouraged her to take the trip with Alma Agee a few years later. Whatever prompted her to go, she didn't like the experience. She so hated the hassle of traveling and the demands of working on unfamiliar terrain that she realized she could never make a career for herself in photojournalism as Cartier-Bresson had. But this left her with no career at all in photography, and as a result she began in the late forties to think of movies as an alternative.

In 1945 she and James Agee had begun shooting movie film candidly in Harlem, and later her friend Janice Loeb took Agee's place on this intermittent project. Not until 1951 did Levitt edit it into its final form, under the title *In the Street*. Meanwhile, she had also collaborated with Loeb and Sidney Meyers on *The Quiet One*, a feature about a black boy for which Levitt shot wild street footage used as intercuts. After these experiences she turned to filmmaking to make a living, working as a free-lance editor and stock-footage researcher on documentary shorts.

Around 1949, Levitt gave up still photography altogether and did no new work for ten years. In this hiatus, as in her work on movies, there is another parallel with Cartier-Bresson's career. Whereas the time spent away from still photography never damaged his reputation, however, it all but eclipsed Levitt's. She realized how neglected she was becoming as a still photographer one day when she saw an illustration based on a photograph she had taken many years before. Since her picture had been copied without her permission, she called up the illustrator to complain. "Oh, I'm sorry," he said, "I thought you were dead." [11]

Levitt tells this story with an obvious pleasure that again suggests her tendency toward self-effacement. Another form this takes is an insistence that she has nothing to say about photography. Like being thought dead, silence is a refuge she can take from unwanted attention. Despite the claim that she is inarticulate, however, the application she submitted for the fellowship from the Modern is one of the few sound statements about street photography actually written by a photographer. It speaks of the way that "those accidental disarrangements" the photographer records in the street "provide a more intense apperception of reality." [12] The only contemporary writing about street photography as astute as Levitt's is an essay on her work that Agee was preparing around this time. It may even be that he helped her with her application for the fellowship; but if her eloquence there owes something to him, the ideas in his own essay owe as much to her.

Although the essay was specifically intended as a text for a book of Levitt's photographs to be called *A Way of Seeing,* the book itself didn't appear until twenty years later, in 1965. This was a misfortune for street photography in general, for in the interim Agee's essay could have helped many photographers who were working independently to recognize the common bond in their pictures. Agee spoke of "luck" as being "one of the cardinal creative forces at work in the universe, one which a photographer has unique equipment for col-laborating with." [13] Like Walter Quirt in his midthirties essay about painting, Agee stressed the artist's need to rely on intuition and feeling rather than intellect. And in one paragraph in particular, he summed up much of photography's development as an art during the previous fifteen years.

"In every other art which draws directly on the actual world," Agee wrote,

the actual is transformed by the artist's creative intelligence into a new and different kind of reality: aesthetic reality. In the kind of photography we are talking about here, the actual is not at all transformed. . . . The artist's task is not to alter the world as the eye sees it into a world of aesthetic reality, but to perceive the aesthetic reality within the actual world, and to make an undisturbed and faithful record of the instant in which this movement of creativeness achieves its most expressive crystallization. Through his eye and through his instrument the artist has, thus, a leverage upon the materials of existence which is unique, opening to him a universe which has never before been so directly or so purely available to artists. . . . The kind of beauty he records may be so monumentally static, as it is in much of the work of Mathew Brady, Eugène Atget, and Walker Evans, that the undeveloped eye is too casual and wandering to recognize it. Or it may be so filled with movement, so fluid and so transient, as in much of the work of Henri Cartier-Bresson and of Helen Levitt, that the undeveloped eye is too slow and too generalized to foresee and to isolate the most illuminating moment. [14]

14: American Classic

If the 1920s were a period of expatriation when American artists flocked to Europe, the thirties were the time of repatriation when many of them felt an urge, or even a duty, to come home again. They found that the French influences they had absorbed were not enough, not by themselves, anyway. Some even began to feel alienated from the culture abroad that they had at first embraced. The drift homeward was actually well under way by 1929, when Ben Shahn, who had lived in Paris off and on for a number of years, returned. Berenice Abbott came back that same year, as had Walker Evans two years earlier.

Shahn's problem was the same as that which Malcolm Cowley in *Exile's Return* attributed to a hypothetical classmate of his at Harvard, a Jewish writer from Brooklyn. Cowley's young writer has a background that contains "street gangs in Brownsville, chants in the Chasidic synagogue, the struggle of his parents against poverty, his cousin's struggle, perhaps, to build a labor union."[1] But he spends his undergraduate years trying to write "Keatsian sonnets about English abbeys, which he had never seen, and nightingales he had never heard."

Like Cowley's hero, Shahn came to the conclusion that he was on the wrong track. "I had seen all the right pictures and read all the right books," he told John Morse in the 1940s. "But it still didn't add up to anything. 'Here I am,' I said to myself, 'thirty-two years old, the son of a carpenter. I like stories and people. The French School is not for me.' "[2] His feeling that he had to return to his American roots, and at least subordinate French influences to that American experience, held true for Abbott and Evans too.

Asked some years ago to sum up her photography, Abbott said, "I think my work is very American. In the first place, I am an American and deeply so. I lived away from this country for a while, which gave me a perspective, then I came back with a kind of nostalgic boom."[3] These sentiments echo those she had expressed almost a half century earlier in a letter to the director of the Museum of the City of New York, Hardinge Scholle, whose support she sought for her project photographing the city's architecture. Having just returned from Europe, she said, "I am overwhelmed by the importance of the American material, so often ignored by our native artists."[4]

Abbott felt the sensations that accompanied return more keenly than many others because she had been away longer and was giving up more to come home. In Paris, after having been a darkroom apprentice to Man Ray, she had become one of the city's most popular portrait photographers among artists and intellectuals. Not only did she leave behind a certain degree of success and bohemian celebrity, but she picked a very inauspicious moment for her repatriation, arriving in mid-1929, just as the stock market crash was about to occur.

Yet neither she nor the others who came back as the Depression began seem to have ever regretted their timing. On the contrary, the atmosphere of national crisis and change in the 1930s made possible a patriotism none could have felt in the 1920s. Having left America because they felt there was no place for them in its culture, many young artists looked upon the collapse of that culture — or, at any rate, of the economic system that supported it — as an opportunity to insert themselves into the society and at last exercise some influence. Looking back on the Depression thirty years later, Shahn claimed, "I felt completely in harmony with the times. . . . I don't think I've ever felt that way before or since."[5]

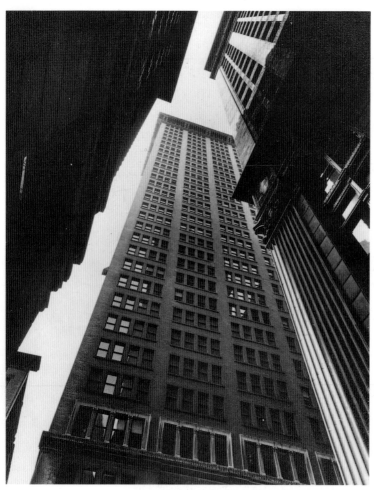

Fig. 14.1
BERENICE ABBOTT
*Canyon, Broadway
and Exchange Place,*
1936

chitecture, was along parallel lines, the WPA underwrote her work in the late thirties as well and provided the assistance of Lincoln Rothschild, the head researcher for the design index.

Cahill wanted American artists to create a "usable past"[6] out of their country's own history, and as part of his campaign he curated at the Modern in 1936 an exhibition on American design whose catalogue urged American painters to cast off French influences. Whether one was a painter or a photographer, the possibility of doing what Cahill urged had its limitations. The Impressionists and the School of Paris were facts of life that artists like Shahn could hardly deny. Behind Shahn's sense of line, and behind the effect that his photography had on that sense, lay Joan Miró and Picasso. Their influence was inescapable. But American artists, including the photographers, could try to naturalize such influences. They could temper them with American alternatives and apply them to uniquely American subjects.

A 1948 study that followed from the kind of work Brooks and Cahill were doing in the thirties was *Made in America,* by John Kouwenhoven, who was a friend of Walker Evans and shared Evans's passion for American architecture. While discussing Charles Sheeler's paintings of Pennsylvania barns, Kouwenhoven made an observation that could as easily refer to Evans, Shahn, Abbott, or any number of street photographers of the period: "Anyone who looks at his work will recognize that although the modes in which he paints have their chief source in France, in post-impressionism and Cubism, the forms which give character to his work are the product of the vernacular tradition."[7]

Shahn's sympathy with the America of the thirties and Abbott's pride in her native land upon her return reflected changes that were occurring everywhere in American intellectual and artistic life. By writing *The Flowering of New England* (1936), for instance, Van Wyck Brooks, whose earlier work had often disparaged American culture, hoped to find a neglected past that could be transmitted as a heritage.

This was what Holger Cahill, the director of the WPA's Federal Art Project, also hoped to create. Cahill's favorite program under the aegis of the project was the Index of American Design, a collective effort to record and catalogue the history of the decorative arts in America. This effort was being carried out primarily with the aid of drawings, watercolors, and other nonphotographic rendering. Yet because the proposal that Abbott submitted to the Museum of the City, an index of urban ar-

How completely Abbott recovered her American enthusiasms upon her return to New York can be seen from some photographs she began taking as soon as she landed. Using a little Kurt-Benzin camera with a 6.5 x 9cm negative that she had bought just before her

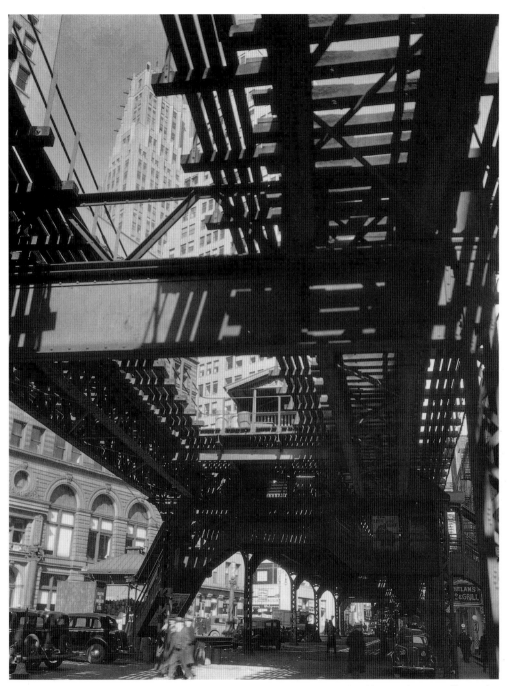

Fig. 14.2
BERENICE ABBOTT
El, Second and Third
Avenue Lines, 1936

departure from France, she wandered the streets looking up at the skyscrapers not like the fashionable photographer she was, an artist returning after nearly a decade's residence in Paris, but as if she were still a girl arriving for the first time from the midwest. The flush of excitement she felt is captured in these pictures by the point of view, which is intensely subjective. We see in it the visitor on whom New York has a dizzying effect, the tourist who, overawed by the scale of the city,

gawks at its tall buildings. She actually made up these snapshots into an album, although not the kind that the tourist keeps as a memento. Hers functioned more as a notebook of rough drafts for the photography she was to do in New York during the following decade (pages 214–215).

In the quotation with which the previous chapter closed, James Agee differentiated the beauties of an Atget or Evans photograph from those found in one by Cartier-Bresson or Levitt. Agee didn't point it out, but the distinction he was making was between the view camera and the hand camera. The difference was significant, especially in America, where Abbott and Evans both extended the view camera's tradition into the 1930s. In Europe, no important street photographer used these large formats once the 35mm was established. The example of Cartier-Bresson and the other photojournalists was overwhelming. But in this country, Evans and Abbott provided an alternative precedent. In fact, the latter used the view camera exclusively for the New York photographs that made her American reputation.

The later versions Abbott did in the larger format recapture the intensity of those first, awestruck impressions of New York, but they also add, besides the gain in image quality we would expect from the increased negative size, a new emotional dimension. The second time around she used the view camera's "swings,"[8] as she called them — the adjustable height and rotation of the front relative to the back — to align all the jutting angles that one sees looking up from the street. Now the ledges and overhangs on the skyscrapers lining Exchange Place neatly interlocked in air (fig. 14.1). The result was that the burst of enthusiasm seen in the small contact prints in the album turned into a more complicated response. Gawking gave way to contemplation. The fervor in the original pictures is still there in the acute angles with which these new views were made; but now a great equanimity is there as well. Meticulous composition becomes a form of composure in the photograph.

The strategy of those pictures that look up at tall buildings or down from on top of them is also to be found in pictures made at street level. One done under an elevated train line, for instance, relies on the same sort of jutting angles and Expressionist graphics (fig. 14.2). The tangle of lines overhead is what imparts a feeling of activity more than the people and traffic, which fill only at the last minute the

nooks and crannies Abbott has left vacant for them in an already busy scene.

This photograph gives a fair idea of the ingenuity with which she was able to solve a problem that plagued her throughout her career. The competition of 35mm imagery put on latter-day view-camera photographers like her a pressure that Atget did not feel. Abbott was always anxious about animating her pictures, stopping action and getting greater depth of field. She complained often about the failure of the manufacturers to supply cameras and films that would give her the range she craved. Yet basically she coped with the problem exactly as Atget, or Hine, had had to. In an article written for *Art Front* magazine in 1936, she praised Atget because he "worked within the limits of his machinery, transmuting these very limitations into positive esthetic virtues."[9] In essence, this is what she did as well.

If Atget had an American counterpart in her affections, it was Lewis Hine. She saw each man as the embodiment of the vernacular tradition in his own country. Her friend Elizabeth McCausland, a critic who had, like Abbott, become aware of Hine through a Beaumont Newhall article, wrote several articles of her own about the older photographer, and in 1938 she helped organize a retrospective of his work at the Riverside Museum. Abbott had used as a portrait camera a Graflex like Hine's, bought in Paris with money borrowed from Peggy Guggenheim. But as a street photographer she was more concerned with architecture than the human subject Hine had emphasized, so she often sacrificed foreground focus to get the background. Technically this was just a reversal of Hine's way of working. Aesthetically it was more radical. It defied the commonsense conventions of photographs to which viewers were accustomed.

In an article about the view camera written for a Graflex handbook, Abbott said that a slight distortion due to the camera's inability to stop motion is "not disturbing."[10] But this under-

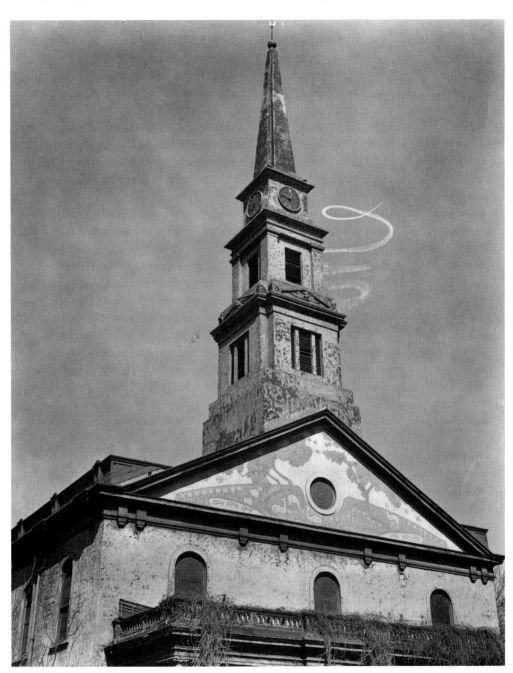

Fig. 14.3
BERENICE ABBOTT
St. Mark's Church with Skywriting, 1937

states the case made by the pictures themselves. The way that she used such effects, they *are* disturbing. That is their intention. Much of the material Abbott published in the book *Changing New York* suggests that she not only tolerated unfocused figures or forms in the foreground but actually went out of her way to include them.

Although the older buildings that might soon be torn down were the ones Abbott expressly set out to document, the distinction of her

photography comes from her eye for the modern. She saw in the relationship between the old structures and the new in New York a unique photographics that her sojourn in Paris had prepared her to recognize. What she responded to when she came home was, as she herself put it, "a new urgency here, for better or worse. America had new needs and new results. There was poetry in our crazy gadgets, our tools, our architecture."[11] She could see in the landscape of old and new together the jerky visual rhythms and reordered space that were to be found in the Modernist work of the artists who were her portrait clients in Paris. The peculiarity of unfocused foregrounds against focused backgrounds was a way to incorporate this into the style of her pictures. It formalized the off-balance quality of the city itself.

Another supposed disadvantage of the view camera — its inversion of the image on the ground-glass back — also encouraged Abbott to experiment in a distinctly modern way. As she explained in her essay about view cameras, "With the image inverted we can compose 'abstractly,' in a sense that the distribution of lines of light and shade in the composition are seen fully. . . . [W]e can, for the time being, forget the subject and think of its design." [12]

Like the limitations of view cameras, the documentation of New York's architecture served for Abbott as a boundary against which she could push. It was a project to which she gave as loose and speculative an interpretation as she did the principles of photography she outlined in her article. This was why it would occur to her, as it did one day in 1937, to photograph a wispy squiggle of skywriting she happened to see drifting out from behind an eighteenth-century steeple (fig. 14.3). While fulfilling her commission from the Museum of the City of New York to document the city, the content of this picture is also something purely figurative. The skywriting is a queer, ingenious conceit for modernity, an abstract notation. Taking a photograph of it was a way of tossing off an epigram on the subject of the modern.

Abbott wasn't the only photographer documenting the city's architecture in the thirties. A man named P. L. Sperr, for instance, was paid a nickel a shot by the New York Public Library for as many pictures of city street addresses as he could take. He took forty thousand. While Abbott never had to stoop to such drudge work herself, she did, unfortunately, sink into a penury close to Sperr's after *Changing New York* was finished. Ap-

proached in the early 1960s about a pictorial history of Wall Street, she agreed to make pictures for ten dollars apiece. When a project on which she had spent her energy did finally come out as a book, such as *Greenwich Village Today and Yesterday* (1949), the result was disappointing. And other projects for which she had higher hopes, like her 1950s documentation of U.S. Highway 1 from Maine to Florida, were never published at all.

The parallel between her own estate and Atget's, for which she had assumed responsibility, could hardly have been lost on her. He too had gone unrecognized as an artist in his own lifetime and continued to be so, she felt, in spite of her efforts on his behalf. Having encountered him in Paris at the end of his life, she had carried his influence back to America with her, after he died, not just as a vision preserved in memory, but physically, in twenty packing cases containing more than fifteen hundred of his negatives and eight thousand prints. This was a Promethean gesture for which she suffered accordingly.

She had come into possession of his archive because his actor friend André Calmette, who had inherited it, didn't really want it. Nor did the French government. In fact, her Atget material would not find a permanent home until the Modern acquired it in the 1960s. Despite a book of his work that she did with publisher Henri Jonquieres in Paris and bookseller Erhard Weyhe in New York, and an exhibition of her holdings at Julien Levy's gallery, by the mid-1930s she felt as if she had failed to get Atget the recognition he deserved. In her 1936 article for *Art Front,* Abbott lamented, "One cannot say of Atget that his work has influenced contemporary photography to any great extent. His work was barely known when he died a decade ago; it is little known now, unfortunately." [13]

But perhaps Abbott wasn't able to appreciate the effectiveness of her own efforts on Atget's behalf. One thing she wasn't taking into account was the importance of her own career, which had been decisively shaped by her exposure to his work. When she had first seen that work, about a decade before she wrote this glum appraisal of his impact, she had been a portrait photographer with no thought of undertaking documentary projects. By the time that the Museum of the City gave her a preliminary exhibition of her New York material in 1934, her ambitions as a photographer were so altered that she could truthfully tell an interviewer from the *New York Sun,* "What Atget did for Paris I want to do for New York." [14]

Nor was she the only photographer whose sense of the medium's possibilities had been transformed by her own attempts to disseminate Atget's influence. His name is one of the three, along with Cartier-Bresson's and Hine's, that crop up everywhere in the reminiscences of American street photographers of the 1930s. A comment made by FSA staffer Theo Jung is typical. When he saw the 1931 show at Julien Levy's gallery, Jung recalled later, "this tremendous group of photographs of the city of Paris . . . turned me over toward that kind of picture." Visiting Europe shortly thereafter, he tried "taking pictures of Vienna . . . after the manner of Atget." [15] Many photographers who saw Atget's work as a result of Abbott's efforts took pictures after his manner. None succeeded quite so magnificently, though, as Walker Evans.

It's possible that early exposure to Atget was not the only way in which Evans and Abbott benefited, more than either ever acknowledged, from knowing each other in the early thirties. They had a lot in common, after all. Both were from the midwest, had been expatriates in Paris during the twenties, and had then returned to New York. After Evans came back in 1927, he took up photography and was soon doing architectural studies just as Abbott would after her return two years later. There are even a couple of instances in which they photographed the same subjects: a doorway on West Thirteenth Street and a house in the Columbia Heights section of Brooklyn. Both subjects reflect an interest the two young photographers shared in period architecture,

and by the early thirties each had a commission that made it possible to pursue this interest outside New York.

Abbott actually made two trips of this kind, both sponsored by Professor Henry-Russell Hitchcock, Jr. The first was to photograph what Hitchcock called, in the title of a 1934 exhibition at Yale, the "urban vernacular" of

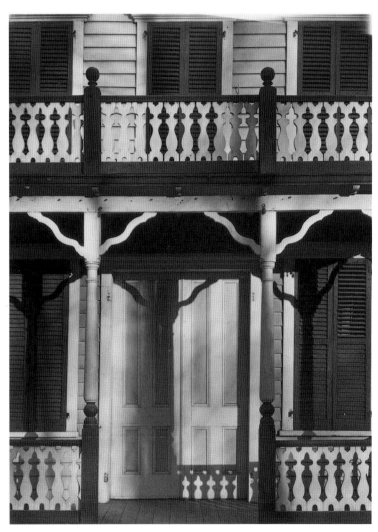

Fig. 14.4
WALKER EVANS
Detail of a Frame House in Ossining, New York, 1931

the antebellum south. The second was for a study of New England houses designed by Henry Hobson Richardson. Evans also made a trip to New England that resulted, like Abbott's, in an exhibition at the Modern. And he too had a sponsor: Lincoln Kirstein, recently graduated from Harvard, who accompanied him as Hitchcock did Abbott. "These houses were found," Kirstein explained in a bulletin issued by the Modern about Evans's trip, "by searching in an automobile with the photographic equipment in the rumble, wherever Evans chanced to be for a sufficient length of time."[16] This is precisely how Abbott explored New York as well, in a Ford roadster with her equipment in the rumble seat.

Some of the parallels between Abbott's career and Evans's during this period were just coincidences, including the overlap in the subject matter of certain pictures. Their photographs of the house in Columbia Heights were actually taken years apart, as were those of the doorway. But similarities in the styles of the pictures and the kind of subjects that caught their eye were not coincidental. They had a common source in Atget. This is especially noticeable where the rendering of shadows is concerned.

In the work of all three, shadow has an architectonics all its own, one that overlays, and sometimes preempts, the pattern made by the buildings themselves. It's clear from the photographs of both Abbott and Evans that they often studied the designs that the shadows of trees or other buildings cast upon whatever building was their subject. Each waited until the shadows were in some stark contrast with the building. The shadows contend against the architecture, nearly obliterating it at times. Both photographers used shadow the way Abbott used selective focus and motion blur, as a subordinate element that could virtually steal the picture from the ostensible subject.

In Evans's pictures made with Kirstein, above all, the hand of Atget can be seen in the sensitivity to shadow. Kirstein himself spoke of how the "brilliant sunlight" on which Evans insisted for his pictures made it seem as if the "houses . . . exist in an airless atmosphere."[17] This was a result of the photographs' having been shot in the clarity of cold weather, when the leaves were off the trees and the sun low in the afternoon sky. Working in the horizontal light of this season was a way of courting shadows, which sometimes fall across the facades of the houses in

Evans's photographs like a pall. They weigh down the houses with a somberness seen, outside of these photographs, only in Atget's. It is as if the gnarled, arthritic limbs of the trees in Atget's pictures were casting their shadows on Evans's.

Like Atget's treks through the suburbs of Paris, those that Evans took around New England eventually arrived at a destination. What Atget found at Sceaux, or in remote, neglected corners of the grounds at Versailles, Evans found in Ossining, New York, when he came upon a group of Victorian summer homes closed up for the winter. The houses are shuttered and banded around by keen shadows of jigsaw Gothic trim hanging under their eaves. The shadow of a porch post bars a door (fig. 14.4). Kirstein compared the "airless atmosphere" of Evans's photographs with the "airless nostalgia" of Edward Hopper's paintings,[18] and it's a good description. There's a feeling of suffocation in both, as there sometimes is in Atget's work. The images of quietness and abandonment Evans made here, and again later in the ruins of Mississippi or Louisiana plantations, take on the kind of desolate power Atget's work has at its best.

In a 1931 issue of *Hound and Horn,* the journal founded by Kirstein when he was still an undergraduate at Harvard, one of six photography books discussed in a review by Evans had been Abbott's Atget book. Evans had praised in Atget's work "a poetry which is not 'the poetry of the street' or 'the poetry of Paris,' but the projection of Atget's person."[19] The attribution of a personal style to a documentary photographer was a novel claim to have made at the time. But Evans had already been thinking about Atget's work for a couple of years, for James Stern, who was later Evans's friend and colleague at *Time* magazine, remembered having originally met him one evening in 1929 at Abbott's apartment in the Hotel des Artistes, in New York. The occasion was a private showing of some of the Atget material Abbott had just brought back from France.

In spite of the obvious debt he owed to Atget, Evans afterward claimed that he was unaware of the aged Parisian's work "until I had been going for quite a while," as he told some undergraduates at Harvard two days before he died.[20] The motive for such denial becomes clear later in his remarks when he admitted that, once he had discovered Atget's work, "I was quite electrified and alarmed." He explained,

> *Every artist who feels he has a style is a little wary automatically of strong work in view. I suppose we are all a little insecure. I don't like to look at too much of Atget's work because I am too close to that in style myself. . . . It's a little residue of insecurity and fear of such magnificent strength and style there. If it happens to border on yours, it makes you wonder how original you are.[21]*

Cartier-Bresson's greatness made Evans nervous too, and for the same reason.

Virtually the only formative experiences Evans would admit to were those with photographers he didn't like, such as Stieglitz, or at least didn't feel threatened by, such as Ralph Steiner. The painter Stefan Hirsch, who gave Evans early encouragement, knew Stieglitz and offered Evans an introduction in 1929. But when Evans visited An American Place, Stieglitz's gallery, the older photographer made only perfunctory comments on his work before sending him away. "I was stimulated by Stieglitz," Evans remembered in later years. "I found him somebody to work against. He was artistic and romantic. It gave me an esthetic to sharpen my own against — a counter-esthetic."[22]

A photograph first published in Stieglitz's magazine *Camera Work* — *Blind Woman*, by Paul Strand (fig. 5.3) — provided a rare instance of an image Evans actually acknowledged as a positive influence. "I said that's the thing to do," Evans admitted. "That really charged me up."[23] And the early photographs of Evans's contemporary Ralph Steiner, who would later become a protégé of Strand's,

were another example of an influence that Evans was willing to own up to.

Working with a small hand camera in the early twenties, Steiner shot a number of subjects that also show up in Evans's early work: billboards, posters peeling off walls, refuse in a vacant lot. Steiner's most original work, though, was a series of whimsical pictures taken from great heights. These are of tiny, lonely figures in a vast, empty landscape of a street, sidewalk, or beach (fig. 14.5). They approach street photography with a wry sense of humor less flamboyant than Cartier-Bresson's and very like Evans's. While Evans never made pictures quite like them, he did try shooting down from above the street occasionally during his first few years as a photographer.

Outside of a few minor or purely negative influences like these, Evans felt that his photography developed by instinct and without specific models. "About 1928 and 1929, I had a few prescient flashes in the street and they led me on," he told an interviewer in 1971. "I found I wanted to get a type in the street, a 'snapshot' of a fellow on the waterfront, or a stenographer at lunch. That was a very good vein. I still work that vein."[24] The key to Evans's own sense of his development is in the phrase "prescient flashes." On another occasion he said,

> *As a matter of fact, I really think I was on the right track right away. And I don't think I've made very many false moves. I now feel almost mystical about it. I think something was guiding me. I really do. I feel that I was doing better than I knew how, that it was almost fate. I really was inventing something, but I didn't know it. . . . I was working by instinct but with a sense — not too clear, but a firm sense — that I was . . . doing something valuable and also pioneering artistically and aesthetically. I just knew it.[25]*

These remarks are suggestive because Evans spoke of the very act of photographing, the moment when one pushed the shutter release, in a way that makes it sound much the same. "I work rather blindly," he explained. "I have a theory that seems to work with me that some of the best things you ever do sort of come through you. You don't know where you

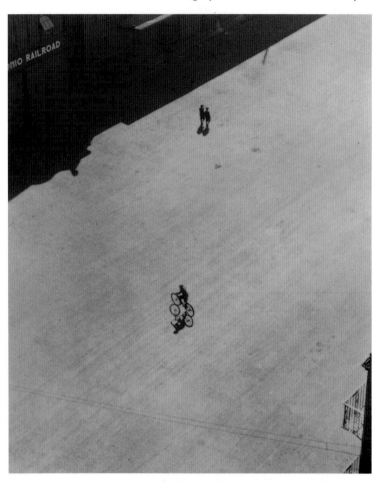

Fig. 14.5
RALPH STEINER
Untitled, 1920s

get the impetus and response to what is before your eyes." [26] It's as if taking pictures were the whole process of the photographer's development in microcosm.

This was how he imagined Atget and Cartier-Bresson to have worked as well. The latter was someone who "has always been a kind of spirit medium: poetry sometimes speaks through his camera." [27] The former too "was a kind of medium. . . . His work sang like lightning through him. He could infuse the street with his own poetry, and I don't think he was even aware of it." [28] The spirit that spoke through the medium of Evans's own camera was the spirit of the times in which he lived. If he sometimes tried to pretend that the oppo-

site was true, that his work was all sui generis, this was only because he knew the variety of sources on which his work drew well enough to be anxious about them.

More than other arts, photography is by nature a medium of contemporary reality. In the pictures of a great photographer, the impression that his culture has made upon his sensibility shows up like light on a negative. For Evans this culture was not only the photographic one of Atget and Cartier-Bresson, but the culture of the thirties in general and of twentieth-century literature and painting as well as photography.

When asked why he took up photography, Evans once said, "I think it came from painters. Several of my friends were painters. And I had a visual education that I had just given myself." [29] The education was obtained in Paris, where, unable to write as he had planned, he spent a good deal of time looking at the new painting. "The School of Paris was so incandescent then," he recalled, "a revolutionary-eye education." [30] It was not only the example of Picasso and Braque that showed Evans the way but, as he himself admitted, his friends back in America, such as Stefan Hirsch, who were also painters.

Like Charles Sheeler, Hirsch was a member of the Precisionist movement, which, although strongly influenced by Cubism, tended to tone down its innovations for an American audience not yet ready to abandon a recognizable world. By veiling new concepts of space with old conventions of seeing, finding in the vagaries of shadow or the ready-made compositions of architecture a naturalistic pretext for abstraction, painters such as Hirsch edged toward the radical aesthetics of their French contemporaries. Evans realized that the strategy this American painting employed, its tempering of abstract vision with realism, could be worked the other way around too. The reality with which the street photographer always begins and from which he can never escape might, nonetheless, be tempered with abstract vision.

There were a few prescient individuals in America, besides the artists themselves, who recognized early on the importance of the changes taking place in the arts in Europe. One of these, perhaps the key one, was Evans's friend Lincoln Kirstein. The Harvard Society for Contemporary Art, which Kirstein cofounded with two other undergraduates in 1928, was the forerunner of the Modern, whose first director, Alfred Barr, wrote articles for Kirstein's *Hound and Horn*. Known later primarily as an impresario of the ballet, Kirstein was actually, like Sergey Diaghilev in Russia, instrumental in modernizing all the arts in his native country and in importing from abroad the most influential new ideas. Kirstein's "articulation of all esthetic matters and their contemporary application . . . ," Evans remarked later, "was immensely helpful and hilariously audacious. Professor Kirstein." [31]

Having gone to Paris to become a writer, Evans could share his frustrated passion for literature with Kirstein, whose *Hound and Horn* had published future literary lions like R. P. Blackmur, Yvor Winters, and Allen Tate. These were the founders of the New Criticism, who championed the sort of young poets Evans liked. "But just look who was publishing then," he exclaimed, referring to his years at Williams College in the early twenties. "That's who I was reading. . . . T. S. Eliot was just coming up. . . . I was right there. I pride myself on that." [32] Thus was Evans able to appreciate Hart Crane's *The Bridge* sufficiently to provide the first edition, published in 1930 by the Black Sun Press, with photographic illustrations worthy of the poem's text.

The fact is that the imagery in Crane's poem abounds with a kind of verbal street photography whose subject is often, as at the beginning of the section entitled "The River," the same found in Evans's work:

> Stick your patent name on a signboard
> brother — all over — going west — young
> man

*Tintex — Japalac — Certain-teed Overalls
ads
and land sakes! under the new playbill
ripped
in the guaranteed corner — see Bert
Williams what?* [33]

The profusion of signs struck Crane's fancy just as it did Evans's or Shahn's or Ralph Steiner's. Crane shared their eye for the poster that was ripped or peeling. And like the real brand names read off the advertisements, the direct address "brother" and the exclamation "land sakes!" are picked out of conversations overheard as the reader passes along the sidewalk. The elliptical, interrupted style of the poetry gives the impression of language transcribed right from the street itself. Such language does in fact appear as direct quotation in another section of the poem, entitled "The Tunnel."

Nor was Crane alone among modern poets in his need to scavenge his imagery from the city streets. Eliot had also incorporated snatches of conversation into *The Waste Land*, the poem Evans would have been reading in 1923 if he was, as he said, keeping up-to-date. (In fact, Evans used a line of this sort from Eliot's poem — " 'Hurry up please, it's time' " — as a caption for a photograph included in a sequence he published in 1930 [page 16]).[34] Eliot poeticized American themes by going to Europe; Crane mythologized America by letting European influences work on him at home. The two poets served as landfalls on opposite sides of the Atlantic, first beacons by which someone making the cultural voyage to Europe and back could get his bearings. When a street photograph puts side by side in the frame gestures or actions that are otherwise unrelated, it is only doing what both Crane and Eliot did with overheard language.

Like the photograph, the quotations from the street in "The Tunnel" section of Crane's poem give the sensation of a chance encounter with reality, yet have the secret order and intended meaning of art. The language of the poem becomes what Evans once said photographs are: "symbolic actuality."[35] "The Tunnel" takes us on a subway ride during which we catch a sentence here and there of the conversations going on around us. Some years later Evans would take his camera down into the New York subways to catch the expressions on people's faces the same way.

Evans felt that photography was "the most literary of the graphic arts,"[36] and his own rise to prominence as a photographer was marked by two literary milestones, Crane's *The Bridge* (1930) and James Agee's *Let Us Now Praise Famous Men* (1941). These works framed Evans's career during the thirties. From his first reproductions in the Black Sun edition of Crane's poem, Evans's reputation advanced steadily; those published with Agee's book were to become the best-known photographs he ever took. His connection with these literary works grew out of his personal relationship with their authors. Evans got to know both men by chance, simply because he lived in the same neighborhood as they — first in Columbia Heights, where Crane rented a room to try to finish his poem, and then a year later in Greenwich Village, where Agee lived after coming down from Harvard.

It's hard to see, on a personal basis, why Evans got along with either man. Their personalities couldn't have been more contrary to his. He may have hit it off with Crane because they had both repudiated the businessman values of their prosperous midwestern fathers, who had been acquaintances in Ohio. Evans got to know Agee, he once explained, "because everybody in Greenwich Village who was serious seemed to know each other in those days." Agee had seen and liked Evans's photography. As Evans recalled, "He . . . talked to me all night every night about [my work]. He was very hard to leave. I used to walk him home. And then he would walk me back home again. And we'd talk all night. He was a great talker,

of course. Indefatigable. He had much more physical energy than I had. I couldn't outlast him."[37]

Crane and Agee were really men of the same type, a literary type very unlike Evans. They were compulsive, loquacious, doomed men who were using themselves up, burning themselves out, at a great rate. Although he could see their genius behind the dissipation and bluster, he himself tended to be introverted, composed, reticent, even taciturn — in short, everything Crane and Agee weren't. One of Evans's favorite words was "oxymoron," a literary term that denotes the combining of contradictory qualities, as in the phrase "deafening silence." He obviously enjoyed this type of dialectic in his personal relationships as much as in art.

In Agee even more than Crane, Evans found someone who confirmed and fed his ideas about art. It's easy to believe that Agee wanted to stay up nights discussing photography. *Let Us Now Praise Famous Men* reflects his enthusiasm. It also suggests that he was articulating the properties of photography for Evans as he later would for Helen Levitt. In order "to represent, to reproduce, a certain city street . . . ," Agee wrote late in the book, "nothing is as important, as sublime, as truly poetic about that street in its flotation upon time and space as the street itself. My medium, unfortunately, is not a still or moving camera, but is words."[38] He was returning here to thoughts he had had at the very beginning of the book, when he was trying to state his aesthetic credo. It was that

in the immediate world, everything is to be discerned . . . with the whole of consciousness, seeking to perceive it as it stands: so that the aspect of a street in sunlight can roar in the heart of itself as a symphony, perhaps as no symphony can: and all of consciousness is shifted from the imagined, the revisive, to the effort to perceive simply the cruel radiance of what is.

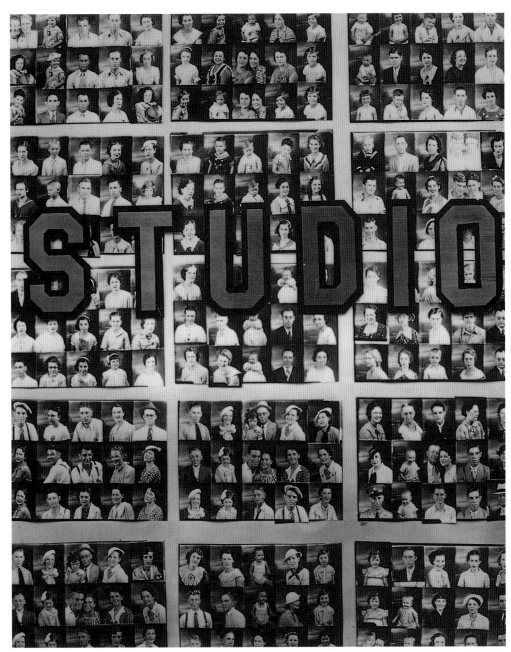

Fig. 14.6
WALKER EVANS
Penny Picture
Display, Savannah,
1936

This is why the camera seems to me, next to unassisted and weaponless consciousness, the central instrument of our time.[39]

In the decade after his collaboration with Agee, Evans's street photography acquired a new sophistication. It became expressive of a new range of emotions to which street photography had scarcely had access before. Agee's influence had much to do with this change. Like Kirstein, Agee helped Evans understand what he was doing.

Agee's guidance came not so much from anything he said about photography, but from his own style as an artist and the advance that that style made on the writing Evans already admired. Agee observed at one point that "one can write only one word at a time . . . lists and inventories merely."[40] At heart his own style is an attempt to reduce writing to a listing process.

Behind the incredible profusion of words in Agee's writing — the sentences that stretch out to a paragraph in length, the endless appositives, the constant use of colons to throw emphasis forward, to build the wave of thought ever higher without letting it break — there is a desire for a kind of austerity. Agee wanted to free his language from rhetoric. Beginning a sentence as if he were Henry James, he would put so much pressure on the Jamesian conventions of prose that all the structure would be squeezed out of them by the sentence's end. The reader is left with mere words, a list. *Let Us Now Praise Famous Men* ends with the section "Notes and Addenda," which is not really addenda at all, but a fitting conclusion to the whole book. In it almost all need to order language is eliminated. The language breaks free of even elementary grammar, turning into a series of nouns lasting two pages and including a passage that begins "shot, pic, pix, angle, contact, leica, candid" and ends "surrealism, photography, photographer, documentary."[41]

For Evans the word "documentary" had a special connotation akin to Agee's experiments with prose. In his interview with Paul Cummings for the Archives of American Art, Evans spoke of having "established the documentary style as art in photography." Then he elaborated, "It's a very important matter. I use the word 'style' particularly because in talking about it many people say 'documentary photograph.' Well, literally a documentary photograph is a police report on a dead body or an automobile accident or something like that. But the style of detachment and record is another matter. That applied to the world around us is what I do with the camera."[42] Evans disowned the documentary photograph per se because it is made out of indifference, without any feeling for the subject. A picture like this is an inhuman object. But when the same type of photograph is made for the opposite reason — in the presence of strong feeling — indifference is transformed into impassivity. It becomes the kind of stoicism seen in Atget's work, a self-restraint that accords dignity to the subject. It gives form to compassion.

Practiced consciously like this, documentation becomes a style, an aesthetic that is at the same time an ethic. Yet behind it the photograph of the dead body or the automobile accident remains, the germ from which it grew. The purpose of such a photograph is to be an itemization, a list of details, a standard article that is itself one item among many. And in Evans's documentary style, that purpose is preserved.

The first two pictures in *American Photographs*, the Evans catalogue published by the Modern in 1938, establish the documentary photograph as the basis for the style of the book that follows. The first picture, *License Photo Studio*, is of the entrance to a street-corner shop. The little identity-card image made there is a variation on the photo document in the police report. On the front of the studio between the words "Photos" and "Applications" are painted two hands that point into a darkened doorway. Through that door, implicitly, lies the rest of the book; and when you turn the page, the second photograph is of a penny picture display that Evans found in the window of a Savannah portrait studio (fig. 14.6).

The row upon row of tiny photographs here — more than two hundred of them, almost all shot against the same background — is another itemization. It's an inventory of people. Of that second photograph Evans said,

> An instinct is touched in it. "This is for me." It's like the meaning of a person. . . . It's uproariously funny, and very touching and very sad and very human. Documentary, very real, very complex. All these people had posed in front of the local studio camera, and I bring my camera, and they all pose again together for me. That's a fabulous fact. I look at it and think, and think, and think about all those people.[43]

The repetitions of "think" suggest a thought for each of the people in his photograph. None lost his individuality for Evans. This list of people functions for him as lists of articles of tenant-farmer clothing do for Agee, or as overheard snatches of conversation for Hart Crane. Making lists or quoting conver-

in Agee's, there are moments when language reduces itself to a kind of listing process, moments in the novels when emotion boils down the already simple, declarative prose until

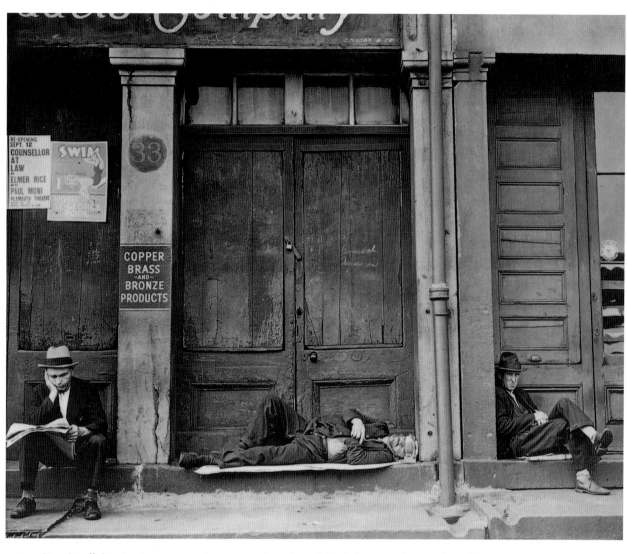

Fig. 14.7
WALKER EVANS
South Street, New York,
1932

sation directly off the street was a way to get right at reality, without mitigation, as photographs can.

Before Evans came to Crane or Agee, or even to photography itself, he had already been predisposed to think of art in documentary terms by the literature he was reading in Paris. He had admired Ernest Hemingway, for instance, but not Scott Fitzgerald. When talking about Hemingway he used the same phrase — "established a style" — that he used for himself.[44] In Hemingway's writing, as

there is nothing left except the naming of names of certain places or people.

Back of Hemingway, Crane, Agee, and everyone else in Evans's pantheon was Gustave Flaubert. "Flaubert's aesthetic is absolutely mine," Evans declared: "Flaubert's method I think I incorporated almost unconsciously, but anyway used it in two ways: his realism and his naturalism both, and his objectivity of treatment; the non-appearance of the author, the non-subjectivity."[45] As John Szarkowski has pointed out, Evans believed completely in

Flaubert's dictum that "art must rise above personal emotions and nervous susceptibilities. It is time to endow it with pitiless method."[46] That is the quality with which Evans endowed photography.

If the unsentimental education Evans gave himself when he was in his twenties began with his discovery at Williams of the most advanced modern poetry, it ended with his 1934 commission from the Modern to photograph the exhibition "African Negro Art." This was a routine assignment that any competent professional could have done; yet the very restrictions the task imposed made it a clarifying experience for Evans. In his documentation of these objects — primitive masks and sculptures confronted one at a time against a neutral, invariable background and in invariable light — he was making his own penny portraits.

The advantage of the method Evans used to document these African pieces he later explained in a proposal to the Metropolitan Museum to give one hundred objects in its collection a similar photographic treatment. He wished to record them, he said, "in such a way that all atmosphere of scholarship, art history, aesthetic theory and analysis; cultural explanation and academic tabulation . . . is absent; so that the pictures are presented solely for the excitement and surprise these things carry in themselves."[47] Depicted in this reductivist manner, and thereby rendered anonymous like the rows of portraits in the studio window later, the African art at the Modern demands a purely human, uncultivated response. While making these photographs, Evans discovered in their subjects a power of imagery that lay beyond the reach of mere art. Here, in the limitations of his assignment, was the "pitiless method" he was looking for.

In 1933, Evans acquired an 8 x 10" view camera, a format with which he had experimented only tentatively earlier. From the six-dollar box camera with which he had taken the pictures of the Brooklyn Bridge published in Crane's volume, he had advanced to a 35mm with adjustable focus, then to two view cameras with small formats — 5 x 7" and 6 x 8" — in 1930. By the time he was ready for the 8 x 10", he was also ready to leave all merely formative experiences behind and get on with his own major work. He himself summed up the process by saying, "When you are young you are open to influences, and you go to them, you go to museums. Then the street becomes your museum; the museum itself is bad for you. You don't want your work to spring from art; you want it to commence from life, and that's in the street now."[48]

This survey of American street photography in the 1930s began in chapter 13, "Collective Vision," by noticing in a picture of Evans's a wit like Cartier-Bresson's. Like a Cartier-Bresson photograph, Evans's picture of the woman wearing a zebra-stripe blouse and standing in a barbershop door relies on a certain formalism (page 22). An amusing, rather touching visual correspondence is being pointed out. The picture has the same gentle irony that Cartier-Bresson's pictures have. But many Evans photographs have neither the formalism nor the gentleness of this one. Other emotions enter in, reducing formal control, creating a less affable mood. Evans didn't always share Cartier-Bresson's love of life. He had more mixed feelings, and consequently his photographs are a more mixed bag. Like the cameras he used, the emotions his pictures display have a wide variety. In fact, the range of equipment was necessary to cover the vacillations of feeling.

The opening section in American Photographs ends with a sequence of three pictures, the first two of which were made at the same time and place, on South Street, in New York. In the first, three derelicts lounge in three adjacent doorways, and the triptych structure gives a certain detachment to the observation the picture makes (fig. 14.7). But in the next picture, Evans moves in on the central figure alone. Without the graphics or distance of the previous pictures, the seedy man unconscious

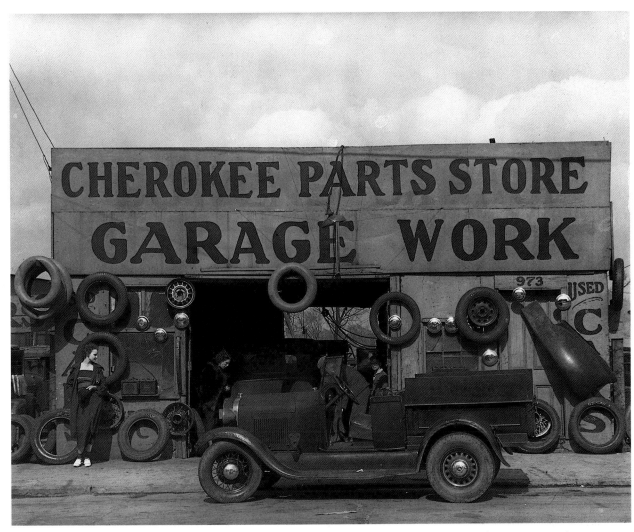

Fig. 14.8
WALKER EVANS
Garage, Atlanta, 1936

on the stoop becomes a brutal, inescapable image.

Cartier-Bresson was capable of a photograph of this sort, especially in America, as the very similar picture he took of a New York derelict shows. But such imagery is not typical of him, whereas it is found throughout Evans's work. Cartier-Bresson's photography contains the full array of human experience, but seldom any ugliness. Life is aesthetic, the way it is in a movie or a play. In Evans's photography the ugliness shows. He was capable of outright nastiness at times. A smear of food enters the mouth of a man at a lunch counter, emphasizing the grossness, the bestiality, of eating (page 16). An American Legionnaire glowers at the camera. A girl in a silly hat looks peevish and stupid. A woman on the street fluffs her hair nervously, self-consciously (page 224). The glove with which she does so — a

quilted gauntlet of sorts — gives the act a heavy, sinister quality.

In these pictures there is no formalism. Evans was taken purely with the gesture for its own sake, for what it betrayed about human nature. He was compiling a catalogue of human grotesqueries. If there is any wit in these pictures, it is of a dry, mordant kind. The only laughter we hear is sardonic, mirthless. Moreover, all four pictures are from 35mm negatives.

What seems to have mollified Evans, to have pulled him back from the brink of this misanthropy, was working with larger formats. Significantly, the picture of the woman in the barbershop door, so like Cartier-Bresson in spirit, was done with an 8 x 10" view camera. There is in this picture an affection for the homeliness in life that Evans might have treated more cruelly with a hand camera. This is what it shares with his other view-camera work. The formalism of that body of work is uniquely Evans's own. It is one that incorporates people as luckily as Cartier-Bresson's but is in intricacy nearer to Atget's. The pictures unroll before our eyes like a scroll containing many scenes.

For example, in an 8 x 10" picture of an auto parts store in Georgia (fig. 14.8), our perception has to move both from side to side and front to back at the same time — from the smartly dressed woman off to the left on the sidewalk in front to the boy illuminated through a square of windshield out back. The dynamics of this picture differ somewhat from those of the woman standing in the barbershop door. This image is slower and more complex. But both are fascinated with the gracelessness of the world.

This quality, which Evans's view-camera pictures all seem to have, is what his love of hand-painted signs and vernacular architecture was about as well. It comes across in the pictures almost as a fellow feeling, as if the cumbersomeness and intractability of the camera itself had taught Evans to respect those properties in the world at large. The 8 x 10" view camera is an instrument whose use instills a sense of life as struggle and compromise. Temperamentally less suited than Atget to such humility, Evans acquired it nonetheless with the help and instruction of Atget's own pictures. Evans's pictures have a stolidity akin to the world they depict. The camera stood flat-footed, braced against life.

Perhaps the picture in which the world mirrors Evans's own mental set most closely is a 4 x 5" he made at a Florida resort in 1941 (pages 236–237). In it another picture is being taken with another small view camera by a local professional who caters to the tourist trade. Evans was enjoying the ambiguity of the situation, the way that the other photographer's work became both a subject and an emblem of his own. The photographer's client, who is posed on a wall by the sea, is really more Evans's subject, since his camera has her attention. The props the other photographer uses — some fake, movie-set palm trees, cardboard pelicans, and a stuffed alligator — all betray the clumsiness of the illusion being created here. The client sits uncomfortably on the wall as the photographer crouches, knock-kneed, behind her camera. A gust of wind blows the hem of her skirt and reveals stockings rolled down around garters.

Many Evans pictures convey, like this one, an awareness that our illusions are hopelessly thin, that our efforts to create them are inadequate, pathetic, even laughable. Things don't work out. Yet these aren't pictures that just poke fun at their subjects. On the contrary, his pictures take a rather philosophical view. There is a fatalism in them, a pessimism tempered by humor. This is a sense of life acquired from modern literature. It is a vision, like modern painting's, sensitive to the passion in even the most ordinary activity, the most futile of gestures. It exacts beauty from the ungainliness of life.

If it is true that Evans's work was strongly affected by the influences around him in the thirties, it is no less true that he himself exerted a powerful influence over others. This too was part of his greatness. Muriel Draper, whose soirees Evans described as the closest thing to a French salon he encountered in New York, felt that Evans held extraordinary sway over the whole company of intellectuals and artists who came to her apartment. Certainly Evans's photography had a kind of magnetic effect on the FSA's staff, and particularly on Roy Stryker, who disseminated Evans's influence.

The staff photographer who felt that influence most profoundly, John Vachon, was the one with the most extensive knowledge of the FSA file. Vachon was the file clerk for several years before getting his own assignments. He himself said, "I was probably, more than any other photographer who ever worked there, imitative, because I had been so exposed to all these other photographers, and particularly

Walker Evans, who had a great influence on me. I went around looking for Walker Evans's pictures. . . . When I'd see the honest-to-God Walker Evans in reality, it was like a historic find." [49] Evans was the only colleague whom American street photographers of the thirties mentioned as an influence in the way they did Atget, Hine, or Cartier-Bresson.

What gave Evans this preeminence, at least at the FSA, was the effect he had on Stryker. His experience with Stryker was uncannily parallel to Hine's. Just as Stryker would not even hire Hine, because he judged him too hard to work with, so did he eventually get rid of Evans for the same reason. (Stryker used a budget cut as a pretext to fire Evans and later advised Edward Steichen against using him when Evans applied for Steichen's Naval Aviation Photographic Unit during World War II.) Like Hine too, Evans educated Stryker through his pictures. "They gave me the first evidence of what we could do," Stryker admitted in his memoir, *In This Proud Land.* [50] Stryker had originally had a more prosaic idea. He had been planning to get photographs of soil erosion, and generally the idea was, as Vachon recalled, to place pictures in Department of Agriculture publications of FSA "clients" who had received funds for "a new barn, or a mule, or something." [51]

Stryker himself explained, a bit vaguely, "Walker Evans's pictures, Ben Shahn's trip [to the mid-south in 1935], all those things began to come back and we began to see the need for doing this, doing that." [52] But the courage of whatever convictions Evans's small-town stuff inspired was lacking until a 1936 trip Stryker took to New York. There Stryker had established a little brain trust of his own that included *Middletown* author Robert Lynd and Ruth Goodhue, the managing editor of *Architectural Forum.* One of them convinced Stryker on this occasion that he should exceed the FSA mandate to make a real record of small-town America. The result was that he began to codify Evans's influence in the form of shooting scripts that he distributed to his staff. By the time he got back to

Washington on the train, he had written the first script. Its point was, in his own words, "Let's begin to cover the main street of America . . . just to see what the heck occurs on it." [53]

After that, if Vachon dutifully traveled with an FSA agent in the field, photographing him as he shook hands with clients in rural Iowa or Nebraska, the reward was a week on his own doing street photography in Omaha. Those were the kind of pictures that were picked up by national magazines, as Vachon's were by *Harper's* or as Russell Lee's of San Augustine, Texas, were by *Travel.*

Sent to San Augustine at the end of the thirties to do a report on an outbreak of hookworm, Lee turned the assignment into a classic study of life in a small town where the town square was still the center of activity. Taking such liberties with routine jobs was itself routine by then. As Jean Lee, who accompanied her husband on the San Augustine trip, explained, "There were some assignments that were continuing: things that made up small towns, signs, the Americana things, all of these were basic assignments that you kept on doing." [54] These were the things Evans had taught Stryker to look out for.

The impact that Evans's photography had on the culture at large can be seen from the recognition he got during his first decade as a photographer. When *Let Us Now Praise Famous Men* came out, Lionel Trilling began a piece on the book in the *Kenyon Review* by saying, "I feel sure that this is a great book." [55] What made it so, in his opinion, was Evans's photographs even more than Agee's text. The cultural establishment that Trilling represented didn't normally take any notice of photography, let alone praise it. Evans's 1938 exhibition at the Modern, besides being an exceptional event for that museum, also met with an exceptional response.

Reviewing *American Photographs* for the *New Republic,* poet William Carlos Williams compared Evans with Atget and said that in

Evans's photographs, "we see what we have not heretofore realized, ourselves made worthy in our anonymity." [56] Even Evans himself, who tended to be glum about any recognition he got, had to admit that the show and catalogue were a "landmark." "Lots of inventors, which is what a stylist is, don't get credit for their inventions," Evans told Paul Cummings. "In this case I did, luckily." [57] There is no better summary of the 1930s than Frederick Lewis Allen's *Since Yesterday,* which was published in 1939. Even at such close range, it was apparent to Allen that Evans was the decade's premier photographer.

Once the decade was over, however, something happened. Evans came to feel that, both for him personally and for the new photography he was pioneering, what had seemed promising beginnings just petered out. Disappointments that he suffered as a photographer during the 1940s left him somewhat embittered, with the consequence that that delicate balance between the merciful and the spiteful in his work was at times upset. To understand the effect on Evans of the setbacks he experienced then, it's helpful to look at an earlier moment in his career when it seemed that he was at a similar impasse.

In 1934, when he had first been ready to leave the museum for the street and throw himself into his own work, his greatest problem was that he as yet had no job with which to sustain such ambitions. He did have a well-connected friend named Ernestine Evans (no relation), who would soon pull strings to get him on staff at the FSA. But before she was able to do so, he wrote her an extraordinary letter while he was on a trip to Florida. Although never finished and mailed, probably because Evans himself realized that it was too angry an outburst, his draft gives us a glimpse of both the scope of his aspirations for his photography and the depth of the frustration he could feel about realizing them. The restiveness and resentments that first welled up here, dark feelings of a sort to which he was always vulnerable, were revived in him

when he found himself in parallel circumstances in the 1940s.

The letter inquires in passing about "Hopkins," a reference to Harry Hopkins, the chief administrator of the WPA, where Ernestine was also apparently trying to get Evans a position. But Evans's thoughts were really elsewhere, on books. "What do I want to do?" he asked rhetorically. "Where did the conversations with the publishers end? I know now is the time for picture books. An American city is best." He then went on to list the contents such a book would have and the cities he would use for his composite picture of urban America. The letter becomes a poison-pen version of the shooting scripts Stryker would do a few years later. "The right things can be found," Evans inveighed,

> in Pittsburgh, Toledo, Detroit (a lot in Detroit, I want to get in some dirty cracks, Detroit's full of chances) Chicago business stuff, probably nothing of New York but Philadelphia suburbs are smug and endless; . . .

> Architecture, American urban taste. Commerce, small scale, large scale. The city street atmosphere, the street smell. The hateful stuff — women's clubs, fake culture, bad education, religion in decay.

> The movies.

> Evidences of what the people of city read, eat, see for amusement, do for relaxation and not get it. [58]

The cities Evans ticked off echo a list that Lincoln Kirstein had made in the 1933 article for the Modern's bulletin concerning the Victorian-house study. At the end of the piece Kirstein observed that while Boston; Greenfield, Massachusetts; Saratoga Springs, New York, et al. had now been covered, "Detroit, Cleveland, Chicago, St. Louis and Philadelphia await the tender cruelty of Evans's camera." [59] "Tender cruelty" has an eloquence especially appropriate because the phrase is, of course, an oxymoron. Evans's favorite figure of speech is indispensable when trying to describe the conflicted feelings that his view-camera photographs entail. What makes his own list of cities in the 1934 letter striking is the loss of the tenderness — only the cruelty remains.

The truth is that even before the thirties were over, Evans began to suffer professional rebuffs that had a disheartening effect on him. The first, which came only a couple of years after he joined the FSA, was Stryker's effort to get rid of him in spite of all that Stryker had learned from his photographs. The trip to the south with Agee in 1936 was a stay of execution, made possible only because *Fortune* agreed to pick up Evans's salary during that period. From the vantage point of the early forties, even that project must have seemed a lost cause, like the south itself. *Fortune* ended up refusing the material; and when it finally appeared as *Let Us Now Praise Famous Men,* the book didn't do very well. Good reviews notwithstanding, it sold only about six hundred copies of its first edition.

Although Evans's 1934 letter asserts that "now is the time for picture books," the tone seems to anticipate the defeats he was to suffer trying to get such books published. A study of antebellum architecture in the south done on an earlier trip with Ben Shahn was never to be published. A maquette of seventy contact prints made in the late forties for a book to be called *Faulkner Country* appeared only as an article in *Vogue.* The book of photographs of works of art at the Metropolitan never saw the light of day either, nor did any of the picture books about American cities defiantly planned in the letter.

The book projects that did come to fruition, besides the Crane poem and the collaboration with Agee, seem to have left Evans with uncertain feelings. When he contributed thirty-one pictures to Carleton Beals's *Crime of Cuba,* a left-wing indictment of the Machado dictatorship, he was able to demand a separate section for his photography and perhaps even to control the sequencing. Candid portraits of dandies, prostitutes, and campesinos that he made for this project during a three-week trip to Cuba in 1933 are among his best early street photography; and his inclusion of three Cuban newspaper photographs of political detainees and assassination victims was a provocative aesthetic experiment. Yet because of the latter aspect of the book in particular, he spoke disparagingly of it afterward, claiming that he had never even read it.

In 1971 Evans said of the Cuba project, "It was a job . . . [at] a time when anyone would do anything for work."[60] Nearly a decade later, in the early 1940s, he was still stuck with the same sort of commission when he did the photography for Karl Bickel's 1942 book, *The Mangrove Coast.* And within another year after its publication, he had to take a job writing book reviews at *Time* because he could no longer support himself as a photographer. He wasn't able to get back to photography for his livelihood until the close of the war. At that point, probably through the good offices of a friend, *Fortune* editor Katherine Hamill, he got the job with *Fortune* that he was to keep for the next two decades.

His position was one that most photojournalists would have envied, for he reported over the heads of the art department directly to the managing editor, who gave him complete freedom. Evans was allowed to propose his own picture stories, then execute them at his leisure. Some of the projects he did at *Fortune* belong with his finest work in any period. Still, as the forties wore on into the fifties, he felt cut off and unappreciated as an artist.

At times Evans has been accused of being arrogant. If he was, his arrogance was the kind that exceptional talent develops as a defense against indifference. Despite the fact that he *did* have the sort of influence outlined earlier, he himself seems to have been unable to appreciate sometimes the importance his work was to have for the medium's history. Perhaps it was just his nature that he couldn't take the amount of satisfaction he might have from that work. Whatever their cause, these feelings of futility eventually took their toll on the photography itself.

By the time the war was over, the animosity heard in the 1934 letter was coming out again in his pictures, especially in a couple of series he did for *Fortune* in the late forties. Although the editors' selections softened the effects somewhat, "Labor Anonymous" (November 1946) and "Chicago: A Camera Exploration" (February 1947) take a rather hard-bitten view of mankind. Evans may even have derived a cynical pleasure at sneaking his misanthropy past his superiors at the magazine, for this only went to prove that people in general (and editors in particular) weren't sensitive to the implications of photographs.

The reason *Fortune* used these series was that each fitted the theme of the issue in which it appeared. Evans accommodated the magazine at least to the extent of attending the editorial meetings where future issues were planned. For both series Evans used the Rolleiflex, with its 2¼ x 2¼" format, which he had employed, along with the 35mm, for street portraits done five years earlier in

Fig. 14.9
WALKER EVANS
Detroit Street Portraits,
1946

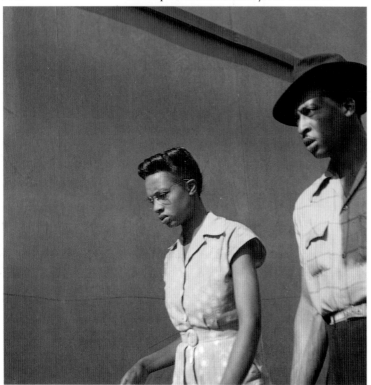

Bridgeport, Connecticut. Technically this format appealed to him as a compromise between 35mm and 8 x 10". While the Rolleiflex had the facility of a hand camera, its negative when blown up could, he felt, be made to look almost as good as an 8 x 10" contact print. The only thing he didn't like about the Rolleiflex was the format's squareness, so he often cropped to achieve an oblong image. In both the Chicago and the labor series, the Rolleiflex gave a distinct and, in his work, new look to the pictures. This was because the camera was held low and aimed up at his subjects.

The effect that Evans achieved using a top viewer is not the one that Hine got with the same point of view. Evans took advantage of the hand-camera design of the Rolleiflex by shooting when his subjects were on the move and, in the Chicago pictures, possibly when he himself was too. Unlike Hine's subjects, who have often paused and are looking directly into the camera, Evans's, if they are aware of the camera at all, notice it only with irritation at the last moment. The consequence is that the heroism that a low angle imparts to Hine's subjects is reduced to mere aggressiveness in Evans's.

Evans probably shot the labor series at quitting time as the workers left their factory or offices. The figures in the pictures are frequently hunched forward with a kind of grim determination, with the bone weariness that eight hours of tedium can produce (fig. 14.9). Not only is the camera pitched low, but, especially in the labor series, the frame is at times turned at an angle. The pictures look as if the camera had been jarred. We can feel an almost physical impact of the photographer with the subject, a collision, a confrontation, as if Evans had purposely bumped into the people he photographed, even though they are in fact often unaware of his presence.

In both series Evans worked in the kind of bright, hard, horizontal sunlight he had favored since the Victorian-house study. In the

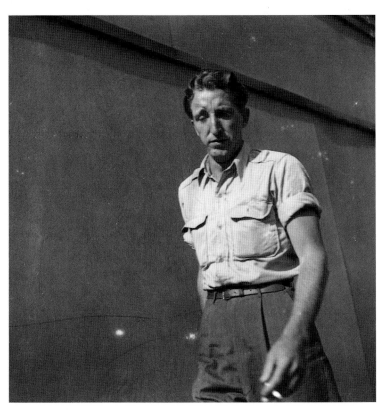

Fig. 14.10
WALKER EVANS
Detroit Street Portraits,
1946

house pictures, however, shadows mitigate the light. In the labor and Chicago pictures, there are no shadows, none of the mystery or atmosphere they create. The light is as pitiless as Evans's Flaubertian method. He caught his subjects as they walked directly into the light (fig. 14.10). It was a strategy that ensured a pinched expression, a grimace, a mood of antagonism.

This mood was characteristic of earlier 35mm pictures but was rendered here with the increased subtlety and craft of ten more years' experience as a photographer. The Chicago street portraits appear to have been made downtown, either in the late afternoon as people emptied out of the office buildings to go home or else at noon as they came out on their lunch hour. They are the photographs of "Chicago business stuff" anticipated in the 1934 letter. The labor series was made in Detroit, and it too seems to hark back to the letter, to the "dirty cracks" Evans said Detroit would let him get in.

The harshness of the pictures is, like most things Evans did, impeccable, above re-

proach. Yet no development in his work was isolated. The key to both his photography and his character is, to return once more to his own word, oxymoron. Every swing of his feelings in one direction was compensated, somewhere else, by a swing the other way. As the humanism of Evans's work in the thirties gave way to the cynicism of the forties, that work passed through a phase where the two impulses were balanced. The result was a set of street photographs begun in the late thirties that are, arguably, Evans's masterpiece: the New York subway series.

A subway *is* a street, of course. It is a thoroughfare along which people pass from place to place. But the feelings displayed on this kind of street differ from those seen in other public places. Here the street is in motion and the people are still. As we see in the Chicago and Detroit pictures, people hurrying along a sidewalk are often tense, keyed up. But on a subway they are passive. Their attention turns inward, and little by little their passivity relaxes the impassivity of the face they usually turn to the world (pages 238, 239).

As James Agee said in a brief introduction to the subway portraits written in 1940, "The simplest or the strongest of these beings has been so designed upon by his experience that he has a wound and a nakedness to conceal, and guards and disguises by which he conceals it. . . . Only in certain waking moments of suspension, of quiet, or solitude, are those guards down."[61] The defenselessness of these New York subway riders protected them from Evans's scorn.

Done between 1938 and 1941, the subway series literally made the transition from one decade to the other in Evans's life. Helen Levitt was seeing a lot of Evans in those days and remembers that Evans was often lethargic. She would drop by his apartment to visit, trying to get him over his mopiness so he would go out and photograph. She felt that if she hadn't done so, he might not have gone out at all. She even rode the subways with him occasionally while he made the pictures for the series, which was supported in 1940 and 1941 by a Guggenheim grant.

Evans would ride the trains with a Contax camera hung around his neck under his coat, its lens peeping out between the buttons and a cable release running down his sleeve to his hand. It was an incredibly constricted way in which to work. "Down in this swaying sweatbox," as Evans described it when he published a selection of the pictures in *Harper's Bazaar* two decades after they were made,[62] he would sit facing his subjects across the aisle. At the time subway cars were lit by bare, dim bulbs that forced Evans to shoot at slow shutter speeds. Levitt helped in the processing of the Double-X negatives, which were so thin that they needed very careful handling to be printed at all. (She tried making some shots on the subway herself with Evans's rig, and she mastered the technique well enough to produce at least a few images, which have more of the sprightliness typical of her work than the dourness characteristic of his.)

The 2¼" Rolleiflex that he would use later for the street portraits may have satisfied Evans as a technical compromise between the 35mm and the view camera. But the real synthesis of the two formats — their emotional reconciliation — came on the subway. There he was using a 35mm hand camera and working in a completely candid way, yet shooting blind at slow speeds as he would have with a view camera. He often had to wait until the train stopped at a station, so that the vibration wouldn't spoil the negative. The only other time that this process occurred, this poised wait for the right moment of stillness, the right expression or gesture, was when he stood beside the 8 x 10". As always, it was a process that moderated between Evans and his subjects.

We see in these subway pictures both Evans's greatness as a photographer and the limits that that greatness imposed on his popularity. It's not fortuitous that the phrase with which William Carlos Williams had praised Evans's photographs in 1938 — "ourselves made worthy in our anonymity" — would have applied even better to the subway series. Williams may have been thinking especially of the sharecropper pictures. Seen in *American Photographs* in the context of Evans's other work from the thirties, those pictures sum up certain aspects of what had come before them and anticipate what was to come after. The attitude toward the subject implicit in them becomes a conception of photography itself in the subway series. An intuitive insight grows into a conscious program.

The subway pictures have something else in common with those of the sharecroppers: neither project was appreciated until twenty years after it was done. In 1942, Evans did draw up a proposal for a book of the subway material to be called *Photographs of Metropolitan Faces*; but this plan, like so many others he had for books, languished. He probably decided not to push the idea because the poor response to *Let Us Now Praise Famous Men*, finally published just as he completed the subway studies, discouraged him about the prospects of finding the public he wanted for his work. *Let Us Now Praise Famous Men* didn't come back into print again until the early 1960s, when it at last achieved the success it deserved. The subway pictures weren't published as a book until 1966, a quarter century after their making. That book was entitled *Many Are Called*, and as Sarah Greenough has pointed out, the emphasis on group shots in Evans's selection for it not only fits in with "the 1960s style of street photography . . . by Frank, Winogrand, Lee Friedlander, and others," but "speaks to the isolation — the anonymity — of the individual within the crowd."[63]

Neither *Let Us Now Praise Famous Men* nor *Many Are Called* made concessions to the popular wisdom of its day. These images had a difficulty, an inaccessibility, that deprived them of the immediate appeal that a picture like Dorothea Lange's *Migrant Madonna* had. Lange's picture serves as an example for two reasons. One is that, as Roy Stryker put it, "when Dorothea took that picture, that was the ultimate. . . . It was *the* picture of Farm Security."[64] No other Depression photograph has been as widely reproduced. The second reason is that Lange's own account of making the picture reveals the difference between her approach to photography and Evans's, and thereby reveals more clearly what his approach was.

Lange's picture was made at the end of an all-night drive, during which she had seen a sign on the side of the highway marking a turnoff to a pea pickers' camp. Having driven quite a way beyond it, she suddenly decided to turn around and go back. "I was following instinct, not reason," she explained later. "I drove into that wet and soggy camp and parked my car like a homing pigeon. I saw and approached the hungry and desperate mother, as if drawn by a magnet. . . . I did not approach the tents and shelters of the other stranded pea-pickers. It was not necessary; I knew I had recorded the essence of my assignment."[65] Evans felt that he was "following instinct" when he photographed too. But by "instinct" he meant a gift for photography rather than telepathy.

Stryker said that Lange's photographs were "pictures you couldn't miss, you couldn't help but like, because she reached out, 'I love you' . . . Russell Lee does the same thing."[66] Lee was another photographer who, Stryker said, had only to "walk down the street and people say, 'Take my picture! I love you!' "[67] The instant images that photography provides encourage a belief in such instant relationships, and this tendency was reinforced in the thirties by the collectivist frame of mind, the conviction that "we're all in this together."

Like Evans's photographs of sharecroppers, Lange's lent themselves to a certain text. John Steinbeck went through the FSA file looking at her pictures of the Okie and Arkie camps when he was doing research for *The Grapes of Wrath*. In contrast to *Let Us Now Praise Famous Men,* Steinbeck's novel was an overnight success. It had the same mass appeal as the photographs Stryker admired in which you could see, as he was quoted as

saying earlier, the "guts still showing" in men's faces. *The Grapes of Wrath* confirmed some of the Depression's most cherished social myths. It invited its middle-class readers to enjoy a false solidarity with the poor that Agee's book, with its constant abrasiveness and challenges to the reader, guarded against.

Evans's photographs also guard against taking too much for granted, against the temptation inherent in all photography to identify too easily with the subject. If Lange's California migrant worker is a Madonna, Evans's portraits of sharecropper Annie Mae Gudger are Mona Lisas, studies of all that is enigmatic in human nature. They refuse to presume upon the brief acquaintance a photograph always represents, even though — or maybe because — Evans had spent considerably more time with his subject than Lange did with hers.

This insight into both photography and human nature is what the subway portraits carried to its ultimate conclusion. In them the unknowability of the subject arrived at in the Gudger portraits becomes a given of the setting itself. The circumstances under which the pictures were made give form to Evans's conviction that no matter how vulnerable and deeply human, the subject of a photograph remains anonymous. Humanity and anonymity constitute the oxymoron on which the pictures are based. Their difficulty lies in their reticence about their subjects and the modesty they display about photographs in general.

As John Szarkowski has pointed out, there is a connection between the subway series, the street portraits in Chicago and Detroit, and a *Fortune* article entitled "Along the Right of Way," for which Evans used a window of a moving train as if it were the frame inside his viewfinder. In each case the photographer limited his choices until, in Szarkowski's words, "all that remained was the freedom to say yes or no."[68] The connection Szarkowski was pointing out among the three series is their automatism. Evans's own conception of the subway portraits was similar, for in his proposal for the book *Metropolitan Faces* he described as "ideal" a situation in which "an impersonal fixed recording machine . . . photographed without any human selection for the moment of lens exposure." [69]

When he chose the photography to be included in a Louis Kronenberger anthology of the arts, Evans ended his selections with, as he put it, a "remote-control, automatic snapshot" of the earth made by NASA. His justification was that "art as an unintentional by-product of technology is none-the-less art." [70] Lincoln Kirstein had said in *American Photographs* that "great photography" always appears to be the "creation" of an "unaided machine," [71] and Evans's own photographs often seem intended to demonstrate the veracity of this point of view. From the subway series on, each further reduction of photography to its bare, mechanical bones moved Evans closer to achieving Flaubert's "pitiless method."

It was to this same end that he turned late in life to yet another automatic picture machine, the Polaroid SX-70. Evans was attracted to the Polaroid because it "reduces everything to your brains and taste. . . . I feel that if you have these things in your head, this is the instrument that will really test it." [72] This comment is an apologia for the subway pictures as well. The things that were in Evans's head when he did that series included snatches of conversation Hart Crane had overheard on the subway, lists of meager possessions James Agee had drawn up, and all the other myriad influences examined earlier.

When he was a young man in Paris, Evans had admired the new painting being done there. But by the time he came to the subway series, he had left "the museum," as he put it. Just before his departure he had studied the African masks that lay behind much of the modern painting he liked. Now he was ready to fashion his own set of primitive masks. Like the ones from Africa, those he made in the subway represent archetypal feeling. What he

admired about Paul Strand's *Blind Woman*, he said, was that it was "brutal." [73] This is the quality that the subway pictures instill in his own work. Out of them he was making his own collection of penny portraits like those in the studio window. He had placed his picture of that window at the beginning of *American Photographs*. In the subway portraits his work achieved its greatest culmination by remaining true to such beginnings.

PART FOUR

Robert Frank
& America Since the War

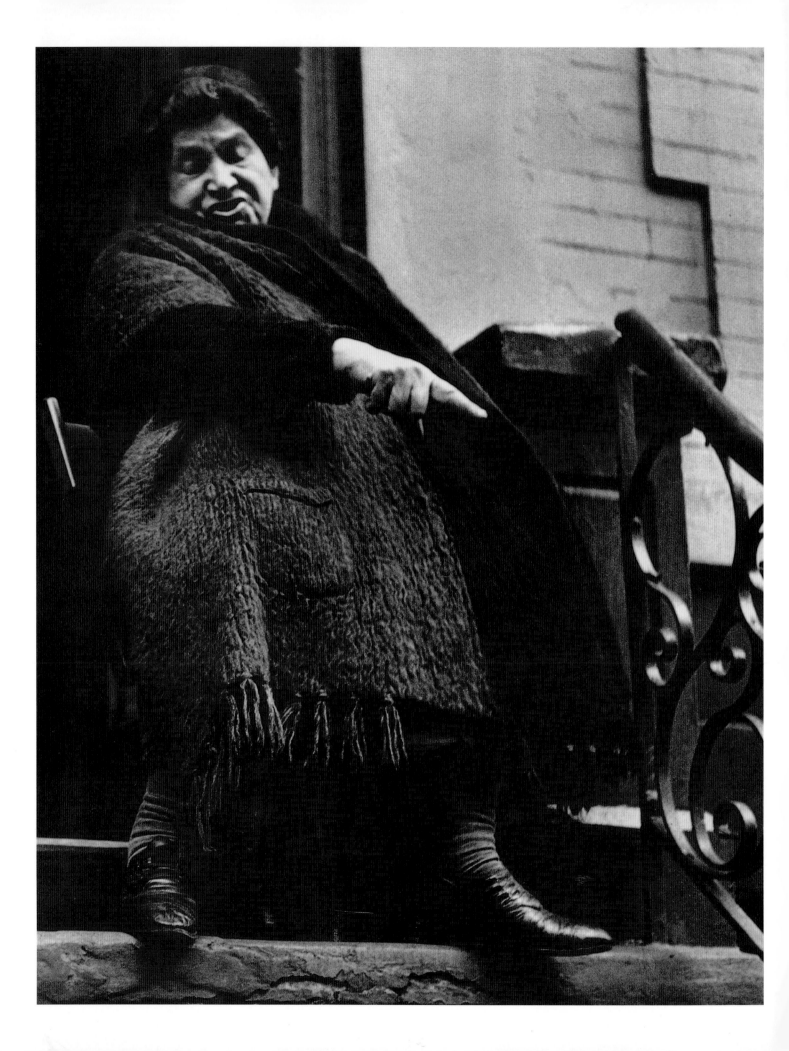

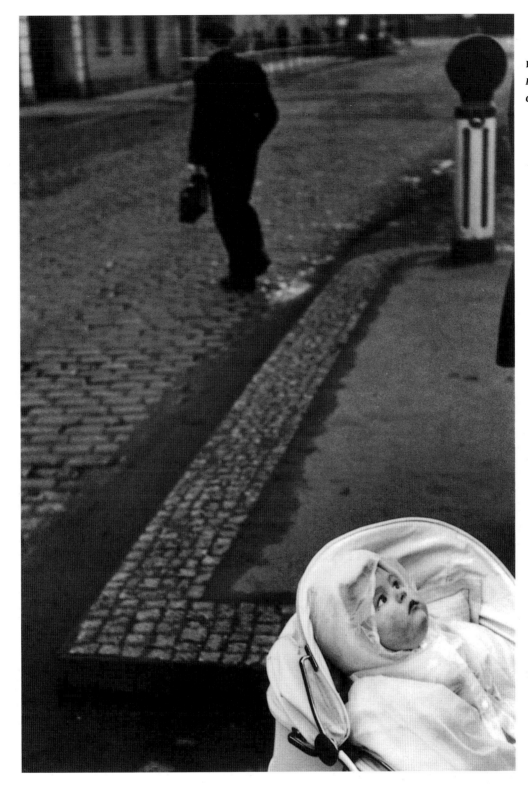

RENÉ BURRI
*Ruhregebiet, West
Germany*, 1960

LISETTE MODEL
*Lower East Side, New
York, c. 1942*

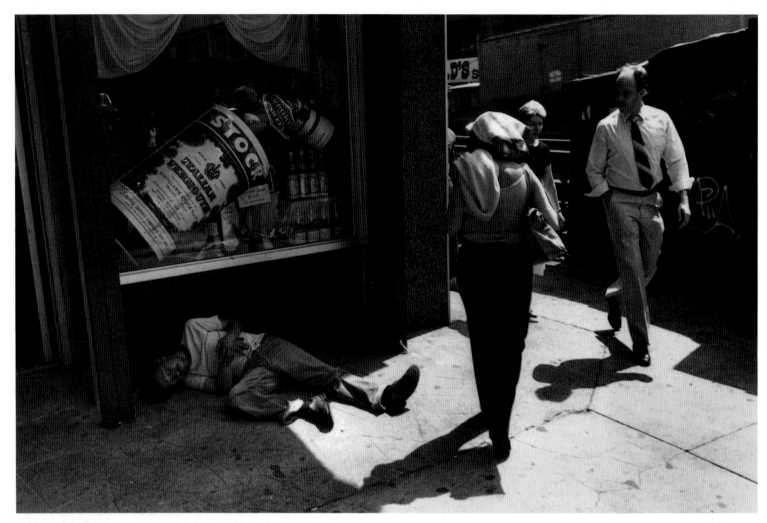

LEE FRIEDLANDER

New York, c. 1963

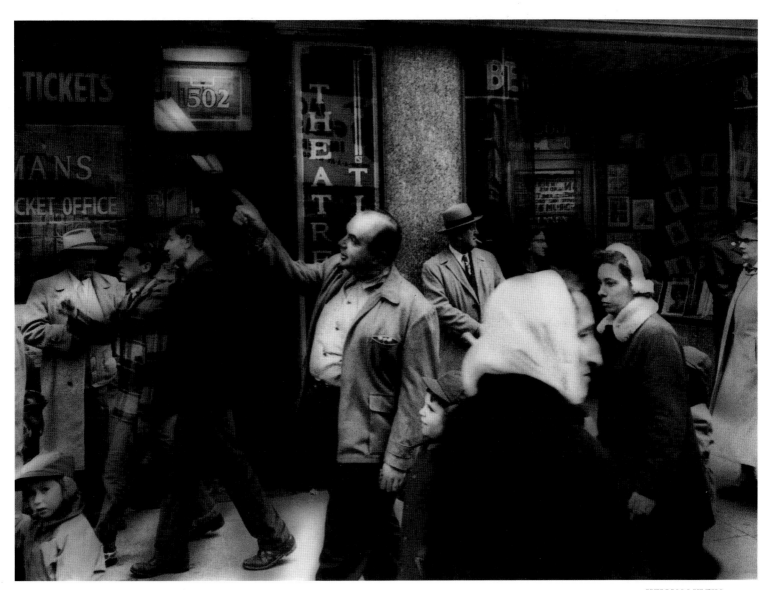

WILLIAM KLEIN
Theater Tickets,
New York, 1955

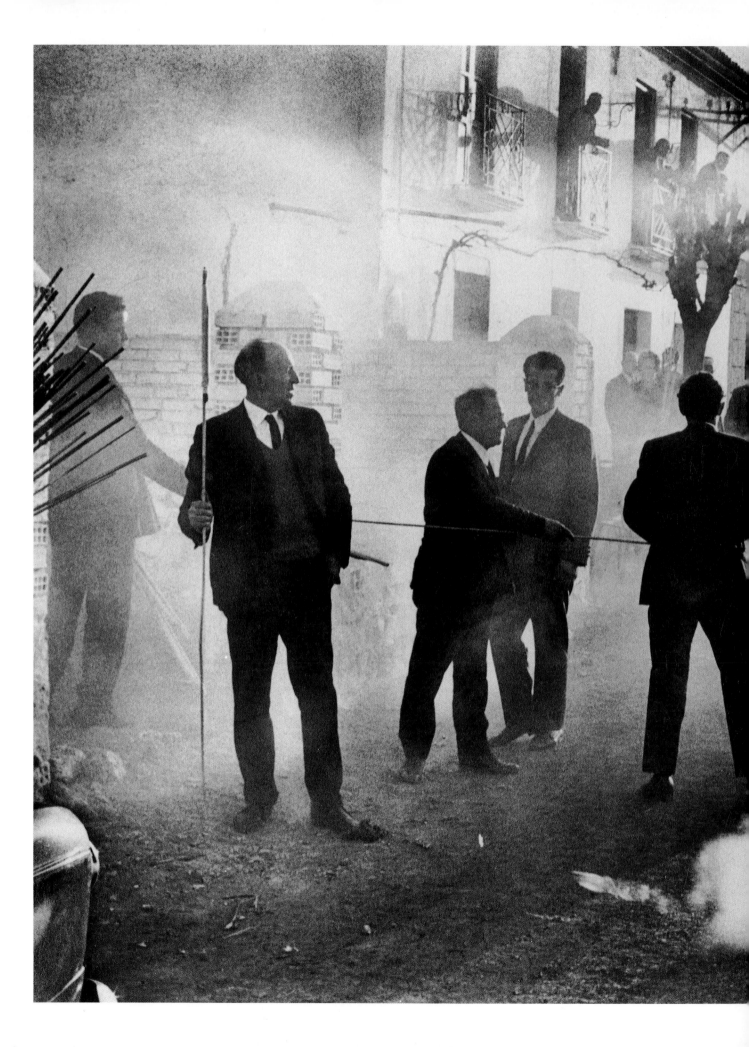

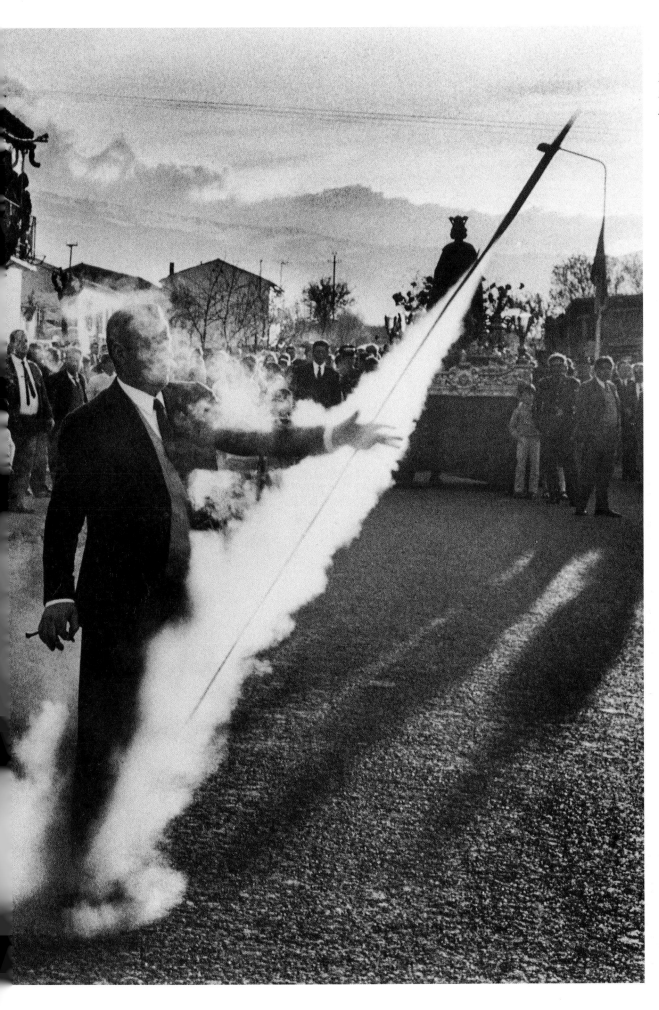

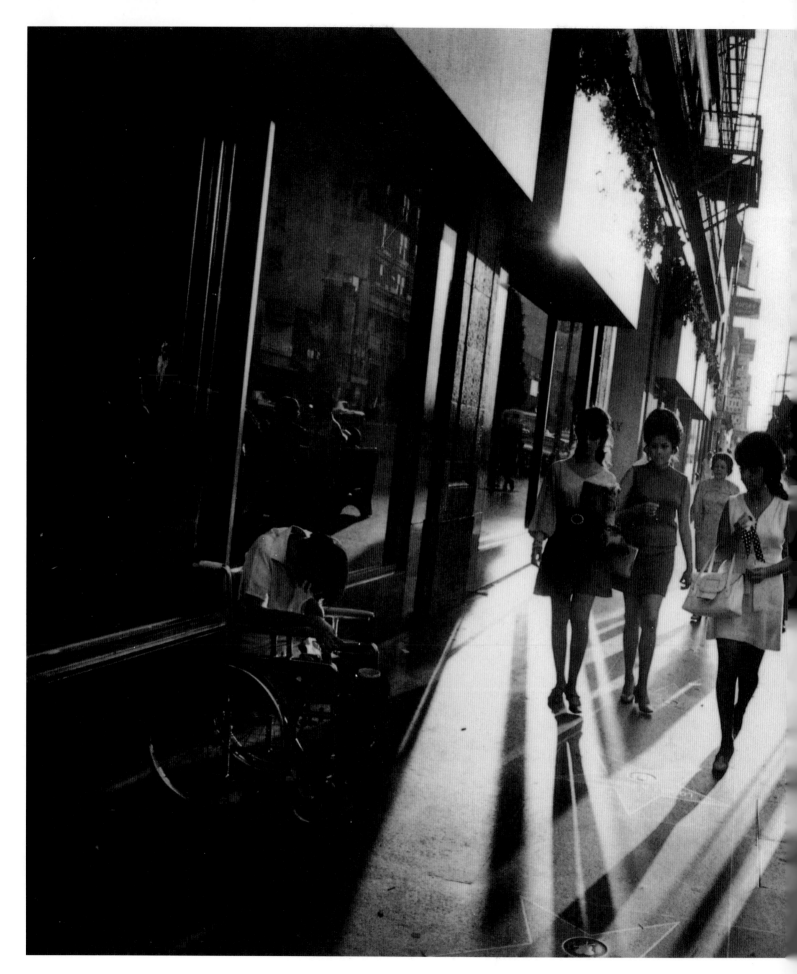

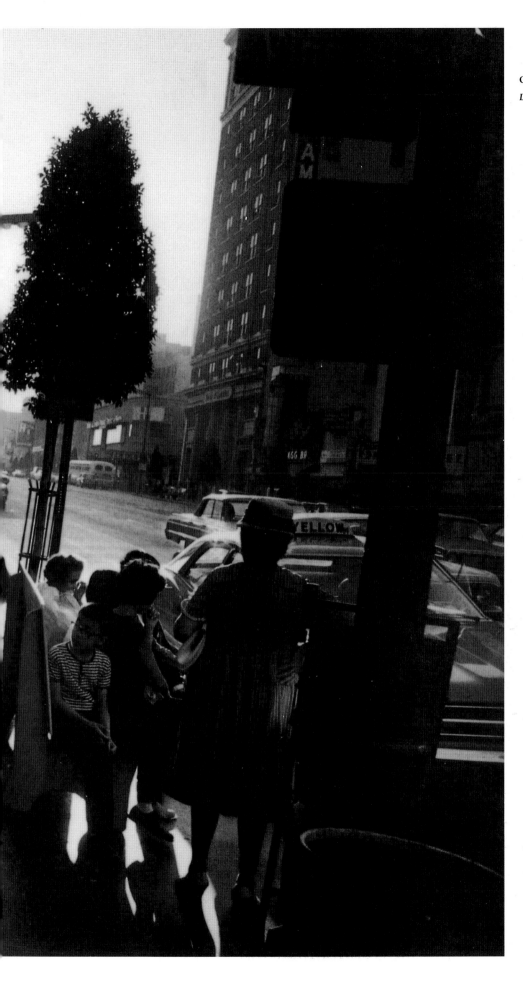

GARRY WINOGRAND
Los Angeles, 1969

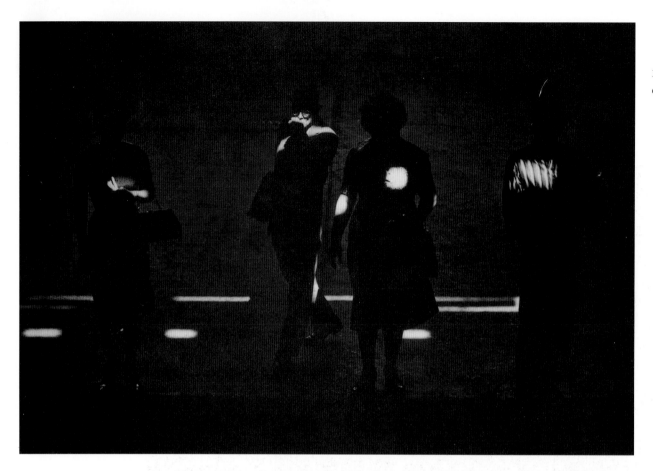

KEN JOSEPHSON
Chicago, 1961

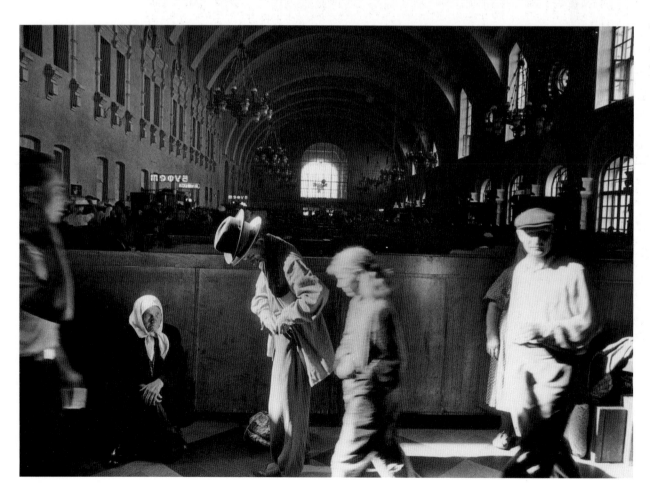

WILLIAM KLEIN
Kiev Railroad Station,
Moscow, 1959

302

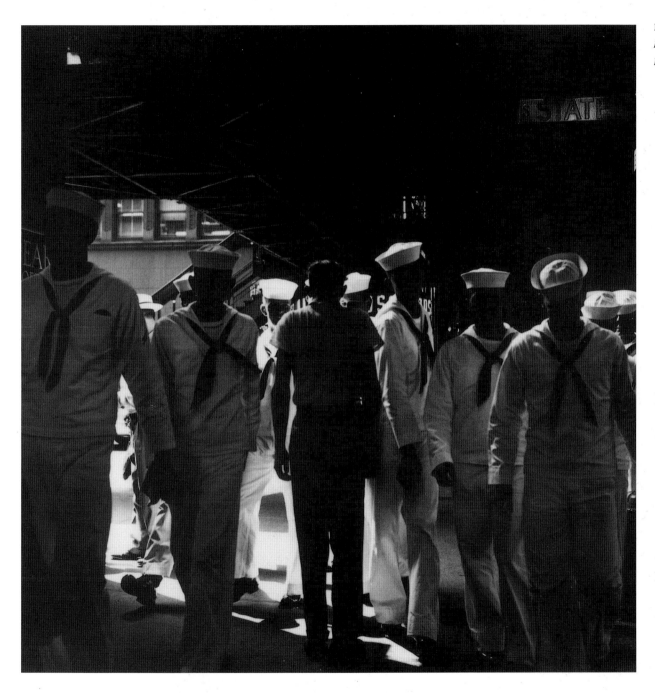

RAY METZKER
*My Camera and I in the
Loop, Chicago, 1964*

303

JOSEF KOUDELKA

Exiles, Spain, 1973

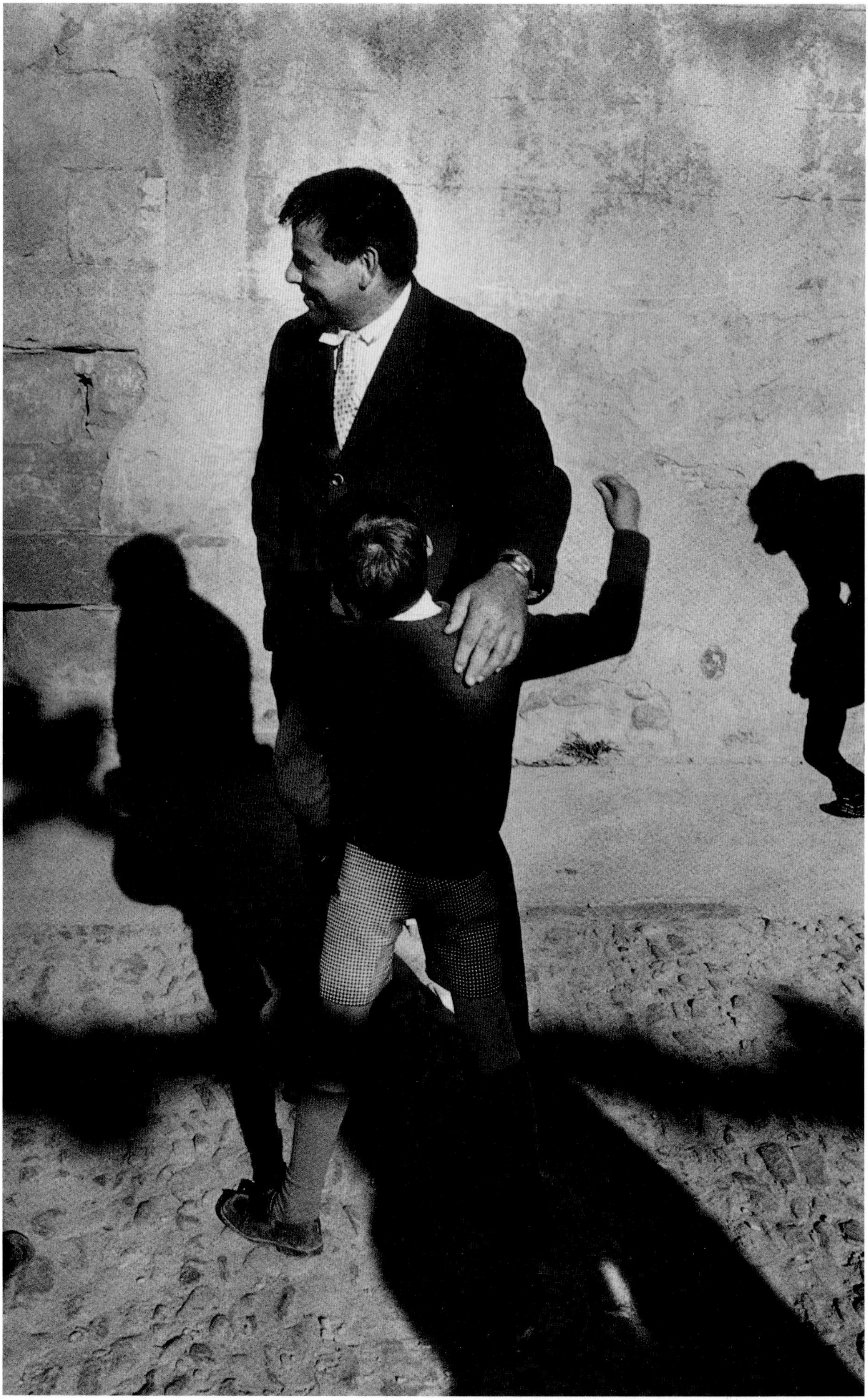

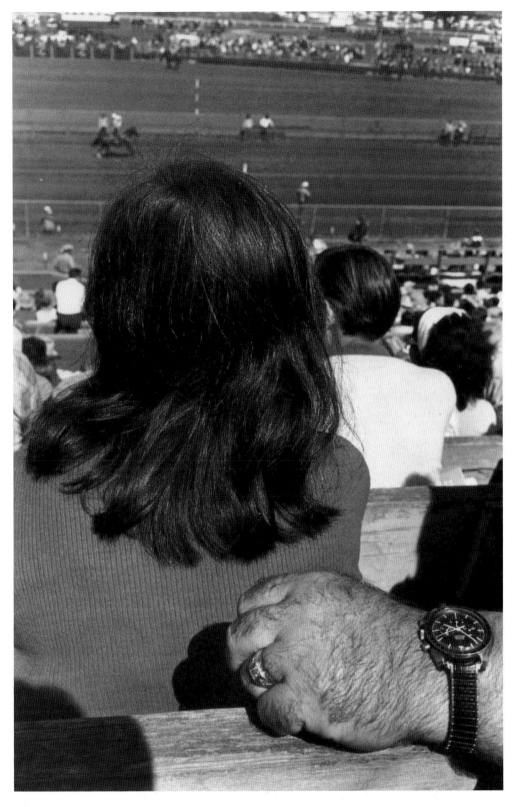

LEE FRIEDLANDER
Salinas, California,
1972

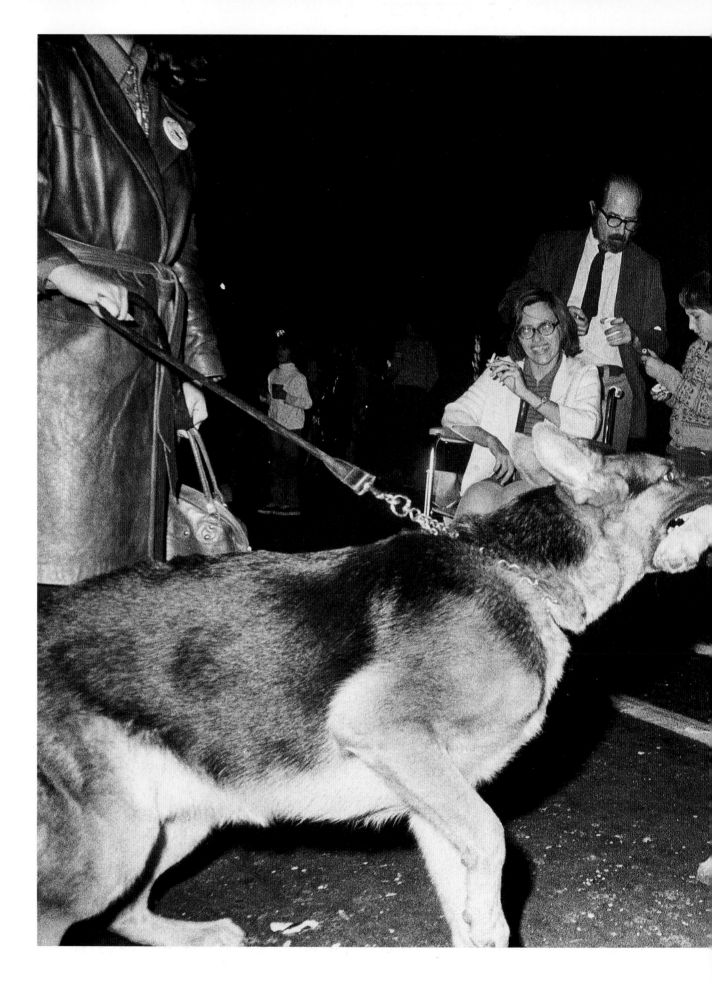

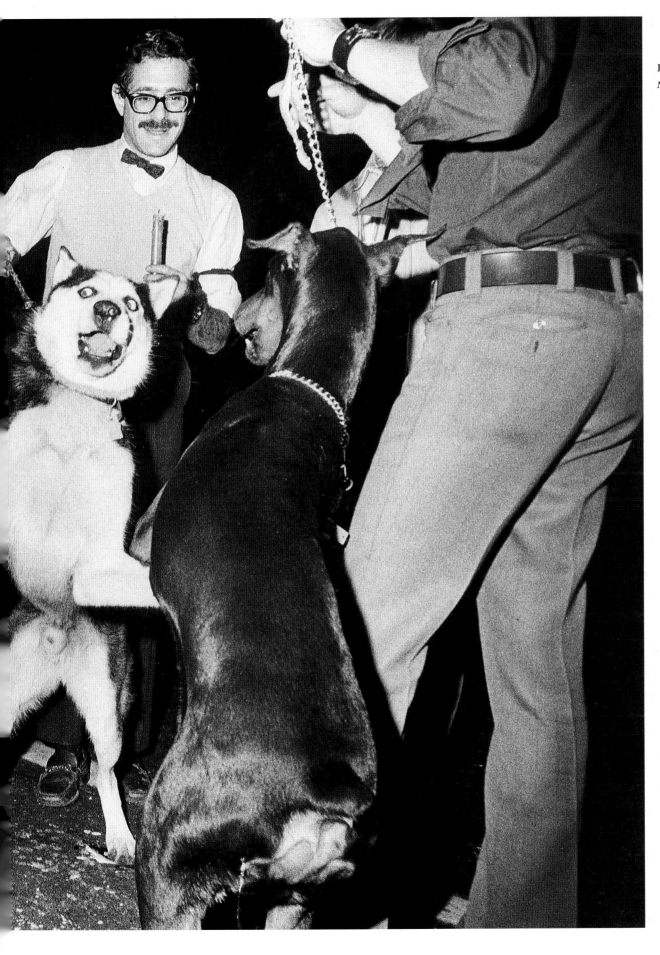

JOEL MEYEROWITZ
New York, 1972

307

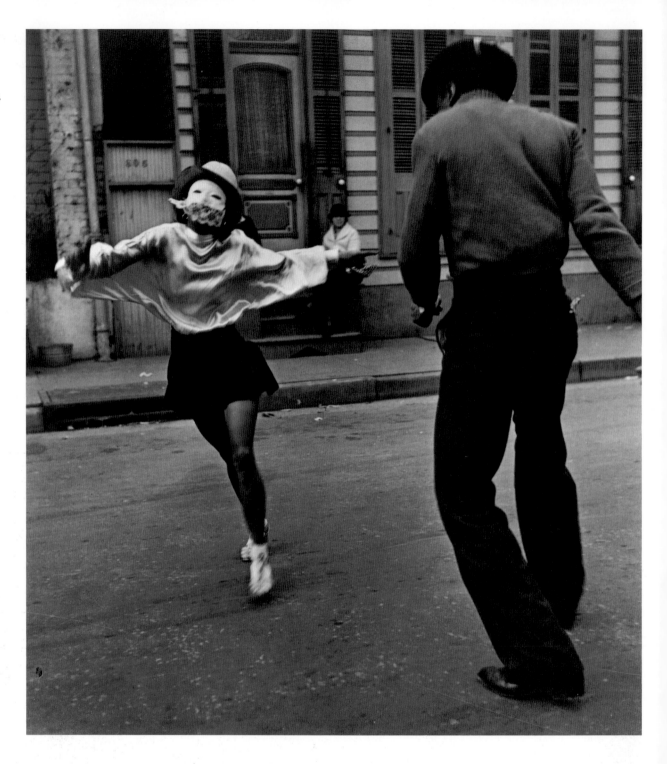

308

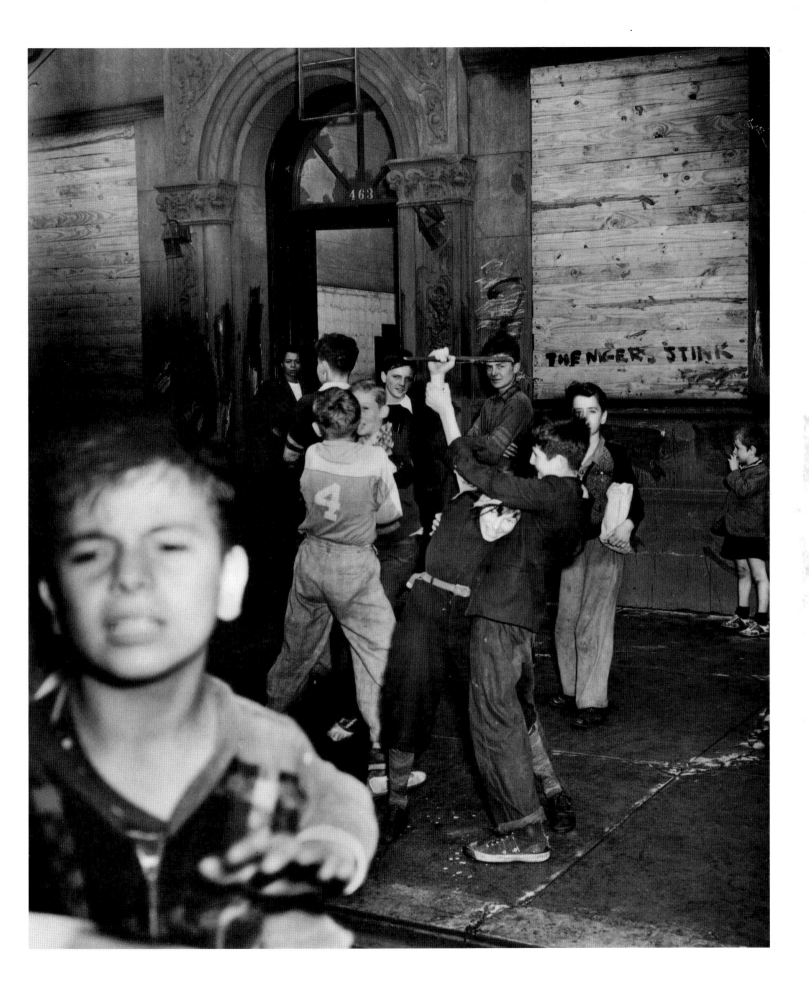

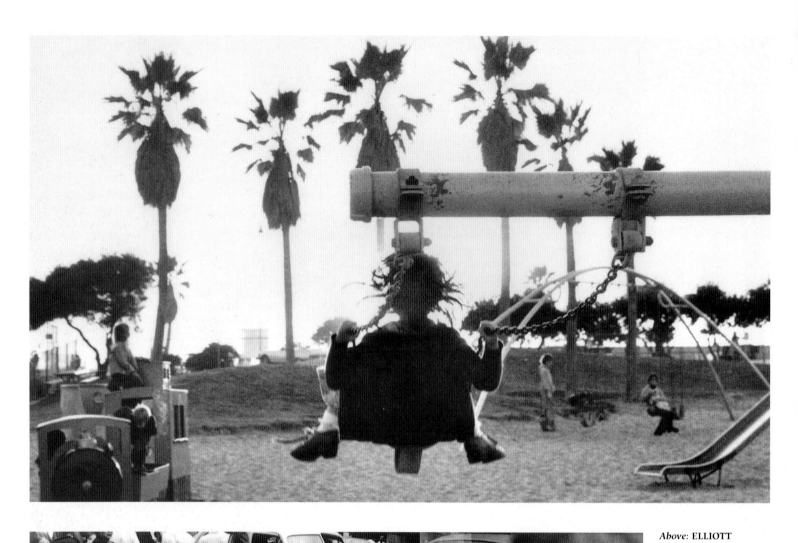

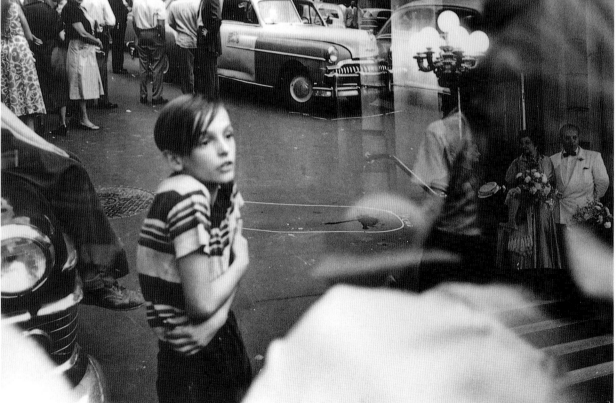

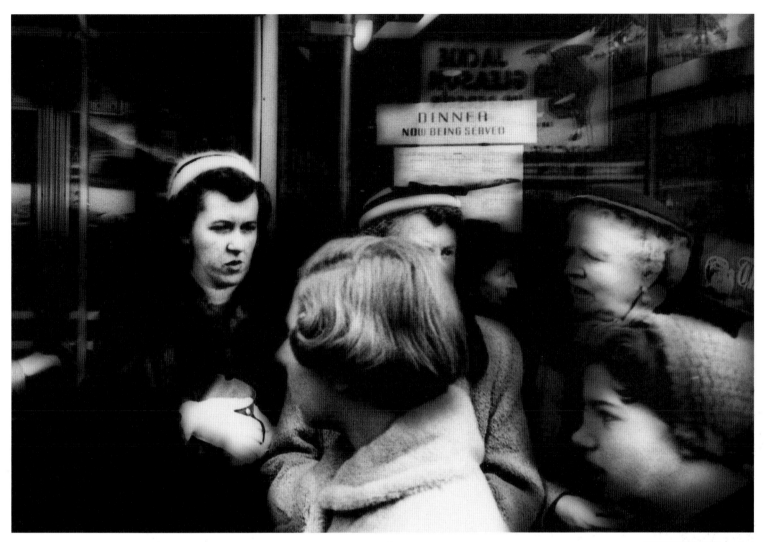

WILLIAM KLEIN
*Dinner Now Being
Served, New York,* 1955

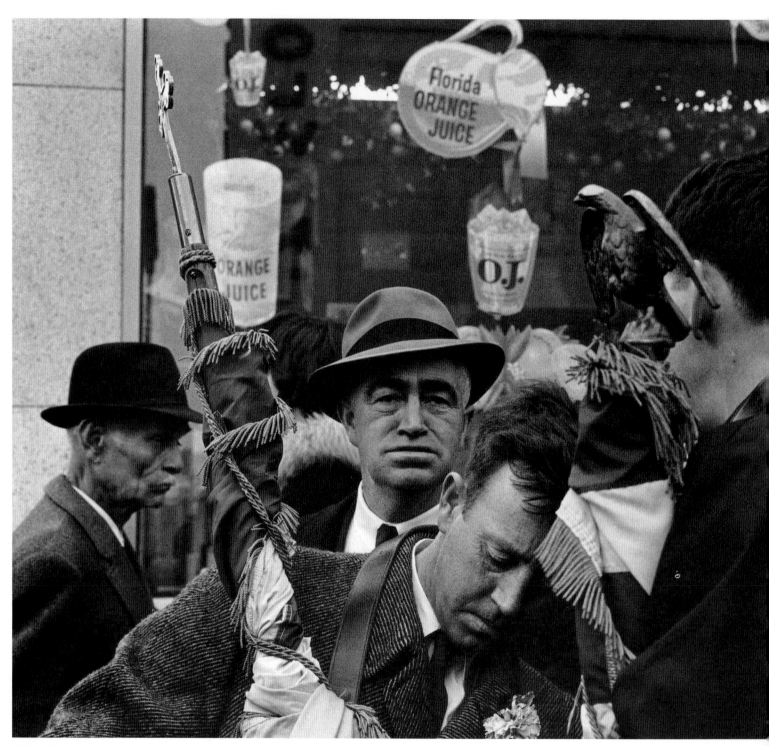

TOD PAPAGEORGE

Parade's End, 1966

312

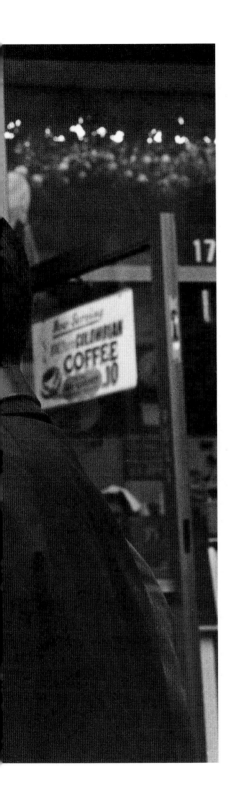

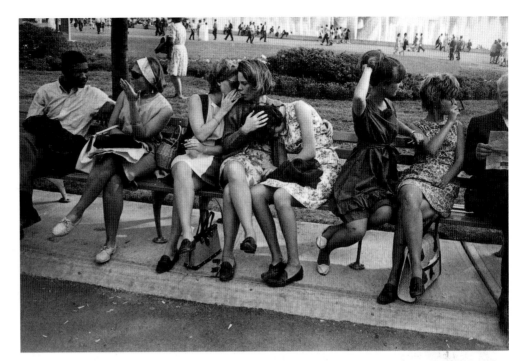

GARRY WINOGRAND
World's Fair, New York,
1964

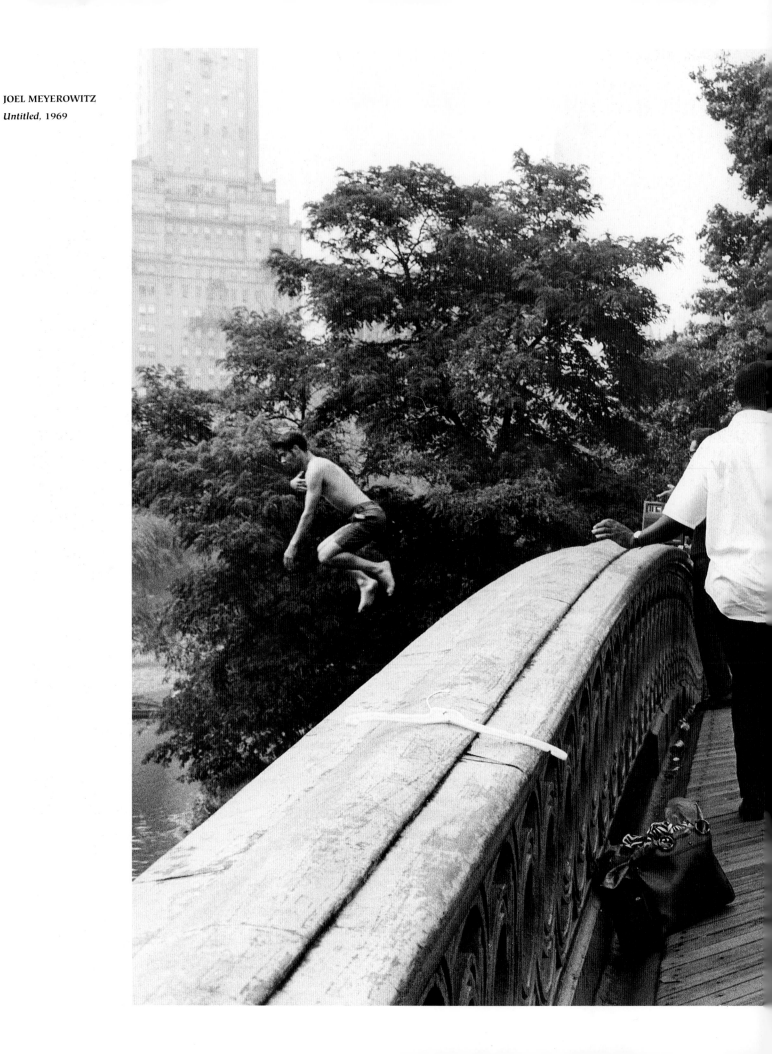

JOEL MEYEROWITZ
Untitled, 1969

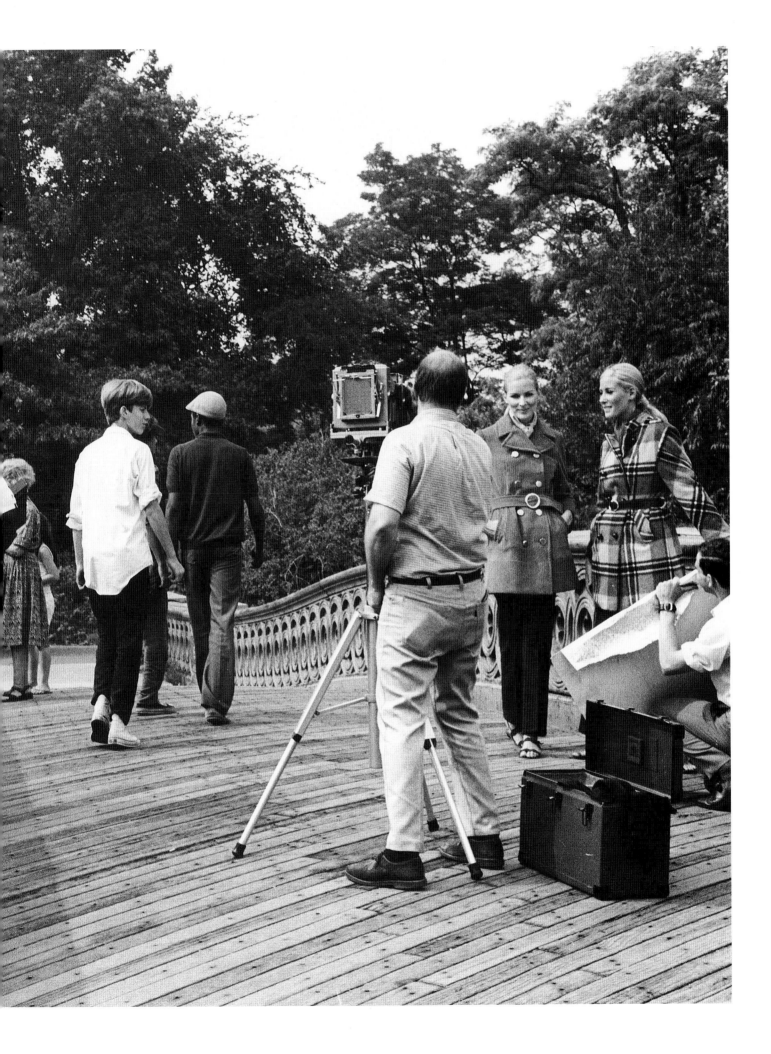

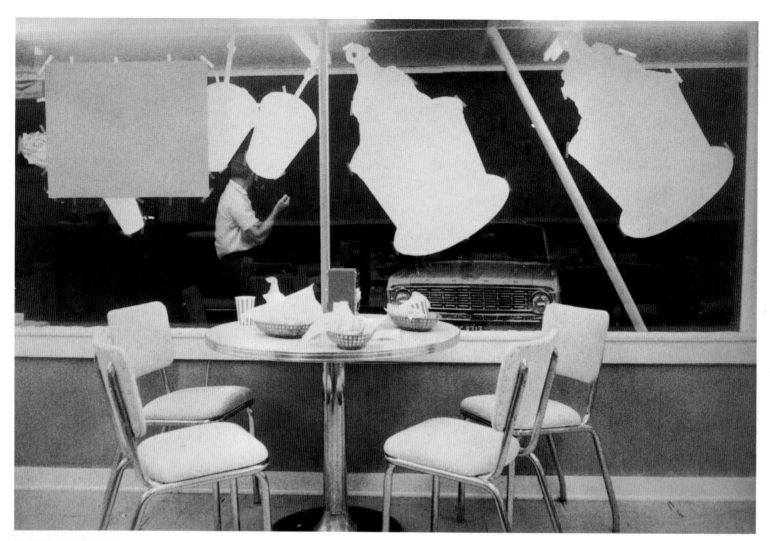

GARRY WINOGRAND
San Marcos, Texas,
1964

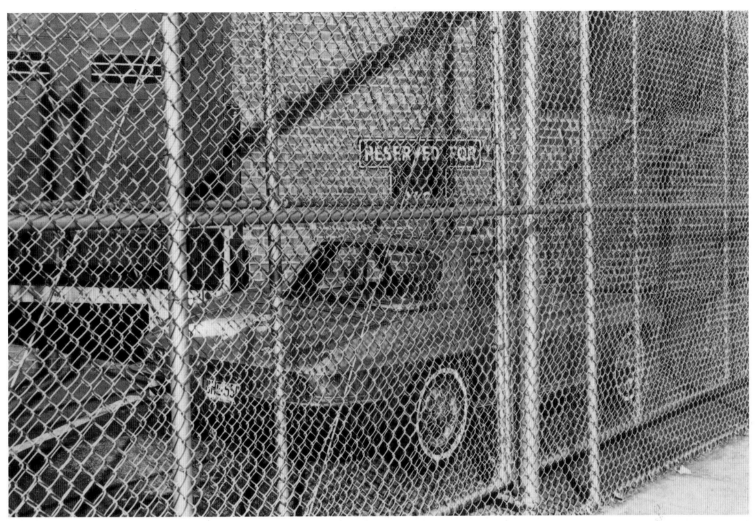

LEE FRIEDLANDER
New York, 1963

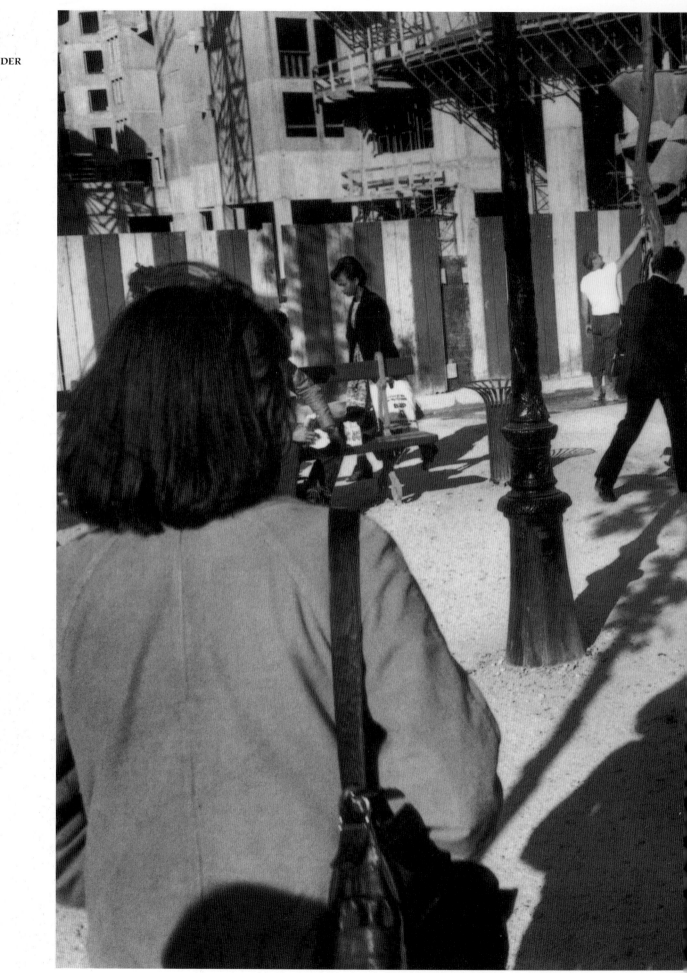

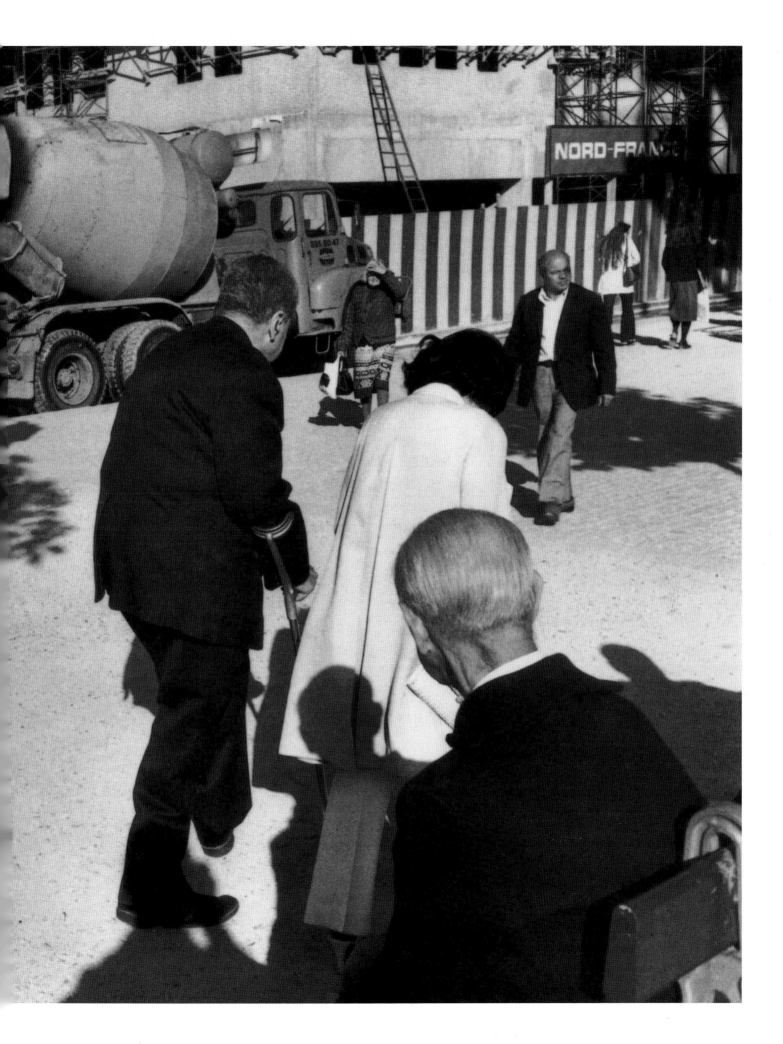

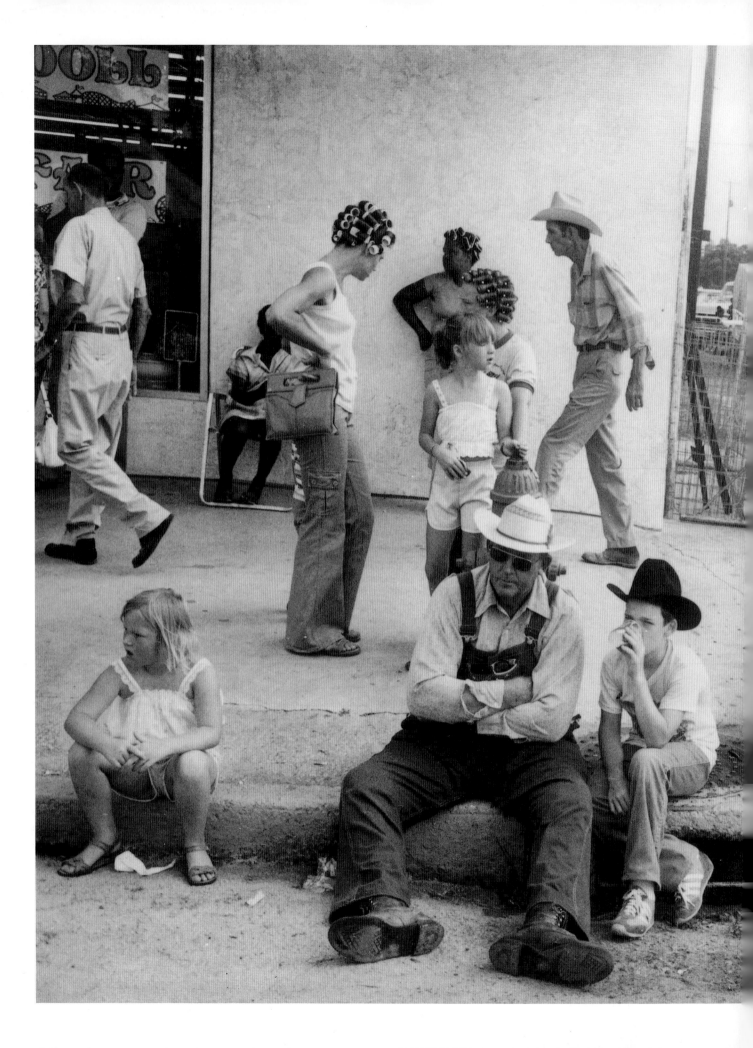

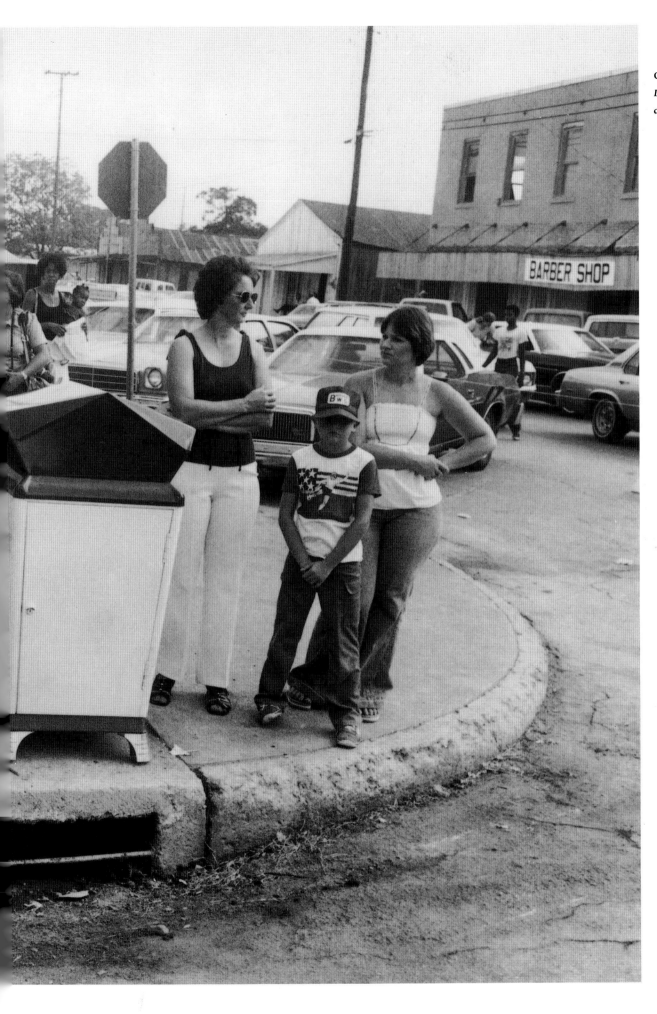

BARBER SHOP

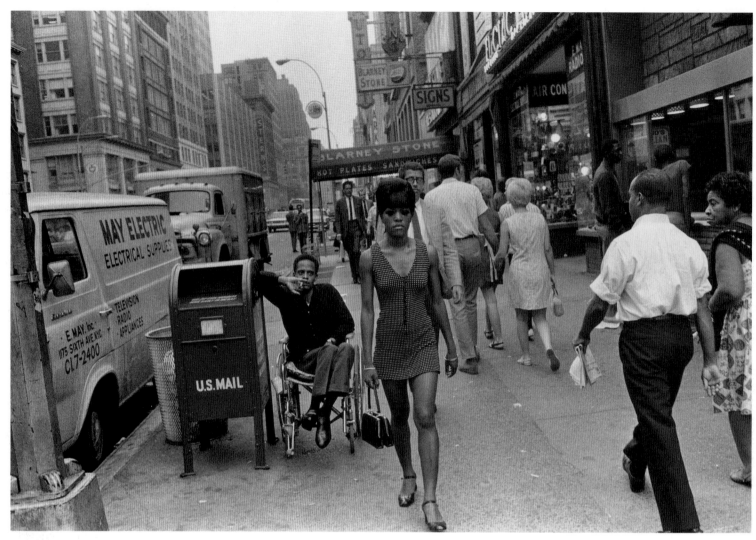

JOEL MEYEROWITZ

New York, 1971

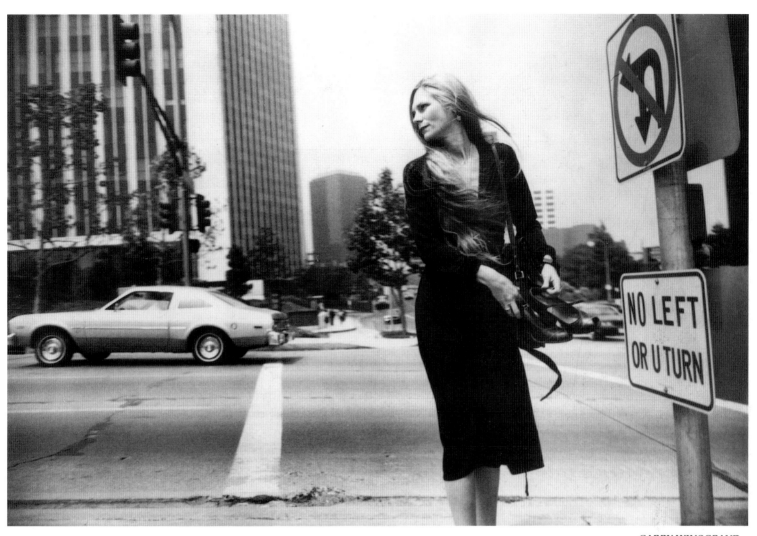

GARRY WINOGRAND
Los Angeles, c. 1980–81

15: Displaced Persons

"To hell with art!" John Gutmann said, talking about a photograph he had made shortly after his 1933 arrival in America from Germany. "What is art anyway? This was much, much bigger than art."[1] Before leaving Germany, he had not felt this way, for he had been an artist himself. The son of a wealthy man (he could remember his father's having been driven around in a chauffeured car), he had had an elite education as a private student of a painter once associated with Die Brücke, the avant-garde group in whose work German Expressionism originated. In 1933, at the relatively young age of twenty-eight, he had had a promising future in the Berlin art world.

But then, with the rise to power of Hitler, he was proscribed from any further public career because he was a Jew. There was nothing to do, he felt, except leave. On the advice of a friend he decided to go not only to America, but all the way to the other side of the continent, to San Francisco. It was as if he were determined to get as far away from the past as possible. In the same spirit he took up a new medium, photography, with which he would ultimately be able to express new attitudes, instilled by his experiences, that were beyond the reach of mere art.

He originally adopted the camera to have a way to support himself on his journey. Because a reporter he knew pointed out that European magazines were always in the market for pictures of America, he bought a Rolleiflex, shot some test rolls, and used the contacts to get a commitment from a Berlin agency, Presse-Photo, for the exclusive rights to his work. Whereas painting was a profession for which he had been trained, photography was an expedient adopted on the spur of the moment. As such it was better suited to the improvised life he would now have to lead.

"To me, photography was a completely new medium," he said, "and I did not . . . feel the urge to transfer to it my ideas about painting."[2]

The photograph that he later exclaimed to be "much bigger than art" was made as part of a series on graffiti. This particular example reads, "To my best pal I ever had. I'm sorry I did you wrong." It's typical of the sort of wall scrawl that attracted Gutmann. Sometimes he documented messages that were obscene or cruel, but more often he was drawn to ones that had a peculiarly American combination of pathos and bathos, a cry in the dark like this apology to a lost friend.

Another subject of this type that caught his attention was a "Date Book" of messages to unknown girls scribbled on the boarded-up mullions of a window. "Hi ya sister! How my doing?" asks one with a street tough's mixture of pushiness and insecurity. Gutmann quickly developed not only an ear for America's slang, as these photographs show, but an eye for her kitsch. The photographs of graffiti blend into a much larger set of images of vernacular signs, advertisements, the covers of girlie magazines, and car accessories.

What obviously amazed and delighted him was the way Americans ran off at the mouth, the machine-gun delivery of their gab, the mile-a-minute graphics of the streets. A newsstand is hung with row upon row of magazine covers that all have scantily clad, physically perfect women on them. A billboard is stacked four stories high with slogans ("Puts spunk in your trunk . . . vigor in your vitals . . . color in your corpuscles"). Headlights, sirens, horns, hood ornaments, reflectors, a speedometer, and coon tails are crammed onto the handlebars of a bicycle. Unable to bear an empty space or a moment's silence, some Americans

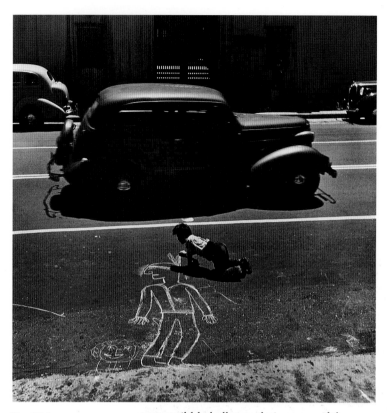

Fig. 15.1

JOHN GUTMANN

The Artist Lives
Dangerously, San
Francisco, 1938

chalk drawing of a Native American on the street as cars whiz by a few feet away (fig. 15.1). Recognizing in hindsight the latent autobiographical significance of this photograph, Gutmann later titled it *The Artist Lives Dangerously*. Like the boy in the street, he did pictures of Native Americans himself, and of all the other minorities that make up America. He saw the country as a stimulating confusion not only of slogans, automobiles, pulp magazines, and signs, but of people.

This was a view that San Francisco enhanced because of its multiracial character as a port city. He photographed blacks both there — for instance, when Count Basie, billed as the "Sepia Swing Sensation," performed with the High Hatters at the 1939 Golden Gate International Exposition — and during Mardi Gras in New Orleans, which Gutmann visited on a 1936–37 tour of the country (page 308). He took pictures of Asians in San Francisco and Indians in Arizona. These were the subjects that made America America for him.

even scribbled all over their cars as if they were the walls of a men's room. "Jeepers Creepers. Lay off!" complains one automobile decorated thus. "Lies are falling thick and fast!" opines another. "The truth marches *on.*"

Gutmann became so fascinated with the visual details of the American scene that he could devote a whole series to the most incidental of subjects, such as license plate holders. The only overview of the country he had that rose above all this visual detail came from the first sight he caught of America when he looked down from the deck of his ship as it landed in San Francisco. There on the pier below him a game of dice was in progress in which the players were Asians, Indians, Mexicans, blacks, and whites. This image of the nation as a kind of ethnic crapshoot stuck with him after he disembarked. Coming to America was a gamble for everybody there, including him.

He didn't get a picture of the scene on the pier, but later he did take photographs that seem to recapture that first impression, particularly one of a Chinese boy making a life-size

For all his efforts to embrace his new country and assume a new identity as a photographer, however, Gutmann wasn't able to escape the past entirely. He himself showed us this with a photograph he took of the swastika hanging prominently beside the American flag during a ceremony in the San Francisco city hall. His pictures also indicate that he watched the invasion of China by Japan from the vantage point of San Francisco's Chinatown and the fall of Spain from the perspective of West Coast leftists (he had thought of going to Spain from Germany before a friend convinced him that some place farther away, like America, would be safer). Even America must have seemed chancy to him, since his main impressions of it before coming had been the films of Charlie Chaplin and the novels of Theodore Dreiser. Both present their heroes as people caught in a kind of continental drift of events over which they have no control.

The art lessons Gutmann had had in Germany may have been forgotten after he left, but the history lesson implicit in his departure

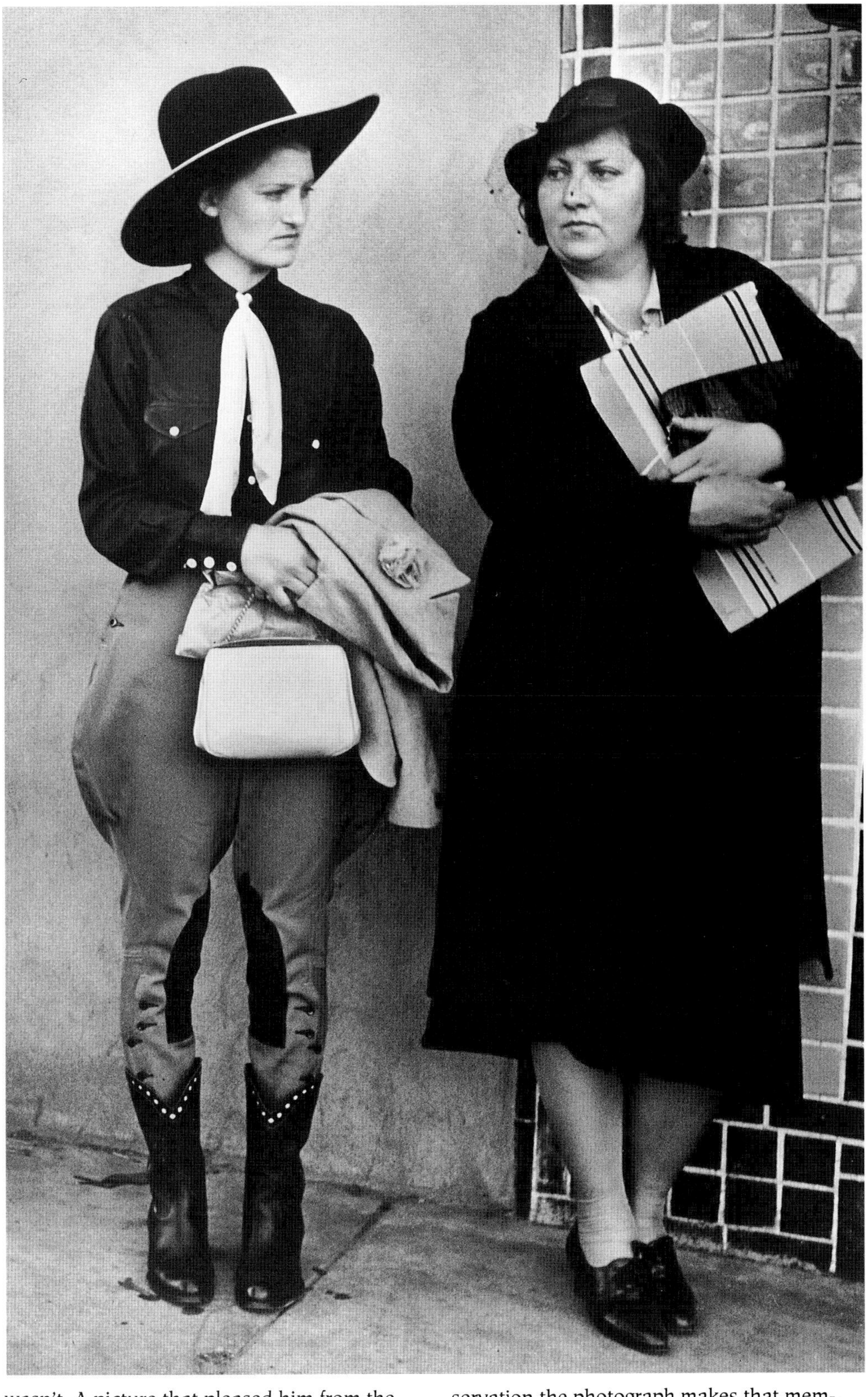

Fig. 15.2
JOHN GUTMANN
Texas Women, 1937

wasn't. A picture that pleased him from the test rolls he shot just before leaving is of a street on which a shop sign advertises SS uniforms for sale. There is a sly irony in the observation the photograph makes that members of this elite Nazi corps do not really come into the world like Athena, goddess of war, springing from the head of Zeus in full battle dress; they are minor functionaries who must buy their work clothes, along with waiters and domestics, from petit bourgeois haberdashers.

When Gutmann came to America, he found that the citizenry here also had a taste for uniforms, and he had a similar temptation as a photographer to demystify what they stood for. In a photograph he took in Texas during his trip around the country, a bowlegged cowgirl in jodhpurs and a ten-gallon hat is standing next to a fat young matron in a frumpy dress (fig. 15.2). They both look uncomfortable and impatient, as if they were waiting for a bus. American uniforms of all kinds caught Gutmann's eye, but in particular those that had military overtones, like drum majorettes'.

He photographed the drill of a high school reserve unit and a shape-up on the waterfront where welders in helmetlike masks stood in a rank as if falling in for inspection. In 1934, he covered the San Francisco general strike, putting emphasis in the pictures on the deployment of the National Guard in the streets. In the Californians' love of the outdoors and sports, he found another unnerving parallel to German culture. He saw Americans embracing the philosophy of *Kraft durch Freude* that the Nazis had exploited so skillfully.

The world depicted in these photographs of his has a nightmare quality. Gutmann has said that America was for him "a kind of surrealist experience. Most everything was a found object."[3] But it seems more accurate to think of his photography as found Expressionism. Despite his determination to make a clean break with his past as a painter, influences from his art education under Otto Müller do seem to creep into his photography at times. With subjects ranging from the High Hatters in San Francisco to an elevator for cars he discovered at a parking lot in Chicago, he shot from a low angle and put the composition on a diagonal, so that it seems to be pitching and yawing in the classic, hallucinatory manner of Expressionism.

Moreover, his photography was given to Gothic touches of a kind that Expressionism often revived, as in a picture he did where a slight blurring of a woman's features makes her face under a heavy veil look like a fleshless skull. Because this death mask looms at us out of the California sunshine, it is just that much more of a shocker. Other photographs, done from San Francisco to New York, used motion blur to similar effect.

That Gutmann was resorting to certain Expressionist techniques in his imagery becomes unmistakable like this only occasionally. The rest of the time the effects of the Expressionist influence are less overt. They become more of a subtext, a hidden agenda, underneath the kind of benign and naturalistic treatment that California seems to invite as a subject. The results were very like those achieved by another group of German refugees who began coming to the West Coast around the time that Gutmann arrived: the movie directors who fled to Hollywood when the Nazis took over the German studio system.

Expressionism had had a longer life in filmmaking than other arts, especially in the work of the dominant figures like Fritz Lang. But the experience of being a refugee — Lang had had to flee from Germany the same year as Gutmann — deflated the grandiosities and Wagnerian profundities toward which his work had tended. German filmmakers like him learned how to indulge in a type of mordant laughter; otherwise, they might have thrown themselves out of hotel windows.

The upshot when they came to America was the emergence of a new movie genre known as film noir, which is decidedly German in look despite its French name. These films all have a mise-en-scène in which the nightmare effects of German Expressionism have, as it were, gone underground. One minute the whole world is pervaded by a darkness that glistens, a kind of stylized evil; the next minute it has a gritty realism to it. In order not to fall victim to his deranged environment, the hero must learn to live by his wits, trusting no

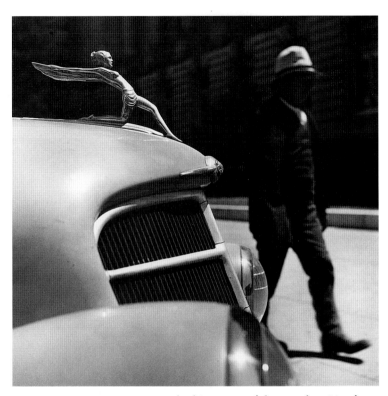

Fig. 15.3
JOHN GUTMANN
Reach, San Francisco,
1938

looked and felt so much like Gutmann's photography was that this kind of cinematic *flânerie* was the only sort the younger, less established filmmakers such as Siodmak and Wilder had done before leaving Germany. In 1929 the two of them collaborated on a quasi-documentary entitled *Menschen am Sonntag*, in which a fictitious plot was interleaved with candid footage of crowds in Berlin's parks and of passersby on the streets. Another experimental film of the period, *Berlin Symphony*, was composed entirely of such material.

Its cameraman, who worked with Lang as well, declared that still photographs made candidly like his shots with a hidden movie camera are "the only type of photography that is really art."[4] The most exciting German street photography of the Weimar era is the street cinematography employed in these two movies. Both give to life in big cities the undertone of sleaziness that would infect the Hollywood films by Lang, Wilder, and the others later, and that can be seen in Gutmann's photographs too.

The background that the street photographer Gutmann shared with all these directors was of course the culture of Berlin. During the period of the Weimar Republic, Berlin was a city of *flâneurs*. Here was where Walter Benjamin learned to appreciate the art of walking through the city that led him to write about nineteenth-century Paris. For the intellectuals and artists who congregated in the cafés on the Kurfürstendamm, the streets were as integral a part of one's cultural life as the high arts of the museum, the opera house, and the publishing house. The prime exemplar of such Berliners was Bertolt Brecht, in whose work street songs played a crucial role. This was the music that entertained the patrons of the city's cabarets, including Gutmann after he arrived in Berlin in the late 1920s.

one and taking none of the usual verities for granted. He has to be someone who knows how to move through the city at night. He becomes a degraded and fugitive *flâneur.*

That's who the passersby in Gutmann's photographs often appear to be as well. The settings or street props that he used — a graffitied wall, the snazzy hood ornament on a car, a display of girlie magazines — were often played against furtive, scurrying figures (fig. 15.3). Each is a shabby éminence grise like the antiheroes in film noir, who are also uncertain presences. Any one of the refugee directors who worked in this genre, from Billy Wilder to Fritz Lang, might have used Gutmann's pictures as insert shots. His imagery is perhaps most compatible with that of Robert Siodmak, whose greatest movie has a title — *Cry of the City* — that fits some of Gutmann's best work, such as his series on graffiti, equally well.

Street movies — melodramas that interwove the stories of people whose paths crossed by chance in the street — were a genre all their own in Germany, going back to the early 1920s. One reason that American film noir

The essence of this sensibility that Gutmann brought with him to America resided not only in the eye and the ear, but in the lip — the *"Berliner Schnauze"*[5] — which curled with dis-

Fig. 15.4

GEORGE GROSZ

A Face in the Crowd,

1932

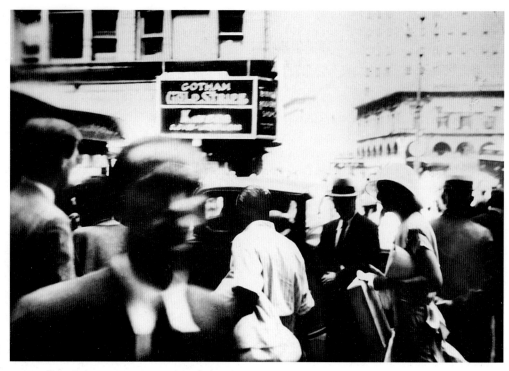

respect for all the pomposity and romantic nonsense in the world. The Berlin lip formed itself into a perpetual oral shrug, an expression with which the wearer sloughed off the pathetic illusions and social hypocrisy he saw around him. "We say no to everything," Kurt Tucholsky remarked about himself and his fellow Berliners in 1919.[6]

Irreverent, absolutely without sentimentality or nostalgia, given to gallows humor, these Berliners reserved their greatest contempt for what they called *"Schmus"* and *"Quatsch,"*[7] for persiflage, hyperbole, flattery, euphemism, grandiloquence, and all other varieties of empty, self-deluding jabber — in short, for kitsch. This was what Gutmann took aim at with his camera when he came to America. He was at once both thrilled and appalled by the visual cacophony of the streets, the ceaseless prattle with which advertisements, magazine covers, and flashy cars assaulted the eye.

The nihilistic culture of Berlin in the twenties turned out to be sound preparation for the life of the refugee in the thirties. Like baggage that has to be abandoned in the rush to get away, Gutmann's aesthetic attitudes were left be-

hind in Germany. But even if he'd wanted to, he couldn't have gotten along without certain social attitudes acquired there.

Nobody was more a Berliner than George Grosz, nor readier to leave when the time came to get out. If Brecht's ballads were the sarcastic voice of Berlin in the Weimar period — the city's wisecracks — then Grosz's cartoons were the disparaging glance Berliners cast at the world. The sour, paranoid view of German society and politics that Grosz took enabled him to be prescient enough about the Nazis to leave Germany for good shortly before the Reichstag fire of 1933.

He landed in New York, which he had first photographed the previous summer as a visitor. His pictures look a great deal like Gutmann's. Shot at Expressionistic angles, revealing the American as a blurry face in a crowd, these photographs convey a strong sense of the disorientation and dismay he felt upon his arrival (fig. 15.4). The implication of these photographs, like that in much of Gutmann's work, is that what was happening back home in Germany had frazzled his view of all societies everywhere. Much of the photography of the postwar period was to be similar in appearance. Beyond being the vision shared by filmmakers and artists or German Jews or Berlin intellectuals, it was the one that belonged to the displaced person.

In the discussion of European photographers earlier, the theme of the displaced person has already arisen. It runs throughout the history of street photography in the twentieth century, from that Kertész picture of fleeing refugees greeting each other to Koudelka's whole career. The most eloquent reflections on the fate of such people were Hannah Arendt's. She saw them as the ultimate modern individuals, human beings who, stripped of the basic legal rights that nationality secures, have only their own inner resources left.

In her characterization of them, they are a kind of absurdist parody of the artist, people trying to live on sensibility alone. They are, at any rate, men and women who have to learn to live by their wits if they are to survive at all. The displaced person is someone who must be able to trust his or her instincts completely, never giving way to that moment's hesitation in which all might be lost. This is a discipline for which the quick reflexes of the street photographer were excellent practice.

Another refugee who had to stoop to hustling, scrambling, and scraping by, and ultimately to street photography to support herself, was Lisette Model. Although she came from Vienna, Model had a background similar to Gutmann's, which gave her a Berliner's perspective on life. She too had come from a wealthy family and studied painting before taking up photography. She had been exposed to avant-garde art and unconventional ideas from the time she was a child, when her favorite playmate was the daughter of composer (and future émigré to Hollywood) Arnold Schönberg. Like Gutmann, Model turned to photography at the suggestion of a friend who pointed out that with the rise of Hitler, it might be useful to have an itinerant profession.

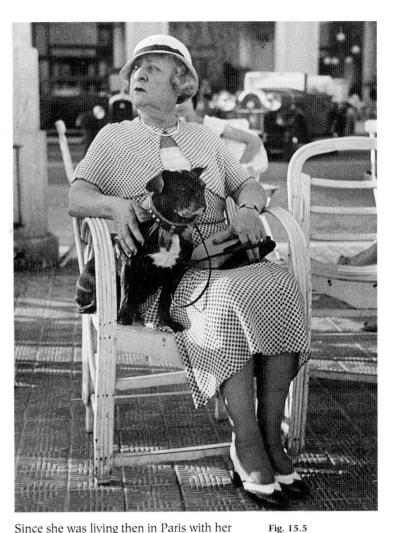

Fig. 15.5
LISETTE MODEL
Promenade des Anglais, Nice, c. 1937

Since she was living then in Paris with her Russian Jewish husband, this seemed to Model a good idea. With some instruction from Kertész's wife, Elizabeth, she set out for the south of France to try her hand at street photography. From the very beginning she sought out subjects who would suggest the corruptness of society. Pictures from the test rolls she shot along the Promenade des Anglais in Nice could easily be taken for caricatures George Grosz had drawn of cabaret goers on the Kurfürstendamm.

Like Grosz, Model saw her subjects as misshapen, almost beastly. A wealthy dowager is photographed at a moment when her face has exactly the same expression as her lapdog's (fig. 15.5). A gambler sunning himself in a chair watches Model with a lizard eye and hands curled like the talons of a pet bird of prey gripping its perch. Model worked often in

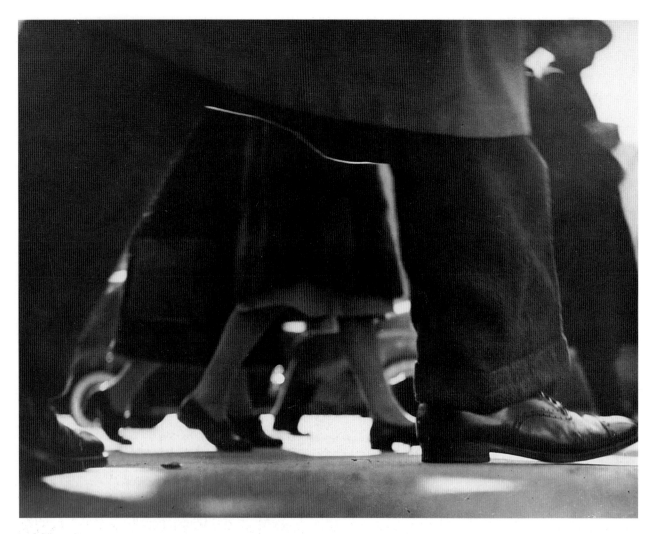

Fig. 15.6
LISETTE MODEL
Running Legs, 1949

the late afternoon, thus giving us the impression that darkness is about to descend on the world in which these people live. When she got back to Paris, she continued her project by making pictures of the poor that complemented those she had done of the rich. She again photographed the obese and the grotesque.

Petite and refined though Model was, her photographs are as aggressive as an assault with a blunt instrument. Nearly all are the most direct of street portraits, head-on confrontations with unattractive subjects. They have a brutal look whose relentless consistency from one picture to the next implies a universal brutishness inherent in man himself. It's a look Model emphasized by always insisting on big (16 x 20"), rough prints. And in America she continued to see the world in

the same terms, photographing both derelicts and society matrons, so that they reflected each other's grossness. She found in American vulgarity the perfect counterpoint to the European decadence she had left behind.

The only change that seems to have come over her photography was in the direction of a greater Expressionism, making her images still more like Gutmann's and Grosz's. Model began photographing reflections of the street in shop windows in a way that makes New York look like the town in which Dr. Caligari lived. She also started a series in which she lowered the camera to the level of the sidewalk to catch the blurry tangle of passing feet (fig. 15.6). This imagery is straight out of the bad dreams of a refugee from Nazism. The pictures have an oppressive, claustrophobic

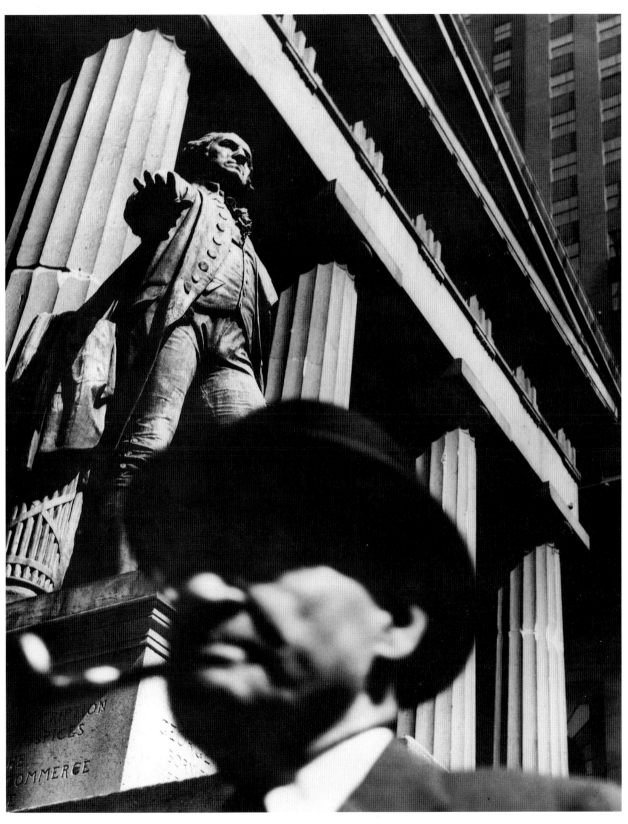

Fig. 15.7
LISETTE MODEL
Wall Street, c. 1945

feeling, as if made by somebody who had lost her footing in a panic in the streets and was being trampled by the crowd.

Some of Model's other pictures from the 1940s, in which she aimed up at passersby at close range, are a variation on the same theme. In one, a banker in a bowler walks under the statue of George Washington on Wall Street (fig. 15.7). The statue extends its hand in what looks like a gesture meant to keep someone on his knees from rising. A massive, grisly figure, so close that he is out of focus, the banker has a shadow like a bandit's mask concealing his eyes. He bears down on Model as if about to run her over. She appears to be literally beneath his notice.

Thus does a misanthropy that began in Nice continue in New York until, in Venezuela in the 1950s, it seems to have come full circle — to have become in effect a vicious circle — in some pictures that she took of life-size voodoo dolls. Sitting up in chairs, these effigies could almost be the mummified corpses of real people. (They look like the slowly decomposing remains of the guests at the Riviera hotels whom Model had photographed in their chairs along the Promenade des Anglais almost twenty years earlier.)

Like Gutmann, Model had a long career as a teacher but a relatively short one as a working photographer. Although she got a steady stream of assignments from *Harper's Bazaar* for a while, those ended by 1951, and virtually all the photographs for which she is known were taken in the thirties and forties. In fact, her entire American reputation was built on those few test rolls shot on the Riviera. That she was praised effusively for such a meager body of work only made her initial success in America seem to her as specious and potentially transient as life had proven to be in Europe.

She mistrusted the fact that the Americans were, as she put it, "making [a] beginner into a star, putting me on a pedestal for something I didn't even know . . . I was doing."[8] Her rough, overenlarged prints were admired in the same fashion, for an artistry to which they did not pretend. When Edward Weston wanted to know how she achieved the effect they had, she told him that she took her film to the corner drugstore to be processed. The sarcastic answer, the grainy prints, the ugly subject matter, and the crude negatives that were often motion-blurred or out of focus were all of a piece. So was the imagery. Like those of Grosz or Gutmann, her pictures match a disregard for art with a disrespect for the world as she saw it.

16: Naturalized Citizens

After she arrived in America, Lisette Model was discovered in 1940 by Ralph Steiner, who was then picture editor of *PM* magazine. He must have thought he was seeing double when she showed him her Nice portfolio — he immediately published it under the title "Why France Fell" — for here was the European counterpart to his star photographer Weegee. The nose for pictures each had was so nearly the same that within a few years it would lead them both to a New York hangout called Sammy's on the Bowery. A dive where the rich sometimes went slumming, Sammy's confirmed Model's view, which Weegee had formed on his own in New York, that the upper classes are a mirror image of the bums and derelicts.

Weegee was one of photography's "boys in the back room," to borrow a phrase that Edmund Wilson used to characterize tough-guy writers like James M. Cain and Raymond Chandler. These were the American novelists in whom émigré movie director Billy Wilder found a kindred spirit, much as émigré photographers Model or John Gutmann did in Weegee. Sammy's had the type of back room Wilson was thinking of — one where a card game was always in progress — and the press room at police headquarters out of which Weegee worked as a crime reporter had an equally seedy atmosphere. Weegee was in effect warming the chair that had been vacated by Jacob Riis, who had taken a photograph of the place that looks a lot like one Gutmann made in Reno, Nevada.

For the novelists, the filmmakers, and the photographers alike, back rooms such as these were a visible metaphor for an impression they had that life in America was a gamble (and the fix might be in). None was more at home there than Weegee, nor was anybody else able to speak the lingo as well as he, to document American life in its own, authentic idiom. In 1944, just as he was about to wind up a ten-year career as a free-lance photographer supplying pictures of fires, crimes, automobile accidents, and the victims of all three to the New York dailies, he gave a lecture at the Modern during which someone in the audience suggested he should put out a book of his pictures. *Naked City* was published the following year and became an instant classic of the genre.

Originally, Weegee had been another kind of street photographer, the sidewalk variety who peddles souvenir snaps to tourists and families on Sunday outings in the park. This promising business had folded suddenly when, after a season of rainy weekends, he couldn't pay the feed bill for the pony named Hypo that he worked with. That was around the end of World War I, and for the next fifteen years he worked as a studio assistant or darkroom technician, trying to find a way to support himself full-time as a photographer. It wasn't until 1935 that he went out on his own again, this time as a newshawk, and succeeded.

Adopting the standard press camera of his day, the Speed Graphic, and using the flashbulbs that had recently replaced the flash powder of Riis's day, Weegee worked very much in the manner of Riis. That is, he shot in the dark, seldom being able to predict what, if anything, he would get. This reliance on blind chance to get some of his most effective pictures is obvious in those he had to take through car windows at the scenes of accidents. He could never be sure whether the flash would bounce off the glass or go through it, or where the reflections and shadows would fall. On one occasion what made a picture was the mirror image, in the open side vent, of a bleeding face inside the car. On another a woman who is herself uninjured, but has killed someone else in a collision, sits behind the wheel of her car in shock (fig. 16.1). In the picture, she reaches for a policeman with an outstretched hand that is oddly cut off by a shadow the flash has created. The severed hand serves as an image of both the car crash itself and her own disconnection from it at this moment.

Fig. 16.1
WEEGEE
(ARTHUR FELLIG)
Accident Victim in
Shock, 1940

Headlines weren't all that Weegee's shots illustrated. Many were meant as human-interest stories. He could stalk intimacy as well as catastrophe, photographing at night with infrared bulbs the lovers on the beach at Coney Island or the smoochers in a Times Square movie theater. In the total darkness of such places he worked as sightlessly as Riis had in cellars with no windows and hallways without gas lamps. He learned to see with his ears like a blind man. "Every time I heard a sigh or a groan in the dark," he said in his autobiography, *Weegee by Weegee*, "I pushed the button."[1] Like Riis too, Weegee invaded tenements at night to take their inhabitants unawares with his flash. Climbing out on a fire escape, he would aim down at the landing below to catch a brood of children or a fat, naked man asleep in the stifling heat.

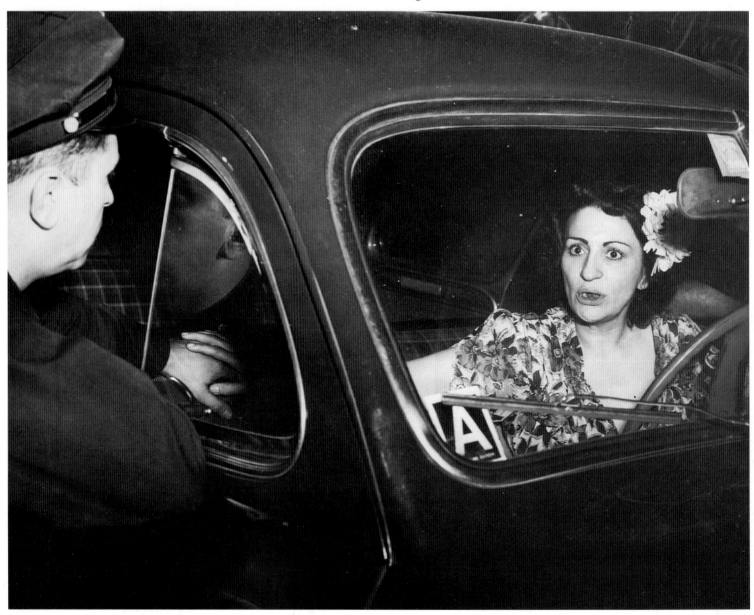

When these pictures were exhibited at the Modern, he was asked how he knew where to find such interesting subjects. "How did I know about them?" he replied. "Hell! That's the way I had slept."[2] He was like Riis not least of all in having come to America as an immigrant — from Austria-Hungary, at age ten — and lived in poverty on the Lower East Side. He even went through a period like Riis's when he was broke and homeless, sleeping on the streets. Where his career differed from Riis's was in the audience for whom his photography was done. The readers of Riis's books and the churchgoers attending his lectures were the middle class, whose conscience he hoped to prick. Weegee's photographs of the poor were made — at least originally — for the poor themselves, the working class who bought the *Daily News* and other lowbrow tabloids in which his reputation was made.

The power of Weegee's photography lay in his ability to reflect the views and emotions of this audience. How strongly he identified with it is obvious on the first page of *Naked City*. The opening chapter is entitled "Sunday Morning in Manhattan," and the photograph on the facing page is of the scene that Weegee began by describing:

> The Sunday papers, all bundled up, are thrown on the sidewalk in front of the still-closed candystores and newspaper stands. New Yorkers like their Sunday papers, especially the lonely men and women who live in furnished rooms. They leave early to get the papers . . . they get two. One of the standard-size papers, either the Times or Tribune . . . and then also the tabloid Mirror . . . to read Winchell and learn all about Cafe Society and the Broadway playboys and their Glamour Girl Friends. Then back to the room . . . to read and read . . . to drive away the loneliness.[3]

This sad sack for whom the high point of the day was going out to get the papers was Weegee's ideal reader, his captive audience. At the same time, the life described here was Weegee's own. He too lived alone in a furnished room, one located in a drab building across the street from police headquarters. Like the fan of gossip columnists he wrote about in this passage, he longed for romance and glamour. That's why he went to Hollywood in the late forties to devote himself to trick shots of show biz celebrities. In the end, he seems to have been less interested in taking pictures than in being in them with movie stars.

In a sense, Weegee's photography was more democratic than Riis's. Weegee's pictures were not only for the people and by the people (since he was one of them himself), but of the people. His subjects were the same as his readers. And yet there was a macabre gulf separating the subjects of the photographs from the photographer and his audience. Despite the affection that the opening paragraph of *Naked City* shows for downtrodden New Yorkers, Weegee's pictures can be absolutely merciless to them. Riis's subjects are pitiful, but Weegee's are worse off. They are laughable, and he was pitiless. He had a knack for catching them at just that instant when pain and defeat had left them goggle-eyed. Although his pictures are full of catastrophes, life in them is never tragic. People are never ennobled by their misery. The human condition falls flat on its puss.

The opening passage of *Naked City* throws on Weegee's pictures a light as eerie and electric as that from his flash. His words contain an empathetic wisdom about why his audience liked his work so much. "People could forget their own troubles reading about others'," he explained.[4] This remark acknowledges that measure of distraction, or even of satisfaction, that human beings can get from seeing their fellow men arbitrarily chosen for suffering. This was what Weegee's photography appealed to, and it was a human capacity that had shaped to a certain degree the history of the 1930s and 1940s. Part of the reason that people who would never have looked at Weegee's pictures in the newspapers pondered them on museum walls after the war

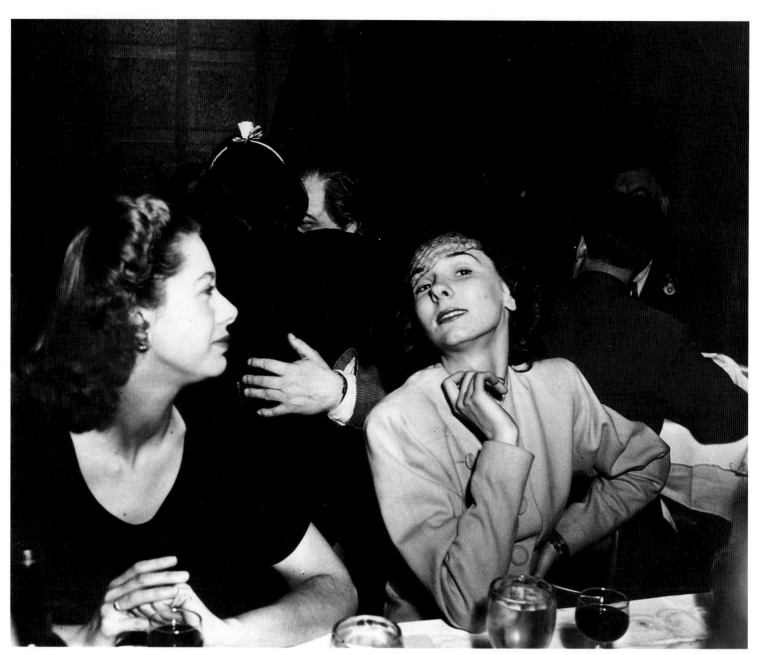

Fig. 16.2
WEEGEE
(ARTHUR FELLIG)
Untitled, c. 1943

may be that they felt a need to grasp the mass psychology such photographs represented.

It was not only at exhibitions, but in the pages of *Vogue,* where Alexander Liberman published Weegee's work after the war, that café society could look at itself in this way. Again, it must be admitted that there was something basically democratic about Weegee's vision. His photography was a great social leveler. It put the rich in as bad a light as the poor. Where the common man was too lively for his own good, his energy

spilling over into violence, high society was seen by Weegee as effete.

The infrared flash he often used for the shots of charity balls and opening nights at the opera that he began making in the early forties highlighted blemishes, accentuated stubble, and transformed a crown in a row of teeth into a dark gap. It turned eyes blank and rendered skin pale and nerveless. To enhance these enervated effects, Weegee tended to shoot at moments when his subjects' faces lacked all animation. His infrared photography made its subjects look like zombies. It implied that high society was the world of the living dead.

The composition of the imagery created in nightclubs and at charity events might almost remind us of Brassaï in the way that it betrays romantic illusions (fig. 16.2). More instructive than occasional similarities between these two photographers, however, are the differences. In Brassaï's best pictures there is a very French rationality, a dialectic that is given visible form by opposing diagonals. The power of Weegee's images is that they are irrational.

Weegee's work relies upon — literally — a killer instinct for pictures. (He once photographed a derelict as the man picked himself up off a sidewalk, stumbled out into traffic, and was run over by a car.) Brassaï's work is imbued with an element of formalism, or at least of balanced composition. The photographs have a center and thereby suggest a certain equanimity in the world that he depicted. Even criminals are convivial here. His vision worked by centripetal force, pulling everything in the frame together, unifying the society in which he lived. Weegee's vision was explosive, blowing the world apart. He showed law-abiding citizens in the aftermath of murder and mayhem. The force in his pictures is centrifugal. The best of them are sheer chaos.

Perhaps his most characteristic images are the reaction shots in which everybody seems to be looking in a different direction. He saw such wacky disorder in all strata of society, from the kids at the scene of a murder to a rehearsal at the Metropolitan Opera. A shot that has a similar effect is of a veritable melee among a gang of teenagers. One anguished face that looms up in the flash too close to the camera to be in focus seems to represent the whole mass of bodies behind (page 309). There is no focus anywhere in this image, even where it is optically sharp. The figures tussling this way and that in the background are all white, while on the wall beyond them

is graffiti reading "The Nigers Stink." The photograph is an image of America as an ethnic free-for-all — not the crapshoot that John Gutmann saw, but the brawl into which the gambling eventually erupts. Here the rules of the game have broken down completely.

If Weegee's street photography differed fundamentally from that of Brassaï and other Parisians, it was because New York was, in contrast to Paris, a tough, graceless town. It demanded another kind of imagery. Brassaï's subjects were all poseurs. Weegee's were schleppers and schlemiels. They made his stumblebum timing and panhandler images (catch as catch can, take what you can get) seem natural. His picture making was done at a pace that matched the historical onslaught, the incessant rush of faces and cultures, that the waves of immigration had represented. He claimed that he went through ten press cameras and five cars in a decade, plus twenty cigars and cups of coffee every night. His philosophy was that "a picture is like a blintz . . . eat it while it's hot."[5]

So he kept pumping them out nonstop until he put himself out of business. "You've been peddling the same pictures to us now for six years," an editor finally told him, "and for all I know, it's the same dead gangster and the same gray fedora lying on the sidewalk. . . . No more dead gangsters." Weegee confessed that in the end, "I had so many unsold murder pictures lying around my room, . . . I felt as if I were renting out a wing of the City Morgue."[6]

A photograph he had made at Coney Island contains within a single frame the transition that occurred in his career at this point, the move from corpses to starlets for his subjects. A crowd has gathered around a drowned man, everyone staring grimly at the body except his girlfriend, who, looking up and seeing a photographer, automatically smiles for the camera (fig. 16.3). In a world where the lure of fame is so strong that it overrides even basic decencies and primal emotions like grief, Weegee knew just where to go once he'd worn out

Fig. 16.3
WEEGEE
(ARTHUR FELLIG)
Coney Island, 1940

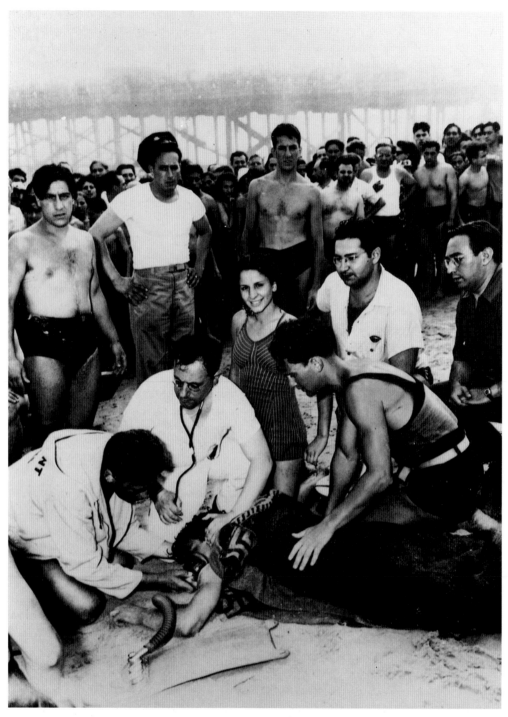

his welcome in New York. He headed for Hollywood.

Weegee was a lot like New York's colorful mayor Fiorello La Guardia, who got into many a photograph by going to fires as often as Weegee himself. La Guardia served as head of the city's government during the decade that Weegee was its premier crime photographer, from the early thirties through the early forties. Like La Guardia, Weegee was something of a Depression hero, a man of the people, a real live New York character. That public image was what he traded on to win entrée to the movie colony. His big break came when columnist-producer Mark Hellinger bought the rights to *Naked City* and made it into a lurid crime melodrama that pioneered the technique of shooting movies on location in the New York streets, the way Weegee had done the photographs. Weegee signed on as a consultant to the movie, and when production on it was completed he closed up his room across from police headquarters to move permanently to the West Coast.

He even became a bit player there in other films noirs, including a remake of Fritz Lang's *M,* in which he played a murder suspect. But the best casting done for him was in a Cary Grant vehicle called *Every Girl Should Be Married.* Weegee played a sidewalk photographer who sells passersby pictures of themselves. He was typecast, in other words, as just the sort of photo hustler he had actually been thirty years earlier when he worked with his pony Hypo.

Of all the street photographers who have worked in New York, from Riis to Weegee and Model, from Robert Frank and William Klein to Garry Winogrand, the only one whose pictures don't seem alienated is Roy DeCarava. There is a certain irony in this, since DeCarava, a black man, might have had better reason than anybody else to feel dispossessed, bitter, and cynical. He doesn't feel that way, because he is the one photographer who is truly at home in the city, or at least in the part of it where he photographs, Harlem. He was born there in 1919, in Harlem Hospital, and has stayed in the neighborhood all his life. DeCarava is such an anomaly that for once comparison to a Parisian seems appropriate. He has found in New York the appealing working-class atmosphere that we think of as belonging only to the *banlieux* of Paris. He is our American Doisneau.

He even sounds like Doisneau when he talks about his pictures, exclaiming over how the subject in one of them, for instance, could be "ugly and brutalizing and . . . beautiful" all at once.[7] Like Doisneau, he finds in the very meagerness of his surroundings the source of their charms, their humanity. The photograph he was speaking about here might have been

any one of the Doisneau-like images he made. In fact, it is of a tenement hallway especially representative of DeCarava's own, unique eye. It is a dim, barren, claustrophobic space; yet as he views it, it is also symmetrical, balanced, almost tranquil in a way. His shots of the streets are often done from the same point of view. He sights down the middle of the street at the woman crossing with her children or kids playing stickball amid traffic. He looks out from between two buildings that frame and center the passersby on the pavement; he looks down the subway steps at the two men standing like sentinels at the ends of the railings on either side.

He has compared the moment he searches for in his photography to the one when the pole-vaulter is at his apogee, "neither going up nor going down. . . . The moment when all the forces fuse, when all is in equilibrium, that's the eternal . . . that's jazz . . . and that's life."[8] The action, like the composition, must be in perfect balance in his photographs. Only in this way can they express DeCarava's sense of the harmony and stability of the world around him.

Often this visual equilibrium is achieved by looking down on the scene, enclosing the subjects in a horizonless world where all conflict and contrast are evened out. Thus do the action in the picture and the backdrop against which it's set attain a certain yin-and-yang quality. The height from which such pictures are usually made is a very specific one, high enough to have an overview and reflect on the scene, but not so high that you become detached from it. This is the view that you get looking out the window of a typical Harlem brownstone or tenement.

In *The Sweet Flypaper of Life,* the 1955 book that DeCarava did with the poet Langston Hughes, watching the world from your window is a special form of entertainment. It is that time when, taking a break from housekeeping in her drab apartment, "a woman gets a chance to set in her window for a minute and look out."[9] The accompanying photograph is of the woman just as Hughes described her, and on the following pages are some of the scenes she sees in the street below. "Yes, you can set in your window anywhere in Harlem and see plenty,"[10] the book reiterates later, again with a picture of somebody perched behind the sill. DeCarava has attempted to create a comparable intimacy and scale in longer views by either using a telephoto lens or blowing up a small part of a negative. He is the only street photographer who can do this without having the results look like snooping. It is as if he wanted to draw the life on the street closer to him by any means he could.

A picture of two boys playing guns in the schoolyard reveals another side of DeCarava's personality as a photographer as well. The image has great significance for him because he spent more than a decade trying to get the print just right. Nothing worked until, he says, "I printed it on the softest paper I could find and pushed it as far as possible on the black end and it came out perfectly."[11] For him, the need to see into the shadows is the paramount consideration: "My concern is always in how I . . . modulate my grays. The emphasis is really not on the black tones. . . . I only use black when there is a black object, when it's solid, when it's a black wall. But space is not black unless there is no light, and since there is always a little bit of light, such space is always dark gray."[12]

Besides the pictures that have readable shadows next to bright sunshine, there are many more in which, as he says, only "a little bit of light" is shown. That he photographs his black subjects in a dark space compels the viewer to adjust his vision, to make subtle distinctions, to see shades of meaning and emotion as well as light. The effect is to humanize subjects who are frequently viewed only as stereotypes in our society. DeCarava doesn't see the world in which he lives in the black-and-white terms to which race relations outside too often reduce it. The civil disturbances of the sixties have a very peripheral and fragmentary place in his life's work. The bulk of it

is, rather, photographs in which his subjects emerge softly from the shadows. What is most striking about his imagery is the exception it makes to the postwar rule of grainy prints, contrasty papers, and a harsh misanthropy among photographers.

17: An American in Paris

When he was growing up in the 1930s on the West Side of Manhattan — Weegee territory — William Klein felt as if he were caught in a vise, being squeezed socially from both above and below. On the one hand, he and his family were the poor relations of a clan of successful lawyers, partners in Louis Nizer's firm, who had connections to the West Coast and show business. Klein was in agony when he had to accompany his badly off parents every year to Thanksgiving dinner at the sumptuous home of relatives from whom his father scraped together a living selling insurance. On the other hand, as a lower-middle-class Jew growing up in a tough Irish-Italian neighborhood, Klein also spent his youth dodging local street gangs. "In rough neighborhoods in New York," as he recalls, "it doesn't do to show you see certain people. It's better not to look."[1] Like the annual ritual of Thanksgiving dinner, the daily ordeal of getting home from school was humiliating. He felt out of place no matter which way he turned.

Although not a displaced person in the sense that someone like Hannah Arendt was, Klein nonetheless shared her feeling that, as she lamented many years after coming to New York, "I somehow don't fit."[2] As a consequence, when the GI Bill provided him with an exit visa in 1948, Klein jumped at the chance to leave America. He went to France to become a painter. He first studied with André Lhôte, but then switched to a man whom he considered a greater master, Fernand Léger. Léger, only recently returned to France, had been yet another of the displaced artists who waited out the war in America.

Klein may not have been accustomed to thinking in political terms before he went to Paris, but he learned to do so under the tutelage of Léger. "He blew my little bourgeois mind," Klein has said.

> Here was a great artist who told us that galleries were dead, easel painting was finished, a socialist who'd been to Russia and America, experimented with film and design, who'd gone his own way against all the Parisian fads and fashions of the time. . . . He wanted us to get out of the studios into

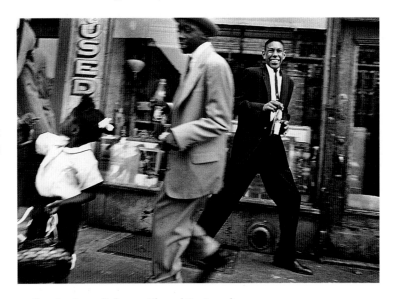

> the streets, or link up with architects as he had with Le Corbusier. He wanted us to be monumental.[3]

Fig. 17.1
WILLIAM KLEIN
Harlem, 1955

Klein threw himself wholeheartedly into the program of work that Léger recommended. He produced wall-size murals that did indeed lead him into a collaboration with an architect, an Italian who saw his abstract paintings at a Milan gallery in 1952 and proposed to use them as freestanding room dividers that would pivot as people entered and exited the space. Before the year was out a prototype room had been constructed, and Klein set about documenting the results with a camera. At one point he bumped one of the panels, causing it to revolve in the middle of the long exposure that the dim interior required. This mischance was to send his career off in a whole new direction.

He was pleased with the motion-blurred image the rotating panel created and tried to duplicate the effect in the darkroom. The patterns that resulted were blown up again in order to be turned into more murals and panels. This success encouraged him to take a further interest in photography, so he began using a Rolleiflex he had won in a poker game in the army to take visual notes.

On one occasion, when he was traveling through the region of Holland where Mondrian had lived during World War I, he photographed barns on which it was the custom to paint the siding dark while outlining window and door frames in white. By doing reversal prints that made these facades look like black outlining on white walls, Klein created in the darkroom an imagery similar to Mondrian's paintings. The following year, 1953, the pictures were used as illustrations for an article about Mondrian, thereby becoming Klein's first published photographs. Images like these expanded his sense of the medium. They carried him from the darkroom out into the everyday world. They provided a link between artistic experiment and straight photography.

The rotating panels were also seen at an exhibition in Paris by *Vogue* art director Alexander Liberman, who offered Klein a contract because, he has explained, Klein was "the first to bring into photography what Léger achieved in art — the glorification of the life and rhythms of the street."[4] The sense of rhythm Liberman mentioned is apparent in a little movie Klein made in 1958, *Broadway by Light.*

This film, which was Klein's first, was proclaimed by Orson Welles to be the first that had ever made color a truly necessary, integral element. Its bold use of neon light owes much to Léger, who had been greatly impressed by the same subject, the electric signs

in Times Square, while he was in exile in New York during the war. Afterward, he began using color as a free-floating wash in his paintings. Like Léger — or like Mondrian in *Broadway Boogie Woogie* — Klein saw the bright lights of Broadway as a kind of visual jazz.

Although Liberman's comparison of Klein and Léger was apt, taking up photography brought to the surface some conflicts Klein had been feeling under Léger's influence. Photography became a way to get out from under the burden of a part of the history of modern art. From the moment he had seen how that spinning panel looked in a time exposure, Klein liked photography's ability to give an impression of movement. He found the set structure in much of modern painting to be confining. His restlessness was already apparent, even in the hard-edged abstraction of the original murals shown in Milan. Their slashing lines and angular, interrupted shapes look like someone's frantic attempt to hack his way out of Analytic Cubism.

At the time, Klein was bored with what he has since called "the same old paintings of circles, squares, and triangles."[5] In his first photographic experiments in the darkroom, he cut these shapes out of black cardboard and literally threw them away. Then he took the cardboard remnants with their geometric holes and passed them, wandlike, over photographic paper. The result was something abstractly Expressionistic that pleased him. He was discarding a formalism basic to earlier modern art, leaving himself free to invent an informal substitute. He was both ridding himself of the fundamentals of drawing, the basic shapes that art students are taught in their first studio class, and adopting in their place the elementary printing techniques — dodging, masking, burning in — that the photography students learn in their first darkroom course. He was reinventing photography to suit himself.

The one thing that Klein hung on to from his time with Léger was not the old painter's aesthetics, but his personality. What he liked about Léger — "this big tough guy," as Klein has affectionately called him — was his feisty, combative nature. In Klein's most vivid recollection, Léger was "a street fighter, a pug, a peasant."[6] Klein could identify with him. Klein's accounts of himself as a photographer are filled with metaphors of brawling and boxing: "Sometimes, I'd take shots without aiming, just to see what happened. I'd rush into

was what he was spoiling for when Liberman offered him a trip to America for *Vogue* in 1954. Klein saw this as a chance to do a photo book, *New York*, about his hometown. "I thought New York had it coming," he has explained, "that it needed a kick in the balls."[9] He was itching for action, like a member of one of those neighborhood gangs he had had to flee from as a boy. "When I returned to New York," he has said, "I

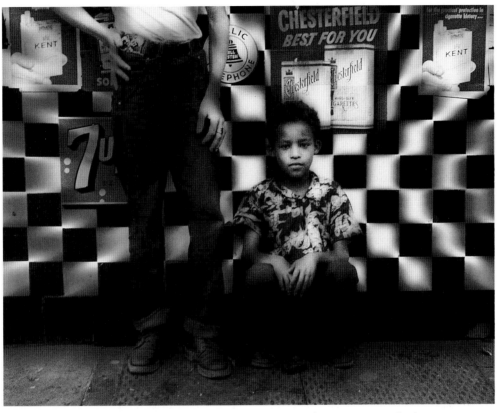

Fig. 17.2
WILLIAM KLEIN
Candy Store,
Amsterdam Avenue,
New York, 1954–55

crowds — bang! bang! . . . It must be close to what a fighter feels after jabbing and circling and getting hit, when suddenly there's an opening, and bang! Right on the button. It's a fantastic feeling."[7]

To qualify for weekend passes when he was in the army, Klein himself competed as a boxer. Since he didn't want to get beaten up, he would try to rig his fights. This tells us more about the kind of scrapper he was than does the mere fact that he got into the ring. He was the kind who doesn't obey the rules. As a photographer, he's just the same. "Anything goes," he says.[8] Street photography appealed to him because it's like a street fight, which

wanted to get even. Now I had a weapon, photography."[10]

Among the laws he broke were Cartier-Bresson's. "I liked Cartier-Bresson's pictures," he says, "but I didn't like his set of rules. So I reversed them."[11] Since Cartier-Bresson had declared the 50mm lens to be the norm for street photography, Klein preferred one with a wide angle. More important, instead of being inconspicuous and unobtrusive with his camera, he used it as a provocation. He stuck it in his subjects' faces. He brandished it at them as if it were a Saturday night special he was using to stick up a liquor store. The rules he could violate by doing so included not only

Cartier-Bresson's, but those by which he himself had had to live as a boy. Now there was nobody he was afraid to look in the eye.

The pictures in which his subjects look back at him set the pace for all his work. They are the superheated core of it. They have an urgent rhythm, a distinctly fifties beat, like the sound of bongo drums. Again refuting Cartier-Bresson, Klein insists, "I never say: 'Don't look at the camera.' " [12] On the contrary, he likes best the subjects who can give as good as they get — the ones who not only return his stare, but react to it, baring to his camera the kind of naked hostility that made his life miserable as a kid. If they won't give him that flash of anger he wants, he makes them look like losers, poor palookas who can't take the punishment that the city dishes out.

The only violence greater than the one he does to New Yorkers is that done to photography itself. His desire to get even with his subjects was only part of the reason that the trip home appealed to him. The rest of it was the opportunity to see how far his ideas about the medium could be pushed. Being the rough, tough town it was made New York the perfect place for Klein to try out his slam-bang style as a photographer. His own explanation of the way he approached picture taking is that "I have always done the opposite of what I was trained to do. . . . Having little technical background, I become a photographer. Adopting a machine, I do my utmost to make it malfunction. For me, to make a photograph was to make an anti-photograph." [13]

One way that he abused his negatives was by allowing movement to smear or fracture the image (fig. 17.1). (The inadequacies of photography at slow speeds and in low light were what first attracted him, after all.) His justification for such effects is that "if you look carefully at life, you see blur. Shake your hand. Blur is a part of life." [14] Klein didn't respect the standards of fine printing any more than he did the ethics of street photography as laid down by Cartier-Bresson. In fact,

there is a certain parallel in his attitudes toward the two.

If his mere presence didn't provoke the aggressive behavior he wanted from a subject, Klein didn't hesitate to meddle in the scene more directly, like the time he suggested to a Puerto Rican woman that she pose holding a toy pistol to the head of her grinning, cross-eyed son. Similarly, if a negative didn't already have motion blur in it, he might jiggle the enlarger head to create some. This is how he activated the image of a solemn child in front of a checkerboard tile wall (fig. 17.2). He moved the head up and down slightly so that in the print the wall would seem to rush at us, to attack us.

Klein "brutalized" his equipment, he says, because he wanted his book to be "as vulgar and brutal as the *News*." [15] He was referring to the *New York Daily News*, which is, like boxing, frequently mentioned in his interviews. In the one he gave to John Halpern he explained,

> *The New York book was a visual diary and it was also a kind of personal newspaper. I wanted it to look like the* News. *I didn't relate to European photography. It was too poetic and anecdotal for me. . . . The kinetic quality of New York, the kids, dirt, madness — I tried to find a photographic style that would come close to it. So I would be grainy and contrasted and black. I'd crop, blur, play with the negatives. I didn't see clean technique being right for New York. I could imagine my pictures lying in the gutter like the New York* Daily News. [16]

He even shot a photograph — as if he were trying his fantasy on for size — of crumpled copies of the *News* thrown in a heap in the subway. The New York tabloid photographer to whom he was paying tribute here was of course Weegee. He and Jacob Riis are the first photographers Klein mentions when asked whose work he admires. Klein recognizes in himself some of that callousness which made

Weegee a great crime photographer. When a terrorist bomb went off in the restaurant on the ground floor of his own apartment building in Paris, Klein and his wife were among the first on the scene. She immediately began helping the wounded, but his impulse, he confesses, was "to grab a camera."[17] With his New York subjects, Klein's relationship is as ambivalent as Weegee's was. He too identifies with the hapless people whom his photographs savage. Like Weegee, he is one of them himself, a reader of the *Daily News,* a wise-assed guy whose only ambition in life is to be able to survive on his street smarts.

The closeness he feels to his subjects, despite his readiness to victimize them, comes out when he talks about snapshot photography. In it, the same people he takes pictures of become the photographers themselves. He loves the results because they are "just photographs, without rules or dogmas."[18] They capture directly the crass innocence at which his own work aims: "I have always loved the amateur side of photography, automatic photographs, accidental photographs with uncentered compositions, heads cut off, whatever. I incite people to make their self-portraits; I see myself as their walking photo booth."[19]

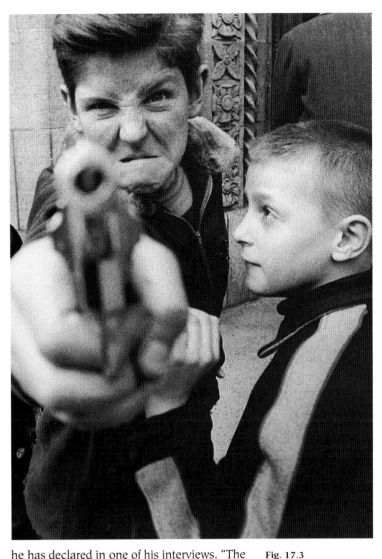

Fig. 17.3
WILLIAM KLEIN
Broadway and 103rd Street, New York,
1954–55

Klein's automatic photography, like the automatic writing of the Surrealists, is produced by a combination of trance and chance. This was what he was getting at in the subtitle of his New York book, *Trance Witness Revels.* The wording is a play on "chance witness reveals," a stock phrase commonly found in the subheads on the front page of papers like the *News.* The pun on "trance" suggests that mixture of obliviousness and vulnerability that Klein not only exploits in his subjects but cultivates in himself. It evokes an image of somebody zonked out on photography.

The double entendre with which his book begins might be thought of as a one-sentence introduction to it. "I believe that I have said in three words what I think about photography,"

he has declared in one of his interviews. "The action of photographing is for me a moment of trance when one can seize several hundred things that are occurring simultaneously and that one senses, that one sees, whether consciously or not."[20] Like a play on words, a photograph should revel in ambiguity. It should go in as many irreconcilable directions as it can, which is precisely what Klein's photographs do when he plunges into a crowd of scowling, gawking, grinning people with his wide-angle lens.

At such moments Klein is, like Weegee (or John Gutmann), the hero of his own film noir. He hears the same voices in the darkness that Robert Siodmak did in his movie *Cry of the City.* Klein has said as much himself: "My

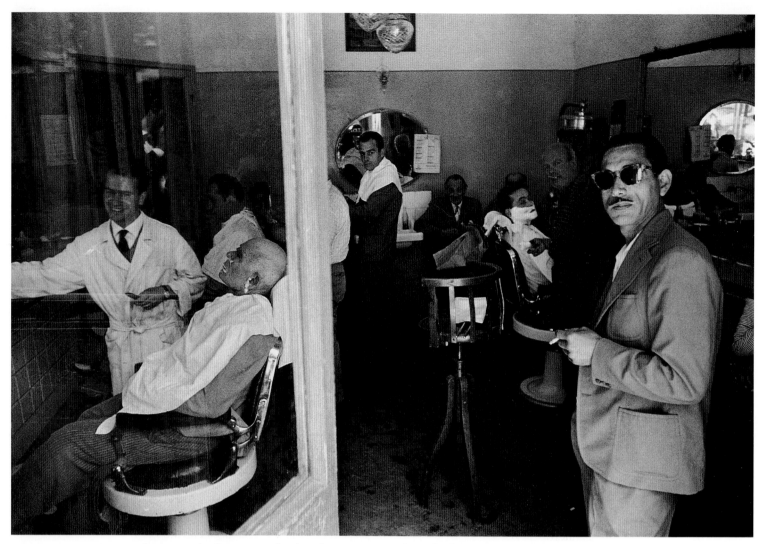

Fig. 17.4
WILLIAM KLEIN
Barbershop, Rome, 1956

photos are the fragments of a shapeless cry that tries to say who knows what. . . . What would please me most is to make photographs as incomprehensible as life."[21] The ambivalence he felt toward New Yorkers instilled in the pictures this ambiguity he craved (page 311).

Although Klein may be, as he says, a walking photo booth for his subjects, a chance for them to take pictures of themselves while he merely holds the camera, their pictures are also portraits of him. What could be a better likeness of Klein with his camera than the photograph he made of a boy sticking a pistol in his face (fig. 17.3)? Like a real mugger, this figure is so menacing that he gets all our attention. We tend to lose sight of the fact that there is another boy in the picture as well. But we have to be aware of the presence of this second subject too, or we miss the point of the photograph.

Where the first subject is the big boy Klein became when he grew up and got his camera, the other is the little boy he once was, somebody scared and quiet who stands there in awe of the violence all around him. Although the smaller boy reaches for his pal's arm as if to stop him from drilling Klein, the gesture is timid. He seems afraid to interfere. Like the many Klein subjects who don't have the nerve to stare down Klein himself, the boy looks dazed. Or maybe, being a chance witness to this shoot-out between his friend and the photographer, he has gone into a trance. The two boys suggest two different sides of Klein's own personality that are at odds with each other. The picture mirrors the sort of self-confrontation out of which all Klein's best work has come.

There's another picture Klein made that he actually calls *Self-Portrait.* It's of a family in Rome whose reactions to his camera range from the friendly to the obscene. Klein had come to Rome in 1956 because filmmaker Federico Fellini, having seen Klein's book *New York*, offered him a job as assistant director on the feature *The Nights of Cabiria*. But when delays arose, Klein figured that he might as well occupy his time in the city by shooting pictures of its street life (fig. 17.4). Maybe a second book could be done on this subject. It turned out that it could, and in 1958 the same Parisian publisher who had picked up *New York* came out with *Rome*.

The one advance it makes over *New York* is not in the quality or style of the pictures, but in the way Klein put them together. There are several places in the book where, as his own designer-editor, he bled into the gutter two pictures on opposite pages to give the illusion of a single image done as a double-page spread. In one instance a woman on an enclosed motor scooter seems to be driving along a wall that is in fact a separate picture. The two images fuse in our minds because the woman in the plastic bubble on the scooter looks just like a statue set into a niche in the wall. This is the way the visual dynamics within an individual street photograph often work as well: a narrative discontinuity is overcome by a symbolic attraction. In laying out his book, Klein was using the association of shapes by which a street photograph is often held together as a visual glue to make two separate photographs work as one.

Weegee had pulled the same stunt a couple of times in *Naked City*, which is undoubtedly where Klein got the idea. But in Weegee's work, all that the device anticipates is the kind of goofy symmetries he would create in some of his trick shots in Hollywood. In Klein's career, this is the beginning of a much more important transition. Now he was blurring the boundaries between photographs much as he had earlier motion-blurred the outlines of the figures in them. It's not surprising that around the time the book was published, he broke out of photography altogether by making his first movie, *Broadway by Light*.

Rome is even more audacious than *New York* in the editing, sequencing, and layout of its pictures. Yet there is to its off-the-wall madness a certain method, one that aims at effects that can be achieved fully only through film-making. Doing books was from the beginning a process that led Klein into the world of movies and toward the conclusion that only there would his ideas be understood. When Paris publisher Robert Delpire passed up a chance to do the New York book, Klein sought advice from the documentary film-maker Chris Marker, who had put out a book Klein admired. He got Klein a contract with his publisher and later gave Klein his chance to get into filmmaking as well.

Klein became active in French movies and television at the moment when the Paris film scene, because of the rise of the New Wave directors, was the most exciting and creative in the world. He fit right in. Besides making shorts, then full-length documentaries, and finally a feature film of his own in 1965, he consulted on Louis Malle's *Zazie in the Metro* in 1960 and in 1967 made the American sequence for *Far from Vietnam*, a joint effort also directed by, among others, his friend Marker and Jean-Luc Godard.

It is fitting that Klein should eventually have ended up a character in a Godard movie when Godard made him the model for the role Yves Montand played, a director who does advertising work to make money, in *Just Great*. Klein and Godard seem to have been especially sympathetic spirits. The hero of Godard's first feature, *Breathless*, is (as the title suggests) someone with the same metabolism that Klein has as a photographer. Godard intended this title as a description not only of his hero's life, but of the movie itself, with its constant jump cuts and dramatic elisions.

This is a style he picked up from the American funny papers, which his hero is reading in the film's opening shot, just as Klein did from growing up with the *Daily News*. "In *New York*," Klein has said, "I wanted to make a photographic comic strip, with pictures running one into the other. This makes the image more difficult to read, but at the same time truer to that series of visual flashes which one can have when walking down the street."[22] The love of this energy that comes off the street is what Klein's work ultimately seems to share with Godard's.

In both movies and still photography, Klein has remained what he was all along, a proto-hipster, a charter member of that postwar generation of artists who wanted to get wired, to charge up their art with the electric energy of amplified music or synthetic drugs or high-speed film. But as he has become more and more involved in movies, the street photography has inevitably lost some of its rock-'n'-roll momentum. In 1964 he published two more books, *Moscow* and *Tokyo*. Each contains work that is as good as his pictures ever get (page 302, bottom). Yet there is less of this in the Russian book than the earlier ones, and less still in the volume from Japan. In these books, as in still more recent work he has done, the photography seems to run out of gas. The pictures begin to look forced.

What turned Klein on to Chris Marker the first time they met was that Marker's office was full of ray guns, flying saucers, and other junk purporting to be from outer space. "A Martian's Martian," Klein has called him with admiration.[23] Klein would gladly go right into orbit himself, for to do so would make him the ultimate outsider of all time. Going to Moscow or Tokyo was just the next best thing. Wherever he is, he has to remain an alien, a displaced person. It's the only way he can function. When he was photographing in New York and at one point found himself in Harlem surrounded by black teenagers, he defused the situation by claiming to be a foreigner. " 'Hey! This guy ain't white. He's *French!*' It was like a passport," Klein says. "I was under assumed papers, posing as a newspaperman, posing as a Frenchman, posing as a photographer."[24]

When he's in America, Klein claims to be French, but when he's in France, he acts like a rude American and gets himself in trouble for it. The first full-length documentary he made, a commission from the French state television network, was never aired; and when the feature *Mr. Freedom* was released, the Ministry of the Interior unsubtly threatened deportation by informing him, "You have abused the hospitality of France!"[25] At times he has been so alienated from France that he has thought of moving elsewhere, or at least wondered why he remains there. The disaffection is, of course, what makes staying on possible. Klein is, in other words, in exactly the position he likes to be, in midair with his camera in his hand, about to lunge half out of control from one thing — a subject, a project, a career, a country — to another.

18: In the American Grain

The only book published in the fifties that would stir up more controversy than William Klein's *New York* was Robert Frank's *Americans,* in which, ironically, there is a picture from a party — a New York charity gala called the Toy Ball — that Klein also photographed. *Vogue* art director Alexander Liberman had sent Klein to cover it, while Frank was there for *Harper's Bazaar.* On Frank's contact sheets there is even a picture of Klein himself. Frank had no idea whom he was photographing, nor did he actually meet Klein on that occasion. Each claims he remained unaware of the other's work until many years afterward.

Be that as it may, there is a basis for comparison between these photographers that lies not only in the provocative first books they published in the late fifties, but in the fact that they would both go from still photography to movies by the early sixties. Yet the contrasts between them are equally interesting. For one thing, they are men of such different temperaments that their work couldn't possibly be as similar as is sometimes imagined. Although their careers seem parallel in certain regards, in others they have gone in opposite directions. The American Klein decided to leave New York for Paris within a year of the time that the European Frank left Paris to sail to New York. The proverbial ships that pass in the night were, almost literally, the ones on which these two men crossed the Atlantic after the war.

In his photographs, as in his speech and his movements, Frank seems to have a different metabolism from Klein. His manner is slower and less self-assured. His pictures are often of moments that are less raucous. He notices a quietness in people that Klein, in more of a hurry, would pass right over. You can find in Frank's photography, for instance, a kind of face in the crowd whose expression might be mistaken for that same blank look of which Klein has often made a picture. But Frank's image is more typically of one of those unexpected moments when life has overwhelmed somebody's feelings, not drained them.

A photograph bearing a strong resemblance to such images by Frank is one of him as a small boy, taken by an automatic camera wired to a target at a shooting gallery. His father had just hit the bull's-eye, and the picture that came back to the son like some incredible, lucky ricochet struck him with a sudden realization that photography was "magic,"[1] as he put it when recalling the incident years later. Before he reached the age of eighteen, he apprenticed himself to a professional photographer in his native Zurich.

But unfortunately, the effect of "magic" wasn't enhanced by the education he got, which was very methodical and very Swiss. A series of assistantships between 1942 and 1946 was capped by a period in the studio of Hermann Eidenbenz, a Basel professional who had done a book about Finland containing flawless reproductions of magnificent mountain scenery. "That book," Frank has said, "put me off perfection for life. . . . You try to make the work good, but it doesn't have to be perfect."[2]

In the fall of 1946, Frank drove his motorcycle to Paris in hopes of becoming a free-lance photographer there. He loved the French capital but couldn't find work, so after a brief re-

---

The authors regret that Robert Frank will no longer permit reproduction of his work except in books that he himself initiates or on which he collaborates.

turn home he set out for America in March 1947. He came armed with a portfolio of prints that he had entitled *40 Fotos*, which got him in the door at *Harper's Bazaar*. Art director Alexey Brodovitch was sufficiently impressed to offer him a place at the studio that the magazine operated for its own photographers. Working first with a 4 x 5" camera there and then outdoors with a Rolleiflex, because Brodovitch encouraged him to experiment, Frank became established as a fashion photographer within a year.

But then, just as he was beginning to succeed in New York, he took off for South America for six months. To this day he doesn't know why he did it. "I just had a feeling I should go" is all he can say.[3] At least part of the reason was that working for *Harper's* didn't make photography magic either. He went first to Lima, Peru, where he found friends, and then gradually made his way up into the Andes by himself. It was a hard trip. Sometimes his money would be swiped, or his film. Traveling in open trucks with the Indians and sleeping on the ground, he got sick from exposure because he hadn't brought the right clothes. Since he couldn't understand local dialects, he couldn't ask for help.

And yet when Frank talks about this trip now, it is obvious that it was one of the happiest periods of his life. "It was a really good time," he says, "the best trip I ever made. I didn't talk to anybody for maybe a month."[4] Because he mentions the muteness of the experience, as if that were what he found so satisfying, his description of the way he lived in the Andes sounds a lot like that which he gives of photography itself.

"Of all the photographs in *The Americans*," he told a group of students in 1971,

I think there were only two or three photographs where I did talk to the person, but most of the time I was absolutely silent, walking through the landscape, through the city, and photographing and turning away.

Well, that is my temperament, to be silent, just looking on. . . . What I liked about photography was precisely this: that I could walk away and I could be silent and it was done very quickly and there was no direct involvement.[5]

The Andes were the first place in which he had this sense of the medium.

Peru was, in his own words, "the beginning of a whole new way of photographing."[6] Frank had used the Leica before, but not in the groping, seeking, innate way he did now. He was traveling light, leaving behind all the baggage of techniques, procedures, and equipment he had lugged with him from Switzerland. "Most of my photographs are . . . seen simply, as through the eyes of the man in the street," he was to tell an interviewer some years later.[7] It's true, too. Beginning in Peru, his way of looking at the world became as elemental as Atget's.

The work from there is intentionally superficial. The pictures are dumb in the sense that they literally say nothing. If he found himself in a situation where there was pushing and shoving — some horseplay perhaps, or a fight — the camera itself began to scuffle. He made pictures in which the figures veer in and out of the frame, and the imagery blurs with incomprehension. To go to a strange land where you don't know anybody and barely speak the language forces you to give up talk, to quit seeking explanations, to live by images alone.

This was the beginning of a symbolic silence into which Frank was to move deeper and deeper as a photographer. Whenever he was photographing, he says, "I felt like I was on the outside looking at something."[8] This was the feeling that his own quietness and isolation in the Andes allowed him to discover. To become a photographer, he had had to leave his home in Switzerland; then, as soon as he began to make a place for himself in New York, he had left there too. Like Model, Gutmann, and Klein, he had not turned into the photographer he wanted to be until he became a complete outsider. He had needed to be a displaced person first.

Frank went off to live among primitive peoples in the Andes because he was trying to make himself primitive as well, to discover an imagery that was prime, mute, prelingual. What he was looking for was not just the originality that all modern artists have sought. He wanted, rather, to become aboriginal. When he went back to New York, he turned his Peruvian material into a handmade book of prints without any text, captions, or even titles. This was the model on which he wanted to base later books, including *The Americans*, for which he also felt that words were unnecessary. Only commercial considerations raised by the publishers forced him to accept the commentaries on the pictures that the book contained.

In the Andes, Frank was able to reclaim for himself the kind of scenery that he thought had been debased in Eidenbenz's book. He photographed the Indians in front of the mountains, the crowns of their fedoras ranged against the peaks, as if these men were the one thing he had never believed he was when he was back home — a part of the landscape itself. Although these Indians may be figures out of a primordial past, they do not recede into a Romantic and mythic one. They are our contemporaries, *Indiens pas morts*, as the title of a 1956 book of photographs by Frank, Werner Bischof, and Pierre Verger put it.

The publisher of this volume, Robert Delpire, had first reproduced Frank's pictures four years earlier in a magazine called *Neuf* that he edited while studying medicine in Paris. The only circulation the pictures had outside of *Neuf* was the still more limited one provided by Frank's handmade books, one of which went to Brodovitch as a token of appreciation. Although the two men grew more cool toward each other once Frank returned from Peru, their relationship set a pattern that Frank would repeat afterward with other mentors — first Edward Steichen, then Walker Evans, whose encouragement was also to be rewarded with a book.

It was a sign of the shift in Frank's interests after Peru that Steichen should have taken Brodovitch's place. Having put Frank in a survey at the Modern in 1950, Steichen asked him two years later to serve as consultant on a couple of new shows the museum was doing, "Post-War European Photography" and "The Family of Man." Researching together in Europe, the two men became so close that when Frank did a new handmade book, entitled *Black, White and Things*, he gave one of the four copies to Steichen. But then, as with Brodovitch earlier, the relationship began to sour. In the early sixties, when Steichen wanted to pair Frank with Harry Callahan for the last in a series of six exhibitions called "Diogenes with a Camera," Frank refused unless the title was changed. It was, but the rift between them was never repaired. Some years later Frank published an article calling Steichen's influence on photography "rather mediocre." [9]

The end of Frank's affection for Steichen came, as it had with Brodovitch, at a point when the photographer was ready to go on to a new phase of his career. Of the three mentors in his life, the only one with whom he didn't eventually have a falling out was the last, Walker Evans. In the rather small world of photography of the early 1950s, it was inevitable that they should find each other sooner or later and become friends, for they were kindred spirits given to a similarly glum view of life. Evans got Frank an assignment from *Fortune* to shoot pictures for an article entitled "The Congressional," about the commuter train between Washington and New York, for which Evans himself wrote the text. Evans also wrote the recommendation that got Frank a Guggenheim fellowship in 1955–56. And just as Frank's friendship with Evans was his most enduring with a mentor, so was the book with which Evans was repaid

— *The Americans* — Frank's most memorable work.

How powerful a document *The Americans* was can be seen from the amount of resistance it met. From the time he first began producing the pictures that would appear in the book, Frank had trouble getting them published. *Pageant* was the only mass-circulation magazine that picked them up, running a spread in the April 1958 issue. *Life* wouldn't touch the work, and the *New York Times* used only one image, a Houston bank interior that Frank considers the most innocuous photograph in the book.

Nor could he find an American publisher, even though the United States was where he really wanted the book to come out. Only Delpire in Paris was eager to do the project, so Frank agreed in 1958; the American edition, by Grove Press, didn't appear until a year later, after the European publication had aroused some controversy. The American edition caused quite a stir too, most of it negative. *Popular Photography* polled its editors to try to reach some kind of consensus. Only one of the seven participating had unreserved praise for the book, which the vast majority condemned outright for being, as Les Barry put it, "an attack on the United States." [10]

The terms in which they denounced the book are instructive, for the very aspect that gives it its power came in for the harshest criticism. While praising the photographs individually, Barry wrote that "editorially, the shots . . . disclose a warped objectivity that gives this book its major limitation." John Durniak concurred: "Frank is a great photographer of single pictures but a poor essayist and no convincing story-teller." [11] Yet the editing, the way Frank selected and sequenced the pictures to create a structure, is what makes his vision of America compelling. The book's fault was to be too effective.

Frank had begun thinking about how to make a photo book when he put together *Black,*

White and Things with the help of Swiss designer Werner Zryd in 1952. Since Peru, he had become less and less interested in the kind of pictures that have an individual impact. Whereas Klein only disobeyed Cartier-Bresson's rules, Frank truly upset them. Cartier-Bresson prized most the single photograph that captures all the human complexities and symbolic possibilities of a situation in one frame. Each picture had to be as complete and self-sufficient as a well-wrought poem. Frank's Modernism was of another sort, and more extreme. He wished to reduce photography not to what was singular, to unity, but to nullity. He wanted to achieve a kind of visual silence equivalent to the stillness that he had experienced so intensely in the Andes.

Although *Black, White and Things* contains no text, it is prefaced by a quotation from Antoine de Saint-Exupéry: "it is only with the heart that one can see rightly/what is essential is invisible to the eye." [12] The lines suggest that Frank wanted to photograph somehow what is beneath the threshold of perception itself. This enigmatic need was also implied by the title he gave to a feature he submitted to a *Life* competition for young photographers in 1951: "People You Don't See." What Frank sought in his photography was not just such overlooked subject matters, but a new style that would be appropriate to them.

Beneath the quotation from Saint-Exupéry in *Black, White and Things*, Frank added a few lines of his own stating that his photography was about "quiet people" and "black events." [13] In the four years since Peru, during which most of the pictures in the new book had been shot either in New York or on extensive trips to Europe, his photography had turned ever darker. Key images from this period are so dim that we can barely make out what is in them. Frank was probing the limits of invisibility. He was as a photographer a lot like the fiddler in one of his own pictures who strokes his instrument in joyous obscurity in the middle of the empty night.

When Helen Gee was opening Limelight, the coffeehouse and photo gallery she ran from 1954 until 1961, she contacted Frank because she wanted to give him the premiere exhibition. During a walk they took to discuss the matter, he had a camera held down at his side with which, she realized, he was shooting constantly while they talked. A contemporary snapshot of him suggests the same thing, for in it his arms are crossed and the camera, resting nonchalantly against his sleeve, looks as if poised to take a vertical. These glimpses of Frank in action seem to show him disciplining himself to do without the one advantage a photographer like Cartier-Bresson was always said to have — a great eye. Frank made compositions that relied upon no eye at all. He took such chancy photographs that it was impossible for any of them to be a masterpiece, or even be able to stand alone as an image.

Gee was perhaps unable to appreciate why Frank responded to her offer with a certain amount of indifference. It was because he was already more fixed on doing books than exhibitions. "Are you the guy who did that book?" he asked Wright Morris before even introducing himself when he went to take a portrait of the novelist for *Time* in the early fifties.[14] He was referring to Morris's 1946 photo text, *The Inhabitants*. A book that made a still bigger impression on him, of course, was Evans's *American Photographs*. The importance of books was that only in them could the true potential of photography as a serial medium be realized.

In *Black, White and Things* there is a page on which four pictures appear of a single subject, an elderly couple who get up from a park bench and slowly walk away under an umbrella. Having shot the first frame from above them, Frank had realized they were about to depart and quickly switched to a wide-angle lens to get the rest. Although continuity of this sort, as if his pictures were a little movie, is rare in Frank's work, this sequence also suggests another cinematic effect, a kind of symbolic montage, that his books often strive to attain.

Consider the way that this page and the one after it, which end the second, or "white," section of the book, repeat a pattern established by the two concluding images of the preceding "black" section. At the end of this white section, the old couple walking away under an umbrella are followed by an image of a line down the middle of a New York City street leading off into the distance. This juxtaposition is much the same as that found at the end of the earlier section, where a picture of a group of people under umbrellas is followed by one of a dirt road running to the horizon on an Andean plain. Since these people under the umbrellas are attending a funeral, that image is, like the one of the old couple walking away alone, an evocation of death. In each section, the effect of the penultimate image is enhanced by the empty road or street disappearing at the horizon that follows.

To say that a photograph is haunting is usually a rather trite metaphor, but in this case it's true. Frank has included the later pictures in part so that the earlier ones will come back to haunt us as we progress through the book. Buried under all the other imagery we have seen since the first section, the photographs with which it closes are revived in our imaginations by the ending of the second section. They become, quite literally, ghost images that our minds impose on the similar sequence we encounter there. We see that they have served as a premonition of the theme of death, of human finality, that Frank wanted the final photographs in both sections to advance.

When a street photographer shoots, he tends to make one exposure after another in rapid succession, varying the composition only slightly each time, looking for the image that will be the best expression of the subject matter. Frank's way of talking is the same; he repeats the important words or phrases over and over in simple declarative sentences. A book by him has a picture grammar that's similar as well. The essential moods and ideas keep returning in a somewhat altered form. By the time he was ready to begin working on

The Americans, the two sides of his personality — the Peruvian and the Swiss, the photographer of primitive, intuitive images and the maker of intricate, highly structured books — were ready to be reconciled. During the years since he had been in South America, he had tried patiently, even methodically, to come to an understanding of what he should do with the mute pictures he took. Now he knew.

In 1949 he had done a little handmade book about Paris for a sixteen-year-old girl who would soon after become his wife. The subjects of the pictures — flowers, folding chairs in the park, gas lamps, et cetera — are all part of the Paris that's for lovers. Frank was not in a dreamy trance when he was doing the shooting, however. On the contrary, he was far more programmatic than in Peru, never wandering aimlessly, carefully studying his contact sheets to see which subjects were working best so he could seek out other examples the next day. When he worked on *The Americans,* his behavior was much the same. He would see certain subjects emerging in the contacts and know where to go — the railroad station or a Woolworth's, a hotel, a diner — to get more pictures that would fit in.

"When I had all I needed," Frank said, "I just knew it — knew to stop and put it together." The longest of several trips he made on the Guggenheim fellowship began in the fall of 1955 and ended the following spring. By the time he got back to New York, he had shot eight hundred rolls of film. Now he chose three hundred negatives to print and arranged the pictures in categories such as "symbols, cars, cities, people, signs, cemeteries," and others. At that point it occurred to him, he says, to "arrange the book into sections, each beginning with a flag." [15]

The Americans goes beyond what Evans had done earlier with his book, or what Klein had accomplished in *New York.* Frank's book is so truly original that it has to teach us how to look at itself. That's one function that the pictures of flags serve. When we come to the second flag we remember that we have seen this subject already, in the book's opening image; and the connection is reinforced when we turn to yet another later on, and another and another. The pattern suggests the existence of subtler, purely symbolic repetitions elsewhere among the pictures. It proposes connections to be made not only from one page to the next, but across the span of pictures from the beginning of the book to the end. The book grows in intensity as we go along, right up to the final picture.

That picture is of Frank's wife, Mary, and his children, half-asleep beside a Texas highway at dawn, seen through the windshield of the 1950 Ford he'd bought to tour the country in. Even if you don't know that you're looking at his own family, the image is filled with pathos because automobiles have gradually been gaining symbolic power throughout the book, bearing down on this ending, giving it an exceptional impact.

All but one of the seven pictures that end *The Americans* are of cars (or, in one instance, a motorcycle). Passing from teenagers petting amid parked cars to newlyweds in Reno, a dejected black couple astride a Harley-Davidson, and finally Frank's wife and kids in the Ford, this closing run of pictures has traced a kind of American romance from courtship through marriage to disillusionment and, in the end, the numbness of family life. The automobile, in whose backseat the Americans of the fifties often had their first sexual experience, becomes a vehicle for Frank's reflections on love American-style.

Even as we began this joyride, we should have had a sense of foreboding about how it would end, for there is an unmistakably morbid side to the appearances that cars make as a theme in the book. The imagery ranges from a car seen earlier parked between two palms and wrapped in a dust cover, so that it looks like a mummified pharaoh lying in state, to the sticker reading "Christ Died for Our Sins" seen in a car window in this closing sequence. All these pictures crowd back at the very end to give the final image an atmosphere as oppressive as that in one in the book's middle, in which a tiny car far in the distance speeds down a New Mexico highway under lowering skies.

Despite Frank's contrapuntal division of the pictures into categories and the book itself into sections tagged with flags, *The Americans* is nowhere near as dialectical in structure as *Black, White and Things*. As the new book was being formed, the fixed divisions found in the earlier one dissolved. The structure became something implicit. The sequences began to seem protean, so that the subjects of one photograph could transform themselves into something new in the next, forever eluding us even as they draw us on.

This way of proceeding is established in the book's opening section when a photograph of two black men at a southern funeral who make duplicate gestures is followed by one at a rodeo of white cowgirls who are twins. A juvenile delinquent in a motorcycle hat in the corner of this second picture becomes, in the next one, an aging army sergeant in uniform. In the same vein, a flag on one page might turn into bunting on the next; a stripe down the middle of a highway turns into the stripes on a flag, and the stars on a flag into little star-shaped lights, and so forth. This slippage between frames results in a kind of metamorphosis. The book takes shape by an inspired free association.

The Americans is, in fact, a very American document. It has the formless, osmotic, improvised structure that Walt Whitman's *Song of Myself* has. Frank could see the country whole in his book — he could take it all in at once, as if by intuition, the way Whitman's poem does — because like Whitman he was able to identify with the people he met on his travels. This too is established in the opening section, where two thirds of the images are of spectators at public events (a parade, a political rally, a funeral, a rodeo) who thereby mirror Frank's own purpose in being there. This suggests that the taking of pictures is also a civic occasion, a patriotic duty of sorts.

Subjects who notice Frank's presence are a motif that returns throughout the book. The wary gaze he fixes on them is mimicked by the way they look right back at him. Each picture in which this occurs is a map of America on which Frank is trying to locate himself, to get his bearings in the human terrain. *He* is the lone individual caught staring amid the landscape that American society forms. By the time he was doing the shooting for his book, Frank had recognized that he himself had a very American character in some respects. Having gone from Switzerland to New York and then Peru, he would later leave photography altogether for movies. He was forever lighting out for the territory, like Huck Finn.

Or like the assorted cowboys that are another motif in this book. They are the ultimate Americans, perennially out of place. Among those he included were ones he had found in Detroit and New York. Restless and rootless like the photographer himself, cowboys had blazed the trail that he now followed. He too went as far west as he could, then drifted back east again. He photographed them from one end of the country to the other — from Detroit or New York to Gallup, New Mexico — taking on their manifest destiny as his own.

There is a picture of Frank, made in New York in 1947, in which he appears as we so often see others in his own pictures — standing on the edge of a crowd watching some event we cannot see. This photograph was taken by Louis Faurer, a colleague of Frank's at *Harper's Bazaar* and the only person from the fashion world whom Frank really liked. Since Faurer commuted from his home in Philadelphia, he sometimes stayed at Frank's studio, where he also used the darkroom while he was on a hot streak photographing around Times Square. During Frank's early days in New York, the two of them spent a lot of time together out on the streets. There Faurer's subject was frequently the witness, the bystander, whom we see in Frank's work as well. Perhaps the attention Faurer paid to these watchful figures stimulated Frank to take an interest in them.

Faurer's best pictures in this period have an almost fictive power, as if they were moments not of reality, but taken from the scenario of some film noir. For instance, Robert Siodmak's *Cry of the City,* which was discussed earlier, is approaching its climax in a scene where a car pulls over to the curb on a side street near Times Square — the area where Faurer himself was photographing in the year the film was released, 1948. In the backseat an unlicensed doctor is operating on a man with a gunshot wound, a fugitive from the police (Richard Conte). "What am I gonna do with him?" his flashy girlfriend (Shelley Winters) calls after the doctor as he emerges and disappears into the darkness, ignoring her question.

When she resumes her night ride with the moaning, semiconscious man, Faurer's pictures might have been used as point-of-view shots, visions of the city that the protagonist, half out of his skull, sees as he looks out the car window. The hallucinations of menace, violence, and crime that Siodmak's character would have are what Faurer's pictures mostly are. One image Faurer made in front of the Plaza Hotel just after a pedestrian was struck by a car — a chalk outline of a body on the pavement has a pool of blood, it seems, where the head is indicated — would have served as a perfect insert shot for the movie (page 310). Perhaps because it really was shot through a car window, Faurer's picture contains a reflection that causes some of the figures to float illogically in the frame and gives his image just the unsteady, woozy feeling *Cry of the City* requires at this point.

Nineteen forty-eight was the year Frank took off for Peru, thereby showing for the first time an ambivalence toward living in New York that was not to end even when he moved to Nova Scotia in 1969. The year after the South American trip, he was gone again, to Europe, where he shared both a studio in Paris and a trip to Italy with Elliott Erwitt. From 1951

until 1953, he was back in Europe once more, with his family, and in 1955 and 1956 he was traveling around America on his Guggenheim grant much of the time. Yet he kept coming back to New York because the city was, among other things, an important resource for him. "That's what New York is great for," he once told a group of students. "You really meet the people you need. You choose them."[16] These included not only Faurer, Steichen, Evans, and others from the world of photography, but painters, writers, intellectuals, and people in the arts in general.

When Frank returned from his travels for *The Americans,* he and Mary rented a place on Third Avenue next door to Alfred Leslie and across a courtyard from Willem de Kooning. Since Europe, Mary had also enrolled in Hans Hofmann's art school, through which she and Frank were both drawn into the circle of Abstract Expressionists that revolved around such meeting places. Frank had much in common with the artists in this group, from displaced Europeans like Hofmann and de Kooning to Westerners like Jackson Pollock and Clyfford Still, aesthetic cowboys who were, Frank saw, as out of place in New York as the rodeo rider he photographed near Madison Square Garden.

De Kooning above all made an impression on him, one strong enough to survive as a vivid memory more than a decade later. Writing a reminiscence of the painter then, Frank recalled how "I could see him from my window; I'd see him with his hands behind his back, his head bent, pacing up and down the length of the studio."[17] Such prowling self-involvement is what somebody who had seen Frank on the street with his camera might have noticed. In Harold Rosenberg's seminal essay, "The American Action Painters," published in 1952, the account of artists like de Kooning or Pollock at work not only sounds like Frank's above, but could be a description of Frank himself as a street photographer. What matters, Rosenberg said, is the "psychic state, concentration and relaxation of the will, passivity, alert waiting." To understand what he's looking at, the viewer of the painting must become "a connoisseur of the gradations between the automatic, the spontaneous, the evoked." [18]

As conceived by this new breed of painter, Rosenberg explained, "a painting . . . is an act . . . inseparable from the biography of the artist. The painting itself is a 'moment' in the adulterated mixture of his life. . . . The new painting has broken down every distinction between art and life." [19] One method of removing the barriers between the two was devised by Pollock when he laid the canvas on the floor. This allowed him to feel as if he were actually standing *in* the painting. Frank did the same thing when he photographed; he stood inside the scene he was making a picture of.

Since "what was to go on the canvas was not a picture but an event," according to Rosenberg,[20] the experiential was more important than the representational. Art was becoming a form of existentialism. De Kooning himself said, speaking of the entire generation of New York painters to which he belonged, that they were very much "in touch with the mood" of the existentialists.[21] The ultimate implication was that the work of art itself was secondary, a mere by-product of the aesthetic experience, and the conclusion to be drawn was that found in Happenings or performance art, where no permanent image remained once the event had passed. Frank's place on Third Avenue was adjacent to Tenth Street, and his friends included the group known as the Tenth Street Painters, among whom was Allan Kaprow. Frank photographed one of the first Happenings that Kaprow staged.

The connection between Frank's photography and Abstract Expressionism extends not only to how the imagery was made, but even, it could be argued, to how it looks. His background and de Kooning's were parallel in a way, and this led them to similar insights into their respective media after the war. Like the photographer's training in Zurich, the

painter's at the Rotterdam Academy had been a stiflingly thorough European education against which he rebelled when he came to America. De Kooning and the other gestural painters were seeking ways to purify their imagery, as Frank did in Peru, by making it more primitive.

The point for them was exactly what it was for Frank: "I didn't work . . . with the idea of perfection," de Kooning said, thus echoing Frank's rejection of Swiss values.[22] Franz Kline, according to Frank O'Hara, expressed similar sentiments against "the dead-end of expertise." [23] In 1947, the year that Frank arrived in America, de Kooning reduced his palette to cheap enamel house paints in black and white, a move soon followed by Kline, Pollock, and Robert Motherwell. Frank matched with his grainy, blurry photographs the splattery, intentionally dirty look that these black and white paintings achieved.

In some instances, Frank's photographs even seem to become what George McNeil, an early supporter of the Abstract Expressionists, said a Pollock painting was: a "mass image." [24] A key photograph in *The Americans* — of a crowd on a New Orleans sidewalk — functions visually, as a surface, in this way. Like action painting, or like Mark Rothko's color-field work, Frank's image is the kind of picture that is overall, without any particular point of focus. In this respect, the photograph draws upon two distinct attitudes toward art that are opposite poles of the Abstract Expressionist movement, just as Cartier-Bresson's imagery earlier represents a union of two sides of Surrealism. Frank's photograph both plunges into the crowd and stands back from it. Like the greatest of the Abstract Expressionist paintings he admired, it is at once both impulsive and disciplined, spontaneous and restrained, gestural and meditative.

Besides being mass images, of course, this picture and the preceding one in the book, which is also from New Orleans, are images of the masses. They are group portraits of the American people, and as such they make an unmistakable political statement. This was the one aspect of *The Americans* that couldn't be missed, even by the editors at *Popular Photography*. By the time he reached New Orleans, Frank no doubt had politics very much on his mind, for earlier in his travels he had had several experiences with pointed political messages.

In Detroit, he had been arrested and held overnight just for having two license plates in his possession, even though one was expired. In Arkansas, the state police detained him again, this time on the grounds that he looked shabby, had cameras in his car, spoke with a foreign accent, and was suspected of being, as he was told point-blank, "a commie."[25] And yet again, as he moved still deeper into the south, some Mississippi teenagers he photographed repeated the charge that he must be a "communist" and told him to go "watch the niggers play."[26]

Whatever larger symbolic or aesthetic significance it may have had, the photograph of the New Orleans trolley made soon after this last incident was first and foremost a documentation of Jim Crow. With the whites sitting up front and the blacks in back, it was a straight record shot of the American apartheid. As a Jew who had grown up in the Europe of the Nazis, Frank was particularly sensitive to the racial prejudice he found here. Certain experiences he had in the United States revived a kind of dread that had been instilled in him by his childhood.

Among the subjects in *The Americans* with whom he could no doubt identify is a little boy in a yarmulke with a lost look on his face. It is an expression similar to Frank's own in the photograph made at that shooting gallery in the late 1930s. Standing at a railing by the water like an immigrant arriving on a ship (the scene is actually a pedestrian way along the East River), the boy gazes out of the lower-right corner of the frame as if looking beyond the picture he is in to the next one in the book.

When we turn the page, we see that the sight he was so quiet before is a huge American flag hanging over a Fourth of July picnic. In the lower-left corner of this photograph is a second boy, who has a somewhat sullen and bad-tempered look on his face and a box of fireworks in his pocket. He is staring back at the first boy across the gulf between the pictures separating two sections of the book. The pages after these are the ones with the New Orleans trolley and sidewalk scenes, two images of American society as a whole.

Remembering what it was like in Zurich during the thirties and forties, Frank told curator and critic Philip Brookman, "I saw fear in my parents. . . . If Hitler invaded Switzerland, and there was very little to stop him, that would have been the end for them. It was an unforgettable situation. I watched the grown-ups decide what to do, when to change your name. It was on the radio every day. You could hear Hitler cursing the Jews, it's forever in your mind."[27]

On account of his background, Frank's feelings about racism in America were all bound up with the legitimate paranoia he had about police states. Because he used to stop by occasionally at the Photo League when he lived opposite its headquarters, on Eleventh Street, he was aware of how the FBI persecuted Sid Grossman. What really shook him about the incident in Arkansas was that the authorities there had forwarded his name to the FBI. Afterward, when he tried to have his file expunged, a lawyer he contacted through Evans advised him to drop the whole matter.

Along with Frank's snapshots of de Kooning, Kline, and other New York artists, there is a picture of writer Norman Mailer, who articulated better than anyone else the political alienation and existential disaffection in which Frank himself shared. Mailer did so best in an article entitled "The White Negro," which came out in *Dissent* in 1957. "No wonder . . . these have been years of conformity and depression," the piece declared. "A stench of fear has come out of every pore of American life. . . . The only courage . . . has been the isolated courage of the isolated individual." In the midst of "this bleak scene," he continued, "a phenomenon has appeared: the American existentialist."

Caught between "instant death by atomic war" and "slow death by conformity," this new man chooses to explore "the rebellious imperatives of the self."[28] Searching frantically for an alter ego, Mailer was, as his title suggests, drawn to American blacks. He identified with them, as Frank did. His "white negro" expresses himself in a "pictorial language" capable of showing us "the immediate experiences of any passing man." He is a *flâneur* on the run who has to keep moving because "in motion a man has a chance, his body is warm, his instincts are quick."[29] With a camera in his hand, he would be Frank himself.

While Mailer's voice may have represented the slashing edge of a new social anger, that of Princeton professor Eric Goldman did not. His was more nearly the establishment view, and his 1956 book *The Crucial Decade: America, 1945–1955* was in many respects a counterpart to Frederick Lewis Allen's popular summary of the thirties, *Since Yesterday*. Yet Goldman also sensed the shift toward existentialism and alienation in America. "A nation accustomed to the categorical yes and no, to war or peace and prosperity or depression, found itself in the nagging realm of maybe," Goldman explained in his first chapter.[30] Writing in the year when Frank was at work on *The Americans*, looking back to the year in which the photographer had arrived from Europe, Goldman explained that because of this malaise he had identified, "in every section of the United States, on all levels of society, the ill-tempered, the mean, the vicious pushed to the fore."[31]

From the photographs he took to the company he kept and the music he liked — which ranged from Johnny Cash to John Coltrane —

Frank was part of a whole culture of alienation on the verge of becoming, in the sixties, the dominant one in America. The nation was about to recognize painters like de Kooning in the only way it knew how, by making them millionaires. Dissenting intellectuals were soon to be legitimized by government agencies as experts, consultants, and overseas ambassadors of the American way. Popular music was going to become ever more openly angry and disaffected. Method actors with terse, dour personalities similar to Frank's — Marlon Brando, James Dean, Montgomery Clift — were already movie stars. Writers like Mailer and Frank's friend Jack Kerouac would be made into media celebrities who appeared on television and in the pages of *Time* and *Life*. *The Americans* was controversial because its subjects could not bear to acknowledge that they themselves were coming to share its vision of them. The book was not really un-American at all. It was *too* American, too prescient and profound a reflection of the country's own bad conscience.

The true white Negroes of the fifties were the Beats, and Frank kept company with them as well. When they were "dragging themselves through the negro streets at dawn," as the second line of Allen Ginsberg's poem *Howl* put it,[32] Frank went along with his camera. He knew Ginsberg first, but it was with Jack Kerouac that he really hit it off when they met not long after *On the Road* was published, toward the end of the decade. Frank must have recognized right away that if the American edition of his own book had to have some kind of text, Kerouac was the person to write it.

On the Road was a book of the same sort. It had been written the way Frank's photographs were taken, spontaneously, and even had the same loose, cyclical structure that the Frank book was given by the periodic reappearance of the Stars and Stripes. In Kerouac's book the euphoria of the road was punctuated every fifty or a hundred pages by an emotional crash that brought him back down to earth; then he would have to drag himself out of his depression again, start over, just as Frank's vision of America did with each new image of the flag.

How well matched they were as observers of the world around them can be seen from the kind of verbal street photography Kerouac was doing long before they ever met. At one point in his 1950 novel, *The Town and the City,* he stands on the curb on Forty-second Street just digging the scene, watching with pleasure the jumble of people passing by on the sidewalk. His one-line profiles of a Methodist minister and a panhandler, a "hairy old Babylonian" on his way to the Turkish baths and a "trim little shopgirl hurrying home . . . to take care of her aged father," are as deftly seen and placed as the profiles in the crowd Frank photographed on the sidewalk in New Orleans. In fact, the spot in which Frank chose to stand was essentially the same position on the curb that Kerouac has taken up here. They were both keeping, in the novel's own words, "the same anxious vigil of the street, from which the watchers of the Street could never turn their eyes without some piercing sense of loss."[33]

In 1958, the two of them took a trip down the East Coast to Florida. It was the culmination of their friendship, which would never bring them this close again except, maybe, when Kerouac improvised a narration for Frank's film *Pull My Daisy* the following year. Ostensibly they were on assignment for *Life,* but in reality the trip was a sentimental journey, a reprise of the road for Kerouac and of *The Americans* for Frank.

During his early travels shooting pictures for the book, Frank had photographed the empty interior of a barbershop in South Carolina; now he steered his friend back there to see it. This time the barber was in. He made them coffee and trimmed Frank's hair. As they rode down the main drag of one little town, Frank was in the driver's seat, hanging out the window to photograph while Kerouac steered.

"O Jeez!" exclaimed some girls on the sidewalk as Frank snapped their picture.[34] With Frank working the pedals and Kerouac's hands on the wheel, the two men were like a couple of car-crazy teenagers playing "spider."

Their whole relationship was complementary — almost symbiotic — in the weird way that this episode suggests. Kerouac brought out Frank's euphoric side, and Frank, in return, sometimes had a sobering effect on Kerouac. Their friendship was based on the attraction of opposites, like Evans's with James Agee and Hart Crane. Kerouac provided Frank with a mythopoeic vision of America much as Crane had Evans. When he ended *On the Road* by having Dean race back and forth maniacally from coast to coast, Kerouac was trying to bridge the continent, to embrace the entire national experience, which was what Crane had attempted with the symbolism of the Brooklyn Bridge.

The success that the publication of *The Americans* and *On the Road* brought to their authors affected the two men in very different ways. Kerouac sank into the brief celebrity he enjoyed with self-destructive dissipation, while Frank took flight from success itself, escaping into filmmaking precisely because it was a new field in which he would have no standing. "I've never been successful at making films, really," he said in 1975. "I've never been able to do it right. And there's something terrific about that. There's something good about being a failure — it keeps you going."[35]

Before *The Americans* was recognized for the classic that it is seen as now, Frank could have done the book again, perhaps done it even better, and kept on doing it until he got the recognition his work deserved. But that's exactly what he didn't want. Speaking of how his attitude toward doing photographic books changed after *The Americans,* he has said, "Then it was intuitive. Now I know. But once you know, you don't have to do it any more. Once you know, all you can do is make it more perfect."[36] Having begun by rejecting the perfectionism of Switzerland, he had eventually grown to share with de Kooning and the other Abstract Expressionists a kind of existential reverence for failure.

The last street photographs he did were a series shot from bus windows in New York in 1958. It was a project a lot like Evans's "Along the Right of Way" for *Fortune,* an article done with pictures made from a train, which Frank admits may have been his inspiration. He has said that what he liked about doing these photographs was that it "forced" him to work in a certain way.[37] He wanted to impose limitations on himself in order to make photography difficult again, and thereby renew it. Twenty years later, he said that these pictures "had to do with desperation and endurance."[38] The former was the state to which his need for a new challenge had reduced him; the latter was the power that photography had always required but no longer aroused in him.

Nonetheless, the bus pictures were not quite the last photographic project he would ever do. As it turned out, he was to undertake at least one more over a decade later when two Japanese publishers approached him about a new book. There was a certain justice to their proposal. It would give his career as a photographer a kind of symmetry and completion, for it didn't entail taking any new pictures. It reduced the medium to editing alone, to only making a book. He called it *The Lines of My Hand,* and in the sequences he created for it, the two images this title suggests — "lines" and "hands" — constantly appear, disappear, transform themselves, and return again just as the themes do in *The Americans.*

In a brief piece written for *U.S. Camera Annual* in 1959, Frank reflected that "it is always the instantaneous reaction to oneself that produces a photograph."[39] In doing this new book, he explored the implications of his own remark. "I really wanted to give [the publishers] something that would tell them about myself," he has said.[40] He began working on *Lines* around the time he completed a film entitled *About Me,* and the film before that, *Con-*

versations in Vermont, had been a cinematic diary of an encounter between himself and his children. *Lines* fit in with his other work at the time because it was, in essence, a personal album.

In a note to one of his publishers, Frank said that he hoped the book would allow the man "to know and to see — how it was — to become like I am."[41] The note appears at the end of the book, superimposed on a photograph of a wall at Frank's house on which he has pinned up letters, announcements, and snapshots that are curling at the edges. This closing spread recalls the way the book opens, with a montage of photographs of more than a dozen friends who have died. Thus does the book both begin and end with a bulletin board of sorts, a haphazard display of personal snapshots, a variation on the idea of the album page. Thus too are Frank's last photographs just like that first one he got as a souvenir when his father hit the bull's-eye at a shooting gallery.

These associations at the end bring us back once again to Frank's title and to the first picture, which is of an outstretched palm, both implying a book in which the photographer's own fate is to be read. *Lines* is an autobiography written in pictures. It is a scrapbook containing many pages on which snaps have been pasted down with the same overlaps and confusions that memory itself often has. By gang-printing pictures on one page, reproducing contact sheets from *The Americans* on another, and showing us a photograph of a postcard rack filled with images or a movie box office pasted with posters somewhere else, Frank purposely made his book into a jumble.

The effect of all these pages filled with imagery is to make the book as a whole into a mass image, like the photographs from New Orleans of the trolley car and the sidewalk full of passersby. Pictures of this type go to the very heart of street photography. The two New Orleans photographs run an entire gamut of emotions, from the meanness in the face of the white woman on the trolley to the anguish of the black man a few seats away. But like Atget, Frank doesn't choose among his subjects. He doesn't emphasize one over another or single out what he wants us to see in either picture. He remains an impassive observer the way Cartier-Bresson does in photographs of crowds in India and China, or Walker Evans in the image of the penny portraits in a studio window. The numerous pages in *Lines* on which photographs are montaged and collaged together are intended only to remind us of the insight into photography as multiplicity that Frank's whole career has represented.

19: The Chicago School

The most important street photographers working in Chicago since the 1950s have created an imagery so uniform, and so unlike that done elsewhere, that for once it seems legitimate to speak of a school of photography. This is not just a metaphor, for there actually is a school — the Institute of Design — at which all the photographers in question have either studied or taught. The ID has been housed since the midfifties in Crown Hall, a quintessential Mies van der Rohe glass box on the campus of the Illinois Institute of Technology. This is not the sort of building that lends itself to the academic tradition of carving words of wisdom on the facade to inspire the students; but if it were, the perfect motto for the institution it contains might be Shakespeare's description of the poet as someone who "gives to airy nothing/A local habitation and a name."

That's what this generation of photographers from the ID has done. László Moholy-Nagy, who founded the institute, instilled in its curriculum the internationalism of the Bauhaus. The Bauhaus philosophy, which he had been instrumental in shaping, advocated a kind of universal vision that would not be limited by regional or national cultures. Moholy-Nagy's own photography, which had been influenced by the Constructivists, tended toward abstraction in the form of photograms and collage pieces. Moreover, the ID faculty who were the mainstays of the photography program after Moholy-Nagy died, in 1946 — first Harry Callahan and then Aaron Siskind — had both developed on their own, before coming to ID, an abstract imagery that was consonant with Bauhaus precepts.

Chicago wasn't the hometown of any of these men, whose work shared a kind of international Modernism and an aspiration to the airy nothing of abstraction. And yet what ultimately came out of the photography program at the ID is an imagery that is unmistakably about Chicago itself, as a place, in the same way that Bill Brandt's pictures are about England or Manuel Alvarez Bravo's about Mexico. For Callahan, Siskind, and students of theirs such as Ken Josephson, Ray Metzker, or Barbara Crane, Chicago was the local habitation in which their Modernist aesthetics could be grounded. As their subject matter, the city gave its name, and a unique form, to their ideas about photography.

Having a transparent lobby usually much smaller in dimensions than the tower on top of it, a skyscraper by Mies seems to float above the ground. Thus does it express, symbolically, its independence from the particular place in which it happens to be located. With its walls of glass, it becomes a structure of pure light. Moholy-Nagy's photograms, which were his earliest experiments with photography, reflect a similar ambition for that medium. On the one hand, a photogram looks like an X ray. It suggests a scientific study of the structure of an object. On the other, it also seems to create an image quite separate from whatever subject was used, to turn subject matter into an abstract pattern of light.

When Moholy-Nagy left the darkroom and began using a camera to make his imagery, doing straight photography of the world outside, his program for the medium remained the same. He believed that photography was "the most reliable aid to . . . objective vision" that had ever been invented.[1] He was following through on the work of German photographers like Karl Blossfeldt and Albert Renger-Patzsch, who had used photography to study the structure of plants, industrial forms, and other concrete phenomena. Like Renger-Patzsch, Moholy-Nagy employed extreme angles to isolate forms. He shot up at people on balconies and down at street scenes, parks, or the footings of bridges and radio towers onto which he had climbed. In every situation, however, he was studying the structure not of the specific subject he photographed, but of light. The result was that an objective vision became a nonobjective one. Light patterns revealed by obtuse angles and the fragmentation of solid forms turned into abstractions. Used as a kind of scientific instrument, the camera corroborated the geometric vision of the Constructivists.

When he arrived in Chicago and opened the New Bauhaus in 1937, the school that was the predecessor of the ID, Moholy-Nagy found a ready disciple in one of his first stu-

Fig. 19.1
HARRY CALLAHAN
Alley, Chicago, 1948

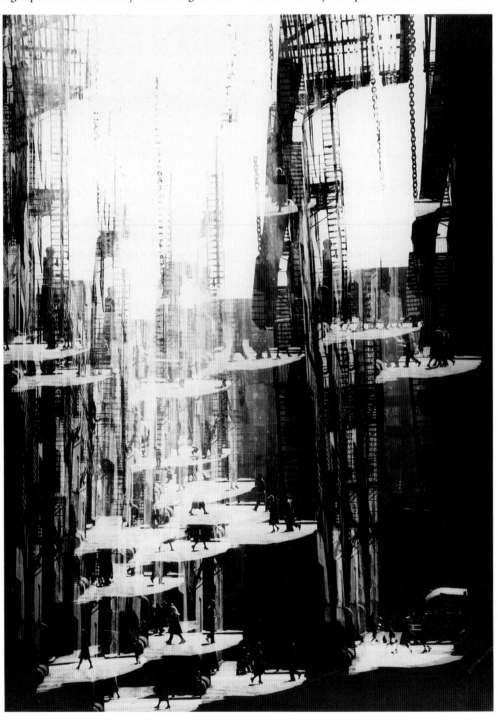

Fig. 19.2
RAY METZKER
Philadelphia, 1967

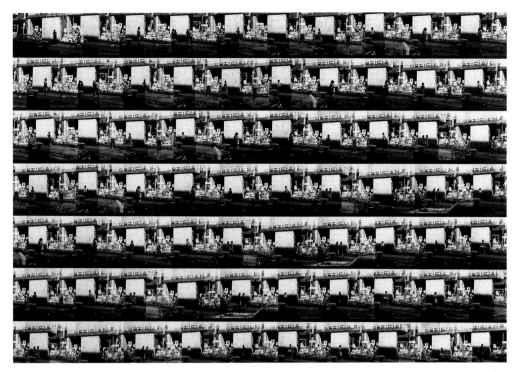

dents, Arthur Siegel. Siegel carried the message of the "new vision," as it was called,[2] back home to Detroit, where he had originally become interested in photography as a member of the Photo Guild. There he communicated his enthusiasm to a colleague at the guild, Harry Callahan. The latter is one of those figures in the history of photography whose work is truly sui generis. He had had no formal training in the medium, and the only job he had in the field before coming to Chicago was as a photo processor in a lab run by General Motors. But he had already begun on his own to do a type of imagery very much in line with Moholy-Nagy's ideas, which served the same function for him that Lincoln Kirstein's did for Evans and that *Zen in the Art of Archery* did for Cartier-Bresson.

Moholy-Nagy's theories clarified for Callahan what he was doing and encouraged him to continue further in that direction. Characteristic of his work at the time were his early experiments combining on a single sheet of photographic paper multiple, overlapping, slightly out of register printings of the same negative (fig. 19.1). Such imagery is both an abstraction of the street and an analysis of the reality found there. It turns the pedestrians

and passing cars into a form of graphic design while at the same time making visible the nervous, jittery energy of crowds and traffic.

By the late 1940s, Callahan was doing multiples in which the subject matter would hardly be recognizable were it not for titles like *Alley* or *Multiple City*. His photographs demonstrated such an extraordinary power in imagery of this sort that others began to be affected by it as well. By the early 1950s, Siegel, then at work on a series entitled "In Search of Myself," was employing a similar technique on color views of Chicago street scenes, and other variations on the theme became one of the staples of work done at the ID.

Multiple printing, montage, and collage were picked up from Callahan by his best students, each of whom has used it extensively at some point in his or her career. In the mid-1960s in Philadelphia, where he had secured a teaching job shortly after graduating from the ID, Ray Metzker did series entitled "Double Frame" and "Composites." The latter, which is perhaps the central project of Metzker's career, juxtaposes or overlaps negatives of street scenes in grids. These sometimes contain hundreds of separate images within a single print, yet remain recognizable as street photographs (fig. 19.2).

Within a couple of years of her graduation, in 1966, Barbara Crane also began doing series in which she utilized the grid, mirror-image printing techniques, and other effects. And Ken Josephson was already making multiple pictures before getting his M.S. degree, which he earned, in part, with a 1959 thesis on this kind of imagery. Josephson's project employed multiple exposure, which Siegel had experimented with a decade earlier and which Crane would use a decade later for a series that combined street portraits with shots of electric signs (fig. 19.3).

Most of the strains of imagery that appear in the work of the ID photographers of the fifties and sixties can be traced back to Callahan. Although he was not the only person who taught photography there, or even the first to do so, he was the one who brought some measure of stability to a program that had been almost too dynamic for its own good. Whereas the turnover in personnel had been constant before he arrived, he stuck with the institute for fifteen years. He originally came to teach not long before Moholy-Nagy died, and he assumed the chairmanship of the program in 1949, when Siegel resigned. He didn't depart until 1961. The only teacher who had a longer tenure was the one permanent member Callahan added to the faculty, Aaron Siskind, who was there from 1951 until 1970.

Siskind's own work during this period suggests that he fit in at the ID because he too was a dedicated abstractionist. Like Callahan, he had begun in the early forties to do a kind of abstract picture very consistent with Moholy-Nagy's Bauhaus philosophy of photography. His close-up photographs of weathered boards and peeling paint are a scrutiny of the phenomenal world so intense that his subjects are isolated, atomized, and ultimately abstracted by the imagery. Siskind was to prove more single-minded than any of the others at ID, for he continued to make essen-

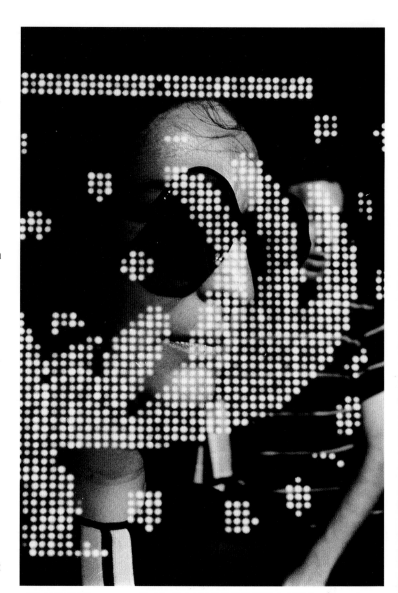

Fig. 19.3
BARBARA CRANE
Neon Series, **1969**

tially the same images until his death, in 1991.

What Callahan hired him to teach was very different: documentary photography of the sort that Siskind had, in practice anyway, largely left behind since being at the Photo League in the thirties (see chapter 12, "Social Uplift"). Yet some of the Chicago work reveals a continuity between that earlier phase of his career and the later one that he was able to instill into the ID curriculum. The kind of pictures he had made in New York, would continue to take in Chicago, and would teach his students to do are head-on, full-frame studies of building facades. From the earliest New York versions of these through the close-ups of peeling paint later, his career developed as if it were a single, steady zoom shot that took decades to complete.

The squared-off graphics of this Chicago phase of Siskind's work, or of similar architectural studies by Josephson and Crane focusing on shadow patterns on siding or reflections in the plate glass exterior of a skyscraper, were very much in line with the Bauhaus imagery being produced at the ID. They seem allusions to the Bauhaus designs of Josef Albers, who began his "Homage to the Square" paintings in 1950 just after quitting the faculty of Black Mountain College, in North Carolina, where Callahan, Siskind, and Siegel all taught in the summer of 1951.

As in this type of image when done by Siegel, Callahan, Metzker, Josephson, or Crane, so too in the street photography that came out of the ID was the landscape of Chicago made to reflect an abstract vision created at the Bauhaus. All these people except Siegel made street photography a key part of their career, as did two others who were at the ID as students, Joseph Sterling and Yasuhiro Ishimoto. The work done by these photographers constitutes the classic imagery of the Chicago School.

Although there are endless variations on it, the main theme of this work is represented by pictures in which people at a distance, alone or in groups, are caught in patches of sunlight against dark, all-but-unfathomable backgrounds (page 302, top; figs. 19.6, 19.7). By blacking out the buildings and other concrete forms, turning their pictures into pure contrasts of sunshine and shadow, the ID photographers who made such imagery were once again confirming the medium as a study of the structure of light.

Street photographs like these are the revival of something else implicit in Moholy-Nagy's work as well. The subjects in them seem to float in the spaces they occupy much the way figures do in early collages by Moholy-Nagy. His spare arrangements with cutouts of peo-

ple pasted down amid a few lines on an otherwise blank page were attempts to schematize new relationships between modern man and modern spaces like cities. New senses of scale and perspective that these compositions illustrate were, Moholy-Nagy felt, becoming ingrained in human consciousness itself, and this he thought that the camera was uniquely suited to reveal. With their white back-

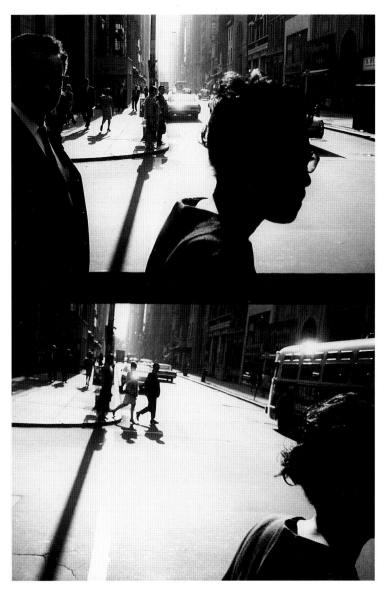

grounds, his collages look as if they might have been the negatives from which the predominantly black ID street photography was printed.

The projects that seem most particularly to elaborate on Moholy-Nagy's vision are Metz-

Fig. 19.4

RAY METZKER

Couplets, Philadelphia,
1968

Fig. 19.5
RAY METZKER
The Loop, Chicago,
1957

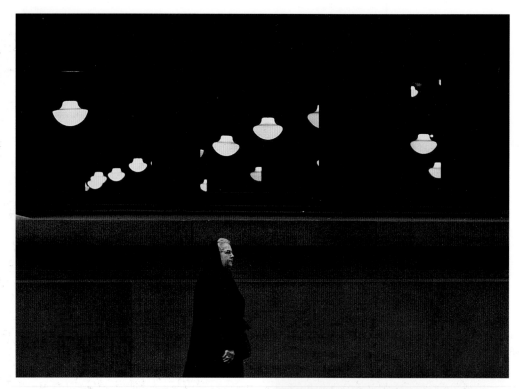

ker's "Double Frame" and "Couplets" series.
Both include pairs of pictures made in such a
way that the seam between the two negatives
is hidden in an area of blackness. The impression is of a single street photograph that
somehow captures the jumps in the sizes of
figures and the other visual discontinuities
Moholy-Nagy was demonstrating. But even
without such optical illusions, street photography at the ID often achieves the same effect.
Created in the universalist spirit of the
Bauhaus, this is a vision that might be applied
to any modern city, or at least to any American city that went through a decline and
depopulation in the postwar period. In
Philadelphia in the early 1980s, Metzker did
a series, entitled "City Whispers," that returns
to the kind of street photography he did in
"My Camera and I in the Loop," his thesis
project at the ID (fig. 19.5).

And yet, no matter how internationalist and
oriented toward aesthetic ideas the work done
at the Institute of Design may have been, it
became a very site-specific art form, a collective vision of the particular city, Chicago, that
was literally the common ground on which
these photographers met. What makes the

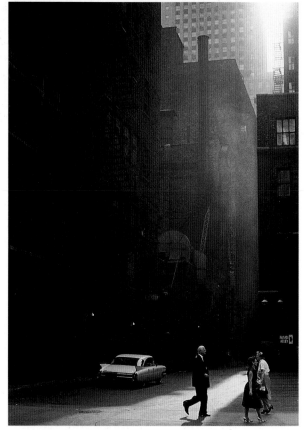

street photography by many different ID
hands comparable is not just the sameness of
the assumptions about the medium and how

Fig. 19.6
YASUHIRO ISHIMOTO
Untitled, 1960–62

Fig. 19.7
HARRY CALLAHAN
Chicago, c. 1953

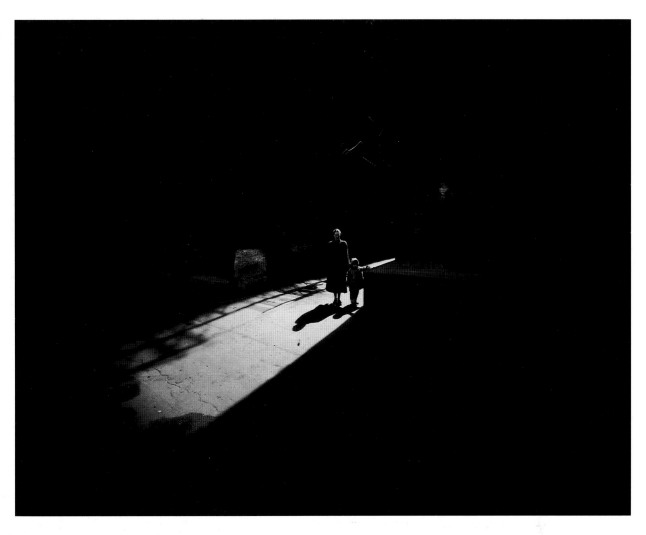

to use it, but the ways in which Chicago as subject matter has infiltrated the work.

This is why the feeling for space and proportion in a Barbara Crane photograph often seems similar to that in one by Metzker. It is the reason that the blank, flat, almost monotonous images of building facades done by Siskind after his arrival in Chicago were anticipated by certain pictures Callahan had made there in the late forties. Even Ishimoto, a nisei who had been interned in a U.S. relocation center during World War II and went to live in Japan after attending the ID in the early 1950s, came all the way back to Chicago in the early 1960s to do a series of street photographs later published as a book with the emphatic title *Chicago, Chicago* (fig. 19.6). It was as if he couldn't find any other place where what he had learned at the ID — the

particular vision of urban life that studying there engendered — made sense.

At one point Callahan had become very disgruntled with the Bauhaus heritage at ID. That was his motivation for wanting, when Siskind was hired, someone with a solid background in documentation. Speaking about the matter years later, he said,

Everything was Bauhaus this and Bauhaus that. I wanted to break it. . . . I got tired of experimentation. I got sick of the solarization and reticulation and walked-on negatives. What I was interested in was the technique of seeing. . . . I introduced problems like "evidence of man," and talking to people — making portraits on the street. . . . I thought [the students] should enter into dealings with human beings and leave abstract photography. I felt that social photography would be the next concern.[3]

Certainly the street photography that came out of the ID has in it a strain of this anti-Bauhaus feeling. In the early fifties Callahan himself began to produce the kind of street portraits he wanted the curriculum to encourage, and a very personal series he did about his family also seems to seek in the concreteness of everyday life some relief from the vagaries of aesthetic theory. The mood established in these pictures of his wife and daughter, nude in furnished rooms with bare walls and no curtains on the windows, is also felt outdoors, in the drab intimacy with which they stand together in the lake, in a deserted park, on a sidewalk, or in a solitary shaft of sunlight that emerges from an alley into a blackened street (fig. 19.7).

Yet a connection is obvious between this sort of image and classic Chicago School street photography, such as a Callahan multiple exposure, which has been influenced by the Bauhaus (fig. 19.1). Even Callahan's street portraits are not finally such a radical departure, for they have an effect very similar to the ID studies of building facades. They have been made at about the same range and with the same confrontational intensity. What finally imparts a distinctive look to all of the street photography, from Callahan's pictures of his wife to his students' pictures of anonymous passersby, is the way in which Bauhaus principles have led to the discovery of something unique to Chicago. In the process of applying Moholy-Nagy's universalist program for photography to the city, these photographers revealed the particularity of the light there.

They took their most characteristic pictures at those seasons of the year and times of day when the light as it passes between the buildings is unlike anything seen in Paris or New York. Only in Chicago does it come into the city, off the flatlands to the west, in quite this way, blasting through the side streets with such force. It seems to move parallel to the ground. It penetrates the Loop all the way to Michigan Avenue. Like the kind of western town where all the buildings on Main Street had a facade two stories tall with a clapboard shed behind, Chicago has high rises along the lake and, just a few blocks beyond, four-story apartment houses or light-industrial buildings that let the sun into the city in the afternoon.

The flatness of the prairie to the west is just a mirror image of the flatness of the lake to the east; between the two, the city is perfectly cross-ventilated with light of an incomparable clarity and forcefulness, which is what the street photography of the Chicago School is really documenting. It is in relation to this light, more than to the skyscrapers, that the people in these photographs so often seem to be diminished in scale. Chicago becomes in these pictures the local habitation and the name given to the airy nothing of Bauhaus vision.

20: Still Going

This final chapter takes the form of a conversation between Colin Westerbeck and Joel Meyerowitz about the latter's memories of his own early days as a street photographer in New York in the 1960s and his association with Robert Frank, Garry Winogrand, Diane Arbus, Lee Friedlander, and others. The talks transcribed here were held over four days in the fall of 1987 in Chicago and, on several briefer occasions later, in both Chicago and New York.

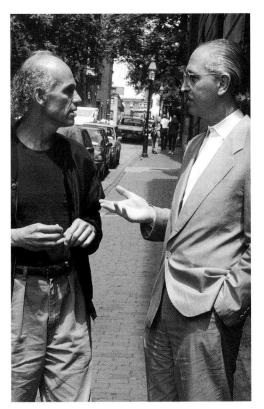

Joel Meyerowitz and Colin Westerbeck, 1993

would take out the French first edition you had of Robert Frank's *The Americans*, which you had looked at so many times that it had fallen apart, and we would lay out Frank's pictures in lines on the floor.

J.M. The funny part of the story behind that copy of *The Americans* is that I knew Frank before I knew the book, or even that he had done it. In the early sixties I was an advertising art director working under a man named Harry Gordon, who sent me one day to supervise a shoot where Robert Frank was going to take pictures of teenage girls in an apartment in Stuyvesant Town. They were going to be doing what teenage girls do when they get together — gossip, comb their hair, put on makeup, try on some clothing, just teenage stuff. And Robert worked with these girls, photographing, just using available light coming through the venetian blinds, or from a desk lamp.

C.W. The name we are giving to this final chapter, "Still Going," was to be the title of the book of your own black-and-white photographs that you were working on when I first met you in 1974. Do you remember? You were trying to condense over a decade of shooting on the street into a book of perhaps seventy pictures — I still have the maquette for it, just in case you decide to publish it someday — and you asked me to come by one afternoon a week to talk about the images you were considering. To give me some idea of how a photographic book ought to look, you

He worked so fast and with such focus that I couldn't believe it. He seemed to be sliding and weaving his way through their lives and around them all the time. Occasionally he would whisper something to one of them, but mostly he made his suggestions physically, in the way he moved. He was just intercepting their movements with the camera. It was a ballet. I thought that to make photographs, you froze everybody before the fact, but Robert never froze them except in the camera. So that was a revelation. I could see the photographs he was making, whereas in the studios I had visited, I never could really.

He was using his body to make photographs, and his timing was precise. I remember when one girl putting on lipstick raised her chin a certain way and pursed her lips, Robert went for that little pout she was making. Suddenly, the girl had become a woman. A moment later she was just a little girl again putting crayon on her mouth, but that split second before she had leapt into womanhood.

Did you talk to Frank at all then?

No, he wasn't someone to be awestruck by because he wasn't *Robert Frank*. He was just Robert Frank, the commercial photographer. Besides, he wasn't so forthcoming. He didn't have much to say. But watching him was truly inspiring. That's what did it for me. The combination of recognizing the captured moment and the physicality of it, of his moving through time. I was grateful that Harry had sent me down because it changed my life. Even though I didn't know anything else existed in photography, I went back and told him I was going to quit in order to take pictures.

I can't tell you why, except that for months I had been yearning to get out of the office. I would stand at the window of the agency's office, which was at 666 Fifth Avenue, and look down to the streets and wish I was out there. So when I quit, I went right out on the streets. Harry lent me a camera. I started to pepper the streets with pictures, though I had no idea that it was something anybody did. I wasn't doing it for any reason except it was exciting to me.

But how did you find out about *The Americans?*

Well, Harry decided a few months later to give up advertising himself to go live in Spain, and when he was unburdening himself of a lot of household goods, he gave me that copy of Frank's book. "I think you'll enjoy this," he said. And wham, there it was, this huge, deep, dark poem about America that gave me something to encounter day after day after day. So that fed me.

How did you get to know Garry Winogrand?

You know, I think that may have been through Harry Gordon too. Harry's wife, Charlotte, was involved in designing the bulletin for WBAI, the commercial-free radio station, and on every cover she'd put a photograph by Garry or by Lee Friedlander or Diane Arbus. So I must have first met Garry, or at least known about his work, through Harry.

Anyway, within a few weeks of the time I quit working for Harry, I was on the subway going up to see my mother in the Bronx, and Garry, this woolly-headed guy, was sitting across from me going to visit the zoo. He was working on the pictures that would later become his book *The Animals*. So we kind of rode up together going in the same direction, and we talked. Then we ran into each other on the streets a few times, and within the first couple of meetings, Garry said, "Why don't you stop by my place and look at some pictures?" That was my introduction to really seeing the bounty of photography.

I went up to this cavern of an apartment he lived in where there were stacks of pictures all over the floor, boxes and boxes stacked up on top of each other, or just stacks of prints one foot, two feet high — piles of a thousand prints each — leaning over on themselves. There seemed to be acres of them, and he would say, "Here, take a look at this," and give me two hundred fifty prints at a chunk. I would sit down with them on my lap and fan my way through them while Garry sat in a chair tapping his feet, chain-smoking, shaking. He would shake so much, the whole place shook. He was nervous, incredibly nervous.

What was your first reaction to that work?

It looked like life was just whizzing by and this guy was snatching at it, and the pictures were funny, funny and crazy, which appealed to me. I had a mocking sense of humor myself because I had been the kind of street kid who hangs around on the corner and watches the people go by. Whether it was a girl on stiletto heels or businessmen in fedora hats carrying briefcases, there was always something to remark about, to pantomime. Someone walks a funny way, they waddle, and you waddled after them for two steps — it was a quick take.

That was what these pictures were, they were quick takes. They were right out of the Three Stooges and the Marx Brothers and the movies of our time. They were all about the things that you couldn't be absolutely sure of because they were so transitory, things that you got a glimmer of, and they made you laugh. Garry was acting out. Right off the streets of the Bronx, and it spoke to me because I had lived there too, only a few blocks away from him.

I love it! You and Winogrand, a couple of little Gavroches from the Bronx.

The kid in *Les Misérables?*

Yeah.

Right, that's it.

Then there were several years when the two of you went out shooting together, didn't you? How did that come about?

Garry loved company. He needed to be out on the street, and he needed company out there with him all the time. It was irresistible. *He* was irresistible. He was so full of, "Let's go! Let's do!" Right from the beginning, he would call in the morning and say, "Listen, I'll meet you at the greasy spoon on Ninety-sixth and Amsterdam: we'll have coffee, we'll go

out, we'll shoot." I was up and ready to go. I was off and running for three intense years — 1962 to 1965 — with this guy, this unstoppable bundle of nerves.

When I first knew you, in the midseventies, I would come along to keep you company when you were shooting sometimes, and Fifth Avenue always seemed the best to me. You could just feel the money and sex and ambition out there every day, surging up and down the street. Did Fifth always seem such a special hunting ground for you street photographers?

Oh yeah. Because Fifth Avenue was the most exciting, and it had the most light. I think Madison was too dark, Park was too wide, Third still had the El in the early sixties, or they were beginning to tear it down — anyway, Third was creepy. Sixth Avenue didn't have much on it. We certainly made some circuits around there, but really Fifth Avenue had the pulse of life, the most vigor, the most beautiful women, the heaviest business action. The mix was best on Fifth. I mean, you got it all, from high fashion to messengers. It just was everything. Pushcarts, pretzel vendors, and limousines. It had the contradictions of life in a big city, and that kind of counterpoint was the stuff of commentary. That's what you could mock, that's what you could wait for, because it was more exciting to see those combinations there.

But the sixties were also the great time for street theater and protest demonstrations. You were all responding to that too, weren't you?

Of course. We went to every public demonstration, every "be-in" in the park, all of the gatherings down in the Forties and Times Square; whenever there were marches, we all went. We really went for two reasons. You lent your body to them because it was right, but also because it was a great place to make photographs. It was chaotic, and it was huge crowds, and the media was there. This notion of the media and the power of the media emerged from those demonstrations.

People would just be milling around when all of a sudden the CBS truck turned on its lights, and the whole thing shifted. Everybody moved toward that truck. They were just turning on their lights to film what was in front of them, but it put a finger on an action, and it created a mass movement, and it created the event, because then the police arrived and the demonstrators arrived, and bam, confrontation. Then the NBC truck turned on its lights. The thing moved up the street. It was like pinball, media pinball.

We all began to see the meaning of the change that represented, how it differed from what photographers like Cartier-Bresson, or like us, would do. The television crews didn't try to come in and not bruise the event. They controlled and directed the event by focusing their cameras. You know, everybody wanted to be in the spotlight, they wanted to be on TV. We began to see that the power was in the hands of the media. Eventually Garry was going to make a book about public relations, which was an interest of his that began with going to those kinds of demonstrations.

I notice you're comparing that New York group you were in to Cartier-Bresson. But his vision is really a long, long way from Winogrand's, don't you think?

Cartier-Bresson's photographs are saying, in a teasing, bemused way, "Look at the modern world. Doesn't it look crazy?" Garry's photographs are saying, "Look at the modern world, it really *is* crazy!" Garry is less interested in the kind of visual coup that Cartier-Bresson is going after.

Winogrand can do that; he can play that delightful formalist game that Cartier-Bresson is so good at when he gets the two old women dressed in black passing underneath the two voluptuous caryatids, or whatever. Winogrand is scoring the same kind of hit when he catches that

pair of rhinoceri nuzzling behind the woman with the sunglasses that have a similar shape [fig. 20.1]. But even if he's coming out of that kind of shooting, he's trying to go someplace else — someplace cruder, deeper and cruder.

Absolutely.

Winogrand wants to see what's left of photography, what the essence of it is, after you give up that kind of formal, French rationality that Cartier-Bresson always hangs on to.

As you pointed out in the chapter on Frank, he was trying to do the same thing. Yet there was also a great difference between the way Robert worked and the way we all did.

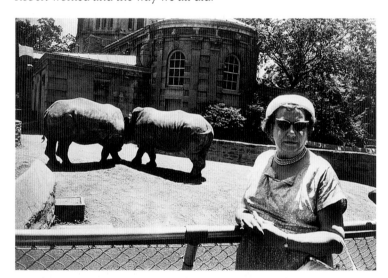

Yes, you see it in the pictures. It's a difference in metabolism.

Fig. 20.1
GARRY WINOGRAND
New York, c. 1963

It's a difference in the ASA at which you're shooting. We were using Tri-X film pushed to 1200 ASA, whereas its normal rating is 400. The reason was to be able to shoot at 1/1000th of a second as much as possible, because if you made pictures on the street at 1/125th, they were blurry. If you lunged at something, either it would move or else your own motion would mess up the picture. I began to work that way after looking at my pictures and noticing that while they had these loose edges, Garry's were crisp. Frank didn't work that way. His pictures were much slower. You could see that he was working at 1/30th and 1/60th and 1/125th.

Frank obviously has a less hyper personality than Winogrand had, or than you do. I envision him moving on the street at a certain pace, with none of that 1200 ASA jitteriness. Was Winogrand literally like that on the street? A few minutes ago you made a wonderful description of him sitting in a chair, twitching, while you looked at pictures. Is that the way he was when he was shooting them as well?

Yeah. Oh yeah. You know, he set a tempo on the street so strong that it was impossible not to follow it. It was like jazz. You just had to get in the same groove. When we were out together, I wasn't watching him — we were both watching the action around us — but I did pick up on his way of working and shooting. You could see what it was in his pictures. They were so highly charged, all you had to do was look at them and you began to assume the physical manner necessary to make pictures. They showed you right away that they were an unhesitating response.

Walking the streets with Garry gave me clues to being ready, to just making sure that I was. I had been a third baseman, so being ready came naturally. I was a quick study on that stuff, darting and twisting and the kind of moves that were necessary to get to a picture.

You know, if you hesitate, forget it. You don't have but a fraction of a fraction of a second. So you have to learn to unleash that. It was like having a hair trigger. Sometimes walking down the street, wanting to make a picture, I would be so anticipatory, so anxious, that I would just have to fire the camera, to let fly a picture, in order to release the energy, so that I could recock it. That's what you got from Garry. It came off of him in waves — to be keyed up, eager, excited for pictures in that way.

You know, the more you talk about Winogrand, the more I find myself wondering whether he wasn't a lot like Cartier-Bresson on some level despite how different their pictures are. His predisposition — or what I called his metabolism before — seems to me pretty similar. Both were men full of nervous impulses who needed photography, maybe, as a way to focus their personalities. On the street something that was in another context a kind of craziness and an irritation to the world, and to himself, suddenly had a usefulness, a coherence, and a purpose.

That was certainly true of Garry. The street gave him someplace to plug in his energy. There he felt that he was necessary to record what was going on. He might be overwound, crazy, but out there everybody was, basically. In his house he was caged. *The Animals* is a great piece of work because it's like him. When we'd meet at the greasy spoon in the morning, Garry would look through the *Daily News*. He'd look at the center spread, at the automobile crack-ups and murders and mayhem from the night before, and it would sort of juice him up to get ready to go out and shoot.

It was the same when he was looking at pictures up in his apartment. He would sit down with a cigarette in his mouth and a chest full of ashes, and he would just flip through a pile of pictures and chuckle and snort and gasp. The whole thing had a kind of animal-like quality to it. Because there wasn't a lot to say about photography. He didn't have a photographic vocabulary yet, but he would grunt his affections for the pictures, and that was the signal, see, that was his visceral reaction to them, and I learned to trust that.

On the street, the same thing. He was restless, like the bear at the zoo. You know how the bear sways back and forth in the cage, how he lumbers up and down? Well, that was Garry.

At the same time, though, Garry could be fiercely articulate about photography, couldn't he? I know he could just from a few occasions I had to talk with him late in his life. There was nothing doltish about him.

Oh, no, far from it. He was Beauty *and* the Beast rolled into one, for he had a tremendous, keen intelligence about photography and a great passion for talking about it. Later on, he was widely respected as a teacher; but he had developed that need to communicate what he knew about the medium long before that. Did you know that he tried to teach a course in photography on his own in the early sixties, in 1963 or 1964, I think it was?

No, I didn't know that.

Yeah. He put a classified in the *Village Voice* or the *Times* or wherever, advertising a course in photography to be taught in his apartment. No one applied.

What a letdown! You've been working for years learning a discipline, and then nobody comes. Well, the whole cult of street photography was four or five people in those days. What were you guys going to do, take lessons from each other?

Well, what we did was this. Garry eventually got two or three people who paid fifty dollars each, so Tod Papageorge and my wife, Vivian, and a few more of us who knew Garry came free, just to fill it out, just to help out. We sat around and talked about photography. There were assignments to make pictures and we tried to make some kind of stimulating dialogue as well.

How did Tod come into the picture?

One day, when I was with Garry, he got a phone call from this guy who said he wanted to be a photographer and could he come up to talk. It turned out that he had come straight to New York from college, where he

had been a literature major, but now he was interested in taking pictures.

How did he know who Winogrand was?

I think he had seen that five-person show at the Modern with Ernst Haas and Jerome Liebling and Garry in it. So he began to hang out with Garry too. There was a long period in 1964–65 when the three of us — Garry, Tod, and me — would go out shooting together, and I believe Tod began doing some of Garry's printing then as well. Garry was progressively pulling away from the darkroom, and my recall is that probably half the pictures in *The Animals* were printed by Tod.

What with this course and you living in the neighborhood and Tod doing printing for him, you all must have been practically camping out in Garry's apartment.

I was, anyway, because he wanted company all the time. He and his wife had split up, and at that time he had his kids. One of them had the nickname Fiddlesticks, because she was fiddly just like him. At the end of the day he would be knocking around his apartment, trying to get dinner together for his kids. He was under tremendous inner pressure. The guy was a pressure cooker. It was like steam was coming out of his ears. In some ways I used to think he was a dragon, a fire-breathing dragon, snorting and gasping, because he had a terrible smoker's cough.

At the end of the day, he and I and the kids would all be in the kitchen of his apartment. Smoke would be pouring out of the broiler, the steak juices would be burning, the creamed spinach would be bubbling, the bottle of Scotch would be on the table, the kids would be yelling, I would be trying to open the window to let the smoke out, and Garry would be having a coughing fit. It was wild, I tell you.

It sounds as if it were beyond wild, some-where nearer to a frenzy or a panic.

You know, Garry always talked about des-peration being his guiding force as a photo-grapher, that when he was desperate to do something and he had reached that kind of fever pitch, some sign came to him, an instinct, and he followed his instinct. Basi-cally a photographer is indecisive ninety-nine percent of the time because you are wandering around waiting for something to happen; but when it does, you better be able to act.

And Garry was at his sharpest when he was under duress?

Well, I don't know about that, but. . . . For in-stance, you'd be at the zoo with him in the late afternoon and he would linger by the seal pond. He's anxious to get home, he's check-ing his watch, he has to go pick up his kids in a little while; but he's lingering at the seal pond and he doesn't know why, he's just stay-ing there. You're saying to him, "Garry, you said you had to go home, get down to the Lower East Side," and he says, "Just wait a few minutes."

Then just when you're really ready to go and the light is fading, the keeper comes out with a huge basket of herrings that he starts flip-ping to the seals, and the seals leap up on the edge of the concrete, a crowd gathers — all of a sudden opportunities for pictures are there. You realize that he stayed beyond the time he should have because he had an instinct to stay. So you learn that if you have an instinct to do something, you should follow that.

One day — this was an incident in partic-ular that I remember — we were going to the zoo heading one way or another, and Garry said, "Let's go to the gorilla cage." The week before, the gorilla had given birth, and it had made headlines in the papers. But this day, we were just wandering, trying to make up our minds where we should go

— the elephants, the snakes, whatever — when Garry decides, the gorilla! And when we get there, there's a little man standing in front of the cage, he takes out of his jacket pocket the centerfold of the *Daily News*. In it there's a picture of the gorilla with the baby in her arms which this little man holds up so the gorilla can see it. He holds out the unfolded newspaper to the gorilla, who reaches for it like a person that wants to read the article, which is, of course, what we're both hoping the gorilla's going to do.

The man holds on to it until the gorilla has it, and then their hands are on either side of the paper, and then he lets go of the paper as the gorilla pulls it into the cage. The gorilla takes a corner of it in her mouth and begins eating it and tearing and rubbing and crackling it up. Garry's standing there, tock-a-tock-a-tock-a-tock, while I'm just looking on. It's his terri-tory, and when you know someone has a territory in a sense, you leave off. You're just there to enjoy it. Had Garry decided to go to the elephant house or the llama cage, we never would have witnessed it. But his in-stinct was to take another look at that gorilla. Timing, intuition. It's the sixth sense that you can't really describe to anybody else.

You don't want to lay too heavy a trip on the mystical side of it, but if you're in a place long enough, whether you're rafting on the Grand Canyon or you are walking down Fifth Av-enue, you begin to learn the river or the streets and to understand something about human behavior there. If you see a flurry in the crowd, or you sense a change in the pres-sure of the crowd, sixty or eighty feet away, you may get yourself up immediately and find out what's happening there. What's going to happen. You begin to predict and project and put yourself in position, and then maybe it comes your way.

That was my greatest lesson from Garry: not how to do something, but *when* to do it. What I watched closely was when he chose to stop, when to take the photograph; the way he followed his instinct, his desperation.

In a situation like that, was there anything distinctive about the way he photographed — how he stood or held himself, or the camera?

There was, in fact. Although he was right-handed, he would put the camera to his left eye. So he had to move the camera across his face, and he would do this thing with his head in a funny way. He would move the camera up in an arc with his right hand while at the same time swiveling his head the opposite direction, almost as if he was starting to look away from what he was, actually, about to photograph. It was very disarming. The camera and his eye would meet just for the moment in a kind of glancing blow.

Do you suppose his famous tilted frame resulted from this arcing motion you say he put on the camera?

I don't know. Maybe.

What about the other ninety-nine percent of the time, the long spells when you were just waiting, keyed up, looking for whatever you were going to photograph next? What did Garry do to keep himself occupied then?

Start an argument, or check his service. He used to check his service every half hour. He'd run to a pay phone; "One second," he'd say, "gotta call my service." He was always in motion. If he stood still a few minutes to talk to you, it could easily turn into an argument about politics or baseball or whatever happened to be bugging him that day. If there was a word to sum up Garry's attitude, it was "abrupt." He had little tolerance for anyone with a point of view that didn't quite agree with his or who couldn't sustain their end of the conversation.

I remember once somebody who came to see him puzzled over his photographs and said he

didn't get them. "You *don't?!*" Garry thundered. He flipped the guy's opinion right back at him. If people blabbered on or weren't quick to get to the point, he cut them short, just cut them. He didn't want to waste his time. He was volatile and hot-tempered, moody and flashy, even downright belligerent at times. He liked arguments. He loved the engagement of them. He loved to get into it. He was a provocateur who was also quick to be provoked.

When you were standing on the street with him, you could suddenly find yourself engulfed in one of these terrifically intense discussions about something. But at the same time that he was talking to you, he was also looking over your shoulder, all the time watching the street, prowling with his eye. And he was unashamed to interrupt a conversation and just leave you flat, for a second, to go tearing off with his camera after something he'd seen.

It sounds as if he was a kind of police scanner when he was out there, his eyes running up and down the street all the time like the automatic tuner, stopping for a minute at any signal it could pick up, then running on, running on.

As you said "scanner," I was thinking "scan." He was scanning the streets, and also scanning his own instincts, constantly.

I've been thinking about these stories you've been telling me, all these impressions I've gotten of how Winogrand behaved on the street — how he'd linger by the seal tank when he knew he should be leaving to pick up his kids, or he'd get into a heated argument about something while at the same time searching the street for pictures, and even the way that his head and his camera would seem to go in two different directions when he was taking a photograph. And it all makes me wonder whether being in a certain state of distraction, of divided attention, didn't help him to see these fleeting,

1/1000th-of-a-second subjects he was looking for.

No, I don't think so, because no one who knew Garry would call him distracted. It wasn't distraction, but *attraction* that made him focus always on the street, no matter what else was going on.

I don't mean that he wasn't totally concentrated when he took the picture itself. But the things he wanted to photograph were so evanescent, so peripheral both visually and socially, that I wonder whether he didn't find he could best catch sight of them out of the corner of his eye. A fragmented consciousness permitted the sort of fragmentary image he was after to filter through.

You know, there's a phenomenon that the military call skewed vision, which is the ability to see something better in low light when you look a bit to one side rather than directly at it. I think Winogrand's habits are an example of how street photography requires a similar tactic.

Yes, when you put it that way. . . . That's possible. The things we were seeking out took an oblique approach. Garry never wanted to look at things head-on. He would get close and make some pictures, then pull back and move around. He circled constantly. All of us did. It was part of the game.

It's funny. The reason Cartier-Bresson preferred overcast conditions was so he could circle and stalk his subjects, without having a particular angle, a given picture, imposed on him by the lighting. As different as his pictures are, they also reflect that need for 360 degrees of latitude in order to find the one permanent image in such transient situations.

Making the picture often seemed to require a very delicate touch because what we were trying to capture was so tentative. Whenever anything happened on the street, he and I would seesaw apart and then kind of collide together again. He would run to make a picture, or I would, and then we would come back to the same spot because afterward there was always the excitement of the brief telling — "Did you see her with that *poodle?*" There was always some quick rehashing of the thing, to fix it a little bit more, because it had been so ephemeral.

I'm struck by your use of the word "delicate." The photography Garry created might be thought of as a type of heart surgery he performed on the street. The surgeon may have to rip flesh or even break ribs to get at the heart; but once it's exposed, he uses the utmost restraint. He gets in there by a kind of brute force, and then disturbs the heart itself as little as possible.

Right. Sometimes you had to elbow your way through a crowd and make a space for yourself, which you could do because you had a determination that nobody else there had. But you had to get through the crowd and into the situation without bruising it.

Wasn't it hard for you to be out on the street with Winogrand, though? He was such an explosive and dominating personality — did he leave you room to find your own pace and style?

I was never threatened by Garry. It was a really healthy thing. He treated me right from the beginning as a fair peer, which was really good, even though my work didn't deserve it in terms of either quantity or, at first, quality. He was encouraging. He saw signs of my humor and my spirit and my openness to things, so he gave me room. The things that he photographed weren't necessarily the same ones that I was interested in. I had from the start a different kind of timing, different distance, different pacing, all of which allowed us to be on the streets together without stepping on each other's toes. It gave us more to share, because there were two of us now look-

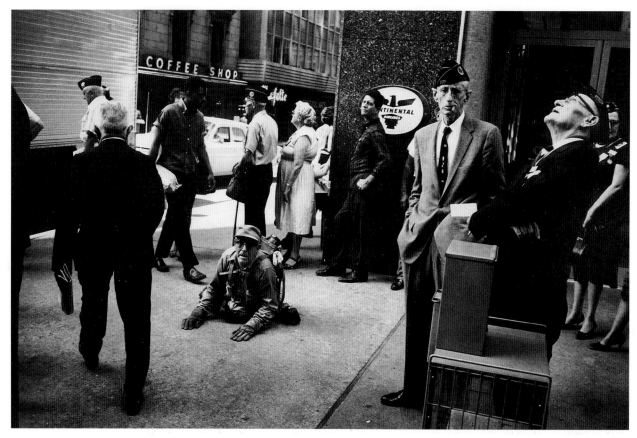

Fig. 20.2
GARRY WINOGRAND
American Legion
Convention, Dallas,
1964

ing at twice as many things. He inspired me without trying to overwhelm me or force me in any way.

I shouldn't be surprised, I suppose, because later he was going to make a career for himself as a teacher, and a damned good one, apparently.

Also, after Tod began to go out with us, there was a kind of herd instinct that took over. When any one of us became alert to something, all three of us did. "What's happening? Garry is moving fast, maybe something's happening for all of us." Or, "Joel's doing this, maybe we should go to that side of the street." There was a mutuality of energy, a play back and forth, a trust that our friendship allowed us to have.

Why was Winogrand drawn to dwarfs, cripples, to marginalized subjects of various kinds? Did he see in such street peo-

ple some kind of reflection, however metaphorical, of himself?

Those pictures are both unflinchingly funny and tragic at the same time [fig. 20.2]. They're tragicomedies, which is what Garry's own life often was.

Yes, it's odd. On the one hand, he has this killer instinct for pictures. You can see in the results that he goes after them like a pit bull. On the other hand, he can be almost sentimental in some of them. He gets away with a certain pathos that a more concerned, humanitarian photographer never would.

Listen, if you can take someone who's both ruthlessly honest and terribly compassionate at the same time, and jam them together in a kind of contradiction — that was Garry. He's the photographer whose pictures are both a slam and an embrace. He's a contradiction, and so the pictures are contradictions. Some of his most poetic pictures have a kind of brutality to them. They are made in that brash, frank, confrontational, aggressive manner, and they're also riddled with a tenderness and poignancy.

It's interesting that Diane Arbus should have been attracted to dwarfs and midgets and the walking wounded of various types as subjects too. What did she think of Winogrand's work?

She didn't like it. I don't think she understood it very well. Or anyway, my memory is that she told me that she couldn't see it.

Why?

I'm not sure. Different attitudes, you know. Garry seemed incredibly casual to people who were making more concrete-looking work. Once when I was down in her little carriage house off Bank Street (I think it was), and we were talking about work, she said that Garry's was too loose for her, too scattered. Cartier-Bresson didn't like *her* work, either. There were so many ideas that were around then. Garry tussled with everybody, and I think it probably unnerved her. His kind of energy, maybe, rubbed her the wrong way.

Nor did Diane hang out with us. I would bump into her occasionally on the street or in the park, and we would walk and talk a bit. A few times, we all went down to her house to see work. But that was it.

Diane was sublime, stealthy, a mystery. She was weird and inwardly focused; she was like a wraith. She kind of hovered off the ground. She was secretive and had long silences, though when she spoke, she was so eloquent that you were mesmerized. It was just impossible not to listen. She was passionate and lyrical. She wrapped words around you. She had a hushed, whispery voice. It was full of sighs. There were poems just dripping out of her mouth, and so the next time

you saw her, you wanted to be near her for a little longer.

You were obviously drawn to her. Why didn't you have more contact with her?

Well, as I say, we would meet on these infrequent occasions by chance and then spend an hour or two with each other just drifting, until she had had enough or until she found something she wanted to do. The one incident I remember that was more elaborate was a time we went away together. I had been talking about the Catskill Mountains, in upstate New York, where I'd been a summer waiter during my teens. It was one of the first places that I myself had gone to photograph when I started out, because a place like that — that too is the street to me. I knew how people behaved, which made it a safe place to work. I spent two or three days and got out of it the first really concrete body of work I did.

Anyway, Diane had said she would love to go there sometime, so one day I said, "Fine, let's go. I'll drive you up there." (I don't know if she even drove.) We went up to Grossinger's because I had once worked with the steward there when he was at another hotel, and I knew that I could get her in behind the scenes, and also get a free meal.

Since we arrived around noon, I took her right to the kitchen and found this steward, who said, "Sure, great to see you, sit down, have a lunch." And the minute we sat down, this crazy came and sat across from us. We were sitting at a long refectory table with the staff, and this heavy-set guy came along looking for a place. There were lots of them everywhere, but he took one look at Diane, sat down opposite her, and within a few minutes he was delivering this loony monologue to her. He was telling her that he was whatever his sign was — a Scorpio or Libra — and what he thought she was (he was right, too) and about how he and his wife had waited for the right moment to make a baby, so the baby would be born under the right sign, and how it was working out real well, and so on. He just began pouring out this story to her.

I was sitting there, he could have told it to me. But it was all directed at her. She had a magnetism that drew this guy out of the flow of people to come and sit by her. After a while, she took him away to make a photograph of him outside someplace. I said, "Well, I'll catch up with you." I didn't go and witness that thing. Later, we went through the whole hotel — the physical director was doing Simon Says or shuffleboard or some game out on the terrace, the dance team was teaching some new steps in the ballroom. Diane had a camera with a flash on it and she just sort of slithered in and out of the dance lesson, the people at the card tables, the ones lounging in the sun. These were for the most part middle- to older-age Jewish people in the Catskills; they were types, the types that you see in her book.

You mentioned the flash mounted on her camera. What about her use of it: how crucial to her pictures do you think it was?

Oh, pretty important, really essential. She really introduced an idea that has of course been picked up by everybody, flash in daylight on the streets. She didn't want to have too much of this situation where faces got dark because the background behind them was lighter. By employing the flash she didn't have to manipulate people who were backlit and turn them around into the sun where she would cast a shadow on them and they would be squinting into the camera. Instead, she could get them unblinking, because if you turn someone around to the sunlight, then they start screwing up their face.

Not only that, but the flash in daylight gave an unnatural feel to the pictures. It gave her subjects a certain fun-house presence, picking up the shine on faces in a way that made them physically gross, even grotesque, or that brought a care-worn quality to them.

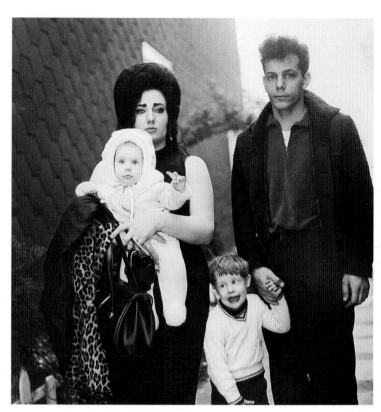

The flash also casts a bizarre light on the account you just gave of how she worked, how she insinuated herself into someone's life. The flash creates an image that looks more like a confrontation than the seduction you describe.

If it was a confrontation, it was a very soft and entangling one. Garry was the bear, and she was the spider. You could see how she got into people's lives. She was genuinely interested in them, and they became entranced by her, enamored of her. She had what would be called, in sixties parlance, good vibes — an aura, charisma, something that emanated from her. If she was next to somebody, near somebody, and she wanted to photograph them, she would send out her interest. It was as if a bloom would just open up, and they would see her, and she would say something to them in hardly an audible way, and they would listen. Because if someone speaks low enough, people listen. There was a kind of incantation in her whisper, and people would go limp.

Fig. 20.3
DIANE ARBUS
A Young Brooklyn Family Going on a Sunday Outing, 1966

Yes, you can literally see that in the pictures. The people in them are limp, often. The posture that she elicits from them is the kind of limpness that you see in the street portrait of the old couple sitting on a bench or the family from Brooklyn where the kid is hanging, goggle-eyed, off his father's hand [fig. 20.3].

You know, if you look at her pictures, the one thing you don't see is resistance. You don't see people chin up, toughing it out, saying, "Here, take my measure, I dare you!" People are giving themselves over to her. When you look at those pictures, their subjects are just flowing out toward her, giving up their mystery. Diane was an emissary from the world of feeling. She cared about these people. They felt that and gave her their secret.

The truth seemed to be that she was usually limp and defenseless herself. In my experience, anyhow, she was always exhausted, searching, sighing. There was a sigh, a profound human sigh deep inside her somewhere: "I can't do it, it's beyond me." But then she would stifle that inner voice, that doubt, enough to lift her spirits so she could go and photograph.

She was always worn out by the demands of working with the camera. She liked to think she was klutzy, that she didn't know how to use this implement, she couldn't print well enough. But that didn't stop her from working. It was part of what she put out around her. It was as if everything was too hard, yet she was doing it all the same, in spite of how hard it was. Even the pressure of her voice, the hushed tones in which she talked, seemed to be saying, "This is too much for me, Joel, this camera, I've got to put the camera down." But she never did.

The most passive and defenseless of her subjects are found among the nudists, I feel, because those people aren't simply nude in the aesthetic sense of the term. They're naked — naked and

vulnerable. They're laid bare not just by their own nudity, but by a kind of collusion with the camera; and (worst of all) they don't even know it [fig. 20.4].

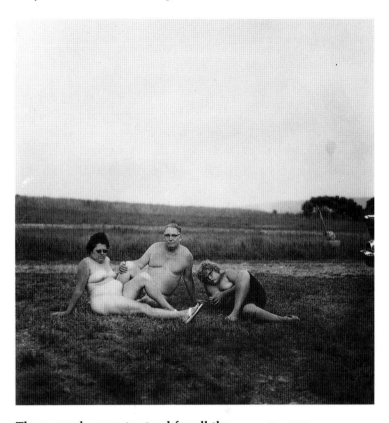

These people seem to stand for all the others in her work, who are also being exposed in some sense by the photograph. It's striking to what extent one set of subjects — fringe groups like nudists or transvestites, or institutionalized people who are retarded — seems to reflect the others. The "ordinary" people she found on the street look as if they live in the same seamless world as the mentally handicapped, the carnival sword swallowers, and the rest.

Diane's world looks everywhere the same because of the way she printed everything. I remember that she had proofs pinned up on a folding screen, maybe four or five panels, that was around her bed in the big main room in her carriage house. That's how she displayed her work there.

Fig. 20.4
DIANE ARBUS
A Family One Evening in a Nudist Camp, Pennsylvania, 1965

She had this funny way of making her prints with black edges. Nobody could figure out how she did it, really, but I thought

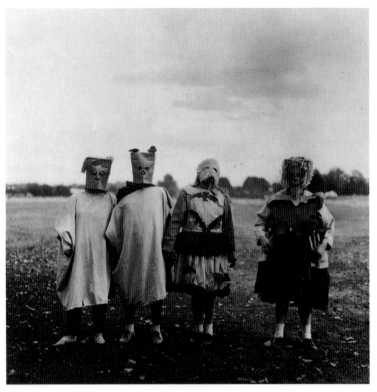

Fig. 20.5
DIANE ARBUS
Untitled (4), 1970–71

I knew. I thought she probably had a piece of glass to hold down the paper she was printing on, and that she had masked the glass with tape or paint. That's why you get those strange, wavy, unfocused edges; if you look closely at them, even in reproduction in the book, you'll see that the bumps and wiggles come always in the same places, as if she was using the same printing matte for every image.

It's a very effective device, as if she had pulled back the enlarger head to reveal the void that exists beyond the confines of the photograph, as if, beyond the photographic frame, you just fell off into indefinite space. I always suspected that the inspiration for those edges came from the work of Richard Avedon, who was of course a close friend of hers, and who was printing his 2¼ negatives so that the Kodak name on the edges showed in the print.

I think Diane was there first. I'll tell you, though, I picked up a clue from her about the portraits that I started to make a number of years ago — that you could allow the subjects the room to liberate themselves for a moment and speak to the camera with their inner self, that that's the thing to photograph, not the surface only, because who cares, you're going to get the surface anyway. But if you could somehow open them up and let them be, as she lets them be. . . .

Where I think she ran into a brick wall was with the people who were institutionalized, because there the inner self was closed to her [fig. 20.5]. I think she spent herself and drove herself crazy with those people because there was no feedback from them. Functional people — the sword swallowers and taxi drivers and so on — were like her. But these others were impenetrable, and I think it must have made her frantic to be on the outside like that with her subjects.

Do you feel that the social consciousness that seems to inhere in the photographs was *in* Arbus herself, that it was any part of her intention with the work? The reason I ask is that I think there was a distinct social overtone to the remarkable success of her posthumous exhibition at the Modern.

That show, in 1972, was the most popular photography exhibition the museum had done since Edward Steichen's "The Family of Man," which the Arbus show was very much the opposite of in spirit. It was grim and rather queasy about life in our time, whereas the earlier show had been very upbeat and sentimental. Arbus's pictures suited the mood of the public, or a part of it, anyway, in the Nixon era, the last stages of the Vietnam War, just as Steichen's editorializing had appealed to the more positive, confident attitudes of a decade and a half earlier.

In fact, one particular image by Arbus, which was very popular and much reproduced at the time, was especially telling, I thought — the one of the skinny kid with the toy grenade in his hand [fig. 20.6]. I always felt that in a funny way that exasperated kid with the grenade was seen by people as an emblematic character. His puny rage, and the way it makes him pull the trigger on that grenade, made him a perfect political cartoon to represent a nation choking on its own bile over Vietnam and greatly diminished in self-image.

I agree that there was a kind of timely social significance to Diane's pictures, though how aware she herself was of that I don't know.

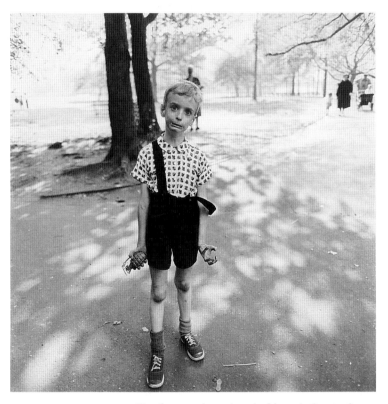

Fig. 20.6
DIANE ARBUS
Child with a Toy Hand Grenade, New York, 1962

You have to keep in mind how intimate the process was by which they were made, even many of the street pictures. She wasn't expanding anybody's horizons, but narrowing down her own focus, homing in on subjects who were enthralled by her because they could feel how personal and private her interest in them was.

You know, I have to say that the reason I think Arbus and Winogrand were the central photographers of that generation —

your generation, the one after Frank's *Americans* — is that they were the ones who were really flying by the seat of their pants, being guided purely by their feelings and intuitions and a kind of subconscious instinct, following through most powerfully on the lead that *The Americans* offered. Whether they felt they were actually being influenced by Frank's example or not, they were still fulfilling a certain promise for the medium that his work held out.

They were trying to make pictures out of a deeper part of their personalities than anyone else had before, the kind of pictures where you remove the constraints of the rational mind. Where Cartier-Bresson would use an elegantly constructed frame as a setting for the one nutty thing he would allow to come into the middle of his picture, Winogrand and Arbus were making pictures that were all nuts. They let the beast get loose in their work.

Diane made the pictures out of her needs, you know, and they took shape from her needs and her curiosity, so we can see the real point, the knife edge of her curiosity, in them. It probes and it sticks us hard and it hurts and it inspires and it's all those sharp things that come when someone needs to do something and they find a way. And it's just the same with Garry. He didn't lean on Robert or Cartier-Bresson or Evans; he was just Garry. The same with her. She created her photographs out of who she was.

What about Lee Friedlander: where did he fit into this New York street scene? Wasn't he out there photographing with all of you sometimes in the sixties?

Oh, yes, in those days we would bump into Lee on the streets too. He was then living out in the country. He didn't photograph with anybody, that wasn't his style. He was very much more a loner than Garry.

Fig. 20.7
LEE FRIEDLANDER
Lafayette, Louisiana,
1968

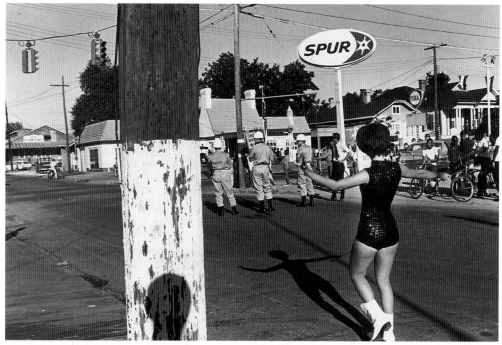

Maybe that's why he photographed his own shadow falling into the scene in so many early pictures, because it was the only company he had out there [fig. 20.7]. "Me . . . and . . . my . . . sha-dow . . ." It was a surrogate for him. He takes pictures of himself everyplace — his reflection in windows, his shadow falling on his subject, or himself as the subject — to identify that he was there. All that stuff points toward a self-consciousness in the work.

I've always thought the number of ways in which his photographs referred back to himself was curious, especially the ones where he seems to have held the camera out and taken his own picture. When Frank holds his camera out at arm's length, it's aimed at the world; doing so is a way of losing himself in an otherness that's out there somewhere. When Friedlander does it, he aims the camera back at himself.

Yeah, he's telling us in his pictures from the very beginning that he's self-involved. The result is work that's coolly intellectual in a way. He's more cerebral than Diane or Garry. They were capable of being dispassionate, even detached. But the hard truths of their needs and urgencies and personalities are what made

their photographs so astonishing. Lee's pictures are less astonishing to me — their complexity hits me first.

Oh, I don't know. I would say that it's Winogrand and Arbus who are truly self-involved. The "urgencies" of their own "personalities" about which you were just speaking make them that way. It's only as a photographer that Friedlander is self-conscious, not as a personality. I think he sees the medium as a form of self-consciousness, and that gesture of aiming the camera back at himself is meant to indicate this. He's always aware of the medium when he's using it. He's always thinking about it, which may be why his career has had such longevity and such a diversity of projects.

More than any other street photographer, he's been able to generalize what he learned on the street, on the road, and apply it to other genres. When you look at the portraits, or even the nudes, you see that it is often the errant detail or the odd, improvised, off-balance feel of the composition that gives the picture its originality. Friedlander has taken the lessons that the street teaches and applied them,

Fig. 20.8
LEE FRIEDLANDER
New York, 1963

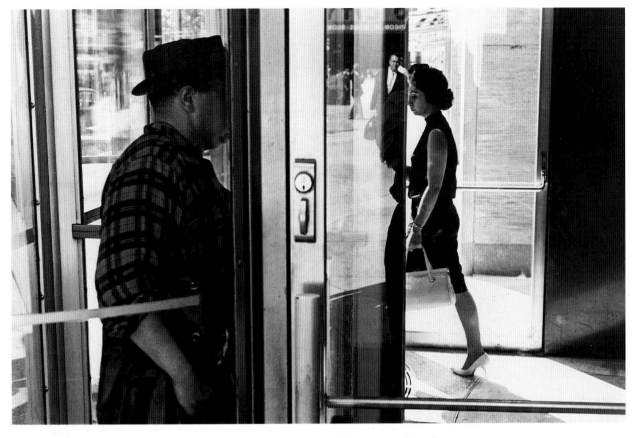

sometimes with great brilliance, to all sorts of other subjects. You above all should appreciate that, since you're the other street shooter from that time who's done it as well.

Do you find Lee's pictures to be as complexly human as Diane's or Garry's? If there is this level of analysis of the medium that you're talking about going on all the time, don't you think it diminishes in his work the amount of conflict and tension — the energy — that really great pictures always need?

Perhaps. But there are contradictions in his pictures too, just as there are in Arbus's or Winogrand's, that make his just as interesting as theirs. You see him in some of the self-portraits; here he is, this stolid, heavy-lidded, empty-looking guy sitting in some cheap motel room somewhere in wrinkled underpants. Then you look at the picture he took of the main drag in a small town or people going around in a revolving door, and the space

is faceted and fragmented in the most pre-cise, intricate way you can imagine. It's really beautiful. The one of the revolving door is like something seen in a kaleidoscope [fig. 20.8]. You can hardly believe that this guy who seems so dopey in the one set of photographs created the controlled, taut compositions in the other set.

Yes, OK, I admit that the best of his images have their own quirky way of looking at the world. But Garry's were revelations about the human comedy and the medium. They came in a sharp jab to the heart/eye. Lee's coolly crept up on you, their delights just came slower, through a different intelligence, that's all . . .

Some of the best pictures in his book *The American Monument* are little essays on the aesthetics of photography in general. They illuminate detail in a way that makes them an object lesson on its impor-tance. He's like Atget in these pictures. You can just feel the calculated way in

Fig. 20.9

LEE FRIEDLANDER

*Commodore John Paul
Jones, West Potomac
Park, Washington,
D.C., n.d.*

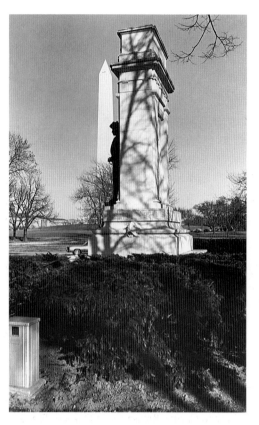

**which he moved from the front of the
monument around to the back until he
saw, pinned in a beam of sunlight like a
butterfly in a specimen case, that little
switch box that turns the floodlights off
and on [fig. 20.9]. This one touch trans-
forms what might have been a humdrum
picture of a dull subject into something
that feels more like a surreptitious
glimpse backstage at an historical drama.**

That image is of a piece with the others he has
made. The pictures all reflect the nature of the
solitary, distant figure who made them. The
planes of the windows, the screen of trees,
and the blossoms on them, the monuments
experienced as objects in space — it does all
have a cumulative power that you could have
seen coming, if you had looked for it, when
Lee was shooting on the streets in New York
like the rest of us.

It was apparent from the Friedlander
photographs that became known in the
early seventies that he was traveling all

over the country. But in fact you did too,
didn't you — and Winogrand as well?
What was the impetus you all felt to go
on the road like that?

Garry and I made our big trips the same summer → 1964. He had a Guggenheim, I think,
and I had taken trips the previous two sum-
mers. I had hitchhiked one year to Mexico
and the second time all through the South
down to Birmingham and all those places, in
'sixty-three. My wife, Vivian, and I had spent
a lot of time just traveling around by thumb.
But in 'sixty-four I wanted to take a trip on
which I would be able to carry more film with
me, so I got an old van that I went around in,
and Garry had a clunker that he may have
gotten from Lee. We crossed paths once or
twice, spent some time in California together.

Robert Frank was the model for these trips.
The idea was that you bought some free time
for yourself, and you took off across America
in search of yourself and what it was like to
be living in this country. Robert's work was an
invitation to do that, the inspiration to go out
and photograph the world at large.

Actually that summer, when I was traveling
around the country, I made some pictures
from the van while I was driving. A couple of
them made a new kind of sense to me. So it
must have been in the back of my mind when
I picked up a car in London in 1966 and
began to travel around Europe. I started to
shoot on the move like that again. Ninety percent of the time I was out of the car and on
my feet when I was photographing, but there
was this little fraction that happened from the
car. Those pictures seemed to me exciting,
risky — just on the edge of perception. I
couldn't wait to see them [fig. 20.10].

When I got back and processed and printed it
all — it was thousands of pictures — the stuff
from the car looked different to me from
everything else. My behavior had changed
when I photographed seated in a moving vehicle, passing through time and space, with
events unfurling outside like a scroll. Every-

Fig. 20.10
JOEL MEYEROWITZ
From the Car, England,
1966

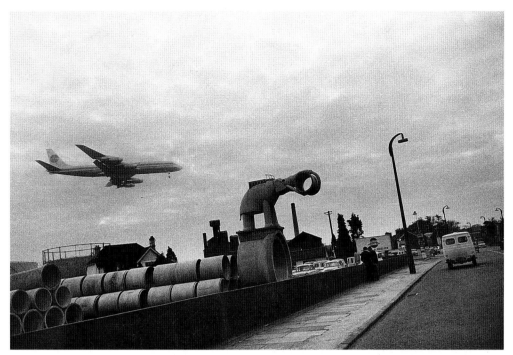

thing was out of control. You could just barely gesture toward it, and you had to do it instinctively, driving with the camera between your legs and then grabbing it and snaring what was out the window. It made for a radical departure for me, but I knew, even before I saw them, that the results were going to be good, that there was something new to look at there. That was the material that was in the one-man show I had at the Modern in 1968.

You had been going out with Winogrand pretty steadily from 1962 until you went to Europe, right?

From 1962 to 1965. Steady. Just about every day. I mean, I thought we were living together. We had our days together, we had our dinner together. Every night. Kids on the weekends. It was a very intense and wonderful period. As good as any period in my life.

This trip to Europe was the first time you'd had a real break from that routine. How did it affect you? Were you able to get back into that groove again when you returned?

Tod, Garry, and I had been a little trio walking the streets together, and even in 'sixty-six,

when I went off to Europe, Garry went with me in a way because I had all the pictures that went into *The Animals,* which I wanted to show to Cartier-Bresson and Delpire, Frank's publisher, so I had a hundred of his pictures that I schlepped around with me. Can you imagine that, having nothing but those pictures to look at for an entire year?

Tod and Garry were hanging out, and when I came back, I couldn't do it anymore. I tried. I did it for four or five months, but I had been my own man for a year, I'd made six hundred rolls of film or more — half color and half black-and-white — and I really felt very different.

Working alone and really finding out what solitude was like, being solitary as a photographer and not having my bulwark of friends around, made a tremendous difference. When I came back, I could feel myself champing at the bit.

When we were all together again walking down the street and he wanted to go left and I wanted to go right, I didn't like how it felt. I really wanted to go right. And there were days when I said, "Well, I'll catch you later at the museum" or something. I would go my own

Fig. 20.11
TONY RAY-JONES
Brook Street, W.1, 1968

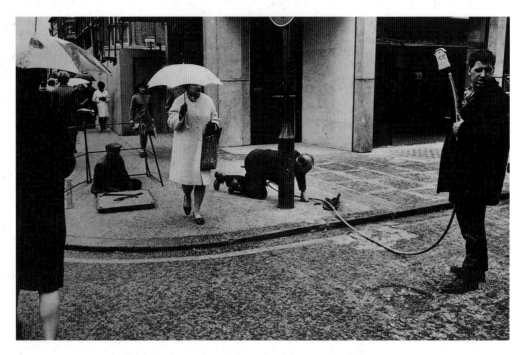

way. I had known that for a year, and I wasn't about to slip back into something that now felt to me like someone else's trip. I was torn, terribly torn emotionally, because I loved Garry and Tod too. But I had to go my own way. You stay in the shadow too long, and you become just a shadow yourself.

Your pictures don't really look like Winogrand's. You had played baseball, been a swimmer, and your pictures are more athletic and graceful than his. There's a Cartier-Bresson side to them. Were there other contacts and alternative experiences, besides the ones with Winogrand, that nurtured that part of your vision when you were just beginning?

Oh, yes. There was a whole parallel development during that time in the early sixties, because I was also out shooting a lot with Tony Ray Jones. He was an English designer who had come down from Yale, where he had been on scholarship, and he was working at Columbia Records. Somehow or other I met him when I was still working in advertising. This was before my time on the street with Garry. Tony was trying to do some photographing himself, shots for record covers or

design jobs — stuff like that, very graphic and jazzy.

When I first went out on the street, I bumped into him one day with his camera. I was shooting color then, and he was too. We talked about the results he was getting, and that started us on a review program. It was a nightly ritual. Tony and I and another photographer we knew would sit and look at each other's slides, one or two rolls at a time, trying to understand what made a photograph. Technically, compositionally, emotionally, temporally. What was right about color that was different? We were looking at both the technique and the act, so that we could refine both our exposures and our timing. In a color slide, after all, you are either right or you are wrong.

Every night we would pick at each other's exposures. Splitting hairs, trying to make exquisite exposure judgments instantaneously. You know — "What did you shoot that at? Why didn't you go slower and have more depth of field, or get closer, so you would have that in focus and that out of focus?" We were analyzing and grinding away at our pictures, and liberating ourselves.

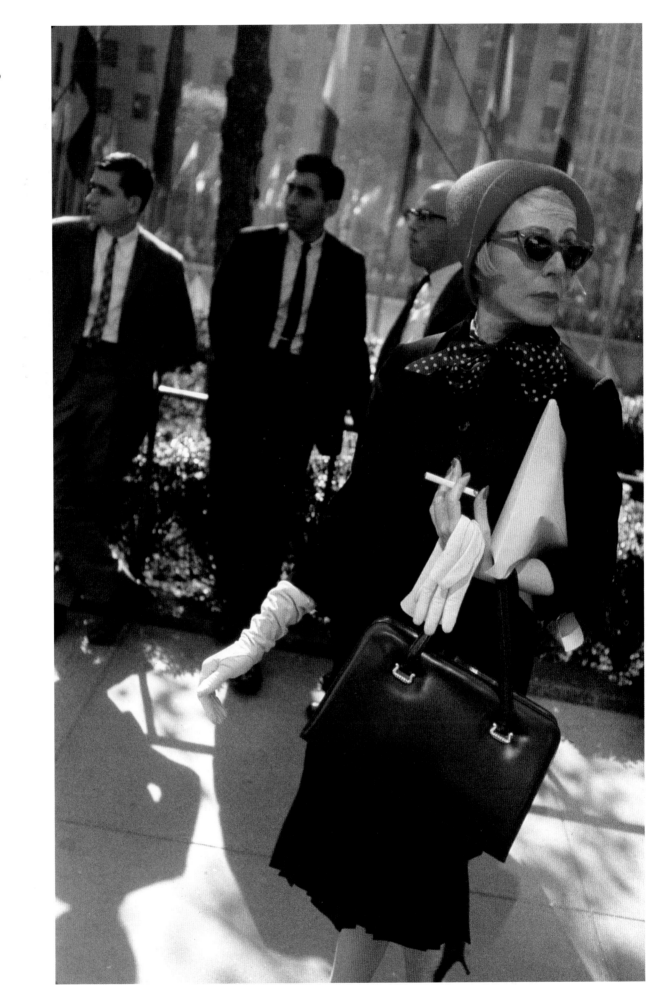

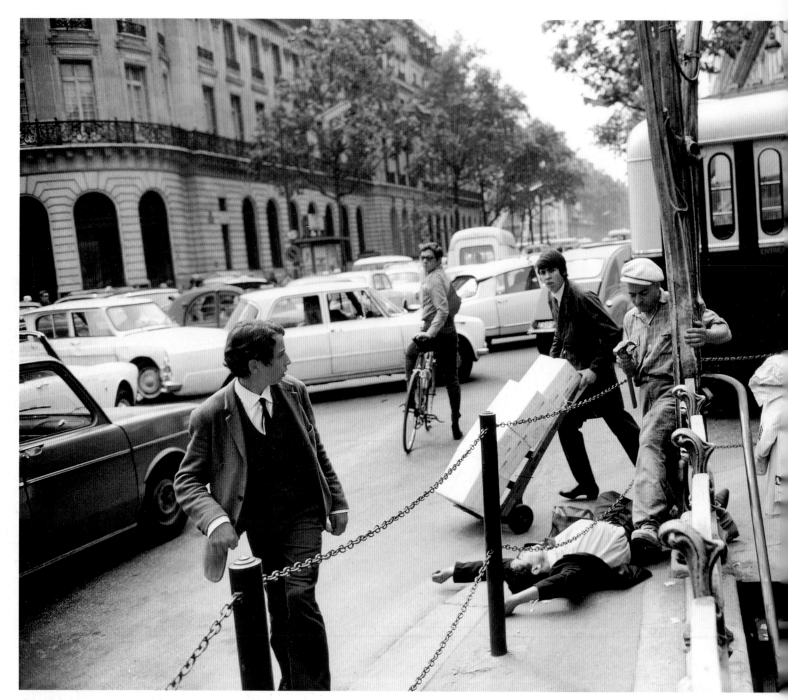

JOEL MEYEROWITZ

Paris, 1967

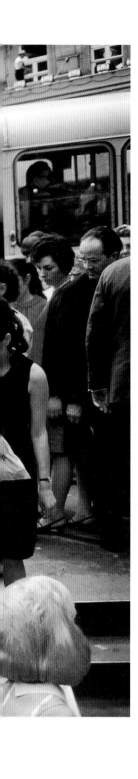

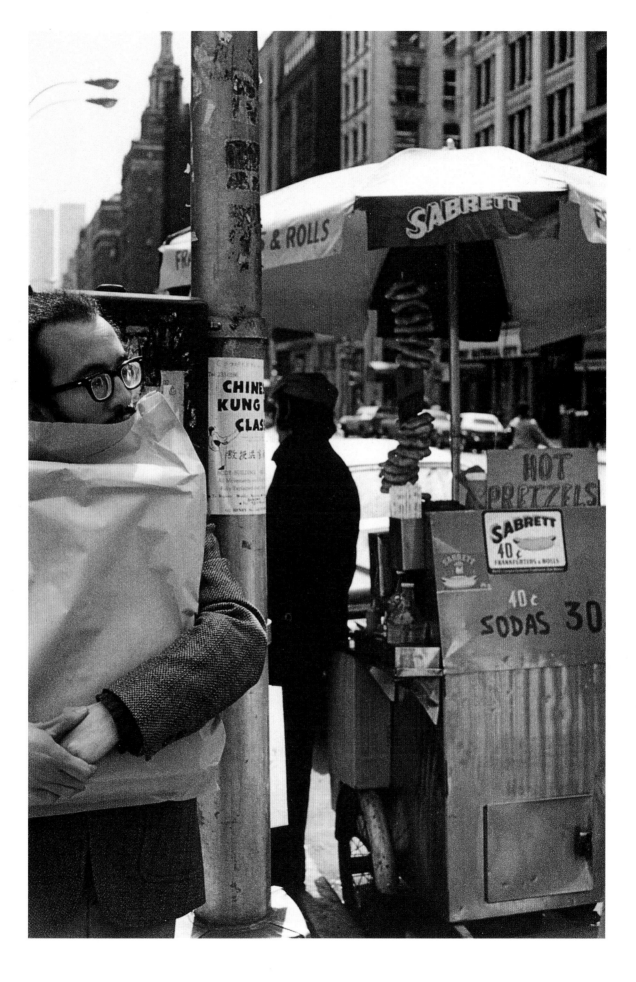

HELEN LEVITT
New York, 1976

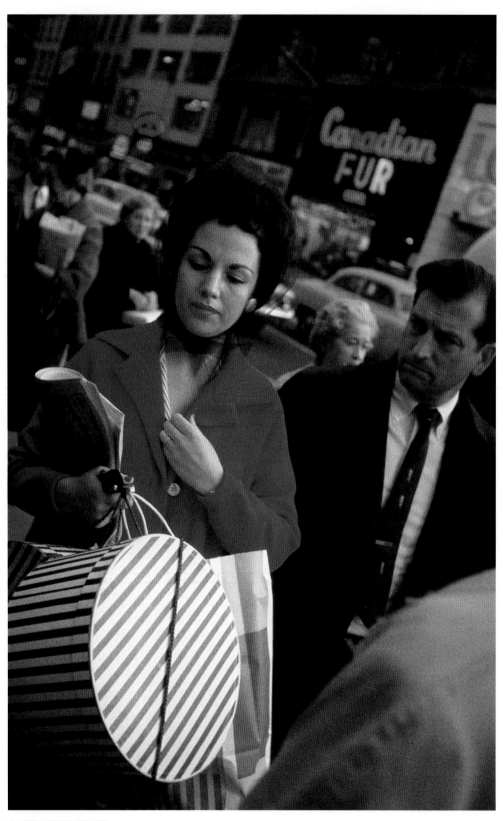

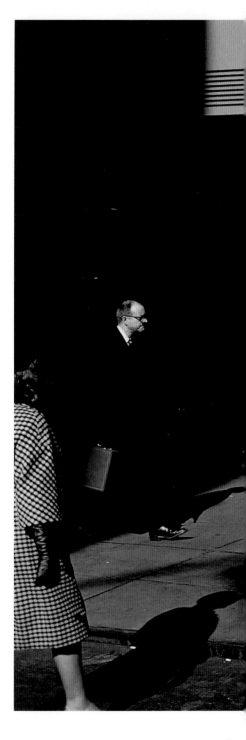

GARRY WINOGRAND
Untitled, c. 1963

396

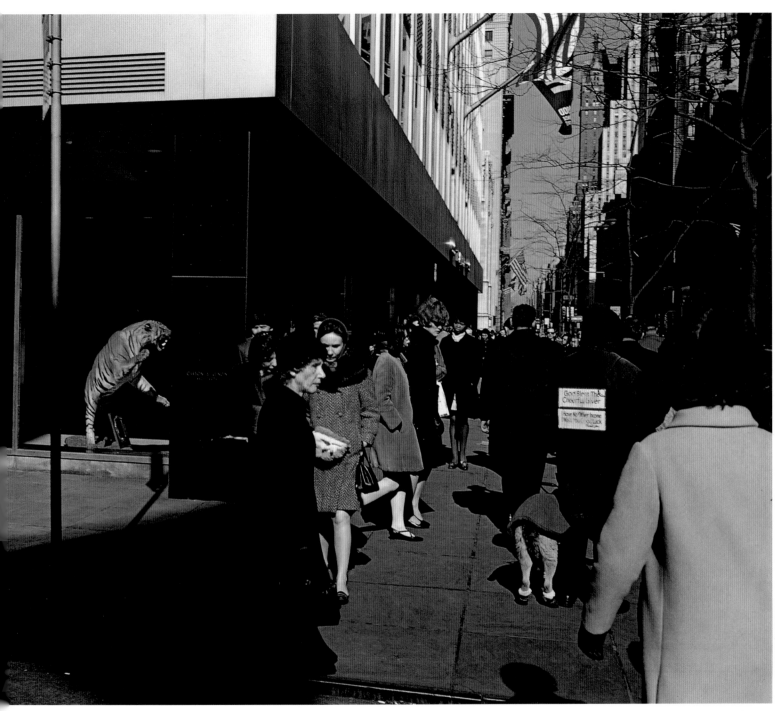

JOEL MEYEROWITZ
Fifth Avenue and
Fifty-second Street,
New York, 1974

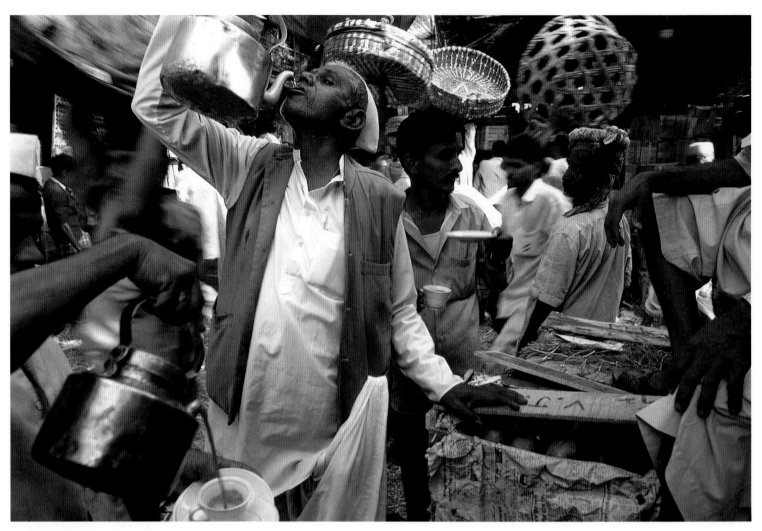

RAGHUBIR SINGH

Untitled, c. 1970s

398

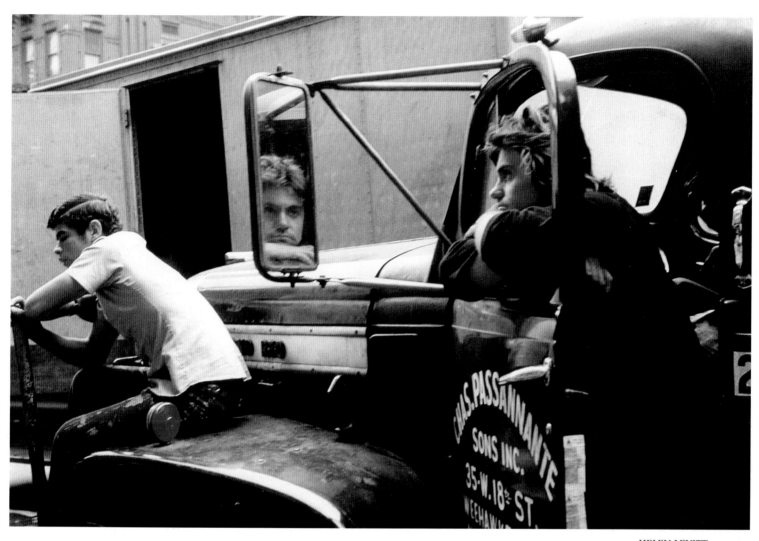

HELEN LEVITT
New York, 1972

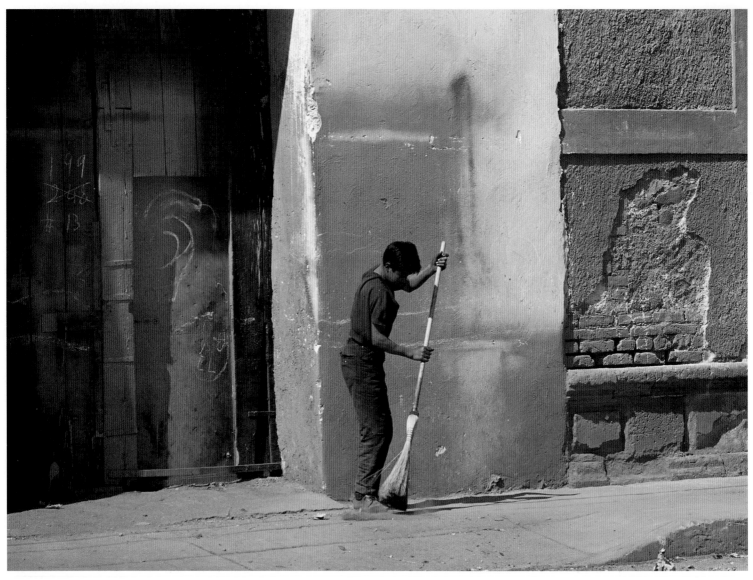

MANUEL ALVAREZ
BRAVO
El Color, 1966

I had this interaction with Tony as a peer, whereas Garry was a really heightened intelligence already. It was just an explosion of commitment to the medium, the way I was working with each of them. I couldn't get enough. The first pictures I showed Garry were color photographs because I didn't have any black-and-white yet. It took me months and months to make those first black-and-white pictures.

Of course, Tony turned then to black-and-white too. He went back to England and did that black-and-white book *A Day Off,* which came out in 1974, two years after he died [fig. 20.11]. I think he needed to go back to Europe to find himself. He really came of age as a photographer there. When he was here, he was struggling to give up the things that he did well. He kept slipping back into that kind of graphic photography that he needed to break loose from. He would get angry with himself when that happened, and he was easily depressed. He was the kind of guy who talked to himself, reprimanded himself: "Don't do this! Don't make that sort of picture!" He allowed himself to get angry, for change. But in the end, I think he had to go back to Europe to achieve it.

You yourself turned primarily to black-and-white for about ten years; yet you never gave up color altogether, and eventually it became the only medium you work in.

I was the only proponent of color photography in that group in New York. I kept on shooting it. In fact, I walked around with two Leicas, one always loaded with color.

Yes, I can remember seeing some work of yours — from Europe, was it? — where you had made virtually the same picture in both black-and-white and color.

That's right. I didn't know it at the time, black-and-white being such a dominant force, but there were a few others out there, some even earlier, who were shooting in color.

Helen Levitt, for instance, and Manuel Bravo in Mexico. there was a young photographer like myself named Raghubir Singh who was photographing all of India. Garry also shot a lot of color, but on assignment and on trips and things like that. He did some wonderful things with it, but he didn't see it as a major force, whereas I believed in it all along and started to lean more and more in that direction. I really started putting the pressure on color, started dropping the black-and-white, in 1971, and by 1972 I was using color exclusively.

Color forced me to behave differently. Its powers of description were greater, but it was also slower. If my subject and I were both in motion, the picture wasn't always sharp, so I tended to photograph from farther away than before.

What did the shift to color have to do with the shift from 35mm to the view camera?

There is a hidden logic in one's evolution, invisible as you're living it but clear and seemingly inevitable years down the road. I always felt color was the most descriptive force in photography's language. But it was slower than black-and-white and so it changed my behavior on the street from instantaneous reaction in the thick of the crowd to a more watchful response at a greater distance. I really wanted to use color to photograph deep space and to hold all the information in the field in focus. Demand leads to frustration leads to experimentation, until one day, in order to get to the descriptive state I felt color was capable of, I found myself using the 8 by 10 and Fifth Avenue turning into Cape Cod.

There haven't been many photographers who could run all up and down the scale, from 35mm to 8 by 10, like that. Was Walker Evans an inspiration to you in this regard?

His precedent was an important one, naturally. You couldn't ignore the significance of what he had done even if you wanted to. It didn't take me long to understand my interest in him, though at first his view-camera pictures seemed to me static and cool. Then the coolness of them and how taut they were began to engage me more. I began to see how playful they were too. I hadn't realized that before. It's also how I came to understand his work more deeply. His is a view-camera mind in a 35mm body.

I can remember a lot of early view-camera pictures of yours that are still very like street photography in spirit. I'm thinking not only of some of the stuff from Cape Cod, but especially of the Empire State Building project, where earlier 35mm pictures on the same theme got mixed in with 8 by 10s, and it would be very hard, judging just by the imagery, to tell them apart.

Maybe you had to wait until your career was ready to mellow in a certain way before the view camera could make complete sense to you. As you know, in the bayscapes and the other pictures where the influence of the street isn't so apparent, I've always thought it was still there, the hidden source, the secret ingredient, that gives your view-camera photographs their particular vitality. You assimilated and absorbed what you learned from over a decade on the street with a Leica until it all became part of the infrastructure of your mind, a basic pathway down which your imagination is guided to a picture, no matter what the subject is or the instrument with which it's taken.

Well, I don't think there's any doubt about that.

What do you think the prospects for street photography are now? Winogrand and Arbus, and Tony Ray Jones, are all dead, unfortunately; and you and Friedlander have gone off into another kind of photography to a large

extent. **All of you followed up on the work of Cartier-Bresson, Evans, and Frank; but no new names seem to be emerging now as prominent as yours, do they?**

Not that I'm aware of, but then the times haven't been very favorable to this idea of photography lately. However, Koudelka still shoots, and Sebastião Salgado. And I had a group of students who still are at it — Mitch Epstein, Babis, Len Jenshel, and Joanne Mulberg. You know, this book is an attempt to show how deeply engrained in photography itself the practice of street photography is. Its potential to stimulate young photographers, and the growth of the medium in general, will come back. It is coming back already after a decade of critical ideas that were unfavorable to it, that seemed to undermine the whole documentary tradition on which street photography is built.

It's been very hard for young American or Western European photographers who do this sort of work to get shows, do books, attract articles, sell prints. . . . I think the ones who do it, the best of them, feel they are just keeping the discipline alive, waiting for attention to return to it. I have in mind somebody like Tom Arndt, who's been working in and out of Chicago for a number of years now. He's out there every day, day in and day out, doing the work for its own sake, keeping the faith.

The street tradition seems to have the greatest currency and activity of late in developing or emerging nations. I'm thinking especially of the photography of Pablo Ortiz Monasterio, Graciela Iturbide, and Pedro Meyer in Mexico, Raghubir Singh in India, Jindřich Streit, Bohdan Holomíček, or Viktor Kolář in [the former] Czechoslovakia, Boris Savelev and others in Russia. In societies where there is instability or a conflict between old ways and new that is being acted out in the streets, street photography has a great deal more urgency than it seems to here.

The street photographers in this country who have been able to get recent recognition are photojournalists also doing books on the third world, such as Alex Webb in *Under a Grudging Sun*, about Haiti. Outside of something like that, the few books of street photography to get done in the last decade or so have been by photographers of your own generation, people whose reputations were established earlier. I mean books like your own *Wild Flowers*, which came out after you'd become known as a view-camera photographer, but which contained a lot of earlier, 35mm work. Or Bruce Davidson's *Subways*, which took outside into a public, streetlike space, and into the medium of color, a kind of vision of New York he'd established for himself before with the black-and-white book *East 100th Street*.

It's true that there doesn't seem to be as much new work coming out as there once was. But I think that as long as there's photography, there'll always be people trying to make street pictures — tough pictures of the kind that Garry and Tod and I were inspired to make twenty-five years ago. "Tough" was a term we used to use a lot. Stark, spare, hard, demanding, tough: these were values that we applied to the act of making photographs.

"Tough" meant the image was uncompromising. It was something made out of your guts, out of your instinct, and it was unwieldy in some way, not capable of being categorized by ordinary standards. So it was tough. It was tough to like, tough to see, tough to make, tough to draw meaning from. It wasn't what most photographs looked like. You couldn't always address it with the familiar terms of other photographs. It was a type of picture that made you uncomfortable sometimes. You didn't quite understand it. It made you grind your teeth.

At the same time, though, you knew it was beautiful, because "tough" also meant that — it meant beautiful too. If you said of a photograph, "Gee, that's tough" or "That's beauti-

ful," it meant that in the moment of making that photograph, *you* were beautiful. It was as if you were graced at that moment. You were in touch with the sudden appearance of beauty and were touched by its purity. That's what made the picture tough. The two words — "tough" and "beautiful" — became synonyms somehow. They were what street photography was all about.

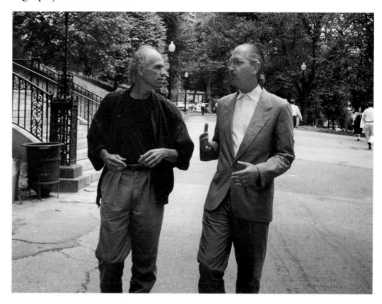

Acknowledgments

Since the authors began to share and explore their mutual enthusiasm for street photography in the late 1970s, so many people have assisted, encouraged, and enlightened us that it would require a whole new text in order to thank them all in detail or explain properly their contributions. But we do wish to acknowledge those whose service and loyalty to our project were most essential.

First and foremost, we would like to thank the photographers themselves whom we were able to talk with and who went out of their way to share their experiences with us. Many were in Paris, where Brassaï and his wife, Gilberte; Henri Cartier-Bresson; Robert Doisneau; William Klein; and Josef Koudelka all gave us their time and hospitality, as did the publisher Robert Delpire and editor Raoul Martinez. There were also important photographers in New York who responded to our inquiries with both patience and passion: Lee Friedlander, André Kertész, Tod Papageorge, and Garry Winogrand. In addition, Barbara Crane and Ken Josephson in Chicago, Bill Brandt in London, and John Gutmann in San Francisco all made themselves available. And even when we could no longer meet with the photographers themselves, their heirs or the executors of their estates — from Dan Weiner's widow, Sandra, to John Hill of the Walker Evans estate, Robert Gurbo from André Kertész's, and Victor Schrager from the Aaron Siskind Foundation — often cooperated with us in valuable ways.

Just as generous with their time were the curators from collections in both the United States and Europe. Museums in New York, where curators shared with us not only their collections but their knowledge of the field, played an especially crucial role in our early research. John Szarkowski gave us free access to both his thoughts about our project and his study room at the Museum of Modern Art, and people who were on his staff, including Peter Galassi, Maria Morris Hambourg, Susan Kismaric, Grace Mayer, and Barbara Michaels, were all unstinting with their time. Equally giving were Mitchell Grubler at the Staten Island Historical Society, Weston Naef at the Metropolitan Museum, and Julia Van Haaften at the New York Public Library.

Curators and archivists in other parts of North America to whom we were also beholden include Cliff Ackley at the Boston Museum of Fine Arts, James Borcoman from the National Gallery of Canada, Robert Doherty at George Eastman House, Roy Flukinger at the University of Texas, Ted Hartwell at the Minneapolis Institute of Arts, Jerald Maddox at the Library of Congress, Davis Pratt at Harvard, Richard Rudisill at the Museum of New Mexico, Amy Rule and Diane Nihlson at the Center for Creative Photography, Marnie Sandweis at the Amon Carter Museum, Anne Tucker of the Houston Museum of Fine Arts, and Paul Vanderbilt at the Wisconsin State Historical Society. Special thanks are due to David Travis of the Art Institute of Chicago for the privileged access he gave the authors early on to two collections of particular interest at his department — those from Alfred Stieglitz and Julien Levy — as well as for the encouragement he gave Colin Westerbeck later to see this project through to conclusion. James N. Wood, the Director of the Art Institute of Chicago, and Jean Tucker of the University of Missouri's Center for Metropolitan Studies in St. Louis have also supported our research from the very beginning, when Mr. Wood was Director of the St. Louis Art Museum.

In Europe, we were extended courtesies and offered insights no less valuable. In England, Brian Coe of the Kodak Museum, Sue Davies of The Photographers Gallery, Raymond Desmond at the India Office Library, and Mark Haworth-Booth from the Victoria and Albert Museum each offered us whatever assistance we needed. In Paris, comparable help came from Pierre de Fenoyl at the Fondation Nationale de la Photographie, Marie de Thezy at the Bibliothèque Historique de la Ville de Paris, Françoise Heilbrun at the Musée d'Orsay, Jean-Claude Lemagny and Bernard Marbot of the Bibliothèque Nationale, and Françoise Reynaud at the Musée Carnavalet.

A number of independent scholars, critics, or editors guided our inquiry and stimulated our thinking too, most notably Gail Buckland, John Coplans, Max Kozloff, Hank O'Neal, Sally Stein, and Clark Worswick in New York, Robert Hershkowitz in London and David Mellor at the University of Sussex, and Molly Nesbit in Paris. Back home, Larry Schaaf from the University of Texas and Alan Trachtenberg at Yale were instrumental in our research as well.

Then there were the dealers and representatives of photo agencies who involved themselves in our work far more than either duty or self-interest would have dictated. One, Jeffrey Fraenkel, was in San Francisco, while the others were all in New York: Anne Cremieux and Melissa Dehncke at Magnum, Bonnie Benrubi, Helen Gee, Howard Greenberg and his assistant Carie Springer, Hans Kraus, Janet Lehr, Larry Miller, Lee Witkin, and Daniel Wolf.

Finally, there were collectors who opened both their personal collections and their notebooks to us, thereby making us privy to knowledge we could not have acquired in any other way at the time. Key were Arnold Crane in Chicago, Martin Sandler in Connecticut, and Sam Wagstaff in New York.

These were the most important photographers, curators, et cetera, who made our research possible; yet there was a whole other kind of support that must be acknowledged as well — that which came from people who helped us both find the money to do the research and get the results published. In the early stages, Elizabeth Topham Kennan gave critical support and guidance to our application for a grant from the National Endowment for the Humanities, Boston scholar Bruce MacDonald made us welcome in his home when we needed a place to stay, and literary agent Hilda Lindley advised us on finding a publisher. The one that saw great promise in our project was Little, Brown, whose loyalty to it over the years has been absolutely essential. This was the case primarily because Janet Swan Bush, Executive Editor of Bulfinch Press, has kept her faith that Bystander would make an important contribution to the field. Two production managers at Little, Brown — Amanda Freymann and Christina Eckerson — have meticulously overseen the preparation and printing of the book. At one point Constance Sullivan played a crucial role as a reader of the manuscript, as did Betty Childs, and more recently, the editing by Deborah Jacobs and book design by Caroline Rowntree made it possible for our ideas to take finished, polished, coherent form as a book. Nor could this book ever have come together without the efforts of our tireless photo researcher, Marvel Maring.

The research for this book was made possible in part by a generous grant from the National Endowment for the Humanities.

Illustration Credits

The authors gratefully acknowledge the following photographers, institutions, agencies, and collections for permission to reproduce the photographs in this book. (Credits are keyed either by page number or figure number.)

Notes

Chapter 1: Before Photography
1. Hugo, *Les Misérables*, vol. 2, 205–206.
2. Flaubert, *Sentimental Education*, 385.
3. Ibid., 383–384.
4. Roger Williams, *The World of Napoleon III*, 99.
5. Goncourt, *Pages from the Goncourt Journal*, 53.
6. Evenson, *Paris*, 21.
7. Fournel, *Ce qu'on voit dans les rues de Paris*, 269–270.
8. Arendt, "Walter Benjamin: 1892–1940," in Benjamin, *Illuminations*, 22.
9. Fournel, *Ce qu'on voit*, 263.
10. Rousseau, *Politics and the Arts*, 125–126.
11. Fournel, *Ce qu'on voit*, 263.
12. Baudelaire, "The Painter of Modern Life," 4, 9.
13. Ibid., 5.
14. Fournel, *Ce qu'on voit*, 261.
15. Milosz, *The Captive Mind*, 61–62.
16. Ibid., 62.
17. Evenson, *Paris*, 138.
18. Rosalind Williams, *Dream Worlds*, 74.
19. Benjamin, "Paris, Capital of the Nineteenth Century," in *Reflections*, 150.
20. Benjamin, "On Some Motifs in Baudelaire," in *Illuminations*, 174–175.
21. Ibid., 193.
22. Baudelaire, *Les Fleurs du Mal*, 98.
25. Hugo, *Les Misérables*, vol. 1, 496–497.

Chapter 2: In the Beginning
1. Quoted in Buckland, *Fox Talbot*, 76.
2. Talbot, *The Pencil of Nature*, plate 6.
3. Quoted in Heilbrun, *Nègre*, 22.
4. Baudelaire, "The Painter of Modern Life," in *The Painter of Modern Life and Other Essays*, 4.
5. Baudelaire, "The Salon of 1846," in *Art in Paris*, 45.
6. Baudelaire, "The Salon of 1859," in *Art in Paris*, 151–152.
7. Nochlin, *Realism*, 36.
8. Ibid., 28, 150.
9. Clark, "The Relations of Photography and Painting," 10.
10. Quoted in Scharf, *Art and Photography*, 209, 184.

Chapter 3: The View from Abroad
1. Quoted in Buckland, *Fox Talbot*, 31.
2. Thomas, *Time in a Frame*, 144.
3. Sobieszek, Robert, "Preface," in White, *John Thomson*, 7. This essay first appeared under the title "John Thomson's Peculiarities of Appearance: Street Life and Topographies" as the text accompanying an exhibition at the Daniel Wolf Gallery, New York, in 1978.
4. Quoted in Jay, *Victorian Cameraman*, 16.
5. Thomson, *Illustrations of China and Its People*, 3: plate 49.
6. Thomson and Smith, *Street Life in London*, 37.
7. Quoted in Desmond, "Photography in India," 12.
8. Ibid.
9. Thomson, *Geographical Journal*, 211.

Chapter 4: Busmen's Holidays
1. Quoted in Hobsbawm, *The Age of Capital*, xx.
2. Zevi, *Alinari*, 22.
3. Quoted in Hiley, *Frank Sutcliffe*, 67.
4. Ibid., 209–210.
5. Sutcliffe, "Landscape with Figures," 42.

Chapter 5: Art for Art's Sake
1. Naef, *The Collection of Alfred Stieglitz*, 10.
2. Demachy, "On the Straight Print," 21, in Green, *Camera Work*, 118.
3. Strand, *Paul Strand*, 142.
4. Ibid.
5. Quoted in Gernsheim, *The History of Photography*, 463.
6. Strand, *Paul Strand*, 142.
7. Quoted in Norman, *Alfred Stieglitz*, 36.
8. Ibid.
9. "Unphotographic Paint," 21.
10. Green, *Camera Work*, 21.
11. Quoted in Norman, *Alfred Stieglitz*, 37.
12. Ibid., 36.
13. Ibid., 80.
14. Strand, *Paul Strand*, 39.
15. Ibid., 19.
16. Ibid.
17. Ibid., 145.
18. Rosenblum, *Paul Strand*, unpaged.
19. Strand, *Paul Strand*, 25.
20. Ibid., 19.
21. Tomkins, "Profiles," 87.
22. Greenough, *Paul Strand*, 37.
23. Martin, *Victorian Snapshots*, 18.
24. Ibid., 17.
25. Irwin, *Pictures of Old Chinatown*, unpaged.
26. Genthe, *Old Chinatown*, 205.
27. Quoted in Hiley, *Frank Sutcliffe*, 138–139.
28. Quoted in Flukinger et al., *Paul Martin*, 33.
29. Sandra Martin, "Samuel Coulthurst," 227.
30. Quoted in Flukinger et al., *Paul Martin*, 35.
31. Ibid.
32. Yellott, "Street Photography," 50.
33. Quoted in Flukinger et al., *Paul Martin*, 35.
34. Ibid., 110.
35. Irwin, *Pictures of Old Chinatown*, unpaged.
36. Keiley, "J. Craig Annan," 18.
37. Quoted in Norman, *Alfred Stieglitz*, 239.
38. Bucquet, "L'appareil à main," 62.
39. Quoted in Hiley, *Frank Sutcliffe*, 132.
40. Hartmann, "On the Possibility of New Laws of Composition," 24–26.

Chapter 6: Documents for Artists
1. Levy, *Memoir of an Art Gallery*, 91.
2. Abbott, symposium, 15 November 1979.
3. Haussmann, in *Histoire générale de Paris*, I, 9.
4. Ibid., 10.
5. Yeats, "Coole Park and Ballylee," in *The Collected Poems*, 240.
6. Quoted in Nesbit, *Atget's Seven Albums*, 5.
7. Benjamin, "The Work of Art in the Age of Mechanical Reproduction," in *Illuminations*, 226.
8. Rewald, *The History of Impressionism*, 175.
9. Nesbit, *Atget's Seven Albums*, 110.

Chapter 7: Children of the Century
1. Peabody, *To Be Young Was Very Heaven*.
2. Lartigue, *Diary of a Century*.
3. Ibid.
4. Ibid. [20].
5. Ibid. [30].
6. Ibid.
7. Lartigue, album, June–July 1909.
8. Lartigue, *Diary of a Century* [52–53]
9. Ibid. [54].
10. Freud, *Civilization and Its Discontents*, 38.

Chapter 8: The Decisive Photographer
1. Thomson, *Democracy in France*, 72; Hughes, *Consciousness and Society*, 337.
2. Levy, *Memoir of an Art Gallery*, 131.
3. Cartier-Bresson, "Henri Cartier-Bresson," 117.
4. Levy, *Memoir of an Art Gallery*, 49.
5. Cartier-Bresson, "Nul ne peut entrer ici s'il n'est pas géomètre," 13.
6. Szarkowski, conversation with Colin Westerbeck and Joel Meyerowitz, May 1979.
7. Kirstein, "Henri Cartier-Bresson," in Cartier-Bresson, *Photographs by Cartier-Bresson*, unpaged.
8. Cartier-Bresson, "Nul ne peut entrer," 13.
9. Newhall, "Cartier-Bresson's Photographic Technique," in *The Photographs of Henri Cartier-Bresson*, 12.
10. Quoted in Norman, "A Visitor Falls in Love," 12.
11. Cartier-Bresson, "Nul ne peut entrer," 13.
12. Kirstein, "Henri Cartier-Bresson," in Cartier-Bresson, *Photographs by Cartier-Bresson*, unpaged.
13. Haas, "Henri Cartier-Bresson," 136.
14. Goldsmith, "Henry Cartier-Bresson Revisited," 139.
15. Capote, Introduction, in Beaton, *The Best of Beaton*, 13.
16. Brinnin, *Sextet*, 110.
17. Capote, Introduction, in Beaton, *The Best of Beaton*, 13.
18. Cartier-Bresson, "Henri Cartier-Bresson, on the Art of Photography," 74.
19. Cartier-Bresson, conversation with Colin Westerbeck, November 1980.
20. Quoted in Cartier-Bresson, *A propos de l'U.R.S.S.*, unpaged.
21. Cartier-Bresson, "Nul ne peut entrer," 13.

22. Breton, *Manifestoes of Surrealism*, 22–23.
23. Ibid., 36–37.
24. Rubin, *Dada, Surrealism, and Their Heritage*, 19.
25. Breton, *Manifestoes*, 20.
26. Cartier-Bresson, "Henri Cartier-Bresson," 198.
27. Breton, *Manifestoes*, 37.
28. Cartier-Bresson, "Nul ne peut entrer," 13.
29. Lhôte, *Treatise on Landscape Painting*, xvi.
30. Lhôte, *Theory of Figure Painting*, 10.
31. Lhôte, *Treatise on Landscape Painting*, 38.
32. Cartier-Bresson, "Henri Cartier-Bresson, on the Art of Photography," 74.
33. Breton, *Manifestoes*, 159–160.
34. Cartier-Bresson, "Henri Cartier-Bresson," 108.
35. Kazin, *New York Jew*, 156.
36. Brinnin, *Sextet*, 105.
37. Ibid., 154.
38. Ibid., 107.
39. Ibid., 108.
40. Ibid., 111.
41. Cartier-Bresson, conversation with Colin Westerbeck, November 1980.
42. Cartier-Bresson, "Henri Cartier-Bresson," 117.
43. Cartier-Bresson, "Nul ne peut entrer," 13.
44. Ibid.
45. Ibid.
46. Cartier-Bresson, "Henri Cartier-Bresson, on the Art of Photography," 74.
47. Herrigel, *Zen in the Art of Archery*, 46.
48. Martinez, conversation with Colin Westerbeck, November 1980.
49. Kirstein, "Henri Cartier-Bresson," in Cartier-Bresson, *Photographs by Cartier-Bresson*, unpaged.
50. Haas, "Henri Cartier-Bresson," 97.
51. Goldsmith, "Henri Cartier-Bresson Revisited," 139.
52. Herrigel, *Zen in the Art of Archery*, 44, 64, passim.
53. Brinnin, *Sextet*, 102.
54. Quoted in Weiss, "Encore at the Louvre," 28.
55. Newhall, "Thoughts on Henri Cartier-Bresson and His Extraordinary Talent," 46.
56. Cartier-Bresson, "Henri Cartier-Bresson," 108.
57. Cartier-Bresson, conversation with Colin Westerbeck, November 1980.
58. Shirer, *The Collapse of the Third Republic*, 109–110.
59. Cartier-Bresson, "Henri Cartier-Bresson, on the Art of Photography," 78.
60. Cartier-Bresson, *The Decisive Moment*, unpaged.

Chapter 9: Hungarian Rhapsody
1. Lorant, symposium at Goethe House, New York, March 1982.
2. Moholy-Nagy, "From Pigment to Light," in Lyons, ed., *Photographers on Photography*, 80.
3. Aigner, "A Life with the Camera," in John P. Aigner, ed., *Lucien Aigner*, 15.
4. Ibid., 17.
5. Ibid., 11.
6. Quoted in Ford, Introduction, in *André Kertész*, 7.
7. Kertész, conversations with Colin Westerbeck, September–October 1980.

8. Quoted in Phillips et al., *André Kertész*, 265.
9. Quoted in *André Kertész*, 22.
10. Quoted in Phillips et al., *André Kertész*, 104.
11. Kertész, *Kertész on Kertész*, 90.
12. Ibid., 38.
13. Brassaï, *The Secret Paris of the Thirties*, unpaged.
14. Quoted in ibid.
15. Miller, Preface, in Brassaï, *Picasso and Company*, ix.
16. Brassaï, conversation with Colin Westerbeck, September 1976.

Chapter 10: Foreign Correspondents
1. Connolly, Introduction, in Brandt, *Shadow of Light*, 11.
2. Quoted in Mark Haworth-Booth, Introduction, in Brandt, *London in the Thirties*, unpaged.
3. Szarkowski, "Bill Brandt," 89.
4. Quoted in Mellor, "Nigel Anderson," 12.
5. Quoted in Mark Haworth-Booth, Introduction, in Brandt, *London*, unpaged.
6. Quoted in "Mass Observation," 1.
7. Alvarez Bravo, in Hill and Cooper, *Dialogue with Photography*, 233.
8. Quoted in Livingston, *M. Alvarez Bravo*, xxi.
9. Castro, "Alvarez Bravo and Mexico," in Livingston, *M. Alvarez Bravo*, xxi.
10. Quoted in Livingston, *M. Alvarez Bravo*, ix.
11. Bravo, letter to Nancy Newhall, 5 July 1943.
12. Quoted in Livingston, *M. Alvarez Bravo*, xii.
13. Kuwabara, *Kineo Kuwabara*, unpaged.

Chapter 11: The Fourth Estate
1. Doisneau, in Hill and Cooper, *Dialogue with Photography*, 95–96.
2. Quoted in Rosenblum, "Robert Doisneau," 136.
3. Doisneau, *Three Seconds from Eternity* [19].
4. Doisneau, in Hill and Cooper, *Dialogue with Photography*, 92–93.
5. Rosenblum, "Robert Doisneau," 136.
6. Doisneau, in Hill and Cooper, *Dialogue with Photography*, 82.
7. Ibid., 107.
8. Ibid., 110.
9. Ibid., 102.
10. Ibid., 95.
11. Ibid., 81.
12. Ibid.
13. Rosenblum, "Robert Doisneau," 137.
14. Sontag, *On Photography*, 134.
15. Doisneau, conversation with Colin Westerbeck and Joel Meyerowitz, November 1980.
16. Sheed, Introduction, in Erwitt, *Recent Developments*, 6.
17. Doisneau, in Hill and Cooper, *Dialogue with Photography*, 98.
18. Quoted in Doisneau, *Three Seconds from Eternity* [33].
19. Quoted in Porter, "Joseph Koudelka," 5.
20. Willy Guy in Koudelka, *Gypsies*, unpaged.
21. Koudelka, conversation with Colin Westerbeck and Joel Meyerowitz, November 1980.

Chapter 12: Social Uplift
1. Quoted in Alland, *Jacob A. Riis, Photographer and Citizen*, 271.
2. Ibid., 158.
3. Quoted in Siegel, "Fifty Years of Documentary," in Lyons, *Photographers on Photography*, 90.
4. Trachtenberg, "Ever — the Human Document," in Hine, *America and Lewis Hine*, 123–124.
5. Quoted in ibid., 118.
6. Stryker, Archives of American Art, 13.
7. Ibid., 32.
8. Quoted in Stryker and Wood, *In This Proud Land*, 14.
9. Rosenblum, Foreword, in Hine, *America and Lewis Hine*, 9.

Chapter 13: Collective Vision
1. Quoted in Meltzer, *Dorothea Lange*, 69–70.
2. Shahn, Archives of American Art, 20.
3. Shahn, "Ben Shahn: An Interview," in Morse, *Ben Shahn*, 133.
4. Soby, *Ben Shahn*, 5.
5. Shahn, Oral History Research Project, 64.
6. Quoted in Rodman, *Portrait of the Artist as an American*, 97.
7. Soby, *Ben Shahn*, 12.
8. Quirt, "On Mural Painting," in O'Connor, *Art for the Millions*, 79–81.
9. Levitt, conversation with Colin Westerbeck, March 1980.
10. Levitt, fellowship application, unpaged.
11. Levitt, conversation with Colin Westerbeck, March 1980.
12. Levitt, fellowship application, unpaged.
13. Levitt and Agee, *A Way of Seeing*, 8.
14. Ibid., 5.

Chapter 14: American Classic
1. Cowley, *Exile's Return*, 31.
2. Quoted in Soby, *Ben Shahn*, 6.
3. Quoted in Mitchell, *Recollections*, 13.
4. Abbott, letter to Hardinge Scholle, 16 November 1931.
5. Shahn, Archives of American Art, 7.
6. Cahill, "American Resources in the Arts," in O'Connor, ed., *Art for the Millions*, 42.
7. Kouwenhoven, *Made in America*, 184.
8. Abbott, symposium, 15 November 1979.
9. Abbott, "Photographer as Artist," 6.
10. Abbott, "The View Camera," 174.
11. Quoted in O'Neal, *Berenice Abbott, American Photographer*, 14.
12. Abbott, "The View Camera," 161–162.
13. Abbott, "Photographer as Artist," 7.
14. Quoted in *New York Sun*, 5 October 1934, 32.
15. Jung, Archives of American Arts, 3–4.
16. Kirstein, "Walker Evans Photographs of Victorian Architecture," 4.
17. Ibid.
18. Ibid.
19. Evans, "The Reappearance of Photography," 126.
20. Evans, "Walker Evans on Himself," 25.
21. Ibid.

22. Evans, "Interview with Walker Evans," 85.
23. Evans, Archives of American Art, 15.
24. Evans, "Interview with Walker Evans," 85.
25. Evans, Archives of American Art, 11–12, 22.
26. Evans, "Walker Evans on Himself," 23.
27. Evans, "Photography," 190.
28. Evans, "Interview with Walker Evans," 88.
29. Evans, Archives of American Art, 10.
30. Quoted in Whitman, "Walker Evans Dies," 40.
31. Evans, "Interview with Walker Evans," 83.
32. Ibid., 8.
33. Crane, The Bridge, 15.
34. Evans, "Mr. Walker Evans Records a City's Scene," 453–456. See also Trachtenberg, Brooklyn Bridge, 188, where this sequence is discussed, although without recognition of the allusion to Eliot. The line itself was one heard in English pubs when the publican had to warn customers of the approach of closing time.
35. Evans, "Photography," 169.
36. Ibid., 190.
37. Evans, Images of the South, 31.
38. Agee and Evans, Let Us Now Praise Famous Men, 212.
39. Ibid., 11.
40. Ibid., 102.
41. Ibid., 416.
42. Evans, Archives of American Art, 34.
43. Evans, "Interview with Walker Evans," 83.
44. Evans, Archives of American Art, 46.
45. Evans, "Interview with Walker Evans," 84.
46. Quoted in Szarkowski, Walker Evans, 11.
47. Evans, project for an art book, unpaged.
48. Evans, "Interview with Walker Evans," 88.
49. Vachon, Archives of American Art, 7–8.
50. Stryker and Wood, In This Proud Land, 7.
51. Vachon, Archives of American Art, 9, 14–15.
52. Stryker, Archives of American Art, 33.
53. Ibid., 32–33.
54. Lee, Archives of American Art, 14–15.
55. Trilling, "Greatness with One Fault in It," 99.
56. Williams, "Sermon with a Camera," 283.
57. Evans, Archives of American Art, 34.
58. Evans, Walker Evans at Work, 98.
59. Kirstein, "Walker Evans Photographs of Victorian Architecture," 4.
60. Quoted in Evans, Walker Evans at Work, 82.
61. Quoted in Evans, "Rapid Transit," 25.
62. Evans, "Walker Evans: The Unposed Portrait," 120.
63. Greenough, Walker Evans, 40.
64. Stryker and Wood, In This Proud Land, 19.
65. Quoted in Meltzer, Dorothea Lange, 133.
66. Stryker, Archives of American Art, 13.
67. Ibid., 32.
68. Szarkowski, Walker Evans, 18–19.
69. Evans, "Photographs of Metropolitan Faces," unpaged.
70. Evans, "Photography," 211.
71. Kirstein, "Photographs of America," in Evans, American Photographs, 191.
72. Evans, Images of the South, 37.
73. Evans, Archives of American Art, 13.

Chapter 15: Displaced Persons
1. Quoted in Gutmann, "John Gutmann," interview by Nancy Stevens, 54.
2. Ibid., 48.
3. Ibid., 50.
4. Quoted in Kracauer, Theory of Film, 183.
5. Quoted in Heilbut, Exiled in Paradise, 3.
6. Ibid., 4.
7. Ibid., x.
8. Quoted in Bosworth, Diane Arbus, 126.

Chapter 16: Naturalized Citizens
1. Weegee, Weegee by Weegee, 117.
2. Ibid., 95.
3. Weegee, Naked City, 14.
4. Ibid., 37.
5. Weegee, Weegee by Weegee, 82.
6. Ibid., 45–46.
7. DeCarava, Photographs, 14.
8. Ibid., 19.
9. DeCarava and Hughes, The Sweet Flypaper of Life, 70.
10. Ibid., 98.
11. DeCarava, Photographs, 10.
12. Ibid., 12.

Chapter 17: An American in Paris
1. Klein, William Klein, Photographs, Etc., 16.
2. Quoted in Heilbut, Exiled in Paradise, 395.
3. Klein, William Klein, Photographs, Etc., 13.
4. Quoted in ibid., 15.
5. Ibid., 15.
6. Ibid., 13.
7. Ibid.,16.
8. Ibid., 7.
9. Ibid., 13.
10. Klein, conversation with Colin Westerbeck, August 1979.
11. Klein, William Klein, Photographs, Etc., 18.
12. Klein, William Klein, photographe, etc., 7.
13. Ibid.
14. Klein, William Klein: Photographs, Etc., 21.
15. Klein, William Klein, photographe, etc., 14.
16. Klein, William Klein, Photographs, Etc., 15–16.
17. Ibid.
18. Ibid., 18.
19. Klein, William Klein photographe, etc., 10.
20. Ibid., 19.
21. Ibid., 10.
22. Ibid.
23. Ibid.
24. Klein, William Klein, Photographs, Etc., 16.
25. Ibid., 22.

Chapter 18: In the American Grain
1. Tucker, Robert Frank, New York to Nova Scotia, 82.

2. Frank, conversation with Colin Westerbeck and Joel Meyerowitz, October 1980.
3. Ibid.
4. Ibid.
5. Frank, The Photo Reporter, 93.
6. Frank, conversation with Colin Westerbeck and Joel Meyerowitz, October 1980.
7. Quoted in Bennett, "Black and White Are the Colors of Robert Frank," 22.
8. Frank, The Photo Reporter, 93.
9. Frank, "Letter from New York (July 1969)," 234.
10. Quoted in Tucker, Robert Frank, New York to Nova Scotia, 36.
11. Ibid.
12. Quoted in Frank, Black, White and Things, unpaged.
13. Ibid.
14. Quoted in Westerbeck, "American Graphic," 8.
15. Frank, conversation with Colin Westerbeck and Joel Meyerowitz, October 1980.
16. Frank, in Janis and MacNeil, eds., Photography Within the Humanities, 53.
17. Frank, "Letter from New York (June 1969)," 202.
18. Rosenberg, "The American Action Painters," 28.
19. Ibid.
20. Ibid., 25.
21. Quoted in Sandler, The Triumph of American Painting, 98.
22. Ibid., 131.
23. Ibid., 257.
24. Ibid., 92.
25. Tucker, Robert Frank: New York to Nova Scotia, 25.
26. Frank, The Lines of My Hand, 69.
27. Tucker, Robert Frank: New York to Nova Scotia, 83.
28. Mailer, "The White Negro," 343–344.
29. Ibid., 353, 355.
30. Goldman, The Crucial Decade, 14.
31. Ibid., 42.
32. Ginsberg, Howl and Other Poems, 164.
33. Kerouac, The Town and the City, 82–83.
34. Kerouac and Frank, "On the Road to Florida," 47.
35. Janis and MacNeil, eds., Photography Within the Humanities, 53.
36. Frank, conversation with Colin Westerbeck and Joel Meyerowitz, October 1980.
37. Ibid.
38. Quoted in Brookman, Robert Frank: Photographer/Filmmaker, unpaged.
39. Frank, "A Statement," 115.
40. Janis and MacNeil, eds., Photography Within the Humanities, 58.
41. Frank, The Lines of My Hand, 111–112.

Chapter 19: The Chicago School
1. Moholy-Nagy, "Photography," in Trachtenberg, ed., Classic Essays on Photography, 166.
2. Traub and Grimes, The New Vision, 12.
3. Quoted in ibid., 45.

Bibliography

Chapter 1: Before Photography

Anderson, Stanford, ed. *On Streets*. Cambridge, Mass.: MIT Press, 1986.

Baudelaire, Charles. *Les Fleurs du mal*. Translated by Richard Howard. Boston: David R. Godine, 1982.

———. *Oeuvres complètes*. Paris: Editions Gallimard, 1961.

———. *The Painter of Modern Life and Other Essays*. Translated by Jonathan Mayne. London: Phaidon Press, 1964.

———. *Paris Spleen*. Translated by Louise Varèse. New York: New Directions, 1970.

Benjamin, Walter. *Illuminations*. Translated by Harry Zohn. New York: Schocken Books, 1969.

———. *Reflections: Essays, Aphorisms, Autobiographical Writings*. Translated by Edmund Jephcott. New York: Harcourt Brace Jovanovich, 1978.

Berman, Marshall. "Baudelaire: Modernism in the Streets." In *All That Is Solid Melts into Air: The Experience of Modernity*, 131–171. New York: Simon and Schuster, 1982.

Biddiss, Michael D. *The Age of the Masses: Ideas and Society in Europe Since 1870*. New York: Harper and Row, 1977.

Charlton, D. G. "French Thought in the Nineteenth and Twentieth Centuries." In *France: A Companion to French Studies*. New York: Pitman, 1972.

Cobban, Alfred. *A History of Modern France*. Vol. 1, *Old Régime and Revolution, 1715–1799*. New York: Penguin Books, 1963.

———. *A History of Modern France*. Vol. 2, *From the First Empire to the Second Empire, 1799–1871*. New York: Penguin Books, 1965.

———. *A History of Modern France*. Vol. 3, *France of the Republics, 1871–1962*. New York: Penguin Books, 1965.

Evenson, Norma. *Paris: A Century of Change, 1878–1978*. New Haven, Conn.: Yale University Press, 1979.

Flaubert, Gustave. *Flaubert in Egypt: A Sensibility on Tour — A Narrative Drawn from Gustave Flaubert's Travel Notes and Letters*. Edited and translated by Francis Steegmuller. Chicago: Academy Chicago Limited, 1979.

———. *Sentimental Education: The Story of a Young Man*. Brentano translation. New York: New Directions, 1957.

Flores, Angel, ed. *An Anthology of French Poetry from Nerval to Valéry in English Translation with French Originals*. New York: Doubleday Anchor Books, 1958.

Fournel, Victor. *Ce qu'on voit dans les rues de Paris*. Paris, 1858.

Galassi, Peter. *Before Photography: Painting and the Invention of Photography*. New York: Museum of Modern Art, 1981.

Girouard, Mark. *Cities and People: A Social and Architectural History*. New Haven, Conn.: Yale University Press, 1985.

de Goncourt, Edmond, and Jules de Goncourt. *Pages from the Goncourt Journal*. Edited and translated by Robert Baldick. New York: Oxford University Press, 1978.

Graña, César. *Bohemian Versus Bourgeois: French Society and the French Man of Letters in the Nineteenth Century*. New York: Basic Books, 1964.

Hamilton, George Heard. *Painting and Sculpture in Europe, 1880–1940*. New York: Penguin Books, 1972.

Hemmings, F.W.J. *Culture and Society in France, 1848–1898: Dissidents and Philistines*. New York: Charles Scribner's Sons, 1971.

Hobsbawm, E. J. *The Age of Capital, 1848–1875*. New York: New American Library, 1979.

———. *The Age of Revolution, 1789–1848*. New York: New American Library, 1962.

Honour, Hugh. *Romanticism*. New York: Harper and Row, 1979.

Home, Alistair. *The Fall of Paris: The Siege and the Commune, 1870–71*. New York: Penguin Books, 1965.

Hughes, Robert. "An Architecture of Grandeur: The Beaux-Arts Tradition Reconsidered." *Horizon* 18 (Winter 1976): 64–70.

Hugo, Victor. *Les Misérables*. 2 vols. Translated by Norman Denny. New York: Penguin Books, 1980.

Lefebvre, Henri. *Everyday Life in the Modern World*. Translated by Sacha Rabinovitch. New Brunswick, N.J.: Transaction Books, 1984.

Loyer, François. *Paris Nineteenth Century: Architecture and Urbanism*. Translated by Charles Lynn Clark. New York: Abbeville Press, 1988.

Milosz, Czeslaw. *The Captive Mind*. Translated by Jane Zielonko, New York: Vintage Books, 1955.

Olsen, Donald J. *The City as a Work of Art: London, Paris, Vienna*. New Haven, Conn.: Yale University Press, 1986.

Pike, Burton. *The Image of the City in Modern Literature*. Princeton, N.J.: Princeton University Press, 1981.

Pinkney, David H. *Napoleon III and the Rebuilding of Paris*. Princeton, N.J.: Princeton University Press, 1958.

Rousseau, Jean-Jacques. *Politics and the Arts: Letter to M. d'Alembert on the Theatre*. Translated by Allan Bloom. Ithaca, N.Y.: Cornell University Press, 1960.

Seigel, Jerrold. *Bohemian Paris: Culture, Politics, and the Boundaries of Bourgeois Life, 1830–1930*. New York: Viking, 1986.

Sennett, Richard. *The Fall of Public Man*, New York: Vintage Books, 1978.

Trilling, Lionel. *Sincerity and Authenticity*. Cambridge: Harvard University Press, 1971.

Williams, Roger. *The World of Napoleon III, 1851–1870*. New York: Collier Books, 1962.

Williams, Rosalind H. *Dream Worlds: Mass Consumption in Late Nineteenth-Century France*. Berkeley: University of California Press, 1982.

Zola, Emile. *The Debacle*. Translated by Leonard Tancock. New York: Penguin Books, 1972.

PART ONE: Eugène Atget and the Nineteenth Century

Boyd, C. D. "Street Photography." *Photoisms* 2 (September 1911): 5–7.

Brodine, Harry A. "Street Scenes." *Photographic Times* (February 1913): 49–53.

Christ, Yvan. *La vie familière sous le second Empire*. Paris: Berger-Levrault, 1977.

Coe, Brian, and Paul Gates. *The Snapshot Photograph: The Rise of Popular Photography, 1888–1939*. London: Ash and Grant, 1977.

Coursaget, René, and Guiton Chabance. *Dans les rues de Paris au temps des fiacres*. Paris: Editions de Chêne, 1950.

Maddow, Ben. "Tears and Misunderstanding." *Aperture* 92 (Fall 1983): 28–36.

Newhall, Beaumont. *The History of Photography: From 1839 to the Present*. New York: Museum of Modern Art, 1982.

"Street Photography." *Bulletin of Photography* 2 (January 1908): 102.

Thomas, Alan. *Time in a Frame: Photography and the Nineteenth-Century Mind*. New York: Schocken Books, 1977.

Thomson, David. *England in the Nineteenth Century, 1815–1914*. Baltimore: Penguin Books, 1950.

Tissandier, Gaston. *A History and Handbook of Photography*. London, 1876.

Trachtenberg, Alan, ed. *Classic Essays on Photography*. New Haven, Conn.: Leete's Island Books, 1980.

Tuchman, Barbara W. *The Proud Tower: A Portrait of the World Before the War, 1890–1914*. New York: Bantam Books, 1967.

Whitehead, Alfred North. *Science and the Modern World*. New York: Mentor Books, 1948.

Williams, H. H. "Shooting in the Streets." *The International Annual of Anthony's Photographic Bulletin* (1889): 281–282.

Yellott, Osborne I. "Street Photography." *The Photo-Miniature: A Magazine of Photographic Information* 2 (May 1900): 48–78.

Zeldin, Theodore. *France, 1848–1945: Ambition and Love*, New York: Oxford University Press, 1979.

———. *France, 1848–1945: Anxiety and Hypocrisy*. New York: Oxford University Press, 1981.

———. *France, 1848–1945: Intellect and Pride*. New York: Oxford University Press, 1980.

———. *France, 1848–1945: Politics and Anger*. New York: Oxford University Press, 1979.

———. *France, 1848–1945: Taste and Corruption*. New York: Oxford University Press, 1980.

Chapter 2: In the Beginning

Baudelaire, Charles. *Art in Paris, 1845–1862*. Translated by Jonathan Mayne. London: Phaidon Press, 1965.

———. *The Painter of Modern Life and Other*

Essays. Translated by Jonathan Mayne. London: Phaidon Press, 1964.

Benjamin, Walter. *Illuminations.* Translated by Harry Zohn. New York: Schocken Books, 1969.

———. *Reflections: Essays, Aphorisms, Autobiographical Writings.* Translated by Edmund Jephcott. New York: Harcourt Brace Jovanovich, 1978.

Clark, Sir Kenneth. "The Relations of Photography and Painting." *Aperture* 3 (1955): 4–14.

French Primitive Photography. Millerton, N.Y.: Aperture, 1969.

DAVID OCTAVIUS HILL
and ROBERT ADAMSON:

Ford, Colin. *An Early Victorian Album: The Photographic Masterpieces (1843–1847) of David Octavius Hill and Robert Adamson.* New York: Alfred A. Knopf, 1976.

Hill, David Octavius, and Robert Adamson. *A Series of Calotype Views of St. Andrews.* Edinburgh, 1846.

Stevenson, Sara. *Hill and Adamson's The Fishermen and Women of the Firth of Forth.* Edinburgh: Scottish National Portrait Gallery, 1991.

Jammes, André, and Eugenia Parry Janis. *The Art of French Calotype, with a Critical Dictionary of Photographers, 1845–1870.* Princeton, N.J.: Princeton University Press, 1983.

CALVERT JONES:

Schaaf, Larry. *Catalogue Five. Sun Pictures: The Reverend Calvert R. Jones.* New York: Hans R. Kraus Fine Photographs, 1990.

———. Conversation with Colin Westerbeck, 27 September 1993.

Marbot, Bernard. *Une Invention du XIXe siècle: La Photographie — expression et technique, collections de la Société Française de Photographie.* Paris: Bibliothèque Nationale, 1976.

CHARLES NÈGRE:

Borcoman, James. *Charles Nègre, 1820–1880.* Ottawa: National Gallery of Canada, 1976.

———. Conversation with Colin Westerbeck and Joel Meyerowitz, May 1981.

Heilbrun, Françoise, and Philippe Néagu. *Charles Nègre, photographe (1820–1880).* Paris: Réunion des Musées Nationaux, 1980.

Jammes, André. *Charles Nègre, photographe (1820–1880).* Choisy-le-Roi: Imprimerie de France, 1963.

Nochlin, Linda. *Realism.* New York: Penguin Books, 1971.

Scharf, Aaron. *Art and Photography.* Baltimore: Penguin Books, 1974.

Sobieszek, Robert A. "Photography and the Theory of Realism in the Second Empire: A Reexamination of the Relationship." In *One Hundred Years of Photographic History: Essays in Honor of Beaumont Newhall,* 146–151. Edited by Van Deren Coke. Albuquerque: University of New Mexico Press, 1975.

WILLIAM HENRY FOX TALBOT:

Arnold, H.J.P. *William Henry Fox Talbot, Pioneer of Photography and Man of Science.* London: Hutchinson Benham, 1977.

Buckland, Gail. *Fox Talbot and the Invention of Photography.* Boston: David R. Godine, 1980.

Harbison, Robert. "Decoding the Cipher of Reality: Fox Talbot in His Time." *Aperture* (Fall 1991): 2–8.

Jammes, André. *William H. Fox Talbot, Inventor of the Negative-Positive Process.* New York: Collier Books, 1973.

Talbot, William Henry Fox. *The Pencil of Nature.* London, 1844–46.

Van Haaften, Julia. " 'Original Sun Pictures': A Check List of the New York Public Library's Holdings of Early Works Illustrated with Photographs, 1844–1900." *Bulletin of the New York Public Library* 80 (Spring 1977): 355–415.

Varnedoe, Kirk. "The Artifice of Candor: Impressionism and Photography Reconsidered." *Art in America* 68 (January 1980): 66–78.

———. "The Ideology of Time: Degas and Photography." *Art in America* 68 (June 1980): 96–110.

Chapter 3: The View from Abroad

Benjamin, Sol. "Views of Japan." *Aperture* 90 (1983): 28–39.

Buckland, Gail. *Fox Talbot and the Invention of Photography.* Boston: David R. Godine, 1980.

Clark, Sir Kenneth. "The Relations of Photography and Painting." *Aperture* 3 (1955): 4–14.

Desmond, Ray. "Photography in India During the Nineteenth Century." In *India Office Library and Records: Report for the Year 1974,* 5–37. London: Foreign and Commonwealth Office, 1976.

Eggan, Fred. "One Hundred Years of Ethnology and Social Anthropology." In *One Hundred Years of Anthropology,* 119–149. Edited by J. O. Brew. Cambridge: Harvard University Press, 1968.

FRANCIS FRITH:

Jay, Bill. *Victorian Cameraman: Francis Frith's Views of Rural England, 1850–1898.* Newton Abbot, England: David and Charles, 1973.

White, Jon E. Manchip, ed. *Egypt and the Holy Land in Historic Photographs: 77 Views by Francis Frith.* New York: Dover Publications, 1980.

Hershkowitz, Robert. *The British Photographer Abroad: The First Thirty Years.* London: Robert Hershkowitz, 1980.

Jones, Gareth Stedman. *Outcast London.* Oxford: Clarendon Press, 1971.

Mayhew, Henry. *London Characters.* London, 1881.

Mennie, Donald. *The Pageant of Peking.* Shanghai: A. S. Watson, 1920.

Nord, Deborah Epstein. "The Social Explorer as Anthropologist: Victorian Travellers Among the Urban Poor." In *Visions of the Modern City: Essays in History, Art, and Literature,* 118–130. Proceedings of the Heyman Center for the Humanities. New York: Columbia University, 1983.

Ollman, Arthur. *Samuel Bourne, Images of India.* Carmel, Calif.: Friends of Photography, 1983.

Rowe, Richard. *Life in the London Streets; or Struggles for Daily Bread.* London, 1881.

Sala, George Augustus. *Gaslight and Daylight, with Some London Scenes They Shine Upon.* London, 1872.

Thomas, Alan. *Time in a Frame: Photography and the Nineteenth-Century Mind.* New York: Schocken Books, 1977.

JOHN THOMSON:

Doty, Robert. "Street Life in London: A Review of an Early Use of Photography in Social Documentation." *Image: Journal of Photography and Motion Pictures of the International Museum of Photography at George Eastman House* 6 (November 1957): 240–245.

Lehr, Janet. "John Thomson, 1837–1921." *History of Photography* 4 (January 1980): 67–71.

Thomson, John. *China and Its People in Early Photographs: An Unabridged Reprint of the Classic 1873/4 Work.* New York: Dover Publications, 1982.

———. *Foo Chow and the River Min.* London, 1873.

———. In *The Geographical Journal* 2 (July–December 1873): 211.

———. *Illustrations of China and Its People: A Series of Two Hundred Photographs, with Letterpress Descriptive of the Places and People Represented.* 4 vols. London, 1873.

———. *The Straits of Malacca, Indo-China and China.* London, 1875.

———. *Street Incidents.* London, 1881.

———. *Through China with a Camera.* London, 1898.

———. *Through Cyprus with a Camera, in the Autumn of 1878.* 2 vols. London, 1879.

Thomson, John, and Adolphe Smith. *Street Life in London.* London, 1877–78.

White, Stephen. *John Thomson: A Window on the Orient.* New York: Thames and Hudson, 1985.

Worswick, Clark, ed. *Imperial China: Photographs, 1850–1912.* New York: Pennwick Publishing, 1978.

———. *Japan: Photographs, 1854–1905.* New York: Pennwick Publishing, 1979.

Chapter 4: Busmen's Holidays

Darrah, William C. *The World of Stereographs.* Gettysburg, Penn.: W. C. Darrah, 1977.

Earle, Edward W. *Points of View: The Stereograph in America — A Cultural History.* Rochester, N.Y.: Visual Studies Workshop, 1979.

Hickey, Kieran, ed. *The Light of Other Days: Irish Life at the Turn of the Century in the Photographs of Robert French.* Boston: David R. Godine, 1975.

Hobsbawm, E. J. *The Age of Capital, 1848–1875.* New York: New American Library, 1962.

Jay, Bill. *Victorian Cameraman: Francis Frith's Views of Rural England, 1850–1898.* Newton Abbot, England: David and Charles, 1973.

Juin, Hubert. *La France 1900 vue par les frères Seeberger.* Paris: Pierre Belfond, 1979.

Lesy, Michael. *Wisconsin Death Trip.* New York: Pantheon Books, 1973.

Mayer, Grace. *Once upon a City: New York from 1890 to 1910.* New York: Macmillan, 1958.

FRANK SUTCLIFFE:
   Hiley, Michael. *Frank Sutcliffe, Photographer of Whitby*. Boston: David R. Godine, 1974.
   Sutcliffe, Frank. "Landscape with Figures." *The Practical Photographer* 11 (August 1904): 42.
   Wagstaff, Sam, Jr. *American Stereographs: A Selection from Private Collections*. New York: Grey Art Gallery, 1980.
   Zannier, Italo. *Verso Oriente: Fotografie di Antonio e Felice Beato*. Florence: Fratelli Alinari Editrice, 1986.
   Zevi, Filippo, ed. *Gli Alinari, fotografi a Firenze — 1852–1920*. Florence: Fratelli Alinari Editrice [1977].

Chapter 5: Art for Art's Sake
Album photographique 1. Paris: Centre Georges Pompidou, 1979.
THOMAS ANNAN:
   Annan, Thomas. *Photographs of Old Closes and Streets of Glasgow 1868/1877*. New York: Dover Publications, 1977.
   ———. *Old Closes and Streets, a Series of Photogravures, 1868–1899*. Glasgow: T. and R. Annan and Sons, 1900.
   ———. *Photographs of Old Closes, Streets, &c., Taken 1868–1877*. Glasgow, 1878–79.
   Bucquet, M. "L'Appareil à main." In *Esthétique de la Photografie*, 61–68. Paris: Photo-Club de Paris, 1900.
SAMUEL COULTHURST:
   Coulthurst, S. I. "The Hand Camera and Hand-Camera Workers." *British Journal of Photography* 42 (27 December 1895): 825–826.
   Martin, Sandra. "Samuel Coulthurst, 1867–1937." *Creative Camera* 193/194 (July-August 1980): 227–237.
ARNOLD GENTHE:
   Genthe, Arnold. *Arnold Genthe, 1869–1942: Photographs and Memorabilia from the Collection of James F. Carr*. New York: Staten Island Museum, 1975.
   ———. *As I Remember*. New York: Reynal and Hitchcock, 1936.
   ———. *Impressions of Old New Orleans*. New York: George H. Doran, 1926.
   ———. *Old Chinatown: A Book of Pictures by Arnold Genthe*. New York: Mitchell Kennerley, 1913.
   Irwin, Will. *Pictures of Old Chinatown*. New York: Moffat, Yard and Co., 1908.
   Kuo Wei Tchen, John, ed. *Genthe's Photographs of San Francisco's Old Chinatown*. New York: Dover Publications, 1984.
Gernsheim, Helmut and Alison. *The History of Photography: From the Camera Obscura to the Beginning of the Modern Era*. New York: McGraw-Hill, 1969.
Green, Jonathan, ed. *Camera Work: A Critical Anthology*. Millerton, N.Y.: Aperture, 1973.
Grey, Howard, and Stuart Graham. *Victorians by the Sea*. London: Academy Editions, 1973.
Hartmann, Sadakichi. "On the Possibility of New Laws of Composition." *Camera Work* 30 (April 1910): 23–26.

Herschel, Sir J.F.W. "Instantaneous Photography." *The Photographic News* 4 (11 May 1860): 13.
Hiley, Michael. *Frank Sutcliffe, Photographer of Whitby*. Boston: David R. Godine, 1974.
Keiley, Joseph T. "J. Craig Annan." *Camera Work* 8 (October 1904): 17–18.
Leos, Edward. "Secret Camera: The Photography of Horace Engle." *History of Photography: An International Quarterly* 1 (January 1977): 17–30.
PAUL MARTIN:
   Flukinger, Roy, Larry Schaaf, and Standish Meacham. *Paul Martin, Victorian Photographer*. Austin: University of Texas Press, 1977.
   Jay, Bill. *Victorian Candid Camera: Paul Martin, 1864–1944*. Newton Abbot, England: David and Charles, 1973.
   Martin, Paul. *Victorian Snapshots*. New York: Arno Press, 1973.
Ranke, Winfried. *Heinrich Zille, Photographien — Berlin, 1890–1910*. Munich: Schirmer/Mosel, 1975.
Sandler, Martin W. *This Was Connecticut: Images of a Vanished World*. Boston: Little, Brown, 1977.
Steichen, Edward. *Steichen: A Life in Photography*. New York: Harmony Books, 1985.
ALFRED STIEGLITZ:
   Eisler, Benita. *O'Keeffe and Stieglitz: An American Romance*. New York: Doubleday, 1991.
   Frank, Waldo, et al., eds. *America and Alfred Stieglitz: A Collective Portrait*. New York: The Literary Guild, 1934.
   Lowe, Sue Davidson. *Stieglitz: A Memoir/Biography*. New York: Farrar, Straus and Giroux, 1983.
   Naef, Weston J. *The Collection of Alfred Stieglitz: Fifty Pioneers of Modern Photography*. New York: Metropolitan Museum of Art/Viking Press, 1978.
   Norman, Dorothy. *Alfred Stieglitz: An American Seer*. Millerton, N.Y.: Aperture, 1973.
   Petersen, Christian A. *Alfred Stieglitz's* Camera Notes. Minneapolis: The Minneapolis Institute of Fine Arts, 1993.
PAUL STRAND:
   Greenough, Sarah. *Paul Strand: An American Vision*. Washington, D.C.: National Gallery of Art, 1990.
   Rosenblum, Naomi. *Paul Strand: The Stieglitz Years at 291 (1915–1917)*. New York: Zabriskie Gallery, 1983.
   Stange, Maren, ed. *Paul Strand: Essays on His Life and Work*. New York: Aperture, 1990.
   Strand, Paul. *Paul Strand*. Zurich: Gallery 'Zur Stockeregg,' 1987.
   ———. *Paul Strand: A Retrospective Monograph*. 2 vols. Millerton, N.Y.: Aperture, 1972.
   ———. *Paul Strand, Sixty Years of Photographs*. Millerton, N.Y.: Aperture, 1976.
   ———. "Photography." *The Seven Arts* (August 1917): 524–526.
Tomkins, Calvin. "Profiles: Look to the Things Around You." *New Yorker* (16 September 1974): 44–94.

KARL STRUSS:
   Harvith, John and Susan. "Karl Struss." *American Photographer* 3 (August 1979): 32–38.
   Struss, Karl. *Karl Struss: Man with a Camera*. Bloomfield Hills, Mich.: Cranbrook Academy of Art, 1976.
"The Sunset of the Old World: A Portfolio from the Work of C. Chusseau Flaviens." *Image: Journal of Photography and Motion Pictures of the International Museum of Photography at George Eastman House* 21 (March 1978): 1–31.
"Unphotographic Paint: The Texture of Impressionism." *Camera Work* 28 (October 1909): 20–23.
Weaver, Mike. *The Photographic Art: Pictorial Traditions in Britain and America*. New York: Harper and Row, 1985.
Yellott, Osborne I. "Street Photography." *The Photo-Miniature: A Magazine of Photographic Information* 2 (May 1900): 48–78.

Chapter 6: Documents for Artists
EUGÈNE ATGET:
   Abbott, Berenice. Symposium, International Center of Photography, New York, 15 November 1979.
   Adams, William Howard. *Atget's Gardens: A Selection of Eugène Atget's Garden Photographs*. Garden City, N.Y.: Doubleday, 1979.
   Borcoman, James. *Eugène Atget, 1857–1927*. Ottawa: National Gallery of Canada, 1984.
   Colloque Atget. Paris: Photographies, 1986.
   Eugène Atget. New York: Pantheon Books, 1985.
   Fraser, John. "Atget and the City." *Cambridge Quarterly* 3 (Summer 1968): 199–234.
   Leroy, Jean. *Atget, magicien de vieux Paris en son époque*. Paris: Pierre Jean Balbo, 1975.
   Nesbit, Molly. *Atget's Seven Albums*. New Haven, Conn.: Yale University Press, 1993.
   ———. "The Use of History." *Art in America* 74 (February 1986): 72–83.
   Szarkowski, John, and Maria Morris Hombourg. *The Work of Atget*. Vol. 1, *Old France*. New York: Museum of Modern Art, 1981.
   ———. *The Work of Atget*. Vol. 2, *The Art of Old Paris*. New York: Museum of Modern Art, 1982.
   ———. *The Work of Atget*. Vol. 3, *The Ancien Regime*. New York: Museum of Modern Art, 1983.
   ———. *The Work of Atget*. Vol. 4, *Modern Times*. New York: Museum of Modern Art, 1985.
Benjamin, Walter. *Illuminations*. Translated by Harry Zohn. New York: Schocken Books, 1969.
Levy, Julien. *Memoir of an Art Gallery*. New York: G. P. Putnam's Sons, 1977.
CHARLES MARVILLE:
   Charles Marville, photographe de Paris de 1851 à 1879. Paris: La Bibliothèque historique de la Ville de Paris, 1980.
   Charles Marville, Photographs of Paris — 1852–1878. New York: French Institute/Alliance Française, 1981.
   Haussmann, Baron Georges-Eugène. In *Histoire générale de Paris*. Vol. 1. Paris: Imprimerie Impériale, 1866.

de Thezy, Marie. "Charles Marville et Haussmann." *Monuments Historiques* 110 (1980): 13–17.

Rewald, John. *The History of Impressionism.* New York: Museum of Modern Art, 1973.

Yeats, William Butler. "Coole Park and Ballylee." In *The Collected Poems of W. B. Yeats,* 239–240. New York: Macmillan, 1956.

PART TWO: Cartier-Bresson and Europe in the Twentieth Century

Barr, Alfred H., Jr. *Cubism and Abstract Art.* New York: Museum of Modern Art, 1974.

Brogan, D. W. *The Development of Modern France, 1870–1939.* Vol. 2, *The Shadow of War, World War I, Between the Two Wars.* New York: Harper and Row, 1966.

Caute, David. *Communism and the French Intellectuals, 1914–1960.* New York: Macmillan, 1964.

Flanner, Janet (Genêt). *Paris Was Yesterday, 1925–1939.* New York: Penguin Books, 1979.

Hughes, H. Stuart. *Consciousness and Society: The Reorientation of European Social Thought, 1890–1930.* New York: Vintage Books, 1977.

Johnson, Paul. *Modern Times: The World from the Twenties to the Eighties.* New York: Harper and Row, 1983.

Lacouture, Jean. *Léon Blum.* Translated by George Holoch. New York: Holmes and Meier, 1982.

Levy, Julien. *Surrealism.* New York: Black Sun Press, 1936.

Lottman, Herbert R. *The Left Bank: Writers, Artists, and Politics from the Popular Front to the Cold War.* Boston: Houghton Mifflin, 1982.

Orwell, George. *Down and Out in Paris and London.* New York: Harcourt Brace Jovanovich, 1933.

Talbott, John E., ed. *France Since 1930.* New York: Quadrangle Books, 1972.

Thomson, David. *Democracy in France Since 1870.* New York: Oxford University Press, 1964.

Tint, Herbert. *France Since 1918.* New York: St. Martin's Press, 1980.

Travis, David. *Photographs from the Julien Levy Collection, Starting with Atget.* Chicago: Art Institute of Chicago, 1976.

Chapter 7: Children of the Century

Freud, Sigmund. *Civilization and Its Discontents.* New York: W. W. Norton, 1962.

JACQUES-HENRI LARTIGUE:

Borhan, Pierre, and Martine d'Astier. *Les Envols de Jacques Lartigue et les débuts de l'aviation.* Paris: Association des Amis de Jacques-Henri Lartigue, 1989.

Delpire, Robert, ed. *Lartigue 8 x 80.* Paris: Musée des Arts Décoratifs, 1975.

Jammes, Isabelle. *Bonjour Monsieur Lartigue.* Paris: Grand Palais des Champs-Elysées, 1980.

Lartigue, Jacques-Henri. *Albums.* Paris: Mission du Patrimonie Photographique.

———. *Boyhood Photos of J.-H. Lartigue: The Family Album of a Gilded Age.* [New York:] Ami Guichard, 1966.

———. *Diary of a Century.* New York: Penguin Books, 1978.

———. *Jacques-Henri Lartigue.* Paris: Le Centre National de la Photographie, 1983.

———. *Le Passé Composé: Les 6 x 13 de Jacques-Henri Lartigue.* Paris: Le Centre National de la Photographie, 1984.

Martin, Marianne W. *Futurist Art and Theory, 1909–1915.* New York: Oxford University Press, 1968.

Novotny, Ann. *Alice's World: The Life and Photography of an American Original — Alice Austen, 1866–1952.* Old Greenwich, Conn.: Chatham Press, 1976.

Peabody, Marian Lawrence. *To Be Young Was Very Heaven.* Boston: Houghton Mifflin, 1967.

GIUSEPPE PRIMOLI:

Palazzoli, Daniela. *Giuseppe Primoli, instantee e fotostorie della Belle Epoque.* Milan: Electa Editrice, 1979.

Vitali, Lamberto. *Un fotografo fin de siècle, il conte Primoli.* Turin: Giulio Einaudi, 1968.

Proust, Marcel. *Remembrance of Things Past.* 3 vols. Translated by C. K. Scott Moncrieff and Terence Kilmartin. New York: Random House, 1981.

Trincere, Yolanda. *Futurism and Photography.* Greenvale, N.Y.: Hillwood Art Gallery, 1984.

Chapter 8: The Decisive Photographer

Aragon, Louis. *Nightwalker (Le Paysan de Paris).* Translated by Frederick Brown. Englewood Cliffs, N.J.: Prentice-Hall, 1970.

Balakian, Anna. *André Breton.* New York: Oxford University Press, 1971.

Becker, Louise F. *Louis Aragon.* New York: Twayne, 1971.

Breton, André. *Manifestoes of Surrealism.* Translated by Richard Seaver and Helen R. Lane. Ann Arbor: University of Michigan Press, 1972.

HENRI CARTIER-BRESSON:

Brinnin, John Malcolm. *Sextet: T. S. Eliot and Truman Capote and Others.* New York: Delacorte Press, 1981.

Capote, Truman. "Introduction." In Cecil Beaton, *The Best of Beaton,* 11–14. New York: Macmillan, 1968.

Cartier-Bresson, Henri. *America in Passing.* Boston: Little, Brown, 1991.

———. *A propos de l'U.R.S.S.* Paris: Editions du Chêne, 1973.

———. *The Decisive Moment.* New York: Simon and Schuster, 1952.

———. *D'une Chine à l'autre.* Paris: Robert Delpire, 1954.

———. *The Europeans.* New York: Simon and Schuster, 1955.

———. "Henri Cartier-Bresson." Interview by Sheila Turner Seed. *Popular Photography* 74 (May 1974): 108, 117, 139, 142, 198.

———. *Henri Cartier-Bresson.* Edinburgh: Scottish Arts Council, 1978.

———. *Henri Cartier-Bresson in India.* New York: Thames and Hudson, 1987.

———. "Henri Cartier-Bresson, on the Art of Photography." Interview by Yvonne Baby. *Harper's* (November 1961): 73–78.

———. *Henri Cartier-Bresson, Photographer.* Paris: Robert Delpire, 1979.

———. *Henri Cartier-Bresson, Photoportraits.* New York: Thames and Hudson, 1985.

———. " 'Nul ne peut entrer ici s'il n'est pas géomètre': un entretien avec Henri Cartier-Bresson." *Le Monde* (5 September 1974): 13.

———. *Photographs by Cartier-Bresson.* New York: Grossman Publishers, 1963.

———. *The World of Henri Cartier-Bresson.* New York: Viking Press, 1968.

———. Conversation with Colin Westerbeck and Joel Meyerowitz, November 1980.

Dupont, Joan. "A Hunter Who Stalked His Prey with a Camera." *New York Times,* 27 September 1982: 17, 39.

Eparvier, Jean. *A Paris sous la botte des Nazis.* Paris: Editions Raymond Schall, 1944.

Galassi, Peter. *Henri Cartier-Bresson, the Early Work.* New York: Museum of Modern Art, 1987.

Goldsmith, Arthur. "Henri Cartier-Bresson Revisited: A Fourteen-Page Portfolio." *35-MM Photography* (1960): 121, 137–140.

Haas, Ernst. "Henri Cartier-Bresson: A Lyrical View of Life." *Modern Photography* 35 (November 1971): 88–97, 134, 136.

Hofstadter, Dan. "Stealing a March on the World." *New Yorker* (23 and 30 October 1989): 59–93 and 49–73.

Kazin, Alfred. *New York Jew.* New York: Alfred A. Knopf, 1978.

Levy, Julien. *Memoir of an Art Gallery.* New York: G. P. Putnam's Sons, 1977.

Martinez, Raoul. Conversation with Joel Meyerowitz, November 1980.

Newhall, Beaumont. *The Photographs of Henri Cartier-Bresson.* New York: Museum of Modern Art, 1947.

———. "Thoughts on Henri Cartier-Bresson and His Extraordinary Talent." *Camera* (October 1955): 46.

Norman, Dorothy. "A Visitor Falls in Love — with Hudson and East Rivers." *New York Post* (26 August 1946): 12.

Nourissier, Françoise. *Vive la France.* Paris: Robert Laffont, 1970.

Soby, James Thrall. "The Art of Poetic Accident: The Photographs of Cartier-Bresson and Helen Levitt." *Minicam* 6 (March 1943): 28–31, 95.

———. "A New Vision in Photography." *The Saturday Review,* 5 April 1947: 32–34.

Stevens, Nancy. "In Search of the Invisible Man." *American Photographer* 3 (November 1979): 62–71.

Szarkowski, John. Conversation with Colin Westerbeck and Joel Meyerowitz, May 1979.

Weiss, Margaret. "Encore at the Louvre: Henri Cartier-Bresson." *The Saturday Review,* 26 November 1966: 23–28.

Herrigel, Eugen. *Zen in the Art of Archery.* Translated by R.F.C. Hull. New York: Vintage Books, 1971.

Hughes, H. Stuart. *Consciousness and Society: The Reorientation of European Social Thought, 1890–1930.* New York: Vintage Books, 1977.

Lhôte, André. *Theory of Figure Painting.* London: A. Zwemmer, 1953.

———. *Treatise on Landscape Painting.* London: A Zwemmer, 1950.

Rubin, William S. *Dada, Surrealism, and Their Heritage.* New York: Museum of Modern Art, 1968.

Shirer, William L. *The Collapse of the Third Republic: An Inquiry into the Fall of France in 1940.* New York: Simon and Schuster, 1969.

Thomson, David. *Democracy in France Since 1870.* New York: Oxford University Press, 1964.

Whelan, Richard. *Robert Capa: A Biography.* New York: Alfred A. Knopf, 1985.

Chapter 9: Hungarian Rhapsody
LUCIEN AIGNER:

Aigner, John P., ed. *Lucien Aigner.* New York: International Center for Photography, 1979.

Aigner, Lucien. *Aigner's Paris.* Stockholm: Fotografiska Museet, 1982.

BRASSAÏ (GYULA HALÁSZ):

Brassaï (Gyula Halász). *Brassaï.* New York: Museum of Modern Art, 1968.

———. "My Friend André Kertész." *Camera* 42 (April 1963): 7–32.

———. *Picasso and Company.* Translated by Francis Price. New York: Doubleday, 1966.

———. *The Secret Paris of the Thirties.* Translated by Richard Miller. New York: Pantheon Books, 1976.

———. Conversation with Colin Westerbeck, September 1976.

———. Conversation with Colin Westerbeck and Joel Meyerowitz, November 1980.

Morand, Paul. *Paris de nuit.* Paris: Edition "Arts et Métiers Graphiques" [1933].

Westerbeck, Colin. "Night Light: Brassaï and Weegee." *Artforum* 15 (December 1976): 34–45.

ANDRÉ KERTÉSZ:

André Kertész. London: Arts Council of Great Britain, 1979.

Corkin, Jane, ed. *André Kertész: A Lifetime of Perception.* New York: Harry N. Abrams, 1982.

Ducrot, Nicolas, ed. *Of New York . . . André Kertész.* New York: Alfred A. Knopf, 1976.

Kertész, André. *André Kertész.* New York: Paragraphic Books/Grossman, 1966.

———. *André Kertész: A Lifetime of Perception.* New York: Harry N. Abrams, 1982.

———. *André Kertész, photographies.* Paris: Bibliothèque Nationale, 1963.

———. *André Kertész: Vintage Photographs.* Chicago: Edwynn Houk Gallery, 1985.

———. *Day of Paris.* New York: J. J. Augustin, 1945.

———. *Hungarian Memories.* Boston: Little, Brown, 1982.

———. *Kertész on Kertész: A Self-Portrait.* New York: Abbeville Press, 1984.

———. *On Reading.* New York: Grossman, 1975.

———. *Washington Square.* New York: Grossman, 1975.

———. Conversations with Colin Westerbeck and Joel Meyerowitz, September/October 1980.

Phillips, Sandra S., David Travis, and Weston J. Naef. *André Kertész: Of Paris and New York.* New York: Thames and Hudson, 1985.

Theodore Fried & André Kertész: An Enduring Friendship. New York: H. V. Allison Galleries, 1987.

Lorant, Stefan. Symposium, Goethe House, New York, March 1982.

Lyons, Nathan, ed. *Photographers on Photography.* Englewood Cliffs, N.J.: Prentice-Hall, 1966.

Chapter 10: Foreign Correspondents
MANUEL ALVAREZ BRAVO:

Alvarez Bravo, Manuel. *Fotografias.* Mexico City: Sociedad de Arte Moderno, 1945.

———. Letter to Nancy Newhall, 5 July 1943. Collection of the Museum of Modern Art, New York.

———. *Manuel Alvarez Bravo.* Mexico: Academia de Artes, 1980.

Hill, Paul, and Thomas Cooper. *Dialogue with Photography.* New York: Farrar, Straus and Giroux, 1979.

Livingston, Jane. *M. Alvarez Bravo.* Boston: David R. Godine, 1978.

Avant-Garde Photography in Germany, 1919–1939. San Francisco: San Francisco Museum of Modern Art, 1980.

BILL BRANDT:

Brandt, Bill. "Bill Brandt." Interview by Ruth Spencer. *British Journal of Photography* 120 (9 November 1973): 1040–1043.

———. *Bill Brandt: Behind the Camera — Photographs, 1928–1983.* Millerton, N.Y.: Aperture, 1985.

———. "Bill Brandt Today . . . and Yesterday." *Photography* (June 1959): 20–33.

———. *Camera in London.* London: Focal Press, 1948.

———. *The English at Home.* London: B. T. Batsford, 1936.

———. *London in the Thirties.* New York: Pantheon Books, 1984.

———. *A Night in London.* London: Country Life, 1938.

———. *Shadow of Light.* New York: Da Capo Press, 1977.

———. Conversation with Colin Westerbeck and Joel Meyerowitz, November 1980.

Szarkowski, John. "Bill Brandt." *Modern Photography* 34 (October 1970): 84–89.

Tichenor, Jonathan. "Bill Brandt." *U.S. Camera Annual* (1950): 17–27.

Campbell, Bryn. Conversation with Colin Westerbeck and Joel Meyerowitz, November 1980.

Davies, Sue. Conversation with Colin Westerbeck and Joel Meyerowitz, November 1980.

Edey, Maitland. "The Photo Essay." *American Photographer* 1 (December 1978): 32–38.

Gidal, Tim N. *Modern Photojournalism: Origin and Evolution, 1910–1933.* New York: Collier Books, 1973.

Henderson, Nigel. *Nigel Henderson.* Nottingham, England: Midland Group, 1977.

Hopkinson, Tom, ed. *Picture Post, 1938–50.* New York: Penguin Books, 1970.

Kuwabara, Kineo. *Kineo Kuwabara: Tokyo 1930's.* Tokyo: Galerie Watari, 1985.

Lax, Eric. "Lorant's Vision." *American Photographer* 12 (June 1984): 60–67,

Lorant, Stefan. Symposium, Goethe House, New York, March 1982.

Man, Felix H. *Man with Camera: Photographs from Seven Decades.* New York: Schocken Books, 1984.

"Mass Observation." *Camerawork* (September 1978): 1.

ROGER MAYNE:

MacInnes, Colin. "Poverty and Poetry in No. 10." *The Observer* (24 January 1962): 24.

Mayne, Roger. "The Realist Position." *Uppercase* 5 (1961).

———. *The Street Photographs of Roger Mayne.* London: Victoria and Albert Museum, 1986.

Mellor, David. "Nigel Henderson." *Camerawork* (September 1978): 12–13.

———, ed. *Germany, the New Photography — 1927–33.* London: Arts Council of Great Britain, 1978.

LÁZLÓ MOHOLY-NAGY:

Bendetta, Mary, and Lázló Moholy-Nagy. *The Street Markets of London.* London: John Miles, 1936.

Hight, Eleanor M. *Moholy-Nagy: Photography and Film in Weimar Germany.* Wellesley, Mass.: Wellesley College Museum, 1985.

Moholy-Nagy, Sybil. *Moholy-Nagy: Experiment in Totality.* Cambridge, Mass.: MIT Press, 1969.

Photographs of Moholy-Nagy from the Collection of William Larson. Claremont, Calif.: Galleries of the Claremont Colleges, 1975.

Ollman, Leah. *Camera as Weapon: Worker Photography Between the Wars.* San Diego: Museum of Photographic Arts, 1991.

Orwell, George. *The Road to Wigan Pier.* New York: Harcourt Brace Jovanovich, 1958.

Osman, Colin. Conversation with Colin Westerbeck and Joel Meyerowitz, November 1980.

Salomon, Erich. *Erich Salomon, Leica Fotografie — 1930–1939.* Berlin: Berlinische Galerie, 1986.

Chapter 11: The Fourth Estate
EDOUARD BOUBAT:

Boubat, Edouard. *Pauses.* Paris: Contrejour, 1983.

George, Bernard. *Edouard Boubat.* New York: Macmillan Publishing, 1973.

Burri, René. *Die Deutschen: Photographien, 1957–1964.* Munich: Schirmer/Mosel, 1986.

ROBERT DOISNEAU:

Doisneau, Robert. *Robert Doisneau's Paris.* New York: Simon and Schuster, 1956.

———. *Three Seconds from Eternity.* Translated by Vivienne Menkes. Boston: New York Graphic Society, 1980.

————. Conversation with Colin Westerbeck and Joel Meyerowitz, November 1980.

Hill, Paul, and Thomas Cooper. *Dialogue with Photography*. New York: Farrar, Straus and Giroux, 1979.

Lepidis, Clement, and Robert Doisneau. *Le Mal de Paris*. Paris: Arthaud, 1980.

Rosenblum, Robert. "Robert Doisneau." *Popular Photography* 80 (January 1977): 108–113, 136–138.

ELLIOTT ERWITT:

Collins, Glenn. "An Erwitt Snapping Tour." *American Photographer* 22 (January 1989): 61–63.

Erwitt, Elliott. *Personal Exposures*. New York: W. W. Norton, 1988.

————. *Recent Developments*. New York: Simon and Schuster, 1978.

JOSEF KOUDELKA:

Koudelka, Josef. *Gypsies*. Millerton, N.Y.: Aperture, 1975.

————. Conversation with Colin Westerbeck and Joel Meyerowitz, November 1980.

Koudelka, Josef, and Milan Kundera. "Invasion: Prague, 1968." *Aperture* (Winter 1984): 6–21.

Porter, Alan. "Joseph Koudelka: A Monograph." *Camera* (August 1979).

Maltête, René. *Au Petit bonheur la France*. Paris: Hachette, 1965.

Paris Magnum, Photographs — 1935–1981. Millerton, N.Y.: Aperture, 1981.

GILLES PERESS:

Kozloff, Max. "Gilles Peress and the Politics of Space." *Parkett* 15 (1988): 6–9.

Parada, Esther. Review of *Telex: Iran. Exposure* (Fall 1985): 42–47.

Peress, Gilles. *Telex: Iran — In the Name of Revolution*. Millerton, N.Y.: Aperture, 1983.

Peress, Gilles, and Curtis Harnack. "Iran Face to Face." *Aperture* (1982): 28–45.

WILLY RONIS:

Ronis, Willy. *Sur le fil du hasard*. Paris: Contrejour, 1980.

————. *Willy Ronis par Willy Ronis*. Paris: Association Française pour la Diffusion du Patrimonie Photographique, 1985.

Sontag, Susan. *On Photography*. New York: Farrar, Straus and Giroux, 1977.

BURK UZZLE:

Uzzle, Burk. *All American*. St. David's, Penn.: St. David's Books, 1984.

————. *Landscapes*. Rochester, N.Y.: Light Impressions, 1973.

ROMAN VISHNIAC:

Capa, Cornell. *Roman Vishniac*. New York: Viking Press, 1974.

Mitgang, Herbert. "Testament to a Lost People." *New York Times Magazine* (2 October 1983): 40–45.

Vishniac, Roman. *Polish Jews: A Pictorial Record*. New York: Schocken Books, 1947.

————. *Roman Vishniac*. New York: Grossman, 1974.

————. *A Vanished World*. New York: Farrar, Straus and Giroux, 1983.

Zwingle, Erla. "Roman Vishniac." *American Photographer* 7 (July 1981): 36–45.

PART THREE: Walker Evans and America Before the War

Allen, Frederick Lewis. *Since Yesterday: The 1930s in America, September 3, 1929–September 3, 1939*. New York: Perennial Library, 1972.

Asch, Nathan. *The Road: In Search of America*. New York: W. W. Norton, 1937.

Brooks, Van Wyck. *America's Coming-of-Age*. New York: Doubleday Anchor Books, 1958.

Johnson, Paul. *Modern Times: The World from the Twenties to the Eighties*. New York: Harper and Row, 1983.

Mumford, Lewis. *The Culture of Cities*. New York: Harcourt Brace Jovanovich, 1970.

Pells, Richard H. *Radical Visions and American Dreams: Culture and Social Thought in the Depression Years*. New York: Harper and Row, 1973.

Rose, Barbara. *American Art Since 1900*. New York: Praeger Publishers, 1976.

Stange, Maren. *Symbols of an Ideal Life: Social Documentary Photography in America, 1890–1950*. New York: Cambridge University Press, 1989.

Sussman, Warren I. "The Thirties." In *The Development of American Culture*, 179–218. Edited by Stanley Coben and Lormer Ratner. Englewood Cliffs, N.J.: Prentice-Hall, 1970.

Terkel, Studs. *Hard Times: An Oral History of the Great Depression*. New York: Pocket Books, 1978.

Trachtenberg, Alan, Peter Neill, and Peter C. Bunnell, eds. *The City: American Experience*. New York: Oxford University Press, 1971.

Chapter 12: Social Uplift

Burckhardt, Rudy. *Mobile Homes*. Calais, Vt.: Z Press, 1979.

Dan Weiner, 1919–1959. New York: Grossman, 1974.

LEWIS HINE:

America and Lewis Hine: Photographs, 1904–1940. Millerton, N.Y.: Aperture, 1977.

Davis, Philip. *Street Land: Its Little People and Big Problems*. Boston: Small, Maynard, 1915.

Gutman, Judith Mara. *Lewis Hine and the American Social Conscience*. New York: Walker, 1964.

Kaplan, Daile. *Lewis Hine in Europe: The Lost Photographs*. New York: Abbeville Press, 1988.

Trachtenberg, Alan. *Reading American Photography: Images as History, Mathew Brady to Walker Evans*. New York: Hill and Wang, 1989.

West Side Studies: Boyhood and Lawlessness. New York: Survey Associates, 1914.

Lyons, Nathan, ed. *Photographers on Photography*. Englewood Cliffs, N.J.: Prentice-Hall, 1966.

JACOB RIIS:

Alland, Alexander, Sr. *Jacob A. Riis, Photographer and Citizen*, Millerton, N.Y.: Aperture, 1974.

Riis, Jacob A. *How the Other Half Lives: Studies Among the Tenements of New York*. New York, 1890.

————. *The Making of an American*. New York: Macmillan, 1901.

Siskind, Aaron. *Harlem Document: Photographs, 1932–1940*. Providence: Matrix Publications, 1981.

Stryker, Roy. Interview by Richard Doud. Archives of American Art, 13 and 14 June 1964.

Stryker, Roy, and Nancy Wood. *In This Proud Land: America 1935–1943 as Seen in the F.S.A. Photographs*. Boston: New York Graphic Society, 1975.

Tucker, Anne. "Photographic Crossroads: The Photo League." *Afterimage* Special Supplement (6 April 1978): 1–8.

————. Conversation with Colin Westerbeck and Joel Meyerowitz, May 1980.

MAX YAVNO:

Caen, Herb. *The San Francisco Book*. Boston: Houghton Mifflin, 1948.

Shippey, Lee. *The Los Angeles Book*. Boston: Houghton Mifflin, 1950.

Yavno, Max. *The Photography of Max Yavno*. Berkeley: University of California Press, 1981.

Chapter 13: Collective Vision

Fleischauer, Carl, and Beverly W. Brannan, eds. *Documenting America, 1935–1943*. Berkeley: University of California Press, 1988.

Hurley, F. Jack. *Portrait of a Decade: Roy Stryker and the Development of Documentary Photography in the Thirties*. New York: Da Capo Press, 1977.

Jung, Theo. Interview by Richard Doud. Archives of American Art, 19 January 1965.

Keller, Ulrich, ed. *The Highway as Habitat: A Roy Stryker Documentation, 1943–1955*. Santa Barbara, Calif.: University Art Museum, 1986.

DOROTHEA LANGE:

Lange, Dorothea. *An American Exodus: A Record of Human Erosion*. New York: Arno Press, 1975.

————. Interview by Richard Doud. Archives of American Art, 22 May 1964.

Meltzer, Milton, *Dorothea Lange: A Photographer's Life*. New York: Farrar, Straus and Giroux, 1978.

Stott, William. "Introduction to a Never-Published Book of Dorothea Lange's Best Photographs of Depression America." *Exposure* (Fall 1984): 22–30.

RUSSELL LEE:

Adams, Mark. "Our Town in East Texas." *Travel* 74 (March 1940): 4–10, 43–44.

Hurley, F. Jack. *Russell Lee, Photographer*. Dobbs Ferry, N.Y.: Morgan and Morgan, 1978.

Lee, Russell and Jean. Interview by Richard Doud. Archives of American Art, 2 June 1964.

HELEN LEVITT:

Dieckmann, Katherine. "Mean Streets." *Art in America* 78 (May 1990): 223–229, 263.

Levitt, Helen. Fellowship application. Museum of Modern Art, New York, 1946.

————. *Helen Levitt.* Washington, D.C.: Corcoran Gallery of Art, 1980.

————. *Helen Levitt, Color Photographs.* El Cajon, Calif.: Grossmont College Gallery, 1980.

————. *In the Street.* Durham, N.C.: Duke University Press, 1987.

————. Conversation with Colin Westerbeck, March 1980.

Levitt, Helen, and James Agee. *A Way of Seeing.* New York: Viking Press, 1965.

Phillips, Sandra S., and Maria Morris Hambourg. *Helen Levitt.* San Francisco: San Francisco Museum of Modern Art, 1991.

Soby, James Thrall. "The Art of Poetic Accident: The Photographs of Cartier-Bresson and Helen Levitt." *Minicam* 6 (March 1943): 28–31, 95.

McKinzie, Richard D. *The New Deal for Artists.* Princeton, N.J.: Princeton University Press, 1973.

O'Connor, Francis V., ed. *Art for the Millions: Essays from the 1930s by Artists and Administrators of the WPA Federal Art Project.* Boston: New York Graphic Society, 1975.

Official Images: New Deal Photography. Washington, D.C.: Smithsonian Institution Press, 1987.

O'Neal, Hank. *A Vision Shared: A Classic Portrait of America and Its People, 1935–1943.* New York: St. Martin's Press, 1976.

BEN SHAHN:

Morse, John D., ed. *Ben Shahn.* New York: Praeger Publishers, 1972.

Pratt, Davis, ed. *The Photographic Eye of Ben Shahn.* Cambridge: Harvard University Press, 1975.

Rodman, Selden. *Portrait of the Artist as an American.* New York: Harper, 1951.

Shahn, Ben. *The Shape of Content.* Cambridge: Harvard University Press, 1957.

————. Interview by Richard Doud. Archives of American Art, 14 April 1964.

————. Interview. Oral History Research Project, Columbia University, New York, 1977.

Shahn, Bernarda Bryson. *Ben Shahn.* New York: Harry N. Abrams, 1972.

Soby, James Thrall. *Ben Shahn*, West Drayton, England: Penguin Books, 1947.

Weiss, Margaret. *Ben Shahn, Photographer: An Album from the Thirties.* New York: Da Capo Press, 1973.

Stott, William. *Documentary Expression and Thirties America.* New York: Oxford University Press, 1973.

Stryker, Roy. Interview by Richard Doud. Archives of American Art, 13 and 14 June 1964.

Stryker, Roy, and Nancy Wood. *In this Proud Land: America 1935–1943 as Seen in the F.S.A. Photographs.* Boston: New York Graphic Society, 1975.

JOHN VACHON:

Vachon, Brian. "John Vachon: A Remembrance." *American Photographer* 3 (October 1979): 34–45.

Vachon, John. Interview by Richard Doud. Archives of American Art, 28 April 1964.

MARION POST WOLCOTT:

Wolcott, Marion Post. Interview by Richard Doud. Archives of American Art, 18 January 1965.

————. *Marion Post Wolcott, FSA Photographs.* Carmel, Calif.: Friends of Photography, 1983.

Chapter 14: American Classic

BERENICE ABBOTT:

Abbott, Berenice. *Changing New York.* New York: E. P. Dutton, 1939.

————. "Documenting the City." *The Complete Photographer* 4 (1942): 1393–1405.

————. "It Has to Walk Alone." *Infinity* 7 (November 1951): 6–7, 14.

————. *New York in the Thirties.* New York: Dover Publications, 1973.

————. "Photographer as Artist." *Art Front* 2 (September-October 1936): 4–7.

————. "The View Camera." In *Graphic Graflex Photography*, 159–175. Edited by Willard D. Morgan and Henry M. Lester. New York: Morgan and Lester, 1940.

————. *The World of Atget.* New York: Horizon Press, 1964.

————. Letter to Hardinge Scholle, 16 November 1961. Collection of the Museum of the City of New York.

————. Symposium, International Center of Photography, New York, 15 November 1979.

————. Interview by Lou Block, 29 November 1967. University of Louisville Archives, Louisville, Ky.

Lanier, Henry Wysham. *Greenwich Village Today and Yesterday.* New York: Harper, 1949.

[McCausland, Elizabeth.] "New York City as Seen in Abbott Photographs." *Springfield Sunday Union and Republican* (21 October 1934): 6E.

McCausland, Elizabeth. "The Photography of Berenice Abbott." *Trend* 3 (March–April 1935): 15–21.

Mitchell, Margaretta, ed. *Recollections: Ten Women of Photography.* New York: Viking Press, 1979.

New York Sun. 5 October 1934: 32.

O'Neal, Hank. *Berenice Abbott, American Photographer.* New York: McGraw-Hill, 1982.

Agee, James. "Plans for Work, October 1937." *Collected Short Prose of James Agee.* Edited by Robert Fitzgerald. Boston: Houghton Mifflin, 1968.

Bergreen, Laurence. *James Agee: A Life.* New York: E. P. Dutton, 1984.

Cowley, Malcolm. *Exile's Return: A Literary Odyssey of the 1920s.* New York: Penguin Books, 1976.

Crane, Hart. *The Bridge.* Paris: Black Sun Press, 1930.

————. *The Complete Poems of Hart Crane.* New York: Doubleday, 1958.

WALKER EVANS:

Agee, James, and Walker Evans. *Let Us Now Praise Famous Men: Three Tenant Families.* Boston: Houghton Mifflin, 1941.

Baier, Lesley K. *Walker Evans at "Fortune," 1945–1965.* Wellesley, Mass.: Wellesley College Museum, 1978.

Beals, Carleton. *The Crime of Cuba.* Philadelphia: J. B. Lippincott, 1933.

Bickel, Karl A. *The Mangrove Coast: The Story of the West Coast of Florida.* New York: Coward-McCann, 1942.

Cummings, Paul. "Walker Evans." In *Artists in Their Own Words: Interviews by Paul Cummings*, 83–100. New York: St. Martin's Press, 1979.

Evans, Walker. "Along the Right-of-Way." *Fortune* (September 1950): 106–113.

————. *American Photographs.* New York: Museum of Modern Art, 1938.

————. "Chicago: A Camera Exploration." *Fortune* (February 1947): 112–121.

————. *Images of the South: Visits with Eudora Welty and Walker Evans.* Interview by Bill Ferris. Memphis: Center for Southern Folklore, 1977.

————. "In Bridgeport's War Factories." *Fortune* (September 1941): 87, 92, 156–162.

————. Interview by Paul Cummings. Archives of American Art, 13 October and 23 December 1971. See also Cummings, Paul. "Walker Evans." In *Artists in Their Own Words: Interviews by Paul Cummings*, 83–100. New York: St. Martin's Press, 1979.

————. "Interview with Walker Evans." Interview by Leslie Katz. *Art in America* (March–April 1971): 82–89.

————. "Labor Anonymous." *Fortune* (November 1946): 152–153.

————. *Many Are Called.* Boston: Houghton Mifflin, 1966.

————. *Message from the Interior.* New York: Eakins Press, 1966.

————. "Mr. Walker Evans Records a City's Scene." *Creative Art* 7 (December 1930): 453–456.

————. "Photographs of Metropolitan Faces." Unpublished book proposal. Collection of the J. Paul Getty Museum.

————. "Photography." In *Quality: Its Image in the Arts*, 169–212. Edited by Louis Kronenberger. New York: Atheneum, 1969.

————. "Portfolio by Robert Frank." *U.S. Camera Annual* (1968): 89–115.

————. Project for an art book. Unpublished book proposal. Collection of the J. Paul Getty Museum.

————. "Rapid Transit." *The Cambridge Review* (20 March 1956): 16–25.

————. "The Reappearance of Photography." *Hound and Horn* 5 (October–December 1931): 125–128.

————. "Robert Frank." *U.S. Camera Annual* (1958): 90.

————. "The Thing Itself Is Such a Secret and So Unimaginable." *Yale Alumni Magazine* 37 (February 1974): 12–16.

————. "Walker Evans: The Unposed Portrait." *Harper's Bazaar* (March 1962): 120–125.

———. "Walker Evans on Himself." *New Republic* (13 November 1976): 23–27.

———. *Walker Evans, Photographs from the Farm Security Administration — 1935–1938.* New York: Da Capo Press, 1973.

Greenough, Sarah. *Walker Evans: Subways and Streets.* Washington, D.C.: National Gallery of Art, 1991.

Kirstein, Lincoln. "Walker Evans Photographs of Victorian Architecture." *Bulletin of the Museum of Modern Art* 1 (1 December 1933): 4.

Lloyd, Valerie. "To Walker Evans, in Praise of His Life, 1903–1975." *British Journal of Photography* 122 (25 April 1975): 348–353.

McBride, Stewart Dill. "Walker Evans." *Christian Science Monitor* 67 (27 May 1975): 18–19.

Meltzer, Milton. *Dorothea Lange: A Photographer's Life.* New York: Farrar, Straus and Giroux, 1978.

Mora, Gilles, and John T. Hill. *Walker Evans: Havana 1933.* New York: Pantheon Books, 1989.

———. *Walker Evans: The Hungry Eye.* New York: Harry N. Abrams, 1993.

Papageorge, Tod. *Walker Evans and Robert Frank: An Essay on Influence.* New Haven, Conn.: Yale University Art Gallery, 1981.

The Presence of Walker Evans. Boston: Institute of Contemporary Art, 1978.

Soby, James Thrall. "The Muse Was Not for Hire." *The Saturday Review* (22 September 1962): 57–58.

Stern, James. "Walker Evans (1903–75): A Memoir." *London Magazine* 17 (August–September 1977): 5–29.

Szarkowski, John. *Walker Evans.* New York: Museum of Modern Art, 1971.

Trachtenberg, Alan. *Reading American Photography: Images as History, Mathew Brady to Walker Evans.* New York: Hill and Wang, 1989.

Trilling, Lionel. "Greatness with One Fault in It." *Kenyon Review* 4 (Winter 1942): 99–102.

Walker Evans and Jane Ninas in New Orleans 1935–1936. New Orleans: The Historic New Orleans Collection, 1991.

Walker Evans at Work: 745 Photographs Together with Documents Selected from Letters, Memoranda, Interviews, Notes. New York: Harper and Row, 1982.

Walker Evans, First and Last. New York: Harper and Row, 1978.

Ward, J. A. *American Silences: The Realism of James Agee, Walker Evans, and Edward Hopper.* Baton Rouge: Louisiana State University Press, 1985.

Whitman, Alden. "Walker Evans Dies." *New York Times* (11 April 1975).

Williams, William Carlos. "Sermon with a Camera." *New Republic* 96 (12 October 1938): 282–283.

Jung, Theo. Interview by Richard Doud. Archives of American Art, 19 January 1965.

Kouwenhoven, John. *Made in America: The Arts in Modern Civilization.* Garden City, N.Y.: Doubleday, 1948.

Lee, Russell and Jean. Interview with Richard Doud. Archives of American Art, 2 June 1964.

Moureau, Geneviève. *The Restless Journey of James Agee.* New York: William Morrow, 1977.

O'Connor, Francis V., ed. *Art for the Millions: Essays from the 1930s by Artists and Administrators of the WPA Federal Art Project.* Boston: New York Graphic Society, 1975.

Shahn, Ben. Interview by Richard Doud. Archives of American Art, 14 April 1964.

Simmonds, Harvey, Louis H. Silverstein, and Nancy Lassalle. *Lincoln Kirstein, the Published Writings, 1922–1977: A First Bibliography.* New Haven, Conn.: Yale University Press, 1978.

Soby, James Thrall. *Ben Shahn.* West Drayton, England: Penguin Books, 1947.

Steiner, Ralph. *A Point of View.* Middletown, Conn.: Wesleyan University Press, 1978.

Stryker, Roy. Interview by Richard Doud. Archives of American Art, 13 and 14 June 1964.

Stryker, Roy, and Nancy Wood. *In this Proud Land: America 1935–1943 as Seen in the F.S.A. Photographs.* Boston: New York Graphic Society, 1975.

Trachtenberg, Alan. *Brooklyn Bridge: Fact and Symbol.* Chicago: University of Chicago Press, 1979.

Unterecker, John. *Voyager: A Life of Hart Crane.* New York: Farrar, Straus and Giroux, 1969.

Vachon, John. Interview by Richard Doud. Archives of American Art, 28 April 1964.

PART FOUR: Robert Frank and America Since the War

Badger, Gerry. "From Humanism to Formalism: Thoughts on Post-War American Photography." In Turner, Peter, ed. *American Images: Photographs, 1945–1980,* 11–22. New York: Penguin Books, 1985.

Bell, Daniel. *The End of Ideology: On the Exhaustion of Political Ideas in the Fifties.* New York: Free Press, 1965.

Dickstein, Morris. *Gates of Eden: American Culture in the Sixties.* New York: Basic Books, 1977.

Gee, Helen. *Photography of the Fifties: An American Perspective.* Tucson: Center for Creative Photography, 1980.

———. Conversation with Colin Westerbeck and Joel Meyerowitz, October 1980.

Hodgson, Godfrey. *America in Our Time.* New York: Doubleday, 1976.

Livingston, Jane. *The New York School: Photographs, 1936–1963.* New York: Stewart, Tabori and Chang, 1992.

Lobron, Barbara. "Limelight Lives!" *Photograph* 1 (February 1977).

Pells, Richard H. *The Liberal Mind in a Conservative Age: American Intellectuals in the 1940s and 1950s.* New York: Harper and Row, 1985.

"The Street." *Camera* 48 (March 1969): 5–49.

Tuchman, Maurice, ed. *New York School: The First Generation — Paintings of the 1940s and 1950s.* Boston: New York Graphic Society, 1977.

Wakefield, Dan. *New York in the Fifties.* Boston: Houghton Mifflin, 1992.

Chapter 15: Displaced Persons

Bosworth, Patricia. *Diane Arbus: A Biography.* New York: Alfred A. Knopf, 1984.

GEORGE GROSZ:

Grosz, George. *George Grosz: Erste Landung/New York 1932.* New York: Kimmel/Cohn, 1977.

Hess, Hans. *George Grosz.* New Haven, Conn.. Yale University Press, 1985.

Schneede, Uwe M. *George Grosz: His Life and Work.* New York: Universe Books, 1979.

Tower, Beeke Sell. *Envisioning America: Prints, Drawings, and Photographs by George Grosz and His Contemporaries, 1915–1933.* [Cambridge, England]: The Museum, 1990.

JOHN GUTMANN:

Gutmann, John. "John Gutmann." Interview by Nancy Stevens. *American Photographer* 6: (May 1981): 48–55.

———. "John Gutmann." Interview by Paul Raedeke. *Photo Metro* 4 (September 1985): 4–17.

———. *The Restless Decade: John Gutmann's Photographs of the Thirties.* Edited by Lew Thomas. New York: Harry N. Abrams, 1984.

Heilbut, Anthony. *Exiled in Paradise: German Refugee Artists and Intellectuals in America, from the 1930s to the Present.* Boston: Beacon Press, 1984.

Kracauer, Siegfried. *Theory of Film: The Redemption of Physical Reality.* New York: Oxford University Press, 1960.

LISETTE MODEL:

Model, Lisette. *Lisette Model.* Millerton, N.Y.: Aperture, 1979.

Porter, Alan. "Lisette Model." *Camera* (December 1977).

Chapter 16: Naturalized Citizens

ROY DECARAVA:

DeCarava, Roy. *Photographs.* Carmel, Calif.: Friends of Photography, 1981.

DeCarava, Roy, and Langston Hughes. *The Sweet Flypaper of Life.* New York: Hill and Wang, 1955.

———. *The Sweet Flypaper of Life.* Washington, D.C.: Howard University Press, 1984.

Leon Levenstein. New York: Photofind Gallery, 1990.

Szarkowski, John. *From the Picture Press.* New York: Museum of Modern Art, 1973.

WEEGEE (ARTHUR FELLIG):

Stettner, Louis, ed. *Weegee.* New York: Alfred A. Knopf, 1977.

Weegee (Arthur Fellig). *Naked City.* New York: Essential Books, 1945.

———. *Naked City.* New York: Da Capo Press, 1975.

———. "Naked Weegee." Interview by Gretchen Berg. *Photography* 1 (Summer 1976).

———. *Weegee by Weegee.* New York: Ziff-Davis, 1961.

Weegee's New York: 335 Photographs, 1935–1960. Munich: Schirmer/Mosel, 1982.
Westerbeck, Colin. "Night Light: Brassaï and Weegee." Artforum 15 (December 1976): 34–45.

Chapter 17: An American in Paris
Heilbut, Anthony. Exiled in Paradise: German Refugee Artists and Intellectuals in America, from the 1930s to the Present. Boston: Beacon Press, 1984.
WILLIAM KLEIN:
Klein, William. Close Up. New York: Thames and Hudson, 1989.
———. Life Is Good and Good for You in New York: Trance Witness Revels. Paris: Editions du Seuil, 1956.
———. Moscow. New York: Crown, 1964.
———. Rome: The City and Its People. New York: Viking Press, 1959.
———. Tokyo. New York: Crown, 1964.
———. William Klein, photographe, etc. Paris: Centre Georges Pompidou, 1983.
———. William Klein, Photographs, Etc. Millerton, N.Y.: Aperture, 1981.
———. Conversation with Colin Westerbeck and Joel Meyerowitz, 9 August 1979.

Chapter 18: In the American Grain
Cassady, Carolyn. Heart Beat: My Life with Jack and Neal. Berkeley, Calif.: Creative Arts, 1976.
ROBERT FRANK:
Arnaud, Georges. "Indiens des Hauts-Plateaux." Neuf (December 1952): 1–34.
———. Indiens pas morts. Paris: Editions Delpire, 1956.
Bennett, Edna. "Black and White Are the Colors of Robert Frank." Aperture 9 (1961): 20–22.
Brookman, Philip. Robert Frank, Photographer/Filmmaker: Works from 1945–1979. Long Beach, Calif.: Long Beach Museum of Art, 1979.
Frank, Robert. Les Américains. Paris: Editions Delpire, 1958.
———. The Americans. New York: Grove Press, 1959.
———. The Americans. Millerton, N.Y.: Aperture, 1978.
———. Black, White and Things. Handmade book of photographic prints [1952].
———. "A Bus Ride Through New York." Camera (January 1966): 32–35.
———. "The Congressional." Fortune (November 1955): 118–122.
———. "The Irretrievable Instant." Camera (March 1968): 4.
———. "Letter from New York." Creative Camera 60 (June–December 1969): 202.
———. The Lines of My Hand. Tokyo: Yugensha, 1971.
———. "One Man's U.S.A." Pageant (April 1958): 24–35.
———. "The Photographer as Poet." U.S. Camera (September 1954): 79–84.
———. In The Photo Reporter (15 November 1971): 93.

———. "Robert Frank Interviewed." Interview by Dennis Wheeler. Criteria 3 (June 1977): 4–7.
———. "A Statement." U.S. Camera Annual (1958): 115.
———. Conversation with Colin Westerbeck and Joel Meyerowitz, October 1980.
Janis, Eugenia Parry, and Wendy MacNeil, eds. Photography Within the Humanities. Danbury, N.H.: Addison House, 1977.
Kerouac, Jack, and Robert Frank. "On the Road to Florida." Evergreen Review (January 1970).
Mann, Margery. "The Americans Revisited." Camera 35 18 (January 1975): 14, 74–75.
Schuh, Gotthard. "Letter to Robert Frank." Camera 36 (August 1957): 339–340.
Stott, William. "Walker Evans, Robert Frank and the Landscape of Dissociation." Arts Canada 192–195 (December 1974): 83–89.
Tucker, Anne. Robert Frank, New York to Nova Scotia. Houston: Museum of Fine Arts, 1986.
Westerbeck, Colin. "American Graphic: The Photography and Fiction of Wright Morris." In Multiple Views: Logan Grant Essays on Photography, 1983–89, 271–302. Albuquerque: University of New Mexico Press, 1991.
Ginsberg, Allen. Howl and Other Poems. San Francisco: City Lights, 1956.
Goldman, Eric F. The Crucial Decade: America, 1945–1955. New York: Alfred A. Knopf, 1956.
Heilbut, Anthony. Exiled in Paradise: German Refugee Artists and Intellectuals in America, from the 1930s to the Present. Boston: Beacon Press, 1984.
Kerouac, Jack. The Book of Dreams. San Francisco: City Lights Books, 1961.
———. The Dharma Bums. New York: Viking Press, 1958.
———. On the Road. New York: Viking Press, 1957.
———. The Subterraneans. New York: Grove Press, 1971.
———. The Town and the City. New York: Harcourt Brace, 1970.
Mailer, Norman. "The White Negro." In The Beat Generation and the Angry Young Men, 342–363. Edited by Gene Feldman and Max Gartenberg. New York: The Citadel Press, 1958.
McNally, Dennis. Desolate Angel: Jack Kerouac, the Beat Generation, and America. New York: Random House, 1979.
Rosenberg, Harold. "The American Action Painters." In The Tradition of the New, 23–39. New York: Grove Press, 1961.
Sandler, Irving. The Triumph of American Painting: A History of Abstract Expressionism. New York: Harper and Row, 1970.

Chapter 19: The Chicago School
HARRY CALLAHAN:
Callahan, Harry. Harry Callahan. New York: Museum of Modern Art, 1967.
———. Harry Callahan Photographs. [Kansas City]: The Hallmark Photographic Collection, 1981.
Szarkowski, John. Callahan. Millerton, N.Y.: Aperture, 1976.

Crane, Barbara. Barbara Crane, Photographs — 1948–1980. Tucson: Center for Creative Photography, 1981.
Ishimoto, Yasuhiro. Chicago, Chicago. Tokyo: Biyutsu Shuppan-sha, 1969.
Josephson, Kenneth. Kenneth Josephson. Chicago: Museum of Contemporary Art, 1983.
Trachtenberg, Alan, ed. Classic Essays on Photography. New Haven, Conn.: Leete's Island Books, 1980.
Traub, Charles, and John Grimes. The New Vision: Forty Years of Photography at the Institute of Design. Millerton, N.Y.: Aperture, 1982.
Tucker, Anne. Unknown Territory: Photographs by Ray K. Metzker. Houston: Museum of Fine Arts, 1984.

Chapter 20: Still Going
DIANE ARBUS:
Arbus, Doon, and Marvin Israel, eds. Diane Arbus. Millerton, N.Y.: Aperture, 1972.
———. Diane Arbus, Magazine Work. Millerton, N.Y.: Aperture, 1984.
Bosworth, Patricia. Diane Arbus: A Biography. New York: Alfred A. Knopf, 1984.
Roegiers, Patrick. Diane Arbus ou le rêve du naufrage. Paris: Texte Chêne, 1985.
Becker, Howard S. "Photography and Sociology." Afterimage 3 (May–June 1975): 22–32.
LEE FRIEDLANDER:
Friedlander, Lee. The American Monument. New York: Eakins Press, 1976.
———. Factory Valleys: Ohio and Pennsylvania. New York: Calloway Editions, 1982.
———. Letters from the People. New York: Distributed Art Publishers, 1993.
———. Like a One-Eyed Cat: Photographs by Lee Friedlander, 1956–1987. New York: Harry N. Abrams, 1989.
———. Self-Portrait. New City, N.Y.: Haywire Press, 1970.
Friedlander, Lee, and Jim Dine. Work from the Same House, Photographs and Etchings. London: Trigram Press, 1969.
JOEL MEYEROWITZ:
Kozloff, Max. "Joel Meyerowitz." Aperture (1977): 32–45.
Meyerowitz, Joel. Bay/Sky. Boston: Little, Brown, 1993.
———. Cape Light. Boston: Museum of Fine Arts, 1978.
———. Redheads. New York: Rizzoli, 1991.
———. St. Louis and the Arch. Boston: New York Graphic Society, 1980.
———. A Summer's Day. New York: Times Books, 1985.
———. Wild Flowers. Boston: Little, Brown, 1983.
TONY RAY-JONES:
Ray-Jones, Tony. A Day Off. Boston: New York Graphic Society, 1974.
———. Tony Ray-Jones. Manchester, England: Cornerhouse Publications, 1990.
RAGHUBIR SINGH:
Singh, Raghubir. Calcutta: The Home and the Street. New York: Thames and Hudson, 1988.

———. *The Ganges.* New York: Aperture, 1992.

———. *Rajasthan: India's Enchanted Land.* New York: Thames and Hudson, 1981.

GARRY WINOGRAND:

Silver, Kenneth E. "The Witness." *Art in America* (October 1988): 148–157.

Szarkowski, John. *Winogrand: Figments from the Real World.* New York: Museum of Modern Art, 1988.

Winogrand, Garry. *The Animals.* New York: Museum of Modern Art, 1969.

———. *Garry Winogrand.* El Cajon, Calif.: Grossmont College Gallery, 1976.

———. *Public Relations.* New York: Museum of Modern Art, 1977.

———. *Stock Photographs: The Fort Worth Fat Stock Show and Rodeo.* Austin: University of Texas Press, 1980.

———. *Women Are Beautiful.* New York: Light Gallery Books, 1975.

———. Conversation with Colin Westerbeck and Joel Meyerowitz, May 1983.

Index